Law and Revolution

LAW and REVOLUTION

The Formation of the Western Legal Tradition

HAROLD J. BERMAN

HARVARD UNIVERSITY PRESS
Cambridge, Massachusetts
and London, England

Copyright © 1983 by the
President and Fellows of Harvard College

All rights reserved

10 9 8 7 6 5 4 3 2

Printed in the United States of America

Library of Congress Cataloging in Publication Data

Berman, Harold Joseph, 1918–
  Law and revolution.

  Includes bibliographical references and index.
  1. Law—History and criticism.   I. Title.
K150.B47   1983   340′.09   82-15747
ISBN 0-674-51774-1

Preface

THIS IS A STORY of origins, of "roots"—and also of "routes," the paths by which we have arrived where we are. The skeptic may read it with nostalgia, retracing in his mind the course by which he came to his alienation. The believer may hope to find in it some guidelines for the future. "The past has revealed to me how the future is built," wrote Teilhard de Chardin.

My own motivation is somewhat more desperate. It is said that a drowning man may see his whole life flash before him. That may be his unconscious effort to find within his experience the resources to extricate himself from impending doom. So I have had to view the Western tradition of law and legality, of order and justice, in a very long historical perspective, from its beginnings, in order to find a way out of our present predicament.

That we are at the end of an era is not something that can be proved scientifically. One senses it or one does not. One knows by intuition that the old images, as Archibald MacLeish says in *The Metaphor*, have lost their meaning.

> A world ends when its metaphor has died.
>
> An age becomes an age, all else beside,
> When sensuous poets in their pride invent
> Emblems for the soul's consent
> That speak the meanings men will never know
> But man-imagined images can show:
> It perishes when those images, though seen,
> No longer mean.

Because the age is ending, we are now able to discern its beginnings. In the middle of an era, when the end is not in sight, the beginning also is hidden from view. Then history does indeed give the appearance, in

Maitland's phrase, of a seamless web. But now that our entire civilization is stretched out before us we can uncover its origins because we know what origins we are seeking.

Similarly, it is because we are emerging from a revolutionary period that we are able more easily to identify the revolutionary eras of the past. Incremental history, "smooth" history, was characteristic of the historical writings of the Darwinian age. Catastrophic history, dominated by social conflict, has been characteristic of the historical writings of the early and middle parts of the twentieth century. Now for the first time we are also beginning to see not only evolution and not only revolution but the interaction of the two as a dominant theme of Western history.

It is impossible not to sense the social disintegration, the breakdown of communities, that has taken place in Europe, North America, and other parts of Western civilization in the twentieth century. Bonds of race, religion, soil, family, class, neighborhood, and work community have increasingly dissolved into abstract and superficial nationalisms. This is closely connected with the decline of unity and common purpose in Western civilization as a whole. Yet there are also some signs of buildup. Perhaps the most hopeful prospect is that of economic, scientific, and cultural interdependence on both a regional and worldwide basis.

What has this to do with law? A great deal. The traditional symbols of community in the West, the traditional images and metaphors, have been above all religious and legal. In the twentieth century, however, for the first time, religion has become largely a private affair, while law has become largely a matter of practical expediency. The connection between the religious metaphor and the legal metaphor has been broken. Neither expresses any longer the community's vision of its future and its past; neither commands any longer its passionate loyalty.

One need not bemoan these changes. They may be a good thing. They are no doubt inevitable. In any case, they mark the end of an era, and since there is no going back, the only question is, "How do we go forward?" Can we find in the group memory of our past experience the resources that may help us to overcome the obstacles that block our way to the future?

What those obstacles are may be learned indirectly from the story told in this book. Among them are a narrowness and a compartmentalization, both of thought and of action, in relation to law itself. We need to overcome the reduction of law to a set of technical devices for getting things done; the separation of law from history; the identification of all our law with national law and of all our legal history with national legal history; the fallacies of an exclusively political and analytical jurisprudence ("positivism"), or an exclusively philosophical and moral jurisprudence ("natural-law theory"), or an exclusively historical and social-economic jurisprudence ("the historical school," "the social theory of law"). We need a jurisprudence that integrates the three traditional schools and goes beyond them. Such an integrative jurisprudence would emphasize that law has to be believed in or it will not work; it involves not only reason and will but also emotion, intuition, and faith. It involves a total social commitment.

In periods of crisis we need a larger vision. Oliver Wendell Holmes, Jr., once said to a class of law students: "Your business as lawyers is to see the relation between your particular fact and the whole frame of the universe." Behind that statement lay Holmes's tragic vision of life, born of the Civil War. He knew that without a universal context particular facts are wholly precarious.

The narrowness of our concepts of law blocks our vision not only of law but also of history. Today people think of law primarily as the mass of legislative, administrative, and judicial rules, procedures, and techniques in force in a given country. The vision of history that accompanies this view of law is severely limited to the more or less recent past and to a particular nation. Indeed, it may even be a vision of no history at all, but only of current policies and values. In contrast, consider the historical implications of concepts of law that prevailed in the past—for example, in eighteenth-century England, as expressed in Blackstone's *Commentaries on the Laws of England,* a book written not only for lawyers but also, and primarily, for all educated people. According to Blackstone, the following kinds of laws prevailed in England: natural law, divine law, the law of nations, the English common law, local customary law, Roman law, ecclesiastical law, the law merchant, statutory law, and equity. Implicit in this catalogue was a view of history not limited to the nation or to the recent past, but a view of overlapping histories—the history of Christianity and Judaism, the history of Greece, the history of Rome, the history of the church, local history, national history, international history, and more. Such a view, by linking Blackstone's readers with various past times, freed them from bondage to any single past as well as to the past as a whole, in some abstract Kantian sense. By the same token it enabled them to anticipate not one single future or some abstract future-in-general, but, once again, various future times. Blackstone himself was very "English" and in many respects quite conservative, but in recognizing the multiformity of the legal tradition in England he recognized the multiformity of history itself.

It has sometimes been noted that too narrow a view of law makes it impossible for scholars of other disciplines—historians, political scientists, sociologists, philosophers—to study it effectively. If law is treated merely as the prevailing rules, procedures, and techniques, it has little interest for social scientists or humanists. It should also be noted that those who lose by this are not only the lawyers but also the social scientists and humanists, who are thus deprived of one of the richest sources of insight into their own disciplines. If our social sciences and humanities have become excessively behavioristic and fragmented, and if our historiography, in particular, has become excessively nationalistic and excessively bound to relatively short time periods, part of the reason is that our legal thought has also become so, and has consequently passed out of the general purview of the professional scholar and hence of the educated public.

It is easier, of course, to complain about the compartmentalization of knowledge than to do something constructive to overcome it. Any effort to reintegrate past times is likely to be understood and judged in terms of the prevailing categories and concepts. To present the history of law in the West as a metaphor of our age is to expect a great deal from readers who have been educated in quite different views of history, of law, and of the West. Yet without a reintegration of the past there is no way either to retrace our steps or to find guidelines for the future.

CONTENTS

Maps and Figures

Law and Revolution

Introduction

THIS BOOK TELLS the following story: that once there was a civilization called "Western"; that it developed distinctive "legal" institutions, values, and concepts; that these Western legal institutions, values, and concepts were consciously transmitted from generation to generation over centuries, and thus came to constitute a "tradition"; that the Western legal tradition was born of a "revolution" and thereafter, during the course of many centuries, has been periodically interrupted and transformed by revolutions; and that in the twentieth century the Western legal tradition is in a revolutionary crisis greater than any other in its history, one that some believe has brought it virtually to an end.

Not all people will want to listen to this story. Many will find the plot unacceptable; they will consider it a fantasy. Some will say that there never was a Western legal tradition. Others will say that the Western legal tradition is alive and well in the late twentieth century.

Even among those who will recognize that the story is true, and that it should be taken seriously, there will be wide differences of opinion concerning the meanings of the words *Western, legal, tradition,* and *revolution.* One purpose in telling the story is to uncover the meanings of those words in a narrative context, that is, in their time dimension. From that standpoint, to attempt to define them in advance would be self-defeating. As Friedrich Nietzsche once said, nothing that has a history can be defined. Nevertheless, an author of nonfiction has an obligation to disclose at the outset some of his prejudices. At the same time it may be useful to attempt, in a preliminary way, to dispel some of the misunderstandings—as I see them—of those who may prejudge the story to be unacceptable.

What is called "the West" in this book is a particular historical culture, or civilization, which can be characterized in many different ways, depending on the purposes of the characterization. It used to be called "the

Occident" and was taken to comprise all the cultures that succeeded to
the heritage of ancient Greece and Rome, as contrasted with "the
Orient," which consisted chiefly of Islam, India, and the "Far East."
Since the end of World War II, "East" and "West" have often been used
to distinguish Communist from non-Communist countries: in "East-
West trade," a shipment of goods from Prague to Tokyo is a shipment
from East to West.

There is another East-West distinction which is less well known today:
the distinction between the eastern and western parts of the Christian
church, which in the early centuries of the Christian era paralleled the
distinction between the eastern and western parts of the Roman Empire.
Although there were differences between the Eastern church and the
Western church from an early time, it was only in 1054 that they split
apart. Their separation coincided with the Western movement to make
the Bishop of Rome the sole head of the church, to emancipate the clergy
from the control of emperor, kings, and feudal lords, and sharply to differentiate the church as a political and legal entity from secular polities.
This movement, culminating in what was called the Gregorian Reformation and the Investiture Struggle (1075-1122),[1] gave rise to the formation of the first modern Western legal system, the "new canon law"
(*jus novum*) of the Roman Catholic Church, and eventually to new secular legal systems as well—royal, urban, and others. The term
"Western," in the phrase "Western legal tradition," refers to the peoples
whose legal tradition stems from these events. In the eleventh and
twelfth centuries, these were the peoples of western Europe, from
England to Hungary and from Denmark to Sicily; countries such as
Russia and Greece, which remained in the Eastern Orthodox church, as
well as large parts of Spain, which were Muslim, were excluded at that
time. In later times not only were Russia and Greece and all of Spain
westernized, but also North and South America and various other parts
of the world as well.

The West, then, is not to be found by recourse to a compass. Geographical boundaries help to locate it, but they shift from time to time.
The West is, rather, a cultural term, but with a very strong diachronic
dimension. It is not, however, simply an idea; it is a community. It implies both a historical structure and a structured history. For many centuries it could be identified very simply as the people of Western
Christendom. Indeed, from the eleventh to the fifteenth centuries the
community of those people was manifested in their common allegiance
to a single spiritual authority, the Church of Rome.

As a historical culture, a civilization, the West is to be distinguished
not only from the East but also from "pre-Western" cultures to which it
"returned" in various periods of "renaissance." Such returns and revivals
are characteristics of the West. They are not to be confused with the

models on which they drew for inspiration. "Israel," "Greece," and "Rome" became spiritual ancestors of the West not primarily by a process of survival or succession but primarily by a process of adoption: the West adopted them as ancestors. Moreover, it adopted them selectively—different parts at different times. Cotton Mather was no Hebrew. Erasmus was no Greek. The Roman lawyers of the University of Bologna were no Romans.

Some Roman law, to be sure, survived in the Germanic folklaw and, more important, in the law of the church; some Greek philosophy also survived, also in the church; the Hebrew Bible, of course, survived as the Old Testament. But such survivals only account for a small part of their influence on Western law, Western philosophy, and Western theology. What accounted for the major part of their influence were the rediscoveries, reexaminations, and receptions of the ancient texts. Even to the extent that the ancient learning may be said to have survived without interruption, it was inevitably transformed. This point is especially important for an understanding of the rediscovery and revival of Roman law: by no stretch of the imagination can the legal system, say, of the twelfth-century free city of Pisa, which adopted many of the rules of Roman law found in the newly rediscovered texts of the Byzantine Emperor Justinian, be identified with the legal system of the empire over which Justinian reigned. The same formulas carried very different meanings.

The West, from this perspective, is not Greece and Rome and Israel but the peoples of Western Europe *turning* to the Greek and Roman and Hebrew texts for inspiration, and *transforming* those texts in ways that would have astonished their authors. Nor, of course, is Islam part of the West, although there were strong Arabic influences on Western philosophy and science—though not on Western legal institutions—especially in the period with which this study is concerned.

Indeed, each of the ancient ingredients of Western culture was transformed by being mixed with the others. The amazing thing is that such antagonistic elements could be brought together into a single world view. The Hebrew culture would not tolerate Greek philosophy or Roman law; the Greek culture would not tolerate Roman law or Hebrew theology; the Roman culture would not tolerate Hebrew theology, and it resisted large parts of Greek philosophy. Yet the West in the late eleventh and early twelfth centuries combined all three, and thereby transformed each one.

Somewhat more controversial is the distinction between the West and the culture of the Germanic and other tribal peoples of Europe before the eleventh century. If West were a geographical term, that earlier culture would have to be included; indeed, one would have to start, as most studies of European history do, with Caesar's Gallic wars, the invasion of the Roman Empire by the Germanic peoples, the rise of the Frankish monarchy, and Charlemagne and Alfred the Great before coming to the Gregorian Reformation, the Investiture Struggle, and what is usually called the High Middle Ages or the Renaissance of the Twelfth Century (though it actually began in the latter half of the eleventh). To speak of the Germanic peoples of Europe as "pre-Western" may sound strange to some ears. Yet there was a radical discontinuity between the Europe of the period before the years 1050–1150 and the Europe of the period after the years 1050–1150.

Finally, it needs to be said in connection with the meaning of the word Western that, at least for the purpose of analyzing and explaining legal institutions, no sharp distinction should be made between Western and "modern"; and further, that modern should be differentiated from "contemporary" by applying modern to the period prior to the two World Wars and contemporary to the period since 1945. One of the purposes of this study is to show that in the West, modern times — not only modern legal institutions and modern legal values but also the modern state, the modern church, modern philosophy, the modern university, modern literature, and much else that is modern — have their origin in the period 1050–1150 *and not before.*

The term "legal," like the term Western, has a history. "Law" these days is usually defined as a "body of rules." The rules, in turn, are usually thought to derive from statutes and, where judicial lawmaking is recognized, from court decisions. From this point of view, however, there could be no such thing as "Western law," since there is no Western legislature or court. (By the same token there could be no such thing as "American law," but only the federal law of the United States and the state law of each of the fifty states.) Such a definition of law is entirely too narrow for any study that embraces the legal systems of all countries of the West in all the various periods of Western history, and which is concerned not only with the law in books but also with law in action. Law in action involves legal institutions and procedures, legal values, and legal concepts and ways of thought, as well as legal rules. It involves what is sometimes called "the legal process," or what in German is called *Rechtsverwirklichung,* the "realizing" of law.

Lon L. Fuller has defined law as "the enterprise of subjecting human conduct to the governance of rules."[2] This definition rightly stresses the primacy of legal activity over legal rules. Yet I would go further by adding to the purpose of the enterprise not just the making and applying of rules but also other modes of governance, including the casting of votes, the issuing of orders, the appointment of officials, and the handing down of judgments. Also the law has purposes other than governance, in the usual sense of that word: it is an enterprise for facilitating voluntary arrangements through the negotiation of transactions, the issuance of documents (for example, credit instruments or documents of title), and the performance of other acts of a legal nature. Law in action consists of people legislating, adjudicating, administering, negotiating, and carrying on other legal activities. It is a living process of allocating rights and duties and thereby resolving conflicts and creating channels of cooperation.

Such a broad concept of law is needed in order to compare, within a single framework, the many specific legal systems that have existed in the West during many centuries. It is needed also in order to explore the interrelationships of these systems with other political, economic, and social institutions, values, and concepts.

I have taken the liberty of defining law in general terms, without reference to the particular legal institutions, values, and concepts that characterize the Western legal tradition. My purpose in doing so has been to answer those who, by defining law too narrowly, namely, as a body of rules, obstruct an understanding of the emergence of the Western legal tradition, of the impact on it of the great revolutions of Western history, and of its present predicament. The concept of law as a particular kind of enterprise, in which rules play only a part, becomes meaningful in the context of the actual historical development of the living law of a given culture.

To speak of a "tradition" of law in the West is to call attention to two major historical facts: first, that from the late eleventh and twelfth centuries on, except in certain periods of revolutionary change, legal institutions in the West developed continuously over generations and centuries, with each generation consciously building on the work of previous generations; and second, that this conscious process of continuous development is (or once was) conceived as a process not merely of change but of organic growth. Even the great national revolutions of the past—the Russian Revolution of 1917, the French and American Revolutions of 1789 and 1776, the English Revolution of 1640, the German Reformation of 1517—eventually made peace with the legal tradition that they or some of their leaders had set out to destroy.

The concept of conscious organic development was applied in the eleventh and twelfth centuries to institutions. In this context the term "institutions" means structured arrangements for performing specific social tasks. Universities, for example, are institutions for transmitting higher education and training professionals; the financial and judicial departments of government are institutions for administering taxation and justice, respectively; the legal system is a structured system of arrangements, one of whose primary purposes is to provide guidance to the various departments of government, as well as to people generally, concerning what is permitted and what is prohibited. In the West in the eleventh and twelfth centuries not only the newly created universities, exchequers and courts, and legal systems were viewed as developing institutions, but even the church came to be so viewed. So also did secular structures such as urban and royal governments. These various institutions were conceived as having an *ongoing* character; they were expected gradually to adapt to new situations, to reform themselves, and to grow over long periods of time. In part, such growth was planned: many cathedrals, for example, were planned to be built over generations and centuries; they had budgets, literally, for a thousand years. In part, the growth was not so much planned as engineered: administrators and legislators revised the work of their predecessors, disciples set out to improve on the work of their masters, the "commentators" succeeded the "glossators." In part, growth seemed less to be planned or engineered than just to happen: for example, architects "combined" Romanesque with Norman, and out of that there "emerged" early Gothic, which "developed" into later Gothic, and so on.

As Robert Nisbet says, no one *sees* a society "grow" or "develop" or "decay" or "die."[3] These are all metaphors. Nevertheless, the belief of people living in a society in a given time that the society is, in fact, growing or developing, or decaying, or dying, is a very real thing. In the formative era of the Western legal tradition the older Augustinian belief that society, the "earthly city," is continually decaying was modified by a new belief that social institutions are capable of birth and growth and reproduction. Moreover, this process was conceived to be one in which successive generations consciously and actively participate. As Goethe said, a tradition cannot be inherited—it has to be earned.

The great English historian F. W. Maitland made use of the biological metaphor of growth to describe the changes that took place in the English law relating to the forms of action in the twelfth century and thereafter. He wrote:

> Our forms of action are not mere rubrics nor dead categories; they are not the outcome of a classificatory process that has been applied to pre-existing materials. They are institutes of the law; they are—we say it without scruple—living things. Each of them lives its own life, has its own adventures, enjoys a longer or shorter day of vigour, usefulness, and popularity and then sinks perhaps into a decrepit and friendless old age. A few are still-born, some are sterile, others live to see their children and children's children in high places. The struggle for life is keen among them and only the fittest survive.[4]

Thus trespass, which Maitland called a "fertile mother of actions," is said to have "given birth to" or "given rise to" or "thrown off"—depending partly on one's taste in metaphors and partly on one's concept of organic continuity — trespass for assault and battery, trespass to chattels, trespass to land, and many other trespass actions. It was also "a source of " trespass on the case, although there the offspring differed very substantially from its progenitor.[5] Scholars have drawn a tree to represent the forms of action, with trunk and branches and dates assigned, like a genealogical tree. Is this just a pedagogical device? Is it perhaps a form of animism?

It may be useful to draw an analogy between the development of law, so conceived, and the development of music. From the eleventh and twelfth centuries on, monophonic music, reflected chiefly in the Gregorian chant, was gradually supplanted by polyphonic styles. Two-part, three-part, and eventually four-part music developed. The contrapuntal style exemplified in the thirteenth-century motet evolved into the harmonic style of the fourteenth-century *ars nova,* exemplified in the ballade. Eventually, counterpoint and harmony were combined. The sixteenth century witnessed the development of the great German Protestant chorales, and these, together with Italian and English madrigals and other forms, provided a basis for opera, which first appeared in Italy at the end of the sixteenth and in the early seventeenth century. Eventually Renaissance music gave way to Baroque, Baroque to Classical, and so on. No good contemporary musician, regardless of how off-beat he may be, can afford not to know this story. There was a time not long ago when a good lawyer was required, in a similar way, to know the story of the development of legal institutions.

Of course, not every change is to be seen as growth. Some changes may be said to cut off growth. One cannot say, for example, that trial by ordeal and trial by battle gave rise to trial by jury, or that the civil action for trespass to land grew out of the appeal of felony. Ordeal, battle, and appeal of felony were tribal and feudal in nature; jury and trespass were royal. Moreover, the former hardly survived the introduction of the latter, whereas the concept of organic growth presupposes that the parent continues to live alongside the offspring. It is different from the concept of causation. Not the ordeal but the abolition of the ordeal gave rise to the jury in criminal cases.

At the same time, conscious growth does not necessarily mean deliberate movement toward particular ideal goals. It means something less than moral progress, though something more than mere change or accumulation. Law reform has been, to be sure, a recurrent feature of the Western legal tradition ever since its formative era. Yet reform itself is seen as part of what I have called the *ongoing* character of the tradition, its self-conscious continuity in time.

The principal characteristics of the Western legal tradition may be summarized, in a preliminary way, as follows:

1. A relatively sharp distinction is made between *legal* institutions (including legal processes such as legislation and adjudication as well as the

legal rules and concepts that are generated in those processes) and *other* types of institutions. Although law remains strongly influenced by religion, politics, morality, and custom, it is nevertheless distinguishable from them analytically. Custom, for example, in the sense of habitual patterns of behavior, is distinguished from customary law, in the sense of customary norms of behavior that are considered to be legally binding. Similarly, politics and morals may determine law, but they are not thought to *be* law—as they are in some other cultures. In the West, though of course not only in the West, law is considered to have a character of its own, a certain relative autonomy.

2. Connected with the sharpness of this distinction is the fact that the administration of legal institutions, in the Western legal tradition, is entrusted to a special corps of people, who engage in legal activities on a professional basis as a more or less full-time occupation.

3. The legal professionals, whether typically called lawyers, as in England and America, or jurists, as in most other Western countries, are specially trained in a discrete body of higher learning identified as legal learning, with its own professional literature and its own professional schools or other places of training.

4. The body of legal learning in which the legal specialists are trained stands in a complex, dialectical relationship to the legal institutions, since on the one hand the learning describes those institutions but on the other hand the legal institutions, which would otherwise be disparate and unorganized, become conceptualized and systematized, and thus transformed, by what is said about them in learned treatises and articles and in the classroom. In other words, the law includes not only legal institutions, legal commands, legal decisions, and the like, but also what legal scholars (including, on occasion, lawmakers, judges, and other officials talking or writing like legal scholars) say about those legal institutions, commands, and decisions. The law contains within itself a legal science, a meta-law, by which it can be both analyzed and evaluated.

The first four characteristics of the Western legal tradition are shared by the tradition of Roman law as it developed in the Roman Republic and the Roman Empire from the second century B.C. to the eighth century A.D. and later. They are not shared, however, in many contemporary non-Western cultures, nor were they present in the legal order that prevailed among the Germanic peoples of Western Europe prior to the eleventh century. Germanic law was embedded in political and religious life and in custom and morality—as law is today in many informal communities such as the school, the neighborhood, the factory, the village. Neither in the Frankish Empire nor in Anglo-Saxon England nor elsewhere in Europe at that time was a sharp distinction made between legal norms and procedures, on the one hand, and religious, moral, economic, political, or other standards and practices, on the other. There were, to be sure, laws, and occasionally collections of laws, issued by kings; but there were no professional lawyers or judges, no professional legal scholars, no law schools, no law books, no legal science. This was true also in the church: canon law was fused with theology, and except for some rather primitively organized collections of canons and the monastic books of penalties for sins, there was nothing that could be called a literature of ecclesiastical law.

5. In the Western legal tradition law is conceived to be a coherent whole, an integrated system, a "body," and this body is conceived to be developing in time, over generations and centuries. The concept of law as a *corpus juris* might be thought to be implicit in every legal tradition in which law is viewed as distinct from morality and from custom; and it is often supposed that such a concept was not only implicit but also explicit in the Roman law of Justinian. However, the phrase *corpus juris Romani* was not used by the Romans but by the twelfth- and thirteenth-century European canonists and Romanists who extrapolated the concept from the work of those who, one or two centuries earlier, had discovered the old Justinian texts and taught them in the European universities. It was the twelfth-century scholastic technique of reconciling contradictions and deriving general concepts from rules and cases that first made it possible to coordinate and integrate the Roman law of Justinian.[6]

6. The concept of a body or system of law depended for its vitality on the belief in the ongoing character of law, its capacity for growth over generations and centuries—a belief which is uniquely Western. The body of law only survives because it contains a built-in mechanism for organic change.

7. The growth of law is thought to have an internal logic; changes are not only adaptations of the old to the new, but are also part of a pattern of changes. The process of development is subject to certain regularities and, at least in hindsight, reflects an inner necessity. It is presupposed in the Western legal tradition that changes do not occur at random but proceed by reinterpretation of the past to meet present and future needs. The law is not merely ongoing; it has a history. It tells a story.

8. The historicity of law is linked with the concept of its supremacy over the political authorities. The developing body of law, both at any given moment and in the long run, is conceived by some—although not by all, and not necessarily even by most—to be binding upon the state itself. Although it remained for the American Revolution to contribute the word "constitutionalism," nevertheless, since the twelfth century in all countries of the West, even under absolute monarchies, it has been widely said and often accepted that in some important respects law transcends politics. The monarch, it is argued, may make law, but he may not make it arbitrarily, and until he has remade it—lawfully—he is bound by it.

9. Perhaps the most distinctive characteristic of the Western legal tradition is the coexistence and competition within the same community of diverse jurisdictions and diverse legal systems. It is this plurality of jurisdictions and legal systems that makes the supremacy of law both necessary and possible.

Legal pluralism originated in the differentiation of the ecclesiastical polity from secular polities. The church declared its freedom from secular control, its exclusive jurisdiction in some matters, and its concurrent jurisdiction in other matters. Laymen, though governed generally by secular law, were subject to ecclesiastical law, and to the jurisdiction of ecclesiastical courts, in matters of marriage and family relations, inheritance, spiritual crimes, contract relations where faith was pledged, and a number of other matters as well. Conversely, the clergy, though governed generally by canon law, were subject to secular law, and to the jurisdiction of secular courts, with respect to certain types of crimes, certain types of property disputes, and the like. Secular law itself was divided into various competing types, including royal law, feudal law, manorial law, urban law, and mercantile law. The same person might be subject to the ecclesiastical courts in one type of case, the king's court in another, his lord's court in a third, the manorial court in a fourth, a town court in a fifth, a merchants' court in a sixth.

The very complexity of a common legal *order* containing diverse legal *systems* contributed to legal sophistication. Which court has jurisdiction? Which law is applicable? How are legal differences to be reconciled? Behind the technical questions lay important political and economic considerations: church versus crown, crown versus town, town versus lord, lord versus merchant, and so on. Law was a way of resolving the political and economic conflicts. Yet law could also serve to exacerbate them.

The pluralism of Western law, which has both reflected and reinforced the pluralism of Western political and economic life, has been, or once was, a source of development, or growth — legal growth as well as political and economic growth. It also has been, or once was, a source of freedom. A serf might run to the town court for protection against his master. A vassal might run to the king's court for protection against his lord. A cleric might run to the ecclesiastical court for protection against the king.

10. There is a tension between the ideals and realities, between the dynamic qualities and the stability, between the transcendence and the immanence of the Western legal tradition. This tension has periodically led to the violent overthrow of legal systems by revolution. Nevertheless, the legal tradition, which is something bigger than any of the legal systems that comprise it, survived and, indeed, was renewed by such revolutions.

Law and History

To follow the story of the Western legal tradition, and to accept it, is to confront implicit theories both of law and of history that are no longer widely accepted, at least in the universities. The theories that do prevail pose serious obstacles to an appreciation of the story.

The conventional concept of law as a body of rules derived from statutes and court decisions — reflecting a theory of the ultimate source of law in the will of the lawmaker ("the state") — is wholly inadequate to support a study of a transnational legal culture. To speak of the Western legal tradition is to postulate a concept of law, not as a body of rules, but as a process, an enterprise, in which rules have meaning only in the context of institutions and procedures, values, and ways of thought. From this broader perspective the sources of law include not only the will of the lawmaker but also the reason and conscience of the community and its customs and usages. This is not the prevailing view of law. But it is by no means unorthodox: it used to be said, and not long ago, that there are four sources of law: legislation, precedent, equity, and custom.[7] In the formative era of the Western legal tradition there was not nearly so much legislation or so much precedent as there came to be in later centuries. The bulk of law was derived from custom, which was viewed in the light of equity (defined as reason and conscience). It is necessary to recognize that custom and equity are as much law as statutes and decisions, if the story of the Western legal tradition is to be followed and accepted.

Beyond that, it is necessary to recognize that law in the West is formed into integrated legal systems, in each of which the various constituent elements take their meaning partly from the system as a whole. Further, each system is conceived to be a developing one; therefore, the meaning of each constituent element is derived not only from what the system has been in the past but also from what it is coming to be in the future. These, too, are not conventional truths of the prevailing "analytical jurisprudence," which postulates a sovereign who issues commands in the form of rules and imposes sanctions for failure to apply them as "he willed" them to be applied — what Max Weber called the "formal rationality" or "logical formalism" of Western law. And this is widely believed to be an accurate description, both by those who are against formalism and by those who are for it. Weber thought it explained the utility of law for the development of capitalism. Such a concept of law is a formidable obstacle to an understanding of the story of the Western legal tradition, which originated in what is usually thought to be the era of feudalism, and which stemmed from the separation of the church from the secular order. The fact that the new system of canon law, created in the late eleventh and twelfth centuries, constituted the first modern Western legal system has been generally overlooked, perhaps just because it does not fit in with the prevailing theories of the nature of law.

If analytical jurisprudence, or, as it is now more often called, legal positivism, is an inadequate theoretical basis for grasping the narrative of the development of Western legal institutions, what theory or theories would provide a better basis? The chief alternatives presented by Western legal philosophy itself are "natural-law theory" and "historical jurisprudence." In addition, in recent times a new school called "sociological jurisprudence" has come to the fore. All of these schools have, of course, many variants. Yet each theory, taken by itself, focuses on only one aspect of the truth. None of them, standing alone, offers a basis for understanding the history of law in the West. The story of the Western legal tradition is itself, in part, a story of the emergence and clash of these various schools of legal philosophy. They do not explain history; it is history that explains them—why they emerged, and why different schools have prevailed in different places at different times.

In the formative era of the Western legal tradition, natural-law theory predominated. It was generally believed that human law derived ultimately from, and was to be tested ultimately by, reason and conscience. According not only to the legal philosophy of the time but also to positive law itself, any positive law, whether enacted or customary, had to conform to natural law, or else it would lack validity as law and could be disregarded. This theory had a basis in Christian theology as well as in Aristotelian philosophy. But it also had a basis in the history of the struggle between ecclesiastical and secular authorities, and in the politics of pluralism. One may compare it with the theory that accompanies the law of the United States, under which any positive law must conform to the constitutional requirements of "due process," "equal protection," "freedom," "privacy," and the like, or lose its validity. "Due process of law" is, in fact, a fourteenth-century English phrase meaning natural law. Thus natural-law theory is written into the positive law of the United States. This does not, however, prevent one from giving a political ("positivist") explanation of it. It is easy enough to show that the state, or the powers that be, or the ruling class, benefits from the due process clause and "wills" it to be.

Similarly, historical jurisprudence—the theory that law derives its meaning and authority from the past history of the people whose law it is, from their customs, from the genius of their institutions, from their historic values, from precedents—has been built into the English legal *system* since the English Revolution of the seventeenth century; yet English legal *philosophy* has swung between positivism and natural-law theory, and historical jurisprudence has had relatively few adherents, at least in the twentieth century. It is Germany—which in contrast to

England created its national law, especially in the nineteenth century, not so much out of its own historic legal institutions as out of a received "alien" Roman law—that has been the homeland of historical jurisprudence, in whose name the greatest German jurists have sung praises to German law as a reflection of the spirit of the German people.

Thus Western legal history has been the breeding ground of a variety of schools of legal philosophy, some of which have been dominant in some times and places and others in others, often for paradoxical reasons—as if in ideological reaction against the existing legal realities. Students of Western legal history must therefore guard against the limitations of each of the individual schools. It would be more appropriate, and more "Western," to use all of them as screens to be placed successively over historical experience rather than to attempt to use history as a buttress for any one of them.

If various schools of legal theory pose obstacles to an understanding or acceptance of the story of the Western legal tradition, far greater obstacles are posed by various theories of history, including legal history. These theories deal with such questions as whether history has a meaning, or direction; whether periodization of history is justified, and if so, on what basis; whether one can speak of "laws of history," or of historical causation in any sense (for example, economic base and ideological superstructure, or primacy of power); and on a somewhat lower level of generalization, with questions concerning the relationship of the history of each individual nation to the history of the West as a whole; the role of the great revolutions in Western history; and the meaning of concepts such as "medieval" and "modern," "feudalism" and "capitalism."

Although the story of the origin and early development of the Western legal tradition can be told without attempting to resolve these large historiographical issues, it is necessary to deal briefly with several theoretical questions concerning history in general and Western history in particular in order to dispel common preconceptions about them. Moreover, the story itself illuminates some of these theoretical questions in a remarkable way.

Questions of meaning and direction in history and related questions of periodization arise inevitably from the dramatic circumstances in which the Western legal tradition came into being. The actors in this drama had no doubt that they were fulfilling an historical destiny. Their confidence does not, of course, in itself refute the position taken by many today that history has no meaning, that changes in history are random, and that any periodization is arbitrary. However, those who go so far as to reject all meaning in history, all direction, and all periodization should not have any greater objection to the story told here than they would have to more conventional accounts that merely attach to the same events and facts less meaning, less direction, and a less strict periodization. If all periodization is arbitrary, then an analysis of the emergence of "modern" legal and political institutions in the "late eleventh century" is no more arbitrary than the conventional analysis which insists that everything before the "sixteenth century" is "medieval" and that there was no radical discontinuity in the period from 1050 to 1150 or 1200. Similarly, people who believe that there are no patterns in the historical development of institutions in the West should be no more dismayed by an account which sees an interaction between revolution and evolution over generations and centuries than they are by accounts that see only revolution or only evolution.

Those who will have most difficulty with the story told here are those who have never directly confronted the problems of meaning and direction and periodization but who uncritically accept the conventional historiography that has been generally taught since the sixteenth century. This view simply assumes that Western history is divided into three periods: ancient, medieval, and modern. Ancient history is the history of Greece and Rome. The decline of Rome, due to the barbarian invasions, produced a medieval age, which lasted roughly from the fifth to the fifteenth century. Then modern times began—some would say with the Renaissance, others would say with the Reformation, still others would say with both. Those who say Reformation may tell a slightly different story. Ancient Israel will be introduced into the picture of the Ancient World. The Middle Ages will be defined by the period between the early Church and Luther's break with Rome. The Protestants, however, will unite with the Humanists in saying that Western art and thought go back to Greece, and Western politics and law go back to Rome. Finally, under the influence of the Enlightenment, all will agree that although Greece and Rome and perhaps ancient Israel form the historical background of Western civilization, the history that really counts is the history of the individual nations—especially the United States, England, France and Germany.

This conception of the past has a great deal of meaning, a great deal of direction, a great deal of periodization. It is, however, quite inconsistent with the best historical research of the last five decades. That research has pushed the "dark ages" back from the period before 1450–1500 to the period before 1050–1100. Even the most conservative historians now distinguish sharply between the Low Middle Ages and the High Middle Ages. Further, the previously postulated continuity of the history of the Germanic peoples in the Low Middle Ages with the history of the Roman Empire, and with Roman and Greek history generally, has been largely discounted. The large-scale revival of Greek philosophy and Roman law in the late eleventh, twelfth, and thirteenth centuries has been shown to be part of a critical turning point in both the history of the

Western church and the history of the European nations, and to have been connected also with the rise of European cities and with other basic social and economic changes.

Here, whatever the proof, many people will experience doubt and frustration. Perhaps they will say to themselves: "Patterns, regularities, in history may be necessary — though they do go beyond the facts — since without them there would be no history. But radical discontinuities are unnecessary, and even unnatural. 'Nature does not make leaps.' But even if Western history has sometimes made leaps, as in the Russian Revolution, the French Revolution, and the Protestant Reformation, still, to say that a radical discontinuity occurred in the very middle of the 'Middle Ages' seems not only unnatural but also unfamiliar. It seems incongruous in view of what we have been taught about the Age of Faith. Why may we not continue to believe that the differences between European society in the year 1500 and in the year 500 resulted from a long series of small incremental changes, with some periods of greater acceleration but without any dramatic changes in a single generation or a single century? Why not continue to believe that the cities were founded (or revived) gradually over ten, or five, or at least three centuries, rather than suddenly over eighty or ninety years; that the pope became supreme judge and legislator in the church gradually over ten centuries, rather than suddenly over three generations; that the emperor and kings of Europe gradually lost their sacral functions and their thaumaturgical character, not as the result of open political and religious conflict but as the result of incremental shifts in attitudes?"

A study of the origins of the Western legal tradition should correct this ideological bias in favor of incremental change. Since law changes more slowly than most other political institutions, one would not usually expect rapid and dramatic changes in a legal system. Nevertheless, one who investigates any of the legal systems of Europe first in the period of 1000–1050 and then in the period 1150–1200 finds a tremendous transformation. This is true, above all, of the law of the church.

To speak of revolutionary change within the Church of Rome is, of course, to challenge the orthodox (though not the Eastern Orthodox) view that the structure of the Roman Catholic church is the result of a gradual elaboration of elements that had been present from very early times. This was, indeed, the official view of the Catholic Reformers of the late eleventh and early twelfth centuries: they were only going back, they said, to an earlier tradition that had been betrayed by their immediate predecessors. The myth of a return to an earlier time is, in fact, the hallmark of all the European revolutions. Luther also preached a return to early Christianity following its betrayal by the papacy. The English Puritans under Cromwell preached a restoration of "ancient English liberties" after one hundred and fifty years of Tudor despotism. The

French Revolution went back to classical antiquity and a state of nature to combat feudalism and aristocratic privilege. The Russian Bolsheviks preached a return to the classless society of primitive tribes before the dawn of property.

A radical transformation of a legal system is, however, a paradoxical thing, since one of the fundamental purposes of law is to provide stability and continuity. Moreover, law—in all societies—derives its authority from something outside itself, and if a legal system undergoes rapid change, then questions are inevitably raised concerning the legitimacy of the sources of its authority. In law, large-scale sudden change—revolutionary change—is, indeed, "unnatural." When it happens, something must be done to prevent it from happening again. The new law must be firmly established; it must be protected against the danger of another discontinuity. Further changes must be confined to incremental changes.

This, at least, has been the course of Western legal development in the wake of the large-scale revolutionary transformations that have periodically overtaken it, starting with that of the late eleventh and early twelfth centuries. A historical dimension has been given to the new legal system established by the revolution. In the first place, the new legal system is considered to be rooted historically in the events that produced it. In the second place, it is considered to have changed not only in response to new circumstances but also according to some historical pattern. The law is considered to be a historical phenomenon; it is considered to have what might be called historicity. It must not only evolve but also must be seen to evolve.

Nevertheless, the historicity of Western law has not prevented the periodic outbreak of violent revolutions that have, to be sure, eventually returned to the historical legal tradition but that have at the same time transformed it and sent it in new directions.

The historicity of law in the West is not to be confused with historicism, in the sense of bondage to the "blind power" (in Nietzsche's phrase) of the past. Not only the adherent of the historical school of legal philosophy but also the positivist and the natural-law theorist, or, for that matter, the cynic who believes that law is simply the will of the stronger—all these are confronting legal institutions and procedures, legal values, and legal concepts and rules that have, in fact, a historical dimension. They derive their meaning in part from their history. It is never enough, in any Western legal system, to attempt to interpret or explain a legal rule (or concept or value or institution) solely by appeal to logic or policy or fairness; it must also be interpreted and explained in part by appeal to the circumstances that brought it into being and by the course of events that have influenced it over time. The dogmatic method, the political method, and the method of equity are always subject to supplementation by the historical method of interpretation. The plurality of the sources of law thus protect historicity and at the same time help to prevent blind historicism.

Blind historicism is also frustrated by the plurality of overlapping histories which constitute Western civilization. It is not "the past" in any monolithic sense that constitutes the historical dimension of law but rather the past times of the various communities in which each person lives and of the various legal systems that those communities have produced. It is only when the different legal regimes of all these communities—local, regional, national, ethnic, professional, polititical, intellectual, spiritual, and others—are swallowed up in the law of the nation-state that "history" becomes tyrannical.

This is, in fact, the greatest danger inherent in contemporary nationalism. The nations of Europe, which originated in their interaction with one another in the context of Western Christendom, became more and more detached from one another in the nineteenth century. With World War I, they broke apart violently and destroyed the common bonds that had previously held them together, however loosely. And in the late twentieth century we still suffer from the nationalist historiography that originated in the nineteenth century and that supported the disintegration of a common Western legal heritage.

The emergence in the nineteenth century of so-called scientific history, that is, of systematic and painstaking research into the facts, intended to show, in Ranke's famous phrase, *wie es eigentlich gewesen ist* ("how it actually was"), coincided with the emergence of the most intense nationalism that Europe had yet experienced. It was simply assumed that history meant national history. History was to be objective, but it was to be the history of the nation. In the twentieth century there has been some change in this respect. The social and economic historians were among the first to break the nationalist barrier and to write about the West as a whole. After World War I this approach was extended by some persons to political history. Even European legal history came to be treated in transnational terms, although English and American legal history remained peculiarly isolated.

It is unfortunate that hardly any attempt has been made to integrate English and American legal history into the panorama of Western legal systems. Such an integration has been made extremely difficult by the insularity of English and American legal historians, who, in addition, have carved up the subject matter of their respective disciplines in such a way as to mystify the stranger who might otherwise wish to intrude. Even for the period in which all the nations of the West, including England, were within the Roman Catholic Church and not only lived under the same system of ecclesiastical law but also had the closest intellectual, cultural and political ties with one another, English law is still treated by many legal historians as though it were outside of European history. These historians are able to sustain their nationalist orientation by concentrating on the so-called common law, that is, the law applied in the royal courts of Common Pleas and King's Bench, and by ignoring the other bodies of law and other jurisdictions that existed in England at the same time. But even the English common law, in this narrow sense, was similar in many ways to the royal or ducal law of Sicily, France, the German duchies, and other countries of Europe.

Edmund Burke once said, "The laws of all the nations of Europe are derived from the same sources." For him, England was part of Europe. By the time legal history had become a matter of scientific inquiry, however, England's historical links with the Continent had been cut. This led to an exaggerated emphasis upon those legal institutions, values, concepts, and rules that distinguish English law from other Western legal systems. Now that England has joined the European Economic Community, a revision of English legal history may occur that will emphasize those legal institutions, procedures, values, concepts, and rules that English law shares with other Western legal systems.

In 1888, in his Inaugural Lecture as Downing Professor at Cambridge University, Maitland raised the question "why the history of English law is not written." His answer was, first, "because of the traditional isolation of the study of English law from every other study," and second, because "history involves comparison and the English lawyer who knew nothing and cared nothing for any system but his own hardly came in sight of the idea of legal history." "One of the causes why so little has been done for our medieval law," he added, "is, I feel sure, our very complete and traditional consecrated ignorance of French and German law. English lawyers have for the last six centuries exaggerated the uniqueness of our legal history . . . I know just enough to say this with confidence, that there are great masses of medieval law very comparable with our own."[8]

Law and Revolution

The Western legal tradition has been transformed in the course of its history by six great revolutions. Three of them—the Russian Revolution, the French Revolution, and the American Revolution—were called revolutions by those who participated in them, although the meaning of the word "revolution" was different in each case. A fourth, the English Revolution, was first called a revolution (the Glorious Revolution) only when it was coming to an end in 1688–89; in its initial stage (1640–1660) it was called the Great Rebellion by its enemies and a "restoration of freedom" by its friends,[9] the second stage (1660–1685) was called the Restoration at the time, although some contemporary writers also called it a revolution. (That was the first modern use of the word *revolution* to identify a major political upheaval; it meant, however, a turn of the wheel back to an earlier system of government.) Thus what most historians now call the English Revolution consisted of three successive "restorations."[10]

The fifth great revolution — still going backward in time — was the Protestant Reformation, which in Germany had the character of a national revolution, starting with Luther's attack upon the papacy in 1517 and ending in 1555 with the frustration of the Emperor by the Protestant League and the establishment of religious peace among the German principalities. The sixth, the Papal Revolution of 1075–1122, which is the subject of this study, was also called a reformation at the time, the *Reformatio* of Pope Gregory VII, generally translated into modern languages as the Gregorian Reform, thereby concealing still further its revolutionary character.

Objections may be raised to calling the German Reformation a revolution, despite the fact that it is often called that by historians of revolutions, including many who are not Marxists. Still stronger objections may be raised to calling the Gregorian Reformation a revolution (or even, perhaps, a reformation). An explanation is therefore in order concerning the use of the word "revolution."

The history of the West has been marked by recurrent periods of violent upheaval, in which the preexisting system of political, legal, economic, religious, cultural, and other social relations, institutions, beliefs, values, and goals has been overthrown and replaced by a new one. There is by no means a perfect symmetry in these periods of great historical change; yet there are certain patterns or regularities. Each has marked
    a fundamental change,
    a rapid change,
    a violent change,
    a lasting change,
    in the social system as a whole.
Each has sought legitimacy in
    a fundamental law,
    a remote past,
    an apocalyptic future.
Each took more than one generation to establish roots.
Each eventually produced
    a new system of law,
    which embodied some of the major purposes of the revolution,
    and which changed the Western legal tradition,
    but which ultimately remained within that tradition.

These upheavals were not, on the one hand, coups d'etat or rebellions, or, on the other hand, long series of incremental changes that were accommodated within the preexisting system. They were fundamental transformations that were accomplished relatively rapidly and with great struggle and passion.

It is appropriate to use the word *revolution* — despite all the abuses to which it has been subjected[11] — to refer to such epoch-making periods, in light of the connotation of violence that is associated with the revolutions of the past two centuries, especially the Russian, the French, and the American. Here "violence" does not refer to the legal force imposed by established governments through police or armies, but to illegal force exerted by individuals and groups against established authority. From the point of view of the history of Western law, it is of special importance to recognize that periodically in Western history such illegal force has been exerted to overthrow the established order, and that eventually those raised to authority as a result of such an overthrow have created new and enduring systems of government and law. The system of government and law of every nation of the West goes back to such a revolution.

The term revolution is used to refer not only to the initial violent events by which a new system is introduced but also to the entire period required for that system to take root. As Eugen Rosenstock-Huessy has emphasized, more than one generation is needed to make a genuine revolution.[12]

The six great revolutions were "total" revolutions in that they involved not only the creation of new forms of government but also new structures of social and economic relations, new structures of relations between church and state, and new structures of law, as well as new visions of the community, new perspectives on history, and new sets of universal values and beliefs.[13] "The reformation of the world," which was a slogan of the Papal Revolution, had an almost exact counterpart in each of the other revolutions. To be sure, much of the old survived, and after some time even more of the old was brought back, but in each revolution the totality — the paradigm — was new.

Thus each of the six revolutions produced a new or greatly revised system of law, in the context of what was conceived as a total social transformation. Indeed, the extent to which its purpose was eventually embodied in new law marks the success of the revolution.

Each revolution represents the failure of the old legal system that the revolution replaced or radically changed. These systems were failures if only in the sense that they were, in fact, replaced or radically changed. One of the first decrees of the Bolshevik government in 1917 was to declare that the entire prerevolutionary legal system was abolished. Henceforth only the decrees of the new government were to be applied, with gaps to be filled by "revolutionary legal consciousness." The French Revolution also discarded, at first, the system of legislation, administration, and adjudication of the ancien régime. In America, after independence was won, democrats fought against the reception of English law by the federal and state courts. In England, the Long Parliament of 1640-41 abolished the Court of Star Chamber, the Court of High Commission, and the other royal "prerogative courts," and this legislation was reenacted by Charles II's Parliament in 1660; together with parliamentary supremacy, a greatly revised common law became England's unwritten constitution. Luther burned the canon law books. Pope Gregory VII denounced the imperial and royal laws by which the Church had been governed—laws which permitted bishops and priests to be appointed to their posts by the secular authorities, church offices to be bought and sold, and the clergy to marry.

The old law was also a failure in another sense: it proved incapable of responding, in time, to the changes that were taking place in society. If the tsarist government had introduced an effective constitutional monarchy and had redistributed the land; if the Bourbon kings had disestablished the church, abolished the remnants of feudalism, and permitted the creation of democratic institutions; if King George III had granted the American colonists all the rights of his English subjects and had, in addition, permitted them to introduce democratic institutions; if the first Stuart kings had accepted the supremacy of Parliament; if the canon law had yielded, in the fifteenth century, to conciliarism and to other pressures for reform; if eleventh-century emperors and kings had given up, in time, their supremacy over the church—if, in short, the inevitable had been anticipated and necessary fundamental changes had been made within the preexisting legal order—then the revolutions would presumably have been avoided. To change *in time* is the key to the vitality of any legal system that confronts irresistible pressure for change. A revolution, in the historical sense of that term, is a rapid, discontinuous, violent change that bursts the bonds of the legal system.

It may be that the failure to anticipate fundamental changes, and to incorporate them in time, is due to an inherent contradiction in the nature of the Western legal tradition, one of whose purposes is to preserve order and another is to do justice. Order itself is conceived as having a built-in tension between the need for change and the need for stability. Justice also is seen in dialectical terms, involving a tension between the rights of the individual and the welfare of the community. The realization of justice has been proclaimed as a messianic ideal of the law itself, originally associated (in the Papal Revolution) with the Last Judgment and the Kingdom of God, then (in the German Revolution) with the Christian conscience, later (in the English Revolution) with public spirit, fairness, and the traditions of the past, still later (in the French and American Revolutions) with public opinion, reason, and the rights of man, and most recently (in the Russian Revolution) with collectivism, planned economy, and social equality. It was the messianic ideal of justice, above all, that found expression in the great revolutions. The overthrow of the preexisting *law as order* was justified as the reestablishment of a more fundamental *law as justice*. It was the belief that the law was betraying its ultimate purpose and mission that brought on each of the great revolutions.

Thomas Kuhn has explained great revolutions in science, such as the Copernican, Newtonian, and Einsteinian revolutions, as the result of crises that occur periodically when those phenomena that cannot be explained in terms of the basic postulates of the established science, and hence are treated as anomalies, are discovered to require new basic postulates. The new basic postulates that are devised to explain as "natural" what were previously though to be merely "anomalous" become, as Kuhn shows, the core of a new scientific "paradigm."[14] The interaction of revolution and evolution in Western law offers a striking parallel to the interaction of revolution and evolution in Western science. In Western law, as in western science, it is presupposed that changes in the data—the "givens," the conditions—will occur, that these changes will be assimilated into the existing system or paradigm, that if they are not assimilated they will be accepted as anomalies, but if too many of them appear to be incapable of such assimilation then at a certain point the system itself will require a drastic change. In science, the old truth may have to give way to a new one. In law, the old justice may have to give way to a new one.

Thus the great revolutions of Western political, economic, and social history represent explosions that have occurred when the legal system proved too rigid to assimilate new conditions. Some writers have treated these historic explosions as a kind of recurrent "cancer" in Western society, a "fever" that must run its course.[15] That, however, is only one side of the story, and not the most important side. They also constituted a great release of energy, which, to be sure, destroyed much of the past but also created a new future. Ultimately, each of the great revolutions may be seen to have been not so much a breakdown as a transformation. Each had to compromise with the past, but each also succeeded in producing a new kind of law that embodied many of the major purposes for which it had been fought.

To emphasize the legal dimension of the great revolutions—their rejection of the preexisting legal order and their ultimate contribution to a new kind of law—does not minimize but, on the contrary, enhances the importance of their political, economic, religious, cultural, and other social dimensions. Fundamental changes in law have inevitably been interlocked with fundamental changes in other structural elements of social life. More particularly, in the Papal Revolution of the late eleventh and early twelfth centuries, the reformation of law was intimately related to the entire range of "very profound and very widespread changes" of that time (in the words of the great social and economic historian Marc

Bloch), which "affected all the graphs of social activity."[16] Moreover, to call this total transformation the Papal Revolution does not limit its scope to such issues as the struggle for papal control over the church and for the freedom of the church, under the papacy, from secular domination, but, on the contrary, includes within its scope all the interrelated changes that took place at that time. The new papal concept of the church, as Joseph R. Strayer has said, "almost demanded the invention of the concept of the State."[17] The revolution in law was closely connected with the revolution *in* the church and the revolution *of* the church, which in turn were closely connected with the revolution in agriculture and commerce, the rise of cities and of kingdoms as autonomous territorial polities, the rise of the universities and of scholastic thought, and other major transformations which accompanied the birth of the West, as it thought of itself—and as it was thought of by others—during the next eight centuries and more. The name "Papal Revolution" is not to be taken narrowly; like the name "Puritan Revolution" applied to English history from 1640 to 1660, it points beyond itself.

The time period of the Papal Revolution is not limited to the relatively few years when it was at its height, so to speak, during the pontificate of Pope Gregory VII, any more than the time period of the Russian Revolution is limited to the few years when Lenin led the Bolsheviks to power and fought off their enemies. One may date the Papal Revolution from 1075—when Gregory proclaimed papal supremacy over the entire church and ecclesiastical independence from, and superiority over, the secular power—to 1122—when a final compromise was reached between the papal and the imperial authority. The repercussions, however, did not cease even then; the forces that were set in motion by these events continued to take effect for centuries.

Many historians shun explanations that involve such long time spans. They would rather attribute given conditions to causes that are contemporary with or that immediately precede those conditions. Yet if the question is posed sharply, it is hard to deny that current conditions are often determined to a significant degree by events that occurred even centuries earlier. For example, if one were to try to explain the crisis of race relations in the United States of America in the second half of the twentieth century, one could not omit the Declaration of Independence of 1776, the resolution of the slavery question in the United States Constitution of 1789, and the Civil War of 1861–1864. Surely the American Revolution set in motion forces that resulted in the emancipation of the slaves and ultimately in the struggle for civil rights.

THE WESTERN CHARACTER OF THE NATIONAL REVOLUTIONS

Like the Protestant Reformation in Germany, the English Revolution, the American Revolution, the French Revolution, and the Russian Revolution were, of course, national revolutions. The Papal Revolu-

tion, by contrast, was a transnational revolution, a revolution throughout Europe in behalf of the clergy, under the pope, against imperial,
royal, and feudal domination. Clearly, the Papal Revolution may be
called Western or European, but is it proper to characterize the national
revolutions in the same way? Two points should be made with respect to
this question that bear directly on an understanding of the Papal
Revolution.

First, all the national revolutions from the sixteenth century on — except the American — were directed in part against the Roman Catholic
(or in Russia, the Orthodox) Church, and all of them transferred large
portions of the canon·law from the church to the national state, thus
secularizing them. Therefore in studying the legal systems, both ecclesiastical and secular, that were created in the late eleventh and the
twelfth and thirteenth centuries under the impact of the Papal Revolution, it must be borne in mind that a great many elements of those
systems eventually passed into the secular law of all the European nations, under the impact of the national revolutions. In this respect, the
national revolutions had an international character.

Second, all the great national revolutions of the West were also, in
their very nature, Western revolutions. Each of them was prepared in
several countries. The Protestant Reformation was prepared by Wyclif
in England and Hus in Bohemia, as well as by active reform movements
in every country of Europe, before it broke out in Germany. The
Puritan movement in England not only was based on the earlier
teachings of the French-Swiss reformer John Calvin, but it also had close
ties with other Calvinist movements in Holland and elsewhere on the
Continent. The Enlightenment of the eighteenth century was an all-
Western phenomenon, which formed the ideological basis not only of
both the American and French revolutions but also of agitation for radical change in England and elsewhere. The Russian Revolution was born
in the international communist movement founded by two Germans; its
roots lay in the Paris Commune of 1870.

Similarly, the national revolutions had enormous all-Western repercussions after they broke out. The immediate effect of their outbreak was
invariably a reaction of fear and hostility in other countries — fear of the
spread of the revolutionary virus, hostility toward the nation that was its
bearer. Eventually, after twenty or thirty years, when the revolution had
settled down in its home country, the other countries accepted a mild
version of it. Thus, after the Lutheran Revolution had subsided in Germany, absolute monarchies with a strong civil service appeared in
England, France, and other countries; after the Puritan Revolution had
subsided in England, constitutional monarchies and quasi-parliamen-
tary institutions emerged on the European continent in the late 1600s
and early 1700s; after the French and American revolutions had subsided, the English enlarged the electorate to include the middle classes in

1832; and after the Russian Revolution had subsided, "socialist" or "new deal" governments appeared in the 1930s in western Europe and the United States.

More important, the legal institutions of the various nations of Europe, although they became more distinctively national and less European from the sixteenth century on, nevertheless retained their Western character. This was true despite the fact that the secular courts and secular law squeezed the ecclesiastical courts and the canon law into an increasingly narrower jurisdiction, and in addition, even the Roman Catholic Church became increasingly nationalized.

Nevertheless, there were many common bonds among the various national legal systems. All these systems share some basic modes of categorization. For example, they all strike a balance between legislation and adjudication and, in adjudication, between code law and case law. They make a sharp division between criminal law and civil law. In all, crimes are analyzed (as they were first analyzed by Abelard in the early twelfth century) in terms of act, intent or negligence, causation, duty, and similar concepts. In all, civil obligations are divided, either expressly or implicitly, into contract, delict (tort), and unjust enrichment (quasicontract). Behind these and many other common analytical categories lie common policies and common values. In the 1930s, for instance, when a statute of National Socialist Germany made punishable as a crime any act that "deserves punishment according to sound popular feeling (*gesundes Volksgefühl*)," this was viewed as a violation of the traditional Western concept of legality; and the Permanent Court of International Justice struck down a similar law of the Free City of Danzig, which was based on the German statute, as contrary to the rule of law (*Rechtsstaat*).

The Pursuit of the Millennium

An important element of each of the great revolutions of Western history was its apocalyptic vision of the future. Each was more than a political program, more even than a passionate struggle to reform the world. Each also represented a belief in, and a commitment to, an eschatology—a messianic dream of an end-time, a conviction that history was moving to a final dénouement. In the case of the Roman Catholic, the Lutheran, and the Puritan revolutions, the eschatology was expressed in biblical terms. The Christian revolutionaries foresaw "a new heaven and a new earth." They envisioned the fulfillment of the prophecy of a thousand years of peace on earth between the Second Coming and the Last Judgment. "And I John saw the holy city, new Jerusalem, coming down from God out of heaven . . . for the former things are passed away. And he that sat upon the throne said, Behold I make all things new." (Rev. 21:1–5). In the case of the American, French, and Russian revolutions, the eschatology was a secular one: a new and final era of freedom and equality, the end of man's long history of oppression, the dawn of a just society.

In his book *The Pursuit of the Millennium,* Norman Cohn has written about a different kind of "revolutionary millenarianism," as he calls it. He has focused attention on the numerous chiliastic movements among the "rootless poor" in Western Europe from the eleventh to the sixteenth century. These included the People's Crusades, the flagellant movements, the heresy of the Free Spirit, some peasant revolts, and the Taborites. Almost all of them were loosely organized, spontaneous, and either anarchistic or communistic or both. "It is characteristic of this kind of movement," Cohn writes, "that its aims and premises are boundless. A social struggle is seen [by the participants] not as a struggle for specific, limited objectives, but as . . . a cataclysm from which the world is to emerge totally transformed and redeemed."[18]

The difference between what Cohn has described and the apocalypticism of the great revolutions—the great *successful* revolutions—of Western history is that the latter's aims and premises were both boundless and bounded; their objectives were not only universal and unlimited but also specific and limited. They were millenarian but they were also well organized and politically sophisticated. Cohn's vivid and perceptive portrayal of millenarian movements of a specific type has led him and others to compare them with the modern revolutionary movements both of the left and of the right.[19] However, the historical roots of at least some of the modern movements, and especially of the Communist "millenarianism" of the nineteenth and twentieth centuries, are to be found not in the wildcat movements that Cohn describes but in the successful revolutions on whose fringes they appeared.

The successful revolutions were also based on a Christian eschatology, which in turn was based on the Judaic vision of history as moving toward a final dénouement, a climax. In contrast to the other Indo-European peoples, including the Greeks, who believed that time moved in ever recurring cycles, the Hebrew people conceived of time as continuous, irreversible, and historical, leading to ultimate redemption at the end. They also believed, however, that time has periods within it. It is not cyclical but may be interrupted or accelerated. It develops. The Old Testament is a story not merely of change but of development, of growth, of movement toward the messianic age—very uneven movement, to be sure, with much backsliding but nevertheless a movement *toward.* Christianity, however, added an important element to the Judaic concept of time: that of transformation of the old into the new. The Hebrew Bible became the Old Testament, its meaning transformed by its fulfillment in the New Testament. In the story of the Resurrection, death was transformed into a new beginning. The times were not only accelerated but regenerated. This introduced a new structure of history, in which there was a fundamental transformation of one age into another. This transformation, it was believed, could only happen once: the life, death, and resurrection of Christ was thought to be the only major interruption in the course of linear time from the creation of the world until it ends altogether.

Thus the Christian concept of renewal is based on the belief in the end of the world. It is also based on the belief that that end is imminent; it is "at hand." "The Christian sense of history," writes Norman O. Brown, "is the sense of living in the last days. Little children, it is the last hour. The whole Christian era is in the last days." "The Christian prayer is for the end of the world: that it may come quickly. The aim is to bring this world to an end; the only question is how. A mistake here might prove quite costly."[20]

Rosenstock-Huessy has shown how the belief in an end-time, the end of the world, has influenced the great revolutions of Western history. Each of those revolutions translated the experience of death and regeneration into a different concept of the nation and of the church.[21] When Christian eschatology was discarded by the Enlightenment and by liberal theology in the eighteenth and nineteenth centuries, a secular eschatology took its place. "No people," Rosenstock-Huessy writes, "can live without faith in the ultimate victory of something. So while theology slept, the laity betook itself to other sources of Last Things"—to the eschatology of Karl Marx, on the one hand, and of Friedrich Nietzsche, on the other.[22]

Before the great reform movement of the eleventh century, the church, both in the East and in the West, had taught that the end-time is not within this world, the material world, but within the spiritual world—not in historical time but in eternity. This was one of the main points of St. Augustine's contrast between the earthly city and the city of God. The earthly city is in perpetual decay. Those who live in the end-time are no longer of this world. For Augustine the same word, *saeculum,* meant "the world" and "time." The *saeculum* was without hope of redemption: it could only be abandoned for the realm of the spirit. St. Augustine and the church, generally, in the first ten centuries, were against revolutionary millenarian movements of the kind described by Cohn, which tried to transform the social and political and economic realities of the here and now into a heavenly kingdom of the spirit. The rebirth of the individual Christian believer as well as the regeneration of mankind were understood to refer only to the eternal soul, which experienced such rebirth or regeneration only by "dying to this world"—above all, through the monastic life.

Similarly, when Christianity first came to the Germanic peoples of western Europe, it was presented as an otherworldly faith, concerned with the sacred and the saintly and having relatively little to say to the existing military, political, and economic power structure, except to devalue it.

In the late eleventh and early twelfth centuries regeneration was for the first time seen as applicable also to the secular society. The reformers put themselves at the beginning and end of a new secular time: they projected backward into the past in order to project forward into the future. They saw themselves at a turning point in history, the beginning of a new age, which they thought would be the final age before the Last Judgment. This was a new interruption within the Christian era; it combined the Greek cyclical idea of a return with the Hebrew idea of linear movement toward a predestined end and the earlier Christian idea of a spiritual birth or a rebirth.

Each of the great revolutions, starting with the Papal Revolution of 1075, made a sharp division between what went before it, "the old," and what came with it and after it, "the new." Each of them also placed the historical old and new within a framework of an original creation, or state of nature, and a final end, an ultimate victory. Without the belief that this world, these times, the secular institutions of human society, could be regenerated—and that such regeneration would lead to the fulfillment of man's ultimate destiny—the great revolutions of Western history could not have occurred.

More specifically, the belief in the capacity of man to regenerate the world, and the necessity for him to do so in order to fulfill his ultimate destiny, provided a basis both for a conscious attack upon the existing order and for the conscious establishment of a new order. The sacred was used as a standard by which to measure the secular order. Thus the eleventh-century reformers began to judge emperors and kings and lords according to principles derived from divine and natural law. The papal party denounced the emperor for betraying the office of ruler of the church and charged that he did not have title to it. It was Daniel's challenge to Nebuchadnezzar: "Mene, mene, tekel, upharsin"—"tekel: thou art weighed in the balances, and art found wanting" (Dan. 5:25, 27). "Freedom of the church," the slogan of the Papal Revolution, was justified as God's will. So also in all subsequent great revolutionary periods of Western history, transcendent standards have been invoked against the existing power structure. When Karl Marx (quoting Proudhon) said, "Property is theft," he was speaking in the Western millenarian tradition: the whole economic and political system was weighed in the balances of the end-time, the *eschaton,* and found wanting.

REVOLUTIONARY LAW

The revolutionary belief in the end of time, the final millennium, helps to account not only for the overthrow of the old law but also for the embodiment of the revolution in a new system of law. This could not happen right away. None of the great revolutions succeeded in abolishing the prerevolutionary law on the first day and establishing a new and permanent system of revolutionary law on the second day. For example, the Bolsheviks in 1917 declared inheritance to be abolished, but at the same time they enacted a decree to the effect that estates up to 10,000 gold rubles would continue to pass to heirs according to the old rules until a system could be worked out for administering smaller estates. It proved impossible, however, to work out a system whereby the state could effectively inherit a cow, household furniture, art objects, or even money. The next resort was to a very high inheritance tax; but this measure eventually conflicted with efforts to promote family stability, and it was easily evaded by gifts in anticipation of death.

Each of the great revolutions experienced an interim period in which new laws, decrees, regulations, and orders were enacted in rapid succession and as rapidly amended, repealed, or replaced. Eventually, however, each of the great revolutions made its peace with the pre-revolutionary law and restored many of its elements by including them in a new system that reflected the major goals, values, and beliefs for which the revolution had been fought. Thus the new systems of law established by the great revolutions transformed the legal tradition while remaining within it.

The Lutheran Reformation, and the revolution of the German principalities which embodied it, broke the Roman Catholic dualism of ecclesiastical and secular law by delegalizing the church. Where Lutheranism succeeded, the church came to be conceived as invisible, apolitical, alegal; and the only sovereignty, the only law (in the political sense), was that of the secular kingdom or principality. It was just before this time, in fact, that Machiavelli had used the word "state" in a new way, to signify the purely secular social order. The Lutheran reformers were in one sense Machiavellians: they were skeptical of man's power to create a human law which would reflect eternal law, and they explicitly denied that it was the task of the church to develop human law. This Lutheran skepticism made possible the emergence of a theory of law—legal positivism—which treats the law of the state as morally neutral, a means and not an end, a device for manifesting the policy of the sovereign and for securing obedience to it. But the secularization of law and the emergence of a positivist theory of law are only one side of the story of the contribution of the Lutheran Reformation to the Western legal tradition. The other side is equally important: by freeing law from theological doctrine and from direct ecclesiastical influence, the Reformation enabled it to undergo a new and brilliant development. In the words of the great German jurist and historian Rudolf Sohm, "Luther's Reformation was a renewal not only of faith but also of the world: both the world of spiritual life and the world of law."[23]

The key to the renewal of law in the West from the sixteenth century on was the Lutheran concept of the power of the individual, by God's grace, to change nature and to create new social relations through the exercise of his will. The Lutheran concept of the individual will become central to the development of the modern law of property and contract. To be sure, there had been an elaborate and sophisticated law of property and of contract, both in the church and in the mercantile community, for some centuries, but in Lutheranism its focus was changed. Old rules were recast in a new ensemble. Nature became property. Economic relations became contract. Conscience became will and intent. The last testament, which in the earlier Catholic tradition had been primarily a means of saving souls by charitable gifts, became primarily a means of controlling social and economic relations. By the naked expression of their will, their intent, testators could dispose of their property after death, and entrepreneurs could arrange their business relations by contract. The property and contract rights so created were held to be sacred and inviolable, so long as they did not contravene conscience. Conscience gave them their sanctity. And so the secularization of the state, in the restricted sense of the removal of ecclesiastical controls from it, was accompanied by a spiritualization, and even a sanctification, of property and contract.

Therefore it is not true to say that Lutheranism placed no limits on the political power of the absolute monarchs who ruled Europe in the sixteenth century. The development of positive law was conceived to rest ultimately upon the prince alone, but it was presupposed that in exercising his will he would respect the individual consciences of his subjects, and that meant respecting also their property and contract rights. This presupposition rested—precariously, to be sure—upon four centuries of history in which the church had succeeded in Christianizing law to a remarkable extent, given the level of the cultural life of the Germanic peoples in the beginning. Thus a Lutheran positivism which separates law from morals, denies the lawmaking role of the church, and finds the ultimate sanction of law in political coercion nevertheless assumes the existence of a Christian conscience among the people and a state governed by Christian rulers.

A slightly later form of Protestantism, Calvinism, also had profound effects upon the development of Western law, especially in England and America. The Puritans carried forward the Lutheran concept of the sanctity of the individual conscience and also, in law, the sanctity of the individual will as reflected in property and contract rights. But they emphasized two elements that were subordinated in Lutheranism: first, a belief in the duty of Christians generally, and not merely Christian rulers, to reform the world;[24] and second, a belief in the local congregation, under its elected minister and elders, as the seat of truth—a "fellowship of active believers" higher than any political authority.[25] The active Puritan congregations, bent on reforming the world, were ready to defy the highest powers of church and of state in asserting their faith, and they did so on grounds of individual conscience, also appealing to divine law, to the Mosaic law of the Old Testament, and to natural-law concepts embodied in the medieval legal tradition. As the early Christian martyrs had founded the church by their disobedience to Roman law, so the seventeenth-century Puritans, including men like John Hampden, John Lilburne, Walter Udall, and William Penn, by their open disobedience to English law laid the foundations for the English and American law of civil rights and civil liberties as expressed in the respective constitutions of the two countries: freedom of speech and press, free exercise of religion, the privilege against self-incrimination, the independence of the jury from judicial dictation, the right not to be imprisoned without cause, and many other such rights and freedoms.[26] Calvinist congregationalism also provided the religious basis for the modern concepts of social contract and government by consent of the governed.[27]

Puritanism in England and America, and Pietism, its counterpart on the European continent, were the last great movements within the institutional church to influence the development of Western law in any fundamental sense. In the eighteenth and nineteenth centuries both the Roman Catholic Church and the various Lutheran denominations continued, of course, to exert pressures upon law in various directions. Undoubtedly, prophetic Christianity continued to play an extremely important part in bringing about law reform—for example, in the abolition of slavery, in the protection of labor, and in the promotion of welfare legislation generally. And undoubtedly, on the other side, organized religion continued to support the status quo, whatever it happened to be. But the significant factor in this regard—in the nineteenth century and even more in the twentieth—was the very gradual reduction of traditional religion to the level of a personal, private matter, without public influence on legal development, while other belief systems—new secular religions (ideologies, "isms")—were raised to the level of passionate faiths for which people collectively were willing not only to die but also to live new lives.

It was the American and French revolutions that set the stage for the new secular religions—that is, for pouring into secular political and social movements the religious psychology as well as many of the religious ideas that had previously been expressed in various forms of Catholicism and Protestantism. At first a kind of religious orthodoxy was preserved by means of a deistic philosophy—which, however, had little of that psychology which is the heart of religious faith. What was religious, in fact, about the great revolutionary minds of the late eighteenth and nineteenth centuries—men like Rousseau or Jefferson—was not their belief in God but their belief in Man, individual Man, his Nature, his Reason, his Rights. The political and social philosophies that sprang from the Enlightenment were religions because they ascribed ultimate meaning and sanctity to the individual mind—and also, it must be added immediately, to the nation. The age of individualism and rationalism was also the age of nationalism: the individual was a citizen, and public opinion turned out to be not the opinion of mankind but the opinion of Frenchmen, the opinion of Germans, the opinion of Americans.

Individualism, rationalism, nationalism—the Triune Deity of Democracy—found legal expression in the exaltation of the role of the legislature and consequent reduction (except in the United States) of the law-creating role of the judiciary; in the freeing of individual actions from public controls, especially in the economic sphere; in the demand for codification of criminal and civil law; in the effort to make predictable the legal consequences of individual actions, again especially in the economic sphere. These "jural postulates" (as Roscoe Pound would have called them)[28] were considered to be not only useful but also just, and not only just but also part of the natural order of the universe. Life itself was thought to derive its meaning and purpose from these and related principles of legal rationality, whose historical sources in theological doctrines of natural law and of human reason are evident.

Liberal democracy was the first great secular religion in Western history—the first ideology which became divorced from traditional Christianity and at the same time took over from traditional Christianity both its sense of the sacred and some of its major values. But in becoming a secular religion, liberal democracy was very soon confronted with a rival: revolutionary socialism. And when, after a century of revolutionary activity throughout Europe, communism ultimately seized power in Russia in 1917, its doctrines had acquired the sanctity of authoritative revelation and its leadership the charisma of high priests. Moreover, the Communist Party had the intimacy, on the one hand, and the austerity, on the other, of a monastic order. It is not accidental that during the purges after World War II, loyal Communists in Europe used to say, "There is no salvation outside the Party."

The jural postulates of socialism, though they differ in many respects from those of liberal democracy, show a common ancestry in Christianity. The Soviet Moral Code of the Builder of Communism, for example, which Soviet school children must learn by heart and which is taken as a basis for Soviet legal policy, contains such principles as: "conscientious labor for the good of society—he who does not work, neither shall he eat"; "concern on the part of everyone for the preservation and growth of public wealth"; "collectivism and comradely mutual assistance—one for all and all for one"; "honesty and truthfulness, moral purity, modesty, and unpretentiousness in social and personal life"; "an uncompromising attitude toward injustice, parasitism, dishonesty, careerism, and money-grubbing"; "an uncompromising attitude toward the enemies of communism"; "fraternal solidarity with the working people of all countries and with all people."[29] Soviet law is strikingly reminiscent of the Puritan code of the Massachusetts Bay Colony, the Body of Liberties of 1641, in its punishment of ideological deviation, idleness, and personal immorality.[30] In addition, the Soviet system places a very strong emphasis on the educational role of law and on popular participation in legal proceedings and in law enforcement—through Comrades' Courts and People's Patrols and by placing persons in the care of the collective of the factory or the neighborhood. Moreover, this is done in the name of an eschatology which foresees the ultimate disappearance of coercion and of law itself as a communist society is created in which every person will treat every other—again, in the words of the Moral Code of the Builder of Communism—as "comrade, friend, and brother." It is by no means inconsistent with this utopian vision that strong measures of coercion and of formal law may be used to bring it about.

The Crisis of the Western Legal Tradition

That the Western legal tradition, like Western civilization as a whole, is undergoing in the twentieth century a crisis greater than it has ever known before is not something that can be proved scientifically. It is something that is known, ultimately, by intuition. I can only testify, so to speak, that I sense that we are in the midst of an unprecedented crisis of legal values and of legal thought, in which our entire legal tradition is being challenged—not only the so-called liberal concepts of the past few hundred years, but the very structure of Western legality, which dates from the eleventh and twelfth centuries.

The crisis is being generated both from within Western experience and from without. From within, social and economic and political transformations of unprecedented magnitude have put a tremendous strain upon traditional legal institutions, legal values, and legal concepts in virtually all countries of the West. Yet in the past there have been periods of revolutionary upheaval which have also threatened to destroy basic elements of the Western legal tradition, and that tradition has nevertheless survived. What is new today is the challenge to the legal tradition as a whole, and not merely to particular elements or aspects of it; and this is manifested above all in the confrontation with non-Western civilizations and non-Western philosophies. In the past, Western Man has confidently carried his law with him throughout the world. The world today, however, is suspicious—more suspicious than ever before—of Western "legalism." Eastern and Southern Man offer other alternatives. The West itself has come to doubt the universal validity of its traditional vision of law, especially its validity for non-Western cultures. Law that used to seem "natural" seems only "Western." And many are saying that it is obsolete even for the West.

The crisis is sometimes viewed in somewhat less apocalyptic terms as a challenge not to fundamental principles of legality as understood in the West for the past nine centuries but rather to the application of such principles to new circumstances of the twentieth century, or at most as a challenge to certain "liberal" or "bourgeois" variants of legality that have prevailed since the eighteenth century, or possibly since the seventeenth or even the sixteenth century. It is said that in all countries of the West, the law is moving away from the individualistic assumptions that accompanied the change from a "medieval" to a "modern" political, economic, and social order, and toward one or another kind of collectivism. From this point of view, the crisis of law in the twentieth century is comparable in scope to earlier crises in the Western legal tradition, such as that which took place after the French Revolution of 1789 or after the English Revolution of 1640, or after the German Revolution of 1517. Just as those revolutions, it is said, inaugurated a new era in which bourgeois or "capitalist" law replaced "feudal" law, so the Russian Revolution of 1917 inaugurated a new era in which "socialist" law is replacing bourgeois or capitalist law.

It is surely true that in the twentieth century virtually all nations of the West have experienced the introduction of pervasive governmental controls over most aspects of economic life. Many countries have nationalized industrial production and have introduced integrated state economic planning. Other countries have adopted some form of state capitalism in which immediate responsibility for production, distribution, and investment is in the hands of large-scale corporate enterprise, subject, however, to direct and indirect controls by state agencies. Lenin's statement of 1921 concerning the Soviet economy is increasingly applicable to other economies as well: "with us, what pertains to the economy is a matter of public law, not private law." In the United States, for example, fields of administrative law such as taxation, labor-management relations, securities regulation, public housing, social security, environmental protection, and a dozen others, which hardly existed before the Great Depression of the early 1930s, have now achieved predominance.

In addition, what was previously conceived to be private law has also been transformed in the twentieth century by the radical centralization and bureaucratization of economic life, of which socialism in one form or another (including state-controlled capitalism) is an aspect or a consequence. Contract law, for example, which has traditionally been viewed in all Western legal systems as a body of rules for giving effect to voluntary agreements according to the intent of the parties, within limits set by broad public policies, has in the twentieth century struggled to adapt itself to a wholly new economic situation in which the detailed terms of the most important kinds of contracts are specifically required by legislation or else set forth in standard forms presented by large-scale business organizations on a take-it-or-leave-it basis. Similarly, in property law, governmental and large-scale corporate interests have intervened to remove from most private owners a very large share of their rights of possession, use, and disposition — that is, of what would in the past have been considered their rights of ownership — while at the same time imposing upon them obligations that are more to be explained in terms of administrative law than in terms of civil law. Throughout the West, corporate, commercial, and industrial property, including housing, is increasingly subject to administrative regulation, while the individual owner may hardly plant a tree or build an extension on his kitchen without governmental permission.

Similarly, tort law, which has traditionally been conceived primarily as a body of rules for compensating losses caused by intentional or negligent misconduct, has been transformed by the rapid spread of liability insurance for harm caused by innocent acts incidental to various forms of economic activity — so-called absolute liability, the grounds for which, and therefore the limits of which, remain largely unclarified. It is said that "general contract law," that is, the body of basic concepts and doctrines which was put forward in the nineteenth century as "the law of contract," applicable to any and all types of contractual transactions, is now dead, and that the principles of liability for breach of contract are to be found increasingly in the law of tort,[31] but others say that the general law of tort, which was also put forward in the nineteenth century, more or less simultaneously with the general law of contract, is equally dead. The division of the whole body of the law into public law and private law, and the subdivision of these into self-contained fields such as civil law, criminal law, administrative law, and the like — was a product of the legal thought of the eighteenth-century Enlightenment and was established by the French Revolution. It spread throughout Europe and ultimately reached the United States. It could not survive the development of socialism in the twentieth century — whether the full-scale socialist planned economy of the Communist countries or the less comprehensive, merely "socialistic" forms of governmental control exercised in the non-Communist countries of the West.

Fundamental changes have taken place throughout the West not only in what has traditionally been called public law and private law but also in what might be called social law, including family law as well as laws affecting race relations, class relations, and relations of the sexes and of the generations. Marriage and divorce have increasingly become largely a consensual matter, while parental power over children has been substantially reduced. As the family has been left more and more to its own devices, social relations of race and class and sex have been more and more subjected to legal restraint, in order to prevent exploitation. These changes have also been associated partly with the socialist movement, although they are only indirectly related to governmental control of the economy. In any event, they, too, constitute legal developments which are not easily reconciled with traditional legal categories.

Criminal law, also, has undergone drastic changes in virtually all countries of the West as a result of the integration and collectivization of the economy, urbanization, mass production, industrialization, and related phenomena. New types of crime have emerged: large-scale theft of corporate property, whether owned by the state or by large corporate enterprise; "white-collar" crime, including tax fraud, embezzlement, and antitrust violations; drug traffic and related urban street crime; and at the other end of the spectrum, political and ideological crimes, which have come to predominate over the "traditional" crimes of murder, rape, burglary, robbery, arson. Critical changes in the nature and incidence of crime have been accompanied by changes of comparable importance in theories of crime and punishment and in practices of law enforcement.

These and other changes in the legal systems of the countries of the West may be called revolutionary not only in the sense that they are fundamental changes that have occurred relatively rapidly but also in the sense that they are a response to a revolutionary political, economic, and social upheaval. In Russia and some other countries, that upheaval has taken the form of a classical type of revolution, in which one kind of political-economic-social order and belief system was violently replaced by another. In other countries the changes have taken the milder form of integration of national life, through technology and communications, through increasing organization into larger units, and through expanding governmental controls. Everywhere, however, this has been much more than a technological revolution; it has also been a political and ideological revolution.

The history of Western law is at a turning point as sharp and as crucial as that which was marked by the French Revolution of 1789, the English Revolution of 1640, and the German Revolution of 1517. The two generations since the outbreak of the Russian Revolution have witnessed—not only in the Soviet Union but throughout the West—a substantial break with the individualism of the traditional law, a break with its emphasis on private property and freedom of contract, its limitations on liability for harm caused by entrepreneurial activity, its strong moral attitude toward crime, and many of its other basic postulates. Conversely, they have witnessed a turn toward collectivism in the law, toward emphasis on state and social property, regulation of contractual freedom in the interest of society, expansion of liability for harm caused by entrepreneurial activity, a utilitarian rather than a moral attitude toward crime, and many other new basic postulates.

These radical changes constitute a severe challenge to traditional Western legal institutions, procedures, values, concepts, rules, and ways of thought. They threaten the objectivity of law, since they make the state an invisible party to most legal proceedings between individuals or corporate entities—the same state that enacted the applicable law and appointed the court. This invisible pressure is increased in Communist countries by virtue of strong central controls not only over economic life, but also over political, cultural, and ideological life; and in non-Communist countries, too, such central controls in the noneconomic sphere have increased, although they have usually been more in the hands of large bureaucratic organizations than of the state as such.

To the extent that the present crisis is comparable to revolutionary crises that have struck the Western legal tradition in the past, the resources of that whole tradition may be summoned to overcome it, as those resources have been summoned to overcome previous revolutionary crises. However, the present crisis goes deeper. It is a crisis not only of individualism as it has developed since the eighteenth century, or of liberalism as it has developed since the seventeenth century, or of secularism as it has developed since the sixteenth century; it is a crisis also of the whole tradition as it has existed since the late eleventh century.

Only four—the first four—of the ten basic characteristics of the Western legal tradition remain as basic characteristics of law in the West.

1. Law is still relatively autonomous, in the sense that it remains differentiated from politics and religion as well as from other types of social institutions and other scholarly disciplines.

2. It is still entrusted to the cultivation of professional legal specialists, legislators, judges, lawyers, and legal scholars.

3. Legal training centers still flourish where legal institutions are conceptualized and to a certain extent systematized.

4. Such legal learning still constitutes a meta-law by which the legal institutions and rules are evaluated and explained.

It is important to stress the survival of these four characteristics of law, since in Russia during the first years of the revolution and again in the early 1930s strong attacks were made—as had been the case in the previous great revolutions—upon the autonomy of law, its professional character, and its character as a learned discipline and a science. In other countries of the West, as well, it was proposed from time to time in the 1920s and 1930s, partly under Marxist—Leninist influence, that law and lawyers should be eliminated, or at least greatly restricted in importance, as unnecessary and harmful to society. In the 1960s and early

1970s the Chinese Revolution took up this cry with great seriousness: all the law schools were closed and almost all lawyers disappeared. Only since the late 1930s in the Soviet Union and the late 1970s in the Chinese People's Republic has "legal nihilism" been denounced.

All of the other six characteristics attributed to the Western legal tradition have been severely weakened in the latter part of the twentieth century, especially in the United States.

5. Law in the twentieth century, both in theory and in practice, has been treated less and less as a coherent whole, a body, a *corpus juris,* and more and more as a hodgepodge, a fragmented mass of ad hoc decisions and conflicting rules, united only by common "techniques." The old meta-law has broken down and been replaced by a kind of cynicism. Nineteenth-century categorizations by fields of law are increasingly viewed as obsolete. Still older structural elements of the law—such as, in England and America, the forms of action by which the common law was once integrated and which Maitland in 1906 said still "rule us from the grave"—are almost wholly forgotten. The sixteenth-century division of all law into public law and private law has had to yield to what Roscoe Pound in the mid-1930s called "the new feudalism." Yet it is a feudalism lacking the essential concept of a hierarchy of the sources of law by which a plurality of jurisdictions may be accommodated and conflicting legal rules may be harmonized. In the absence of new theories that would give order and consistency to the legal structure, a primitive pragmatism is invoked to justify individual rules and decisions.

6. The belief in the growth of law, its ongoing character over generations and centuries, has also been substantially weakened. The notion is widely held that the apparent development of law—its apparent growth through reinterpretation of the past, whether the past is represented by precedent or by codification—is only ideological. The law is presented as having no history of its own, and the history which it proclaims to present is treated as, at best, chronology, and at worst, mere illusion.

7. The changes which have taken place in law in the past, as well as the changes which are taking place in the present, are viewed not as responses to the internal logic of legal growth, and not as resolutions of the tensions between legal science and legal practice, but rather as responses to the pressure of outside forces.

8. The view that law transcends politics—the view that at any given moment, or at least in its historical development, law is distinct from the state—seems to have yielded increasingly to the view that law is at all times basically an instrument of the state, that is, a means of effectuating the will of those who exercise political authority.

9. The source of the supremacy of law in the plurality of legal jurisdictions and legal systems within the same legal order is threatened in the twentieth century by the tendency within each country to swallow

up all the diverse jurisdictions and systems in a single central program of legislation and administrative regulation. The churches have long since ceased to constitute an effective legal counterweight to the secular authorities. The custom of mercantile and other autonomous communities or trades within the economic and social order has been overridden by legislative and administrative controls. International law has enlarged its theoretical claim to override national law, but in practice national law has either expressly incorporated international law or else has rendered it ineffectual as a recourse for individual citizens. In federal systems such as that of the United States, the opportunity to escape from one set of courts to another has radically diminished. Blackstone's concept of two centuries ago that we live under a considerable number of different legal systems has hardly any counterpart in contemporary legal thought.

10. The belief that the Western legal tradition transcends revolution, that it precedes and survives the great total upheavals that have periodically engulfed the nations of the West, is challenged by the opposing belief that the law is wholly subordinate to revolution. The overthrow of one set of political institutions and its replacement by another leads to a wholly new law. Even if the old forms are kept, they are filled, it is said, with new content, they serve new purposes, and they are not to be identified with the past.

The crisis of the Western legal tradition is not merely a crisis in legal philosophy but also a crisis in law itself. Legal philosophers have always debated, and presumably always will debate, whether law is founded in reason and morality or whether it is only the will of the political ruler. It is not necessary to resolve that debate in order to conclude that as a matter of historical fact the legal systems of all the nations that are heirs to the Western legal tradition have been rooted in certain beliefs or postulates: that is, the legal systems themselves have presupposed the validity of those beliefs. Today those beliefs or postulates—such as the structural integrity of law, its ongoingness, its religious roots, its transcendent qualities—are rapidly disappearing, not only from the minds of philosophers, not only from the minds of lawmakers, judges, lawyers, law teachers, and other members of the legal profession, but from the consciousness of the vast majority of citizens, the people as a whole; and more than that, they are disappearing from the law itself. The law is becoming more fragmented, more subjective, geared more to expediency and less to morality, concerned more with immediate consequences and less with consistency or continuity. Thus the historical soil of the Western legal tradition is being washed away in the twentieth century, and the tradition itself is threatened with collapse.

The breakdown of the Western legal tradition springs only in part from the socialist revolutions that were inaugurated in Russia in October 1917 and that have gradually spread throughout the West (and throughout other parts of the world as well), albeit often in relatively mild forms. It springs only in part from massive state intervention in the economy of the nation (the welfare state), and only in part from the massive bureaucratization of social and economic life through huge centralized corporate entities (the corporate state). It springs much more from the crisis of Western civilization itself, commencing in 1914 with the outbreak of World War I. This was more than an economic and technological revolution, more even than a political revolution. If it had not been, Western society would be able to adapt its legal institutions to meet the new demands placed upon them, as it has done in revolutionary situations in the past. Western society would be able to accommodate socialism — of whatever variety — within its legal tradition. But the disintegration of the very foundations of that tradition cannot be accommodated; and the greatest challenge to those foundations is the massive loss of confidence in the West itself, as a civilization, a community, and in the legal tradition which for nine centuries has helped to sustain it.

Almost all the nations of the West are threatened today by a cynicism about law, leading to a contempt for law, on the part of all classes of the population. The cities have become increasingly unsafe. The welfare system has almost broken down under unenforceable regulations. There is wholesale violation of the tax laws by the rich and the poor and those in between. There is hardly a profession that is not caught up in evasion of one or another form of governmental regulation. And the government itself, from bottom to top, is caught up in illegalities. But that is not the main point. The main point is that the only ones who seem to be conscience-stricken over this matter are those few whose crimes have been exposed.

Contempt for law and cynicism about law have been stimulated by the contemporary revolt against what is sometimes called legal formalism, which emphasizes the uniform application of general rules as the central element in legal reasoning and in the idea of justice. According to Roberto M. Unger, with the development of the welfare state, on the one hand, and of the corporate state, on the other, formalism is yielding to an emphasis on public policy both in legal reasoning and in the idea of justice.[32] Policy-oriented legal reasoning, Unger writes, is characterized by emphasis upon broad standards of fairness and of social responsibility. He connects this shift in "post-liberal" Western legal thought with a change in beliefs concerning language. "Language is no longer credited with the fixity of categories and the transparent representation of the world that would make formalism plausible in legal reasoning or in ideas about justice," he writes.[33] Thus described, the revolt against legal formalism seems both inevitable and benign. Yet what is to prevent discretionary justice from being an instrument of repression and even a pretext for barbarism and brutality, as it became in Nazi Germany? Unger argues that this is to be prevented by the development of a strong sense of community within the various groups that comprise a society. Unfortunately, however, the development of such group pluralism is itself frustrated by some of the same considerations that underlie the attack on legal formalism. Most communities of more than face-to-face size can hardly survive for long, much less interact with one another, without elaborate systems of rules, whether customary or enacted. To say this is not to deny that in the late nineteenth and early twentieth centuries, in many countries of the West, there was an excessive concern with logical consistency in the law, which still exists in some quarters; the reaction against it, however, loses its justification when it becomes an attack on rules per se, and on the Western tradition of legality which strikes a balance among rule, precedent, policy, and equity — all four.

The attack on any one of these four factors tends to diminish the others. In the name of antiformalism, "public policy" has come dangerously close to meaning the will of those who are currently in control: "social justice" and "substantive rationality" have become identified with pragmatism; "fairness" has lost its historical and philosophical roots and is blown about by every wind of fashionable doctrine. The language of law is viewed not only as necessarily complex, ambiguous, and rhetorical (which it is) but also wholly contingent, contemporary, and arbitrary (which it is not). These are harbingers not only of a "post-liberal" age but also of a "post-Western" age.

Cynicism about the law, and lawlessness, will not be overcome by adhering to a so-called realism which denies the autonomy, the integrity, and the ongoingness of our legal tradition. In the words of Edmund Burke, those who do not look backward to their ancestry will not look forward to their posterity.

This certainly does not mean that the study of the past will save society. Society moves inevitably into the future. But it does so by walking backwards, so to speak, with its eyes on the past. Oliver Cromwell said, "Man never reaches so high an estate as when he knows not whither he is going." He understood the revolutionary significance of respect for tradition in a time of crisis.

Toward a Social Theory of Law

Two words that have shaped modern man's thinking about the past have made it difficult to capture the meaning of the Western legal tradition.

The first word is "medieval" (or Middle Ages). This came into use in the sixteenth century to characterize, on the one hand, the period between early Christianity and the Protestant Reformation and, on the other hand, the period between classical antiquity and the "new humanism" (the Renaissance, as it was first called by Michelet three hundred years later). The word medieval was pleasing also to supporters of the Catholic Counter-Reformation, because it implied not only that Protestantism was an innovation but also that Roman Catholicism had a continuity unbroken since at least the time of Constantine. Eventually the word proved convenient also for the nationalistic historiography of the nineteenth century, for it seemed to define the period between the decline of the Roman Empire and the rise of the sovereign national states.

How surprising it is, then, to discover that virtually all of the modern Western legal systems originated right in the middle of the Middle Ages!

The second word to conjure with is "feudalism," which came to be identified as the social-economic formation of the Middle Ages. The medieval age of feudalism was contrasted with the modern age of capitalism. Capitalism was associated with individualism and Protestantism, as feudalism was associated with traditionalism and Catholicism.

The concept of feudalism is almost as highly charged with hidden ideological assumptions as the concept of the Middle Ages. The adjective feudal, derived from the concrete noun fief (*feod*), had technical, political, economic, and legal meanings from the eleventh century on; but the abstract noun feudalism, referring to the total social-economic system, was only invented in the eighteenth century.[34] The French Revolution purported to abolish feudalism (*féodalité*) and feudal society (*la société féodale*). A decree of August 11, 1789, proclaimed: "The National Assembly totally abolishes the feudal regime." As Marc Bloch has said, "How could one thenceforth deny the reality of a system which it had cost so much to destroy?"[35] Bloch's irony is justified by the later statement of a leading English Marxist historian, Christopher Hill. In attacking the view that feudalism ended when serfdom ended, in the sixteenth century, Hill remarked, "If feudalism is abolished with serfdom, then France in 1788 was not a feudal state, and there never has been a bourgeois Revolution in the sense of a Revolution which overthrew the feudal state."[36] In other words, feudalism could not possibly have ended two hundred years before 1789; if it had, the French Revolution would have been fought in vain, and even more serious, Marxist theory would be wrong.

Thus all the ideologies of the nineteenth century, including Marxism, conspired to minimize, deny, or ignore the deep roots of modern Western institutions and values in the pre-Protestant, prehumanist, prenationalist, preindividualist, and precapitalist era; and all conspired to conceal the break in Western history that took place in the late eleventh and twelfth centuries. This false periodization of Western history not only led to many errors on the part of conventional historians concerning the movement of history from a medieval to a modern age but also confounded the social theorists' efforts to trace lines from a modern to a "new" (socialist, postliberal, postmodern) society.

The belief that Western society developed from an age of feudalism to an age of capitalism often carries with it an implication that the basic structure of a social order is economic, and that law is part of an "ideological superstructure" used by those who have economic power as a means of effectuating their policies. However, the Western legal tradition cannot be understood simply as an instrument of domination, whether economic or political; it must be seen also as an important part of the basic structure of Western society. It is both a reflection and a determinant of economic and political development. Without constitutional law, corporation law, contract law, property law, and the other fields of law that developed in Western Europe from the twelfth to the fifteenth centuries, the economic and political changes of the seventeenth to the nineteenth centuries, which contemporary social theorists have identified with capitalism, could not have taken place.

Moreover, the word feudalism may be used to obscure the fact that Western legal institutions and values in their formative period of development often challenged the prevailing political and economic system. There were recurrent struggles between law and feudal class oppression, between law and the power of urban magnates, between law and ecclesiastical interests, between law and royal domination. Serfs who escaped to the cities claimed their liberty, under urban law, after a year and a day. Citizens rebelled against their urban rulers in the name of constitutional principles declared in the city charters. Barons demanded ancient rights and privileges from kings. Princes and popes fought one another, each claiming that the social-economic power of the other was being exercised in violation of divine and natural legal rights, against the spirit of the laws, and even against their letter. In these and other struggles law was invoked against prevailing material facts and conditions; it was turned against the very social structure that had mothered it, so to speak.

Similarly, in Western history law has been invoked periodically against the prevailing political and moral values of society—the very values which may be said to have fathered it, and which it is supposed to share. Law is summoned to protect the dissident, the heretic, although the political authorities and public opinion itself condemn dissent or heresy. Law may protect the collective against a dominant individualism, or the individual against a dominant collectivism. This loyalty of the law to its own values is hard to explain in terms of an instrumental theory that views legal institutions as merely a tool of the dominant class or of the political elite.

Law—in Western history, at least—cannot be wholly reduced either to the material conditions of the society that produces it or to the system of ideas and values; it must be seen also, that is, in part, as an independent factor, one of the causes, and not only one of the results, of social, economic, political, intellectual, moral, and religious developments.

The first task of a social theory of law today—almost a century and a half after Karl Marx and almost a century after Max Weber—is to escape from oversimplified concepts of causation and of law. Whatever philosophers may wish to say about idealism and materialism, from a historical point of view the fact that Hegel was wrong in supposing that consciousness determines being does not mean that Marx was right in saying that being determines consciousness. In history, in real life, neither "determines" the other; usually they go together; when they do not, it is sometimes one and sometimes the other that is of decisive importance. A social theory of law should stress the interaction of spirit and matter, of ideas and experience, in its definition and analysis of law. It should bring the three traditional schools of jurisprudence—the political school (positivism), the moral school (natural-law theory), and the historical school (historical jurisprudence)—together in an *integrative* jurisprudence.

The second task of a social theory of law today is to adopt a historiography that is appropriate to legal history, rather than a historiography that is derived principally from economic history, the history of philosophy, or other kinds of history. A social theory of law must confront the fact that legal systems began to be constructed in the West in the late eleventh and twelfth centuries, and that some of the basic characteristics of those legal systems have survived the great national revolutions of the sixteenth to the twentieth centuries. Another fact to be confronted is that the first modern Western legal system was the canon law of the Roman Catholic Church, and that that legal system had many characteristics in common with what contemporary social theorists call the secular, rational, materialistic, individualistic legal systems of liberal capitalist society. The dualism of ecclesiastical and secular jurisdictions is a distinctive if not unique feature of Western culture. A social theory of law must surely offer an explanation of this. Such an explanation would have to deal also with the Western concept of plural corporate groups within the secular jurisdiction, each with its own law, and of the relationship of that pluralism to the dualism of the secular and ecclesiastical. This is a historiographical, not only a sociological, problem, since it involves an interpretation of the great revolutions of Western history, through which the national states have swallowed up a large part of the jurisdiction of the church, and ultimately a large part of the jurisdiction of the various corporate groups within the secular order as well.

Such a historiography would lead to a *general* social theory that sees

Western history not primarily as a series of transitions from feudalism to capitalism to socialism but rather as a series of transitions from plural corporate groups within an overarching ecclesiastical unity to national states within an overarching but invisible religious and cultural unity, and then to national states *without* an overarching Western unity, seeking new forms of unity on a world scale.

Taking this historical perspective, a social theory *of law* would be concerned with the extent to which the Western legal tradition has always been dependent, even in the heyday of the national state, on belief in the existence of a body of law beyond the law of the highest political authority, once called divine law, then natural law, and recently human rights; and the extent to which this belief, in turn, has always been dependent on the vitality of autonomous legal systems of communities within the nation (cities, regions, labor unions), as well as communities crossing national boundaries (international mercantile and banking associations, international agencies, churches).

In addition, it is a task of a contemporary social theory of law to study the fate of law in periods of revolutionary change, not so much in order to examine the rapid substitution of new laws for old but rather in order to examine the ways in which foundations are or are not laid for a stable and just legal order in the future, after the revolution has settled down.

Finally, a social theory of law must move beyond the study of Western legal systems, and the Western legal tradition, to a study of non-Western legal systems and traditions, of the meeting of Western and non-Western law, and of the development of a common legal language for mankind. For only in that direction lies the way out of the crisis of the Western legal tradition in the late twentieth century.

PART I

The Papal Revolution

and

the Canon Law

1 | The Background of the Western Legal Tradition: The Folklaw

AN HISTORIAN IS KEENLY AWARE of the danger of speaking about "origins." Wherever one starts in the past, there are always earlier beginnings — a fact which may testify to the continuity of the entire history of the human race. In the famous words of Maitland's opening paragraph in Pollock and Maitland's *History of English Law,* "Such is the unity of all history that anyone who endeavors to tell a piece of it must feel that his first sentence tears a seamless web. The oldest utterance of English law that has come down to us has Greek words in it; words such as *bishop, priest,* and *deacon.* If we search out the origins of Roman law we must study Babylon . . . A statute of limitations must be set; but it must be arbitrary. The web must be rent."

Despite this warning, I am prepared to argue that there are seams, there are new things under the sun, and where one starts is not necessarily arbitrary. More particularly, it is a principal thesis of this book that there was a time when what is known today as a legal system — a distinct, integrated body of law, consciously systematized — did not exist among the peoples of Western Europe, and that at the end of the eleventh century and in the early twelfth century and thereafter legal systems were created for the first time both within the Roman Catholic Church and within the various kingdoms, cities, and other secular polities of the West.

The term legal system is used here to mean something narrower and more specific than law in general, or what may be called a "legal order." There was a legal order in every society of the West prior to the eleventh and twelfth centuries, in the sense that there were legally constituted authorities that applied law. Indeed, at no time in their history did the peoples of Western Europe lack a legal order: the earliest written records are collections of laws, and Tacitus, writing in the first and second centuries A.D., describes Germanic assemblies that acted as courts. Also the church from very early times had declared laws and had established procedures for deciding cases. Yet, the legal rules and procedures which were applied in the various legal orders of the West in the period prior to the late eleventh and early twelfth centuries were largely undifferentiated from social custom and from political and religious institutions. No one had attempted to organize the prevailing laws and legal institutions into a distinct structure. Very little of the law was in writing. There was no professional judiciary, no professional class of lawyers, no professional legal literature. Law was not consciously systematized. It had not yet been "disembedded" from the whole social matrix of which it was a part. There was no independent, integrated, developing body of legal principles and procedures clearly differentiated from other processes of social organization and consciously articulated by a corps of persons specially trained for that task.

In the late eleventh and early twelfth centuries all this changed "with marvellous suddenness," to use Maitland's phrase. In every country of the West there were created professional courts, a body of legislation, a legal profession, a legal literature, a "science of law." The primary impulse for this development came from the assertion of papal supremacy over the entire Western church and of the independence of the church from secular control. This was a revolution, declared in 1075 by Pope Gregory VII; the papal party and the imperial party fought it out in bloody wars for almost fifty years, and it was only after almost one hundred years, in 1170, that the martyrdom of Thomas Becket sealed the final compromise in England.

In the following centuries the folklaw of the peoples of Europe seemed to disappear almost completely. New sophisticated legal systems were constructed, first for the church and then for the secular political orders — canon law, urban law, royal law, mercantile law, feudal and manorial law. Eventually, in the period from the sixteenth to the twentieth centuries, a series of great revolutions — the German Reformation, the English Revolution, the American Revolution, the French Revolution, the Russian Revolution — transformed the Western legal tradition, leaving its Germanic "background" farther and farther behind.

Nevertheless, Western concepts of law — and perhaps more important, Western attitudes toward law — cannot be understood unless they are seen partly in terms of what they first emerged *from* and reacted *against*. Especially now, in the last part of the twentieth century, when the West is less sure of its legal tradition than ever before, it is important to recall what that tradition originally replaced. Surely if new ways are being sought to overcome or supplement Western "legalism," they should be considered in the light of the Germanic alternative, which, although it was once rejected, still remains beneath the surface of our historical memory.

Moreover, although the jurists of the new era denounced the "irrational" features of the old customs and subjected them to drastic revision, Germanic law was not wholly rejected, and the parts that were rejected were not dropped all at once. The new jurisprudence was not a creation ex nihilo. It was a conscious reaction against the past (often in the name of a still older past), but it was also a re-creation of preexisting institutions and ideas.

More than that, Germanic law provided a necessary foundation for the new legal tradition that superseded it. Perhaps the clearest evidence in support of this paradoxical truth may be found in the new legal developments within the church. In the late eleventh and early twelfth centuries the church in the West achieved for the first time a legal identity independent of emperors, kings, and feudal lords. There was a separation of the church from the secular authorities and a separation of ecclesiastical law from other modes of ecclesiastical control. A hierarchy of ecclesiastical courts was established, culminating in the papal curia. All this was quite new, as was the emergence within the church of a legal profession, legal scholarship, legal treatises, and a body of legislative and judge-made law. Yet all this would have been impossible if a preexisting community, the *populus christianus,* had not been formed in Europe between the fifth and eleventh centuries. During that time Europe consisted of a multiplicity of tribal, local, and feudal (lordship) units, which, however, came to share a common religious faith and a common military loyalty to the emperor, and, outside the empire, to kings. The emperor or king was considered to be the sacred representative of the faith among all the peoples of his empire or kingdom. He was called the vicar of Christ. (The pope did not then claim that title but called himself the vicar of St. Peter.) The preexisting community of faith and loyalty was not only a necessary precondition for the later emergence of the new separate legal identity of the church under the papacy; it was also a necessary foundation for that legal identity, since without it there would have been no underlying social reality to be legally identified.

Similarly, the Germanic folklaw, which was basically tribal, local, and feudal (or protofeudal), based on blood feud and composition of blood feud, with ordeals, oath-helping, and other procedures—all of which came under attack in the late eleventh and early twelfth centuries—was a necessary foundation for the secular legal systems which replaced it. The necessary foundation was, once again, the communitarian character of the society which the older folklaw had helped to maintain. The new law, in contrast to the old law, was learned, sophisticated, systematized; but it could not have come into being, and it could not have continued to exist, without the foundation of structured, close-knit Germanic communities, with their strong emphasis on interdependence, comradeship, mutual responsibility, and other communitarian values.

Tribal Law

The earliest known legal orders prevailing among the peoples of
northern and western Europe were mainly tribal in character. Every
tribe or "stem" (*Stamm*) had its own law: the Franks, Alemanns, Frisians,
Visigoths, Ostrogoths, Burgundians, Lombards, East Saxons, Vandals,
Suevi, and other peoples that were eventually combined in the Frankish
Empire, embracing much of what later became Germany, France, and
northern Italy; the Angles, West Saxons, Jutes, Celts, Britons, and
other peoples of what later became England; the Danes, Norwegians,
and other Norsemen of Scandinavia and later of Normandy, Sicily, and
elsewhere; and many others, from Picts and Scots to Magyars and Slavs.
In the period from the sixth to the tenth centuries, the legal orders of all
these peoples, though largely independent of one another, were nevertheless remarkably similar. On the one hand, the basic legal unit within
the tribe was the household, a community of comradeship and trust
based partly on kinship and partly on oaths of mutual protection and service. Violation of the peace of the household by an outsider would lead
to retaliation in the form of blood feud, or else to interhousehold or
interclan negotiations designed to forestall or compose blood feud. On
the other hand, there were territorial legal units consisting typically of
households grouped in villages, villages grouped in larger units often
called hundreds and counties, and hundreds and counties grouped in
very loosely organized duchies or kingdoms. In the local territorial communities, the chief instrument of government and law was the public
assembly ("moot," "thing") of household elders. Besides kinship and local
territorial communities, there were also various kinds of lordship
(feudal) bonds, often formed by households "commending" themselves to
great men for protection.[1]

At the head of the tribes and of the local and feudal communities stood
royal and ecclesiastical authorities. In the course of time the larger territorial and religious units represented by these higher authorities became
more and more important. Kings continued to be called kings of a
people— *Rex Francorum* ("King of the Franks"), *Rex Anglorum* ("King of
the Angles")—until the twelfth century, but similar terms were also used
to refer to vaguely defined political territories, such as Francia and
Anglia. Also the church, though ultimately subject to emperors, and to
kings within their respective domains, was recognized as a wider
spiritual community which, though wholly without organizational unity,
transcended all secular boundaries. Nevertheless, prior to the latter half
of the eleventh century royal and ecclesiastical authorities did not attempt to alter in any fundamental way the essentially tribal and local and
feudal character of the legal orders of Europe. This may seem less
strange if it is understood that the economy of Europe at the time was

also almost wholly local, consisting chiefly of agriculture and cattle-raising, with subsidiary hunting; population was sparse, and there were virtually no towns with more than a few thousand people; commerce played only a small role, and communications were very rudimentary. What is strange from an economic or geopolitical point of view is not the weakness of central royal and ecclesiastical *law,* but the strength of central royal and ecclesiastical *authority.*

It was the central royal authority, inspired by ecclesiastical counselors, which was responsible for issuing the written collections (or "codes," as they later came to be called) of tribal and local laws that provide a great deal of what is known today about the folklaw of that period.

With the final disintegration of the Western Roman Empire in the fifth century, what little there had been of the great fabric of Roman law in the Germanic kingdoms diminished and in many places virtually disappeared. In other places, however, notably among some of the peoples in northern Italy, in Spain, and in southern France, the memory as well as some of the terminology and rules of Roman law survived. This was a simplified, popularized, and corrupted Roman law, which modern scholars have called "Roman vulgar law" to distinguish it from the more sophisticated Roman law of the earlier classical and postclassical periods. Roman vulgar law has been described as "a law averse to strict concepts and neither able nor inclined to live up to the standards of classical jurisprudence with respect to artistic elaboration or logical construction."[2] Even the most advanced "Romanist" legal collections of the time, such as that of the seventh-century Visigothic kings, consisted only of miscellaneous provisions, grouped together broadly according to subject but lacking both conceptual unity and the capacity for organic evolution.[3] Perhaps the chief historical importance of these scattered survivals of Roman law is that they helped preserve the idea that law should play a role in the ordering of political and social relationships.[4] Also the church retained many remnants of Roman law as well as of biblical law; and consequently upon his conversion to Christianity a Germanic tribal leader would often promulgate a set of laws consisting largely of the customs of his people.

The earliest of the surviving *leges barbarorum* ("laws of the barbarians"), as they are called by historians to distinguish them from *leges Romanae,* was the law of the Salic Franks, the Lex Salica, issued by the Merovingian king Clovis shortly after his conversion to Christianity in 496.[5] It starts by listing monetary sanctions to be paid by a defendant to a plaintiff for failure to respond to the plaintiff's summons to appear in the local court. It also lists monetary sanctions to be paid by wrongdoers to injured parties for various kinds of offenses, including homicides, assaults, thefts. These are typical provisions of primitive law; one of their principal purposes was to induce the parties to a dispute to submit to a decision of the local assembly (the hundred court) instead of resolving their dispute by vendetta, or else to provide a basis of negotiations between the household of the victim and that of the offender. Sometimes, however, they did not have even that effect. The injured party, in the words of one of the Anglo-Saxon laws, might either "buy off the spear or bear it." The prevalence of private warfare was connected with the great difficulty of bringing a person accused of wrongdoing to trial or getting witnesses to testify or enforcing a judgment.

The earliest of the Anglo-Saxon legal compilations was the Laws of Ethelbert, promulgated about 600 A.D. Ethelbert, ruler of Kent, had married a Christian and, according to tradition, had been converted to Christianity by Pope Gregory's emissary, the monk Augustine, in 597. Ethelbert's laws are remarkable for the extraordinarily detailed schedules of tariffs established for various injuries: so much for the loss of a leg, so much for an eye, so much if the victim was a slave, so much if he was a freeman, so much if he was a priest. The four front teeth were worth six shillings each, the teeth next to them four, the other teeth one; thumbs, thumbnails, forefingers, middle fingers, ring fingers, little fingers, and their respective fingernails were all distinguished, and a separate price, called a *bot*, was set for each. Similar distinctions were made among ears whose hearing was destroyed, ears cut off, ears pierced, and ears lacerated; among bones laid bare, bones damaged, bones broken, skulls broken, shoulders disabled, chins broken, collar bones broken, arms broken, thighs broken, and ribs broken; and among bruises outside the clothing, bruises under the clothing, and bruises which did not show black.[6]

If the act of the defendant caused death, the price to be paid to the kin of the deceased was called *wer* (or *wergeld*). Much of the written Germanic (including Frankish and Anglo-Saxon) law was concerned with setting different measures of wergeld for different classes of people.

Somewhat more sophisticated than the Laws of Ethelbert was the so-called Edict of the Lombard chieftain, or king, Rothari, written down in 643, seventy-five years after the Lombards had moved from what is now Hungary and Yugoslavia to what is now northern Italy. Of the 363 articles in the edict almost 140 deal with penal measures. For the murder of a free man or free woman by a free person, compensation of 1200 shillings (*solidi*) was required, whereas the price for the death of a household servant was only 50 solidi, and for a slave 20. (Murder of a free person by an unfree person was "compensated" by death.) Various prices were stated for hitting someone on the head, cutting off someone's hair, breaking various named parts of the skull, gouging out the eyes, cutting off a nose, breaking a nose, boxing an ear, breaking arms (with distinction made between simple and compound fractures), cutting off arms, fingers, toes. The little finger of a free man was worth 16 solidi, that of the half-free four, and that of a slave only two.[7]

The institution of fixed monetary sanctions payable by the kin of the wrongdoer to the kin of the victim was a prominent feature of the law of all the peoples of Europe prior to the twelfth century, and indeed of every Indc-European people at some stage of its development, including the peoples of India, Israel, Greece, and Rome. It is also an important part of the law of many contemporary primitive societies.[8]

It is, in many respects, a very sensible system. The threat of heavy financial burdens upon the wrongdoer and his kin is probably a more effective deterrent of crime than the threat of capital punishment or corporal mutilation (which succeeded pecuniary sanctions in Europe in the twelfth and thirteenth centuries), and at least equally as effective as the modern sanction of imprisonment; and it is surely less expensive for society. Moreover, in terms of retributive justice, not only is the wrongdoer made to suffer, but in addition—in contrast to today's more "civilized" penology—the victim is thereby made whole.

Yet the system cannot be satisfactorily explained on utilitarian grounds alone, at least insofar as the Germanic peoples of Europe are concerned. It was part of a whole ideology, a whole world view, and that world view helps to explain not only its sensible features but also those which may not have been so sensible—for example, the marked differentiation of payments for the slaying of persons belonging to different classes, the enormous size of the payments in many cases, the liability of kindred for wrongdoing regardless of their fault, and the fixed tariffs for injuries regardless of the actual cost to the victim.

In functional terms, the institution of monetary sanctions for crime, payable by the kindred of the wrongdoer to the kindred of the victim, is to be judged, not primarily by the extent to which it served to deter or to punish or to compensate for crime, but primarily by the extent to which it served to forestall interfamily vendettas and, more particularly, by the extent to which it facilitated negotiation and mediation between hostile families. Ideologically, however, both the institution of the blood feud and the institution of monetary compensation as a replacement of the blood feud are to be explained, in Germanic societies, by the high value placed upon honor as a means of winning glory (*lof,* "praise") in a world dominated by warring gods and by a hostile and arbitrary fate (*wyrd*). Honor, for Germanic man, meant "getting even"; only by getting even could he conquer the forces of darkness that surrounded his life.[9] The fixed schedules of payments provided a standard for evening accounts.

Lof was gained when a person took what others defended, as it was lost when others took what he or she defended. Therefore bot was, in its origins, essentially punitive and only secondarily compensatory. It was the retribution imposed by one household or kin group upon another. The challenge to lof was particularly great in cases of homicide, because the dead could never recover their own lost honor; the duty rested entirely with their kinsmen, whose first instinct was to resort to vengeance. Originally, the life or limb of the assailant himself, or of another member of his household, was demanded (in biblical terms "an eye for an eye, a tooth for a tooth"), or if the offense had been caused by a nonhuman agent such as a beast or a tree, the offending agent itself might be required to be forfeited (so-called noxal surrender). The substitution of fixed rates of payment gave dignity to a settlement short of violence, while not altering the basic raison d'être of the remedy, which was the redemption of the honor of the household and the kin.

Bot and wer were thus related to *mund,* which was the protection extended by the household to persons and groups associated with it, and to *frith,* which was the peace of the household. The king's mund and frith were like any other man's, only better. The laws of Ethelbert, for example, provided that the king's *mundbyrd,* that is, the penalty for violating the king's mund, should be fifty shillings and a ceorl's (commoner's) mundbyrd should be six shillings.[10] Mund was violated, and bot or wer was to be paid, when, for example, an outsider slept with a serving maid of the household or slew someone on the premises of the household. Closely related to bot and wer and mund and frith were three other Germanic legal institutions: the surety (*borh*), the pledge (*wed*), and the hostage.[11] A kinsman might act as a surety for a man who agreed to pay wer but could not pay the full amount at once; or the debtor might give a valuable object in pledge; or he might send a hostage to live and work in the enemy household until the price was paid. All these legal devices reflected both the solidarity of the household and the substitution of tribute for vengeance in interhousehold or interclan strife.

In addition to the settlement of disputes by blood feud and by interhousehold or interclan negotiations, the Germanic peoples from earliest times held public assemblies (moots) to hear and decide disputes. However, jurisdiction in most types of cases depended on the consent of the parties. Even if they consented to appear, they might not remain throughout, and even if they remained, the moot generally could not compel them to submit to its decision. Thus the procedure of the moot had to assume, and to help create, a sufficient degree of trust between the parties to permit the system to operate, just as the procedure for interhousehold or interclan negotiations, with its reliance upon sureties, pledges, and hostages, had to assume, and to help create, such a degree of trust. Yet it is clear that both the trial before the assembly and the negotiations between the households or clans were apt to be intensely hostile in character. "The two sides faced each other with implacable hostility, determined to make no concessions and to forgive and forget nothing."[12]

The polar relationship between vengeance (blood feud) and pacification (composition of blood feud) in Germanic folklaw is an example of the intense dialectic of mistrust and trust which exists in many contemporary kinship societies. Claude Lévi-Strauss has written that "observers have often been struck by the impossibility for natives of conceiving a neutral relationship, or more exactly, no relationship. We have the feeling—which, moreover, is illusory—that the absence of definite kinship gives rise to such a state in our consciousness. But the supposition that this might be the case in primitive thought does not stand up to examination. Every family relatonship defines a certain group of rights and duties, while the lack of family relationship . . . defines enmity." Lévi-Strauss quotes the following passage from Marcel Mauss: " 'Throughout a considerable period, and in a large number of societies, men met in a curious frame of mind, with exaggerated fear and an equally exaggerated generosity which appear stupid in no one's eyes but our own . . . There is either complete trust or complete mistrust. One lays down one's arms, renounces magic, and gives everything away, from casual hospitality to one's daughter or one's property.' "[13]

In Germanic society, the "trust-mistrust" syndrome was closely related to the overriding belief in an arbitrary fate, and this belief, in turn, was reflected above all in the use of the ordeal as a principal method of legal proof. The two main types of ordeal were those of fire and water, the former for persons of higher rank, the latter for the common people. Originally, these were invocations of the gods of fire and water, respectively. Those tried by fire were passed blindfolded or barefooted over hot glowing plowshares, or they carried burning irons in their hands, and if their burns healed properly they were exonerated. The ordeal of water was performed either in cold water or in hot water. In cold water, the suspect was adjudged guilty if his body was borne up by the water contrary to the course of nature, showing that the water did not accept him. In hot water he was adjudged innocent if after putting his bare arms and legs into scalding water he came out unhurt. A later, more subtle ordeal, used chiefly by the clergy, was that of the morsel: an ounce of bread or cheese was eaten, with the adjuration, "Close, O Lord, this man's stomach so that he cannot swallow this bread (cheese) if he has sworn unjustly." If he could not swallow or keep down the bread or cheese, he was guilty. Such primitive lie detectors may have worked quite well. In any event, there was a considerable resistance to the abolition of ordeals in the thirteenth century.

The ordeal was a characteristic example, in Peter Brown's words, of the "mingling of the sacred and the profane," a "blurring of the borderline between the objective and the subjective in human experience." It relied on a sacred and dramatic rite to determine the judgment of God; yet it was "mercifully slow" and "allowed room for maneuver and the evolution of a situation." The outcome was usually subject to interpretation by consensus of the community. Thus small face-to-face groups, largely nonliterate, could deal with problems of violence, deceit, or witchcraft in a manner consistent both with belief in the supernatural and with practical communal needs.[14]

The system of trial by ordeal was combined with, and sometimes replaced by, trial by ritual oaths ("compurgation"). First came the fore-oaths. For example, a party claiming bot for the theft of cattle would swear: "By the Lord, before whom this relic is holy, so I prosecute with full folkright, without fraud and without deceit, and without any guile, as was stolen from me the cattle [designating them] that I claim, and that I have attached with [the defendant]."

The opposing party would then swear a denial of this claim. For example: "By the Lord, I was not at rede nor at deed, neither counselor nor doer, where were unlawfully led away [the complainant's] cattle." Or, "As I cattle have, so did it come of my own property, and so it by folright my own is, and my rearing."[15]

These oaths opened the lawsuit. The moot would then decide which party should be allowed to give the oath of proof. On the appointed day both parties would appear, and the party allowed to give the oath would swear to a set formula. To complete his oath, however, he would have to have a number of compurgators, or oath helpers, swear to supporting formulas. The number of required oath helpers depended on their *wer* and on the offense being tried. They might swear, for example: "By the Lord, the oath is clean and unperjured [the complainant or the defendant] has sworn."[16]

All the fore-oaths, denials, final oaths, and supporting oaths had to be repeated flawlessly, "without slip or trip," if they were to succeed. All were cast in poetic form, with abundant use of alliteration. For example, an oath used in suits affirming title to land reads as follows: "So I hold it as he held it, who held it as saleable, and I will own it—and never resign it—neither plot nor plough land—nor turf nor toft—nor furrow nor foot length—nor land nor leasow—nor fresh nor marsh—nor rough ground nor room—nor wold nor fold—land nor strand—wod nor water."[17]

The formality of proof and its dramatic character were connected with the fact that the law was almost entirely oral. "So long as law is unwritten," Maitland states, "it must be dramatized and acted. Justice must assume a picturesque garb or she will not be seen." Maitland's remark echoes that of the nineteenth-century German historian and linguist Jakob Grimm, who speaks of the "sensuous element" in Germanic law, as contrasted with the more abstract or conceptual element which is prominent in more "mature" legal systems.[18] The expression of legal rules in poetic images helped to stamp them on the memory. Among common phrases were "unbidden and unbought, so I with my eyes saw and with my ears heard," "foulness or fraud," "house and home," "right and righteous," "from hence or thence." The law was contained in a multitude of proverbs. The earliest Irish law was expressed in the form of poetry.

The dramatic and poetic qualities of Germanic law were associated with the plasticity of its substance. "Men were especially prone to express provisions relating to time and space in such a naive and inexact way as left room for chance in particular cases. It is often declared that something shall be the rule as far as a cock walks or flies, a cat springs, or a stone or hammer is thrown, or as one can reach with a sickle. A law shall endure so long as the wind blows from the clouds and the world stands . . . or so much land shall be acquired as can be ridden round in a certain time on horse or ass, turned over with the plow, or covered with hides."[19] This "naive and inexact" manner of expression was well suited to the needs of peoples who had not yet acquired a scientific outlook with its subject-object dualism. For the peoples of Europe in the Germanic era, life was much less compartmentalized than it later became, much more a matter of total involvement; hence poetic and symbolic speech, which is closely associated with the whole being and with the unconscious, was more appropriate than prosaic and literal language, especially on solemn occasions involving the law.

Some examples of the symbolic and ceremonial character of Germanic law are the transfer of land by the handing over of twig and turf or hat and glove or by the touching of the altar cloth or the bell rope; the leaving of the house key upon the bier of her dead husband by a widow who wished to free herself from liability for his debts; the use of the staff in legal transactions (for instance, its delivery in a contract of pledge); the handclasp as the usual confirmation of pledges of faith and of contracts; and the use of various ceremonials in seating oneself when taking possession of land or of an office.[20]

The dramatic and poetic elements of Germanic law — its mimetic elements — elevated legal speech above ordinary speech and thereby put a distance between law and ordinary life. Of course it is necessary in all societies that law be separated from the daily routine by ritual, by ceremony, and by belief reflected in ritual and ceremony — the belief in the power of certain words put in certain ways to bring about certain effects denominated as "legal." This kind of magic is necessary if law is to work. Yet each age has its own magic, reflecting its particular concept of ultimate reality. The Germanic concept postulated an essentially arbitrary fate at the center of life, and Germanic legal magic reflected that concept.

The Germanic trial was a symbolic continuation of the blood feud. The parties hurled oaths at each other instead of blows. The outcome of the ordeal, like the outcome of battle itself, was the decision of fate, of wyrd. As James Gordley has put it, "The ceaseless conflict of households bent on gaining *lof* at the expense of each other was a cosmological principle in which all forces of nature joined."[21] Ultimately the arbitrary force of wyrd was decisive. In the words of an Anglo-Saxon poem:

> Good against evil; youth against age;
> Life against death; light against darkness;
> Army against army; foe against foe;
> Hostile with hostile shall always fight
> Contending for land and avenging wrongs
> A wise man must ponder this world's strife.[22]

The same word, *dom* (doom) — judgment — was used to refer to a decree of wyrd and to the outcome of a trial. In the words of Beowulf:

> Often Fate saves
> an undoomed man, if his courage is good.[23]

This was the heroic side of Germanic law: it was foe against foe locked in a deadly struggle for honor, yet each prepared to accept wyrd's decree, however bitter it might be.

But there was another side, the community of comradeship and trust represented within the household itself. And this community carried over to the whole tribe or folk. The moot acted like a household. It had its peace, its frith (in modern German, *Friede*). It assembled not only to decide disputes but also to give advice and to consult and discuss problems in an amicable way. It was concerned with establishing justice (*riht;* in modern English, "right"; in modern German, *Recht*). The wise men, the *witan* ("knowing ones," "witnesses"), gave their opinions in an effort to hold the assembly of households together. Also the tribe, the folk, sought to protect itself by acting collectively against wrongdoers: the judicial outcry — called in Anglo-Saxon law the "scream" or the "hue and cry" ("out! out!") — was the signal for all to join in the pursuit of the offender. A corollary of this was the characteristic penalty of outlawry in the case of the most serious offenses; theoretically, at least, none were permitted to communicate with the outlaw and he died from starvation and exposure.

The symbolism of mund and frith — protection and peace — which characterized the household and the folkmoot was at the same time the symbolism of surety, pledge, and hostage: it was the symbolism of the oath and of the dramatic performing of handshakes and other ceremonial acts of peace. By swearing oaths that placed them under the protection of the gods, and later of God, the parties acquired the degree of trust necessary to enable them to submit, when they did, to compurgation and the ordeals or to accept sureties, pledges, and hostages for bot and wer. They could not violate their oaths without threatening the very basis of household and tribal life, which was itself founded on oaths.

The importance of the household within the tribe should not obscure the growing importance also of bonds of lordship and bonds of territorial community. From earliest times there was a hereditary aristocracy, and in time lordship by service became as important as lordship by blood. "Loyalty to a lord had been a consistent theme of epic poetry," writes H. R. Loyn. "From the reign of Alfred [871–900]"—and, it should be added, among the Franks at least from the reign of Charlemagne a century earlier—"it became the cardinal moving spirit in the moulding of society. You shall fight for your kinsman when he is attacked except against your lord: that we do not permit, said a law of Alfred. Under his successors the lordless man was treated as more and more of an anomaly. Society was held together by bonds of loyalty from man to lord and from lord who was also a thegn [the royal servant in the localities] to king."[24] Just as bonds of lordship led up to the king as great lord, so the bonds of territorial community led up to the king as ruler of the whole land. Yet as Loyn says, "There was no conflict between kindred power and secular lordship,"[25] and similarly there was no conflict between kindred power and territorial community. The household of the lord was similar to households within the tribal community, and the household of the king as ruler of the whole land was also similar to households within the tribal community. All were caught up in the paradigm of wyrd and lof, mund and frith, bot and wer, borh and wed; all were founded on oaths of mutual protection and service. All were part of a legal order which resolved conflict by the "binary opposites" (in Lévi-Strauss's phrase) of feud or composition of feud, proof being by ordeal or by compurgation.[26] Other characteristic institutions of this legal order were judicial outcry when an offense was discovered (in Latin, *clamor,* from which is derived the legal word "claim"; in Anglo-Saxon, *hcream,* from which is derived the word "scream"); outlawry, involving forfeiture of all goods and liability to be killed by anyone with impunity; and noxal surrender, that is, surrender to the victim of the object or slave by which the offense had been committed.

Legal historians have given to this type of law the name Archaic Law. In its main outlines, it was characteristic not only of the Germanic peoples in the period prior to the late eleventh century but also of all Indo-European peoples, from Kent to Kashmir, at one time or another in their development. Of course, there were a great many local differences from place to place and a great many changes over time; nevertheless, there was a common legal style.[27]

Dynamic Elements in Germanic Law: Christianity and Kingship

The Germanic folk assembly, or moot, not only issued dooms
(judgments) in particular cases but also issued general decrees, which
were likewise called dooms. The dooms, however, were not considered
to be legislation in the modern sense; they were regarded rather as
divinely inspired affirmations of ancient custom. They were the will of
the gods—or, after the introduction of Christianity, the will of God.
They had an objective reality. The wise men of the assembly were not
called legislators but law speakers. The law which they spoke was binding because it was old; it was old because it was divinely instituted.
"Right" changed slowly and surreptitiously; overt changes in the legal
order required very strong justification. "Even the amendment of law
[was] thought of as a judgment, a speaking out of that element of law
hitherto unrevealed, an act of judgment of the folk through its witan."[28]

Two closely interconnected factors, however, made for conscious,
overt change: one was the influence of Christianity on legal concepts; the
other was the development of the kingship as a translocal and transtribal
institution, uniting large areas containing various peoples.

One might suppose that the new religion which gradually spread
through Europe between the fifth and tenth centuries would have
threatened the very existence of the Germanic folklaw, founded as it was
in tribal myths of warring gods; in worship of rivers, woods, and moun-
tains; in concepts of the divine descent of the tribal kings; in absolute
loyalty to kinship and lordship ties; and in an overriding belief in fate.
Christianity replaced the old myths with the gospel of a universal
creator, father of all men, who once appeared on earth in the form of his
son, Jesus Christ, worship of whom brings freedom from bondage to all
earthly ties, freedom from fate, freedom from death itself. These new
ideas must have seemed strange and abstract to Germanic men.

Yet Christianity also taught a more practical doctrine—that hills,
valleys, forests, rivers, rocks, wind, storm, sun, moon, stars, wild
beasts, snakes, and all the other phenomena of nature were created by
God to serve man and were not haunted (as the Germanic peoples
believed) by hostile supernatural deities, and that therefore it was possible for the wandering, warring tribes to settle on the land without fear.
This was both preached and lived out in the fifth, sixth, seventh, and
eighth centuries by tens of thousands of monks, who themselves settled
in the wilderness, first as hermits and then in monastic communities,
and who attracted many others to join them in tilling the soil. Thus
Christian monasticism was one of the factors contributing to the
emergence of the European peasantry. Spreading across Europe from
Ireland and Wales, the monastic movement fought the superstitions of

nature that dominated Germanic religions, and it opposed to the pagan calendar, based on nature and the four seasons, a Christian calendar based on biblical events and the lives of the saints.[29]

Moreover, Christianity appealed to the Germanic peoples by its concept of a community, the church, which transcended kindred, tribe, and territory. On the one hand, Christianity, in contrast to Germanic paganism, treated kings not as descendants of gods but as human beings, subject like all other human beings to punishment by God for their sins. On the other hand, the Germanic rulers remained the supreme religious heads of their respective peoples, appointing bishops and dictating liturgical and other religious matters. In addition, they could begin to make wider claims to the allegiance of people of other kindreds, tribes, and territories: to bring them to the true faith, or, if they were already converted, to unite them in the true church.

In general, Christian beliefs and practices had a great appeal to Germanic man. They brought him, for the first time, a positive attitude toward life and toward death, a larger purpose into which to fit the tragedies and mysteries of his existence. Beside Christianity the old pagan myths seemed harsh and bleak. One can sense the passion in King Alfred's words, in the famous "Addition" to his translation of Boethius, "I say, as do all Christian men, that it is a divine purpose that rules, and not fate." At the same time, the Christian cosmology and the Christian ethic were not easy for Germanic man to grasp. If taken seriously, they threatened to undermine not only his former system of beliefs but also his entire social order.

Yet why, if Christianity constituted a threat to Germanic social institutions, did it succeed in making converts among Germanic tribal chiefs and ruling families? The question rests on a false premise. Christianity did not, at first, constitute a threat to Germanic social institutions.

It is important not to confuse Germanic Christianity with modern Western Christianity, whether Roman Catholic or Protestant. It was, in fact, much closer to Eastern Orthodoxy—both as it was then and as it still is in some countries today. Germanic Christianity was hardly concerned with the reform of social institutions. Nor was it primarily oriented toward ecclesiastical unity and ecclesiastical power. Its message concerned the life of the world to come—heaven and hell—and preparation for that life through prayer and through personal humility and obedience.[30] The highest Christian ideals in the first thousand years of church history, both in the East and in the West, were symbolized above all by the lives of holy men and by monasticism, with its emphasis on spiritual withdrawal from the temporal world. But apart from monasticism, the church as an organization was almost wholly integrated with the social, political, and economic life of society. It did not stand opposite the political order but within it. Religion was united with politics and economics and law, just as they were united with one another. Ecclesiastical and secular jurisdictions were intermingled.

The church taught sanctity and produced saints; this was something new for the peoples of northern and western Europe, who had previously glorified only heroes. But the church did not oppose heroism and heroes; it only held up an alternative, a higher ideal. Similarly, the church did not oppose blood feud and ordeals; it only said they could not bring salvation, which came from faith and good works. The majority of bishops and priests of the church became, in fact, wholly involved in the corruption and violence that characterized the age; this was inevitable, because they were generally appointed by leading politicians from among their friends and relatives. Christianity was Germanized at the same time that the Germanic peoples were Christianized.[31] It is true that the monastic movement, by its example as much as its doctrine, attempted to teach Christian ideals of sacrifice and service and love of one's neighbor—and, at the same time, improved techniques of agriculture—to the Germanic peoples. But the monasteries that sprang up all over Europe between the sixth and tenth centuries, at first each with its own rule, offered no program of secular law reform; they offered, instead, an ascetic life of work and prayer, in preparation for the life of the world to come. This, too, had the effect of devaluing Germanic legal institutions without replacing them.

Indeed, Christianity supported the Germanic legal institutions of ordeal and compurgation by reinforcing the Germanic concept of divine immanence that underlay them. It was presupposed both by Germanic religion and by the Christianity which initially replaced it that supernatural powers were immanent within the natural sphere, and that the world accessible to the senses was, in Marc Bloch's words, a "mask behind which the truly important events take place." The *judicium dei* was based on the belief in such immanent, indwelling supernatural powers.[32] It was only when the church shifted its emphasis to a transcendent God, who inspires man to imitate him, that ordeals, oath helpers, duels, and trial by champions gave way to a "rational" procedure for finding truth by questioning witnesses.

This is not to say, however, that Christianity prior to the eleventh century had no positive effect whatever on the folklaw of the European peoples. On the contrary, it produced substantial changes. In the first place, conversion to Christianity gave an impetus to the writing down of the tribal customs: one sees this in the Salic Law adopted by Clovis, the first Christian king of the Franks; in the Laws of Ethelbert, ruler of Kent, who was the first Christian king in England;[33] and four centuries later in the *Russkaia Pravda* of the first Christian princes of Kievan Russia.[34] For one thing, Christianity brought writing, and writing made it possible to fix customs (and especially customary monetary sums) that might otherwise have been uncertain. This facilitated the negotiation of dispute settlements; also it strengthened the incipient jurisdiction of public authorities to punish the most serious forms of crime. In addition, the sacred writing of the Bible suggested a way of attaching a new kind of sanctity to custom—the writing was itself a ritual. In the second place, the writing down of the customs gave an opportunity to make some subtle—as well as some not-so-subtle—changes in them. The Christian clergy, who became the king's advisers, and who had the gift of writing, wanted protection. Indeed, the monks in particular needed special protection since they were, in a sense, outside the tribal system; they were to some extent a people without kin. (The "secular clergy"—nonmonks—were generally married.) It is no accident that the Laws of Ethelbert begin: "Theft of God's property and the Church's, to be compensated twelvefold."

Nor were all the changes which Christianity wrought in the folklaw attributable to political factors. In the long run, moral factors probably played an even greater part. The Germanic "codes" contain strong exhortations in favor of more just and more humane legal values. The Laws of King Alfred, for example, start with the Ten Commandments and a restatement of the laws of Moses, a summary of the Acts of the Apostles, and references to the monastic penitentials and to other laws of the church. Alfred's laws themselves, although largely consisting of a recapitulation of earlier collections, contain such striking provisions as: "Doom very evenly: doom not one doom to the rich, another to the poor; nor doom one to your friend, another to your foe."[35]

Christianity broke the fiction of the immutability of the folklaw. Gradually, between the sixth and the eleventh centuries, Germanic law, with its overwhelming biases of sex, class, race, and age, was affected by the Christian doctrine of the fundamental equality of all persons before God: woman and man, slave and free, poor and rich, child and adult. These beliefs had an ameliorating effect on the position of women and slaves and on the protection of the poor and helpless. Also Christianity had an important effect on judicial proof by oaths, since the swearing of oaths began to take Christian forms and was supported by ecclesiastical sanctions. Oaths were administered by priests in churches, at altars, on relics, and through appeals to divine sanctions against falsehood; and false swearing was subject to discipline through ecclesiastical penances. Indeed, oaths took a place alongside ordeals as a principal mode of trial. Ordeals were retained for trial of those who had no kin to swear for them (or who for some other reason failed to produce the necessary oath helpers), and for those of ill repute whose oaths were wholly unreliable, as well as for certain designated crimes; but in other cases an equally common method of proof came to be that of compurgation. As before, oath helpers were drawn chiefly from kinfolk, and there remained a strong element of loyalty in it, which is implicit in the concept of oath-*helping*. But the church added the risk of offending God by perjury, and the duty, if one did perjure himself, to confess the sin to his priest and be subjected to penitential discipline. Moreover, not only the false swearing of oaths but also all other obstructions of justice were considered to be sins subject to penitential discipline. For example, persistence in blood feud after a reasonable offer of satisfaction was an offense against God which was to be confessed to a priest and atoned for by fasting and other forms of penance.

Christianity also enhanced the role of kingship in the development of the folklaw during the period prior to the late eleventh century, and especially the king's responsibility to see that tribal justice was tempered with mercy and that the poor and helpless were protected against the rich and powerful. In the eighth, ninth, tenth, and eleventh centuries, Frankish and Anglo-Saxon kings were considered to be appointed by God to act as judges in extraordinary cases. As they moved about their realms—and they were continually moving, for there were few means of communication—they heard cases for mercy's sake: cases of widows or orphans or men who had no families to protect them, or no lords; cases of the very worst crimes for which no money payment could make satisfaction. This was part of their spiritual jurisdiction as patriarchs of their people.

Politically, too, Christianity served to transform the ruler from a tribal chief (*dux*) into a king (*rex*). Once converted to Christianity, the king no longer represented only the deities of his tribe: he represented, in addition, a universal deity whose authority extended to all tribes, or at least to many tribes. He became, in effect, the head of an empire. Christianity was a unifying ideology. Under its banner Charlemagne, who ruled the Franks from 768 to 814, and who was crowned Emperor in 800, mobilized the various people of his empire into a unified army for wars against Arabs, Saxons, Danes, and Slavs, while across the Channel Mercian kings (and a century later the Saxon king Alfred the Great) established military hegemony over the various races of England and ultimately drove out the Scandinavian invaders. The universality of the imperial kingship came to prevail—at least for various periods of time—over tribal, local, and household loyalties: a universality based not only on military power but also on the spiritual authority of the king (or emperor) as head of the church. Charlemagne called church councils and made church law—even before he agreed to be crowned Emperor by the Bishop of Rome. As Christopher Dawson has put it, "Charles regarded the Pope as his chaplain, and plainly tells Leo III that it is the King's business to govern and defend the Church and that it is the Pope's duty to pray for it." Similarly, Alfred was head of the church in England.[36] As stated in the laws of Ethelred (about 1000 A.D.), "A Christian king is Christ's deputy among Christian people and he must avenge with utmost diligence offenses against Christ."[37] On the whole, despite some tensions between popes and emperors, the clergy supported the imperial concept, including imperial leadership of the church itself.

Both the royal authority and the ecclesiastical authority were dynamic factors in the development of legal institutions. Especially from the eighth century on, the kings extended their peace—their household law—beyond their own families, courts, friends, servants, and messengers. Even in the sixth and seventh centuries they had made very strong efforts to regulate and limit the blood feud; they had, for example, exacted payment from persons and households for certain offenses even when their own royal household peace had not been violated. Gradually, more and more offenses became triable before the king. Treason, intentional homicide, and adultery were made capital offenses. In the eighth and ninth centuries the Frankish emperors, and in the ninth and tenth centuries the Anglo-Saxon kings as well, openly undertook responsibility for maintaining the king's peace throughout their territories. In the oath composed by Archbishop Dunstan of Canterbury for the coronation of King Edgar in 973, Edgar swore that "true peace" should be assured to all "Christian people" in his kingdom, that robberies and "all unrighteous deeds" should be forbidden, and that "justice and mercy" should govern all judgments.[38] The Frankish emperors had for some time sworn similar oaths. Eventually, ways were found to implement such oaths through the appointment of royal officials to supervise local assemblies and through other administrative devices for maintaining royal influence over the tribes and localities. In addition, an incipient feudalism, in which the king had the role of chief lord, served to reinforce his peacekeeping function.

Kings and bishops issued new laws and held court. The needs of the royal and ecclesiastical bureaucracy generated new legal institutions, more sophisticated than those of the tribal, local culture. For example, royal delegates summoned inquests (juries) and interrogated witnesses. Royal edicts as well as ecclesiastical decisions and decrees come to constitute an important source of law. Thus an official law (*Amtsrecht,* as Rudolph Sohm called it) grew up alongside the folklaw (*Volksrecht*).[39] The official law and many features of the folklaw were influenced by the Roman law as it existed in the territories conquered by the invading Germanic peoples. Many Roman rules were kept: for example, that an immoral or unlawful transaction should be void, that a sale or gift made under violence or threat should be invalid, that a debtor in default should pay interest on his debt. There was, in effect, a reception—and at the same time a vulgarization—of Roman law.[40] A modern analogy is the reception of a Western type of law in Japan and China in the late nineteenth and early twentieth centuries—a Western type of law which governed certain official and upper-class relations but which left virtually unaffected the traditional legal order among the people as a whole.

So in Europe, until the latter part of the eleventh century, the basic contours of the folklaw remained tribal and local, with some feudal elements. The kinship bond continued to provide the primary definition and the primary guarantee of a person's legal status.[41] The kings took little initiative in making the folklaw. There was virtually no royal law of contract, or of property, or of landlord and tenant, and very little royal law of crime and tort. When kings did succeed in establishing some degree of administration of the localities by royal delegates, the latter either tended to be swallowed up by the localities which they were supposed to administer in the king's behalf or else they became their own masters. The written collections of laws which kings occasionally promulgated, setting forth customs that needed to be better known or more firmly established, were not legislation in the modern sense but were rather exhortations to keep the peace and do justice and desist from crime. The king had to beg and pray, as Maitland put it, for he could not command and punish. Indeed, Germanic laws contain provisions stating that when a person has exhausted his opportunities in the local courts, he should *not* go to the king for a remedy.

Undoubtedly, one factor in the weakness of the central authority was economic and technological: despite some increase in commerce and some growth in the number and population of towns during the eighth, ninth, tenth, and early eleventh centuries, despite the improvement of agricultural technology, despite the growth of handicrafts and a general advance in the arts and in learning, the economy remained almost entirely local and the existing technology did not permit efficient communication between the center and the periphery. These economic and technological factors were connected with underlying religious and political factors: the legitimacy of the central authority was based on Christianity, whose world outlook was in sharp conflict with that of Germanic tribalism, with its belief in honor and fate; and at the same time the central authority lacked a concept of the independent role of law as a means of effectuating Christian concepts and values and of rationalizing and controlling social, economic, and political processes. The dynamic elements of the law were unsystematized and weak; the static elements predominated. Law was conceived primarily as an expression of the unconscious mind of the people, a product of their "common conscience" (in the words of Fritz Kern),[42] rather than primarily as a deliberate expression of conscious reason or of will. It was, in that respect, like art, like myth, like language itself.

Penitential Law and Its Relation to the Folklaw

Deeper insight into the nature of the legal order which prevailed in Europe prior to the late eleventh century may be gained by examining more closely the system of penances introduced by the Western Church, or rather, the churches, for despite the great prestige of the Bishop of Rome as *primus inter pares* ("first among equals"), there was as yet no separate, corporate, organized Roman Catholic Church in the West, no unified legal entity, but rather an invisible spiritual community of individual bishoprics, local churches, and monasteries subordinate to tribal and territorial and feudal units as well as to kings and emperor.

The system of penances originated in the monasteries. Each monastic community had its own miniature legal order, its own "rule" of work and prayer and of administration and discipline. Each was independent, subject only to the ultimate control of the bishop of the diocese. Starting in the sixth century, various leading abbots wrote collections of rules, called "penitentials," assigning specific penances for various sins.[43] At first, varying numbers of strokes or blows were assigned for various forms of misconduct; in time physical sanctions became more diversified and non-physical sanctions were added. The usual penance came to be fasting at certain times, to which there were added alms, good works, and compensation of victims. Thus Christian monasticism, without denouncing the old communal methods of dispute resolution and punishment, offered its own procedures, which were more concerned with the care of souls than with the appeasement of vengeance.

Soon penitentials came to be written not only for the discipline of monks but for the discipline of the whole Christian people. By the eleventh century there were scores of such penitentials circulating among the clergy of the peoples of the West. They spread (like the monastic movement itself) from Ireland, Wales, and Scotland to the Anglo-Saxon and Frankish kingdoms, including the eastern territories of the Frankish empire, to Spain, to Lombardy, to Rome itself, and to Scandinavia as well. They were unofficial collections of rules compiled by individual clerics, and were intended not to bind but rather to guide priests in their treatment of persons who confessed their sins. They differed widely in character in different places and in different centuries.

The earliest sources of the Western penitentials are to be found in the practice of the church in the first centuries of the Christian era, both in the East and in the West, to require public penance for heinous sins. In the early centuries all penitents were required to present themselves at a certain time or times during the year to the bishop, who in a solemn and elaborate church ceremony sentenced them, according to the gravity of their sins, to varying terms of fasting and deprivation of the sacraments. For example, the fourth-century Canonical Letters of Basil the Great listed various penances for various sexual or marital offenses, such as rape, adultery, second marriage ("digamy"), and incest; for religious offenses such as magic, idolatry, and violation of graves; and for what at a much later period would be called secular offenses, such as homicide of various kinds, theft, perjury, abortion, and infanticide. The sacrament of penance was supposed to effectuate a permanent reconciliation with God and neighbor. Therefore there was only one penance, just as there was only one baptism; as a result, penance came generally to be postponed until the end of life.[44]

The practice of public penance survived only fitfully in the West after the fifth century. Under Celtic influence it was largely replaced by private penance, which could be repeated at will, with secret confession by each individual to a priest and secret imposition of the duty to perform penitential acts. The types of offenses covered by the Western penitentials were derived from the earlier Eastern models, but new types were added. "Secular" crimes were also sins; in fact, the words "crime" and "sin" were used interchangeably. The penitentials often distinguished between major sins, called "chief crimes" (*capitalia crimina*) and minor sins (*peccata minora*). The chief, or capital, crimes were not defined in terms of acts but rather in terms of states of mind or motivations; there were usually seven — pride, envy, unchastity, anger, bitterness (*accidia*, sometimes called *tristitia seculi*, "sadness of the world"), gluttony, avarice.[45] In the case of a particular type of act — say, homicide — the penance varied according to the motivation of the actor when he committed the act, as well as according to other circumstances. The particular penance imposed by the priest was left to his own discretion, guided by the penitentials.

The penitentials established no trial procedure, although in time they came to indicate the types of questioning that priests should use. The procedure was that of the confessional. Penances were applicable to sins which were confessed to a priest. Typically, the confession was informal and private, and the priest was under a sacred duty not to divulge it. However, in some penitentials (especially Frankish penitentials of the ninth and tenth centuries, which opposed the Celtic tradition in this respect), public penance was preserved for notorious sin.[46] But whether public or private, the penitential system rested ultimately on the consent of the individual offender to confess and to do penance — and, of course, on the strong social pressure of the community which evoked such consent.

Although the penitentials usually stated the penance for a given sin in terms of a certain number of days, months, or years of fasting, they also provided for a great variety of alternative types of atonement. These included prayers and vigils, reading of psalms, and pilgrimages. They also included compensation of victims and assistance of their relatives; thus in cases of beating the offender might be required to pay for medical treatment of the victim, to do his work, and to make compensation. Property that was stolen or property fraudulently obtained or withheld was subject to restitution.[47] Also from an early time the practice developed of permitting substitution of one type of penance for another in cases of necessity. For example, if a person was too ill to fast he might be permitted to substitute a certain number of readings of psalms. Eventually, commutation into monetary payments was introduced, after the fashion of the folklaw, and the payments could be made by kinfolk in exceptional cases. This led to various forms of penance by proxy, including vicarious penance by priests through singing of masses in behalf of the sinner. Commutation of long sentences of fasting and prayer sometimes took bizarre forms, such as sleeping in water, on nutshells, or with a dead body in the grave, or reciting a psalm seven times while standing with arms extended like a cross (called "honest cross-vigil").

Modern historians of the canon law have charged that such devices reduced repentance and grace to "an artificial formality." It is important to recognize, however, that the system of penances did not have the same significance in the Germanic era that it acquired later. For one thing, money payments for offenses and group atonement were central features of Germanic law. For another, prior to the late eleventh century penitential discipline had not become a scientific system of rules and procedures. The absolute duty to confess before taking the sacrament of holy communion had not been established. The sacraments in general had not yet been legalized. The penitential system left great leeway for variations of method, and even of principle, among the various bishoprics and monasteries and even, possibly, the parishes. Above all, the priest was not conceived to have the power himself to absolve the penitent from the consequences of his sin. At most, he could pray that as a result of the penance, God or St. Peter or one of the other saints would absolve the sinner. Only in the post-Germanic period, that is, the late eleventh and twelfth centuries, after the church had established itself as a legal entity, after the legal concept of representation had been fully developed, and after the sacraments had become legalized, would it become possible for the priest to say, "Ego absolvo te."[48]

The basic conception of the penitentials was that penance was medicine for the soul. Thus the Penitential of Burchard of Worms, about 1010 A.D., opens with the following words: "This book is called 'the Corrector' and 'the Physician,' since it contains ample corrections for bodies and medicines for souls and teaches every priest, even the uneducated, how he shall be able to bring help to each person, ordained or unordained; poor or rich; boy, youth, or mature man; decrepit, healthy, or infirm; of every age; and of both sexes."[49] The idea of punishment was subordinated to the idea of cure; and cure was envisioned as the establishment of a right relationship to God, that is, to life as a whole, including the life of the world to come. The ultimate penance was excommunication, which signified deprivation of the right to participate in the sacraments of the church (including communion, marriage, burial, and others); this purported to cut off—temporarily—the relationship of the sinner to God and to the church until by faith and works he had prepared himself for reconciliation. It was an extreme measure, which had an effect similar to outlawry, since curses were heaped not only on the offender but also, prospectively, on anyone who came to his assistance. For the most part, the penances were more subtle. There was a general theory, which derived from medical concepts of the time, that "contraries are cured by their contraries." "The duty of a physician is to cool what is hot, to warm what is cold, to dry what is moist, and to moisten what is dry." [50] This found reflection, for example, in the provision of the Penitential of Columban that "the talkative person is to be sentenced to silence, the disturber to gentleness, the gluttonous to fasting, the sleepy fellow to watchfulness." [51] For the shedding of blood, renunciation of weapons was normally required; for unchastity, abstention from marital intercourse.

Yet a wide variety of variations and substitutions were permitted, depending on the individual offender. As the preface of the Penitential ascribed to Bede states:

> For not all are to be weighted in one and the same balance, although they be associated in one fault, but there shall be discrimination for each of these, that is: between rich and poor; freeman, slave; little child, boy, youth, young man, old man; stupid, intelligent; layman, cleric, monk; bishop, presbyter, deacon, subdeacon, reader, ordained or unordained; married or unmarried; pilgrim, virgin, canoness, or nuns; the weak, the sick, the well. He shall make a distinction for the character of the sins or of the men; a continent person or one who is incontinent, wilfully or by accident; [whether the sin is committed] in public or in secret; with what degree of compunction [the culprit] makes amends by necessity or by intention; the place and times [of offences]. [52]

"In this way," Bishop Mortimer states, "casuistry and moral theology found their way into canon law." [53]

The law of penance, codified in the penitentials, contrasted sharply in many respects with the folklaw as it had developed since pre-Christian times. The folklaw was concerned primarily with the control of the blood feud; the penitential law of the church was concerned primarily with the care of souls. The folklaw based its sanctions for harm principally on the extent of harm; the penitential law of the church based its sanctions for harm principally on the character and degree of the offense. The folklaw rested fundamentally on concepts of honor and fate; the penitential law of the church rested fundamentally on concepts of repentance and forgiveness. The folklaw was directed primarily toward the repression or forestalling of violent conflict within the tribal, local, and lordship community; the penitential law of the church was directed primarily toward the preservation of the spiritual welfare of the community of the faithful and the preparation of their individual souls for eternal life.

Yet despite these contrasts, the penitential law and the folklaw belonged to the same culture. All major "secular" offenses — homicide, robbery, and the like — were also sins to be atoned for by penance; and all major "ecclesiastical" offenses — sexual and marital sins, witchcraft and magic, breaking of vows by monks, and the like — were also crimes prohibited by the folklaw and subject to secular sanctioning. Indeed, the "secular" authorities who administered the criminal law were in fact largely the clergy. One cannot speak, therefore, of a separation of secular and spiritual law, or of secular and ecclesiastical law, in this period of Western history. The folklaw and the penitential law covered the same ground, so to speak. Of course, they covered it in different ways. The writings of the time, from the sixth to the early eleventh centuries, referred to the two ways in terms of "worldly law," or "man's law," on the one hand, and "God's law," on the other. But what are called today the state and the church were both equally concerned with each kind of law. A good illustration of this may be found in a provision of the laws of the Anglo-Saxon King Ethelred: "And he who henceforth in any way violates right laws of God or man, let him expiate zealously . . . as well through divine penance as through worldly correction."[54] Thus the penitential laws were enforced by the king and declared by him to be applicable to all offenses, whether against God or man. Another illustration may be found in the address of one of the Missi Dominici sent out by Charlemagne to check on local administration. "We have been sent here," he begins, "by our Lord, the Emperor Charles, for your eternal salvation, and we charge you to live virtuously according to the law of God, and justly according to the law of the world."[55] Frankish and Anglo-Saxon kings often issued laws requiring ecclesiastical penances to be enforced against violators of worldly law.

The folklaw, having only weak means of enforcement, needed the support of the penitential law in order to maintain its own sanctity, and especially to maintain the sanctity of the oaths on which the folklaw came to rest. Beyond that, the penitential law reinforced the folklaw's emphasis on negotiated settlement, and strongly encouraged the "trust" side of the "trust-mistrust" syndrome. The penitentials appropriated the Germanic word for compensation (in Anglo-Saxon, bot) as the word for penance. Bot was paid for injury to God; sometimes it was called god-bot in the Anglo-Saxon penitentials and also in Anglo-Saxon law generally, and sometimes just bot. The verb form, *gebete,* meant "repent of," "expiate," "atone for." The bot imposed by priests for sins against God had elements of atonement and expiation as well as of restitution. The offer of a reasonable bot to the victim or his kinfolk was thus an offer of reconciliation which he or they had to respect. Also it was an offer which the sinner was required to make and the victim or kinfolk to accept — not by the folklaw but by divine law. It is not surprising that the folklaw bot became permeated with concepts of atonement and reconciliation drawn from the penitential bot. As late as the second decade of the twelfth century, a manual called *Laws of Henry the First* (*Leges Henrici Primi*) repeatedly emphasized that English law preferred friendly settlement to litigation, *amor* or *amicitia* to *judicium*. This was a time when the old system of folklaw was being challenged by new ideas of legality. The unknown author, who was probably an ecclesiastic in the court of the English king, followed the tradition of the penitentials when he wrote: "All causes are . . . preferably to be settled by friendly concord [*pax*]." "Those whom the county court finds in dispute with each other it shall bring together in friendly agreement [*amor*] or it shall let a judgment stand in settlement between them." "But if an oath of reconciliation [*juramentum pacationis*] is demanded, the offender shall swear . . . that if the accuser were in the same position . . . he would accept the offer of compensation or renounce any amends." "If anyone makes amends to another for his misdeed . . . and afterwards for the purpose of effecting a friendly accord [*amicitia*] with him offers him something along with an oath of reconciliation [*pacis*], it is commendable of him to whom the offer is made if he give back the whole thing and not retain any suggestion of the affront [*contumelie*] to himself." "Where any of them has the choice . . . of amicable agreement . . . this shall be as binding as a legal decision [*judicium*] itself." "Concerning disputes between neighbours . . . they shall meet at the boundary court of their lands, and the person who makes the complaint first shall have justice first. If a dispute ought to be taken elsewhere, they shall proceed to the court of their lord . . . and in his court friendly agreement shall bring them together [*eos amicitia congreget*] or a formal judgment shall stand between them [*sequestret judicium*]; if the situation be otherwise they shall proceed to their hundred court if need be." "For it is a rule of law that a person who unwittingly commits a wrong shall consciously make amends. He ought, however, to be the more accorded mercy and compassion at the hands of the dead man's relatives the more we understand that the human race grows sick with the harshnesses of a cruel fortune and with the melancholy and wretched lamentation of all."[56]

More than a century before the *Leges Henrici Primi* a code of Ethelred had stated: "Where a thegn has two choices, love or law" — that is, composition or judgment — "and he chooses love, it shall be as binding as judgment."[57] Doris M. Stenton writes that the importance of this statement, which reappears in Latin in the *Leges Henrici Primi,* lies in the fact that a judicial decision is "likely to leave one party dissatisfied and in mind to make trouble." She goes on to note that, in records of Anglo-Saxon lawsuits of the tenth and eleventh centuries, "it is remarkable how often a party who has been completely successful in the pleadings comes at last to a compromise leaving his opponent possessed for life of the land at issue."[58] What Lady Stenton writes of Anglo-Saxon law is confirmed by reports of Frankish and other European cases of the time. As Stephen White states, disputes both in England and on the Continent in the tenth and eleventh centuries were often concluded by formal compromises symbolized by the exchange of gifts, which were clearly tokens of friendship and mutual trust; he adds that such formal settlements were often reached through the good offices of mediators, sometimes referred to as "friends and neighbors."[59]

One should not, however, exaggerate the influence of the penitentials, or of the church's law of penance, on the folklaw in the period from the sixth to the tenth centuries. The Christian division between God's law and the world's law certainly encouraged and supported some of the softer tendencies of the world's law, and especially what Max Gluckman, referring to contemporary primitive societies, has called "the peace within the feud."[60] But Christianity did not, in those centuries, alter the Germanic folklaw in its fundamental structure. It could not do so, if only because the church as an institution — outside the monasteries — was wholly integrated into Germanic society. Viewed in the abstract, the conflict between the Christian world view and the Germanic was incredibly sharp: *caritas* against honor, mercy against fate, a peaceful and harmonious natural order against a natural order haunted by demonic forces, eternal salvation against sacred temporal values associated with kinship and kingship. But the conflict in world views was not carried over into social action. With regard to social institutions, Christianity at that time took — for the most part — an essentially passive position. Even after the development under Charlemagne of the concept of the king as ruler of the "Christian empire," pagan social institutions continued to prevail. The kingship, Wallace-Hadrill writes, "has been transformed into an office with duties and rights defined by churchmen . . . Should we now call kingship Christian rather than Germanic? I think that it is still Germanic; warfare still holds a prime place in western society: it is still a way of life as much as a means of survival or expansion."[61] Similarly, with regard to criminal law, property law, and even matrimonial law, the ties of kinship continued to predominate and to be enforced ultimately by blood feud and composition. The church preached marriage by consent of the spouses, but many parents continued to have their offspring married in childhood. The church desacralized nature and made it a sin to practice magic or to be superstitious, but Germanic man continued to believe in demons and powers in rocks and trees and to practice his magic and superstitions, and indeed the church eventually assimilated many of the pagan supersititions and — especially in the law — clothed them with Christian formulae and rituals.

Viewed from the perspective of the year 1100 or 1150, the folklaw of the peoples of northern and western Europe in the year 1000 appears quite primitive. In 1000 there was no professional legal scholarship. There was no class of trained lawyers to act as judges, advocates, or advisers in ecclesiastical, royal, city, manorial, mercantile, or other courts. There was no concept of law as a body of principles, a *corpus juris,* in which diverse and contradictory customs and laws were reconciled. There were no textbooks on law and no professors to gloss them. There was no concept of law as an object of study distinct from theology and philosophy; indeed, theology and philosophy were themselves not yet conceived as distinct scholarly disciplines.

Moreover, seen from the perspective of the twelfth century, the institutions of legislation and adjudication of the peoples of northern and western Europe in the year 1000 were very rudimentary. Although kings issued laws, they did so only rarely, and largely in order to reaffirm or revise preexisting customs. The lawmaking authority of popes, metropolitans, and bishops was also largely restricted to occasional reaffirmance or revision of preexisting rules laid down in Scripture or by the church fathers or by church councils. There was no idea that royal or ecclesiastical authorities had the task of systematically developing a body of statutory law. The so-called codes, whether of worldly law or of God's law, were incomplete collections of specific customs, or specific rules, elliptical in character, without definitions of principles or concepts. Similarly with regard to adjudication, there were no professional courts, that is, courts staffed with professional judges, and no idea that cases should be decided according to a developed system of general principles. There were, of course, established rules and procedures for punishing offenses, for compensating for harm, for enforcing agreements, for distributing property on death, and for dealing with many other problems related to justice. Each of the peoples of Europe had its own rather complex legal *order.* But none had a legal *system,* in the sense of a consciously articulated and systematized structure of legal institutions clearly differentiated from other social institutions and cultivated by a corps of persons specially trained for that task.

Not only the style of the early European folklaw but also its content seems primitive by the standards of the Western legal tradition as it has developed since the eleventh and twelfth centuries — and indeed it was expressly condemned as barbaric by the later jurists. In the twelfth century and thereafter, the earlier "magical-mechanical" modes of proof by ordeal and compurgation and battle were finally denounced and replaced. Kinship responsibility and self-enforcing local and feudal customs gave way to more "rational" standards of procedural and substantive law. The church's law of penance, as manifested in the penitentials of the sixth to tenth centuries, also seemed primitive to the canon lawyers of the eleventh and twelfth centuries, and they subjected it to far-reaching changes.

Yet if a different and broader perspective is adopted — not the perspective of the Western legal tradition as it later developed, but the perspective of the legal concepts and legal institutions of non-Western cultures — the negative features of the earlier folklaw are less striking than its positive features.

As in many non-Western cultures, the basic law of the peoples of Europe from the sixth to the tenth centuries was not a body of rules imposed from on high but was rather an integral part of the common consciousness, the "common conscience," of the community. The people themselves, in their public assemblies, legislated and judged; and when kings asserted their authority over the law it was chiefly to guide the custom and the legal consciousness of the people, not to remake it. The bonds of kinship, of lordship units, and of territorial communities *were* the law. If those bonds were violated, the initial response was to seek vengeance, but vengeance was supposed to give way — and usually did — to negotiation for pecuniary sanctions and to reconciliation. Adjudication was often a stage in the reconciliation process. And so peace, once disrupted, was to be restored ultimately by diplomacy. Beyond the question of right and wrong was the question of reconciliation of the warring factions. The same can be said also of the law of many contemporary so-called primitive societies of Africa, Asia, and South America, as well as of many ancient civilizations of both the past and the present.

Before the professionalization and systematization of law, more scope was left for people's attitudes and beliefs and for their unconscious ideas, their processes of mythical thought. This gave rise to legal procedures which depended heavily on ritual and symbol and which in that sense were highly technical, but by the same token the substantive law was plastic and largely nontechnical. Rights and duties were not bound to the letter of legal texts but instead were a reflection of community values, a living law which sprang, in Fritz Kern's words, "out of the creative wells of the sub-conscious." Kern recognized that the customary law of this early period of European history was often "vague, confused, and impractical, technically clumsy," but that it was also "creative, sublime, and suited to human needs."[62] These characterizations, too, are applicable to the legal concepts and processes of many contemporary nonliterate cultures of Africa, Asia, and South America, as well as to complex, literate, ancient civilizations such as those of China, Japan, and India.

Thus many characteristics of the Germanic folklaw that to Western eyes appear to be weaknesses may to non-Western eyes appear to be strengths. The absence of law reform movements, of sophisticated legal machinery, of a strong central lawmaking authority, of a strong central judicial authority, of a body of law independent of religious beliefs and emotions, of a systematic legal science — are only one side of the coin. The other side is the presence of a sense of the wholeness of life, of the interrelatedness of law with all other aspects of life, a sense that legal institutions and legal processes as well as legal norms and legal decisions are all integrated in the harmony of the universe. Law, like art and myth and religion, and like language itself, was for the peoples of Europe, in the early stages of their history, not primarily a matter of making and applying rules in order to determine guilt and fix judgment, not an instrument to separate people from one another on the basis of a set of principles, but rather a matter of holding people together, a matter of reconciliation. Law was conceived primarily as a mediating process, a mode of communication, rather than primarily as a process of rule-making and decision-making.

In these respects, Germanic and other European folklaw had much in common with certain Eastern legal philosophies. In the Sufi tradition of the Middle East, one of the stories told of the Mulla Nasrudin depicts him as a magistrate hearing his first case. The plaintiff argues so persuasively that Nasrudin exclaims, "I believe you are right." The clerk of the court begs him to restrain himself, since the defendant is yet to be heard. Listening to the defendant's argument, Nasrudin is again so carried away that he cries out, "I believe you are right." The clerk of the court cannot allow this. "Your honor," he says, "they cannot both be right." "I believe you are right," Nasrudin replies.[63] Both are right, yet both cannot be right. The answer is not to be found by asking the question, Who is right? The answer is to be found by saving the honor of both sides and thereby restoring the right relationship between them.

In the tradition of peoples of Asia who have lived under the strong influence of both Buddhist and Confucian thought, social control is not to be found primarily in the allocation of rights and duties through a system of general norms but rather in the maintaining of right relationships among family members, among families within lordship units, and among families and lordship units within local communities and under the emperor. Social harmony is more important than "giving to each his due." Indeed, "each" is not conceived as a being distinct from his society — or from the universe — but rather as an integral part of a system of social relationships subject to the Principle of Heaven. Therefore in the ancient civilizations of Asia the traditional, collective, and intuitive sides of life were emphasized, and the intellectual, analytical, and legal sides were fused with and subordinated to them.[64]

This was true also of the peoples of Europe before the great explosion of the late eleventh and early twelfth centuries. The folk myths which dominated their thought prior to (and after) the introduction of Christianity did not make a sharp division between magic and logic or between fate and the rules of criminal law. Nor did Christianity—an Eastern religion—make a sharp division between faith and reason.

But is it possible to say that law exists in a society whose social order reflects an "Eastern" concept of the fusion, or harmony, of all aspects of social life? Does law exist, for example, among the Tiv of northern Nigeria, who have a system of social control which rests on clan and lineage loyalties, clan reprisals, and ritual reparation to avoid punishment by supernatural sources, but who have no distinct governmental institutions, no courts, and no word in their language for law?[65] They accept certain rules as binding upon them, certain decisions as authoritative, and certain procedures for declaring these rules and decisions effective. Does the fact that *they* do not distinguish these procedures and decisions and rules from religion, politics, economics, and family life, and do not call them "law," mean that *we* should not call them law? May we not say that among the Tiv—and in many other societies—*what we call law* is wholly diffuse, wholly interwoven with religious, political, economic, family, and other social institutions and processes? A. S. Diamond, who defines law as rules of conduct whose breach is regularly met by sanctions imposed by the community through regular procedures, states categorically that "the Tiv have no law." For Diamond, with his Western orientation, "law in the full sense of that word" consists of "rules of conduct enforceable by an organ of the state"; this definition would also almost rule out Germanic law (including Anglo-Saxon and Frankish law), of which Diamond indeed says that it is only "near the beginnings of law."[66]

The paradigm of a social order in which law is largely diffuse, largely embedded in religious, political, economic, family, and other social institutions and processes—and the thesis that such a social order preceded, historically, the development of the legal systems of Western civilization—was advanced more than a century ago in the writings of Sir Henry Maine. Maine wrote that the ancient Roman, Greek, and Hindu law codes, both in the East and the West, "mingled up religious, civil, and merely moral ordinances without any regard to differences in their essential character," and that "the severance of law from morality and religion from law belong only to the *later* stages of mental progress."[67] To answer these statements, as Diamond does, by asserting that the early codes contain very little "religious matter," that they are "entirely secular," and that they "show no confusion between law and religion" begs the question of what is law and what is religion.[68] Maine argued, in effect, that rules which might appear to a modern observer to be "en-

tirely secular"—for example, that one who slays a freeman should pay
100 shillings wergeld and one who slays a nobleman should pay 300 shillings wergeld—were in fact wholly bound up with the moral and
religious rules of the society. It is not sufficient to say that such a rule is
to be distinguished from modern legal rules only insofar as there was an
absence of centralized government or other specific "legal machinery" for
enforcing it (as Dennis Lloyd has argued),[69] or that the mode of enforcement of the rule (by ordeal or compurgation) was religious but the rule
itself was secular (as Diamond would have it).[70] The important point is
that the whole Germanic system of rules of pecuniary compensation for
injuries was part of the paradigm of wyrd and lof, wer and bot, mund,
frith, borh, wed—part of the system of *fate* and *honor* which fused law
with religion, politics, economics, clan and household loyalties. Diamond reduces his own argument to absurdity when he contends that
much of the Hebrew law of the Old Testament is also "secular law,"
wholly distinct from religion. The Hebrews never recognized such a distinction and would have denounced it; for them every word of the Bible
was sacred.

It is my contention that the folklaw of the peoples of Europe in the
sixth to tenth centuries was merged with religion and morality, and yet it
was law, a legal order, a legal dimension of social life; and further, that it
makes sense to identify as a legal dimension of social life the shared sentiment of the members of any community—even a family or neighborhood or school—that they are bound by mutual rights and duties that
derive from an authority recognized by them. As soon as a child invokes
the principles of equality, consistency, and adherence to a promise or
rule—to argue, for example, that he has a right to a certain toy because
his brother had it earlier and because they always take turns with it and
because it is *his* and because his father said so—then it makes sense to
speak of an appeal to Right or to Law. Such an argument may be discouraged by some systems of child rearing, especially those strongly influenced by the Confucian ethic. Yet the fact that the argument has to be
discouraged is some evidence that it reflects a principle that is inherent in
social ordering.

It is not that a family—or a village—governed by the Confucian ethic
has no law, but rather that the legal dimension of its life is wholly subordinated to the nonlegal, the *fa* to the *li*.[71] It is not that the Tiv lack law,
but that their legal rights and duties are wholly interwoven with religious
and other institutions and values. And what links the folklaw of the Germanic peoples of Europe to these and other non-Western legal orders is
the fact that the folklaw was subordinated to kinship and lordship and
kingship loyalties and interwoven with the heroic struggle for honor in a
universe ruled by fate.

If a single phrase can be used to describe what all these various legal

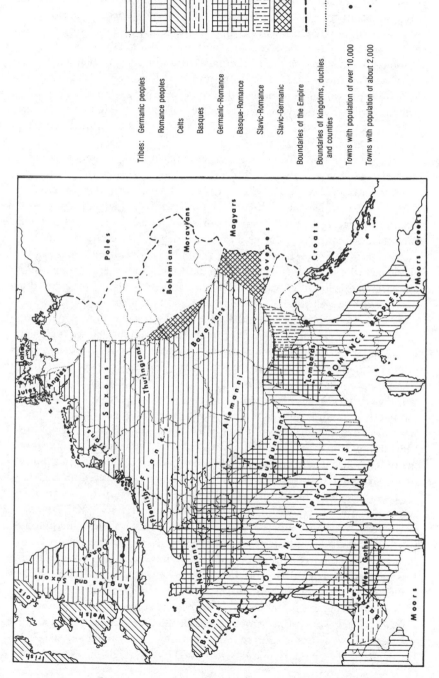

Map 1. Western Europe circa 1050.

orders have in common, it is the sanctity of custom. Custom is sacred and its norms are sacred. In Sophocles' words, "these laws are not for now or for yesterday, they are alive forever; and no one knows when they were shown to us first" (*Antigone*). In this type of legal order, law is not something that is consciously made and remade by central authorities; there may be occasional legislation, but for the most part law is something that grows out of the patterns and norms of behavior, the folkways and the mores, of the community. Moreover, in this type of legal order, custom is not subjected to conscious and systematic and continuous rational scrutiny by jurists. Custom is so sacred that it might not even be called sacred; it is simply unquestioningly and unquestionably respected.

Yet the Germanic folklaw does not fit easily into the model or archetype of Customary Law—or, indeed, into any other model or archetype, including Archaic Law and primitive law—if only for the reason that it came under the influence of Christianity. The emergence of Christianity and its spread across Europe was a unique event, which cannot be explained by any general social theory. By contradicting the Germanic world view and splitting life into two realms, Christianity challenged the ultimate sanctity of custom, including the ultimate sanctity of kinship, lordship, and kingship relations. It also challenged the ultimate sanctity of nature—of the water and fire of the ordeals, for example. It challenged their *ultimate* sanctity, however, without denying their sanctity altogether; on the contrary, the church actually supported the sacred institutions and values of the folk (including the ordeals). The church supported them and at the same time challenged them by setting up a higher alternative—the realm of God, God's law, the life of the world to come. When life was split into two realms, the eternal and the temporal, the temporal was thereby depreciated in value but not otherwise directly affected. The split took place not in the life of society but in the human soul. Yet social life was *in*directly affected in important ways. The basic structure of the folklaw remained unaltered, but many of its particular features were strongly influenced by Christian beliefs.

If all traces of Christianity could be subtracted from the Germanic folklaw, it might well fall into one or more of the archetypes of legal orders which have been offered by social theorists. It would fall squarely into Archaic Law, together with the Roman law in the time of the Twelve Tables, early Hindu law, and ancient Greek law. It would fall less squarely into primitive law. It might be viewed as a type of law characteristic of an incipient feudalism. It would surely be an example of Customary Law. Such models as these, however, are only partly applicable to the legal institutions of the Frankish, Anglo-Saxon, and other peoples of Europe in the sixth to tenth centuries. They make no place for the penitentials, or the religious laws issued by kings, or the central role of the clergy in all phases of government. Above all, Christianity attached a positive value to law which is in sharp contrast to attitudes toward law that are characteristic of religions or philosophies of other societies whose general institutional structure is comparable to that of the Christianized peoples of Europe.

If however, one compares the situation of the church in the Germanic-Frankish period of European history with that of the Mosaic priesthood in the tribal period of the history of Israel, one is struck by the ambivalence of the church's attitude toward law and by its otherworldliness. In fact, it was an essential part of the Christian faith of that time to deny the value of attempting to reform in any fundamental way the law of this world. The world's law was believed to be just and even sacred. It failed only if it was compared in value with God's law, which alone could save the wicked from hellfire.

It was this attitude toward law, and toward the relation of the church to the world, that changed dramatically in the late eleventh and the twelfth centuries. The church set out to reform both itself and the world by law. It established itself as a visible, corporate, legal entity, independent of imperial, royal, feudal, and urban authorities. Autonomous bodies of law were articulated, first within the ecclesiastical polity and then within the various secular polities, in part to maintain the cohesion of each polity, in part to achieve the reform of each, in part to keep an equilibrium among them all. These new developments were only possible, however, because the foundations for them had been laid in the earlier period. It was then that a basis was established for the formation of stable communities; that basis was the integrated *populus christianus* in which there was neither a separation of church from state nor a separation of law from other modes of social control. From a sociological and historical point of view, the existence of such an integrated society was a necessary prerequisite to the later creation of diverse, autonomous, competing systems of law, ecclesiastical and secular. Without that prior integration, new legal systems would have been seen as merely mechanical and bureaucratic, and they would have been incapable of achieving their ultimate purposes of cohesion, reform, and equilibrium.

In the late twentieth century the prehistory of the Western legal tradition takes on special significance. Western society during the past two generations has been characterized increasingly by fundamental divisions of race, class, the sexes, and the generations. Bonds of faith have grown weak and bonds of kinship and of soil have given way to vague and abstract nationalisms. With the breakdown of stable communities, the West no longer has confidence in law as a way of protecting spiritual values against corrupting social, economic, and political forces. There is, of course, no returning to the past—least of all, to the remote beginnings of Western civilization. Yet it is important, in a time of skep-

ticism, for the skeptics, above all, to ask by what historical route
Western man has come to his present predicament, and to confront their
own nostalgia for an earlier age when people really believed that "peace
vanquishes law, and love vanquishes justice."

2 | The Origin of the Western Legal Tradition in the Papal Revolution

A MONG THE PEOPLES of western Europe in the period prior to
the eleventh century, law did not exist as a distinct system of
regulation or as a distinct system of thought. Each people had,
to be sure, its own legal order, which included occasional legal enactments by central authorities as well as innumerable unwritten legal rules
and institutions, both secular and ecclesiastical. A considerable number
of individual legal terms and rules had been inherited from the earlier
Roman law and could be found in the canons and decrees of local ecclesiastical councils and of individual bishops as well as in some royal
legislation and in customary law. Lacking, however, in both the secular
and the ecclesiastical spheres, was a clear separation of law from other
processes of social control and from other types of intellectual concern.
Secular law as a whole was not "disembedded" from general tribal, local,
and feudal custom or from the general custom of royal and imperial
households. Similarly, the law of the church was largely diffused
throughout the life of the church—throughout its structures of authority
as well as its theology, its moral precepts, its liturgy—and it, too, was
primarily local and regional and primarily customary rather than centralized or enacted. There were no professional judges or lawyers. There
were no hierarchies of courts.

Also lacking was a perception of law as a distinct "body" of rules and
concepts. There were no law schools. There were no great legal texts
dealing with basic legal categories such as jurisdiction, procedure,
crime, contract, property, and the other subjects which eventually came
to form structural elements in Western legal systems. There were no
developed theories of the sources of law, of the relation of divine and
natural law to human law, of ecclesiastical law to secular law, of enacted
law to customary law, or of the various kinds of secular law—feudal,
royal, urban—to one another.

The relatively unsystematized character of legal regulation and the relatively undeveloped state of legal science were closely connected with the prevailing political, economic, and social conditions. These included the predominantly local character of tribal, village, and feudal communities; their relatively high degree of economic self-sufficiency; the fusion of authorities within each; the relative weakness of the political and economic control exercised by the central imperial and royal authorities; the essentially military and religious character of the control exercised by the imperial and royal authorities; and the relative strength of informal community bonds of kinship and soil and of military comradeship.

In the late eleventh, the twelfth, and the early thirteenth centuries a fundamental change took place in western Europe in the very nature of law both as a political institution and as an intellectual concept. Law became disembedded. Politically, there emerged for the first time strong central authorities, both ecclesiastical and secular, whose control reached down, through delegated officials, from the center to the localities. Partly in connection with that, there emerged a class of professional jurists, including professional judges and practicing lawyers. Intellectually, western Europe experienced at the same time the creation of its first law schools, the writing of its first legal treatises, the conscious ordering of the huge mass of inherited legal materials, and the development of the concept of law as an autonomous, integrated, developing body of legal principles and procedures.

The combination of these two factors, the political and the intellectual, helped to produce modern Western legal systems, of which the first was the new system of canon law of the Roman Catholic Church (then regularly called for the first time *jus canonicum*). It was also at that time divided into "old law" (*jus antiquum*), consisting of earlier texts and canons, and "new law" (*jus novum*), consisting of contemporary legislation and decisions as well as contemporary interpretations of the earlier texts and canons. Against the background of the new system of canon law, and often in rivalry with it, the European kingdoms and other polities began to create their own secular legal systems. At the same time there emerged in most parts of Europe free cities, each with its own governmental and legal institutions, forming a new type of urban law. In addition, feudal (lord-vassal) and manorial (lord-peasant) legal institutions underwent systematization, and a new system of mercantile law was developed to meet the needs of merchants engaged in intercity, interregional, and international trade. The emergence of these systems of feudal law, manorial law, mercantile law, and urban law clearly indicates that not only political and intellectual but also social and economic factors were at work in producing what can only be called a revolutionary development of legal institutions. In other words, the creation of modern legal systems in the late eleventh, twelfth, and early thirteenth centuries was not only an implementation of policies and theories of central elites, but also a response to social and economic changes "on the ground."

Religious factors were at work, as well. The creation of modern legal systems was, in the first instance, a response to a revolutionary change within the church and in the relation of the church to the secular authorities. And here the word "revolutionary" has all the modern connotations of class struggle and violence. In 1075, after some twenty-five years of agitation and propaganda by the papal party, Pope Gregory VII declared the political and legal supremacy of the papacy over the entire church and the independence of the clergy from secular control. Gregory also asserted the ultimate supremacy of the pope in secular matters, including the authority to depose emperors and kings. The emperor— Henry IV of Saxony—responded with military action. Civil war between the papal and imperial parties raged sporadically throughout Europe until 1122, when a final compromise was reached by a concordat signed in the German city of Worms. In England and Normandy, the Concordat of Bec in 1107 had provided a temporary respite, but the matter was not finally resolved there until the martyrdom of Archbishop Thomas Becket in 1170.

The great changes that took place in the life of the Western Church and in the relations between the ecclesiastical and the secular authorities during the latter part of the eleventh and the first part of the twelfth centuries have traditionally been called the Hildebrand Reform, or the Gregorian Reform, after the German monk Hildebrand, who was a leader of the papal party in the period after 1050 and who ruled as Pope Gregory VII from 1073 to 1085. However, the term "Reform" is a serious understatement, reflecting in part the desire of the papal party itself—and of later Roman Catholic historians—to play down the magnitude of the discontinuity between what had gone before and what came after. The original Latin term, *reformatio*, may suggest a more substantial break in continuity by recalling the sixteenth-century Protestant Reformation. Another term used to denote the same era, namely, the Investiture Struggle, is not so much an understatement as an oblique statement: by pointing to the struggle of the papacy to wrest from emperor and kings the power to "invest" bishops with the symbols of their authority, the phrase connects the conflict between the papal and imperial (or royal) parties with the principal slogan of the papal reformers: "the freedom of the church." But even this dramatic slogan does not adequately convey the full dimensions of the revolutionary transformation, which many leading historians have considered to be the first major turning point in European history, and which some have recognized as the beginning of the modern age.[1] What was involved ultimately was, in Peter Brown's words, "the disengagement of the two spheres of the sacred and the profane," from which there stemmed a release of energy and creativity analogous to a process of nuclear fission.[2]

Church and Empire: The Cluniac Reform

Prior to the late eleventh century, the clergy of Western Christendom —bishops, priests, and monks—were, as a rule, much more under the authority of emperors, kings, and leading feudal lords than of popes. For one thing, most church property belonged to those very emperors, kings, and feudal lords. As lay proprietors, they not only controlled church lands and incomes but also appointed persons—often selected from among their close relatives—to the bishoprics and other ecclesiastical offices which were part of their property. Such power of appointment to ecclesiastical offices ("benefices") was often very lucrative, since those offices usually carried the obligation to provide revenue and services from the lands which went with them. Thus a bishopric was usually a large feudal estate, with manorial lords to administer the agricultural economy and to carry out military duties, and with peasants to provide the labor. A lesser church office within the bishopric—an ordinary village parsonage, for example—might also be a lucrative property; the patron would be entitled to a share of the agricultural produce and of the income from various kinds of economic services.

In addition to its political-economic subordination, the church was also subject in its internal structure to the control of leading laymen. Emperors and kings called church councils and promulgated church law. At the same time, bishops and other prominent clergy sat in governmental bodies—local, baronial, and royal or imperial. The bishopric was often a principal agency of civil administration. Bishops were important members of the feudal hierarchy. Marriage of priests, which was very widespread, brought them into important kinship ties with local rulers. Emperors and kings invested bishops not only with their civil and feudal authority but also with their ecclesiastical authority. Thus there was a fusion of the religious and political spheres. A dispute over the jurisdiction of a bishop might end up at Rome or in a regional synod, but it might also end up in the court of a king or of the emperor.

The system was similar to that which prevailed in the Eastern Roman Empire, and which was later denounced in the West as Caesaropapism.

It is not strictly correct, however, to speak of the kings and emperors of western Europe in the sixth to eleventh centuries as "laymen." That is what the pope called them after 1075, but before then they had had undisputed religious functions. It is true that they were not clergy; that is, they were not ordained priests. Nevertheless, they were "deputies of Christ," sacral figures, who were considered to be the religious leaders of their people. They were often said to be men made holy by their anointment and to have healing powers. The emperor, especially, claimed to be the supreme spiritual leader of Christendom, whom no man could judge, but who himself judged all men and would be responsible for all men at the Last Judgment.[3]

The empire of Charlemagne or of Henry IV is not to be confused with the earlier Roman Empire of Caesar Augustus or of Constantine. Although an illusion of continuity with ancient Rome was maintained, the Carolingian term "empire" (*imperium*) referred not to a territory or a federation of peoples but rather to the nature of the emperor's authority, which was in fact very different from that of the earlier Roman emperors. Unlike Caesar, Charlemagne and his successors did not rule their subjects through an imperial bureaucracy. There was no capital city comparable to Rome or Constantinople — indeed, in sharp contrast to Caesar's city-studded empire, Charlemagne and his successors had hardly any cities at all. Instead, the emperor and his household traveled through his vast realm from one principal locality to another. He was constantly on the move, traveling in France, Burgundy, Italy, Hungary, as well as in his Frankish-German homeland. In an economy which was almost entirely local, and in a political structure which gave supreme power to tribal and regional leaders, the emperor had both the military task of maintaining a coalition of tribal armies which would defend the empire against enemies from without and the spiritual task of maintaining the Christian faith of the empire against a reversion to paganism. He ruled by holding court. He was first and foremost the judge of his people. When he arrived in a place he would hear complaints and do justice; he was also the protector of the poor and weak, the widows, the orphans.

The empire was not a geographical entity, but a military and spiritual authority. It was not called the Roman Empire until 1034, and it was not called the Holy Roman Empire until 1254.

In the tenth and early eleventh centuries there was a strong movement to purge the church of feudal and local influences and of the corruption that inevitably accompanied them. A leading part in this movement was played by the Abbey of Cluny, whose headquarters were in the town of that name in southern France. Cluny is of special interest from a legal point of view because it was the first monastic order in which all the monasteries, scattered throughout Europe, were subordinate to a single head. Prior to the founding of Cluny in 910, each Benedictine monastery had been an independent unit ruled by an abbot, usually under the jurisdiction of the local bishop, with only a loose federal connection with other Benedictine monasteries. The Cluniac monasteries, on the other hand, which may have numbered well over a thousand within a century after the order was founded, were all ruled by priors under the jurisdiction of the Abbot of Cluny. For this reason Cluny has been called the first translocal corporation;[4] ultimately it served in this respect as a model for the Roman Catholic Church as a whole.

Cluny's importance as a model of translocal, hierarchial, corporate government was matched by its importance in supporting the first peace movement in Europe. In a number of synods held in different parts of southern and central France near the end of the tenth century, the idea of a Peace of God was given official sanction not only by the clergy but by secular rulers. The peace decrees of the various synods differed in detail, but in general they all forbade, under pain of excommunication, any act of warfare or vengeance against clerics, pilgrims, merchants, Jews, women, and peasants, as well as against ecclesiastical and agricultural property. Moreover, they generally made use of the device of the oath to secure support; that is, people were asked to swear collectively to support the peace. At the Council of Bourges in 1038, for example, it was decreed that every adult Christian of the archdiocese should take such an oath and should enter a special militia to enforce the peace. In addition to the protection of noncombatants, the peace movement, which spread throughout most of western Europe, came to include a prohibition of warfare on certain days. Authored by Abbot Odilo of Cluny (994-1049), the Truce of God suspended warfare at first from Saturday noon until early Monday morning, and later from Wednesday evening until Monday morning as well as during Lent and Advent and on various saints' days.

The efforts of Cluny and the church generally to exempt certain classes of people from military service and from attack on their person or property, and to restrict fighting to certain times, could be only partly successful in an age of violence and anarchy such as the tenth and eleventh centuries. The importance of the peace movement for the future, however, and especially for the future of the Western legal tradition, was enormous, for the experience of collective oath-taking by groups in the name of peace played a crucial role in the founding of cities in the late eleventh century and thereafter, in the formation of guilds within cities, and in the promulgation of legislation by dukes, kings, and emperors through the so-called ducal or royal peace and through the "land peace" (*pax terrae, Landfriede*).

Above all, the Cluniacs and other reforming houses sought to raise the level of religious life by attacking the ecclesiastical power of feudal and local rulers, which was manifested particularly in the buying and selling of church offices (called "simony") and also in the related practices of clerical marriages and clerical concubinage (called "nicolaism"), through which bishops and priests were involved in local and clan politics. For these efforts to succeed, however, the support of a strong central power was needed. The papacy would have been far too weak for this purpose; at this time popes were, in fact, subordinate to the nobility of the city of Rome. The Cluniacs successfully sought the support of the emperors, Charlemagne's successors, who governed the area including what is now western Germany, eastern France, Switzerland, and northern Italy. The emperors, in turn, were glad to have Cluny's support, as well as that of other reform movements; with such support, in time, they wrested from the nobles of Rome the power to appoint the pope.

Contrary to modern ideas of the separateness of the church and the state, the church in the year 1000 was not conceived as a visible, corporate, legal structure standing opposite the political authority. Instead, the church, the *ecclesia*, was conceived as the Christian people, *populus christianus*, which was governed by both secular and priestly rulers (*regnum* and *sacerdotium*). Long before Charlemagne consented to be crowned emperor by the pope in 800, his devoted servant Alcuin, the English scholar and ecclesiastic, had referred to him as ruler of the *imperium christianum* ("Christian empire"), and Charlemagne himself in 794 had called a "universal" church council at Frankfurt at which he promulgated important changes in theological doctrine and ecclesiastical law. Some historians argue that Pope Leo III made Charlemagne emperor, but it is closer to the truth to say that Charlemagne made Leo pope; and in 813 Charlemagne crowned his own son emperor without benefit of clergy.[5] In fact, later German emperors required the pope, on his election, to swear an oath of loyalty to the emperor. Of the twenty-five popes who held office during the hundred years prior to 1059 (when a church synod for the first time prohibited lay investiture), twenty-one were directly appointed by emperors and five were dismissed by emperors. Moreover, it was not only the German emperors who controlled bishops within their domain. The other rulers of Christendom did the same. In 1067 William the Conqueror issued a famous decree asserting that the king had the power to determine whether or not a pope should be acknowledged by the church in Normandy and England, that the king made ecclesiastical law through church synods convened by him, and that the king had a veto power over ecclesiastical penalties imposed on his barons and officials.

Imperial and royal control of the church was needed to emancipate it from the corrupting influences of baronial and local politics and economics. However, this basic aim of the Cluniac Reform faced an insuperable obstacle: the clergy were so thoroughly enmeshed in the political and economic structure at all levels that they could not be extracted from it. Under the aegis of the great reforming emperors of the tenth and eleventh centuries, the monastic orders could be cleansed and the papacy could be strengthened, but the church as a whole could not be radically reformed because it was not independent. Simony and nicolaism remained burning issues.

Nicolaism (clerical marriage) was not only a moral issue, in the narrow sense, but also a social and political and economic issue. Marriage brought the priesthood within the clan and feudal structure. It also involved the inheritance of some church offices by priests' sons and other relatives. This, at least, placed some limits upon simony (sale of ecclesiastical beneficies). If no church offices were to be heritable, could appointment (investiture) continue to be left in lay hands? More fundamentally, were emperors and kings spiritually qualified to make the large number of new appointments to high clerical offices that would be required if priests could no longer marry and have heirs to succeed them? And what about lower clerical offices that were to be filled at the behest of feudal lords?

There had always been a certain tension associated with the subordination of the clergy, and especially the papacy, to persons who, however dignified and even sacred their offices, were not themselves ordained priests. At the end of the fourth century, St. Ambrose, Bishop of Milan, had said, "Palaces belong to the emperor, churches to the priesthood"; and he had excommunicated Emperor Theodosius, lifting the curse of anathema only after the emperor had done penance. A century later Pope Gelasius I had written to the Emperor Anastasius: "Two [swords] there are, august emperor, by which this world is chiefly ruled, the sacred authority of the priesthood and the royal power . . . If the bishops themselves, recognizing that the imperial office was conferred on you by divine disposition, obey your laws so far as the sphere of public order is concerned . . . with what zeal, I ask you, ought you to obey those who have been charged with administering the sacred mysteries [in matters of religion]?"[6] This was the original "two swords" doctrine: the priesthood administered the sacred mysteries, but the emperors made the laws, including the ecclesiastical laws. Among the Franks, kings and emperors had often depended on the support of popes and had acknowledged their superiority, and that of bishops generally, in matters of faith. The idea of ecclesiastical autonomy had deep roots in scriptural authority as well. Yet in fact Frankish emperors, and in the tenth and eleventh centuries German emperors as well as French and English kings—plus Spanish, Norse, Danish, Polish, Bohemian, Hungarian, and other rulers — governed bishops even in matters of religious doctrine, just as the Byzantine emperors had done. Moreover, they invested clergy with the insignia of their clerical offices: Frankish emperors and kings bestowed upon bishops the ring and pastoral staff that symbolized their episcopal authority, and uttered the words, "Accipe ecclesiam!" ("Receive the church!"). This placed both the secular sword and the spiritual sword in the same hand. The justification was that emperors and kings were consecrated, sacral rulers, "deputies of Christ." There were many bishops, of whom the Bishop of Rome was primate (first among equals), but there was only one emperor, and within each kingdom only one king.

The Bishop of Rome had the title "deputy of St. Peter." Only in the twelfth century did he acquire the title "deputy of Christ." Only then was the emperor compelled to relinquish that title. As deputy of Christ, the pope claimed to wield both swords—one directly, the other indirectly. Now there were many secular rulers but only one pope.

The primacy of the Bishop of Rome among the other bishops of the church had been asserted as early as the fourth, and possibly even the third, century, and had occasionally—though by no means always—been acknowledged by other leading bishops. Primacy, however, could mean many different things. As long as the church in the West remained largely decentralized and under the control of local lay rulers, papal authority was inevitably weak and was closely linked with imperial authority, which was also weak. The occasional struggle of local bishops and local churches to emancipate themselves from local lords might thus take the form of appeal to either imperial authority or papal authority or both. Only rarely did conflict escalate to higher levels. A striking example was the great forgery of the mid-ninth century known as the Pseudo-Isidore, or False Decretals. This was a huge collection of letters and decrees, falsely attributed to popes and councils from the fourth century on; it was directed against the efforts of the Archbishop of Rheims, supported by the emperor, to prevent his clergy from having recourse to Rome to decide disputes. The fact that for this purpose the author had to concoct a multitude of documents tells something of the nature of episcopal authority in the church at that time and before. In fact, the Pseudo-Isidore was not composed in Rome and was not generally accepted by the popes until over two hundred years later, when the papal party used it to justify aims quite different from those of the original text. In the latter part of the ninth century Pope Nicholas I (856-867) did assert papal authority not only over archbishops and bishops, declaring that their sees could not be filled without his consent, but also over emperors, declaring that kings were not entitled to sit in judgment over priests and that priests were exempt from the jurisdiction of kings. Again, however, such assertions were more important for the future than for their own time. They did not change the reality of imperial, royal, and local lay lordship over the church. Indeed, in the latter ninth, the tenth, and the early eleventh centuries, the prestige of the papacy was at its lowest ebb, and it was the emperors who attempted to raise it.

The primacy of the Bishop of Rome among other bishops also gave the king of the Germans a reason to take his armies down across the Alps every few years to reassert his imperial claim to be protector of Rome against the Lombard and Tuscan and Roman nobility.

The spiritual authority of the emperors became increasingly anomalous in the eleventh century, as simony and nicolaism proved too deeply rooted for them to overcome. In 1046 the subordination of the bishops of Rome to the emperor became not only anomalous but scandalous when Henry III, upon arrival in Rome to celebrate his imperial coronation, saw to it that three rival popes were deposed and a fourth elected. His appointee died after a few months in office, and a second appointee died a few weeks later—both said to have been poisoned by factions in Rome that resented imperial intervention in the affairs of the city.[7] A third appointee, Leo IX (1049-1053), though a close kinsman and friend of Henry III, rejected the concept of the papacy as a bishopric of the emperor, and asserted not only his own independence but also his power over all other bishops and clergy, even outside the empire.

During Leo's reign a group of his protégés—led by Hildebrand—formed a party which proposed and promoted the idea of papal supremacy over the church. Among its techniques was widespread publicity for the papal program. Eventually a large polemical literature which included many hundreds of pamphlets, was circulated by partisans of various sides. One historian has called this period "the first great age of propaganda in world history."[8] The papal pamphlets urged Christians to refuse to take the sacraments from priests living in concubinage or marriage, contested the validity of clerical appointments made in return for money payments, and demanded the "freedom of the church"—that is, the freedom of the clergy, under the pope, from emperor, kings, and feudal lords. Finally, in 1059 a council in Rome called by Pope Nicholas II declared for the first time the right of the Roman cardinals to elect the pope.

The Dictates of the Pope

It was Hildebrand who in the 1070s, as Pope Gregory VII, turned the reform movement of the church against the very imperial authority which had led the Cluniac reformers during the tenth and early eleventh centuries. Gregory went much farther than his predecessors. He proclaimed the legal supremacy of the pope over all Christians and the legal supremacy of the clergy, under the pope, over all secular authorities. Popes, he said, could depose emperors—and he proceeded to depose Emperor Henry IV. Moreover, Gregory proclaimed that all bishops were to be appointed by the pope and were to be subordinate ultimately to him and not to secular authority.

Gregory had been well prepared to ascend the papal throne. He had been the dominant force in the reigns of the popes Nicholas II (1058-1061) and Alexander II (1061-1073). Also, in 1073 at the age of fifty, he was ready to exercise the enormous will and pride and personal authority for which he was notorious. Peter Damian (1007-1072), who had been associated with him in the struggle for papal supremacy since the 1050s, once addressed him as "my holy Satan," and said: "Thy will has ever been a command to me—evil but lawful. Would that I had always served God and Saint Peter as faithfully as I have served thee."[9] A modern scholar has described Gregory as a man with an overpowering sense of mission, who pressed his ideas with "frightening severity and heroic persistence . . . regardless of the consequences to himself or to others [and who] had, to say the least, the temper of a revolutionary."[10]

Once he became pope, Gregory did not hesitate to use revolutionary tactics to accomplish his objectives. In 1075, for example, he ordered all Christians to boycott priests who were living in concubinage or marriage, and not to accept their offices for the sacraments or other purposes. Thus priests were required to choose between their responsibilities to their wives and children and their responsibilities to their parishioners. As a result of opposition to this decree, there were open riots in churches and beating and stoning of those who opposed clerical marriage. One writer, in a pamphlet entitled "Apology against Those who Challenge the Masses of Priests," stated that Christianity was being "trampled underfoot." "What else is talked about even in the women's spinning-rooms and the artisans' workshops," he asked, "than the confusion of all human laws . . . sudden unrest among the populace, new treacheries of servants against their masters and masters' mistrust of their servants, abject breaches of faith among friends and equals, conspiracies against the power ordained by God? . . . and all this backed by authority, by those who are called the leaders of Christendom."[11]

Lacking armies of its own, how was the papacy to make good its claims? How was it to overcome the armies of those who would oppose papal supremacy? And apart from the problem of meeting forceful opposition, how was the papacy to exercise the universal jurisdiction it had asserted? How was it effectively to impress its will on the entire Western Christian world, let alone Eastern Christendom, over which some claims of jurisdiction were also made?

An important aspect of the answers to these questions was the potential role of law as a source of authority and a means of control. During the last decades of the eleventh century, the papal party began to search the written record of church history for legal authority to support papal supremacy over the entire clergy as well as clerical independence of, and possible supremacy over, the entire secular branch of society. The papal party encouraged scholars to develop a science of law which would provide a working basis for carrying out these major policies. At the same time, the imperial party also began to search for ancient texts that would support its cause against papal usurpation.

There was, however, no legal forum to which either the papacy or the imperial authority could take its case — except to the pope or the emperor himself. This, indeed, was the principal revolutionary element in the situation. In 1075 Pope Gregory VII responded to it by "looking within his own breast" and writing a document — the *Dictatus Papae* (*Dictates of the Pope*) — consisting of twenty-seven terse propositions, apparently addressed to no one but himself, including the following:

1. That the Roman church is founded by the Lord alone.
2. That the Roman bishop alone is by right called universal.
3. That he alone may depose and reinstate bishops.
4. That his legate, even if of lower grade, takes precedence, in a council, over all bishops and may render a sentence of deposition against them.
7. That to him alone is it permitted to make new laws according to the needs of the times.
9. That the pope alone is the one whose feet are to be kissed by all princes.
10. That his name alone is to be recited in churches.
11. That he may depose emperors.
16. That no synod should be called general without his order.
17. That no chapter or book may be regarded as canonical without his authority.
18. That no judgment of his may be revised by anyone, and that he alone may revise [the judgments] of all.
21. That the more important cases of every church may be referred to the Apostolic See.
27. That he may absolve subjects of unjust men from their [oath of] fealty."[12]

This document was revolutionary—although Gregory ultimately managed to find some legal authority for every one of its provisions.[13]

In December 1075 Gregory made known the contents of his Papal Manifesto, as it might be called today, in a letter to Emperor Henry IV in which he demanded the subordination of the emperor and of the imperial bishops to Rome. Henry replied, as did twenty-six of his bishops, in letters of January 24, 1076. Henry's letter begins: "Henry, king not through usurpation but through the holy ordination of God, to Hildebrand, at present not pope but false monk." It ends, "You, therefore, damned by this curse and by the judgment of all our bishops and by our own, go down and relinquish the apostolic chair which you have usurped. Let another go up to the throne of St. Peter. I, Henry, king by the grace of God, do say unto you, together with all our bishops: Go down, go down [*Descende, descende*], to be damned throughout the ages." The letter of the bishops is in a similar vein, ending: "And since, as you did publicly proclaim, no one of us has been to you thus far a bishop, so also shall you henceforth be pope for none of us."[14]

In response, Gregory excommunicated and deposed Henry, who in January 1077 journeyed as a humble penitent to Canossa, where the pope was staying, and waited three days for the opportunity to present himself barefoot in the snow and to confess his sins and declare his contrition. Thus appealed to in his spiritual capacity, the pope absolved Henry and removed the excommunication and deposition. This gave Henry a chance to reassert his authority over the German magnates, both ecclesiastical and secular, who had been in rebellion against him. The struggle with the pope, however, was only postponed for a short time. In 1078 the pope issued a decree in which he said: "We decree that no one of the clergy shall receive the investiture with a bishopric or abbey or church from the hand of an emperor or king or of any lay person, male or female. But if he shall presume to do so he shall clearly know that such investiture is bereft of apostolic authority, and that he himself shall lie under excommunication until fitting satisfaction shall have been rendered."[15] The conflict between pope and emperor broke out again and the Wars of Investiture resulted.

The first casualties of the Wars of Investiture were in the German territories, where the emperor's enemies took advantage of his controversy with the pope to elect a rival king, whom Gregory eventually supported. However, Henry defeated his rival in 1080 and moved south across the Alps to besiege and occupy Rome (1084). Gregory appealed for help to his allies, the Norman rulers of southern Italy—Apulia, Calabria, Capua, and Sicily. The Normans' mercenaries drove the imperial forces from Rome, but then proceeded to loot and sack it with the savagery for which they were notorious. Henry continued to face revolts from the German princes; and when he died in 1106, his own son was leading a rebellion against him. That son, as Emperor Henry V, occupied Rome in 1111 and captured the pope.

The immediate political issue of the Wars of Investiture was that of the power of emperors and kings to invest bishops and other clergy with the insignia of their offices, uttering the words, "Accipe ecclesiam!" Behind this issue lay the question of loyalty and discipline of clergy after election and investiture. These issues were of fundamental political importance. Since the empire and the kingdoms were administered chiefly by clergy, they affected the very nature of both the ecclesiastical authority and the imperial or royal authority. Yet even more was involved—something deeper than politics—namely, the salvation of souls. Previously, the emperor (or king) had been called the deputy ("vicar") of Christ; it was he who was to answer for the souls of all men at the Last Judgment. Now the pope, who had previously called himself the deputy of St. Peter, claimed to be the sole deputy of Christ with responsibility to answer for the souls of all men at the Last Judgment. Emperor Henry IV had written to Pope Gregory VII that according to the church fathers the emperor can be judged by no man; he alone on earth is "judge of all men"; there is only one emperor, whereas the Bishop of Rome is only the first among bishops. This indeed was orthodox doctrine that had prevailed for centuries. Gregory, however, saw the emperor as first among kings, a layman, whose election as emperor was subject to confirmation by the pope and who could be deposed by the pope for insubordination.[16] The argument was put in typical scholastic form: "the king is either a layman or a cleric," and since he is not ordained he is obviously a layman and hence can have no office in "the church." This claim left emperors and kings with no basis for legitimacy, for the idea of a secular state, that is, a state without ecclesiastical functions, had not yet been—indeed, was only then just being—born. It also arrogated to popes theocratic powers, for the division of ecclesiastical functions into spiritual and temporal had not yet been—indeed, was only then just being—born.

Ultimately, neither popes nor emperors could maintain their original claims. Under the Concordat of Worms in 1122, the emperor guaranteed that bishops and abbots would be freely elected by the church alone, and he renounced his right to invest them with the spiritual symbols of ring and staff, which implied the power to care for souls. The pope, for his part, conceded the emperor's right to be present at elections and, where elections were disputed, to intervene. Moreover, German prelates were not to be consecrated by the church until the emperor had invested them, by scepter, with what were called the "regalia," that is, feudal rights of property, justice, and secular government, which carried the reciprocal duty to render homage and fealty to the emperor. (Homage and fealty included the rendering of feudal services and dues on the large landed estates that went with high church offices.) Prelates of Italy and Burgundy, however, were not to be invested by the scepter and to undertake to render their homage and fealty to the emperor until six months after their consecration by the church. The fact that the power of appointment had to be shared—that either pope or emperor could, in effect, exercise a veto—made the question of ceremony, the question of procedure, crucial.

In England and Normandy, under the earlier settlement reached at Bec in 1107, King Henry I had also agreed to free elections, though in his presence, and had renounced investiture by staff and ring. Also, as later in Germany, he was to receive homage and fealty before, and not after, consecration.

The concordats left the pope with extremely wide authority over the clergy, and with considerable authority over the laity as well. Without his approval clergy could not be ordained. He established the functions and powers of bishops, priests, deacons, and other clerical officials. He could create new bishoprics, divide or suppress old ones, transfer or depose bishops. His authorization was needed to institute a new monastic order or to change the rule of an existing order. Moreover, the pope was called the "principal dispenser" of all church property, which was conceived to be the "patrimony of Christ." The pope also was supreme in matters of worship and of religious belief; and he alone could grant absolution from certain grave sins (such as assault upon a clerk), canonize saints, and distribute indulgences (relief from divine punishment after death). None of these powers had existed before 1075.

"The Pope," in the words of Gabriel LeBras, "ruled over the whole church. He was the universal legislator, his power being limited only by natural [law] and positive divine law [that is, divine law laid down in the Bible and in similar documents of revelation]. He summoned general councils, presided over them, and his confirmation was necessary for the putting into force of their decisions. He put an end to controversy on many points by means of decretals, he was the interpreter of the law and granted privileges and dispensations. He was also the supreme judge and administrator. Cases of importance—*maiores causae*—of which there never was a final enumeration, were reserved for his judgment."[17] None of these powers had existed before 1075.

Gregory declared the papal court to be "the court of the whole of Christendom."[18] From then on, the pope had general jurisdiction over cases submitted to him by anyone—he was "judge ordinary of all persons." This was wholly new.

Over the laity the pope ruled in matters of faith and morals as well as in various civil matters such as marriage and inheritance. In some respects, his rule in these matters was absolute; in other respects, it was shared with the secular authority. Also, in still other matters which were considered to belong to the secular jurisdiction, the papal authority often became involved. Prior to 1075 the pope's jurisdiction over the laity had been subordinate to that of emperors and kings and generally had not been greater than that of other leading bishops.

The separation, concurrence, and interaction of the spiritual and secular jurisdictions was a principal source of the Western legal tradition.

The Revolutionary Character of the Papal Revolution

The term revolution, as applied to the great revolutions of European history, has four main characteristics which, taken together, distinguish it from reform or evolution, on the one hand, and from mere rebellions, coups d'etat, and counterrevolutions and dictatorships, on the other. These are its *totality*, that is, its character as a total transformation in which political, religious, economic, legal, cultural, linguistic, artistic, philosophical, and other basic categories of social change are interlocked; its *rapidity*, that is, the speed or suddenness with which drastic changes take place from day to day, year to year, decade to decade as the revolution runs its course; its *violence*, which takes the form not only of class struggle and civil war but also of foreign wars of expansion; and its *duration* over two or three generations, during which the underlying principles of the revolution are reconfirmed and reestablished in the face of necessary compromises with its initial utopianism, until the grandchildren of the founding fathers themselves acknowledge devotion to their grandparents' cause. Then evolution can take place at its own pace, without fear of either counterrevolution from the right or the radicalism of a new left.[19]

THE TOTALITY OF THE PAPAL REVOLUTION

The search for a basic cause of historical change, and the very division of causes into basic causes and secondary causes, may obscure the fact that great revolutions do not occur without the coincidence of a great many different factors. The classification of these factors into political, economic, cultural, and other categories is a matter of convenience of exposition. To give a true picture, however, the exposition must show the necessary interconnections among the factors. Otherwise, the most important point is missed, namely, that such revolutions are experienced as total events.

Thus the Papal Revolution may be viewed in political terms, as a massive shift in power and authority both within the church and in the relations between the church and the secular polities; also it was accompanied by decisive political changes in the relations between western Europe and neighboring powers. The Papal Revolution may also be viewed in socioeconomic terms as both a response and a stimulus to an enormous expansion of production and of trade and to the emergence of thousands of new cities and towns. From a cultural and intellectual perspective, the Papal Revolution may be viewed as a motive force in the creation of the first European universities, in the emergence of theology and jurisprudence and philosophy as systematic disciplines, in the creation of new literary and artistic styles, and in the development of a new social consciousness. These diverse political, economic, and cultural movements may be analyzed separately; yet they must also be shown to have been linked with one another, for it was the linking of them all that constituted the revolutionary element in the situation.

Political changes. The major political shifts in power and authority within the church and in its relations with secular rulers have been described in preceding pages. It is necessary here, however, to state briefly some of the political changes that took place at the same time in relations between western Europe and neighboring powers.

For centuries there had been constant military incursions into Europe from the north and west by the Norsemen, from the south by the Arabs, and from the east by the Slavs and Magyars. The whole of Western

Christendom "was a beleaguered citadel which only survived because its greatest enemy, Islam, had reached the end of its lines of communication, and its lesser enemies (the Slavs, the Hungarians, and the Vikings) were organized only for raids and for plunder."[20] It was the role of the emperor to mobilize soldiers, especially knights, from among the various peoples of the empire, to resist by military force these pressures from the outside. He also had enemies within — to the west the French kings were not always friendly, and across the Alps the princes of northern Italy were openly hostile. Thus Europe was turned in upon itself, with its main axis running from north to south. At the end of the eleventh century, however, the papacy, which for at least two decades had been urging secular rulers to liberate Byzantium from the infidels, finally succeeded in organizing the First Crusade (1096-1099). A second crusade was launched in 1147 and a third crusade in 1189. These first crusades were the foreign wars of the Papal Revolution. They not only increased the power and authority of the papacy but also opened a new axis eastward to the outside world and turned the Mediterranean Sea from a natural defensive barrier against invasion from without into a route for western Europe's own military and commercial expansion.[21]

The crusades had a counterpart in the extensive migration into northern and eastern European territories (the Netherlands, Scandinavia, Poland, Hungary, and other regions) which took place in the late eleventh and the twelfth centuries. Here, too, the papacy played a leading part, especially through the Cistercian monastic order, founded in 1098. The Cistercians, who were ardent supporters of papal policy, were known for their agricultural expertise, managerial skill, and colonizing zeal. They were particularly adept in the development of implements useful in clearing wilderness areas.

Socioeconomic changes. Political changes of such magnitude could not have occurred without comparable changes in the economy and in the social structure connected with the economy. Such changes did take place, but it is difficult to determine their relationship to the political changes. In some instances they appear to have been causes, in others conditions, and in still others effects.

The late eleventh and the twelfth centuries were a period of great acceleration of economic development in western Europe. As R.W. Southern has put it, "That moment of self-generating expansion for which economists now look so anxiously in underdeveloped countries came to Western Europe in the late eleventh century."[22] New technological developments and new methods of cultivation contributed to a rapid increase in agricultural productivity and to a consequent expansion of trade in agricultural surpluses in the countryside.[23] These factors, in turn, facilitated a very rapid increase in population; although reliable figures are scarce, it seems likely that the population of western

Europe as a whole increased by more than half, and possibly doubled, in the century between 1050 and 1150, whereas in the preceding centuries, under conditions of subsistence agriculture and military invasions, it had remained virtually stationary and at times had even declined. The expanding population spilled over into many hundreds and even thousands of cities and towns that emerged in western Europe for the first time since the decline of the Roman Empire in the fourth and fifth centuries.

The emergence of cities and towns is perhaps the most striking socioeconomic change of the late eleventh and the twelfth and thirteenth centuries. In the year 1050 there were probably only two settlements in western Europe — Venice and London — with a population of more than ten thousand, and perhaps two dozen others with a population of more than two thousand (see map 1). (In 1050 Constantinople, in contrast, had hundreds of thousands of inhabitants.) Almost all settled places were either villages or else fortified places with or without an adjoining market. The term *civitas* ("city") was reserved for the seats of bishoprics. The cities of Sicily and southern Italy were still Byzantine and Arab, not Western. Rome was exceptional — less for its size, which was not much greater than that of other major bishoprics, than for the numerous noble families congregated there. In the following two centuries great trading and manufacturing centers sprang up all over western Europe, some with populations over 100,000, dozens with populations over 30,000, hundreds with populations over 10,000. By 1250 some 5 to 10 percent of the population of western Europe — perhaps three or four million people — lived in cities and towns (see map 3).

The merchant class, which in 1050 had consisted of a relatively few itinerant peddlers, increased sharply in numbers and changed drastically in character in the late eleventh and the twelfth centuries, first in the countryside and then in the cities and towns. Commerce overland and overseas became an important aspect of western European economic and social life (as it had been in the eastern Mediterranean, continuously, for over a thousand years). Fairs and markets became important economic and social institutions. Credit, banking, and insurance developed, especially in long-distance trade. Concomitant with the growth of commerce was the growth of manufacture of handicrafts, and this was accompanied by the widespread formation of craft guilds. Often the guilds played a major role in city or town government.

The expansion of commerce and the growth of cities in the eleventh and twelfth centuries have led many twentieth-century economic and social historians, among them Henri Pirenne, to place the origins of Western capitalism in that period. Yet the same period is also considered by many to be the high point of feudalism. In fact it was in that period — especially the twelfth and thirteenth centuries — that the manorial system became almost universal in western European agriculture; before then, a substantial percentage of peasants were living in villages as autonomous landholders, working their own land. Also in that period the character of the feudal bond between lord and vassal was substantially changed by the introduction of the practice of substituting monetary payments for military and other feudal obligations.

Cultural and intellectual changes. In the late eleventh and the twelfth centuries western Europe experienced not only political and economic explosions but also a cultural and intellectual explosion. This was the time when the first universities were created, when the scholastic method (as it later came to be called) was first developed, when theology and jurisprudence and philosophy were first subjected to rigorous systematization. This period marked the beginning of modern scientific thought.[24]

It was also the period of transition first to Romanesque and then to Gothic architecture; it was the age when the first great European cathedrals were started — St. Denis and Notre Dame de Paris, Canterbury and Durham.

This was the age when Latin as a scholarly language was modernized and when vernacular languages and literature began to take their modern form. It was the period of great epic poetry (the *Song of Roland*, the Arthurian epics) and of courtly lyrics and romances (the writings of Bernard de Ventadour).[25] It was a time of remarkable growth of literacy among the laity, and of the earliest development of national cultural sentiments in most of the countries of western Europe.

Three other basic changes in social consciousness contributed to the transformation of the cultural and intellectual life of the peoples of western Europe in the late eleventh and the twelfth centuries: first, the growth of the sense of corporate identity of the clergy, its self-consciousness as a group, and the sharp opposition, for the first time, between the clergy and the laity; second, the change to a dynamic concept of the responsibility of the church (considered primarily as the clergy) to reform the world, the *saeculum* (considered primarily as the lay world); and third, the development of a new sense of historical time, including the concepts of modernity and progress.

THE RAPIDITY AND VIOLENCE OF THE PAPAL REVOLUTION

In trying to comprehend the full dimensions of the changes that took place during the eleventh and twelfth centuries, one may lose sight of the cataclysmic character of the events that were at the heart of the Papal Revolution. These events may be explained, ultimately, only by the totality of the transformation; but they must be seen initially as the immediate consequence of the effort to achieve a political purpose, namely, what the papal party called "the freedom of the church" — the liberation of the clergy from imperial, royal, and feudal domination and their unification under papal authority. By placing that political purpose, and the events that followed immediately from the effort to realize it, in the context of the total transformation, one can see that what was involved was far more than a struggle for power. It was an apocalyptic struggle for a new order of things, for "a new heaven and a new earth." But at the same time, the political manifestation of that struggle, where power and conviction, the material and the spiritual, coincided, is what gave it its tempo and its passion.

Rapidity is, of course, a relative matter. It may seem that a transformation which began in the middle of the eleventh century and was not secured until the latter part of the twelfth century, or possibly the early part of the thirteenth century, should be called gradual. However, the length of time which it takes a revolution to run its course is not necessarily the measure of its rapidity. The concept of rapid change refers to the pace at which drastic changes occur from day to day or year to year or decade to decade. In a revolution of the magnitude of the Papal Revolution, life is speeded up; things happen very quickly; great changes take place overnight. First, at the start of the revolution—in the *Dictatus Papae* of 1075—the previous political and legal order was declared to be abolished. Emperors were to kiss the feet of popes. The pope was to be "the sole judge of all" and to have the sole power "to make new laws to meet the needs of the times." The fact that many of the features of the old society persisted and refused to disappear did not change the suddenness of the effort to abolish them or the shock produced by that effort. Second, new institutions and policies were introduced almost as suddenly as old ones were abolished. The fact that it took a long time—several generations—for the revolution to establish its goals did not make the process a gradual one.

For example, it was part of Pope Gregory VII's program, at least from 1074 on, that the papacy should organize a crusade to defend the Christians of the East against the Turkish infidels. Until his death in 1085 he promoted that idea throughout Europe, although he was never able to get sufficient support to bring it about. Only in 1095 did his successor and devoted follower, Pope Urban II, succeed in launching the First Crusade. One may say, then, that it took a long time—over twenty years—to accomplish this change, which literally turned Europe around and united it in a collective military and missionary expedition to the East. But in another sense, the change from a precrusading Europe to a crusading Europe came with shocking rapidity. From the first moment the crusade became a declared objective of the papacy, the reorientation proceeded, continually producing new hopes, new fears, new plans, new associations. Once the First Crusade was undertaken the pace of change accelerated. The mobilization of knights from virtually every part of

Western Christendom, their journeys across land and sea and, finally, the innumerable military encounters, were a compression of events into a time span that came and went with extraordinary speed. Moreover, it was not only on the ground, so to speak, that the crusades represented an acceleration of the pace of events. It was also so in the realm of high politics. For example, the papacy tried to use the crusades as a means of exporting the Papal Revolution to Eastern Christendom. The pope declared his supremacy over the entire Christian world. The schism between the Eastern and Western churches, which had reached a climax in 1054 in the famous theological controversy over the *filioque* clause in the creed,[26] took the form of violence and conquest. Also in 1099 Western knights entered Jerusalem and founded there a new kingdom, the Kingdom of Jerusalem, subordinate, at least in theory, to the papacy. History was moving very fast indeed! Although almost fifty years elapsed before the Second Crusade was launched, and another forty years from the end of the Second Crusade to the Third, these time spans, too, must be considered in the light of the continual agitation that was generated both by anticipation of them and by the remembrance of them. Throughout the twelfth century there was a widespread feeling that a crusade might come at any time.

And so with the principal aim of the revolution, expressed in the slogan, "the freedom of the church": it was not something that could be achieved overnight — indeed, in its deepest significance it was not something that could be achieved ever — yet the very depth of the idea, its combination of great simplicity and great complexity, was a guarantee that the struggle to achieve it would be, on the one hand, a prolonged one, over decades and generations and even centuries, and on the other hand, a cataclysmic one, with drastic and often violent changes occurring in rapid succession. For freedom of the church meant different things to different people. To some it meant a theocratic state. To others it meant that the church should renounce all its feudal lands, all its wealth, all its worldly power; this, indeed, was proposed by Pope Paschal II in the early 1100s, but was quickly rejected both by the Roman cardinals and by the German bishops who supported the emperor. Or it might mean something quite different from either of these extreme alternatives. The fact that its meaning kept changing from 1075 to 1122 was one of the marks of the revolutionary character of the times.

Apart from the crusades, the violence of the Papal Revolution took the form of a series of wars and rebellions. The papal and the imperial or royal sides used both mercenaries and feudal armies. There were many violent popular rebellions, especially in cities, against the existing authorities — against ruling bishops, for example, who might be appointees and supporters of either the emperor or the pope.

It is doubtful that the rapidity of the Papal Revolution can be separated from its violence. This is not to say that if the struggle could have been carried on without civil war—if Henry IV could have been persuaded not to resist Gregory by armed force, or Gregory not to summon his Norman allies in defense—the events would have lost their rapid tempo. Nevertheless, in the Papal Revolution, as in the great revolutions of Western history that succeeded it, the resort to violence was closely related to the speed with which changes were pressed as well as to their total or fundamental character. It was partly because of the rapidity of the changes and partly because of their totality that the preexisting order was unwilling and unable to make room for them; and so force, in Karl Marx's words, became "the necessary midwife" of the new era.

Force, however, could not give a final victory either to the revolutionary party or to its opponents. The Papal Revolution ended in compromise between the new and old. If force was the midwife, law was the teacher that ultimately brought the child to maturity. Gregory VII died in exile. Henry IV was deposed. The eventual settlement in Germany, France, England, and elsewhere was reached by hard negotiations in which all sides renounced their most radical claims. What can be said for force is that it took the experience of civil war in Europe to produce the willingness of both sides to compromise. The balance was struck, ultimately, by law.

THE DURATION OF THE PAPAL REVOLUTION

The totality of the transformation of Western Christendom in the late eleventh and the twelfth centuries, its rapidity, and its violence would not in themselves justify its characterization as the first of the great revolutions of Western history, if the revolutionary movement had not endured for several generations.

At first, the long duration of a revolution may seem to contradict its speed and violence; in fact, however, it is partly because of the speed and violence of the changes, as well as their totality, that their underlying principles must be reconfirmed and reestablished by successive generations. Moreover, the basic goals of the revolution must be preserved in the face of necessary compromises with its initial utopianism. Just as the totality of the transformation distinguishes a revolution from reform, and just as the rapidity and violence distinguish it from evolution, so the transgenerational character of the great revolutions of Western history distinguishes them from mere rebellions, coups d'état, and shifts in policy, as well as from counterrevolutions and military dictatorships.

The Papal Revolution was the first transgenerational movement of a programmatic character in Western history. It took almost a generation, from about 1050 to 1075, for the papal party to proclaim the program to be a reality. Then followed forty-seven years of struggle before another pope could reach an agreement with another emperor on the single question of papal versus imperial investiture of bishops and abbots. It took even longer for the respective criminal and civil jurisdictions of the ecclesiastical and secular powers within each of the major western European kingdoms to be defined. In England it was not until 1170, the year of Becket's martyrdom—ninety-five years after Gregory's *Dictatus* and sixty-three years after Henry I, the English king, had yielded on the investiture issue—that the Crown finally renounced its pretension to be the supreme ruler of the English clergy. Ultimately compromises were reached on a whole range of issues involving not only the interrelationship of church and state but also the interrelationship of communities within the secular order—the manorial system, the lord-vassal unit, the merchant guilds, the chartered cities and towns, the territorial duchies and kingdoms, the secularized empire. The children and grandchildren of the revolution enacted its underlying principles into governmental and legal institutions. Only then was it more or less secure for succeeding centuries. Indeed, it was never wholly secure; there were always disputes at the boundaries of the ecclesiastical and secular powers.

Social-Psychological Causes and Consequences of the Papal Revolution

Mention has been made of three aspects of the new social consciousness that emerged during the eleventh and twelfth centuries—a new sense of corporate identity on the part of the clergy, a new sense of the responsibility of the clergy for the reformation of the secular world, and a new sense of historical time, including the concepts of modernity and progress. These all had a strong influence on the development of the Western legal tradition.

The first aspect, the corporate self-consciousness of the clergy (it would be called *class* consciousness today) was essential to the revolution, both as cause and as consequence. Of course, the clergy had always had some sense of their own group identity; yet it was at best a sense of spiritual unity, a unity of belief and of calling, and not a sense of political or legal unity. Politically and legally, the clergy prior to the eleventh century had been dispersed locally, with very few links to central ecclesiastical authorities. Even the sense of spiritual unity was flawed by the sharp division between the "regular" clergy and the "secular" clergy; the regular clergy were the "religious" ones, the monks and nuns, who having died to "this world," lived out their membership in the Eternal City; the secular clergy were the priests and bishops, who were almost wholly involved in the political, economic, and social life of the localities where they lived.

More than any other single factor, the Cluniac Reform laid the foundation for the new sense of corporate political unity among the clergy of Western Christendom. The zeal of the reformers helped to give a new consciousness of common historical destiny to both the regular and the secular clergy. In addition, Cluny provided a model for uniting the clergy in a single translocal organization, since all Cluniac houses were subject to the jurisdiction of the central abbey.

In adopting the principal aims of the Cluniac Reform, including the celibacy of the priesthood and the elimination of the purchase and sale of church offices, the papal party in the 1050s and 1060s appropriated the moral capital of the earlier movement, including the clerical class consciousness that it had helped to develop. To those older aims was joined the new cry for "the freedom of the church"—that is, its freedom from control by "the laity." This was both an appeal to clerical class consciousness and a stimulation of it. Moreover, by the very act of denouncing imperial control of the church, Gregory shattered the old Carolingian ideal. The clergy were confronted with a choice between political unity under the papacy and political disunity among new national churches, which would have inevitably arisen in the various polities of Europe if the papacy had lost the battle. The investiture struggle made that clear. Ultimately the question of investiture was settled by separate negotiations between each of the principal secular rulers, representing his secular polity, and the papacy, representing the entire clergy of Western Christendom. The Papal Revolution itself thus helped to establish the clerical class consciousness on which it was based.

The clergy became the first translocal, transtribal, transfeudal, transnational class in Europe to achieve political and legal unity. It became so by demonstrating that it was able to stand up against, and defeat, the one preexisting universal authority, the emperor. The emperor had no such universal class to support him. From the twelfth century to the sixteenth the unity of the clerical hierarchy in the West could only be broken by a few powerful kings. Even the Norman kings of Sicily, who in the twelfth and thirteenth centuries were able to exclude papal control over a clergy nominally subordinate to Rome, agreed to submit to the pope any disputed elections of bishops.

The term "class" has been used here to describe the clergy partly to emphasize that the Papal Revolution, like the German (Protestant) Revolution, the English Revolution, the French and American revolutions, and the Russian Revolution, involved the interactions not only of individuals or elites but also of large social groups that performed major functions in the society. The validity of the Marxian insight that a revolution involves class struggle, and the rise of a new ruling class, need not commit one to the narrow Marxian definition of class in terms of its relation to the means of production of economic wealth. The clergy in western Europe in the late eleventh and twelfth centuries did, in fact, play an important role in the production of economic wealth, since the church owned between one-fourth and one-third of the land; bishops and abbots were lords of manors with the same economic interests as their nonecclesiastical counterparts; the struggle against lay investiture was in part a struggle to wrest economic power from lay lords and to transfer it to the church. However, it was not primarily the economic interests of the clergy that gave them their class character. It was, rather, their role as producers of spiritual goods—as father confessors, as performers of marriage ceremonies, as baptizers of infants, as ministers of last rites, as preachers of sermons, and also as expounders not only of the theology of Western society but also of its basic political and legal doctrines.

The growth of the class consciousness of the clergy was associated with the second aspect of the new social consciousness of the eleventh and twelfth centuries—the development of a new sense of the clergy's mission to reform the secular world. On the one hand, the new tendency to identify the church primarily with the clergy, the "hierarchy," led to a sharp distinction between the clergy and the laity. On the other hand, this distinction carried the implication that the clergy were not only superior to, but also responsible for, the laity. In other words, the class consciousness of the clergy was at the same time a social consciousness in the modern sense, a conscientiousness with respect to the future of society.

This was reflected in a sharp change in the meaning of the word "secular." In classical Latin, *saeculum* meant "an age," "a time," "a generation," or "the people of a given time" (as in "the younger generation"); it also came to mean "a century." The church fathers in the second, third, and fourth centuries used saeculum to refer to the world of time—the "temporal" world—as contrasted with the eternal kingdom of God. (The world of space, *mundus*, was another thing.) In the writings of St. Augustine, for example, as Peter Brown has pointed out, saeculum meant "existence," that is, the sum total of transitory human existence, past, present, and future, from the fall of Adam to the Last Judgment. Professor Brown has written: "For St. Augustine, this *saeculum* is a profoundly sinister thing. It is a penal existence . . . it wobbles up and down without rhyme or reason . . . There are no verbs of historical movement in the City of God, no sense of progress to aims that may be achieved in history. The Christians are members of a far country . . . they are registered aliens, existing, on sufferance, *in hoc maligno saeculo.*"[27]

Contrary to what is sometimes supposed, St. Augustine did not identify the City of God with the Christian Church as such, nor did he identify the Earthly City with the Roman Empire or with the state in general. For him both the Church and the Empire were living in evil times, the saeculum. The Christian, however, was distinguished by the fact that he yearned ardently—again in Brown's words—"for a country that is always distant but made ever present by the quality of his love and hope."[28] Thus for St. Augustine the true Christian, whether priest or layman, lived in both "cities," that is, in both the earthly and the heavenly society.[29]

The negative view of the saeculum reflected in the writings of St. Augustine and, indeed, of most Christian thinkers in the first thousand years of the church's history, contributed to a sharp division between the regular clergy and the secular clergy. The former lived farther away from the saeculum and closer to the City of God. That may be why, in the late eleventh and early twelfth centuries, the papal party, which championed the secular as well as the regular clergy, often preferred to speak of the "temporal" rule of emperors and kings, and of "temporal" law, rather than of "secular" rule and "secular" law, although the two terms were synonymous. Temporal, or secular, was a pejorative term; it meant time-bound, the product of the decay and corruption of human existence, especially in the sphere of political rule; it was now made applicable to all laymen. The antonym of temporal (or secular) was "spiritual." All clergy were now called *spirituales* ("spiritual ones"). In a famous letter Gregory VII wrote:

> Who does not know that kings and princes derive their origin from men ignorant of God who raised themselves above their fellows by pride, plunder, treachery, murder—in short by every kind of crime—at the instigation of the Devil, the prince of this world, men blind with greed and intolerable in their audacity? . . . Kings and princes of the earth, seduced by empty glory, prefer their own interests to the things of the spirit, whereas pious pontiffs, despising vainglory, set the things of God above the things of the flesh . . . The former, far too much given to worldly affairs, think little of spiritual things, the latter, dwelling eagerly upon heavenly subjects, despise the things of this world.[30]

The imperial authority, according to its enemies, lacked spiritual, that is, holy or "heavenly," qualities. One of Gregory's propagandists addressed the emperor as follows: "you say that your authority has stood unchallenged for seven hundred years, and so you would have a right to it by prescription? But no more than a thief is able to transfer title to stolen goods can the devil transfer property rights to an unjust power."[31]

And again: "The least in the kingdom of the spiritual sword is greater than the Emperor himself, who wields [only] the secular sword."[32]

The Papal Revolution started with this attempt by the papacy to reduce the Holy and Most Christian Emperor—who for centuries had played the leading role in the life of the church—to the status of a simple layman, lower than the lowest priest. The fact that emperors and kings, being laymen, wielded only the secular sword, that is, were responsible only for temporal affairs, the things of this world, placed them in subordination to those who wielded the spiritual sword and were responsible for spiritual affairs, and who "dwell eagerly upon heavenly subjects"; for the laity were inferior to the clergy in matters of faith and morals, and the secular was less valuable than the spiritual.

Yet Gregory VII and his supporters never doubted that secular government, though subordinate to the church in spiritual matters and even — though only indirectly — in secular matters, represented divine authority, that the power of the secular ruler was established by God, and that secular law flowed ultimately from reason and conscience and must be obeyed. Despite his harsh denunciation of secular rulers, Gregory was full of hope for the future of secular society — under papal tutelage. In this, he and his followers were poles apart from St. Augustine.

Indeed, the most radical of the papal claims, namely, that not only the spiritual sword but the temporal sword, too, belongs ultimately to the church, which confers it on the secular ruler, contains a paradox. In the words of John of Salisbury, the king "is a minister of the priestly power, and one who exercises that side of the sacred offices which seems unworthy of the hands of the priesthood."[33] Unworthy — nevertheless, sacred. The very division between the spiritual and the secular — which the church ardently maintained when claiming its freedom, but often violated when seeking to expand its power — provided defenses against the papal attempt to assert jurisdiction over the sinfulness attributed to secular rulers pursuing secular policies.

Ultimately, compromises were reached in the struggle between the papalists and their opponents. It was out of that struggle and those compromises that Western political science — and especially the first modern Western theories of the state and secular law — were born. As K.J. Leyser has written, "Political ideas in the classical sense only appear in the polemics of the eleventh and early twelfth centuries incoherently, in flashes . . . There [was at that time] no theory of the secular state as such, but as a result of the great crisis it was all ready to be born."[34]

The new meanings of secular were derived from the struggle between supporters of the secular and spiritual authorities, respectively. Those who denied altogether the papacy's distinction between secular and spiritual, and who insisted on maintaining the sacral character of imperial or royal rule, were generally defeated. But the actual boundaries between the two realms — the specific allocations of functions — were worked out by reconciliation and compromise between opposing forces. They could not, by the very nature of the problem, be defined abstractly.

Closely related to both the clergy's sense of corporate identity and its sense of mission to reform the world was a third aspect of the new social consciousness that emerged in the eleventh and twelfth centuries, namely, a new sense of historical time, including the concepts of modernity and of progress. This, too, was both a cause and a consequence of the Papal Revolution.

A new sense of time was implicit in the shift in the meaning of *saeculum* and in the new sense of mission to reform the world. A relatively static view of political society was replaced by a more dynamic view; there was a new concern with the future of social institutions. But there was also a fundamental revaluation of history, a new orientation toward the past as well as the future, and a new sense of the relationship of the future to the past. The distinction between "ancient" and "modern" times, which had occasionally been made in previous centuries, became common in the literature of the papal party. In the twelfth century there appeared the first European historians who saw the history of the West as moving from the past, through stages, into a new future—men such as Hugo of St. Victor, Otto of Freising, Anselm of Havelberg, Joachim of Floris, and others. These men saw history as moving forward in stages, culminating in their own time, which some referred to as modern times or modernity (*modernitas*). Joachim of Floris and his disciples considered that a new age of the Holy Spirit was about to replace the age of the Son, which had come to an end. Otto of Freising wrote that secular history had entered into sacred history and was intertwined with it.[35]

Like the English Revolution of the seventeenth century, the Papal Revolution pretended to be not a revolution but a restoration. Gregory VII, like Cromwell, claimed that he was not innovating, but restoring ancient freedoms that had been abrogated in the immediately preceding centuries. As the English Puritans and their successors found precedents in the common law of the thirteenth and fourteenth centuries, largely passing over the century or more of Tudor-Stuart absolutism, so the Gregorian reformers found precedents in the patristic writings of the early centuries of the church, largely passing over the Carolingian and post-Carolingian era in the West. The ideological emphasis was on tradition, but the tradition could only be established by suppressing the immediate past and returning to an earlier one. Writings of leading Frankish and German canonists and theologians of the ninth and tenth centuries were simply ignored. In addition, the patristic writings were interpreted to conform to the political program of the papal party, and when particular patristic texts stood in the way of that program they were rejected. Faced with an obnoxious custom, the Gregorian reformers would appeal over it to truth, quoting the aphorism of Tertullian and St. Cyprian, "Christ said, 'I am the truth.' He did not say 'I am the custom.'" Gregory VII quoted this against Emperor Henry IV.

Becket quoted it against King Henry II. It had special force at a time when almost all the prevailing law was customary law.

It is the hallmark of the great revolutions of Western history, starting with the Papal Revolution, that they clothe their vision of the radically new in the garments of a remote past, whether those of ancient legal authorities (as in the case of the Papal Revolution), or of an ancient religious text, the Bible (as in the case of the German Reformation), or of an ancient civilization, classical Greece (as in the case of the French Revolution), or of a prehistoric classless society (as in the case of the Russian Revolution). In all of these great upheavals the idea of a restoration—a return, and in that sense a revolution, to an earlier starting point—was connected with a dynamic concept of the future.

It is easy enough to criticize the historiography of the revolutions as politically biased and, indeed, purely ideological. This, however, is to impose on revolutionaries the standards of objectivity asserted by modern historical scholarship, which is itself a product of its times and has its own biases. Moreover, it is important to recognize that the revolutionaries were perfectly aware that they were reinterpreting the past and adapting historical memories to new circumstances. What is significant is that at the most crucial turning points of Western history a projection into the distant past has been needed to match the projection into the distant future. Both the past and the future have been summoned, so to speak, to fight against the evils of the present.

The Rise of the Modern State

The Papal Revolution gave birth to the modern Western state—the first example of which, paradoxically, was the church itself.

As Maitland said a century ago, it is impossible to frame any acceptable definition of the state which would not include the medieval church. By that he meant the church after Pope Gregory VII, since before his reign the church had been merged with the secular society and had lacked the concepts of sovereignty and of independent lawmaking power which are fundamental to modern statehood. After Gregory VII, however, the church took on most of the distinctive characteristics of the modern state. It claimed to be an independent, hierarchical, public authority. Its head, the pope, had the right to legislate, and in fact Pope Gregory's successors issued a steady stream of new laws, sometimes by their own authority, sometimes with the aid of church councils summoned by them. The church also executed its laws through an administrative hierarchy, through which the pope ruled as a modern sovereign rules through his or her representatives. Further, the church interpreted its laws, and applied them, through a judicial hierarchy culminating in the papal curia in Rome. Thus the church exercised the legislative, administrative, and judicial powers of a modern state. In addition, it adhered to a rational system of jurisprudence, the canon law. It imposed taxes on its subjects in the form of tithes and other levies. Through baptismal and death certificates it kept what was in effect a kind of civil register. Baptism conferred a kind of citizenship, which was further maintained by the requirement—formalized in 1215—that every Christian confess his or her sins and take Holy Communion at least once a year at Easter. One could be deprived of citizenship, in effect, by excommunication. Occasionally, the church even raised armies.

Yet it is a paradox to call the church a modern state, since the principal feature by which the modern state is distinguished from the ancient state, as well as from the Germanic or Frankish state, is its secular character. The ancient state and the Germanic-Frankish state were religious states, in which the supreme political ruler was also responsible for maintaining the religious dogmas as well as the religious rites and was often himself considered to be a divine or semidivine figure. The elimination of the religious function and character of the supreme political authority was one of the principal objectives of the Papal Revolution. Thereafter, emperors and kings were considered—by those who followed Roman Catholic doctrine—to be laymen, and hence wholly without competence in spiritual matters. According to papal theory, only the clergy, headed by the pope, had competence in spiritual matters. Nevertheless, for several reasons this was not a "separation of church and state" in the modern sense.

First, the state in the full modern sense—that is, the secular state existing in a system of secular states—had not yet come into being, although a few countries (especially the Norman Kingdom of Sicily and Norman England) were beginning to create modern political and legal institutions. Instead, there were various types of secular power, including feudal lordships and autonomous municipal governments as well as emerging national territorial states, and their interrelationships were strongly affected by the fact that all of their members, including their rulers, were also subject in many respects to an overarching ecclesiastical state.

Second, although emperor, kings, and other lay rulers were deprived of their ecclesiastical authority, they nevertheless continued to play a very important part—through the dual system of investiture—in the appointment of bishops, abbots, and other clerics and, indeed, in church politics generally. And conversely, members of the clergy continued to play an important part in secular politics, serving as advisers to secular rulers and also often as high secular officials. The Chancellor of England, for example, who was second in importance to the King, was virtually always a high ecclesiastic—often the Archbishop of Canterbury or of York—until the sixteenth century.

Third, the church retained important secular powers. Bishops continued to be lords of their feudal vassals and serfs and to be managers of their estates. Beyond that, the papacy asserted its power to influence secular politics in all countries; indeed, the pope claimed the supremacy of the spiritual sword over the temporal, although he only claimed to exercise temporal supremacy indirectly, chiefly through secular rulers.[36]

Thus the statement that the church was the first modern Western state must be qualified. The Papal Revolution did lay the foundation for the subsequent emergence of the modern secular state by withdrawing from emperors and kings the spiritual competence which they had previously exercised. Moreover, when the secular state did emerge, it had a constitution similar to that of the papal church — minus, however, the church's spiritual function as a community of souls concerned with eternal life. The church had the paradoxical character of a church-state, a *Kirchenstaat*: it was a spiritual community which also exercised temporal functions and whose constitution was in the form of a modern state. The secular state, on the other hand, had the paradoxical character of a state without ecclesiastical functions, a secular polity, all of whose subjects also constituted a spiritual community living under a separate spiritual authority.

Thus the Papal Revolution left a legacy of tensions between secular and spiritual values within the church, within the state, and within a society that was neither wholly church nor wholly state. It also, however, left a legacy of governmental and legal institutions, both ecclesiastical and secular, for resolving the tensions and maintaining an equilibrium throughout the system.

The Rise of Modern Legal Systems

As the Papal Revolution gave birth to the modern Western state, so it gave birth also to modern Western legal systems, the first of which was the modern system of canon law.

From early centuries on, the church accumulated a great many laws — canons (that is, rules) and decrees of church councils and synods, decrees and decisions of individual bishops (including the Roman pontiff), and laws of Christian emperors and kings concerning the church. The church in the West also produced many Penitentials (handbooks for priests), containing descriptions of various sins and the penalties attached to them. All these laws were considered to be subordinate to the precepts contained in the Bible (both the Old and New Testaments) and in the writings of the early church fathers — men such as Polycarp of Smyrna, Tertullian of Carthage, Gregory of Nyssa, and Augustine of Hippo.

These authoritative writings, in which the canons were merged, had contributed to the gradual establishment throughout Western Christendom, between the sixth and tenth centuries, of a common body of theological doctrine, a common worship service (in Latin), a common set of rules concerning major sins (such as killing, breaking oaths, stealing), and a common ecclesiastical discipline and structure. Everywhere priests heard confessions and dispensed the sacraments to their flocks; everywhere bishops ruled priests, consecrated churches, and arbitrated disputes within their respective dioceses; everywhere bishops were responsible to their primates (metropolitan bishops of provinces and regions), and all bishops owed loyalty to the Bishop of Rome as first among equals. There was, however, no book or series of books in existence in the year 1000 which attempted to present the whole body of ecclesiastical law or, indeed, systematically to summarize any part of it. There were, to be sure, a considerable number of collections of canons, and particularly canons of church councils and decrees of leading bishops. Usually these collections were simply arranged chronologically within broad categories of sources (canons of councils, letters of popes, sayings of the fathers), but in some collections there was also a division into a number of topics (Ordination, Church Courts, Liturgy, Marriage, Heresy, Idolatry). Hardly any of these collections were recognized as valid everywhere; almost all of them had only regional significance.

The decentralized character of ecclesiastical law prior to the late eleventh century was closely related to the decentralized character of the political life of the church. As a rule, bishops were more under the authority of emperors, kings, and leading lords than of popes; and even in those spiritual matters in which secular authorities did not intervene, a bishop usually had a considerable autonomy within his own diocese.[37] The universality of the church did not rest primarily on a political or legal unity but on a common spiritual heritage, common doctrine and worship, and a common liturgy. Such political and legal unity as it had was connected, above all, with the preservation of its spiritual universality. In this respect the Western Church was like the Eastern Church. Its law, being largely interwoven with theological doctrine and with the liturgy and the sacraments, was concerned only secondarily with organizational matters and the authority of bishops, and hardly at all with rules of property law, crime and tort, procedure, inheritance, and the like. In these secondary and tertiary concerns the law of the church was often wholly merged with secular law, and secular law was itself largely diffused in political, economic, and social custom.

In the wake of the Papal Revolution there emerged a new system of canon law and new secular legal systems, together with a class of professional lawyers and judges, hierarchies of courts, law schools, law treatises, and a concept of law as an autonomous, integrated, developing body of principles and procedures. The Western legal tradition was formed in the context of a total revolution, which was fought to establish

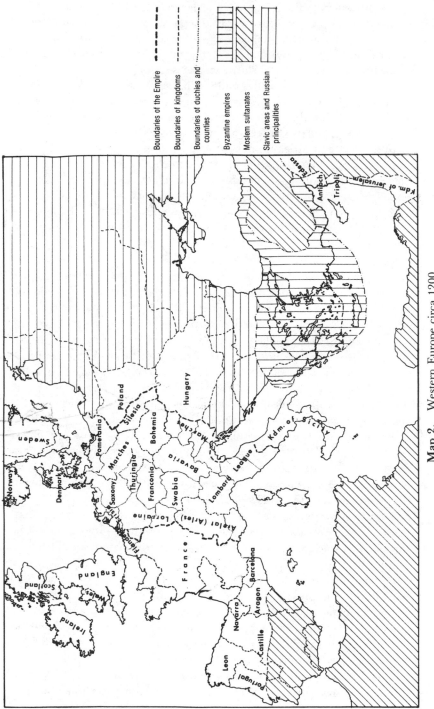

Boundaries of the Empire
Boundaries of kingdoms
Boundaries of duchies and counties
Byzantine empires
Moslem sultanates
Slavic areas and Russian principalities

Map 2. Western Europe circa 1200.

"the right order of things," or "right order in the world."[38] "Right order" signified a new division of society into separate ecclesiastical and secular authorities, the institutionalization of the ecclesiastical authority as a political and legal entity, and the belief in the responsibility of the ecclesiastical authority to transform secular society.

The dualism of ecclesiastical and secular legal systems led in turn to a pluralism of secular legal systems within the ecclesiastical legal order and, more specifically, to the concurrent jurisdiction of ecclesiastical and secular courts. Further, the systematization and rationalization of law were necessary in order to maintain the complex equilibrium of plural competing legal systems. Finally, the right order of things introduced by the Papal Revolution signified the kind of systematization and rationalization of law that would permit reconciliation of conflicting authorities on the basis of synthesizing principles: wherever possible, the contradictions were to be resolved without destruction of the elements they comprised.

To summarize, the new sense of law and the new types of law that emerged in western Europe in the wake of the Papal Revolution were needed as means: (1) to control by central authorities a widely dispersed population with diverse group loyalties; (2) to maintain the separate corporate identity of the clergy and add a new legal dimension to their class consciousness; (3) to regulate relations between competing ecclesiastical and secular polities; (4) to enable secular authorities to implement in a deliberate and programmatic way their proclaimed mission of imposing peace and justice within their respective jurisdictions; and (5) to enable the church to implement in a deliberate and programmatic way its proclaimed mission to reform the world.

The most important consequence of the Papal Revolution was that it introduced into Western history the experience of revolution itself. In contrast to the older view of secular history as a process of decay, there was introduced a dynamic quality, a sense of progress in time, a belief in the reformation of the world. No longer was it assumed that "temporal life" must inevitably deteriorate until the Last Judgment. On the contrary, it was now assumed—for the first time—that progress could be made in this world toward achieving some of the preconditions for salvation in the next.

Perhaps the most dramatic illustration of the new sense of time, and of the future, was provided by the new Gothic architecture. The great cathedrals expressed, in their soaring spires and flying buttresses and elongated vaulted arches, a dynamic spirit of movement upward, a sense of achieving, of incarnation of ultimate values. It is also noteworthy that they were often planned to be built over generations and centuries.

Less dramatic but even more significant as a symbol of the new belief in progress toward salvation were the great legal monuments that were built in the same period. In contrast not only to the earlier Western folklaw but also to Roman law both before and after Justinian, law in the West in the late eleventh and twelfth centuries, and thereafter, was conceived to be an organically developing system, an ongoing, growing body of principles and procedures, constructed—like the cathedrals —over generations and centuries.

3 | The Origin of Western Legal Science in the European Universities

MAITLAND CALLED THE twelfth century "a legal century." It was more than that: it was *the* legal century, the century in which the Western legal tradition was formed. The great revolutionary events that inaugurated that tradition, however, and the first great legal achievements, occurred not in the twelfth but in the last decades of the eleventh century—the *Dictates* of Pope Gregory VII and the centralizing administrative measures of the Norman rulers of Sicily, England, and Normandy, the scholarly achievements of the great canon lawyer Ivo of Chartres (1040-1116) and of the great Roman lawyer Irnerius (about 1060-1125).

The emergence of modern Western legal systems in the late eleventh and the twelfth centuries was closely related to the emergence of the first European universities. There, for the first time in western Europe, law was taught as a distinct and systematized body of knowledge, a science, in which individual legal decisions, rules, and enactments were studied objectively and were explained in terms of general principles and truths basic to the system as a whole. Trained in the new legal science, successive generations of university graduates went into the chanceries and other offices of the emerging ecclesiastical and secular states to serve as counselors, judges, advocates, administrators, legislative draftsmen. They applied their learning to give structure and coherence to the accumulating mass of legal norms, thus helping to carve new legal systems out of the older legal orders which previously had been almost wholly diffused in social custom and in political and religious institutions generally.

Of course, law in the usual sense of legal data, such as legal rules and procedures, cannot constitute a science, any more than matter or animal behavior can constitute a science. Legal science, if it exists, must be the scientific study of such legal data, the scientific body of knowledge *about* law, just as physical or biological science is the scientific study of, or body of knowledge about, matter or animal life. Yet there are important differences, from the point of view of science, between legal data, or any other social data, and physical data, arising from the fact that the participants in social activities are conscious of what they are doing, and their consciousness is an essential part of the data. Moreover, the consciousness may itself have, or seek to acquire, the characteristics of a science. The actors may ascribe to their own observations of what they themselves are doing the qualities of a systematic, objective, verifiable body of knowledge. That, in fact, is what happened in law in the late eleventh and twelfth centuries: the legal rules, concepts, decisions, and procedures remained data, and in that sense just the opposite of a science, but the consciousness of participants in legal activities came to include a systematic study of them, and the accumulation of a body of knowledge about them, which had some of the qualities of a science. In addition, the science, the body of knowledge *about* law, was treated as part of the legal data themselves. Understanding was merged with interpretation, and interpretation with application. For example, the scientific observation that the Decalogue prohibits killing but that other passages in the Bible indicate that killing may be justified when committed in self-defense or excused when committed accidentally, is itself a statement of an applicable legal principle, namely, that killing is prima facie illegal (according to the Bible) but that it may be justified or excused in particular circumstances. The fact that the observation itself is, or may become, the law—part of the very thing that is being observed—distinguishes legal science from natural science. Indeed, that is probably one of the reasons why in the twentieth century the phrases "legal science" and "science of law" have almost disappeared from English and American usage, although in French, German, Italian, Russian, and other languages these phrases continue to be widely used. In those languages the word for science carries a broader connotation and one can distinguish more easily between law and meta-law, law as it is practiced and law as it is conceived—between *Recht* and *Rechtswissenschaft*, *droit* and *la science du droit*.

To say that in the late 1000s and the 1100s law began to be taught and studied in the West as a distinct science, at a time when the prevailing legal orders were only beginning to be disembedded from politics and religion, raises a number of questions. What did the first law teachers teach? How was it possible to teach law when the prevailing laws and legal institutions, both ecclesiastical and secular, were largely local and customary and largely merged in religious beliefs and practices and in political, economic, and social life generally?

The answer sounds curious to modern ears. The law that was first taught and studied systematically in the West was not the prevailing law; it was the law contained in an ancient manuscript which had come to light in an Italian library toward the end of the eleventh century. The manuscript reproduced the enormous collection of legal materials which had been compiled under the Roman Emperor Justinian about 534 A.D. — over five centuries earlier.

The Roman law compiled under Justinian in Constantinople was a highly developed, highly sophisticated legal system, very different from the Germanic folklaw. It had at one time prevailed in the Western Roman Empire as well as the Eastern. In 476, however, the last of the Western emperors was deposed, and long before that, Roman civilization had been superseded in the West by the primitive tribal civilizations of the Goths, the Vandals, the Franks, the Saxons, and other Germanic peoples. After the sixth century Roman law survived in the West only in fragments, although it continued to flourish as a system in the Eastern Empire, called Byzantium (including southern Italy). Some of its individual rules and concepts appeared in the occasional enactments of Western ecclesiastical and secular authorities as well as in the customary law of the peoples inhabiting what are today France and (northern) Italy. Also the Carolingian and post-Carolingian idea of the succession of the Frankish king to the authority of the Roman emperors fostered the survival of individual maxims and principles of Roman law, especially some concerning imperial authority. Some of the loosely organized collections of laws promulgated by the Germanic kings contained a considerable number of Roman legal rules and concepts. But Roman law as such, that is, as a system, had a very limited validity in western Europe when Justinian's work was discovered in Italy. The texts had disappeared. The terms had acquired new meanings. There were no Western counterparts to the Roman magistrates (praetors), legal advisors (jurists), or advocates (orators). The prevailing legal institutions were largely Germanic and Frankish. Thus it was the body of law, the legal system, of an earlier civilization, as recorded in a huge book or set of books, that formed the object of Europe's first systematic legal studies.

It was of critical importance, however, that the jurists who studied these ancient texts believed, as did their contemporaries generally, that that earlier civilization, the Roman Empire, had survived until their time, in the West as well as in the East. It had survived in a special sense — in a new form, as the soul of a person might survive the body. More than that, they believed it had a universal and permanent quality. They took Justinian's law not primarily as the law applicable in Byzantium in 534 A.D., but as the law applicable at all times and in all places. They took it, in other words, as truth — the way they took the Bible as truth and the works of Plato and (later) Aristotle as truth. Although, for example, what was written in Justinian's compilation about ownership of land had nothing to do with the regulation of feudal property rights prevailing in 1100 in Tuscany or Normandy, this did not mean that it was not "the law." It was, in fact, the *true* law, the ideal law, the embodiment of reason. Moreover, Tuscany and Normandy themselves were thought to be the continuation of Rome, just as the church, or Christendom, was thought to be the continuation of Israel. The discovery in about 1080 of a copy of Justinian's compilation was received in the same spirit as that in which the discovery of a copy of a long-lost supplement to the Old Testament might have been received. Thus the author (or authors) of the great thirteenth-century summa on English law, Bracton's *Treatise on the Laws and Customs of England,* quoted something like five hundred passages from Justinian's Digest, without attribution, simply taking it for granted that they were "the law" in England, even though many of them might not have been applicable in the king's courts.[1] Indeed, Bracton actually had to argue that the English customs applicable in the kings' courts constituted a "law" as real as that contained in the ancient Roman texts.

Two other ingredients were also necessary to the creation of the Western legal tradition. One was the method of analysis and synthesis which was applied to the ancient legal texts — a method which in modern times has been called, somewhat disparagingly, "scholasticism." The second was the context in which the scholastic method was applied to the books of Roman law — namely, the university.

These three elements — the discovery of the legal writings compiled under the Roman Emperor Justinian, the scholastic method of analyzing and synthesizing them, and the teaching of law in the universities of Europe — are at the root of the Western legal tradition. The Roman law gave all Europe (including England) much of its basic legal vocabulary. The scholastic method has remained a predominant mode of legal thought throughout the West to this day. The universities brought together legal scholars — teachers and students — from all over Europe, brought them into contact not only with one another but also with teachers and students of theology, medicine, and the liberal arts, and made them a calling or, in today's terminology, a profession.

The Law School at Bologna

The newly discovered texts of Roman law were copied and began to be studied in various cities of Italy and elsewhere near the end of the eleventh century. Students would come together and hire a teacher for a year to expound them; the legal form adopted was that of a partnership (in Roman law, *societas*) of professor and students. One teacher in particular, named Guarnerius but known historically as Irnerius, who began teaching at Bologna in northern Italy in about 1087, gained preeminence, and students flocked to him from all over Europe.[2] His school survived his death. Modern estimates of the number of law students at Bologna at any one time in the twelfth and thirteenth centuries range from 1,000 to 10,000.[3]

Being aliens, most of the students were in a precarious legal situation. For example, any alien might be liable for the debts of any of his fellow countrymen. A Bolognese merchant with a claim against a London merchant could exact damages from any of the English law students at hand. To protect themselves against these and other hazards, the students banded together in "nations," on the basis of their ethnic and geographical origin — the Franks, Picards, Provençals, Alemanns (Germans), Angles, Spaniards, and others, altogether some twenty or more nations. Finally, they united in two corporate bodies, or guilds, one comprising all students from north of the Alps and the other all those from south of the Alps, with each of the two groups being organized in the form of a *universitas* — a term of Roman law then given the meaning of an association with legal personality or, in today's terminology, a corporation. The professors were not members of the student universitas.

The virtues of incorporation were obvious to the students of Bologna, teenagers who by medieval standards were mature young men ready for an active political life. United, they could bargain effectively with the city government and also dominate the administration of the school. Bologna was the archetype of the medieval student-controlled institution of higher learning — in contrast to the professorially controlled university that was founded a little later in Paris. The name "university" was ultimately given to all such institutions. Originally, the term applied to the university in today's sense, that is, the entire institution or enterprise, was *studium generale* ("general education"), signifying education available and accredited generally, not only locally. It was not necessary that there be several "departments": a faculty of theology or of law might itself be called a studium generale.

The student universitas, or corporation, or guild, received from the city of Bologna a charter which permitted it to make contracts with the professors, to regulate the rents of student lodgings, to determine the kinds of courses to be taught and the material to be covered in each, to set the length of lectures and the number of holidays, to regulate prices for the rent and sale of books. The professors were paid directly by the students in their respective classes.

The student guild was also given wide civil and criminal jurisdiction over its members. Thus students were exempted from the civil disabilities of alienage and acquired, in effect, an artificial citizenship of their own.

The charter of Bologna provided that the student guild should be responsible for "the cultivation of fraternal charity, mutual association and amity, the care of the sick and needy, the conduct of funerals and the extirpation of rancor and quarrels, the attendance and escort of our candidates for the doctorate to and from the place of examination, and the spiritual welfare of members."[4]

The professors formed their own association, the college of teachers, which had the right to examine and admit candidates for the doctorate — and to charge examination fees. Since the doctor's degree was in effect an admission into the teaching profession, the professors retained the power to determine the membership of their own guild, but that was about all. If the students felt that a professor was not fulfilling his teaching duties, they would boycott his classes and refuse to pay him. And if a lecture did not begin promptly when the opening bell rang, or if it concluded before the closing bell, or if the course of lectures was not covered by the end of the term, the professor was fined by the student guild.

The governing board of the student university was a general council, to which each "nation" elected two members. The general council elected the rector, each nation having the right to nominate a candidate for that post. The rector had to be at least twenty-four years old and had to have been in residence for five years. The baccalaureate (bachelor's) degree was awarded by the rector. A committee of students, called Denouncers of Professors, was appointed by the rector to report professorial irregularities.

The general council ruled by majority vote. Large issues were acted on by an assembly ("congregation") of all the students, attendance at which was compulsory, with each student having the right to speak and to vote. The general council had the power to enact university statutes. The statutes regulated the economic affairs of the institution, including fees and salaries, cost of renting books, housing, and conditions of money lending; they also regulated both student and professorial discipline as well as many aspects of the curriculum. A major limitation on student self-government, however, was the rule that no statute adopted by the assembly could be changed until twenty years after it had been enacted except by unanimous consent of both the students and the professors.

The source of student power was in part economic. The students — either sons of wealthy families or else supported by foundations (usually monasteries) — brought a very large income to the city. If they were dissatisfied they could easily migrate, taking the professors with them. Since the dormitories, dining halls, and lecture halls were owned by the city or by local entrepreneurs rather than by the students, the departure of the students could cause a severe economic crisis. In later times the professors came to be paid by the city and were bound by oath to the city not to depart. This development brought a sharp decline in student control over the university.

The ecclesiastical hierarchy also played an important role in controlling legal education. Except in the Italian cities, education throughout Europe in the twelfth century was supervised by the ecclesiastical rather than by the secular authority. However, in 1219, more than a century after Bologna had been started, the pope decreed that nobody there should be installed in the office of teaching (that is, should receive the degree of doctor) without being examined by, and receiving a license from, the Archdeacon of Bologna. In fact, the archdeacon (or in the case of other Italian universities, under similar papal decrees, the bishop) did not himself ask questions but rather presided over the examination. Nevertheless, the papal decree of 1219 deprived the doctors of their independent role in granting degrees, and the church's *licentia docendi* ("licence to teach") was henceforth required in Italy as elsewhere. In many parts of Europe the remote control of universities by bishops led to periodic student revolts.

Historically more significant than episcopal control of the universities, however, was their relative freedom from such control, as compared with preexisting educational institutions. Prior to the eleventh century, formal education in Europe had been carried on almost exclusively in monasteries. In the eleventh and twelfth centuries, cathedral schools were formed and gradually achieved preeminence. The cathedral being the seat of the bishop, the cathedral school was under his immediate supervision, just as the monastic school was under the immediate supervision of the abbot. A teacher would hardly dare to contradict his bishop or his abbot. The University of Bologna, on the other hand, is said to have been founded when Matilda, Duchess of Tuscany and friend of Pope Gregory VII, invited Irnerius to teach Roman law there. For over a hundred years, then, the teaching at Bologna was free of direct ecclesiastical control. There was, to be sure, substantial indirect pressure; Irnerius himself is said to have been excommunicated because he supported the imperial cause against the papacy. Yet, in general, Bolognese jurists were free to support opposing views concerning the extent to which various provisions of Roman law justified imperial and papal claims. Meanwhile, in Paris in the early 1100s, Peter Abelard dared to contradict his bishop and to teach a "countercourse" against him. It was out of this confrontation that the University of Paris emerged in the twelfth century.[5] Thus the European universities established themselves from the beginning as educational institutions where professors were free to take opposing positions. This was in contrast to the earlier system, known since antiquity, under which each school had been dominated by a single teacher or a single theory.

Bologna was also, from the beginning, a university in the sense that it was a graduate school; that is, most of the students had previously received an education in the liberal arts, usually at a monastic or cathedral school. There the curriculum consisted of the seven "liberal arts": grammar, rhetoric, logic (also called dialectics), arithmetic, geometry, astronomy, and music. However, many of the schools concentrated on the first three, called the trivium, based chiefly on the Bible, the writings of the church fathers, and some parts of Plato, Aristotle, Cicero, and other Greek and Roman writers. Study of the liberal arts was a prerequisite, from the twelfth century on, to the study of the new "sciences" of law, theology, and medicine. (When, as at Paris, liberal arts became a fourth university discipline, its study remained a prerequisite to the other three.) Bologna did not at first embrace a faculty other than law, and when eventually other faculties were formed there, there was no constitutional connection among them except that all students received their degrees from the same chancellor, the Archdeacon of Bologna.

The Bologna system of legal education was transplanted to many other cities throughout Europe, including Padua, Perugia, and Pisa, Salamanca and Montpellier and Orléans, Prague, Vienna, Cracow, and Heidelberg.[6] Most universities north of the Alps, however, although they followed Bologna's law curriculum and teaching methods, adopted the type of organization initiated at Paris, where doctors and students of all four faculties—theology, law, medicine, and the arts—were embraced in a single body and made subject to a common head and a common government.[7] At Oxford, Vacarius, who had been trained at Bologna, taught Roman law in the mid-1100s, although apparently a law faculty as such was not established at Oxford (and another at Cambridge) until the next century.

The Curriculum and Teaching Method

What was taught from the beginning at Bologna was the text of the Roman law compiled by Justinian's jurists in the sixth century. Indeed, it is likely that the law school was founded primarily for the purpose of studying that text.

The manuscript consisted of four parts: the Code, comprising twelve books of ordinances and decisions of the Roman emperors before Justinian; the Novels, containing the laws promulgated by Emperor Justinian himself; the Institutes, a short textbook designed as an introduction for beginning law students; and the Digest, whose fifty books contained a multitude of extracts from the opinions of Roman jurists on a very wide variety of legal questions. In a modern English translation, the Code takes up 1,034 pages, the Novels 562 pages, the Institutes 173 pages, and the Digest 2,734 pages.[8]

The outlook of the European jurists of the late eleventh and the twelfth centuries dictated that they treat all these writings as a single body.

Primary importance, however, was attached not to the Institutes, which was a kind of short primer of Roman law, and not to the Code or the Novels, which laid down specific imperial statutes and decrees, but to the Digest, also called the Pandects. The Digest was a vast conglomeration of the opinions of Roman jurists concerning thousands of legal propositions relating not only to property, wills, contracts, torts, and other branches of what is today called civil law, but also to criminal law, constitutional law, and other branches of law governing the Roman citizen. It was "municipal" law (*jus civilis,* "the law of the city"), covering everything except "the law of nations" (*jus gentium*), which applied also to non-Romans and which was only touched on incidentally. The Digest was not a code in the modern sense; it did not attempt to provide a complete, self-contained, internally consistent, systematically arranged set of legal concepts, principles, and rules. It was only in the West, after the founding of the universities, that the Digest, together with the Code, Novels, and Institutes, came to be called Corpus Juris Civilis—"the body" of civil law.

The legal propositions which the Digest set forth were very often "holdings" (as they would be called today) in actual cases. Others were statements ("edicts") of magistrates, called praetors, of how they would rule in prospective cases: for example, "The praetor says, 'If you or your slaves have forcibly deprived anyone of property which he had at that time, I will grant an action only for a year, but after the year has elapsed I will grant one with reference to what has [subsequently] come into the hands of him who dispossessed the complainant by force.' " Such propositions are then followed by quotations from opinions of various jurists. For instance, concerning that statement of the praetor, the jurist Ulpian is quoted as saying: "This interdict was established for the benefit of a person who has been ejected by force, as it is perfectly just to come to his relief under such circumstances. This interdict was devised to enable him to recover possession . . . This interdict does not have reference to all kinds of violence but only to such as issued against persons who are deprived of possession. It only relates to atrocious violence, and where the parties are deprived of the possession of soil, as, for instance, to a tract of land, or a building, but to nothing else." Other jurists also comment on the same interdict—for example, Pomponius is quoted as saying: "If, however, you are ejected by armed force, you will be entitled to recover the land, even if you originally obtained possession of it either by force (*vi*), or clandestinely (*clam*), or under a precarious title (*precario*)."[9]

The Roman jurists, as John P. Dawson has written, directed most of their attention "not to theoretical synthesis, but to the consistent and orderly treatment of individual cases . . . Their whole impulse was toward economy, not only of language, but in ideas. Their assumptions were fixed, the main purposes of the social and political order were not to be called in question, the system of legal ideas was too well known to require much discussion. They were problem-solvers, working within this system and not called upon to solve the ultimate problems of mankind's needs and destiny. They worked case by case, with patience and acumen and profound respect for inherited tradition."[10]

Professor Dawson notes the Roman jurists' "intense concentration on specific cases," sometimes hypothetical but often drawn from actual litigation. "The cases," he says, "are briefly stated, likewise the jurists' own conclusions. No elaborately reasoned justification was needed, for to persons outside the elite group the jurist's own authority was enough and those inside would understand the reasons well enough. There were many assumptions that were unspoken or merely hinted at and that have only been disclosed through centuries of later patient study. The primary task of the jurists as they conceived it was to provide solutions for cases that had arisen or might arise, testing and revising their central ideas by observing their effects on particular cases."[11]

Law students in Europe today, who study Roman law as it has been systematized by university professors in the West since the twelfth century, find it hard to believe that the original texts were so intensely casuistic and untheoretical. They are taught to show that *implicit* in the myriad of narrow rules and undefined general terms was a complex system of abstract concepts. It is this very conceptualism of Roman law that is held up by way of contrast to the alleged particularism and pragmatism of English and American law. But that is to view the Roman law of Justinian through the eyes of later European jurists; it was they who first drew the conceptual implications — who made a theory of contract law out of particular types of Roman contracts, who defined the right of possession, who elaborated doctrines of justification for the use of force, and who, in general, systematized the older texts on the basis of broad principles and concepts.

The curriculum of the twelfth-century law school consisted in the first instance of the reading of the texts of the Digest. The teacher would read — and correct — the language of the handwritten text, and the students would follow it in their (usually rented) manuscript copies and would make the necessary corrections. The term lecture, meaning "reading," was applied to this exercise. Some students who could not afford to buy or rent copies of the Digest would learn it by heart.

Since the text was very difficult, it would have to be explained. Therefore, after reading the text the teacher would "gloss" it, that is, interpret it, word by word, line by line. (*Glossa*, in Greek, means both "tongue," or "language," and "unusual word.") The glosses, dictated by the teacher, were copied by the student between the lines of the text; as they became longer, they spilled over into the margins. Soon the written glosses had authority almost equal to that of the glossed text itself. In about 1250 the *Glossa Ordinaria* of Accursius became the standard authoritative work on the Digest as a whole. Thereafter came the "post-glossators," or "commentators," with their "commentaries" on the texts and the glosses.

The glosses were of several kinds. Some (called *notabilia*) gave short summaries of the contents of the passage glossed. Others (nicknamed *brocardica*) were statements of broad legal rules (maxims) based on the part of the text that was being glossed. In addition, the teachers would annotate the text by classifications called *distinctiones*: they would start with a general term or broad concept and would divide it into various subordinate species, which in turn would be divided and further subdivided, with the writer "following these ramifications of sense and terminology into the most minute details."[12] Finally, in addition to making "distinctions," the teacher would pose *quaestiones*, testing a broad doctrine by its application to particular problems or "questions."

The curriculum and the form of lectures and disputations were described by the statutes of the university. One surviving introduction to a lecture by a medieval law professor goes as follows:

> First I shall give you summaries of each title [of the Digest] before I proceed to the text. Second, I shall pose as well and as clearly and as explicitly as I can the examples of the individual laws [given in the title]. Third, I shall briefly repeat the text with a view to correcting it. Fourth, I shall briefly repeat the contents of the examples [of the laws]. Fifth, I shall solve the contradictions, adding general principles commonly called "brocardica" and distinctions or subtle and useful problems [*quaestiones*], with their solutions, so far as the Divine Providence shall enable me. And if any law shall seem deserving, by reason of its celebrity or difficulty, of a Repetition, I shall reserve it for an evening Repetition.[13]

In addition to the readings of the texts and the glosses, and the analysis of them through distinctions and questions, the curriculum at Bologna and other medieval law schools included the *disputatio*, which was a discussion of a question of law in the form of a dispute between two students under the guidance of a professor or else a dispute between professors and students. It has been compared to a modern moot court, but the questions were always questions of law, not actual or hypothetical situations of fact.

As time went on, the law curriculum at Bologna, Paris, Oxford, and other universities of Europe expanded to include more than the Roman law contained in the Corpus Juris Civilis. The principal new subject added in the latter half of the twelfth century was the newly developed canon law of the church. In contrast to Roman law, canon law was current, prevailing law, replenished by decrees of popes and church councils and applied by ecclesiastical courts. Also, as the secular legal systems of the cities, principalities, and kingdoms of Europe developed — usually under the guidance of jurists trained at Bologna or elsewhere — the curriculum was enriched by references to current problems of secular law. In analyzing the texts of Justinian, the professors would introduce legal questions of current practical significance and would analyze them in the light of the Roman texts as well as of the canon law.

Thus the revival of the study of Roman law of an earlier time led to the analysis of current legal problems. Roman law served at first as an ideal law, a body of legal ideas, taken as a unified system; current legal problems, previously unclassified and inchoate, were analyzed in its terms and were judged by its standards. In a sense, Roman law played a role for the medieval legal mind similar to that which legal history played for the modern Anglo-American legal mind from the seventeenth to the early twentieth century. It gave a perspective for analyzing prevailing laws, and it provided ideals for testing the validity of prevailing laws. This is not to say that Roman law was thought to be something other than prevailing law. It prevailed alongside newer laws, and in a sense *over* them. But it had a fundamental quality which they lacked. The newer laws were in the flux of becoming; the rules of Roman law were present to be concorded.

The Scholastic Method of Analysis and Synthesis

Underlying the curriculum and the teaching methods of the law schools of Bologna and of the other Western universities of the twelfth and thirteenth centuries was a new mode of analysis and synthesis, which later came to be called the scholastic method. This method, which was first fully developed in the early 1100s, both in law and in theology, presupposes the absolute authority of certain books, which are to be comprehended as containing an integrated and complete body of doctrine; but paradoxically, it also presupposes that there may be both gaps and contradictions within the text: and it sets as its main task the summation of the text, the closing of gaps within it, and the resolution of contradictions. The method is called "dialectical" in the twelfth-century sense of that word, meaning that it seeks the reconciliation of opposites.[14]

Both in law and theology, and later in philosophy, the scholastic mode of analysis and synthesis was promoted by the method of teaching in the university, particularly the method of glossing the text and posing questions for disputation. "The principal books of law and theology were the natural outgrowth of university lectures."[15] In other words, science — scholarship — came from teaching, and not vice versa.

At the very time that Western jurists were beginning to create what they conceived to be a science of law, Western theologians were beginning to create what they conceived to be a science of theology. Indeed.

Peter Abelard (1079-1142), who was the first to use the word "theology" in the modern sense, meaning a systematic analysis of the evidence of divine revelation,[16] was also one of the great pioneers of scholastic logic and is sometimes called the father of scholasticism. Abelard sought by means of scholastic methods of analysis and synthesis to apply rational criteria for judging which revealed truths were of universal validity and which were of only relative validity. This was not, then, the kind of fundamentalism which takes all the words of the text as being equally true under all circumstances; the whole is taken to be true, and within the whole the parts are assigned various shades of truth. Indeed, one of the most important books of Abelard, *Sic et Non* (*Yes and No*), merely documents by successive quotations a list of over 150 inconsistencies and discrepancies in the Bible and in the writings of the church fathers and other authorities, assuming them all to be true and leaving it to the reader to try to harmonize them.[17]

In law, the scholastic method took the form of analyzing and synthesizing the mass of doctrines, many of them in conflict with others, found in the law of Justinian as well as in secular authorities. As in the case of theology, the written text as a whole, the Corpus Juris Civilis, like the Bible and the writings of the church fathers, was accepted as sacred, the embodiment of reason. But the emphasis on reconciliation of contradictions gave the twelfth-century Western jurist a greater freedom and flexibility in dealing with legal concepts and rules than his Roman predecessors had had. Like them, he was, to be sure, concerned, in Professor Dawson's words, with the "consistent and orderly treatment of individual cases." But he was also concerned, as they were not, with finding "elaborately reasoned justifications" and a "theoretical synthesis." And in seeking justifications and synthesis he often sacrificed the narrower kind of consistency that the Romans had prized.

The Relation of Scholasticism to Greek Philosophy and Roman Law

The method of the twelfth-century European jurists was a transformation of the methods of dialectical reasoning characteristic of ancient Greek philosophy and of classical and postclassical Roman law. "Dialectic" in Greek means "conversation" or "dialogue." Ancient Greek philosophers referred to the "art of conversation" (*tekhne dialektike*) as a method of reasoning; indeed, Plato viewed it as the only sure method of arriving at knowledge of the truth, which he called "science" (*epistémé, scientia*). The Socratic dialogues reported by Plato involved three basic "dialectical" techniques: (1) the refutation of an opponent's thesis by drawing from it, through a series of questions and answers, consequences that contradict it or that are otherwise unacceptable; (2) the deriving of a generalization—again by questions and answers—from a series of true propositions about particular cases; (3) the definition of concepts by the techniques of distinction, that is, repeated analysis of a genus into its species and the species into their subspecies, and synthesis, that is, repeated collection of species into their genus and the genera into larger genera. Through such reasoning Plato sought to achieve sure knowledge of the nature of Goodness, Justice, Truth, Love, and other "Forms" existing, as he thought, in the universe, independent of humanity.

Aristotle greatly refined Plato's concepts of dialectical reasoning. He distinguished, first, between reasoning from premises that are known to be necessarily true (such as "all men are mortal" or "fire burns") and reasoning from premises that are generally accepted, or propounded by experts, but are nevertheless debatable (such as "man is a political animal" or "philosophy is desirable as a branch of study"). Only the latter kind of reasoning is dialectical, according to Aristotle, and since its premises are disputable it is not capable of arriving at certainty but only at probabilities. The former kind of reasoning, on the other hand, called "apodictic," is alone capable of demonstrating necessary truths since only from indisputable premises can indisputable conclusions be drawn.

Aristotle also refined and developed the Platonic conception of science. He was the first to use the term in the plural to refer to "a whole series of separate and distinct 'sciences,' all of which possess certain methods and certain distinctions in common, but each of which has its own distinctive *archai* or 'principles' [literally, "beginnings"] and its own determinate subject matter."[18] Each also has its own method of investigation, "growing out of the subject matter itself,"[19] although all share in common the method of observation and hypothesis. Aristotle thus divided Platonic "science" into physics, biology, geometry, ethics, politics, metaphysics, and other types. Medicine, however, remained for Aristotle an "art" (*tekhne*), since it applied scientific truths but did not itself lead to the demonstration of such truths. Law was not even treated as an art by Aristotle, but was dissolved into ethics, politics, and rhetoric.

In both apodictic and dialectical reasoning, Aristotle said, either inductive or deductive logic may be applicable. (In this, too, he differed from Plato, for whom truth was obtainable only from deductive logic, that is, by reasoning from the general to the particular rather than from particulars to the general.) Nevertheless, in Aristotle's view inductive logic is to be preferred in dialectical reasoning, since it is clearer and more convincing to most people, whereas in apodictic reasoning deductive logic is appropriate to certain kinds of science (such as mathematics) but not to others (such as biology). Inductive logic moves from experience either to certainty or to probability by finding the common element in the particular cases that have been observed. For example, if one observes that the skilled pilot is the best pilot and the skilled charioteer is the best charioteer, one may conclude that as a general principle the skilled man is the best man in any particular activity.[20] But this general observation only becomes "scientific," in Aristotle's sense, when the principle that underlies it, that is, the cause of it, is recognized, so that the premises of the argument can be seen to be necessarily true.

The distinguishing feature of dialectical reasoning, however, is not that it is partial to inductive logic, for, as Aristotle showed, apodictic reasoning also inclines toward the inductive method in many fields. Dialectical reasoning is distinguished above all by the fact that it does not start with "propositions," that is, with declarative statements that must be either true or false, from which "scientific" conclusions can be drawn, but rather with "problems," or "questions," about which people may differ, although ultimately the disputed question will be resolved conclusively by a proposition, or first principle, in favor of one side or the other if valid methods of dialectical reasoning are used.[21]

Aristotle's distinction between apodictic and dialectical reasoning was accepted by the Stoics of the third century B.C. and thereafter. However, the Stoics viewed dialectical reasoning not as a method of arriving at first principles but as a method of analyzing arguments and defining concepts by distinction and synthesis of genus and species. And they lacked Aristotle's overriding concern for systematic exposition; with them dialectics became an independent discipline, not essentially different from logic but with strong elements also of rhetoric and grammar.

It was in its Stoic form, with the writings of Plato and Aristotle in the background, that Greek dialectics was imported into Rome in the republican period (second and first centuries B.C.). There it was taken up by the educated classes, including jurists, who applied it for the first time to prevailing legal institutions. The Greeks had never attempted such an application. The reasons for that are complex. The Greek cities did not experience the rise of a prestigious class of jurists entrusted with the development of law. Adjudication was by large popular assemblies, and those who argued before the assemblies practiced a mode of declamation that relied less on legal argument than on appeals to moral and political considerations. Moreover, the Greek philosophers did not recognize legal rules as starting points for reasoning. They professed an allegiance to a higher philosophical truth, attainable by observation and reason alone.[22] Legal rules and decisions were, for them, not *authorities* to be accepted, or at least to be reckoned with, as embodiments of the community's sense of justice; they were instead merely *data* to be used, or not used, in constructing their own philosophical theories. Thus Greek philosophers would gladly debate questions concerning the nature of justice and whether a ruler should govern by law or by his own will, but they considered it unimportant to debate whether, for example, the law should give a remedy to an owner of goods against one who had bought them in good faith from another who had fraudulently persuaded the owner to part with them. When they did consider such questions of civil law, they generally treated them as matters of personal ethics. Conversely, questions of constitutional law were generally treated as matters of politics.

Indeed, Platonic thought attributed a transcendent reality to the idea of justice that inhibited the entrusting of its execution to lawyers. Only the seeker after wisdom, the *philosophos*, was capable of governing, and then only when he had succeeded in his search and become a knower. In Carl Friedrich's words, "The very transcendency of justice precludes [for Plato] its realization in a constitutional order." He adds that as a result constitutional law in the Western sense of the term "was unknown at Athens."[23]

In Rome, on the other hand, a prestigious class of jurists came into existence quite early. From the fifth century B.C. on, priests (pontiffs) kept records of various legal remedies ("actions") available for various causes. Thereafter there emerged the practice of electing each year praetors who, in the form of an annual edict, declared general rules of law applicable to private disputes, and who received individual complaints concerning violations of rights laid down in the edict. The praetor would transmit such a complaint to a judge, who was a layman appointed by the praetor ad hoc, with instructions to hold a hearing and, upon proof of the facts alleged in the complaint, to grant a remedy. In addition to praetors and judges there existed a third group of laymen who participated in legal proceedings, the advocates, who argued before the judges. Finally, and ultimately most significantly, there were the jurists (also called jurisconsults). These were the only professionals. It was their chief task to give legal advice—to praetors, to judges, to advocates, to litigants, to clients wishing to engage in legal transactions.[24]

The Roman jurists were intensely practical in their approach to law. Their importation of Greek dialectical reasoning in the second and first centuries B.C., although it was the first scholarly inroad into Roman law, was not the intermarriage of Roman law with Greek philosophy that took place over a thousand years later in the universities of western Europe. The Roman jurists refused to adopt the Hellenistic system of education; legal training continued to consist chiefly of very informal, individual apprenticeship in the house of an older practitioner. "The [Roman] jurisconsults did not discuss with their pupils basic conceptions like justice, law, or legal science, though to the Greeks these seemed problems of the highest, nay almost of sole importance. The student was plunged straight into practice, where he was faced with the everrecurrent question: What, on the facts stated, ought to be done?"[25] Nevertheless, it was in this period—before the great flowering of so-called classical Roman law in the first to third centuries A.D.—that jurists first attempted systematically to classify Roman law into its various kinds (genera and species) and with precision to define general rules applicable to specific cases.

Perhaps the earliest example of the systematic application of dialectical reasoning to law was the treatise on jus civile by the Roman jurist Q. Mucius Scaevola, who died in 82 B.C.[26] In this work, which is said to have "laid the foundations not merely of Roman, but of European, jurisprudence,"[27] civil law was classified into four main divisions: the law of inheritance, the law of persons, the law of things, and the law of obligations. Each of these was subdivided: inheritance into testaments and intestate succession; persons into marriage, guardianship, free status, paternal power, and some other divisions; things into possession and nonpossession; obligations into contracts and delicts. These were further subdivided: for example, contracts were subdivided into real contracts, purchase and sale, letting and hiring, and partnership, while delicts were subdivided into assault, theft, and damage to property.[28] Under the various genera and species, each of which was characterized by its governing principles, legal materials were reproduced—above all, the decisions of praetors in particular cases, but also legislative enactments, authorities from older collections of documents, and also authorities from the oral tradition. The major task which the author set for himself was to present "definitions," as he called them,[29] that is, precise statements of the legal rules implicit in decisions of cases.

In the work of Q. Mucius Scaevola and his fellow jurists of the second and first centuries B.C., not only the classification system but also the method of arriving at the formulation of specific rules was dialectical in the broad Greek sense. Questions were posed, various answers of jurists were collected, and the author's own solutions were offered. For example, an earlier jurist had summarized various decisions concerning the scope of the law of theft by saying that one who borrowed a horse was guilty of theft if he took it to a place other than that agreed when he received it, or if he took it further than the place agreed. Q. Mucius Scaevola reviewed the same decisions, and others, and achieved a broader and at the same time a more precise formulation: whoever receives a thing for safekeeping and uses it, or receives it for use and uses it for a purpose other than that for which he receives it, is guilty of theft.[30] This definition includes not only loans but deposits, and it substitutes "thing" for "horse."

As Professor Stein writes, "Following the Aristotelian techniques [Q. Mucius] saw his task as that of explaining what actually happened in legal proceedings."[31] He sought to achieve that task by subdivision of genera and species until he reached specific decisions, classified them, and then was able to explain them by finding "a form of words that included all the relevant categories and excluded all others."[32] His aim, and that of other jurists who followed him, was to declare the preexisting law and to define its precise limits.[33] However, the breadth of generalization was in inverse ratio to its sophistication. One would not look to the Roman jurists of the republican period for a discussion of legal concepts; "indeed the notion of a concept was not found in their mental equipment."[34]

Subsequently, in the classical and postclassical periods (first to fifth centuries A.D.), the Roman jurists refined and developed the dialectical techniques that had been applied by their republican predecessors, without changing them fundamentally. There was a tendency toward somewhat greater abstraction. In the first part of the second century they began to speak expressly of "rules" (*regulae*) and not only of "definitions." The difference between the two terms is a subtle one. The definitions seem to have been more closely connected with the cases which they generalized. The rules, though derived from cases, were capable of being considered separately. Sometimes they were collected in "books of rules," which were especially useful to the numerous minor officials of the Roman Empire. Also a few law schools were founded in this period, and although their orientation remained intensely practical, they undoubtedly contributed to a tendency to search for broader rules. Aristotelian concepts of the "nature" of a thing were used, for example, to summarize rules concerning what may be omitted from the express terms of agreements of purchase and sale: it was said that terms that "naturally belong" to the case require no express agreement.[35] However, only one kind of term was given as "naturally belonging" to all types of purchase and sale—namely, that the vendor had title; various other specific implied warranties (as they would be called today) for individual types of purchase and sale were then listed separately—for example, that an animal is healthy, or that a slave is not in the habit of running away. Sometimes common rules were developed to govern diverse types of transactions—for example, diverse types of contracts, such as sales and leases. Only occasionally would Roman jurists go so far as to postulate broad principles that seemed to embrace the entire law. Thus Gaius, the great jurist and law teacher of the mid-second century, wrote that agreements concluded "against the rules of the civil law" are invalid, thereby implying, but only implying, what was first spelled out in the twelfth century by the scholastic jurists of the West: that the law forms a whole system, a whole "body."

This implication was also present in some very broad regulae which, when abstracted from the cases for which they were first generalized, have the form of succinct epigrammatic statements of fundamental legal principles. In Justinian's Digest the concluding Title 50.17, "Concerning various rules of the ancient law," collects 211 such broad rules: for example, "No one is considered to defraud those who know and consent," "In doubtful matters the more benevolent interpretations should be preferred," "Good faith confers as much on a possessor as the truth, whenever the law (*lex*) offers no impediment." However, as Stein has shown,[36] these "legal maxims," as they came to be called in the twelfth century, have a wholly different meaning when taken as abstract principles from that which they had in the context of the types of cases in which they were originally uttered and which are often reproduced in the earlier parts of the Digest. Thus the first of the rules just quoted referred originally to the case of one who acquires something from a fraudulent debtor with the consent of the creditors: the creditors may not later claim that they were defrauded. The second originally referred to legacies; the "more benevolent interpretations" are those that are more benevolent to legatees. The third originally referred to the good-faith possessor of another's slave; if the slave has stolen from another, the victim has an action against the possessor. In 530 A.D. Justinian issued a constitution clarifying the older law on the subject. This constitution is the lex which is obliquely referred to in the concluding phrase of the regula.

This collection of 211 bare statements of abstract rules of the ancient law was not intended by Justinian to deceive anyone into believing that these rules had a meaning independent of the concrete situations to which they were originally applied. The very first regula makes this clear: the jurist Paul is quoted as having said, "A rule is something which briefly relates a matter . . . By means of a rule a short account of matters is passed on and . . . if it is inaccurate in any respect, it loses its effect." In other words, rules must not be considered outside the contexts of the cases which they summarize. This is also shown by the fact that each rule is preceded by a citation to its original context. Moreover, with the exception of the first one, the rules are arranged unsystematically, and some of them contradict one another.[37] Justinian added the regulae partly, at least, as an ornamental index to his great collection. It is also likely that they were intended to be useful in argument, possibly as presumptions that could be used to shift the burden of proof. Finally, they served a didactic purpose as an aid to memorizing the vast text. Certainly no Roman jurist treated them as abstract principles. Indeed, the entire Title 50.17 of the Digest must have demonstrated beyond a doubt to the Roman lawyers of Justinian's time the validity of the famous rule of Javolenus, also contained in Title 50.17, "All rules [*definitiones*] in civil law are dangerous, for they are almost always capable of being distorted." (That, too, was probably aimed at a specific definition.)[38]

The classical and postclassical Roman jurists thought of a legal rule as a generalization of the common elements of decisions in a restricted, specified class of cases. Only by thus limiting the scope of legal rules did they hope to achieve their objective of using Greek methods of classification and generalization as a rational basis for deciding cases. The Greeks had never attempted any such rationalization of legal decisions and rules; for them, dialectical reasoning was a technique for deriving valid philosophical conclusions — "propositions" — from agreed premises. The Romans converted the Greek dialectic from an art of discovery to an art of judging.

It is important to distinguish Roman legal casuistry from the legal casuistry of the western European jurists of the eleventh and twelfth centuries and thereafter, as well as from the case method of analysis practiced by English and American common lawyers to this day. On the one hand, the Romans did not use cases in order to illustrate principles or to test them by going back a step, so to speak, in order to see their applications. On the other hand, they reduced their cases to bare holdings, without treating them in their fullness — without discussion of ambiguities or gaps in their fact situations, or alternative formulations of the legal issues involved.[39] Max Weber undoubtedly went too far when he referred to the classical Roman jurists' use of rules as a "merely paratactic and visual association of the analogy."[40] Yet their failure to articulate the assumptions and deeper reasons on which the analogies were founded — indeed, their failure even to define the most important legal terms[41] — led to a narrowness, or woodenness, in case analysis; and this was just what the Roman jurists wanted! When Cicero argued for a more complex systematization of the law, with clear definitions and abstract legal rules, the jurists "answered these strictures by polite silence."[42] They had no reason to try to transform the Roman genius for consistent adjudication into a philosophical system. They had every reason to be suspicious of the applicability of the higher ranges of Greek philosophy to the practical needs of adjudication.

The western European jurists of the eleventh and twelfth centuries carried the Greek dialectic to a much higher level of abstraction. They attempted to systematize the rules into an integrated whole — not merely to define elements common to particular species of cases but also to synthesize the rules into principles and the principles themselves into an entire system, a body of law or corpus juris.

One of the techniques the scholastic jurists used to achieve this objective was to treat the Roman *regulae*, found in Title 50.17 of the Digest and elsewhere, as legal "maxims," that is, as independent principles of universal validity. The word "maxim" was drawn from Aristotelian terminology; it referred to a "maximum proposition," that is, a "universal." The Roman writer Boethius (480–524 A.D.), from whose Latin translations and commentaries Western scholars from the sixth to the mid-twelfth centuries learned their Aristotle, wrote that Aristotle postulated certain self-evident propositions, and that from these "maximum, that is, universal . . . propositions . . . the conclusions of syllogisms are drawn."[43] In the twelfth century the great logician Peter Abelard, in his

Dialectica, described such a maximum proposition as one that summarizes the meaning and the logic common to the particular propositions that are implied in it. For example, from the propositions "if it is man it is animal," "if it is rose it is flower," "if it is red it is color," and other similar propositions in which a species is antecedent to a genus, "the maximum proposition is induced that what is said of a species may be said of a genus." "The maxim," Abelard wrote, "contains and expresses the sense of all such consequences and demonstrates the mode of inference common to the antecedents."[44] In the same way the jurists of Bologna, contemporaries of Abelard, induced universal principles from the implications of particular instances. This was just the opposite of the older Roman concept of a rule as merely "a short account of matters"; it was assumed instead that the whole law, the entire jus, could be induced by synthesis from the common characteristics of specific types of cases. A similar logic was used centuries later by English and American lawyers to derive general rules from particular judicial decisions. Contemporary logicians call it "existential generalization."[45] It rests on the general principle of inference that if an individual object *a* of a collection *M* has the property *F*, then it can be said of the collection *M* that some or at least one of the objects in it have or has the property *F*. The twelfth-century scholastic jurists went farther than the Anglo-American common lawyers, however, in their belief that every legal decision or rule is a species of the genus law. This made it possible for them to use every part of the law to build the whole, and at the same time to use the whole to interpret every part.

It was this belief and this method that characterized the approach by which the scholastic jurists analyzed and synthesized the rediscovered texts of Justinian. Here Aristotelian dialectics—even before the translation of Aristotle's principal works on logic—was carried over to law at a level of synthesis far higher than that of the Roman jurists whose writings were being studied.[46]

Yet there was another side to it. Aristotle had denied the apodictic character of dialectical reasoning. It could not achieve certainty because its premises were uncertain. The twelfth-century jurists of western Europe, on the contrary, used the Aristotelian dialectic for the purpose of demonstrating what is true and what is just. They turned Aristotle on his head by conflating dialectical and apodictic reasoning and applying both to the analysis and synthesis of legal norms. In contrast to the earlier Roman jurists and the earlier Greek philosophers, they supposed that they could prove by reason the universal truth and universal justice of authoritative legal texts. For them, the edicts and *responsa* of Roman law, taken both individually and as a whole, constituted what they certainly had not constituted in the minds of the Roman lawyers themselves—a written natural law, a *ratio scripta*, to be taken, together with the Bible, the patristic writings, and the canons of the church, as sacred. Since Roman legal norms were true and just, they could be reasoned from, apodictically, to discover new truth and justice. But since they contained gaps, ambiguities, and contradictions, they had to be reasoned from dialectically as well; that is, problems had to be put, classifications and definitions made, opposing opinions stated, conflicts synthesized.

This was the first systematic application of St. Anselm's famous motto, *Credo ut intelligam* ("I believe in order that I may understand"). Aristotle's contradiction between dialectical reasoning and apodictic reasoning was itself resolved. The dialectical method became the scientific method in law—as it eventually became the scientific method in other branches of learning, including the natural sciences.

The scholastic jurists differed from the Greek philosophers not only in their belief that universal legal principles could be derived by reasoning from authoritative texts but also in their belief concerning the nature of such universal principles. Plato had postulated that universals exist in nature—that the idea of justice or beauty, the idea of a triangle, the idea of color, the idea of a rose, and other general ideas in people's minds are imperfect reflections of "paradigms" or "forms" that exist in external reality. This "realist" view of universal ideas, as it was later called in the West (today it would be called "idealist"), was not entirely shared by Aristotle, although most of the differences between Aristotle and Plato were concealed in the only versions of Aristotle's works known in the West until near the end of the twelfth century, namely, the translations and commentaries of Boethius.[47] Thus Western Christian philosophers had taken both Plato and Aristotle to be realists. Although some of these philosophers had raised some questions concerning the "reality" of universals, the first sharp and systematic attack on the realist position was taken in the eleventh and twelfth centuries, above all by Abelard. He denied the external reality of the common characteristics that define a class of individual substances. He argued that only the individual substances exist outside the mind, and that universals are names (*nomina*) invented by the mind to express the similarities or relationships among individual things belonging to a class. Some "nominalists" denied that universals have any meaning at all; Abelard, however, asserted that the names do have meaning, in that they characterize the individuals in the class, but that they do not "exist" except as they are attributed to individuals. Thus "goodness," and "society," and "color," and "rose" are not to be found either in the physical world or in some ideal world of forms; rather they are general qualities that the human intellect attributes to good acts, or to individual people living in social relations with one another, or to particular pigments, or to individual roses.

Nominalism played an indispensable role in the movement to systematize law. For realism in the Platonic sense, however convincing it might be as metaphysics, was wholly alien to the effort of twelfth-century jurists to classify, divide, distinguish, interpret, generalize, synthesize, and harmonize the great mass of decisions, customs, canons, decrees, writs, laws, and other legal materials that constituted the legal order of the time. To have postulated, in Platonic style, the external reality of justice, equality, consistency, procedural regularity, and other universal principles, and to have attempted to deduce from them specific legal rules and institutions, would have been a futile academic exercise. Such an abstract system would have been of no use to the emerging polities, ecclesiastical or secular.

What was needed was the Greek genius for classification and generalization but without the belief that the classifications and generalizations reflect the realities of the external world — without, in short, Platonic naturalism. In law, such naturalism could not go much beyond the casuistic *regulae* of the Roman jurists. The nominalists, on the other hand, although they shared with the realists a deep concern to establish general principles and to prove the validity of general concepts, nevertheless denied that such principles and concepts exist *as such*. The nominalists believed that universals are produced by the mind, by reason and will, and therefore can be revised by reason and will, but that at the same time, they inhere in the particulars that they characterize, and can therefore be tested by those particulars. Extreme nominalism would deny that "the whole is greater than the sum of its parts," but a more moderate nominalism, such as that of Abelard, asserts that the whole is *in* the parts, holding them together, so that the parts taken in isolation from one another (rather than as parts) are not so great as the parts taken in relation to one another. Thus the parts are not, strictly speaking, derived from the whole (deduction), nor is the whole, strictly speaking, derived from the parts (induction), but rather the whole *is* the parts interacting with one another. Therefore nominalism such as Abelard's was congenial to the systematizing and synthesizing of law; for in law there can be no such separation of the whole and the parts, the general and the particular, the form and the substance, the ends and the means, as is inherent in realist philosophies.

The paradoxes implicit in the combining of universals and particulars were closely related to the paradoxes implicit in the combining of apodictic and dialectical reasoning. Both were closely related, in turn, to the paradoxes implicit in the scholastic synthesis of faith and reason. The scholastic dialectic was more than a method of reasoning and more than a way of organizing thought. Its criteria were moral as well as intellectual; it was a way of testing justice and not only truth. Thus the scholastic antitheses included not only general versus special, object versus subject, argument versus reply, but also strict law versus dispensation in exceptional cases, precept versus counsel, absolute rule versus

relative rule, justice versus mercy, divine law versus human law. These
and similar "oppositions" were used as a means of logical reconciliation
of contradictory texts, but they were also used for shaping the legal institutions of both the church and the secular society in such a way as to
manifest alternative values. For God himself was conceived to be a God
both of justice and of mercy, both of strict law and of equity. The
paradoxes of divine justice were for the first time systematically applied
to human laws. Thus scholasticism was not only a method but a
jurisprudence and a theology.

The Application of the Scholastic Dialectic to Legal Science

Probably the most striking single example of the role of the scholastic
dialectic in the formation of Western legal science is the great treatise of
the Bolognese monk Gratian, written about 1140 and entitled
characteristically, *A Concordance of Discordant Canons*.[48] This work, which
in a modern edition fills over 1400 printed pages,[49] was the first comprehensive and systematic legal treatise in the history of the West, and
perhaps in the history of mankind—if by "comprehensive" is meant the
attempt to embrace virtually the entire law of a given polity, and if by
"systematic" is meant the express effort to present that law as a single
body, in which all the parts are viewed as interacting to form a whole.

Prior to the previous century (the eleventh) there had been no effort to
collect all the laws of the church into a single book or books, and in such
partial collections as existed the laws (typically called *canones*, "rules")
were arranged chronologically. About 1012, however, Burchard, Bishop
of Worms, made a very large collection, called a *Decretum*—it runs to
some five hundred pages in a printed edition—arranged not
chronologically but according to various categories, including the
episcopacy, ordained persons, churches, baptism, the Eucharist,
homicide, incest, monks and nuns, witches, excommunication, perjury,
fasting, drunkenness, laymen, accusers and witnesses, fornication,
visitation of the sick, penance, and contemplation (in that order).[50] Burchard did not distinguish law from theology and did not attempt to present any explicit theory or theories of law. He set forth, without comment, scriptural texts, canons of ecumenical and local councils, decrees
of popes, rules contained in various penitentials, and other sources.
Then in 1095 Ivo, Bishop of Chartres, made another such collection,
also called a *Decretum*, and a few years later he made still another, called
Panormia. Both of these included more commentary than had ever been
given before and were broader in their coverage, including a large
number of rules concerning theft, certain types of voluntary transactions, possession, adjudication, and a variety of other matters.[51] In the
Prologue to his *Decretum*, Ivo stated that he was attempting to unite the

ecclesiastical rules "into one body." He was one of the first to set forth conflicting passages in the authorities and to suggest some standards by which they could be reconciled. Admonitions, he said, should yield to statements of law, and indulgences should not be given the force of general rules. Also, it should be considered whether a particular canon is revocable or irrevocable, and whether it was intended that dispensations from it should be granted under certain circumstances.

Gratian built on Ivo's work.[52] He also had before him the work of the glossators of the Roman law, above all his fellow citizen Irnerius. By the time of Gratian, Irnerius and his followers at the law school of Bologna had for some decades been cross-indexing and glossing the Roman texts, and formulating general principles to explain them. Gratian, however, pursued a method of systematization different from that of any of his predecessors. Unlike the Romanists, he did not have a predetermined text but had to dig out for himself, from many written sources, the canons that he wished to systematize. He collected and analyzed approximately 3800 canonical texts, including many from early periods of church history. But he did not group them according to the conventional categories either of earlier canonical collections (ordination, marriage, penance, and so forth) or of Roman law (persons, things, obligations, succession, crimes, and so forth).

His categories were, on the one hand, more comprehensive: the first part of his work was arranged in 101 divisions (*distinctiones*), of which the first 20 analyzed and synthesized authoritative statements concerning the nature of law, the various sources of law, and the relationship between the different kinds of law, while the next 81 dealt with the jurisdiction of various offices within the church and other rules concerning ecclesiastical personnel. Gratian's categories were, on the other hand, more functional than those that had previously been used in legal literature. In the second part of his work he set forth 36 specific complex cases (*causae*), within each of which he posed difficult problems (*quaestiones*). These he analyzed by presenting patristic, conciliar, and papal authorities pro and con, reconciling the contradictions where possible or else leaving them unresolved, offering generalizations, and sometimes harmonizing the generalizations.[53] The third part reverted to the form of distinctiones; and Gratian inserted still another section presented in the form of distinctiones in the second part. These variations affected the symmetry of the work but not its basic integrity as a restatement of the law.

The best example of his more comprehensive method of analysis and synthesis is found in the first twenty distinctiones, in which various kinds of law are identified (divine law, natural law, human law, the law of the church, the law of princes, enacted law, customary law), and the relationships among them are defined. Gratian did not, of course, invent these categories: the Roman jurists had adapted to their own use Aristotelian distinctions between natural law and positive law, universal law and national law, customary law and enacted law; and the distinction between divine and human law had always existed within the church. But Gratian was the first to explore systematically the legal implications of these distinctions and to arrange the various sources of law in a hierarchical order. He started by interposing the concept of natural law between the concepts of divine law and human law. Divine law is the will of God reflected in revelation, especially the revelation of Holy Scripture. Natural law also reflects God's will; however, it is found both in divine revelation and in human reason and conscience. From this Gratian could conclude that "the laws [*leges*] of princes [that is, of the secular authorities] ought not to prevail over natural law [*jus naturale*]."[54] Likewise ecclesiastical "laws" may not contravene natural "law."[55] "*Ius*," he wrote, "is the genus, *lex* is a species of it."[56]

Gratian also concluded that, as a matter of natural law, "princes are bound by and shall live according to their laws."[57] This principle had been declared also by Ivo and Burchard. In its strict form — that kings are "bound" by their laws — it was not a part, however, of older Roman and Germanic law. There were passages in the earlier texts to the effect that a good prince or emperor ought, as a moral matter, to observe his own laws, but it was generally stated that, as a matter of *law*, he was absolved from them.[58] Under the new theory, on the contrary, although the lawmaker could change the old laws in a lawful manner, he could not lawfully disregard them at will.

Moreover, the laws (*leges*) and enactments (*constitutiones*) of princes were, according to Gratian, to be subordinate to ecclesiastical leges and constitutiones.[59] Further, customs (*consuetudines*), he wrote, must yield not only to natural law but also to enacted laws, whether secular or ecclesiastical.[60]

The theory that customs must yield to natural law was one of the greatest achievements of the canonists. When Gratian lived, most law in the West was customary law; that is, most legal norms were binding not because they had been promulgated by political authorities, whether ecclesiastical or secular, but because they were practices accepted as binding by the communities in which they prevailed. Enacted laws were relatively rare. Also, enacted laws were still justified, for the most part, as restatements of preexisting custom. The theory of Gratian and his fellow canonists provided a basis for weeding out those customs that did not conform to reason and conscience. Elaborate criteria were developed to determine the validity of a custom: its duration, its universality, its uniformity of application, its reasonableness — tests still used in the twentieth century. This meant that custom lost its sanctity; a custom might be binding or it might not.

Thus the canon lawyers "marked off," in the words of Gabriel Le Bras, "from the principles of eternal validity the variable elements of the law, which had been suggested by particular circumstances, whether of time, place, or persons, and enforcement of which other conditions might render unreasonable. This amounted to the recognition of the relativity of rules and provided a technical method of harmonizing contradictions."[61] Two contradictory rules could both be true if, in the words of Gratian's Prologue to the *Concordance of Discordant Canons*, they related to a law which was "variable" and the contradiction was due to a dispensation in a special case.

Gratian's emphasis on natural law and on reason was derived in part from Greek, especially Stoic, philosophy. In addition, the newly rediscovered Roman law of Justinian included many references to and remarks about natural law and equity, but it had not developed those concepts into any sort of system. The sources of law were classified but they were not organized into a hierarchy or pattern. The Roman lawyers were not philosophers, and the Greek philosophers were not lawyers; but in the twelfth century the canonists and Romanists of western Europe combined the Greek capacity for philosophy with the Roman capacity for law. In addition, they deepened the earlier concepts of reason and equity by adding to them the Judaic and Christian concept of conscience, which they related to mercy and love.

Moreover, they specifically identified the division between positive law and natural law as a division between lex, that is, an enacted law, and jus, or the system of justice, of right. Not only princes and other secular authorities but also ecclesiastics—popes, local councils, bishops—enacted individual leges and constitutiones. But the body of jus, whether it was the body of Roman law (*corpus juris Romani*), as it then came to be called, or the new body of canon law (*corpus juris canonici*), as it came to be called a century later, was sacred; and the validity of an enacted law depended on its conformity to the body of human law as a whole, which in turn was to conform to both natural law and divine law.

The subordination of positive law to natural law was reinforced by the dualism of secular and ecclesiastical law as well as by the coexistence of conflicting secular authorities. The church claimed that secular laws which contradicted the law of the church were invalid. Princes did not always yield to that claim. Nevertheless, they themselves made similar claims with respect to laws of competing secular authorities (such as feudal lords or city councils) and occasionally to laws of competing ecclesiastical authorities. Given plural legal systems, victims of unjust laws could run from one jurisdiction to another for relief in the name of reason and conscience.

The laws of the church itself were to be tested by their conformity to natural law. Gratian wrote: "Enactments, whether ecclesiastical or secular, if they are proved to be contrary to natural law, must be totally excluded."[62] However, only rarely was anyone in a position to say authoritatively that an ecclesiastical enactment was contrary to natural law, for the pope was not only the supreme legislator in the church but also the vicar and representative of Christ on earth. In the twelfth and thirteenth centuries, at least, most of the men who served as officials and judges and counselors of kings and emperors were clerics who owed at least half of their allegiance to the pope. Nevertheless, secular authorities did sometimes challenge ecclesiastical enactments on the ground that they were contrary to natural law.

The theory of the relativity of rules was thus based partly on the politics of competing legal systems. But it was also based partly on the scholastic dialectic, which provided a method for placing both customary laws and enacted laws within a larger theoretical framework of the nature and sources of law.

A good example of Gratian's second principal method of systematization — the method used in the second part of his work, specifically, the analysis and synthesis of conflicting solutions to a particular legal "question" — is his discussion of whether or not priests should read profane literature.[63] After posing the problem, Gratian quotes the statements of church councils, church fathers, and others, as well as examples from Scripture and church history, all tending to show that priests should not read profane literature, and then he quotes similar authoritative statements and examples to the opposite effect. After giving each authoritative statement or example, Gratian introduces his own interpretation. Thus he starts with the pronouncement of the Carthaginian Council, "A bishop should not read the books of the heathen." In his gloss he notes that nothing is said about books of heretics, which may be read "carefully, either of necessity or for some special reason." He comments further on the word "necessity," interpreting it as signifying that priests may read the books of heretics "in order that they may know how to speak correctly." A more significant gloss accompanying the statement of the question itself sums up the interpretation of all the authorities against reading profane literature: "pleasure alone seems to be forbidden." Ultimately Gratian offers his conclusion, "solving the contradiction" by stating that anyone (and not only priests) ought to learn profane knowledge not for pleasure but for instruction, in order that what is found therein may be turned to the use of sacred learning. Thus Gratian used general principles and general concepts to synthesize opposing doctrines — not only to determine which of two opposing doctrines was wrong, but also to bring a new, third doctrine out of the conflict.[64]

Many other examples could be given to show how the scholastic method was applied to particular legal problems in order to reconcile

contradictions among authoritative texts and to bring forth new doctrines from them. The following example, drawn not only from Gratian
but from other canonists and from Romanists of the twelfth and thirteenth centuries, shows the similarities between the legal technique of
the scholastic jurists and modern legal technique. Both the Old Testament and the New Testament forbid killing; yet both give examples in
which the use of force is approved. Roman law, on the contrary,
although it did not purport to lay down moral standards, contained the
rule, *Vim vi repellere licet* ("Force may be used to repel force"). Like
Roman legal rules generally, this was not conceived as embodying a
general principle or concept but was limited to the specific types of situations in connection with which it was found, chiefly the rule of Lex
Aquilia that a man could use physical force to protect his property from
seizure. The European jurists of the twelfth and thirteenth centuries
converted the Roman law rule into a general principle, which they jux-
taposed with the so-called pacifistic utterances of Jesus ("turn the other
cheek"), and from the opposing maxims they developed a general concept of justification for the limited use of force applicable to a whole
series of interrelated categories systematically set forth: force necessary
to execute the law, to defend oneself, to defend another, to protect one's
own property, to protect another's property. These principles were applied not only to civil and criminal law but also to political and
theological questions concerning a "just war."[65]

These are rather simple examples of the scholastic technique of posing
a *quaestio* relating to contradictory passages in an authoritative text,
followed by a *propositio* stating authorities and reasons in support of one
position, followed by an *oppositio*, stating authorities and reasons for the
contrary view, and ending with a *solutio* (or *conclusio*) in which it is shown
either that the reasons given in the oppositio are not true or that the propositio must be qualified or abandoned in light of the oppositio. Usually,
the scholastic method of posing "disputed questions" was much more
complex.[66] The teacher or writer would often pose not one but a series of
interconnected problems, one after the other. Arguments were then
made on opposite sides, as though by a plaintiff and a defendant in a
lawsuit. The pros and the cons would be "arranged in two battle
fronts."[67] In support of each argument, rules of law were cited;
sometimes dozens of such *allegationes* were made to support a single argument pro or con. Most of the characteristic terms of the argument, as
Hermann Kantorowicz has shown, were derived from the available
literature on Greek dialectics or from the Roman law texts of Justinian,
or from both.[68] What was wholly new, when the method was first invented by the jurists in the second quarter of the twelfth century,[69] was
the putting together of all these terms in a highly complex structure
resembling pleading and argumentation in difficult cases in court. The

resemblance was not accidental; Kantorowicz believes that the style was first developed in litigation and then imitated in the classroom and in the literature—just as the style of the English Yearbooks of 1280–1535 was probably derived from student notes of arguments in cases in the king's courts.[70] But that still leaves the question why argument in court took the form of a whole battery of positions pro and con, with multiple citations, intricate regulations, and complex syntheses. Surely an important part of the answer is that "the *quaestiones disputatae* were the chief link between the written law of Justinian and its application in the contemporary courts of justice. Thus was developed the courage to draw audacious analogies, to handle far-flung principles of equity, to fill the *lacunae* of the law by intuition and imagination. Therefore, the historical importance of these questions as a dynamic factor in the adaptation of the Roman law to changed and everchanging views and conditions was great indeed."[71] The same audacity, and the same techniques, were applied in adapting Biblical, patristic, and canonical principles to the new conditions of life.

In addition to elaborating general legal principles that underlay the rules applicable to concrete cases, the jurists of the twelfth and thirteenth centuries, both canonists and Romanists, also defined general concepts, such as the concept of representation, the concept of the corporation, and the concept of jurisdiction. Here again, while the Roman law of Justinian provided the basic terminology and the Greek dialectics of Plato and Aristotle provided the basic method, the combination of the two—in a wholly different social context—produced something quite new. For example, the Roman jurists had laid down various rules under which a slave could act in behalf of his master, as his agent, and the master would be liable, but they had offered no general definition of agency or of representation. Similarly, they had stated a variety of situations in which a group of people were to be treated as a collective unit, such as a *societas* ("partnership"), but they had offered no general definition of group or corporate personality and they had not developed the idea of limited liability. Justinian's Roman law lacked even a general concept of contract; it provided for certain specific types of contracts, but they were not subordinated to a general concept of binding promises, so that an agreement which fell outside the types of contracts named by law was ipso facto not a contract.[72]

It would be wholly incorrect to say that there were no general concepts in the Roman law of the time of Justinian and before; on the contrary, Roman jurists eagerly discussed situations in which a contract would be void because of "mistake," situations in which the enforcement of an informal obligation was required by "good faith," and various other types of situations in which legal results involved a reference to concepts. Indeed, Roman law from early times was permeated by such concepts as ownership, possession, delict, fraud, theft, and dozens of others. That was its great virtue. However, these concepts were not treated as ideas which pervaded the rules and determined their applicability. They were not considered philosophically. The concepts of Roman law, like its numerous legal rules, were tied to specific types of situations. Roman law consisted of an intricate network of rules; yet these were not presented as an intellectual system but rather as an elaborate mosaic of practical solutions to specific legal questions. Thus one may say that although there were concepts in Roman law, there was no concept of a concept.

In contrast, the European jurists who revived the study of Roman law in the eleventh and twelfth centuries set out to systematize and harmonize the huge network of Roman legal rules in terms both of general principles and of general concepts, using methods similar to those which their colleagues in theology were employing to systematize and harmonize the Old and New Testaments, the writings of the church fathers, and other sacred texts. The jurists took as a starting point the concept of a legal concept and the principle that the law is principled.

This amounted to much more than the addition of a philosophical dimension to the more practical style of the Roman texts; it fundamentally changed the very meaning of everyday legal questions, such as, "What are my rights if my debtor does not pay up?" The Roman rules might still be cited, but they would be subject to interpretation in the light of their perceived underlying purposes and their perceived relationship to other parts of the whole system. For example, whereas the Roman rule might require the debtor to pay even if he had a valid counterclaim, leaving him to pursue his remedy against the creditor in a separate action, the European Romanists and canonists would apply the concept of mutuality of contractual obligation, based ultimately on the principle of good faith.

The conceptualization of general legal terms, like the formulation of general principles underlying the legal rules, was closely related not only to the revived interest in Greek philosophy but also to developments in theology; and both the philosophical and the theological aspects were closely related to the great changes in political, economic, and social life which constituted the Papal Revolution. Above all, it was the coexistence and competition of newly emerging, centralized polities, ecclesiastical and secular, that made it important to articulate the principles. Thus the church in the eleventh century was the first collective to call itself a corporation (*universitas*). The authority of bishops and priests, formerly derived solely from the sacrament of ordination, was held to be derived also from jurisdiction: they were for the first time appointed with the consent of the papacy ("by grace of God and of the Apostolic See") and could be removed only by the papacy. A bishop was viewed as an official of the corporate church. His "jurisdiction" included the power and duty to try cases in his court, under the rules of a universal body of procedural and substantive law, with an automatic right of appeal by the losing party to the papal curia.

A similar process of conceptualization took place in the development of secular legal systems. The same terms, derived largely from Roman law, were used in the articulation of general principles and eventually in the formation of general concepts. The principles and concepts were then used as a basis for extrapolation of new applications. This development revolutionized the science of law. It meant that the meaning of a legal rule could be tested, and its validity proved, by showing its organic consistency with the principles and concepts of the system as a whole.

Law as a Prototype of Western Science

The scholastic jurists created a legal "science," in the modern Western sense rather than the Platonic or Aristotelian sense of that word. For Plato, science was knowledge of the truth derived by deduction from the general to the particular. Aristotle, although he emphasized the method of observation and hypothesis, nonetheless focused on finding the true cause or necessity that produces a certain substance or conclusion; for him, the ultimate model of a science was geometry. For modern Western man, the very certitude of mathematics, the fact that it is based on its own inner logic rather than on fallible human observation, makes it appear more like a language or a philosophy than a science. Modern Western science, unlike Aristotelian science, focuses on formulating hypotheses that can serve as a basis for ordering phenomena in the world of time, and hence in the world of probabilities and predictions rather than certitudes and necessities. The science of the scholastic jurists was just that kind of science. It used a dialectical mode of establishing general legal principles by relating them to particulars in predication. It was not, to be sure, an "exact" science, like modern physics or chemistry; nor was it susceptible to the kind of laboratory experimentation that is characteristic of many (though not all) natural sciences, although it did utilize its own kinds of experimentation. Also, it was concerned with constructing a system out of observed *social* phenomena—legal institutions—rather than observed phenomena of the world of matter; nevertheless, like the natural sciences that developed in its wake, the new legal science combined empirical and theoretical methods.

A science, in the modern Western sense of that word, may be defined by three sets of criteria: methodological criteria; value criteria; and sociological criteria. By all three sets of criteria, the legal science of the twelfth-century jurists of western Europe was a progenitor of the modern Western sciences.

METHODOLOGICAL CHARACTERISTICS OF LEGAL SCIENCE

A science in the modern Western sense may be defined in methodological terms as: (1) an integrated body of knowledge, (2) in which particular occurrences of phenomena are systematically explained, (3) in terms of general principles or truths ("laws"), (4) knowledge of which (that is, of both the phenomena and the general principles) has been obtained by a combination of observation, hypothesis, verification, and to the greatest extent possible, experimentation. However, (5) the scientific method of investigation and systematization, despite these common characteristics, is not the same for all sciences but must be specifically adapted to the particular kinds of occurrences of phenomena under investigation by each particular science. This definition rejects the view now popular among many, especially in the United States and England, that only methods appropriate to the natural sciences, and, above all, physics and chemistry, can properly be called scientific.

By all five of the criteria listed above, the scholarly researches and writings of the Italian, French, English, German, and other jurists of the late eleventh, the twelfth, and the thirteenth centuries, both canonists and Romanists, constituted a science of law. The phenomena studied were the decisions, rules, customs, statutes, and other legal data promulgated by church councils, popes, and bishops, as well as by emperors, kings, dukes, city magistrates, and other secular rulers, or that were found in Holy Scripture, the Roman law texts of Justinian, and other written sources. These legal materials were treated by the jurists as data to be observed, classified, and systematically explained in terms of general principles and general concepts of truths. The explanations were subject to verification in terms of both logic and experience. To the extent that positive examples of their application could be adduced, and the effects measured, a kind of experimentation was also involved.

The originality of the twelfth-century jurists' contribution to scientific thought lay in their construction of general principles that were consistent with the evidence, and their use of those principles to explain the evidence and to extrapolate from it. They were the first Western scholars to see and develop not only empirical tests of the validity of general principles but also empirical uses for such principles. That the empirical data they examined were existing laws, customs, and decisions did not make their achievement any less astonishing. The available alternative method, derived from Platonic thought as it was then understood, was to use general principles (ideal Forms) to validate theological, cosmological, and political doctrines. But since the Platonic method required the rejection of evidence that did not correspond to the ideal Forms, it would have been ill suited to the harmonization of existing laws, customs, and decisions.

To take a specific example, the jurists observed that in all the various legal systems under examination the question arose whether one who was forcibly dispossessed of his goods has the right to take them back by force. One solution was reached by interpretation of the Roman law texts of Justinian, where it appears that the Roman praetor had decreed that one who has been forcibly dispossessed of his land (nothing is said about goods) may not take it back by force after a certain period of time has elapsed. The twelfth-century jurists concluded that this rule is equally applicable to goods, since the same purposes are involved in both classes of cases. Further, it had been laid down by certain church councils and in individual ecclesiastical cases that a bishop forcibly ousted from his bishopric must not resort to force to recover it. A bishopric, it was noted by the twelfth-century jurists, includes not only rights in land but also rights in goods and, in addition, rights in perquisites — rights in rights ("choses-in-action"). Such instances gave rise not only to analogies but also to hypotheses. It appeared that underlying the various rules was a basic legal principle — nowhere stated in the law but stated at this time by the legal scientists to explain the law — that persons whose rights are violated are required to vindicate them by legal action rather than by "taking the law into their own hands." This hypothesis was verified logically by the proposition that it is a basic purpose of law to provide an alternative to force as a means of settlement of disputes. It was further verified by experience, including experience of the circumstances that had given rise to the rule, namely, the disorder and injustice that resulted when disputes over rights in land, goods, and choses-in-action were settled by a series of violent acts of dispossession, first by one of the disputants and then by the other. Such experience reached the level of experimentation when the jurist was able to compare the consequences of diverse legal rules and of changes in legal rules. Rules that were considered unsatisfactory sometimes were amended or repealed or fell into disuse. Rules that were considered satisfactory were often continued. Such "experiments" lacked the exactness of laboratory tests; yet they were a kind of social experimentation, a "laboratory of history" — what modern scientists would call "natural experiments." To use modern terminology, experience, including the experience of applying rules in concrete cases, was viewed as a process of constant feedback concerning the validity both of the rules and of the general principles and concepts that were thought to underlie them.

Of course, the science of law was at the mercy of politics: lawmakers could and often did disregard the jurists' findings. In practice, logic and experience were often sacrificed to power, prejudice, and greed. That however, is a different matter and does not detract from the scientific nature of twelfth-century legal scholarship.

The verification of general legal principles by logic and experience constituted legal science at its highest intellectual levels; usually, however, the legal scientist of the twelfth century, like his counterpart today, was concerned with what was called much later "legal dogmatics," that is, the systematic working out of the ramifications of legal rules, their interconnections, their application in specific types of situations. To go back to the example of forcible dispossession: once a principle had been established forbidding a person to recapture his property by force, knotty questions arose concerning the remedy of the person forcibly dispossessed. Should he be restored to possession even if he had previously taken possession by force, and even if the person dispossessing him was the true owner? Were the remedies to be the same with respect to goods as with respect to land? Was there a time limit within which the victim of the dispossession might lawfully defend his rights by force ("hot pursuit")? Such questions were not viewed by the jurists primarily as moral or as political questions but rather as legal questions; that is, they were questions to be resolved on the basis of the interpretation of legal authorities — decisions, rules, customs, statutes, scriptural texts, authoritatively laid down. The authoritative texts were taken as objectively given; an attempt might be made to show that they were contrary to reason or that they were not useful or that they were historically conditioned, and thus to undermine their authority, but if they withstood the challenges they had to be accepted. They were "facts," and the jurists' task was to organize and make sense out of them. Their methods of doing so were not essentially different from those later used by natural scientists to explore and synthesize other kinds of data.[73]

In addition to the methodology developed by legal science for the discovery and verification of principles implicit in decisions, rules, concepts, and other legal data, another methodology was developed for the discovery and verification of facts in the course of legal proceedings. The proof of facts in court was closely connected with new developments in the study of rhetoric. Rhetoric had not yet become the art of persuasion by appeal to emotion and by ornamentation in speech; it still retained its older Aristotelian connotation of persuasion by appeal to reason. In the twelfth century the emphasis was placed on methods of proof. The concept of the hypothesis was put forward by the rhetoricians to supplement the dialectical concept of the thesis (quaestio). Proof of hypotheses was understood to require the presentation of evidence, which in turn implied the notion of probable truth. This led to the development of a scale of probabilities, in which presumptions played an important role as a form of logic. It also led to rules for avoiding distortion and errors in the presentation and evaluation of evidence. The parallels with law were stressed: a well-known treatise of the twelfth century, *Rhetorica Ecclesiastica*, stated that "both rhetoric and law have a common procedure." The same treatise defined a case (causa) as a "civil dispute concerning a certain statement or a certain act of a certain person."[74] Thus the legal concept of a case was associated with the rhetorical concept of the hypothesis. The same treatise also stated that to find the truth of a disputed matter four persons were required: a judge, a witness, an accuser, and a defender. The judge was to see to it that the rules of argumentation were not violated, and especially the rules of relevancy and materiality. By the early thirteenth century exclusionary rules had been developed to prevent the introduction of superfluous evidence (matters already ascertained), impertinent evidence (having no effect on the case), obscure and uncertain evidence (from which no clear inferences could be drawn), excessively general evidence (from which obscurity arose), and evidence contrary to nature (which was impossible to believe).[75] Alessandro Giuliani has shown that this system of "artificial reason" of the law was discarded in most countries of Europe after the end of the fifteenth century and replaced by "natural reason," which emphasized mathematical logic, but that it was retained in the English common law through the efforts of Edward Coke, Matthew Hale, and their successors, despite the contrary efforts of Thomas Hobbes and others.[76]

The comparison between legal reasoning and scientific reasoning and the assertion that legal reasoning was a prototype of modern scientific reasoning in the West rest upon contemporary views of science that are not universally accepted. Usually the dawn of modern science is dated from about the time of Galileo, five centuries later. Moreover, Galileo, Kepler, Descartes, Leibniz, Newton, and other leaders of what is now considered the classical period of modern science all shared an antipathy for "medieval scholasticism," even if they shared nothing else. However, it is important that their antipathy was not directed at scholasticism as such but rather at the failure of the scholastics to develop a mathematical framework of explanation. As Alexander Koyré has shown, Galileo and other major thinkers of the seventeenth century took mathematics to be the model for all true scientific explanations.[77] Mathematics and its laws, like Platonic Forms in an earlier era, came to constitute the ideal language of modern science. In the nineteenth century, the scholastic method was also attacked from other directions: its emphasis on the purposes of the subject matter being investigated was criticized, as well as its lack of emphasis on the predictive value of its findings. Nevertheless, neither seventeenth-century science nor nineteenth-century science would have been possible without the scientific method first developed by the jurists of the twelfth century.[78]

VALUE PREMISES OF LEGAL SCIENCE

Although science, in the modern Western sense, has usually been defined only in methodological terms, there has been an increasing recognition that it must also be defined in terms of the attitudes, convictions, and fundamental purposes of those engaged in the scientific enterprise. One may, indeed, speak of a scientific code of values,[79] which includes: (1) the obligation of scientists to conduct research with objectivity and integrity, and to evaluate their own and one another's work solely on the basis of universal standards of scientific merit; (2) the requirement that scientists adopt a position of doubt and of "organized skepticism" toward the certitude of their own and one anothers' premises and conclusions, together with a tolerance of new ideas until they are disproved, and a willingness publicly to acknowledge error; and (3) a built-in assumption that science is an "open system," that it seeks "increasingly close approximations to the truth rather than final answers," and that "science cannot be frozen into a set of orthodox conceptions . . . but is an ever-changing body of ideas with varying degrees of plausibility."[80]

Many would doubt the likelihood, or even the possibility, that a "lawyer" could meet these three standards. His objectivity, integrity, and universality seem questionable, since he is called by both political and private partisans to promote and justify their interests. Further, if he is to be skeptical of his own conclusions he may place difficulties in the way of their acceptance, and it is often part of his professional responsibility to persuade people to accept them. The same difficulty obstructs the concept of legal science as a body of ever changing ideas: society itself seems to demand that "law" be something more than that. Finally, during the period when not only the authority and power of the papacy but also its dogmatism were at their height, it seems incredible that lawyers — even though they might have been legal scholars and not practitioners (in fact many of them were both) — or, indeed, any other pursuers of knowledge, could have had the disinterestedness and open-mindedness that is at the basis of the code of values of modern Western science.

These doubts raise fundamental questions concerning the freedom not only of legal science in the twelfth century but of any science in any society.[81] The scientific code of values is always precarious; it must always be defended against political and ideological pressures from without and from prejudices and partisanship on the part of scientists themselves. What is striking about the twelfth century is that at the very climax of the movement to centralize authority and power in the church, and at the very time when dogma itself first became legalized and heresy defined in terms of criminal disobedience,[82] there emerged the belief that the progress of science depends on the freedom of scientists to take opposing points of view on matters of scientific truth. It was presupposed that such dialectical reasoning from contradictory positions would result in a synthesis, and that the synthesis would correspond to authoritative declarations of the true faith; nevertheless, it was also presupposed that the dialectical reasoning must proceed scientifically or else it would be worthless. Thus at the same time that unorthodox doctrines were being legally proscribed, and heretics who persisted in "disobedience" were being put to death, the values of scientific objectivity, disinterestedness, organized skepticism, tolerance of error, and openness to new scientific truths were not only proclaimed but given expression in the very form of the new sciences that then emerged. The two opposing movements—toward authority and toward rationality—were in fact closely interconnected.

Doubts concerning the capacity of lawyers to adhere to scientific values rest on several misconceptions. It is true, of course, that when a lawyer is an advocate for a party or cause, he must act as a partisan and not as a scientist. However, this role is an essential part of legal proceedings in which opposite points of view are presented to a tribunal charged with making a decision. Indeed, the legal proceedings themselves are, in one sense, scientific, since the contest is designed to bring before the tribunal all relevant considerations. In a trial, the court is supposed to decide the case "objectively," on the basis of "the evidence" presented in behalf of the disputants. Yet even in instances when that ideal is realized, a trial, or legislative debate, or any other such legal proceeding, has other characteristics that are quite unscientific. For one thing, the tribunal must act under the pressure of given time limits, whereas the scientist may wait indefinitely until he is ready to draw conclusions. Beyond that, the tribunal is a political body; it stands too close to community prejudices and pressures to maintain the "distance" required of scientists.

However, it is neither the legal practitioner nor the tribunal (whether it be a judicial or legislative or administrative body), but the law teacher or legal scholar who is asked to adhere to the scientific code of values. He, too, has difficulties in doing so—greater difficulties, perhaps, than scholars in fields that are more remote from everyday political, economic, and social life. Yet by the same token he may be more aware of the outside pressures upon him as well as of the inside pressures of his own passions and prejudices, and hence may be better able than others to resist them, or at least more sensitive to the precariousness of his own scientific freedom.

The value premises of science, including legal science, were implicit in the dialectical method of analysis and synthesis of legal problems created by the scholastic jurists of the eleventh and twelfth centuries. The intense concentration on contradictions in the law, on dialectical problems, and the intense effort to reconcile them by legal principles and concepts on ascending levels of generalization, could only succeed, as a method, by adherence to the very values that characterize science itself: objectivity, integrity, universalism, skepticism, tolerance of error, humility, openness to new truth—and, one should add, a special time sense that is associated with the coexistence of contradictories. Since it was believed that the whole of law was informed by a common purpose, a *ratio*, it was taken for granted that the paradoxes would ultimately be resolved; meanwhile, the corps of jurists would patiently cope with the uncertainties that the paradoxes created.

In speaking of the "value premises" of science, one cannot ignore the fact that, at least in Western civilization, where science has flourished more than in any other culture (indeed, some would say it has flourished *too* much), the objectivity, skepticism, openness, and general spirit of rationalism that characterize scientific inquiry have stemmed from a complex relationship between the sacred and the profane. On the one hand, a belief in the sacredness, or potential sacredness, of all things, such as existed among the Germanic peoples and also in Eastern Christianity, inhibits objective, skeptical, open, rational investigation. Thus it was no accident that the first Western sciences emerged at the time when there was a separation between ecclesiastical and secular polities. On the other hand, they first emerged precisely in the ecclesiastical sphere, not the secular — in canon law and in theology itself. Western theologians of the late eleventh and twelfth centuries — Anselm, Abelard, and others — did not hesitate to subject the evidence of divine mysteries to systematic, rational, and even skeptical examination. Anselm sought to prove "by reason alone," without the aid of faith or revelation, not only the existence of God but also the necessity of his incarnation in Christ. Abelard exposed the self-contradictions in sacred writings — a first step toward scientific Biblical criticism. Similarly, the canon lawyers examined openly the contradictions in the canons of the church. Proceeding from an objective analysis of the prevailing law, they concluded that even the pope, Christ's deputy, was subject to deposition if found to be a heretic or if guilty of a crime that was a scandal to the church.

The conclusion seems inescapable that what gave rise to scientific values was not the carving out of a sphere of life — the secular, the temporal, the material — which could be investigated without risk to religious beliefs, but rather a new attitude toward the sacred itself. The church, though still understood to be the "mystical body of Christ," was viewed as also having a visible, legal, corporate identity and an earthly mission to reform the world. The emphasis shifted from sacredness in the sense of otherworldliness to the incarnation of the sacred, which meant its manifestation in the political, economic, and social life of the times. That, in turn, made it necessary to examine the sacred, the spiritual, with scientific value premises. Only when the effort was made to study God objectively, and God's laws, did it become possible to attempt to study secular life, and secular laws, objectively — and eventually nature and nature's laws.

Nevertheless, there was, of course, an obvious tension between the sacred and the profane in the theology of the church and in the canon law, which existed also in other branches of learning and which inevitably imposed severe restrictions on scientific value premises. It is hardly necessary to recall the repressive measures taken against scientists who departed from official dogma. The original thinker, the innovator, ran severe risks of condemnation; the heretic might be executed. It is of little comfort, yet it is important, to know that the very tension that caused such repression also made possible the first growth of science in the West.

Sociological Criteria of Legal Science

In addition to its methodology and its value premises, a science, in the modern Western sense of that word, must be defined in terms of sociological criteria. There are certain social preconditions that not only are indispensable to its existence but also help to form its character. These include: (1) the formation of scientific communities, usually coextensive with the various disciplines, each of which has a collective responsibility for the conduct of research, the training of new recruits, the sharing of scientific knowledge, and the authentication of scientific accomplishments within the discipline and outside it;[83] (2) the linking of the various scientific disciplines in larger scholarly communities, and especially in universities, whose members share a common concern for both the advancement of learning and the education of the young, as well as a common implicit assumption that all branches of knowledge rest ultimately on the same foundations; and (3) the privileged social status of the communities of scientists, including a high degree of freedom of teaching and research, which is correlative to their high degree of responsibility to serve the cause of science itself, its methods, its values, and its social function.

That Western legal scholarship was, in the twelfth century, and still is, a collective enterprise, and that legal scholars did, and still do, form a community of shared interests and concerns will scarcely be seriously disputed. That legal scholars also formed, and still form, a profession, in the sense that the individual members have a public responsibility and are pledged to place the advancement of their discipline above their personal self-interest or profit, is perhaps only slightly less obvious. These truisms of Western historical experience may also be applicable to all sciences wherever and whenever they have existed. But what has been especially characteristic of Western science, including legal science, since the twelfth century is its close historical connection with the institution of the university; science was born in the university and the university bestowed upon it its precarious heritage of freedom of teaching and research.

Here is another key to the solution of the question why modern

Western scientific concepts and scientific methods emerged in the late eleventh and early twelfth centuries. The universities emerged then. This may seem simply to put the question back one step, but it does more: it removes the question from the realm of history of ideas to the realm of history of communities. The scientific methodology and the values that characterize science in the modern Western sense are to be explained *not* in terms of the unfolding of ideas in some Platonic or Hegelian sense, but as social responses to social needs. It takes more than the progressive translation of the works of Aristotle to explain why, in the year 1150, possibly ten thousand students from all over Europe could be found in the town of Bologna in northern Italy studying legal science.[84] They were there because society made it possible—indeed, made it urgent—that they be there; more than that, the same social conditions inevitably played a critical part in determining the nature of the legal science that they were there to study.

The scholastic dialectic and consequently modern science, including legal science, were produced by the contradictions in the historical situation of western European society in the late eleventh and twelfth centuries, and by the overwhelming effort to resolve those contradictions and to forge a new synthesis. They were produced, above all, by the revolutionary upheaval which separated the ecclesiastical and secular jurisdictions and thus made the reconciliation of opposites an acute necessity at virtually all levels of social life. A learned profession of jurists emerged in western Europe—first mainly in the church and eventually, in varying degrees, in the cities and kingdoms—in response to the need to reconcile the conflicts that raged within the church, between the church and the secular authorities, and among and within the various secular polities. Formed primarily in the universities, the legal profession produced a science of laws; that is, the jurists constituted a community in which legal science was the expression of the community's reason for being. Through its science, the legal profession helped to solve the contradictions in the social and historical situation of western Europe by solving the contradictions *between* that situation *and* the preexisting legal authorities. Legal science was, in the first instance, an institutionalization of the process of resolving conflicts in authoritative legal texts.

The presence of important islands of Jewish and Islamic culture in the midst of Christendom contributed to the need for a dialectical method of analysis and synthesis of contradictions as well as to the need for a legal resolution of social conflict. Surprisingly, however, there seem to have been virtually no direct contemporary Jewish or Islamic influences on the development of Western legal systems in their formative era, that is, in the late eleventh and twelfth centuries. There were, to be sure even at that early time, important direct Arabic influences on astronomy, mathematics, medicine, art, and probably also on certain specific governmental institutions and practices (especially in the Norman Kingdom of Sicily), as well as important direct Jewish influences on Biblical studies and theology; and of course the historical influence of Judaism on Christianity was enormous, since the Church claimed Abraham as its founder and the Jewish Bible as its heritage. Yet so far as scholarship has thus far revealed, neither the Talmud nor the Koran seems to have made any impact on the first great lawmakers and jurists of the West.[85]

The principal social characteristics of Western legal science in its formative period, especially as they were influenced by the universities, may be summarized as follows:

In the first place, the universities helped to establish the transnational character of Western legal science. As David Knowles has said, "For three hundred years, from 1050 to 1350, and above all in the century between 1070 and 1170, the whole of educated Europe formed a single and undifferentiated cultural unit. In the lands between Edinburgh and Palermo, Mainz or Lund and Toledo, a man of any city or village might go for education to any school, and become a prelate or an official in any church, court, or university (when these existed) from north to south, from east to west. It is the age of Lanfranc of Pavia, Bec, and Canterbury [Lanfranc was William the Conqueror's chief adviser and archbishop of Canterbury]; of Anselm of Aosta, Bec, and Canterbury [Anselm succeeded his former teacher, Lanfranc, under William's successor]; of Vacarius [a famous professor of Roman law] of Lombardy, Canterbury, Oxford, and York; of John of Salisbury, Paris, Benevento, Canterbury, and Chartres [an intimate associate and counselor of kings, archbishops, and popes, "the most accomplished scholar and stylist of his age"]; . . . of Nicholas Brakespeare of St. Albans, France, Scandinavia, and Rome [the son of English peasants, who became Pope Hadrian IV]; of Thomas of Aquina, Cologne, Paris, and Naples . . . In this period a high proportion of the most celebrated writers, thinkers, and administrators gained greatest fame and accomplished the most significant part of their life's work far from the land of their birth and boyhood. Moreover, in the writings of many of them, there is not a single characteristic of language, style, or thought to tell us whence they sprang. True, we are speaking only of a small educated minority, to which the land-owning aristocracy in general, many monarchs, and even some bishops, did not belong. The world of Church and State was often rent by schisms and wars, while the bulk of the population, fast rooted in the soil, knew nothing beyond the fields and woods of their small corner. But on the level of literature and thought there was one stock of words, forms, and thoughts from which all drew and in which all shared on an equality. If we possessed the written works without their authors' names we should not be able to assign them to any country or people."[86]

What Knowles writes of scholarship in general in that period was equally applicable to legal scholarship in the field of canon and Roman law. These were disciplines without national boundaries. They were taught in the universities to law students gathered from all the countries of Europe. They all, of course, spoke Latin, which was the universal Western language not only of the law but also of teaching and scholarship, as well as of worship and theology.

Second, in addition to giving legal scholarship a transnational character, the European universities helped to give the law itself a transnational terminology and method. The graduates of the university law schools went back to their own countries, or moved to other countries, where they served as ecclesiastical or lay judges, practicing lawyers, legal advisers to ecclesiastical, royal, and city authorities and to lords of manors, and as administrative officials of various kinds. To the extent that they were involved with canon law, they could use their university training directly; to the extent that they were concerned with secular law, they applied to it the terminology and the method of the Roman and canon law that they had studied.

Third, the legal method which was taught in the European universities was one which made possible the construction of legal systems out of preexisting diverse and contradictory customs and laws. The techniques of harmonizing contradictions, coupled with the belief in an ideal body of law, an integrated structure of legal principles, made it possible to begin to synthesize canon law and then feudal law, urban law, commercial law, and royal law.

Fourth, the universities exalted the role of the scholar—the scientist—in the shaping of the law. The law was to be found primarily in the ancient texts, and hence it was necessary to have a class of learned men who could explain the texts to those who wished to be introduced to their mysteries. The doctor, that is, the university teacher, became the authoritative expositor of the "true rule." This, too, gave a universality to legal science that helped to overcome the contradictions of laws.

Fifth, the juxtaposition of law and other university disciplines—especially theology, medicine, and the liberal arts—also contributed a breadth to law studies that would otherwise have been lacking. The scholastic method was used in all the disciplines; also the subject matter of all the disciplines overlapped. Thus the law student could not help knowing that his profession was an integral part of the intellectual life of his time.

Sixth, law, though linked to other university disciplines, also was separate and distinct from them; it was no longer, as it had been before the rise of the universities, a branch of rhetoric, on the one hand, and of ethics and politics, on the other. While in the Roman Empire the autonomy of legal thought had been maintained by practitioners, especially praetors and professional legal advisers, in western Europe that autonomy was maintained by the universities.

Seventh, the fact that law was taught as a university discipline made it inevitable that legal doctrines would be criticized and evaluated in the light of general truths, and not merely studied as a craft or technique. Even apart from the universities, the church had long taught that all human law was to be tested and judged by divine law and moral law; but the university jurists added the concept of an ideal human law, the Roman law of Justinian's books, which—together with the Bible, the writings of the church fathers, the decrees of church councils and popes, and other sacred texts—provided basic legal principles and standards for criticizing and evaluating existing legal rules and institutions. These inspired writings of the past, and not what any lawgiver might say or do, provided the ultimate criteria of legality.

Eighth, the Western universities raised the analysis of law to the level of a science, as that word was understood in the twelfth to fifteenth centuries, by conceptualizing legal institutions and systematizing law as an integrated body of knowledge, so that the validity of legal rules could be demonstrated by their consistency with the system as a whole.

Ninth, the universities produced a professional class of lawyers, bound together by a common training and by the common task of guiding the legal activities of the church and of the secular world of empires, kingdoms, cities, manors, and merchant and other guilds. The law students themselves, initially at least, formed a corporation, a guild, and although upon graduation they scattered to many countries, they remained bound together informally by their common training and their common task.

It is true that in England in the fourteenth century there grew up alongside the university law schools of Oxford and Cambridge a different mode of legal education, in the Inns of Court. Nevertheless, in England as in other countries of Europe the system of university law teaching established in the twelfth century had a profound influence on legal thought. It is also true that the growth of nationalism in modern times has made inroads into the transnational character of Western legal education, and that the links between law and other university disciplines have been substantially weakened. Yet something of the Bologna tradition, and something of the scholastic dialectic, survive nine centuries later—even in the law schools of America. Indeed, they have spread throughout the world. Only in the latter part of the twentieth century have they come to be seriously challenged.

The new legal methodology that emerged in the West in the late eleventh and the twelfth centuries—its logic, its topics, its style of

reasoning, its levels of generalization, its techniques of interrelating particulars and universals, cases and concepts — was an essential part of the
conscious systematization of law as an autonomous science. This, in
turn, was an essential part of the creation of autonomous legal systems
for the new polities that emerged from the Papal Revolution: the new
church-state, the emerging secular kingdoms, the chartered cities and
towns, the newly systematized feudal and manorial relationships, the
translocal community of merchants. The emphasis on conflicting,
authoritative legal texts, and on their reconciliation by means of general
principles and concepts, was a creative intellectual response to the felt
need to reconcile the sharply conflicting elements that coexisted and
competed within the social structure. To recognize the legitimacy of
each of the contradictory elements (ecclesiastical and secular, royal and
feudal, feudal and urban, urban and guild) and yet to recognize the
structural unity of the total society (Europe, the West, Western
Christendom), of which they were parts, and to find a genuine synthesis,
that is, a way of dealing with the ambiguities and conflicts without
destroying the autonomy of the factors that constituted them — that was
the revolutionary challenge of the times. And that was the challenge
which was confronted in legal science by the glossators and the
canonists, just as it was confronted in the development of the new legal
systems that were created with the help of that science.[87]

By the same token, however, the new Western legal science was much
more than an intellectual achievement — much more than a method of
reasoning or a method of organizing thought. Its criteria were moral as
well as intellectual. The form expressed substantive values and
policies.[88] The reconciliation of opposing legal rules was part of a larger
process of attempting to reconcile strict law and equity, justice and
mercy, equality and freedom.

Above all, the effort to combine these conflicting norms and values
was seen in the eleventh and twelfth centuries as part of an even more
formidable reconciliation — the reconciliation of God and man. More
than anything else, it was the new vision of his own ultimate destiny that
first led Western man to have faith in legal science.

4 | Theological Sources of the Western Legal Tradition

I T IS IMPOSSIBLE to understand the revolutionary quality of the Western legal tradition without exploring its religious dimension. It has been said that the metaphors of the day before yesterday are the analogies of yesterday and the concepts of today. So the eleventh-century legal metaphors were the twelfth-century legal analogies and the thirteenth-century legal concepts. The legal metaphors that lay at the foundation of the legal analogies and concepts were chiefly of a religious nature. They were metaphors of the Last Judgment and of purgatory, of Christ's atonement for Adam's fall, of the transubstantiation of bread and wine in the sacrament of the eucharist, of the absolution of sins in the sacrament of penance, and of the power of the priesthood "to bind and to loose"—that is, to impose or remit eternal punishment. Other legal metaphors were chiefly feudal, though they had religious over-tones—metaphors of honor, of satisfaction for violation of honor, of pledge of faith, of reciprocal bonds of service and protection. All of these metaphors were part of a unified structure of rituals and myths. (The word "myth" is used here not in the old sense of "fable" but rather in the opposite, now widely accepted, sense of "sacred truth.")[1]

What such an exploration shows is that basic institutions, concepts, and values of Western legal systems have their sources in religious rituals, liturgies, and doctrines of the eleventh and twelfth centuries, reflecting new attitudes toward death, sin, punishment, forgiveness, and salvation, as well as new assumptions concerning the relationship of the divine to the human and of faith to reason. Over the intervening centuries, these religious attitudes and assumptions have changed fundamentally, and today their theological sources seem to be in the process of drying up. Yet the legal institutions, concepts, and values that have derived from them still survive, often unchanged. Western legal science is a secular theology, which often makes no sense because its theological presuppositions are no longer accepted.

A bizarre example may shed light on the paradoxes of a legal tradition that has lost contact with its theological sources. If a sane man is convicted of murder and sentenced to death, and thereafter, before the sentence is carried out, he becomes insane, his execution will be postponed until he recovers his sanity. Generally speaking, this is the law in Western countries and in many non-Western countries as well. Why? The historical answer, in the West, is that if a man is executed while he is insane he will not have had the opportunity freely to confess his sins and to take the sacrament of holy communion. He must be allowed to recover his sanity before he dies so that his soul will not be condemned to eternal hellfire but will instead have the opportunity to expiate his sins in purgatory and ultimately, at the Last Judgment, to enter the kingdom of heaven. But where none of this is believed, why keep the insane man alive until he recovers, and then kill him?

The example is, perhaps, of minor importance in itself; but what it illustrates is that the legal systems of all Western countries, and of all non-Western countries that have come under the influence of Western law, are a secular residue of religious attitudes and assumptions which historically found expression first in the liturgy and rituals and doctrine of the church and thereafter in the institutions and concepts and values of the law. When these historical roots are not understood, many parts of the law appear to lack any underlying source of validity.

Last Judgment and Purgatory

Christianity inherited from Judaism the belief in a God who is both a loving father and a righteous judge—a paradoxical God, who combines both mercy and justice. On the one hand, God punishes evil and rewards good: man is accountable to Him for his acts. On the other hand, God takes pity on man's weakness and spares him the full deserts of his disobedience. God "desires not the death of a sinner but rather that he should turn from his wickedness and live."[2]

Christianity also inherited from Judaism the belief that at the end of history God will come to judge the nations of the world, including the souls of all people who have ever lived. In the Old Testament the Last Judgment is awaited with joy: to be sure, many will be punished, but at the same time the messianic age of peace and justice and love will be introduced.[3] Similarly, in Christian doctrine it is declared that at the end of time Christ will return "to judge the living and the dead," and that this will inaugurate his reign of peace and justice and love in the world.[4] However, the threat of eternal punishment, and the corresponding emphasis on repentance and forgiveness, are stronger in the New Testament than in the Old. Jesus declares that at the end of history, "when the Son of Man comes in his glory," "all nations will be assembled before him," and he will separate all men into two groups: those who, while on earth, ministered to the needs of the hungry, the sick, the naked, the stranger, and the prisoner will be given eternal life, while those who neglected them will be cast into "the eternal fire" and "eternal punishment."[5]

The belief that God is a righteous judge, and that Christ will return as a judge, played an important part in the development of the legal values of the Eastern as well as the Western Church. In the early centuries, when the church consisted principally of numerous small communities of secret believers, legal values were largely dissolved in moral and religious values. High standards of conduct were proclaimed, and informal procedures for settlement of disputes among Christians were established, but there was no effort to create a new Christian legal system. Questions concerning the relation of law to Christian faith were cast chiefly in terms of the attitudes which Christians should take toward Judaic law and toward Roman Law. Judaic law was not considered by the early church to be binding on gentile Christians, and the observance of it was not considered to be a path to salvation; although conceived to be a historical continuation of the Jewish people, the church embraced other peoples as well, each with its own law. Nevertheless, the Biblical law (though not the rabbinic law) was binding in another sense, that is, as a revelation of the moral standards that God had set for man. "The Law is sacred," St. Paul wrote to the Church at Rome, "and what it commands is sacred, just, and good" (Rom. 7:12). This meant that Christians should internalize the Biblical law, should believe in their hearts the truths it embodied, and should do good out of faith and hope and love rather than because of legal commands or sanctions.

Similarly, the church in the first three centuries respected Roman law but rejected its absolute authority. On the one hand, it was believed that "the powers that be are ordained of God" (Rom. 13:1). On the other hand, an immoral law was not considered to be binding in conscience, and indeed there might be a positive duty to disobey it. The principle of civil disobedience was in fact inherent in the experience of the early church, since Christian worship was itself illegal.

Thus the Judaic-Christian belief that God is a judge — and a legislator as well, for the Bible takes an "activist" position on divine adjudication — was at first considered in the church to be related almost solely to such ultimate concerns as the nature and destiny of man, the struggle in his soul between the forces of light and the forces of darkness, the explanation of human suffering, the meaning of life and death. There was no effort, indeed no opportunity, to reform the law of the state to conform to divine law.

The conversion of Emperor Constantine in 313 A.D. and the establishment of Christianity as the official imperial religion raised in stark terms the question whether Christianity had anything positive to contribute to the ruler's role as supreme judge and supreme legislator in his domain. The question was rendered especially acute by the belief that the emperor was head of the church and represented Christ on earth. The answer that was given was not essentially different from the answer given to the same question upon the conversion of the Germanic kings in the fifth, sixth, and seventh centuries. Christianity was received as an apocalyptic faith, not as a social program. Yet it had certain implications for social reform which could not be avoided even by the most otherworldly of its adherents. The Christian emperors of Byzantium considered it their Christian responsibility to revise the laws, as they put it, "in the direction of greater humanity."[6] Under the influence of Christianity, and also under the influence of Stoic and neo-Platonic ideas adopted by Christian philosophy, changes were made: (1) in family law, giving the wife a position of greater equality before the law, requiring mutual consent of both spouses for the validity of a marriage, making divorce more difficult (which at that time was a step toward women's liberation), and abolishing the father's power of life or death over his children (*patria potestas*); (2) in the law of slavery, giving a slave the right to appeal to a magistrate if his master abused his powers and even in some cases the right to freedom if the master exercised cruelty, multiplying modes of manumission of slaves, and permitting slaves to acquire rights by kinship with freemen; (3) in the relation between strict law and equity, strengthening the concept of equity and tempering the strictness of general prescriptions. Finally, (4) the great collections of law compiled by the Emperor Justinian and his successors in the sixth, seventh, and eighth centuries were inspired in part by the belief that Christianity required that the law be systematized as a necessary step in its humanization.

The effort to eliminate from the law those of its features which were repugnant to a Christian ethic suffered, in the East as in the West, from the absence of a vision of what kind of legal order a Christian ethic required. In the West, prior to the twelfth century, this defect was compounded by the absence of a consciously systematized body of law: there was no professional class of lawyers and judges, there were no law schools, no legal literature, and very little legislation. By and large, law in the West consisted of customary norms and procedures, and these were diffused in political, economic, and social institutions generally. In Byzantium, on the contrary, there was a distinct legal heritage, founded on Greek concepts of the supremacy of natural reason and on the Roman sense of order. There were lawyers and judges, a legal literature, law schools, and a developed system of legislation and administration. Yet during most of Byzantine history the Roman legal system was in decay; the movement to reform it "in the direction of greater humanity" lacked the necessary driving power to be effective. Law schools came and went. The changes enacted by one emperor were repealed by the next. There was little organic development. The level of legal analysis of the classical jurists of the second and third centuries was never equaled by their Christian successors. Justinian forbade commentaries on his collection of laws; ironically, it fell more or less into oblivion when the official language of the empire was changed from Latin to Greek shortly after his death. Despite its generally humanizing influence on the law, Eastern Christianity may indeed have ultimately exerted, on the whole, a negative effect upon Byzantine legal science, since it robbed Roman law of its ultimate significance while offering no alternative system of justice in this world.

As long as the Last Judgment was understood solely as the inauguration of divine rule in the world to come, imminent or already present, it did not inspire the creation of parallel legal institutions for the interim period on earth. The vision was essentially apocalyptic rather than prophetic. This was characteristic of the church of the first millennium, both in the East and in the West. Christian faith was represented above all in the monastic life, where men and women who had "died to this world" sought to live impeccable lives in the heavenly kingdom. The church did not usually stand in a critical or reforming posture toward the world: the fundamental hopelessness of secular life in a decaying "terrestrial city" was accepted, and the return of the Messiah "to judge the living and the dead" was awaited patiently and faithfully.

In the early part of the eleventh century, however, belief in the Last Judgment acquired a new significance in the West through the development of a parallel belief in an intermediate judgment upon individual souls at the moment of their death, and an intermediate time of "purging" between the death of each individual Christian and the final coming of the divine judge. The Last Judgment continued to refer to the time when all souls that had ever lived would be resurrected, judged, and admitted together to the kingdom of God or else consigned, with the devil, to eternal punishment. Purgatory, however, was conceived as a *temporal* condition of punishment of *individual* Christian souls: having been baptized, they were freed from the debt of "original" (or natural) sin; nevertheless, justice required that they suffer punishment in time, after death, for "personal" (or actual) sins not fully expiated during their life on earth. Except in rare cases, no expiation on earth was sufficient to absolve a soul from liability to further expiation after death. Expiation meant payment of a price, not gradual reformation: the soul remained guilty (indebted) until the full price was paid.

In the Eastern Church there was — and is — no generally accepted doctrine of expiatory suffering of the soul after death and before the Day of Judgment, although there were (and are) prayers for the dead.[7] In the West as well, prior to the eleventh century, the idea of purgatory, although introduced as early as the fifth century and reinforced by the monastic penitentials, did not have the doctrinal significance that it later acquired. It was not a necessary part of Christian faith, nor was it clearly articulated or defined.

Shortly after the year 1000 a new holiday was created in the West, called All Souls' Day, which is still celebrated by Roman Catholics each year on November 2, the day after All Saints' Day. (All Saints' Day is celebrated in both the East and the West, but All Souls' Day is celebrated only in the West and mainly in the Roman Catholic Church.) The Abbot of Cluny, Odilo, conceived the idea of the holiday, and Cluny brought about its general adoption. It was a day to celebrate the community of all souls who had ever lived or ever would live, who were visualized as trembling before the Judge on the last day of history. Meanwhile, Christian souls on earth and in purgatory anticipated that day with their prayers for mercy. Rosenstock-Huessy has written eloquently about this holiday as a shared vision of death which united Western Christendom. "The liturgical readings for All Souls emphasize the utter naught that is man. Man is like Job, like grass, like a shadow. Yet God thinks highly enough of him to fix His eyes upon him and to call him to judgment . . .the idea of Judgment . . . revealed man's dignity, his claim not to be thrown into the fire like a weed, but to be judged . . . the army of Christian soldiers marches with irresistible faith before the Saviour who was their comrade, and is now their judge. The triumphant outcry in the mass for the dead on All Souls runs: 'I know that my Redeemer liveth, and I shall rise on the Last Day.' "[8] The great hymn *Dies irae* ("Day of Wrath") was written in the thirteenth century to express the thoughts and emotions of All Souls' Day. The theme that runs throughout is the conflict of justice and mercy and their ultimate reconciliation by divine judgment at the end of time.

Prior to that final judgment, however, the Christian soul remained in purgatory until fully purged by suffering. The punishments of purgatory were meted out to all Christians except the very few who were in heaven (the saints) or in hell (the unrepentant), and every one in purgatory was punished, regardless of rank, in accordance with his sins. As the Last Judgment was conceived as a great universal democracy, so purgatory was conceived as a great Christian democracy. In the vivid account of Dante Alighieri (1265–1321), popes and emperors suffered there together with serfs and brigands. The only principle that distinguished the fate of one from that of another was the allocation of punishment according to the gravity of personal sins.

The idea of a Last Judgment presupposes that life is more than mere flux, that it has a purpose — and more than that, that man is responsible for the realization of that purpose. One's whole life on earth is something to be accounted for at the Last Judgment. But the accounting does not necessarily proceed according to an elaborate system of rules and standards. The idea of purgatory, on the other hand, presupposes that the accounting does proceed according to an elaborate system of rules and standards. Individual sins are to be weighed, and the penalties in purgatory are to be allocated according to the gravity of each sin. Moreover, the church, and more specifically the pope, is considered to have jurisdiction over purgatory. The pope administers the so-called Treasury of Merits; he may distribute merits in purgatory equivalent to the time period of penance that would be required on earth to expiate the penitent's sins—provided, however, that the penitent's soul is in the same condition it would have been in if he had done the required penance. This means, in effect, that the time to be spent in purgatory can be reduced by clerical decision.[9] With the emergence of papal monarchy at the end of the eleventh century, the Council of Clermont under Pope Urban II granted the first "plenary indulgence," absolving all who would go on the First Crusade from liability for punishment in purgatory for sins committed prior to their joining the holy army of crusaders.

The liturgy of All Souls' Day and the doctrine of Purgatory provide an important link between theology and jurisprudence in Western Christendom. Sin had formerly been understood to be a condition of alienation, a diminution of a person's being; it now came to be understood in legal terms as specific wrongful acts or desires or thoughts for which various penalties must be paid in temporal suffering, whether in this life or the next. The more fundamental understanding of sin as a separation from God and from neighbor came to play only a secondary role. What specific sinful acts or desires or thoughts were to be punished, and by what kinds or degrees of temporal suffering, was to be established primarily by the moral law revealed by God first in Scripture (divine law) and second in the hearts and minds of men (natural law); but it was to be further defined by the positive laws of the church. Such ecclesiastical laws were to be derived from and tested by divine law.

Eventually the legalization, so to speak, of life after death resulted in a substantial reduction of the significance of the Last Judgment itself. The logical implication was drawn that all who were in purgatory would in fact be purged of their guilt; having paid the full price, they would automatically enter the kingdom of heaven. Thus it was assumed that the vindication of the law must have a happy ending. By the same token, however, those who chose to remain outside the system—the unrepentant Christian and also those infidels who had consciously rejected Christianity—were condemned to eternal punishment from the moment of death. Thus the role of God at the Last Judgment became a ministerial one, at least with respect to the souls of all who died before Christ's Second Coming. Man was beginning to take the center of the stage. His freedom of choice was becoming the determining factor in his progress toward salvation. The route was charted by a system of punishments and rewards that extended from this world through the next, until the final goal was reached.

The Sacrament of Penance

The new vision of purgatory, which exercised so powerful an influence on the religious imagination of the West in the eleventh and twelfth centuries and thereafter, was accompanied by important liturgical developments relating to the sacrament of penance. Prior to the eleventh century, penance in the West, as in the East, consisted essentially in penitential works leading to reconciliation of the penitent with God, with the community of the faithful, and with those whom he or she had offended.[10] Only occasionally was it called a sacrament. In the course of the eleventh and twelfth centuries, however, in the West, penance began regularly to be called a sacrament, and at the same time the focal center of its sacramental character shifted away from acts of reconciliation. It became sufficient for the penitent to confess his sins to a priest, with genuine contrition, in order to obtain absolution from the eternal punishment in hell to which every Christian was liable, after death, for mortal sins not confessed and repented of. The priest would usually insist also that the penitent agree to perform penitential works in the future. These would help to expiate the temporal punishment, both in this life and, after death, in purgatory, to which every Christian was liable for venial sins as well as for mortal sins confessed and repented of.

Although the sacrament was still called "penance" (*poenitentia*), the penitential works, which were postponed and to that extent dissociated from contrition, confession, and absolution, were for the first time expressly identified with "punishment" (*poena*) for previous sinful acts. The leading eleventh-century tract on the subject, *Concerning True and False Penance*, which had a strong influence on later theological and legal writings, identifies poenitentia with *poenam tenere*, "to undergo punishment."[11] The author states: "Properly speaking, punishment (*poena*) is a hurt (*laesio*) which punishes and avenges (*vindicat*) what one commits . . . Penance (*poenitentia*) is therefore an avenging (*vindicatio*), always punishing in oneself what he is sorry to have done."[12] This was an important shift in emphasis away from the earlier meaning of penance as works of contrition symbolizing a turning from sin and toward God and neighbor.

The priest's power of absolution was said to derive from Christ's transfer to St. Peter of "the keys of the kingdom," with "the power to bind and to loose" (Matt. 16:19). This had been originally understood solely as the power to impose or remit eternal punishment. In the eleventh and twelfth centuries, however, the power to impose punishment in the form of penitential works was said to derive from the same source: by confession, eternal punishment could be converted into temporal punishment.[13] This was a far cry from the "charismatic" penance of the East, with its emphasis on healing and spiritual counsel;[14] it was also far removed from the penitential discipline that had been practiced in the monasteries of the West from the sixth to the eleventh centuries (and which had also been extended outside the monasteries), for that earlier discipline had been much less formal and had retained to a far greater extent the "Eastern" character. Also in that earlier period penitential discipline was entirely local and varied from place to place. Finally, while in the East, as in the earlier period in the West, the priest invoked divine forgiveness but could not himself declare the sinner to be absolved, after the Papal Revolution a new formula was introduced in the West: *Ego te absolvo* ("I absolve you"). This was at first interpreted as the priest's certification of God's action, resulting from contrition and confession. In the twelfth century, however, it was interpreted as having a performative, that is, a sacramental, as well as a declarative, effect.[15]

The Sacrament of the Eucharist

In the eleventh and twelfth centuries the commemoration of the eucharist or last supper was also rigorously defined and systematized; at the same time it was raised in importance to become the primary Christian sacrament, the principal symbol of membership in the church.

The question of the meaning of the eucharist began to be hotly debated in the 1050s and 1060s, when Lanfranc, then head of the Abbey of Bec in Normandy, and later Archbishop of Canterbury under William the Conqueror, challenged the interpretation offered by the head of a rival monastic school, Berengar of Tours. Berengar's fame is based chiefly on his persistence in defending his views for some thirty years, not only against Lanfranc but against the whole papal party, including Pope Gregory VII. Berengar argued that the effectiveness of the sacrament, its grace-giving power, does not depend on the transformation of the bread; the bread, he argued, remains bread, but it is also the "figure" and "likeness" of Christ when it is offered and received in the proper manner. Lanfranc, using the Aristotelian categories of substance and accidents, persuaded the First Lateran Council to denounce Berengar's views and to affirm that in the sacrament the substance of the bread is miraculously transformed into the "true" body of Christ at the time it is consecrated.[16] Theoretically, no one need participate but the priest. In the next century Lanfranc's theory—later called "transubstantiation"—was expressed liturgically by the introduction of the ritual of the elevation of the host: before the bread is lifted up, the ceremonial words, "This is my body," effectuate the transformation.[17]

Also in the twelfth century it came to be generally required that the sacrament of the eucharist, which previously had been partaken of only occasionally or rarely by laymen, be taken by them at least annually, at the Easter season, and that it be preceded by the sacrament of penance. By 1215 the Fourth Lateran Council made this requirement applicable universally to all Christians. The eucharist (holy communion) became the symbol of membership in the church as a corporate body; and excommunication, that is, the deprivation of the right to take communion, became the chief means of expulsion from membership.

The relationship of these changes in liturgical doctrine and ritual to the Papal Revolution and to the new prerogatives of the priesthood is apparent.[18] In this connection it is helpful, once again, to consider the liturgy of the Eastern Church. In that church today, as in the West prior to the late eleventh and twelfth centuries, not the eucharist but baptism is considered the most important sacrament.[19] Baptism is seen as the great Christian mystery in which man, once and for all, dies to himself, renounces the devil, and is reborn as a citizen of the heavenly kingdom. It is baptism above all which saves men from demons and from death. The doctrines of "transubstantiation" and "real presence" were adopted by many Eastern theologians in the eighteenth century and thereafter, but they have never played a central role in Eastern thought. Moreover, the liturgy of the eucharist in the Eastern Church, as in the West prior to the eleventh and twelfth centuries, is linked not to membership in a visible, corporate church but to communal fellowship with the risen Christ.[20]

It was also in the eleventh and twelfth centuries that the celebration of the eucharist in the West first became highly ritualized. In addition, the number of sacraments, which hitherto had been unlimited, was reduced to seven, and each was subjected to its own liturgical rules.[21] These developments were also connected with the establishment of the corporate legal structure of the church. The sacraments were not valid unless performed correctly, and their correct performance usually required the expert offices of the ecclesiastical hierarchy. (Marriage was an exception — until the sixteenth century.) A sacrament was said to be effective *ex proprio vigore* ("by its own force") if it was correctly performed by an authorized person. Thus in the case of the eucharist, Christ's presence, the source of grace, was considered to be effected by the words and acts of consecration, rather than by invocation of the Holy Spirit, as in the Eastern Church then and today.

The New Theology: St. Anselm's Doctrine of Atonement

Upon these metaphors and analogies, concepts were built, first in theology and then in law.

It was in the same crucial century of the Papal Revolution, roughly from 1050 to 1150, that great systematizers of Christian doctrine, theologians in the modern sense, emerged in western Europe for the first time: St. Anselm (1033–1109), Lanfranc's great successor both at Bec and at Canterbury; Peter Abelard (1079–1142); Peter Lombard (1100–1160); and many others. Indeed, the word "theology" itself was applied for the first time by Abelard to the systematic study of the evidence of the nature of the divinity.

Of course, these men built on the works of previous thinkers, including the church fathers, especially St. Augustine (345–430), and a few outstanding Western writers of the intervening period. However, they transformed those works in a fundamental way.[22] For the previous thinkers, including St. Augustine, "theology" had meant divine wisdom, prayerful reflection on the meaning of Holy Scripture, or, more precisely, the mystical intuition of God and his attributes; to a lesser extent it had meant the interpretation of decrees of church councils and of bishops, especially concerning the sacraments. Theology in the new sense, that is, as a rational and objective analysis and synthesis of the articles of faith and of the evidence of their validity, began with the writings of St. Anselm, especially his ontological proof of the existence of God (written about 1078) and his demonstration "by reason alone" of the necessity of the incarnation (written about 1097). The new theology received an important impulse a generation later from Abelard's use of the dialectical method of reconciling contradictions in authoritative texts; thereby it became possible to explain the paradoxes of Christian faith in a manner intended to be convincing to reason and yet consistent with revelation. Finally, about 1150 Peter Lombard, who had been a student of Abelard's, wrote the *Libri Sententiarum* (*Books of Sentences*), the first comprehensive treatise on systematic theology; it remained the principal theological textbook of the West even after St. Thomas Aquinas, over a century later, wrote his *Summa Theologica*.

The revolution in theology that accompanied the revolution in legal science rested on an analytical division between reason and faith and, in particular, on the belief that it was possible to demonstrate by reason alone what had been discovered by faith through divine revelation. This was the premise of St. Anselm's proof of the existence of God, the *Proslogion*, which he subtitled *fides quaerens intellectum* ("faith seeking understanding"), and in which he proclaimed what became the great motto of his age: *Credo ut intelligam* ("I believe in order that I may understand").[23] For Anselm, "to understand" meant to understand with the intellect, to know the reasons for, to be able to prove. Rational demonstration was considered important both for its own sake and as a means of persuading the nonbeliever, but above all as a means of maintaining the consistency, and hence the validity, of Christian dogma.

It has been argued—by Karl Barth, for example—that in Anselm's view rational proof meant a proof peculiar to the object of faith; and therefore for the believer to address unbelievers rationally was to address them as if they shared the same theological beliefs. This interpretation neglects the fact that Anselm applied the same criteria of proof to the existence of God, or to the necessity of his incarnation in Christ, that were applied at the time — by him and by others — to other phenomena of experience. The *ratio* applied by Anselm to the divine mysteries was not, in fact, peculiar to those mysteries. It was the ratio of feudal legal concepts of satisfaction of honor and of canonist legal concepts of punishment for crime. These concepts were presented as objective truths open to be understood by the rational minds of unbelievers as well as of believers.

In dealing scientifically, so to speak, with what had hitherto been considered to be divine mysteries, knowable only when reason was wholly integrated with intuition, experience, and faith, the "rationalists" of the eleventh and twelfth centuries were driven to the objectification of general categories of thought. This was the time not only of the realists, who believed that truth, justice, humanity, righteousness, sin, and other universals had an independent existence, but also of the nominalists, who, although they insisted that universals exist only in the mind, nevertheless were compelled by the very terms of the argument to deal with them *as if* they had an objective existence. For the nominalists, justice and sin, for example, were categories created by the mind, mere ideas, and not external realities; nevertheless, they were capable of being studied by the mind with the same rationality, and in that sense objectivity, as other phenomena. The nominalists did not say, as the Eastern Church said, and as had been said prior to the eleventh century in the West, that justice and sin were not to be understood as universals at all, but rather as manifestations of the struggle between God and the devil for the soul of every man. In the East sin was personified, not conceptualized. Earlier Western theology, too, though it had adhered in general to the Platonic view of the objective existence of ideas, had nevertheless been unable to separate universal sin — except by a personification — from the particular sinners in whom it was found. Sin was not considered to be an entity but rather a relationship between man and God. Moreover, Man with a capital "M" — Adam — was not considered to be dissociable from individual men and women. Neither humanity nor sin was seen as an objective universal reality that existed apart from its concrete manifestations.

Anselm, on the contrary, was concerned in his writings to convert the mysteries of Christian faith into a logic understandable and convincing to a religiously neutral intellect. His proof of the existence of God was essentially a proof that the very thought processes of man presuppose the existence of an absolute goodness. His later and much more daring effort to prove the necessity of the incarnation went even farther: it sought to demonstrate by logic that the very destiny of man is a reflection of the moral and legal structure of the universe.

In *Cur Deus Homo* (*Why the God-Man*) Anselm set out to prove "by necessary reasons" and "by reason alone," apart from revelation — *Christo remoto* ("Christ aside") — that the sacrifice of the Son of God was the only possible means by which atonement could be made for human sinfulness.[24] The argument, in the briefest possible terms, went like this: God created man for eternal blessedness. This blessedness requires that man freely submit his will to God. Man, however, chose to disobey God, and his sin of disobedience is transmitted by inheritance to everyone. Justice requires either that man be punished in accordance with his sin, or else that he make satisfaction for the dishonoring of God. As for punishment, none would be adequate; at the very least, man would have to forfeit the blessedness for which he was created, yet that would only frustrate God's purpose once again. As for satisfaction, there is nothing man can offer to God that would be valuable enough to restore his honor. Thus man cannot, though he ought to, atone for his sin. God can (since he can do anything), but he ought not to. Since only God can and only man ought to make an offering which would constitute satisfaction, it must be made by a God-Man. Therefore the God-Man, Jesus Christ, is necessary, who both can and ought to sacrifice himself and so pay the price of sin, reconcile man to God, and restore creation to its original purpose.

Anselm's theory of the atonement, although never officially adopted by the church, became the predominant view in the West, not only from the twelfth to the fifteenth century but also (with modifications) in later times, and not only in Roman Catholic but also (with modifications) in Protestant thought. Moreover, it was this theory that first gave Western theology its distinctive character and its distinctive connection with Western jurisprudence.

The theory, whether or not it was consciously intended as such, was in fact an explanation of the contemporaneous liturgical development: the exaltation of the sacrament of the eucharist as the primary Christian sacrament and the interpretation of the eucharist as an experience of the real presence of the crucified Christ.

Once again, this new doctrine of atonement may be contrasted with Eastern Christian doctrine and liturgy, which is essentially similar to that which had prevailed in the West prior to the Papal Revolution. For the Eastern Church the crucifixion had then and still has no significance apart from the resurrection. The atonement is seen as part of a continuum of incarnation-crucifixion-resurrection: liturgically, the resurrection is a central part even of the celebration of the last supper. The Christian "dies and rises with Christ." Christ is seen primarily as the conqueror of death. In the Roman Catholic theology of St. Anselm, on the other hand, and in the Roman Catholic liturgy of the eleventh and twelfth centuries, redemption was identified chiefly with the crucifixion.[25] The resurrection was explained as a necessary sequence to the crucifixion. Christ was seen primarily as the conqueror of sin.

The striking difference between these closely interrelated conceptions of Christ's mission was manifested in religious art. Since the eleventh and twelfth centuries, Roman Catholic religious art has emphasized Christ on the cross, and the stations of the cross. In contrast, the icons of the Eastern Church have typically shown the resurrected Christ "trampling down the devil and his host, raising Adam and Eve, and freeing the patriarchs from bondage."[26] Similarly, Western portrayals of Christ prior to the eleventh century, even when showing him on the cross, had almost invariably portrayed him as a triumphant figure, a heavenly ruler as well as a redeemer.[27]

Moreover, Eastern Christian art has reflected the theology of the Eastern Church, and also the theology of the West between the sixth and tenth centuries, in its emphasis on transcendence (or "otherworldliness," as it is called in the West). This is a theology centered in heaven, in man's "ascent to the infinite," in man's deification. The emphasis is on God the Father, the Creator. Christ has shown mankind the way to him. The icons reflect this. But Western theology of the eleventh and twelfth centuries shifted the emphasis to the second person of the Trinity, to the incarnation of God in this world, to God the Redeemer. God's humanity in Christ took the center of the stage. This was reflected in the papal amendment of the Nicene Creed by the proclamation that the Holy Spirit "proceeds" not only "from the Father" but also "from the Son" (*filioque*).[28] God the Father, representing the whole of creation, the cosmic order, is incarnate in God the Son, who represents mankind. By the *filioque* clause, God the Holy Spirit, who is identified in the Nicene Creed with the church, was said to have his source not only in the First Person but also in the Second Person of the Trinity — not only in creation but also in incarnation and redemption.

Thus the church came to be seen less as the communion of saints in heaven and more as the community of sinners on earth. Rationalism itself was an expression of the belief in the incarnation of divine mysteries in human concepts and theories. God was seen to be not only transcendent but also immanent. This was reflected in the more "realistic" paintings of the Holy Family as well as in the Gothic architecture which was the great artistic symbol of the new age in the West.

It was not transcendence as such, and not immanence as such, that was linked with the rationalization and systematization of law and legality in the West, but rather incarnation, which was understood as the process by which the transcendent becomes immanent. It is no accident that Christianity, Judaism, and Islam, all three of which postulate both a radical separation and a radical interconnection between God and man, also postulate that God is a judge and lawgiver and that man is governed by divine law. Nevertheless, the distinctive features of the Western concepts of human law that emerged in the eleventh and twelfth centuries—as contrasted not only with Judaic and Islamic concepts but also with those of Eastern Christianity—are related to the greater Western emphasis on incarnation as the central reality of the universe. This released an enormous energy for the redemption of the world; yet it split the legal from the spiritual, the political from the ideological.

Anselm's conception of the atonement was a perfect myth for the new theology. Its emphasis was on the humanity of the Son of God, who suffered death as a propitiation for sin and thereby made it right for God to forgive and at the same time gave man the capacity to accept forgiveness and hence to be redeemed.

The Legal Implications of the Doctrine of the Atonement

Anselm's theory also laid the foundation for the new jurisprudence. It did so by answering the question why either satisfaction or punishment is required, why God in his mercy cannot forgive man's sin freely, as a matter of grace. The answer was that this would leave the disturbance of the order of the universe, caused by sin, uncorrected, and that an uncorrected disorder would constitute a deficiency in justice. The just order of the universe, the *iustitia* or righteousness of God, requires that the price be paid. Mercy, said Anselm, is the daughter of justice; it is derived from justice and cannot work against justice.[29] It is the mercy of God that lets man live, and indeed offers him redemption, although man has willfully betrayed the sacred trust of Paradise. But God does not act arbitrarily; his mercy is subject to his justice, just as his justice is subject to his *rectitudo*, his "right ordering."

It is interesting to compare this language with that of the tract *Concerning True and False Penance*, written perhaps forty to fifty years before *Cur Deus Homo* and well known to Anselm. The earlier work is in the older theological and moral tradition (also the Eastern Christian tradition) of refusing to subordinate God's mercy to his justice or his justice to his mercy. The author writes: "For God is merciful and just, preserving mercy in justice and also justice in mercy." "The just [judge] should be merciful justly." "He should have mercy with justice . . . and justice in mercy."[30] Yet the author distinguishes between justice and mercy in his analysis of punishment. "For justice alone condemns," he writes.[31] Further, he attacks "the error of those who presume forgiveness without penance," that is, without punishment, on the ground that they in effect justify evil and give a "license to sin."[32] God's grace is not to be cheapened in this way. Thus the new theory of "true and false penance" paved the way for Anselm's argument that the rational order of the universe requires that sins always be punished.[33]

Anselm is often charged with having adopted a "legal" or "legalistic" view of the atonement. He has also been defended against this charge on the ground that his criteria of justice (iustitia) are essentially moral criteria rather than legal criteria.[34] Neither of these views is quite adequate. Surely Anselm was not legalistic in the sense of being concerned with the technicalities of a divine law of sin and penance or crime and punishment. For him, as for his predecessors, iustitia was the word used for the Biblical term which is translated "righteousness." Anselm was concerned to explore the fundamental character of God's righteousness.

He was equally concerned, however, with the way in which God's justice, or righteousness, manifests itself in specific acts and norms. He was not willing to sacrifice a particular decision or rule, derived from justice, on the altar of an inconsistent principle, however attractive. In *Cur Deus Homo*, Anselm's pupil is led to say: "If God follows the method of justice, there is no escape for a miserable wretch; and God's mercy seems to perish." Anselm replies: "You asked for reason, now accept reason."[35] However broadly Anselm conceived justice, reason required that he stop at the boundary of grace. God is bound by his own justice. If it is divinely just for a man to pay the price for his sins, it would be unjust, and therefore impossible, for God to remit the price. In *Cur Deus Homo* Anselm's theology is a theology of law.[36]

Before the time of Anselm (and in the Eastern Church still) it would have been considered wrong to analyze God's justice in this way. It would have been said, first, that these ultimate mysteries cannot be fitted into the concepts and constructs of the human intellect; that reason is inseparable from faith — one is not the servant of the other, but rather the two are indivisible; and that the whole exercise of a theology of law is a contradiction in terms. And second, it would have been said that it is not only, and not primarily, divine justice that establishes our relationship with God but also, and primarily, his grace and his mercy; that it is his grace and mercy, and not only his justice, which explains the crucifixion, since by it mankind was ransomed from the power of the devil and the demons of death — the very power which had procured the slaying of Jesus in the first place but which then itself was finally conquered through the resurrection.

Eastern Orthodoxy, in fact, never developed theories concerning merits, satisfaction, purgatory, and supererogatory works. Such theories were considered legalistic in the East. The doctrine of eternal damnation was also rejected. Sin was viewed primarily as the fallen state of a person's soul, not as an act committed in violation of divine law. Similar ideas prevailed in Germanic Christendom prior to the Papal Revolution.

Seen thus from an earlier perspective (and today from an Eastern perspective), Anselm's theory is a legal one in the sense that it explains both human suffering and divine forgiveness in terms of a single framework of justice and right ordering. Human suffering is seen as a price paid for man's disobedience. More fundamentally, God's remission of eternal punishment, despite the infinite wrong that man has done to him, is made right, made legal, by the only possible sacrifice commensurate with the sin. Thus redemption was explained essentially in terms of a legal transaction.

Theological Sources of Western Criminal Law

Anselm's theory that satisfaction was required for man's dishonoring of God reflected preexisting legal concepts more than the new legal concepts that were soon to be superimposed on it. Anselm conceived satisfaction in terms of the kind of self-abasement by which a serf appeases a lord whom he has dishonored. Christ's self-sacrifice was not presented—as it was later, especially after the Reformation—in terms of punishment for crime (Christ being the substitute), but rather in terms of penance in the older sense, that is, in the sense of works of contrition, leading to reconciliation of the victim with the offender.[37] Because Christ as the representative of man had offered himself as a propitiation for man's sin, God's honor was restored and he could be reconciled to man. This expressed a leitmotiv of criminal law among the people of Europe in the period before and during the eleventh century. A crime was not generally conceived as an offense directed against the political order as such, or against society in general, but rather as an offense directed against the victim and those with whom he was identified—his kinfolk, or his territorial community, or his feudal class. It was also an offense against God—a sin. A normal social response to such an offense was vengeance on the part of the victim or of his kinship (or other) group. At the same time, tribal and local and feudal law between the sixth and eleventh centuries placed great emphasis on penance, restitution of honor, and reconciliation—as an alternative to vengeance. In addition, royal law and imperial law of that earlier time were based on similar concepts and consisted largely of customary rules and procedures protecting the rights of the royal or imperial household and of the persons under its protection. Occasionally kings would issue "codes" of law, restating and revising the customary law, but, on the whole, royal or imperial jurisdiction over crimes was extremely limited. The relative lack of a universal criminal law—and the predominance of local customs—only emphasizes the fact that crime was considered for the most part to be an offense against other people—and at the same time an offense against God—rather than an offense against an all-embracing political unit, whether the state or the church.

The same was true in the monasteries, whose penitentials—codes of sins and penances—formed an important source of the new canon law of crimes of the twelfth century. Offenses by monks were confessed and punished, secretly, preliminary to the reintegration of the offender into the local monastic community. For the most part, each monastery had its own penitential rules. These rules also came to be applied very widely to the laity in the ninth, tenth, and eleventh centuries.

Penance, restitution of honor, and reconciliation: these were the stages through which atonement for crime or sin had to pass. The alternative was blood feud, or outlawry, or excommunication.

And so the atonement was presented by Anselm as an act of penance ("oblation") and reconciliation, in which the God-Man offered himself as a sacrifice. Yet the argument ultimately depended on another premise which was not fully articulated, namely, that a punishment (and not only a penitential satisfaction) was required by divine justice, not for man's original sin, or "natural sin" (as Anselm preferred to call it), but for "personal sins" ("actual sins") committed by baptized Christians. By the sacrament of baptism they had the benefit of Christ's atoning sacrifice—the infinite debt of their original sin was paid; however, liability for their subsequent sins remained, and that liability, it was implied, they must themselves assume, by undergoing punishment.

That implication was derived from the sharp distinctions that were drawn: (1) between universal original *sin*, which was removed by baptism, and "actual" *sins* subsequently committed by individual Christians; and (2) between satisfaction, which was a payment sufficient to restore the victim's honor, and punishment, which was a payment commensurate with the gravity of the offense. Anselm expressly rejected the alternative of punishment as an appropriate sanction for original sin, since, he said, to be commensurate with the offense it would have required man's total destruction. God, who "has made nothing more valuable than a rational creature capable of enjoying him," did not want man utterly to perish, and so he permitted his honor to be restored by the self-sacrifice of his Son.[38] Thus God has forgiven mankind its state of sinfulness: the human race is absolved from the consequences of its inherited tendency toward greed, pride, power, and other forms of contempt of God. God accepts man as he is. But this very absolution imposes an added responsibility on each individual not to choose voluntarily to do those things that are prohibited. If he does so choose, he is to be punished for it—not destroyed, not hated, but made to pay a price commensurate with the offense, that is, with the illegality. In contrast with mankind's (Adam's) original sin, the actual sins of individual, baptized, penitent Christians need not entail their destruction in order to be commensurate with the illegality; they may be expiated by temporal punishments in this life and in purgatory. Even those consigned to eternal punishment are not totally destroyed.

The new concepts of sin and punishment based on the doctrine of the atonement were not justified in Germanic terms of reconciliation as an alternative to vengeance, or in Platonic terms of deterrence and rehabilitation, or in Old Testament terms of the covenant between God and Israel—though elements of all three of these theories were present. The main justification given by Anselm and by his successors in Western theology was the concept of justice itself. Justice required that every sin (crime) be paid for by temporal suffering; that the suffering, the penalty, be appropriate to the sinful act; and that it vindicate ("avenge") the particular law that was violated. As St. Thomas Aquinas said almost two centuries after Anselm's time, both criminal and civil offenses require payment of compensation to the victim; but since crime, in contrast to tort, is a defiance of the law itself, punishment, and not merely reparation, must be imposed *as the price for the violation of the law.*[39]

This is usually called a "retributive" theory of justice, since it rests on the premise that a "tribute," that is, a price, must be paid to "vindicate" the law. In the United States the retributive theory has often been associated with the avenging of the victim rather than the avenging of the law—which is quite another matter. I would call the former "special retribution" and the latter "general retribution." Historically, it was in the wake of the Papal Revolution that Western man experienced the substitution of general retribution (the vindication of the law) for special retribution (the vindication of the honor of the victim) as the basic justification of criminal law. Yet the phrase "general retribution" does not exhaust the depth of the change. The doctrine of the atonement added other dimensions to the ideas of tribute and vindication. On the one hand, the sinner who broke the law was, indeed, considered to be not only a sinner but also a criminal, a lawbreaker, and hence liable not only to repent but also to pay a price for the violation of the law; but on the other hand, the lawbreaker, the criminal, was also a sinner, whose guilt consisted not only in the fact that he broke the law but also, and more significantly, in the fact that he voluntarily chose to do evil. Thus there was a strong emphasis on the moral (or rather, the immoral) quality of his act, that is, his sinful state of mind when he committed it.

At the same time the association of crime with sin, and of punishment with atonement, gave the criminal or sinner a certain dignity vis-à-vis his accusers, his judges, and his other fellow Christians. They, too, were sinners; they, too, were candidates for unknown torments in purgatory and eventual admission to the kingdom of heaven. This alleviated the element of moral superiority that generally accompanies a retributive theory of justice. For example, the executioner was required to kneel down before the condemned man at the last moment and to ask his forgiveness for the act he was about to commit. Thus, although the association of crime with sin created an infinite responsibility on the part of the criminal toward God, the attribution of sin to all members of society, including the law abiding, served somewhat to de-emphasize self-righteous indignation as a component part of criminal law.[40] All Christians shared a common, sinful humanity.

The belief in the moral equality of all the participants in legal proceedings provided a foundation for a scientific investigation of the state of mind of the accused. In the tract *Concerning True and False Penance,* the author developed the remarkable theory that a judge who examines a person should put himself in that person's position in order to discern what he knows and to elicit from him, by subtle questioning, that which he may wish to conceal even from himself.

> For one who judges another . . . condemns himself. Let him therefore know himself and purge himself of what he sees offends others . . . Let him who is without sin cast the first stone (John 8:7) . . . for no one is without sin in that it is understood that all have been guilty of crime . . . Let the spiritual [that is, ecclesiastical] judge beware lest he fail to fortify himself with science and thereby commit the crime of injustice. It is fitting that he should know how to recognize what he is to judge. Therefore the diligent inquisitor, the subtle investigator, wisely and almost cunningly interrogates the sinner about that which the sinner perhaps does not himself know, or because of shame will wish to hide.[41]

Finally, the doctrine of the atonement gave a universal significance to human justice by linking the penalty imposed by a court for violation of a law to the nature and destiny of man, his search for salvation, his moral freedom, and his mission to create on earth a society that would reflect the divine will. There were marked similarities here with the Judaic concept of the covenant which God had entered into with his chosen people. From that covenant were derived the Ten Commandments and the multitude of Biblical laws based thereon. Each of those laws was sacred; every violation was a breach of the covenant. In the Western view of the atonement, God had entered into a new covenant, now with all mankind, represented in a person who was both human and divine, the God-Man. Under the new covenant, however, the Biblical law was dissolved: man's sinfulness was wiped out by Christ's sacrifice. Henceforth baptized Christians were able to live righteous lives without any need for law. Yet despite this newfound grace, they voluntarily chose to do evil. And so a new kind of law was needed — human law, not sacred in the old sense, though inspired by the Ten Commandments as well as by other Biblical texts. Human law would judge men on earth, leaving to God's sacred justice the judgment of their eternal souls. Yet it was also the mission of human law to help prepare men's souls for their eternal destiny. The priesthood in particular, being God's representatives on earth, had the task not only of caring for souls through the administration of the sacraments, including penance, but also of promulgating and enforcing rules of ecclesiastical law and cooperating in the promulgation and enforcement of rules of secular law; and these ecclesiastical and secular laws, though human and not divine, were nevertheless intended to reflect the divine will and hence to have an ultimate validity. Therefore—to vindicate that ultimate validity—violations had to be punished. "The law must keep its promises."[42]

The Canon Law of Crimes

The new theology was reflected in a new system of criminal law, created by the canonists of the eleventh and twelfth centuries, which differed substantially from "God's law," that is, the penitential law, that had previously prevailed in the Western Church, as well as from the "worldly law" (or "man's law ") that had prevailed, alongside the penitential law, in the tribal, local, feudal, and royal or imperial legal orders.

In the earlier period the words "crime" and "sin" had been used interchangeably. Generally speaking, not only were all crimes sins but all sins were also crimes. There was not a sharp distinction in underlying nature between offenses to be atoned for by ecclesiastical penance, on the one hand, and offenses to be dealt with by kinship negotiations (or blood feuds), by local or feudal assemblies, or by royal or imperial procedures, on the other hand. Homicide, robbery, and other major violations of man's law were considered to be at the same time violations of God's law; conversely, sexual and marital offenses, witchcraft and magic, sacrilege, and other major violations of God's law were considered to be at the same time violations of man's law. The clergy played a predominant role in "secular" adjudication, and the supreme royal or imperial authority was itself considered to have a sacral and sacerdotal character. In the church, however, there was no regular system of adjudication of crimes, such as developed after the Papal Revolution; the system of ecclesiastical penances was administered chiefly by local priests and monks, whose purpose was not punishment as such but care of souls, renewal of moral life, and restoration of a right relationship with God. Similarly, the primary purpose of secular sanctioning was not punishment as such but satisfaction of honor, reconciliation, and restoration of peace.

In the late eleventh and the twelfth centuries a sharp procedural distinction was made, for the first time, between sin and crime. This happened partly because the ecclesiastical hierarchy succeeded in withdrawing from the secular authorities jurisdiction over sins—thereby, incidentally, giving the word "secular" a new meaning. Any act punishable by royal or other "lay" officials was henceforth to be punished as a violation of secular law and not as a sin, that is, not as a violation of a law of God. When the secular authority punished for robbery, for example, it was to punish for the breach of the peace, for the protection of property, for the offense against society. In this world, it began to be said, only the church has the jurisdiction to punish for sins—thereby, incidentally, giving the word "church " a new meaning, connected with such terms as "hierarchy," "in this world," "jurisdiction," "punishment for sins."

A gross exception, however, to the principle of the division between ecclesiastical and secular jurisdictions was contained in the law applicable to heretics. In the twelfth and thirteenth centuries, heresy, which previously had been only a spiritual offense, punishable by anathema, became also a legal offense, punishable as treason. The inquisitional procedure was used for the first time to expose it, and the death penalty was for the first time made applicable to it. The gist of the offense was dissent from the dogmas of the church. If the accused was willing to swear an oath to adhere to those dogmas, he was to be acquitted, although he was still subject to penances if he had sworn the oath only because of torture or other duress. If he persisted in heresy he remained liable to prosecution in the church courts and to transfer to the secular authorities for execution. Thus the church overcame its aversion to the shedding of blood by engaging in it only indirectly. This was an "anomaly" on which eventually—in the sixteenth century—the entire "model" foundered.

The church divided its authority over sins into two parts: (1) sins that were judged in the "internal forum" of the church, that is, by a priest acting under the authority of his *ordination*, especially as part of the sacrament of penance; and (2) sins that were judged in the "external forum" of the church, that is, by an ecclesiastical judge acting under the authority of his *jurisdiction*. The latter were called by the twelfth-century canon lawyers criminal sins, or ecclesiastical crimes, or simply crimes. A criminal sin was a violation of an ecclesiastical law.

The principle that a criminal sin is a violation of an ecclesiastical law carried with it necessarily the principle that what is not a violation of an ecclesiastical law is not actionable in an ecclesiastical court. This was expressed in the twelfth century by Peter Lombard in the following way: "There is no sin if there was no prohibition."[43] The use of the past tense—"was"—is striking. Here was the beginning of a long and winding jurisprudential path in the Western legal tradition, which culminated in the principle expressed in the eighteenth century in the Enlightenment and in the French Revolution's Declaration of the Rights of Man and the Citizen: *Nullum crimen, nulla poena sine lege*—"No crime, no punishment without a law," that is, without a previously enacted statute defining the crime and fixing the punishment.

From the principle that every criminal sin is a violation of an ecclesiastical law it does not necessarily follow, however, that every violation of an ecclesiastical law is a criminal sin. A sin is an offense against God. Only in a society in which all laws are divine is every violation sinful. That was so in ancient Israel, under the Mosaic law. It was true also among the Germanic peoples of Western Europe prior to the eleventh century. An offense against a kinship group or a local community or a feudal relationship was also an offense against God (or prior to Christianity, the gods). This is shown by the fact that the normal mode of trial of offenses was by appeal to the supernatural — usually by ritual oath or by ordeal. The clergy were involved; the sacrament had to be taken before the divine judgment was invoked. The words "sin" and "crime" were used interchangeably both in the "worldly law" and in the "divine law." In the late eleventh and the twelfth centuries, however, theologians and jurists of western Europe distinguished between sins which were offenses against God alone and which God alone would judge — for example, secret sins of thought or desire — and sins which were also offenses against the church and which the church, viewed as a corporate entity, a political-legal institution, had jurisdiction to judge through its own courts. Criminal sins differed from other sins in that their sinfulness, that is, their offensiveness to God, was measured by standards of ecclesiastical law applied by ecclesiastical judges acting under authority of their jurisdiction — rather than by standards of divine law applied by God himself through priests acting under authority of their ordination.

The theoretical foundation for the new law of ecclesiastical crimes was laid by Abelard in his *Ethics,* some decades before it was given a more detailed legal formulation by Gratian, the great founder of the science of canon law.[44] Abelard set forth three main conditions that were required to make a sin cognizable in the ecclesiastical courts:

First, it must be a grave sin. The starting point for determining its gravity was the traditional division between mortal sins (literally, sins involving death, that is, spiritual death), and venial sins (pardonable sins, light sins). Following Abelard, the twelfth-century canonists said that only a mortal sin can constitute a crime and, further, that not all mortal sins constitute crimes, but only those mortal sins which, under the circumstances of their commission, were sufficiently grave to merit criminal punishment at the order of an ecclesiastical court. Greed, for example, is a mortal sin; but the greed required to justify a criminal prosecution in a given case might have to be more than ordinary greed.

Second, the sin must be manifested in an external act. Sinful thoughts and desires are punishable by God and are cognizable in the "heavenly forum" (as Abelard called it) of the church in the sacrament of penance, including confession; but they are not to be punished as such in the "earthly forum" of the church, that is, by an ecclesiastical court. Abelard put this on the ground that only God can see directly into the mind and heart and soul of a person, and that human judges can only know what is externally manifested. It came to be universally accepted that "the church does not adjudicate matters that are hidden." This, in turn, led to the rule of canon law—which eventually came to be the rule also of the secular legal systems of the West—that mere preparation of a crime (even to the extent of assembling the means to commit it) is not punishable; there must be at least an attempt, that is, an external act commencing the course of criminal conduct. There were two striking exceptions to this rule: treason and heresy.

The canonists also defined the kinds of intent and the kinds of causal connection that were required for an external act to be criminal. They distinguished between "direct intent" (knowledge that the act would produce the particular illegal result—for example, a homicide—coupled with the desire to cause the result) and "indirect intent" (knowledge that the illegal result would occur but no desire to accomplish it—for example, the reluctant killing of a guard in order to escape). They also distinguished between intent (of either kind) and negligence (as in the case where the actor lacked knowledge that the result would occur, but if he had been diligent he would have known). With regard to causation, they distinguished between remote causes (*causae remotae*) and proximate causes (*causae proximae*). They discussed complex cases—actual and hypothetical—of intervening causes. For example, a cleric throws a stone intending to frighten his companion; the companion, in avoiding it, runs into a rock and is badly hurt; as a result of the negligence of his father and of a doctor, he dies. Was throwing the stone a proximate cause of the death? There were countless such examples. A student of any one of the modern Western legal systems will be familiar with this mode of analysis of criminal conduct in terms of the difference between intent and negligence, various kinds of intent, and various kinds of causal connections.

Third—according to Abelard (and the canonists followed him in this as well)—the act must be vexatious to the church. It must be a "scandal" to the ecclesiastical polity. The law should not punish even morally evil acts unless they are also harmful to the society whose law is being applied. This, too, seems wholly modern.[45] Thus the canonists determined, for example, that a breach of a simple promise, though morally reproachable, is not sufficiently vexatious to the church to justify the imposition of criminal sanctions.

What was not modern in the new canon law of crimes was the use of external indicators not only to determine guilt in the modern sense (was the act a crime? did the accused commit it?) but also to measure the sinfulness of the accused. Abelard went farther than his successors in attempting to eliminate the question of sinfulness: he argued that the gravity of the sin should be *presumed* from the external indicators. In other words, in Abelard's view the ecclesiastical court should not make a specific inquiry into the attitudes, the motivations, and the character of the accused except insofar as such an inquiry was necessary to determine his violation of ecclesiastical law, that is, whether his act was sufficiently immoral and sufficiently harmful to the church to constitute an ecclesiastical crime and whether he had the requisite intent to commit it, whether there was the requisite causal connection, and whether the other legal requirements of guilt were established. His sinful mind (attitudes), heart (motivations), and soul (character), which were known directly to God, could only be known to the ecclesiastical court through external signs; and therefore, Abelard argued, only the external signs should be examined by the court. Stephan Kuttner points out that this reasoning might have led Abelard to a concept of crime totally emancipated from sin and totally free from theology (*theologiefrei*), but that Abelard did not take the final step to reach that concept.[46] Instead, he used a conclusive presumption, that is, a fiction, to bridge the gap between crime and sin. He postulated that the tests available to earthly judges, despite their limitations, will yield a result that approximates the result reached by God—and that it is hopeless to seek more than such an approximation.

Abelard's view that sinfulness may be presumed and only presumed, and therefore ignored, was rejected by the church.[47] The canon lawyers were concerned above all with measuring the offense against God. They saw the "external indicators" as God-given devices for that purpose, but they also went beyond them to a specific inquiry into the mind and heart and soul of the accused. They recognized that ecclesiastical law is applied in the earthly forum of the church, not in the heavenly forum, and that therefore it must proceed according to the criteria of objectivity and generality; nevertheless, they saw no essential conflict but rather a basic harmony between those criteria and the criteria of divine justice. Following their conceptions of God's own procedures, they were interested to determine *both* whether the accused intentionally committed a morally and socially offensive act in violation of a law *and* to what extent he thereby revealed a depraved mind and heart and soul.

The two types of inquiry were not, in fact, separate. In order to evaluate the act it was necessary to analyze the actor's intent. This led to an examination of the freedom of his will. The canonists developed the rules—now familiar to all Western legal systems—that a person may be excused from criminal liability if he acted while he was out of his mind, or asleep, or drunk, or mistaken, provided: (1) that as a result of his condition he could not know that what he was doing was wrong, and (2) that he had not wrongfully brought himself into such a condition (as, for example, by voluntary intoxication). Clearly, an inquiry into the freedom of will of the accused which leads to a consideration of whether he wrongfully brought himself into a condition in which he should have known that he might commit a morally evil, socially harmful, illegal act is at least compatible with, if it does not necessarily lead to, an examination of a man's whole personality. Such an inquiry will almost inevitably pass from questions of intent and knowledge to questions of attitude and motivation and character. From the canonists' point of view this was highly desirable, since it was the sinfulness of the actor himself, and not only the criminality of the act, which ultimately justified the ecclesiastical court in taking jurisdiction over criminal sins once the division had been made between secular and ecclesiastical criminal law.

The intimate connection between crime and sin in the canon law is also apparent in the rules which were first systematically developed in the twelfth century concerning justification and excuse for acts otherwise criminal. It was accepted that a person who intentionally attacks another may be justified by self-defense or by defense of others, or he may be excused because he was exercising disciplinary authority, or he may be immune from criminal liability because of his youth or because of some other incapacity. Here, too, the canonists (relying in part on the Justinian texts) created modern criminal law, but not for modern reasons. What they were concerned with above all was not the guilt but the sin.[48] Again, the evaluation of justifications and excuses for acts merged with the evaluation of motivations, attitudes, character.

A case that was widely discussed in the twelfth and thirteenth centuries may illuminate these considerations. Robbers broke into a monastery, knocked out two monks, and stole their clothes. The monks regained their strength and overpowered and tied up the robbers. One of the brothers went to notify the head of the chapter, leaving the other to guard the robbers. The captives began to free themselves, whereupon the brother who had been left behind killed them in order not to be killed by them. The case was brought to Alexander III, the famous twelfth-century jurist pope, who declared both the tying up of the robbers and the killing of them to be criminal sins. The brothers had offended against the meekness which was required of them as monks and also against ecclesiastical discipline. They had neglected Jesus' precept that if a man takes your coat you should let him have your cloak as well. Kuttner reports: "Many canonists cited this Decretal as an argument against the admissibility of the killing of a thief by a cleric or against the right of a cleric to undertake armed opposition for protection of goods or in general against the use of force in self-defense on the part of any who (like monks) strive for evangelical perfection. It was probably more accurate, however, to interpret the decision of Alexander, in the concrete circumstances of the case, according to the general doctrine of self-defense and not to treat it as a problem of [justification for] killing a thief; for the second monk had attacked the robbers not for the sake of the goods but in defense of his life . . . [However,] this situation of self-defense had been created by the previous tying up of the robbers, and that had been inadmissible, since before then the first attack had already been warded off and the monks could have escaped in another way. Thus the tying up could be seen . . . as a *culpa praecedens* [preceding guilt] for the defensive killing; and so Alexander's decision was harmonized with the general theory of [the privilege of] self-defense.[49]

This case is an example of the close connection between crime and sin—that is, between offenses against the legal order of the church and offenses against God—in the canon law. As a matter of criminal law, without reference to sin, one may justify a rule which permits a person to kill another in order to prevent the other from killing him. Similarly, one may justify a rule which does not permit a person to kill another, but imposes criminal liability, where the killing is committed in order to prevent the other from stealing goods. Pope Alexander III's decision, however, introduces two additional factors.

First, the killer is a cleric, indeed, a monk. It was a firm principle of canon law that a cleric who commits a criminal act commits a greater sin than a layman who commits the same criminal act. Moreover, a monk is not an ordinary cleric but one who has "died to this world" and undertaken a life of perfection. He is therefore held to still higher standards.

Second, the ordinary rule justifying homicide when committed in necessary defense of one's own life is subject to an important qualification introduced by the canonists: one who defends himself must not have wrongfully created the danger from which he seeks to escape by violent means. This was viewed in legal terms as "preceding guilt," but the legal fiction is obvious since the alleged crime is not the wrongful creation of a danger of a subsequent attack but rather the homicide beyond the limits of justifiable self-defense. An analogy may be made with the rule that one who, while in a drunken stupor, kills another may nevertheless be liable for murder since he is not excused by voluntary intoxication. Judged on the basis of external indicators, such a person should be liable not for intentional homicide but for intentionally drinking with knowledge that he might fall into a drunken stupor and kill someone. If by a fiction he is convicted, however, of intentional homicide—though he had no intent to kill—one is justified in saying that the "real crime" is the *sin* of drunkenness.

The canon lawyers invented a word to distinguish the quality of legal sinfulness from legal guilt, that is, from the guilt implicit in the legal tests of guilt, such as gravity of the evil act, intent to commit it, proximate causation. They had taken the word "guilt" from the Roman legal term *culpa*. But the quality of sinfulness of a person who committed a criminal sin they described by a new term, *contemptus*, which, though never defined, was used to signify contempt, scorn, defiance, obstinacy, presumptuousness, or, from the opposite point of view, pride or exaltation of self. Thus Adam's sin was self-exaltation, which manifested itself in contemptuous defiance of God's law.[50]

In emphasizing the subjective factors of criminal responsibility, the canonists used distinctions that had been made in the earlier Roman legal science, but they developed those distinctions into complex and elaborately articulated concepts. Such Roman terms as *imputabilitas* ("imputability"), *culpa* ("guilt" or "fault"), and *dolus* ("malicious intent," "willfulness") were systematically analyzed in terms of the precise state of mind of the actor (subjective aspect) and of the detailed circumstances of the act (objective aspect). Roman criminal law, in contrast, especially in the earlier period but also at the time of Justinian, was not greatly concerned with the moral quality of the specific criminal act; it was concerned, rather, with what is called today the protection of interests and the enforcement of policies. Much of the Roman law of crimes was elaborated by analogy to rules of property, contract, and tort. In the postclassical period, as imperial power increased, the kinds of misconduct to which imperial punishment was applicable also increased, as did the severity of criminal sanctions. Yet this development was not accompanied by an emphasis on the punishment of immorality (sin) as such. It was in the Western monastic penitentials that moral indignation and moral reform first became a matter of central *legal* concern, and it was on the monastic practice of "minute and detailed analysis of the circumstances of the sin . . . [and] the precise investigation in any given case of the intention . . . and of the external circumstances of the act," that the canonists of the late eleventh and the twelfth centuries founded their doctrines of the subjective and objective aspects of crime.[51]

Both the unity and the complexity of the new canon law of crimes are striking. Here, on the one hand, was an integrated theory of criminal law which both supported and explained the practice of the church in disciplining its own army of clergy and in maintaining moral and ideological standards among the laity as well. Here also, on the other hand, were complex distinctions between divine law (including divine criminal law) and human law; in human law between ecclesiastical law and secular law; and in ecclesiastical law between the sin and the crime of each criminal sin. Moreover, the most burning distinction of all, both from a theoretical and from a practical point of view, was the one between the church's role in disciplining its own army of clergy and its role in maintaining moral and ideological standards among the laity. The clergy were subject to trial in ecclesiastical courts for any type of crime. Murder, theft, arson, assault—indeed, any act proscribed by any secular authority, whether tribal or local or feudal or royal or imperial—might fall within the competence of the ecclesiastical courts if committed by a cleric. Wholly apart from the technical questions of concurrent jurisdiction, every serious breach of the peace could be either a secular crime or an ecclesiastical crime if it was committed by a member of the clergy. Undoubtedly this is to be explained politically: the church as a political-legal entity sought to maintain control over its functionaries. It is also to be explained theologically and ethically, or, as would be said in a later age, ideologically: the clergy were the elite, and what for a layman might be merely a breach of the peace might be for a cleric a breach of a still higher obligation.

Whatever explanation is adopted, however, there was a serious practical legal question for the church: was the *definition* of "secular" crimes — murder, theft, arson, and the like — committed by clerics to be left to the secular authorities, or was the church to supply its own definitions of such crimes? The answer to this question adds another dimension to the analysis of the relation between crime and sin. The church did not attempt to define particular secular crimes. It did, however, give its own definitions of the conditions under which secular crimes became criminal sins when committed by clergy; for example: when they were of sufficient moral gravity and sufficient vexatiousness to the church, when they were committed intentionally, when they proximately caused the prohibited result, when they were not justified by self-defense or one of various other justifications, when they were not excused by official authorization or one of various other privileges, *and when they manifested the contemptus of the accused.*

The relevance and materiality of the inquiry into sinfulness becomes still more apparent when one recalls that the chief sanctions imposed by ecclesiastical courts upon clergy were degradation (that is, permanent deprivation of all ecclesiastical offices and rights), deposition from particular ecclesiastical offices, suspension from celebration of the sacraments, alms, amends to injured persons, certain exercises of piety such as fasting and pilgrimage, and for the very worst offenders, excommunication. Excommunication could take a variety of forms, ranging from exclusion from participation in the sacraments to total exclusion from the church (which was equivalent to total ostracism). However, the ecclesiastical court could suspend the penalty of an excommunication on condition that the offender make good in any of a variety of ways the harm which he had caused — including compensation to the victim as well as charitable acts such as gifts to the poor or a pilgrimage to a holy shrine.

Thus, if one thinks only of the church's jurisdiction over the clergy, it is the "crime" side rather than the "sin" side of the canon law of crimes that is the more striking.

With respect to the other part of ecclesiastical criminal jurisdiction, that is, jurisdiction over the laity, the church as a matter of its own affirmative policy (and not as the result of any diffidence on its part) asserted only a restricted competence. Generally speaking, violence among the laity was to be controlled by secular criminal law; that, above all, was what the secular authority was for. Laymen were criminally liable in ecclesiastical courts only for acts falling roughly within the following categories: heresy, sacrilege, sorcery, witchcraft, usury, defamation, certain sexual and marital offenses (homosexuality, adultery, and others), desecration of religious places by theft or otherwise, and assaults upon clerics. In other words, the church insisted on its competence over certain types of crimes of laymen involving strong moral and ideological elements and (usually) no violence, as well as violent crimes against church property and clergy. Once again, the element of sinfulness in the offense was a very important basis for the church's claim to jurisdiction over it.

Also with regard to the laity, the ecclesiastical sanctions were more moral and economic than physical: alms, amends, fasting, good works, and ultimately excommunication, as well as excommunication suspended on condition that the offender compensate victims, perform charitable acts or works of piety, and so on. Indeed, the principle of reparation led the canon law to make some compromises with the principle of sinfulness: a financial liability was sometimes imposed upon innocent third parties related to the guilty ones—heirs, families, corporations, and associations—especially in cases where economic interests of the church had been criminally infringed.

The Western law of crimes emerged from a belief that justice in and of itself, justice *an sich*, requires that a violation of a law be paid for by a penalty, and that the penalty should be appropriate to the violation. The system of various prices to be paid for various violations—which exists in all societies—was thought to justify itself; it was justice—it was the very justice of God. This idea was reflected not only in criminal law but in all branches of the new canon law from the twelfth century on, and it was reflected more and more in the various branches of the new secular legal systems that began to develop contemporaneously. Contracts, it was said, must be kept, and if they were not, a price must be paid for their breach. Torts must be remedied by damages equivalent to the injury. Property rights must be restored by those who had violated them. These and similar principles became so deeply embedded in the consciousness—indeed, in the sacred values—of Western society that it became hard to imagine a legal order founded on different kinds of principles and values. Yet contemporary non-Western cultures do have legal orders founded on different kinds of principles and values, and so did European culture prior to the eleventh and twelfth centuries. In some legal orders, ideas of fate and honor prevail, of vengeance and reconciliation. In others, ideas of covenant and community dominate; in still others, ideas of deterrence and rehabilitation.

Western concepts of law are in their origins, and therefore in their nature, intimately bound up with distinctively Western theological and liturgical concepts of the atonement and of the sacraments. The new church holiday, All Souls' Day, introduced in the eleventh century, symbolized Western man's vision of the Last Judgment as a universal "Law Day," when all souls that have ever lived are to come before Christ the Judge to account for their sins and to be eternally convicted or acquitted. On this foundation, there was built a new conception of purgatory: baptized Christians who had died penitent could be assured that their natural propensity to sin was already forgiven, and that their actual sins would be fully expiated by proportional punishment in this life and the next, prior to the final day. Christ, in this conception, was no longer seen primarily as the Judge but as the divine Brother whose sacrifice on the cross served to reconcile God and man. The new emphasis on atonement was linked, in turn, with a new symbolism in the celebration of the sacrament of the eucharist: the performance of certain acts and the utterance of certain words by the priest were considered to effectuate the transformation of the bread into the spiritual body of Christ. Thus the atonement, with its paradoxical consequence of divine forgiveness and divine punishment, was repeatedly reenacted and incorporated in the lives of the faithful. With divine justice so understood, it seemed to be a natural step to create a parallel concept of human justice. As God rules through law, so ecclesiastical and secular authorities, ordained by him, declare legal principles and impose appropriate sanction and remedies for their violation. They cannot look directly into men's souls, as God can, but they can find ways to approximate his judgment.

Yet the foregoing analysis is subject to an important qualification. The steps in the derivation of Western jurisprudence from the theology of the eleventh and twelfth centuries were not so natural as they may have seemed to those who took them. The movement from Anselm to Abelard to Gratian was at every stage a product not of reason alone but of the tension between reason and faith, the scientific and the mystical, the legal and the visionary. Anselm's own faith in reason was accompanied by a profound piety and a poetic awareness of grace. He said that reason would only prove what faith already knew, and that his analysis "by reason alone" was intended for intellectual "delight." Similarly, Abelard the skeptical scholastic was at the same time Abelard the devout believer as well as the passionate lover and popular love-song writer of Europe. Gratian's great legal treatise was itself filled with the most imaginative mythological devices for reconciling the irreconcilable — for the sake of justice and the greater glory of God.

When one thinks of the twelfth century as the great century of the construction of legal institutions and legal concepts, one must think also of
St. Bernard of Clairvaux, archenemy of Abelard, whose saintliness was
as renowned throughout Western Christendom as Abelard's adventures
were notorious. In 1129 at the council of Reims, presided over by Pope
Innocent II, Bernard denounced the study of Roman law — the only kind
of law then being studied systematically, since Gratian's treatise (which
introduced canon law into the university curriculum) was still a decade
away — and the council prohibited monks from studying it. (Although
this prohibition was repeated at the Council of Clermont in 1130 and the
Council of Tours in 1163, Roman law continued to be widely taught to
nonmonks and even to some monks.) Bernard also denounced the
legalism of the papal court and called for a return to spirituality. Modern
Eastern Orthodox theologians regard Bernard as having been an ally at
a time when the predominant voices in Western theology were hostile to
their beliefs.

One cannot understand Abelard without Bernard, or Bernard without
Abelard. Nor can one understand the fundamental change in theology
and in jurisprudence which took place in the West in the late eleventh
and the twelfth centuries without recognizing that it took part of its
character from the more mystical and romantic tendencies of the age.
These tendencies were symbolized not only by the lives and teachings of
men such as St. Bernard but also by the cult of the Virgin Mary (who,
above all, would intercede with the Supreme Judge, for mercy's sake, in
behalf of sinners)[52] and by the rise of chivalry and courtly love.[53] In the
law itself, mercy asserted itself as a principle under the Graeco-Roman
name *aequitas* ("equity"). In "canonical equity" the rigor of the strict law
was to be mitigated in exceptional cases where good faith, honesty, conscience, or mercy so required.[54]

The struggle and tension between rational, scientific, and formalist attitudes, on the one hand, and mystical, poetic, and charismatic attitudes, on the other, help to explain why it took three generations for
the new jurisprudence to establish itself and centuries more for it to run
its course, and why ultimately it was in turn challenged by subsequent
revolutions.

Behind these competing attitudes there stood the revolutionary subdivision of Western society into two political realms, the ecclesiastical and
the secular, and the further subdivision of the secular realm into royal,
feudal, urban, and other polities. The belief in a God of justice who
operates a lawful universe, punishing and rewarding according to principles of proportion, mercifully mitigated in exceptional cases, corresponded to the belief in a complex social unity, Christendom, in which
the dialectic of interacting realms and polities was regulated by a similar
kind of justice-based-on-law and law-based-on-justice, with mercy play-

ing an exceptional role. Moreover, behind the complex dialectical unity in space stood a historical dialectic in time — a revolutionary break between ancient and modern and an evolutionary development of the modern. As each man moved through this life into purgatory, and through purgatory to the Last Judgment, reaping the rewards and punishments of his choices between good and evil, so the various communities in which he lived moved through time toward the fulfillment of their respective destinies. And their movement, too, was responsive to law. This, indeed, was the fundamental concept of the Western legal tradition to which the theological metaphors and analogies gave birth — the concept of a society that has the power to transform itself in time by the rapid and continuous infusion of divine and natural law into ecclesiastical and secular legal institutions.

In the sixteenth century and thereafter, the legalism of the Roman Catholic Church was subjected to sharp attack by various forms of Protestantism. Martin Luther denounced the concept of a visible corporate church united by law; he burned the books of canon law, partly in order to symbolize his belief that the true church can have no legal character whatever, that it is an invisible communion of the faithful.

Nevertheless, Luther also had a passionate belief in the value of law, that is, the secular law of the Prince, the law of the State, which he simply assumed would be the law of a Christian Prince. Thus the Roman Catholic belief in the infusion of divine and natural law into legal institutions was carried on by Lutheranism, but only into secular legal institutions and not into ecclesiastical. The church henceforth appeared as a purely spiritual community coextensive with a particular secular order, whereas between the eleventh and fifteenth centuries many secular orders had coexisted and interacted within the *una sancta ecclesia*. Yet for Protestantism, in both its Lutheran and Calvinist forms, God remained a God of justice, and the body of ecclesiastical and secular law of "medieval" Europe (as it came to be called in the sixteenth century) was to a large extent carried over into the law of the "modern " state.

With the transfer of the principal lawmaking and law-enforcing functions to the sole jurisdictions of the national state, the foundation was laid for the separation of jurisprudence from theology and ultimately for the complete secularization of legal thought. This did not occur at once, since the predominant system of beliefs throughout the West remained Christian. It is only in the twentieth century that the Christian foundations of Western law have been almost totally rejected.

This twentieth-century development is a historical consequence of the Western belief, of which St. Anselm was the first exponent, that theology itself may be studied independently of revelation. Anselm had no intention of exalting reason at the expense of faith. Yet once reason was separated from faith for analytical purposes, the two began to be separated for other purposes as well. It was eventually taken for granted that reason is capable of functioning by itself, and ultimately this came to mean functioning without any fundamental religious beliefs whatever.

By the same token, it was eventually taken for granted that law, as a product of reason, is capable of functioning as an instrument of secular power, disconnected from ultimate values and purposes; and not only religious faith but all passionate convictions came to be considered the private affair of each individual. Thus not only legal thought but also the very structure of Western legal institutions have been removed from their spiritual foundations, and those foundations, in turn, are left devoid of the structure that once stood upon them.

5 | Canon Law: The First Modern Western Legal System

T
O ASSERT THAT a *system* of canon law was created—or, to put it another way, that the law of the church became systematized—for the first time in the century and a half between 1050 and 1200 is not to deny that a legal *order* had existed in the church from its early beginnings. The New Testament itself, especially in the Epistles of St. Paul and the Acts of the Apostles, gives evidence that there were within the Christian community legally constituted authorities that declared and applied rules concerning matters of doctrine, worship, morality, discipline, and ecclesiastical structure.[1] Also, from the earliest times, elders (bishops) had judged disputes between Christians and imposed sanctions for offenses committed by them. The first-century *Didache*, the third-century *Didascalia Apostolorum* (*Teachings of the Apostles*), and the fourth-century *Constitutiones Apostolorum* (*Enactments of the Apostles*) contained many ecclesiastical rules intended to regulate conduct and to serve as a basis of ecclesiastical adjudication.[2] Also in the third and fourth centuries, local ecclesiastical councils (synods) in North Africa and in Arles issued laws, and in 325 the first general (ecumenical) council met at Nicaea and adopted many laws.[3] At that time the Greek word *kanon*, which meant originally a straight rod, then a measuring stick, and eventually a rule or norm, began to acquire the technical legal meaning of a law promulgated either by a synod or by an ecumenical council or even by an individual bishop. ("Canon" came to be used also to designate the authentic, or "canonical," list of books composing the Holy Scriptures as well as persons lawfully accepted, or "canonized," as saints. Still another meaning refers to the "canons"—of a cathedral chapter authorized by the local bishop to serve as ministers.)

Over the centuries the canons issued by synods and ecumenical councils, as well as by individual bishops, multiplied, and occasionally they were brought together in unofficial collections, which also contained rules laid down in Scripture and in the writings of the church fathers as well as individual decretal letters and decisions of patriarchs, popes, and bishops, together with rescripts and enactments of Roman emperors and other rulers concerning the church.[4] None of these collections reflected the existence of a self-conscious legal system. None of them purported to be complete or universal. In the earlier compilations the contents were arranged chronologically; eventually some were loosely arranged under various subject headings, including some of a legal nature. They all combined legal rules with moral injunctions, theological doctrines, and liturgical formulas. Nevertheless there were many rules, whether or not included under legal headings, that concerned legal matters, such as (1) church finances and property—for example, tithes, charitable bequests, rights of possession, use, and disposition of church lands and buildings; (2) ecclesiastical authority—for example, powers of appointment to church offices, procedures for settlement of disputes among clergy, disciplinary sanctions; (3) relations between ecclesiastical and secular authorities—for example, exemption of clergy from trial by secular courts in certain types of cases; (4) crime—for example, lists of penances to be imposed for various kinds of offenses, including homicides and perjury; and (5) marriage and family relationships—for example, marriage impediments, legitimacy of children, dissolution of the matrimonial bond.

These ecclesiastical laws, both in the West and in the East, were heavily influenced by Roman law. Various concepts and rules of classical and postclassical Roman law were carried over, especially in matters of property, inheritance, and contracts. In addition, the compilations of Justinian and his successors in the East contained a great many imperial regulations concerning liturgy and theology as well as ecclesiastical authority.[5] In the West also, ecclesiastical regulations were issued frequently by kings and emperors; indeed, the Frankish emperors claimed to inherit the mantle of Roman imperial authority over the church. Moreover, in the clan-dominated culture of western Europe the church was considered to be a bearer of Roman law, and the eighth-century "code" of the Ripuarian Franks, the Lex Ribuaria, contained the provision: *Ecclesia vivit jure Romano* ("the church lives by Roman law"). This meant that to the extent each person carried the law of his clan with him, and was to be judged according to it wherever he went, the church was deemed to carry with it the Roman law.

In addition, the laws of the church during the first millennium of its history bore the strong influence of the Bible, especially the Old Testament. From the Bible the church derived the authority of the Ten Commandments and of many other moral principles formulated as divine commands. Beyond that, the Bible transmitted the pervasive belief in a universal order governed by the God who was both supreme legislator and supreme judge. As heir to the tradition of Israel, the church took seriously the numinous character of law, its pervasiveness in the divine order of creation. Moreover, many specific rules of conduct contained in the Old and New Testaments, as well as many Biblical examples and metaphors, were carried over into ecclesiastical canons.

Of course, the legal concepts and rules that prevailed in the church in the West from the fifth to the tenth centuries were influenced not only by Roman law and Biblical law but also, and especially, by the folklaw of the Germanic peoples, with its emphasis on honor, oaths, retribution, reconciliation, and group responsibility.

The existence, prior to the eleventh century, of a great many ecclesiastical laws, governing a wide variety of relationships both within the church and between the church and the secular authorities, has led many scholars to doubt the thesis of Rudolph Sohm, the great German legal historian, that the "old Catholic" church law, as he called it, was essentially sacramental, spiritual, and theological in nature, and that only after Gratian's treatise did canon law become truly "legal" in the modern sense.[6] Sohm said that prior to the twelfth century the church was essentially a spiritual or sacramental community, not a legal community. Yet, as Stephan Kuttner has pointed out, the "interlacing of the 'spiritual' and the 'material,' corporative side of the Church is as old as the Church herself and . . . is grounded in the dual nature of the Church as a spiritual communion and as a corporate society at the same time . . . When Sohm failed to see the operation of the 'legal' element in the earlier canon law, this is due in part to his denial of the basic dualism, i.e., of the existence of a sacramental and a jurisdictional element in the law of the primitive and the ancient church."[7]

Despite these qualifications, what is true and important in Sohm's thesis can perhaps be rescued. It is generally recognized that prior to the late eleventh century the material and corporative sides of the church were fused, to a much greater extent than they were later, with its spiritual and sacramental sides. Professor Kuttner would perhaps agree that the "basic dualism" of which he speaks, which became so prominent in the century after the reign of Pope Gregory VII, was not *felt* to be basic in the earlier period—at least not to nearly the same degree. Distinctions between the sacred and the profane were much less pronounced. The jurisdictional element of the church's law was viewed as an integral part of the sacramental element, which embraced not only such liturgical events as baptism, marriage, and ordination but also an undefined variety of moral and spiritual acts and rites. This was connected with the high degree of heterogeneity and the intensely local character of the churches in pre-Gregorian Christendom.

More particularly, the "interlacing" (to use Kuttner's term) of ecclesiastical law with liturgy and theology was so strong that it apparently did not occur to anyone to separate out the legal aspects and to transform them into a system. Indeed, in the collections of ecclesiastical laws that were compiled prior to the late eleventh century, legal rules were wholly mixed up with rules (and nonrules) concerning worship and faith. The term "canon law" (*jus canonicum*) was not regularly used before the twelfth century, and the phrase *jus ecclesiasticum* was applied to that part of imperial or royal or feudal law that governed ecclesiastical relations. There were ecclesiastical *laws*, a legal *order* within the church, but no *system* of ecclesiastical *law*, that is, no independent, integrated, developing body of ecclesiastical legal principles and procedures, clearly differentiated from liturgy and theology.

The systematization of the laws of the church in the late eleventh and the twelfth centuries was closely related to the Papal Revolution in all its aspects. As early as 1050, at the very start of the reform movement, a collection of canons and other texts, the *Collection of 74 Titles*, was published, which went back to decretals of early popes and Roman councils to give a legal basis for papal supremacy over the church and for ecclesiastical independence from secular authority. This was followed by other similar collections — of Anselm of Lucca, Cardinal Deusdedit, and other leading reformers. In the period after the death of Pope Gregory VII and before Gratian many new collections appeared. In the 1090s the works of Ivo of Chartres represented the first effort to portray the whole law of the church in a coherent form — a *Pannormia* ("all law") as he called it. This great burst of legal scholarship testifies not only to the emergence of a cohesive group of canon lawyers but also to the importance attached to canon law by the leaders of the Papal Revolution. This development was closely connected with the proclamation by the papacy of its right to legislate. Gregory VII asserted for the first time the power of the pope to "create new laws in accordance with the needs of the times."[8] The new laws, called decretals, issued by him and his successors were not viewed simply as incremental additions to the preexisting canons but as something new. Thus a revolutionary periodization was introduced into the history of ecclesiastical law, and it became possible to summarize the laws on the basis of that periodization. This summarizing movement culminated in 1140 in the great treatise of Gratian, which was immediately recognized as both a definitive summary of what was called the *jus antiquum* and an integration of it with what was called the *jus novum*. The phrases "old law" and "new law," which are usually attributed to the period just after Gratian, were actually implicit in his division of the legal sources of canon law into two groups, the (old) conciliar canons and the (new) papal decretals. Gratian's pupil Huguccio developed the doctrine that "a decretal prevails over a canon," since the pope promulgates decretals "from certain knowledge, according to law."[9] Thus the system of canon law, as conceived by Gratian, rested on the premise that a body of law is not a dead corpse but a living corpus, rooted in the past but growing into the future. Contrary to what is sometimes supposed, this concept of legal evolution was not an invention of Edmund Burke, Friedrich von Savigny, and the "historical school" of the eighteenth and nineteenth centuries;[10] it was a basic presupposition of Western jurists—and nonjurists—from the late eleventh and the twelfth centuries on, first in the ecclesiastical sphere and then in the secular.

These interrelated elements—(1) the periodization into old law and new law, (2) the summarization and integration of the two as a unified structure, and (3) the conception of the whole body of law as moving forward in time, in an ongoing process—are defining features of the Western legal tradition.

Gratian's book, which was viewed as part of the ongoing process of the law itself, received almost immediate recognition as an authoritative statement of the canon law. Besides taking a place alongside the Roman law texts as a principal object of study in the European law schools, it was cited as authoritative by popes, church councils, and ecclesiastical courts. Being relatively loosely organized and open-textured, it was designed to be glossed and summarized; and glosses, commentaries, treatises, and monographs on it soon appeared in abundance.

On the foundation provided by Gratian's work it was possible to build an edifice not only of scholarly glosses and summaries but also of judicial decisions and legislation. Pope Alexander III (1159-1181), himself a famous jurist (under the name Rolandus Bandinelli) and a former pupil of Gratian, issued seven hundred decretals which have been preserved, in addition to others which have not been preserved. Many of these were, in effect, holdings in decided cases, that is, rules of law which were the necessary implication of the decisions. Pope Alexander III summoned the Third Lateran Council in 1179, and Pope Innocent III, an equally distinguished jurist, summoned the Fourth Lateran Council in 1215; from these councils there emerged hundreds of new laws. (The councils were held in the Lateran Palace in Rome, which was also used as the cathedral church.) In the last decade of the twelfth and the first decades of the thirteenth century five major systematic compilations of decretals were prepared. Finally, in 1234 under Pope Gregory IX there appeared a comprehensive collection of decretals, containing about two thousand sections, which summarized and systematized the work of almost a century; together with Gratian's *Decretum*, the *Decretals* of Gregory IX remained the basic corpus of the canon law of the Roman Catholic Church until the adoption of the *Code of Canon Law* of 1918.[11]

These compilations were glossed, commented upon, and summarized by legal scholars; indeed, the popes officially issued the compilations directly to the universities. In these aspects, too—the close relationship between legal scholarship and legal practice, and the dialectical character of legal scholarship manifested in the glossing and summarizing of authoritative texts — the new developing system of canon law exerted a formative influence on Western concepts of the nature of a legal system.

The systematization of canon law was not, however, merely an intellectual matter. The tensions between the old and the new, the whole and the parts, or theory and practice could not have been harmonized by books and lectures alone, although legal science played an extremely important role in the harmonizing process. Nor could theology alone, or theology and jurisprudence together, have maintained the integrity of the legal system. It was necessary also that harmonizing elements be built into the positive law itself.

The Relation of Canon Law to Roman Law

It is sometimes said that the new system of canon law was an "offspring" of the Roman law of Justinian,[12] and that "the great codifications that make up the *Corpus Juris Canonici* were patterned on those that make up the *Corpus Juris Civilis*."[13] At the very least, such statements require the modification that it was not the Roman law of sixth-century Byzantium, but the revivified and transformed *Romanist* law of eleventh- and twelfth-century Christendom, to which the parentage of canon law must be traced. Yet even with this modification, the idea that canon law was somehow modeled on Roman law involves serious misconceptions. The canonists used Roman law abundantly — as Roman law was understood in their time — just as they used Biblical law, and just as they used Germanic law; they used them all as sources. Thus one may speak, in a qualified sense, of the "romano-canonical" legal system. Also the canonists shared with the Romanists of their day the same basic theories concerning the nature and functions of law and the same basic methods of analysis and synthesis of opposites — theories and methods which were as much borrowed from them by the Romanists as by them from the Romanists. Indeed, not only theories and methods but also many specific legal concepts and institutions were taken over into contemporary Roman legal science from the new science of canon law.[14]

The comparison of Roman law and canon law in the late eleventh, the twelfth, and the thirteenth centuries is confounded by the fact that canon law was the positive law of the church, while Roman law was not the positive law of any specific polity in the West. Roman law was, of course, the positive law of the Roman Empire in Byzantium; but that was not Roman law as the Western Romanists understood it — it was not the *corpus juris Romani*. In the West, Justinian's Roman law was considered to be an ideal law, a written embodiment of reason, *ratio scripta*, whose principles ought to govern all legal regulation everywhere, both in the church and in the secular polities. Jurists turned to Justinian's texts as they turned to the Mosaic law and as they later turned to Aristotle, as sources of positive law. It is true that from the time of Charlemagne, Western emperors claimed succession to the authority of the ancient Roman emperors; and with the discovery of the Justinian texts, the Western emperors relied upon them—as did the popes—for support. But the "Holy Roman Empire of the German Nation"[15] was governed by the laws laid down by Western emperors, which were superimposed on tribal (clan), local, feudal, urban, mercantile, ecclesiastical, and other particular laws. Rules and concepts and institutions of Roman law only became the positive law of the Western Empire, just as they only became the positive law of the Western Church, if they were expressly incorporated into that positive law by legislation or juristic interpretation. Roman law was called "a handmaiden of canon law": it could equally have been called a handmaiden of imperial law and a handmaiden of the positive law of the emerging secular kingdoms and city-states. It was, however, always a handmaiden; those scholars err who suppose that Western jurists believed that the Eastern Roman Empire of Justinian somehow continued to exist in the West as a political reality.[16]

Perhaps the most significant difference between Roman law and canon law in the West was the fact that Roman law, with certain rare exceptions, was treated as finished, immutable, to be reinterpreted but not to be changed.[17] Canon law, by contrast, although also handed down from the past, was not finished, it was continually being remade. It had a quality of organic development, of conscious growth over generations and centuries. This gave it a somewhat disorderly character, which has perhaps made it less appealing than Roman law as an intellectual discipline,[18] but surely more interesting from both a moral and a political point of view. For its "disorderliness" as a science was a necessary part of its dynamic quality as a system—its movement from past to future. The existence of such a time dimension is an essential attribute of modern Western legal systems.

Constitutional Foundations of the Canon Law System

The harmonizing, or structural, elements of the canon law, which helped to make it an independent, integrated, developing system, were derived in part from the constitution of the church, as that constitution was understood in the late eleventh and the twelfth centuries. The word "constitution" is used here, in its modern sense, to refer to the location and limits of sovereignty, the process of selection of rulers, the allocation of legislative, administrative, and judicial powers, the scope of governmental authority, and the basic rights and duties of subjects. This usage may seem anachronistic, since the church not only lacked a formal constitution in the eleventh and twelfth centuries, but it also had not yet systematized its constitutional law. The nearest the canonists of that time came to creating a subsystem of constitutional law within the body of canon law was their development of a law of corporations and their application of corporation law to the ecclesiastical polity. Nevertheless, certain fundamental constitutional principles were generally recognized, and these underlay the new system of canon law as a whole.

Building on the Gregorian Reform, and especially on Gregory's *Dictates* of 1075, the canonists of the late twelfth and the thirteenth centuries attributed supreme governance (*imperium*) in the church to the pope. The pope was head of the church; all other Christians were its limbs, its members. He had full authority (*plenitudo auctoritatis*) and full power (*plenitudo potestatis*).[19] Although in practice his powers were limited — they increased only gradually, especially in the thirteenth and fourteenth centuries — nevertheless, in law, from the time of Gregory VII, the pope was the supreme legislator, the supreme administrator, the supreme judge. He could make laws, impose taxes, punish crimes. He could establish and suppress bishoprics. He could dispose of ecclesiastical benefices and had final authority with respect to the acquisition, administration, and alienation of all church property. All actions and decisions of church officers or bodies — for example, decisions of ecclesiastical courts or disputed elections of bishops — could be appealed to him. In addition, he was a universal judge of first instance; any Christian could resort to him in any matter requiring judicial resolution, and he had sole cognizance of so-called major causes, such as cases involving the deposition of bishops or the determination of disputed articles of faith. He had supreme authority to excommunicate those who were recalcitrant. He alone could summon a general council, and its decisions took effect only after he confirmed them. Finally, he was the supreme teacher in the church, having a decisive voice in the definition of ecclesiastical dogmas and the determination of the rules of the liturgy and other matters of worship. Also in the twelfth century the pope acquired the sole power to canonize saints.

These powers did not attach to the pope because he was the Bishop of Rome, but they attached to the Bishop of Rome because he was pope; that is, they attached to him not by virtue of his ordination (*potestate ordinis*) but by virtue of his jurisdiction (*potestate jurisdictionis*). Indeed, the Archdeacon Hildebrand was elected Pope Gregory VII even though he had not yet been ordained a priest, let alone a bishop. Once he was pope, his opinions in matters that came before him *as pope* were to be preferred, in Gratian's phrase, to those of such revered theologians as St. Augustine and St. Jerome. But, Gratian added, in matters concerning the interpretation of Scripture, the opinions of St. Augustine or St. Jerome were to be preferred to those of the pope. After all, said Gratian, the pope might be a heretic.[20] His power to decide doctrinal disputes derived not from superior spiritual qualities but solely from his jurisdiction as supreme officer of the church.[21]

The sharp distinction between ordination and jurisdiction, made for the first time in the late eleventh and the twelfth centuries, was one of the fundamental constitutional principles of the Church of Rome. Ordination was a sacrament, that is, a sacred symbol of divine grace. By ordination every priest received from God the authority to say mass, to celebrate the eucharist, to hear confessions and administer penance, and to perform other sacramental and priestly rites; a bishop, by virtue of ordination, could also ordain priests and consecrate other bishops. Jurisdiction, on the contrary, was a power conferred by the church as a corporate legal entity. It was the power to govern by law—to "speak law" (*jus dicere*) within the limits established by law. By virtue of jurisdiction every bishop held supreme legislative, administrative, and judicial authority within his diocese, subject to the pope, just as the pope, by virtue of jurisdiction, held supreme legislative, administrative, and judicial authority within the church as a whole. Such authority, derived from jurisdiction, could be exercised by anyone to whom it had been lawfully delegated. The pope could appoint a deacon, for example, to sit as a judge in a dispute between two bishops. This power had not existed before the Papal Revolution.

Thus the *imperium* and the *auctoritas* or *potestas* of the pope, though supreme and full, were identified also as his *jurisdictio*, which meant that they were legal in nature. But that, in turn, meant that there were legal limits to their exercise.

Those legal limits were implicit in the mode of selection of the pope as well as of the subordinate bishops, abbots, and other ecclesiastical officers. Before the Papal Revolution the appointment of popes, bishops, and abbots had been substantially controlled by emperors, kings, princes, or feudal lords. One of the first events leading to the Papal Revolution was the decree of a church council at Rome, called by Pope Nicolas II in 1059, conferring on the cardinals of Rome—bishops and priests of neighboring dioceses, who also performed some liturgical and other functions in the great basilicas in Rome—the principal role in selecting a pope.[22] A century later a decree of Alexander III gave the cardinals sole power to choose a new pope, and in 1179 the Third Lateran Council made the number of required votes a two-thirds majority. (Under the decree of Nicholas II, a simple majority had sufficed, but it was a qualified majority, that is, a majority of "the greater and sounder part" of the electors.) Once elected, the pope ruled for life (unless he resigned, as one pope did); but when there was a vacancy, not only politics but also law played a significant part in the choice of a successor, and this undoubtedly contributed to the concept of papal responsibility to the church. Papal elections were often hotly contested.

Sometimes there were rival popes. In fact, in all but 82 of the 278 years from 1100 to 1378, legitimate popes were forced to live outside the city of Rome.[23]

The cardinals were, to be sure, appointed by the pope; nevertheless, in the course of time they acquired some independence. They governed the church during an interregnum in the papacy. Great offices in the church were reserved to them. It became a matter of customary law for the pope to obtain their consent, as a body, to the creation of new bishoprics, the transfer of a bishop from one see to another, and the appointment of abbots, as well as various other important matters. At times, tension became acute as the College of Cardinals sought to extend its powers and popes resisted such attempts.[24]

As the pope was elected by the cardinals, so a bishop was elected by the chapter of the cathedral, that is, by the canons and other clergy who lived and worked in the capital of the diocese; and an abbot was elected by the monks of the monastery. That the pope could hear appeals in behalf of losing candidates in disputed elections of bishops and abbots is an indication of papal control. Yet in theory, at least, only if the electors had been negligent or if there had been a divided election or if for some other reason the proper procedure had been violated, could the pope take action. And in practice the priests of the cathedral chapter, or the monks of the abbey, generally played an important part. If their will was flouted they could make a great deal of trouble. Here, too, the electoral principle—prior to its gradual decline and virtual disappearance in the fourteenth and fifteenth centuries—helped to preserve the constitutional character of the papal monarchy and of the hierarchical chain of authority.

Not only the electoral principle and the necessity to accommodate the cardinals, bishops, and clergy generally but also the very complexity of the ecclesiastical system of government served as a substantial limitation upon papal absolutism. Although legislation was their sole prerogative, popes in the twelfth and thirteenth centuries nevertheless felt the need to summon general councils periodically to assist them in the lawmaking process. These were Europe's first legislatures. Similarly with respect to administration, the papacy developed a highly efficient bureaucracy of specialists in various fields (see figure 1). The papal chancery was in charge of drafting and issuing documents, including writs initiating judicial cases, and of keeping records of decrees, regulations, and decisions of the papal government; the chancellor was the keeper of the papal seal. The papal exchequer, called the Apostolic Chamber, operated both as a treasury for papal revenues and as a ministry of finance; in addition, the chamber had its own court for civil and criminal cases connected with taxation and other financial affairs. The papal court of general jurisdiction, both original and appellate, was called, in the twelfth century, the consistory; the pope himself presided over it. As papal jurisdiction expanded, the popes began to appoint judicial auditors (cardinals, bishops, or simple chaplains), whose decisions were binding, subject to papal ratification. In the thirteenth century the auditors became a permanent court, called the Audience of the Holy Palace, which deliberated as a body (often divided into sections), and at the end of that century a separate court of appeals was established for civil and criminal cases. (In the fourteenth century a supreme court was established, eventually named the Rota.) In addition, the papal household had a "penitentiary," which heard cases in the "internal" forum, that is, cases of sins to be dealt with not as criminal or civil offenses but by way of confession and penance. The Grand Penitentiary heard appeals from penances administered by bishops, and he administered censures and absolutions reserved to the pope.

The papal government also operated, at the regional and local level, through papal legates as well as through other appointees and subordinates. From early times popes had occasionally appointed delegates to act in their behalf, but it was only after the Papal Revolution that such delegates became a regular instrument of papal government.[25] There were three kinds: the proctorial legate, who was sent out to a locality or region with "full right" to act in place of the pope, under either a general or a special mandate; the judge-delegate, who exercised the judicial power of the papacy in particular cases; and the nuncio, who until the sixteenth century had only a limited capacity to represent the pope, for example, to transmit messages, gather information, or negotiate and conclude agreements on particular matters. Of these, the proctorial legate was the most powerful; he was sometimes authorized to preside over bishops in council and to bring sentences of deposition against them. However, decisions of all these types of papal legates were subject to appeal to the pope himself.

Popes also exercised authority through other officers, especially papal collectors (of revenues) and papal bankers (who raised loans).

Moreover, archbishops and bishops, as well as heads of the major religious orders and of those individual monasteries that came directly under papal authority, were also in one sense the pope's officers. From the end of the eleventh century on, they were required at installation to swear an oath of loyalty to the pope. His approval was necessary for their appointment, and all their decisions were subject to his review.

Yet bishops were more than the pope's officers, both in theory and in practice. Each was also supreme on his own level of authority. Even after the Papal Revolution, every bishop remained the supreme judge, legislator, and administrator in his own diocese—unless the pope intervened. Therefore, it is only half the truth to say that the pope ruled the whole church through a corps of bishops; the other half of the truth is

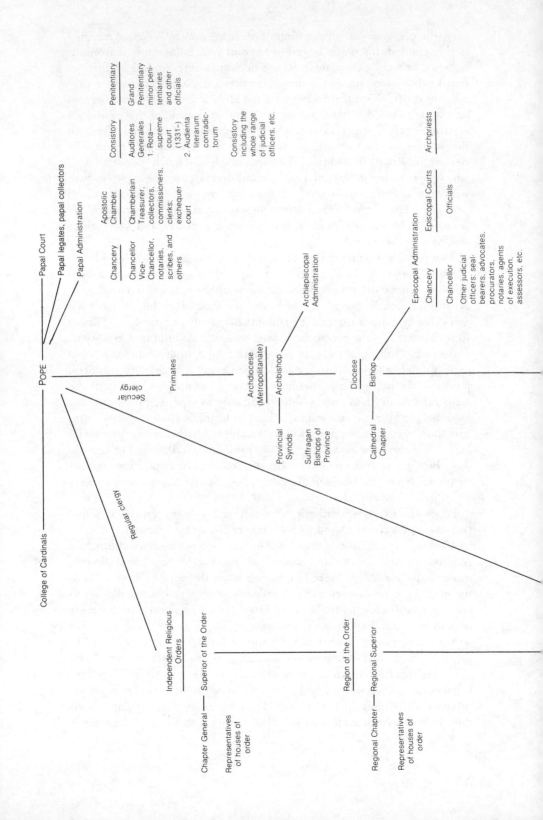

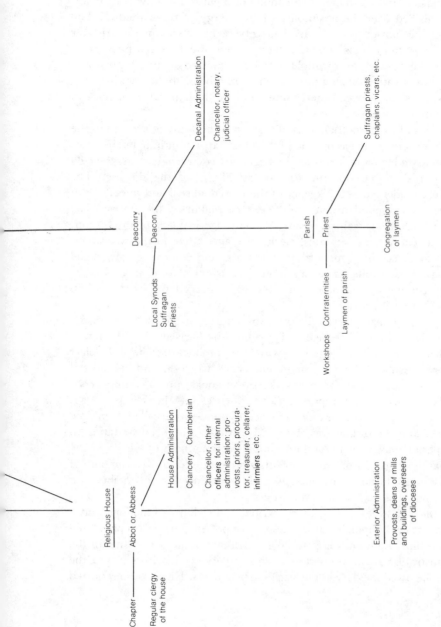

Figure 1. Structure of the Western church state, 1100-1500. Levels of authority and religious life are marked by a horizontal line, with the institution named above and the head named below.

Note: Institutions of representation or consent are shown at the left of the head of the authority level. Institutions of administration are shown at the right of the head of the level. The membership of an institution is generally given beneath the name of the institution.

that the bishops ruled their respective dioceses subject to the pope. They too had imperium, auctoritas, and potestas jurisdictionis—though not of the same plenitude. The pope had to reckon with them; he could not merely order them about.

At the same time, the bishop was surrounded in his diocese by various functionaries, who in practice wielded considerable countervailing power. The canons of the cathedral chapter elected the bishop just as the cardinals elected the pope. The canons also elected a provost or dean, who presided over the assemblies of the clergy of the cathedral. The chapter had power to try its own members, before its own courts, for disciplinary infractions. The chapter's consent was required for various acts by the bishop—for example, for the alienation of church property. Privileges of cathedral chapters varied from diocese to diocese; in many places, tensions between the chapter and the bishop led to appeals to Rome by one side or the other.

Officers of the bishop's household began to multiply at the end of the eleventh century, just as officers of the papal curia multiplied. The archdeacon assumed more power as chief executive officer; generally selected by the bishop, he ran the day-to-day affairs of the diocese. The chancellor emerged as the keeper of the episcopal seal and the officer in charge of correspondence and of the external affairs of the diocese. The "official" (*officialis*), trained in law, sat as judge in place of the bishop. Judicial seal-bearers, notaries, clerks of court, advocates, procurators, agents for executing court orders, assessors, and other types of judicial or quasi-judicial officers emerged in the bishop's court, just as archpriests, coadjutors, and other types of clergy emerged to assist the bishop in his liturgical functions.

As the pope had intermediate agents for ruling the dioceses, so the bishops had intermediate agents for ruling the parishes. For the larger parishes, the bishop (together with the archdeacon) would select deacons, each with his own small chancery, his clerk, and his judicial officer, to supervise the property, keep the books, provide support for priests in need, and report serious offenses of the clergy. Also, assemblies of priests of the diocese—local synods—were called from time to time, and the bishop was supposed to make an official visitation to each parish once a year. As the bishops swore an oath of fidelity to the pope at their ordination, so the priests were required to swear an oath of fidelity to the bishop. The bishops could also send nuncios to check up on the parishes and to transmit orders.

At the parish level, too, there existed a division of functions and a system of checks upon arbitrary exercise of power. The parish priest had responsibility both for the spiritual government of the parish and for the administration of its property. To his superiors—his bishop and the pope—he owed the duty to pay ecclesiastical taxes. He was also required by canon law to maintain continuous residence in his parish. At the same time, especially in the larger parishes, the priest was surrounded by assistants, clerical and lay, whose needs and wishes he could not safely ignore. Suffragan priests helped him, especially in the conduct of the liturgy. Chaplains, who might be clergy or just simple parishioners, supervised charitable works in the parish and were often charged with the instruction of children. "Confraternities" of faithful Christians in the parish were dedicated to devotion, charity, and penitence; Le Bras calls them "cells of devout Christians . . . little parishes within the larger parish."[26] They generally held annual assemblies. There also originated in the twelfth century the practice of forming "workshops" (*fabricae*) of laymen to help administer the property of the parish; these were often resented by both the parish priest and the bishop.[27]

Thus, although all governmental powers within the church were gathered ultimately into the hands of the papacy, papal autocracy was limited by the division of functions within the bureaucracy at the top level as well as by the hierarchical, or pyramidal, character of ecclesiastical government as a whole. These limitations certainly fell short of the modern concepts of separation of powers and of federalism;[28] yet they constituted important checks on absolutism and at the very least fostered habits and traditions of government that popes were, for the most part, reluctant to abuse. A formal, legal, bureaucratic structure was created which was a complete innovation in Germanic Europe. Government was separated from personal loyalty of man to lord. Complex interorganizational relationships developed which were in striking contrast not only to tribal but also to feudal institutions, and even to the earlier imperial institutions, whether Byzantine or Frankish. The very complexity and specificity of the structure was a source of constitutional principles. "With a government as delicate and over-extended as that of the medieval Church, consensus was absolutely critical."[29]

Constitutionalism in ecclesiastical government was facilitated above all by the limitation upon the scope of ecclesiastical authority itself. These limitations were imposed in part by the theory of the dualism of ecclesiastical and secular authorities and in part by the practice of resistance by the secular authority to ecclesiastical abuses and excesses. It is true that some popes and some canon lawyers, especially in the thirteenth and early fourteenth centuries, made extravagant claims of unlimited ecclesiastical competence to legislate not only in matters of faith, doctrine, cult, sacraments, church offices, and clerical discipline but also in matters of contract, property, and crimes of all kinds, and even in matters of secular politics. Yet on the whole the church, after the Concordat of Worms of 1122, came to accept in theory as well as in practice substantial limitations upon the scope of its authority. The very separation of ecclesiastical and secular authority was a constitutional principle of the first magnitude, which permeated the entire system of canon law.

In addition, within the church itself, viewed as a polity separate from secular polities, there were theoretical as well as practical limitations upon arbitrariness, whether of the papacy or of the episcopal princes. In the first place, it was accepted that the church as a visible institution had been founded by Christ himself, and that he and the apostles, and later the church fathers and the ecumenical councils of the first seven centuries, had endowed it with definite, unchangeable norms of belief and of conduct. Even at the height of papal power a standard canonist gloss stated that "it would be dangerous to commit our faith to the will of a single man."[30] It was understood that neither a pope nor a general council could change the dogma of the church or introduce a new dogma at will. "New teachings were to be tested against existing dogma, but beyond that, only such doctrines were to be declared which were already implicit in the existing treasury of teachings of the Church and which presented themselves as an organic development of the existing foundation of beliefs."[31]

More concretely, popes and general councils as well as bishops and local councils were specifically limited in the scope of their authority by both divine law and natural law. It is true that no one was authorized to reverse or overrule a papal decree that violated divine law or natural law. The only recourse was to political action, or else to civil disobedience. Nevertheless, the canon lawyers laid a legal foundation for such resistance. Gratian wrote that "a pope can be judged by no one, unless he is caught deviating from the faith."[32] This left the way open, as Brian Tierney has said, for a theory of deposition of a pope on grounds of heresy.[33] Later canonists added other grounds, including dissipation of church property, and at the end of the twelfth century the theory was developed by Huguccio that a pope could be tried and deposed for any notorious fornication, robbery, sacrilege, or other notorious crime that gave scandal to the church.[34]

Further, it was said by canonists of the twelfth and thirteenth centuries that the pope might not act contrary to the "state" (*status*) of the whole church, and that he might not enact a law to the prejudice of its "general state" (*generalis status ecclesiae*), that is, its character, its general welfare or public order, or, as it would be called in later centuries, its constitution.[35] Even Pope Innocent IV (1243-1254), one of the most authoritarian of papal monarchs, admitted the possibility of disobeying a pope if he should command an unjust thing by which the status ecclesiae could be disturbed, as for example, if his command should contain heresy.[36]

Theories of constitutional limitations upon papal absolutism were weakened by the lack of an available tribunal to challenge the papacy.

No trial or deposition of a pope took place until the early fifteenth century, when the Council of Constance deposed two rival popes and recognized the resignation of a third. Nevertheless, even at the height of papal power, such theories of limitation had a firm basis in social, economic, and political conditions, which were strongly conducive to local autonomy. To quote Tierney: "In spite of the persistent tendency towards papal centralization, the whole Church, no less than the secular states, remained in a sense a federation of semi-autonomous units, a union of innumerable greater or lesser corporate bodies." Tierney mentions bishoprics, abbeys, colleges, chantries, guilds, religious orders, congregations, and confraternities, all of which "exercised substantial rights of self-government."[37]

Thus the canonists' identification of imperium with jurisdictio corresponded to the living constitution of the ecclesiastical polity. The church was a *Rechtsstaat*, a state based on law. At the same time, the limitations placed on ecclesiastical authority, especially by the secular polities, as well as the limitations placed upon papal authority within the church, especially by the very structures of ecclesiastical government, fostered something more than legality in the Rechtsstaat sense, something more akin to what the English later called "the rule of law."

Corporation Law as the Constitutional Law of the Church

The principle of jurisdictional limitations upon power and authority was a fundamental constitutional principle underlying the new system of canon law of the late eleventh and twelfth centuries. Yet an analysis of the ways in which the jurisdictional principle was applied requires a consideration not of constitutional law as such but rather of corporation law. According to the canonists, it was the church as a corporate legal entity that conferred jurisdiction upon individual ecclesiastical officers (pope, bishops, abbots), and it was the law of corporations that determined the nature and limits of the jurisdiction thus conferred.

The term "corporation" (*universitas;* also *corpus* or *collegium*) was derived from Roman law, as were many of the terms used to define it and many of the rules applicable to it. Yet there are substantial differences between the corporation law of the Romans and that of the twelfth-century western European jurists.

According to Roman law at the time of Justinian,[38] the state as such (still called *populus Romanus*) was considered to be a corporation, but its rights and obligations were regulated administratively rather than in the courts and it was not subject to the civil law; however, the imperial treasury did have rights of ownership and other civil rights and obligations, and could sue and be sued in the ordinary courts. Also municipalities were corporations, with the right to own property and make contracts, to receive gifts and legacies, to sue and be sued, and, in general, to perform legal acts through representatives. Similarly, many private associations, including organizations for maintaining a religious cult, burial clubs, political clubs, and guilds of craftsmen or traders, were considered to be corporations, although the extent of their rights depended on privileges and liberties granted by the emperor. In 313, when Christianity became the official religion of the empire—and to a certain extent before that time—churches and monasteries were added to the list of associations that were considered to have the capacity to receive gifts and legacies as well as to have property and contract rights generally and the right to act as legal persons through representatives. In addition, the legislation of Justinian recognized charitable societies such as hospitals, asylums, orphanages, homes for the poor, and homes for the aged as having legal capacity to receive gifts and legacies for special purposes, with a general right of supervision preserved in the bishop of the diocese. (Neither in the East nor in the West was the concept of a corporation as a legal entity applied, prior to the late eleventh century, to the whole church—the Church Universal.)

The Roman jurists, with their intense hostility to definitions and theories, did not address in general terms the question of the relationship of the universitas to the ensemble of its members. The Digest stated epigrammatically: "What is of the corporation is not of individuals," and again, "If something is owed to a corporation it is not owed to individuals; nor do individuals owe what the corporation owes." However, many questions—such as whether a corporation derives its existence and its powers from a grant by a public authority or from the will of its founders or from its own nature as an association, what powers are exercised by its officers and what cannot be done by them without the consent of the members, and how the officers are to be chosen and how and why they may be dismissed—were not discussed by the Roman jurists. Even the phrases "legal person" and "legal personality" were rarely used by them, and were never analyzed. Only in retrospect can one discern several implicit principles of Roman corporation law that became explicit in Western legal thought in the twelfth century when corporation law first began to be systematized. Two of these were, first, the principle that a corporation has legal capacity to act through representatives, and second, the principle that the rights and duties of the corporation are distinct from those of its officers.

Roman rules of corporation law were carried by the church into the Germanic communities of western Europe. They had to compete, however, with Christian concepts of the corporate nature of ecclesiastical communities and also with Germanic concepts of the corporate nature of associations generally. St. Paul had called the church the body or corpus of Christ (1 Cor. 12:27), and he wrote to the Galatians: "for you are all

one in Christ Jesus" (Gal. 3:28). Other Christian metaphors for the
church were "wife," "spouse," "mother." All such personifications were
meant to apply to the fellowship of believers, "the communion of saints,"
"the congregation of the faithful." Although it was accepted that all
Christians everywhere formed a spiritual body, the main emphasis was
on the spiritual unity of individual churches or individual dioceses. In
that connection it was further emphasized that the prelate of the individual church — the parish priest or the bishop or some other shepherd
of the flock — was united with his church in a spiritual marriage. As
Christ was believed to be married to the Church Universal, so the bishop
or priest was believed to be married to the local church. He represented
it as the head represents the rest of the body. These Christian ideas were
diametrically opposed to the ideas implicit in the treatment of churches
as corporations under Roman law. This is not to say that under the
Roman Empire or under Germanic emperors and kings the church opposed giving to individual churches the status of corporations under
Roman law. On the contrary, it eagerly sought the protection of that
status. Yet it was at least anomalous that under Roman law the Christians who composed an ecclesiastical corporation bore no responsibility
for acts performed by prelates in the name of the corporation and for its
benefit; and it was even more anomalous that the prelates themselves
were considered to act only as agents and not, for example, as constituent members or partners within the association.

Germanic concepts of association bore some resemblance to Christian concepts of the church as "one person," a *corpus mysticum*. As Otto
von Gierke, the great historian of Germanic law, emphasized, the Germanic household, or warrior band, or clan, or village was conceived to
have a group personality which all the members shared; its property was
their common property and they bore a common liability for its obligations. However, according to Gierke the *Genossenschaft* ("fellowship")
derived its unity and its purpose not from a higher authority, whether
divine or human, but solely from within itself, that is, solely from the
voluntary coming together of the members to achieve an end set by
themselves.[39]

The twelfth-century canonists utilized earlier Roman, Germanic, and
Christian concepts of corporate entities in developing a new system of
corporation law applicable to the church. To some extent they harmonized the three competing sets of concepts. They did so, however, not
as an abstract exercise in legal reasoning but in order to achieve practical
solutions to actual legal conflicts that arose in the wake of the Papal
Revolution: legal conflicts between the church and the secular polities as
well as legal conflicts within the church. At the same time, they looked
for the interrelationships among these legal conflicts and sought to

systematize the underlying principles by which they were to be resolved.

The following questions illustrate the kinds of practical issues that arose in litigation in the twelfth century.

Is the head of a corporation (say, a bishop) required to consult its members (the chapter) before making a decision to sue or to answer a charge in court? Is he required not only to consult them but also to obtain their consent? What about a decision to alienate property, or a decision to confer privileges of various kinds?

Can a chapter repudiate a settlement with an opposing party made by a bishop without its consent?

How is the consent of a chapter to be expressed?

Who is to exercise the powers of the head of a corporation during a vacancy, that is, when the head has died or resigned or been dismissed?

If the clergy of a chapter may act on behalf of their bishop if he becomes incapable through illness or old age, may they do so also if he is neglectful?

Can a corporation commit crimes? Can it commit torts? Is it liable for the crimes or torts of its officers?

May an ecclesiastical corporation be formed without the permission of the pope?

If a corporation loses all its members, does it continue to exist? If not, may it be revived by one or more applicants who qualify for membership?

What happens to the property of a corporation that ceases to exist?

May a corporation create law for its members? May it select a magistrate to exercise lawmaking power in its name? May it select a judge to decide cases in its name?

May a corporation to which property has been given for a particular purpose lawfully decide to use that property for another purpose?

And a final question: would the answers to those questions be different if the corporation were not a bishopric or an abbey or some other local body, but the entire Church of Rome, headed by the sole vicar of Christ on earth?

Such practical legal questions arose once the church in the West declared itself to be a corporate legal entity — an *universitas* — independent of emperors, kings, and feudal lords. What is most striking about these questions is, first, their legal formulation; second, the high degree of conscious interrelationship among them; and third (related to the second), the systematic character of the answers that were eventually given, that is, the resort to a conscious systematization of corporation law in order to arrive at a set of satisfactory solutions.

The body of corporation law developed in the Roman Catholic Church in the course of the late eleventh, the twelfth, and the thirteenth centuries may be characterized as a subsystem within the system of canon law as a whole. It differed substantially from the corporation law of the Romans as found in the texts of Justinian. In the first place, the church rejected the Roman view that apart from public corporations (the public treasury, the cities, churches) only collegia recognized as corporations by the imperial authority were to have the privileges and liberties of corporations. In contrast, under canon law any group of persons which had the requisite structure and purpose—for example, an almshouse or a hospital or a body of students, as well as a bishopric or, indeed, the Church Universal—constituted a corporation, without special permission of a higher authority.[40] Second, the church rejected the Roman view that only a public corporation could create new law for its members or exercise judicial authority over them. In contrast, under canon law any corporation could have legislative and judicial "jurisdiction" over its members. Third, the church rejected the Roman view that a corporation could only act through its representatives and not through the ensemble of its members. Instead, canon law required the consent of the members in various types of situations. Fourth, the church rejected the Roman maxim that "what pertains to the corporation does not pertain to its members." According to canon law, the property of a corporation was the common property of its members, and the corporation could tax its members if it did not otherwise have the means of paying a debt.[41]

These and various other rules and concepts of canon law seem to reflect Germanic ideas of the corporation as a fellowship, with a group personality and a group will, in contrast to the Roman idea of a corporation as an "institution," whose identity is created by a higher political authority.[42] Other rules and concepts of canon law, however, seem to reflect the "institutional" idea of the corporation. Thus, every corporation had to have a head (usually called a rector or prelate in an ecclesiastical corporation and a president or governor in a lay corporation), who was empowered to perform acts which the corporation could not accomplish itself (such as administration of property and adjudication of disputes), and who had rights distinct from those of the corporation. The head of the corporation, as well as other officers, was viewed as a species of guardian or tutor, and the corporation as a kind of ward or minor.[43] In contrast to the rule of Roman law, canon law imposed civil and criminal liability on a corporation when a majority of its members consented to a wrongful act, but in contrast to Germanic law the wrongful acts of officers of a corporation could not be imputed to the corporation itself.[44] Thus a city could be placed under ecclesiastical ban for the crimes of its citizens but not, theoretically, for the crimes of its officers.

What has been said thus far may seem to support the thesis put forward by Gierke that the corporation law of the medieval church wavered between the Germanic concept of the corporation as a group personality and the Roman concept of the corporation as an artificial institution (*Anstalt*). (Gierke went on to argue that in the fourteenth century the Roman concept won out, with disastrous consequences for Europe because absolutist theories were ultimately built upon it.)[45] Gierke's thesis is weakened by the fact that the medieval canonists themselves were apparently not aware of either of the two concepts.[46] It is even more seriously impaired by the fact that both concepts are greatly overdrawn. It is doubtful that corporate personality in a legal sense can ever emerge solely from within a group; its existence always depends partly on the recognition of it by those outside — in other words, by the larger society of which it is a part. It is equally doubtful that corporate personality in a legal sense can ever be imposed solely by action of society, or the state, without the prior existence of a group of people having common interests and the capability of acting as a unit.

Tierney emphasizes that it was not until the thirteenth and fourteenth centuries — that is, two centuries after the systematization of the canon law of corporations had begun — that the canonists developed a "coherent theory of corporation law," and that even then they were "not interested in philosophical problems of a corporation's essence."[47] These two points help to make clear that the system — and eventually a "coherent theory" — of corporation law was a legal response to the actual situation and the actual problems that confronted the church, and not a prior intellectual construct to which that situation and those problems were somehow adapted. Yet it would be wrong to suppose that the new canon law of corporations did not, from the beginning, rest on philosophical presuppositions. For the most part the canonists accepted the moderate nominalist position that a group cannot have a personality or a will distinct from that of its members.[48] This philosophical position differs from both the romantic theory of Gierke and the positivist theories that Gierke fought against. Moreover, it is a philosophical position that is particularly suited to the construction of a system of corporation law, since it provides a neutral philosophical basis for raising crucial legal questions concerning the distribution of powers between the officers and the members of a corporation.

Thus if the corporation is understood to be the totality of its parts *taken as parts*, it becomes easy to consider the rights and duties of the members as members, and of the head as head, and the relationships between those two sets of rights and duties. This approach was implicit in the legislation of the late eleventh and early twelfth centuries which Gratian summarized when he stated that a bishop, as the head of the church in his diocese, needed the cooperation of the members, that is, the chapter, in conferring benefices and privileges, in alienating church property, and in judging cases.[49] Some decades later Pope Alexander III confirmed and extended these rules, stating that in various types of cases the "advice" or "consent" of the chapter was required.[50] "The chapter" was understood to consist of the clergy. In amplifying the meaning of advice and consent, later canonists distinguished among three different spheres of rights: rights principally of the corporation as such, rights principally of individual members or officers as individual members or officers, and rights of the corporation and an individual member or officer in common. Thus it was said that if an attorney or other agent is to be appointed in a matter that touches principally the prelate, he should be appointed by the prelate with the consent of the chapter; but if the matter touches principally the chapter, he should be appointed by the chapter with the advice of the prelate; and if the matter touches both in common, he should (as in the first case) be appointed by the prelate with the consent of the chapter.[51] A later canonist explained these rules more generally: the consent of the chapter is necessary whenever the action concerns the corporate body as a whole, since the bishop and chapter together form that body.[52] Here Christian metaphors were used: the bishop was married to his church just as the pope, as vicar of Christ, was married to the Church Universal. However, the church as a corporate entity was identified legally as the clergy; it was the chapter, not "the congregation of the faithful," whose consent was to be obtained.[53]

Analysis of the powers of the head and members of ecclesiastical corporations, including especially cathedral chapters (bishoprics), led to the development in the twelfth and thirteenth centuries of a legal theory of limitations upon the power of ecclesiastical and secular rulers to act alone, without the advice and consent of their counselors and chief subordinates. Here a maxim of Roman law was seized upon, transformed, and raised to the level of a constitutional principle: "What concerns everyone ought to be considered and approved by everyone."[54]

Limitations on Ecclesiastical Jurisdiction

Prior to the late eleventh century ecclesiastical jurisdiction—in the broad sense of legislative and administrative as well as judicial competence—lacked precise boundaries. There was considerable overlapping between the competence of ecclesiastical authorities and that of secular authorities. Also within the church there was no clear division between matters that came before a priest or bishop in his capacity as father confessor and dispenser of penitential remedies, on the one hand, and matters that came before him as an ecclesiastical administrator or judge, on the other. Everything he did was supposed to stem from his ordination; it was ordination, and not jurisdiction, that gave him his authority. At the same time, his undivided authority as an ordained priest or bishop was subordinate in many respects to the authority of emperors, kings, and barons. Emperors, kings, and barons appointed and dominated—and often overruled—popes, bishops, and priests. It was the Papal Revolution, with its liberation of the clergy from the laity and its emphasis upon the separation of the spiritual from the secular, that made it both necessary and possible to place more or less clear limits upon, and hence to systematize, ecclesiastical jurisdiction.

Characteristically—and here legal science elucidated the positive law—such jurisdiction was said to be divided into two types: jurisdiction over certain kinds of persons (*ratione personarum*, "by reason of persons") and jurisdiction over certain kinds of conduct or relationships (*ratione materiae*, "by reason of subject matter"). The church claimed "personal jurisdiction" over: (1) clergy and members of their households; (2) students; (3) crusaders; (4) *personae miserabiles* ("wretched persons"), including poor people, widows, and orphans; (5) Jews, in cases against Christians; and (6) travelers, including merchants and sailors, when necessary for their peace and safety. This was the famous—or notorious—*privilegium fori* ("privilege of court" or "benefit of clergy"), against which secular rulers struggled hard, and often with some success.

Clergy were forbidden by canon law to waive the privilege of ecclesiastical jurisdiction; however, in practice they were subjected to secular justice in certain types of crimes and certain types of civil actions. There were also some recognized exceptions to ecclesiastical jurisdiction over crusaders and over students; and they could waive such jurisdiction if they wished. Personae miserabiles, who prior to the Papal Revolution had been treated primarily as wards of emperors and kings, were thereafter subject also to ecclesiastical jurisdiction, principally in cases where the secular authorities did not offer adequate protection to them. The same was true with regard to Jews and travelers (including merchants and sailors): the church did not attempt to eliminate but only to supplement imperial or royal jurisdiction over them.

The personal jurisdiction of the church extended, in principle, to all types of cases in which these six classes of persons were involved, although the principle sometimes yielded to the competing interests of the secular authorities. The "subject-matter jurisdiction" of the church, by contrast, extended in principle to all classes of persons, laymen as well as clerics, in certain types of cases, although—again—there were qualifications and exceptions. The principal types of cases over which the church claimed jurisdiction were so-called spiritual cases and cases connected to spiritual cases. Spiritual cases were chiefly those arising out of: (1) administration of the sacraments; (2) testaments; (3) benefices, including administration of church property, patronage of church offices, and ecclesiastical taxation in the form of tithes; (4) oaths, including pledges of faith; and (5) sins meriting ecclesiastical censures. It was on this jurisdictional foundation that legal science in the twelfth century began to develop various branches of substantive law, including family law (on the foundation of jurisdiction over the sacrament of marriage), the law of inheritance (on the foundation of jurisdiction over testaments), property law (on the foundation of jurisdiction over benefices), contract law (on the foundation of jurisdiction over pledges of faith), and criminal and tort law (on the foundation of jurisdiction over sins). Presupposed was the jurisdiction of the church over its own jurisdiction; on this basis it constructed the body of corporation law.

The church also extended its jurisdiction to other kinds of causes by offering it to all who wished to choose it. This was done through a procedure called prorogation, whereby parties to any civil dispute could, by agreement, submit the dispute to an ecclesiastical court or to ecclesiastical arbitration. Such an agreement might take the form of a clause in a contract renouncing in advance the jurisdiction of a secular court and providing for recourse to an ecclesiastical court or to ecclesiastical arbitration in the event of a future dispute arising out of the contract. Because of the primitive character of most secular procedure in the twelfth and thirteenth centuries, parties to civil contracts often wrote in such renunciation clauses.

In addition, according to canon law any person could bring suit in an ecclesiastical court, or could remove a case from a secular court to an ecclesiastical court, even against the will of the other party, on the ground of "default of secular justice." Thus the church ultimately offered its jurisdiction and its law to anyone and for any type of case, but only under exceptional circumstances, that is, when justice itself, in the most elementary sense, was at stake. It was understood that normally there were two distinct kinds of jurisdiction, the ecclesiastical (spiritual) and the nonecclesiastical (secular). Indeed, if *all* questions had fallen normally within the ecclesiastical jurisdiction, it would have been meaningless to speak of jurisdiction: there would have been nothing with which to contrast it. Even if just all *legal* questions had fallen within the ecclesiastical — or any other single — jurisdiction, it would only have been meaningful to speak of competence (what is and what is not subject to legal regulation), and not of any other aspect of jurisdiction. It was the conscious restriction of ecclesiastical jurisdiction, and therefore of nonecclesiastical jurisdiction as well, to certain classes of persons and certain types of cases that made it both necessary and possible to define jurisdiction and to give it its place as a basic structural element of the system of canon law.

It was, in fact, the limitations placed upon the jurisdiction of each of the polities of Western Christendom, including the ecclesiastical polity, that made it both necessary and possible for each to develop not only laws but also a *system* of laws, and more than that, a system of *law*. A ruler whose jurisdiction is unlimited may rule by laws, but he is not likely to have either the will or the imagination to bring his laws into a coherent, integrated intellectual system, with a complex structure of principles, including principles for regulating the application of principles to specific kinds of cases. In the West, the competition and cooperation of rival limited jurisdictions not only required each to systematize its law but also gave each a basis for doing so. That basis was provided in part by the overarching dialectical unity that held all the individual systems together, however loosely, and in part by the distinct interests and resources of each community having such a system.

Competition and cooperation between rival limited jurisdictions not only made necessary and possible the systematization of law but also led to the legal formulation and resolution of some of the most acute political and moral problems of the time. The tendency to convert political and moral questions into legal questions, which Alexis de Toqueville perceived to be characteristic of America in the early nineteenth century, existed, albeit to a lesser degree, in Western society as a whole after the late eleventh and the twelfth centuries. This has contributed to the excessive legalism of the West, compared with many other civilizations; it has also contributed to its relative success in achieving freedom from political and moral tyranny.

6 | Structural Elements of the System of Canon Law

THE NEW SYSTEM of canon law that was created in the eleventh and twelfth centuries embraced only those kinds of legal relations that fell within the jurisdiction of the church as a corporate legal entity. Other legal relations fell within the respective, overlapping jurisdictions of various secular polities, including kingdoms, feudal domains, and autonomous cities and towns. Every person in Western Christendom lived under both canon law and one or more secular legal systems. The pluralism of legal systems within a common legal order was an essential element of the structure of each system.

Because none of the coexisting legal systems claimed to be all inclusive or omnicompetent, each had to develop constitutional standards for locating and limiting sovereignty, for allocating governmental powers within such sovereignty, and for determining the basic rights and duties of members. In the canon law system, these constitutional standards were expressed primarily in terms of corporation law, including the law of corporate jurisdiction over particular classes of persons and particular types of subject matter.

Out of the system of ecclesiastical constitutional law there gradually developed relatively coherent bodies of substantive rules pertaining to other fields of law as well. Thus there gradually developed, out of the church's jurisdiction over the sacraments, a body of law pertaining to marriage; out of the church's jurisdiction over testaments, a body of law pertaining to inheritance; out of the church's jurisdiction over benefices, a body of law pertaining to property; out of the church's jurisdiction over oaths, a body of law pertaining to contracts; out of the church's jurisdiction over sins, a body of law pertaining to crimes and torts. There also developed, in connection with these five types of jurisdiction, a body of rules of judicial procedure. These bodies of law were not conceptualized in the same way that autonomous branches of law came to be conceptualized in later centuries; the canonists of the twelfth and thirteenth centuries did not attempt to organize each branch of law — property, contract, crime, and so forth — as a self-contained set of rules stemming logically from various principles and doctrines, which stemmed in turn from a general theory of property, a general theory of contract, a general theory of crime and punishment, and so forth. The canon law of the twelfth and thirteenth centuries was less abstract, less "logical." Its categories had grown out of the jurisdiction of the ecclesiastical courts and out of the legal problems confronting those courts, rather than out of the speculative reasoning of academic jurists. Like the developing English royal law of the same period, the canon law tended to be systematized more on the basis of procedure than of substantive rules. Yet after Gratian, canon law, unlike English royal law, was also a university discipline; professors took the rules and principles and theories of the cases into the classroom and collected, analyzed, and harmonized them in their treatises. And so subsystems of law did emerge, though without the high degree of autonomy and doctrinal consistency that developed later.

Each of the subsystems or fields of law manifested its own structural elements, and each manifested in a different way the structural elements of the system as a whole. The canon law of crimes, for instance, was founded on concepts of sin which affected all the other fields of canon law. In the other fields as well, one can identify pervasive features that helped to define canon law as a modern legal system.

The Canon Law of Marriage

From earliest times, the church had a great deal to say about marriage and the family.[1] In pagan cultures in which polygamy, arranged marriages, and oppression of women predominated, the church promoted the idea of monogamous marriage by free consent of both spouses. In the West this idea had to do battle with deeply rooted tribal, village, and feudal customs. By the tenth century ecclesiastical synods were promulgating decrees concerning the matrimonial bond, adultery, legitimacy of children, and related matters; nevertheless, children continued to be married in the cradle and family relations continued to be dominated by the traditional folkways and mores of the Germanic, Celtic, and other peoples of western Europe. In the folklaw of the European peoples, as in the classical Roman law, marriage between persons of different classes (for example, free and slave, citizens and foreigners) was prohibited. Also divorce was at the will of either spouse — which usually meant, in practice, at the will of the husband. There were not even any formal requirements for divorce. Paternal consent was required for a marriage to be valid. Few obligations between the spouses were conceived in legal terms.

It was the great upheaval of the late eleventh and twelfth centuries, symbolized by the Papal Revolution, that made it possible to effectuate to a substantial degree ecclesiastical policy concerning marriage and the family. Social and economic factors — of which the Papal Revolution was both a cause and an effect — played a crucial part: population movements, the rise of the cities, and the rapid spread of the manorial system helped to break down earlier social formations. Political changes also had an important role: the formation of a single, separate ecclesiastical state headed by the papacy gave the clergy a kind of political power that they had never had before, and in addition the establishment of the universal celibacy of priests helped to lessen their personal involvement in tribal kinship relations. Equally important were the legal changes through which ecclesiastical policy concerning family relations was implemented, for without the systematization of the canon law it would not have been possible to communicate that policy effectively or to secure allegiance to it or to make it work.

As long as ecclesiastical laws on marriage and the family were largely hortatory, they did not have to be either precise or complete. After they became fully binding, they had to be both. Since all family relationships were henceforth to be based, in legal practice and not only in theory, on the sacrament of marriage, it became necessary to determine the precise nature of that sacrament. The church had long held that no formality was required to effectuate a marriage; the two parties were themselves "ministers of the sacrament of marriage." (The presence of a priest was first made obligatory in the sixteenth century; the common law marriage of English and American law is, in fact, a survival of canon law marriage as it existed before the Council of Trent.) Yet the absence of formality left open the question of exactly how and when a marriage was concluded. Some of the earlier texts had indicated that it was concluded from the moment of the exchange of promises. Others had indicated that it was not concluded until it had been consummated by sexual intercourse. Gratian argued that the traditional analogy between human marriage and the mystical marriage of Christ and the Church required that there be a physical union, a *copula carnalis*, before the sacrament was complete. Nevertheless, he also stressed the element of free consent, including consent to the physical union. Ultimately, the canon law distinguished among: (1) an exchange of promises to be married in the future, constituting a contract of betrothal, which could be broken in certain cases by either party and could always be dissolved by mutual consent; (2) an exchange of promises to be married in the present, constituting a contract of marriage; and (3) consent to intercourse following the marriage, constituting consummation of the marriage. Although the contract was deemed to be concluded with "words in the present," it remained vulnerable to dissolution until it had been consummated.

The rules concerning consent to a marriage were developed into a whole body of contract law. The consent must have been given with a free will. A mistake concerning the identity of the other party, or a mistake concerning some essential and distinctive quality of the other party, prevented the consent and hence nullified the marriage. Duress also nullified the marriage by interfering with the freedom of consent. It was also ruled that a marriage could not be validly contracted under the influence of fear or fraud.

Here were the foundations not only of the modern law of marriage but also of certain basic elements of modern contract law, namely, the concept of free will and related concepts of mistake, duress, and fraud. In particular, the canonists were able to find a solution to the problem of mistake, which had greatly vexed the Roman jurists quoted in the Digest, by focusing on the question whether the mistaken party would have entered into the marriage if he or she had known the truth.

Canon law also laid down conditions necessary for the validity of a marriage, apart from consent. In the twelfth and thirteenth centuries the regulations as to age imposed by Roman law were maintained in general, but exceptions were permitted in the light of local custom, provided that the parties were able to beget children and to understand the nature of the act they were performing. Impotence at the time of marriage was a cause of nullity, however. Also a marriage between a Christian and a heathen was void, since baptism was a necessary condition for participation in any sacrament. But the church recognized the validity of a marriage between a Catholic and a heretic or a person who had been excommunicated. It also recognized the validity of a marriage between two slaves or between a freeman and a slave or serf.

Canon law in the twelfth and thirteenth centuries simplified and relaxed the earlier rules concerning marriage impediments based on consanguinity and affinity. Also penal impediments such as adultery and abduction were relaxed: the adulterers could cure their crime by marrying, the abductor could marry if he set the *rapta* free. However, the marriage of priests, which had been valid under the earlier canon law, was declared to be void.

Where the parties married in good faith, without knowledge of an impediment, the canonists held that the children of the marriage were legitimate and that the marriage itself was valid up to the day it was declared null; this was called a putative marriage. Moreover, a marriage could not be annulled without a legal action, and restrictions were placed on those who could bring such an action: if there were no near relatives, preference was given to persons of known prudence. But there was no statute of limitations governing an action for annulment of a marriage, and the party seeking annulment was not barred from bringing an action simply because he had brought one before and had lost.

In addition to annulment on the ground of lack of consent or impediments, the church permitted judicial separation, called *divortium*, on the ground of fornication, apostasy, or grave cruelty. However, divorce in the modern sense was not permitted; the sacramental bond, once validly entered into, was considered indissoluble until the death of one of the spouses. There were two exceptions to this: first, a nonconsummated marriage was dissolved by the entry of one of the parties into a religious order, and could in any case be dissolved by the pope; and second, under certain circumstances a convert to Christianity might divorce his or her spouse who remained heathen.

Finally, canon law offered considerable protection — as contrasted with the folklaw of the society in which it first developed — to the female partner in the marriage. "Before God the two parties to marriage were equal and this doctrine of equality was first taught by Christianity. In practice it meant, above all, that the obligations, especially that of fidelity, were mutual. Nevertheless, the husband was head of the household, and in virtue of his position as such, he might choose the place of abode, reasonably correct his wife, and demand from her such domestic duties as were consonant with her social position."[2] Although the church, for the most part, accepted the severe restrictions placed by secular law upon women's property rights (and their civil rights generally), nevertheless, to protect the widow it insisted that no marriage could be contracted without a dowry, that is, the establishment of a fund which could not be reduced in value during the marriage.

As a subsystem of the canon law, the church's law of marriage rested in part upon a tension between the concept of the marriage sacrament as a voluntary union of two persons in the presence of God and the concept of the marriage sacrament as a legal transaction within the legal system of the church as a corporate entity. On the one hand, there was an emphasis upon the internal disposition of the marriage partners and their personal desires and responses; on the other hand, there was an emphasis upon the institutional authority of the church and upon conformity to social custom and social policy, both ecclesiastical and secular. This tension was reflected in the questions which the ecclesiastical courts had to answer, such as whether a marriage is invalid because of mistake, fraud, or duress; whether a husband may abandon an adulterous wife; whether a wife who marries another, thinking her first husband is dead, must return to the first man when he reappears; and whether a clandestine marriage, contracted with no third party present, is valid. The tension was also reflected in many of the answers which the ecclesiastical courts gave to such questions. It came out clearly in the resolution of the question of the validity of clandestine marriages. On the one hand, as Gratian stated, "marriages secretly contracted are prohibited by all the authorities" and are unlawful. On the other hand, such marriages are valid if they can be proved by the confession of both spouses. But if the will of one of the parties has changed, the judge is not to give credence to the confession of the other. Thus the strong policy of social betrothals and of external obligations was affirmed, while the sanctity of sacramental consent was also maintained. Yet the solution — resting as it does on a fiction in the law of evidence — though "systematic," was hardly perfect.

The systematization of family law was made possible by focusing attention upon the jurisdiction — in the most elementary sense of the power *jus dicere* ("to speak law") — of the ecclesiastical authorities over the administration of the sacrament of marriage. The whole structure of substantive family law was formed primarily in terms of "marital causes," which included validity of marriage, nullity of marriage, breach of marriage (*divortium*), clandestine marriage, promises of marriage, separation from bed and board, legitimacy of children, and marital property. Out of the jurisdiction over marital causes there developed a relatively integrated subsystem of legal standards, principles, concepts, and rules within the system of canon law as a whole. For example, since marriage and not blood relationship was the basis of the family, adopted children of a marriage were to have equal rights with natural children. Children born out of wedlock, however, were "illegitimate" and subject to disabilities, although they could be legitimated by subsequent marriage. While the subsystem of family law had its own structural features, it also shared the structural features of the whole system of canon law. Besides having many important elements in common with contract law, it shared with feudal law — and with ordination — the basic concept of the capacity voluntarily, by a sacred vow, to enter into an indissoluble, lifelong relationship whose terms were fixed by law — in modern terminology, the power by contract to create a status.

The Canon Law of Inheritance

The folklaw of the Germanic peoples of Europe did not provide for testamentary succession.[3] Devolution upon heirs of the rights and duties of a decedent was regulated initially by tribal custom, later also by village custom, and still later also by feudal custom; the main concern was that the family or household or fief should survive the death of its individual members, and especially of its head. Under early Germanic law, only when a person had no heir could he appoint one with the consent of the tribal council or chief. Most of the property belonged to the family or tribe and was not subject to distribution on the death of a member. The personal belongings of the decedent were distributed to the surviving spouse and children, with a portion reserved to himself, to be buried with the corpse or burned with it as part of the funeral rights.

With the introduction of Christianity, the dead man's portion was no longer buried or burned with the corpse; instead, it was distributed for pious works, for the benefit of the dead man's soul. Customs varied throughout Europe, but typically the property subject to distribution was divided into thirds: one-third for the clan chieftain or king, one-third for the heir, and one-third as "God's portion."

The clergy, of course, had a great interest in God's portion. Particularly when a person was known to be about to die, a priest was apt to be present to remind him of his duty to atone for his sins and to leave his belongings for religious or charitable uses, such as the building of a chapel or relief of the poor. Throughout Europe the rule was introduced that a dying man's "last words" were to be given legal effect, whether or not they were reduced to writing. A Latin phrase was attached to the practice: *donatio causa mortis* ("gift in anticipation of death"). It was not exactly a will, although in most cases it had the same effect. In the rare event that the dying man recovered, the gift lost its effect.

Another form of gift to take effect on death was the "post obit gift": with respect to certain land, called "bookland," a "book" was drawn up in which the owner would state, "I give the land after my death to . . . " This, as Maitland says, was not a will in the modern sense, since: (1) it was not revocable; (2) it was not ambulatory, that is, it did not apply to what the donor might own at the time the gift became effective; and (3) it did not provide for any representative of the donor at his death or any other procedure for administration of his estate.[4]

It was partly on the basis of the Germanic Christian gift *causa mortis* and post obit gift that the twelfth-century canonists created a new law of wills—and partly on the basis of the classical Roman law of testaments, which was known to the church and used by the church from early times. The Romans had a law of intestate succession that was similar to that of the Germanic folklaw, in that its primary purpose was to provide a successor to the head of the household (*pater familias*). Roman law, however, spelled out the legal aspects of succession much more fully. The inheritance itself was called a *universitas juris*, a single complex legal unit; this comprised the *familia* itself, with its ancestral privileges and obligations, its property, its slaves, and all the legal rights and duties of the decedent. All this devolved upon the heir instantaneously at the death of the decedent. However, from the time of the Twelve Tables, Roman law also provided that the "universal succession" of the heir to the legal personality of the decedent could be governed, alternatively, by a testament. Initially, the purpose of the testament was to counteract the rules of intestate succession in instances when those rules were unsuitable to a particular family situation; in other words, the same basic purpose motivated the introduction of the Roman testament that motivated the rules of intestate succession, namely, the continuation of the family household by the transmission of the legal personality of the decedent to his heir (or to coheirs). The primary purpose was not to give individuals the power to effectuate their will after death; the primary purpose was to protect the social unit.

In the course of centuries, the Roman testament changed its character. The extremely elaborate formalities of the early period— a fictitious sale of the familia, with copper coins and scales and ritual formulas—gave way to signatures and seals of seven witnesses and subscription of the testator. Indeed, under certain circumstances an oral will could be valid. Also the heir was given the right to abstain from the inheritance, as he might well want to do if its liabilities exceeded its assets. Most important, special legacies and codicils in favor of individual beneficiaries multiplied, tending to weaken the heir's position (since he assumed the testator's obligations); and a wide variety of substitutions and default clauses were introduced. These developments in the direction of freedom of testation also favored the church in the Roman Empire. By the time of Justinian, bequests to the angels and the saints or to the poor or to other pious causes were awarded to appropriate churches or to bishops to administer.[5]

Nevertheless, the Roman testament, though it fulfilled the three tests of the modern will listed by Maitland, lacked a fourth quality that was fundamental in the law of wills as it developed in the West in the late eleventh and twelfth centuries in the wake of the Papal Revolution. The new quality was the sanctity of the testator's wishes insofar as those wishes were linked with the preservaton of his soul: the "testament" became a "will," but it was a religious will.

The canonists treated the very making of a will as a religious act, and the will itself as a religious instrument. Typically it was made in the name of the Father, Son, and Holy Spirit. In Maitland's words, "The testator's first thought is not of the transmission of an *hereditas*, but of the future welfare of his immortal soul and his mortal body. The soul he bequeathes to God, the Virgin and the saints; his body to a certain church. Along with his body he gives [to] his mortuary . . . one of the best chattels that he has; often, if he is a knight, it will be his war-horse . . . Elaborate instructions will sometimes be given for the burial; about the tapers that are to burn around the bier, and the funeral feast . . . Then will come the pecuniary and specific legacies. Many will be given to pious uses; the four orders of friars are rarely forgotten by a well-to-do testator; a bequest for the repair of bridges is deemed a pious and laudable bequest; rarely are villeins freed, but sometimes their arrears of rent are forgiven or their chattels are restored to them. The medieval will is characterized by the large number of its specific bequests. The horses are given away one by one; so are the jewels; so are the beds and quilts, the pots and pans. The civilian or canonist names his precious books; the treasured manuscript of the statutes is handed on to one who will love it . . . On the other hand, the testator has no stocks, funds and securities to dispose of; he says nothing, or very little, of the debts that are owed to him, while of the debts he owes he says nothing or merely desires that they be paid."[6]

In the twelfth century the canonists established a body of rules for determining the validity of wills and for interpreting and enforcing them. In contrast to Roman law, testamentary formalities were minimized. Not only were "last words" spoken to one's confessor on one's deathbed treated as full-fledged testaments, but oral wills generally were considered valid. The Roman requirement of signatures and seals of seven qualified witnesses yielded to the rule stated in a decretal letter of Pope Alexander III to the Bishop of Ostia: "We decree as permanently valid the testaments which your parishioners may make in the presence of their priest and of three or two other suitable persons."[7] In addition, individual bequests to pious causes were valid, according to another regulation of Alexander III, if witnessed by two or three persons. Thus canon law added charitable bequests to the two kinds of testaments which also under Roman law were exempt from the usual legal requirements, namely, testaments of soldiers and sailors in active service and testaments of parents conferring a benefit on those descendants who would have received property in the absence of a testament.

The canonists also strengthened the protection of the surviving spouse and children against disinheritance by the testator. Roman law had provided that an heir could not be deprived of his "legitimate share"; this was originally fixed at one-fourth of what he would have received if the testator had died without a will, and later was raised to one-third (or one-half, if the testator was survived by five or more children). However, the heirs entitled to this share were the children and grandchildren or, if there were none, the parents, but not the wife. Canon law increased the share and included the wife within the protection, but not the grandchildren or the parents of the decedent. If a wife and children survived, neither could be deprived by will of more than one-third of the property subject to disposition by will; if only a wife or only children survived, she or they were entitled to one-half.

Even more important than changes in the Roman substantive law of testaments were the changes made by the canonists in the administration of estates. They created in the twelfth century the new institution of the testamentary executor. On the testator's death, instead of the acceptance of the inheritance by the heir, followed by his "entering upon" it and carrying out the instructions of the testament, the person appointed in the will as executor took possession of all the property subject to distribution. It was not the heir but the executor who exercised the rights of the testator and incurred his obligations. He could sue the testator's debtors in the secular courts; legatees, however, had to make their claims against him in the ecclesiastical courts. The legitimate share of wives and children also could only be enforced against the executor in the ecclesiastical courts.

The fact that the making of a will was a religious act explains the church's assumption of jurisdiction over intestacy as well. The church, in fact, considered intestacy to be in the nature of a sin. If a man died intestate, it was likely that he had died unconfessed. Moreover, the goods of the intestate ought to be distributed for the welfare of his soul. Thus the goods of the intestate were at the disposal of the ecclesiastical judge, that is, the bishop or his deputy, the "official." The bishop might trust the next of kin of the intestate to do what they thought best for his soul, but they had no claim to inherit anything more than their "legitimate part." Under the new canon law, the part that could not be taken from the wife and children by will was also the part that they inherited without a will; and all other kin had no right of inheritance at all unless the decedent had named them in a will. Thus the church claimed jurisdiction over intestate succession not only in order to protect the decedent's widow and orphaned children but also, for the good of his soul, to distribute the residue of his estate for charitable purposes.

In time, the ecclesiastical courts developed the practice of appointing an administrator to distribute the property of one who had died intestate. His functions were similar to those of the testamentary executor. The medieval canonical system of administration of decedent's estates by executors and administrators has survived in English and American law, whereas on the continent of Europe there was a return, in the sixteenth century and thereafter, to older Roman concepts whereby the estate was transferred to the heirs and administered by them, under judicial supervision, whether the decedent had died testate or intestate.

The institutional role of the priesthood was central. Priests heard "last words," witnessed wills, served as executors and administrators, and received bequests as trustees for religious bodies or for carrying out charitable works.

The institutional role of the eclesiastical court—the bishop or his deputy—was also central. Executors and administrators were required to render an account to the ecclesiastical court. Trustees for religious or charitable purposes were under the supervision of the ecclesiastical court. All disputes over inheritance were subject to the jurisdiction of that court (although some of them were also subject to the jurisdiction of secular courts).

The canon law of inheritance constituted a direct intervention by the church in feudal economic and political relations. The secular authorities offered strenuous resistance, especially with respect to ecclesiastical claims of jurisdiction over devises of land. In England and Normandy, for example, the secular courts in the twelfth century condemned the post-obit as well as the deathbed gift of land. Of the latter, Glanvill's treatise (1187) stated that "it may be presumed that one who when sick unto death has begun to do, what he never did while in sound health, namely, to distribute his land, is moved to this rather by his agony than by a deliberate mind."[8] But perhaps that was not the most important aspect of the matter, since deathbed gifts of chattels were not condemned, and devises of land generally (whether by "last words" or by a carefully considered, unagonized, written testament) were also prohibited—not only in England but throughout the West—under feudal law (though not under urban law). Feudal law was, in fact, hostile to the devise of land, whether for charitable or noncharitable purposes.

In the case of devises to the church, would-be testators—with ecclesiastical assistance—found various ways to circumvent the prohibition. One was the gift of land to a religious corporation with reservation of a life estate in the donor. This was, in form, an *inter vivos* gift, which was at that time permitted, but it had the same effect as a will. The secular authorities eventually responded with statutes of mortmain ("dead hand") prohibiting all gifts of land to religious bodies. Other schemes were then tried. The landholder would not give the land but would surrender it to the religious corporation to be held by it as feudal lord, the transferor to continue to occupy it as vassal; after his death there was no one to enter and claim it but the religious corporation. Or the landholder would lease the land to the religious corporation for a thousand years, reserving the right to remain on it until his death. These devices, too, were eventually struck down. Finally, the church hit upon the device of the trust ("use"). Title to the land was conveyed to a lay person to be held by him as trustee for the religious corporation, which, after the donor's death, would have the use of the land and the right to all profits derived from it; and provision was made for a new trustee to succeed a trustee who died. Such "uses" had been widely utilized since the twelfth century for the benefit of religious orders that were forbidden to "own" property. Eventually they became a means not only of conveying land for charitable purposes during the landholders's lifetime but also of establishing what was in effect a charitable bequest or devise.

The story of the early development of the law of charitable trusts tells a great deal about the formation of the Western legal tradition. Even more clearly than in the case of family law, the canon law of inheritance was shaped by the need to take into account the secular law, which, by its emphasis on the political significance of land tenure, drove the church to focus its law of wills on chattels and to find other means of obtaining gifts of land. In England, at least, the ecclesiastical courts established a virtually exclusive jurisdiction over succession to chattels, both testate and intestate; this continued even after the English Reformation, and it has given the English and American law of inheritance a character different from that of the countries of continental Europe. In all the countries of the West, however, including England, ecclesiastical jurisdiction over succession to land was subordinated to secular jurisdiction. In fighting for gifts of land, the church made use of new legal concepts and new legal instruments. These included the modern concept and instrument of the trust, which passed over into English secular law through the equitable jurisdiction of the chancellor, but which between the twelfth and the fifteenth centuries was part of the law of all the countries of Europe, insofar as all were subject to ecclesiastical jurisdiction. Both the charitable bequest of chattels and the gift of land for the use of religious bodies in perpetuity involved the obligation of executors or trustees to effectuate the desires of donors in the interest of beneficiaries. And they both involved the enforcement and supervision of such obligation by the ecclesiastical courts.

The law that came out of the ecclesiastical jurisdiction over inheritance had not only its own structural elements but also some of the structural elements of the canon law as a whole. The wishes of the testator were sacred, since in making a will he was performing a religious act; by the same token, however, they were subject to the moral standards of the church as interpreted by the ecclesiastical authorities. A bequest for an immoral purpose—for example, a bequest to a heretic—was void. Yet a bequest that would normally have been void for vagueness—for example, because of the uncertainty of the beneficiary, or of the amount of the legacy, or of the purpose of the testator, or of the means of carrying out his intention—was enforced if it was a charitable bequest. A bequest "for the poor" or "for the worship of God" or merely "to charity" was valid. If a trustee was not named, the ecclesiastical court would appoint one. If an unincorporated association or a corporation incapable of holding property was named as legatee, the court would appoint a trustee to administer the bequest in its behalf. These are still rules of the law of trusts in the United States.

Where the wishes of the testator could not be fulfilled because of physical impossibility (for example, if the legatee was no longer alive), or because of illegality (for example, if the legatee was a heretic, or the devise was illegal under the secular law), the ecclesiastical court would carry out the testator's intention "as near as may be possible" (in Norman French, *cy pres*, "as near as"). Another legatee, similar to the one named, would be found. Some equivalent of the land, or some rights in it, would be given to the legatee. The doctrine of cy pres still prevails in the United States.

The canon law of wills was founded on the jurisdiction of the church and of church courts over the religious act of making a will. Freedom of testation was conceived essentially as the freedom to contribute to religious and charitable causes, although it inevitably involved also the freedom to bequeath one's belongings to relatives and friends. The welfare of the decedent's soul was at stake in every bequest. In addition, the welfare of the beneficiaries of the bequest was at stake, especially in the case of religious and charitable bequests. The canon law of intestate succession, however, though founded partly on the jurisdiction of the church and of church courts over the welfare of the decedent's soul, was also founded partly on their jurisdiction over widows and orphans. On these two jurisdictional foundations the canon law reintegrated the surviving Germanic and Roman legal institutions into a new body of inheritance law. There was a dialectical tension—which remains to this day—between the law of wills (inherited only in part from Roman law) and the law of intestate succession (inherited only in part from Germanic folklaw).

Thus to speak of the canon law of inheritance as a subsystem within the system of canon law as a whole is to recognize that its structural unity, like that of the whole canon law, was founded on the conscious concordance of discordant elements.

The Canon Law of Property

The ecclesiastical courts could hardly claim so extensive a jurisdiction over property relations as they exercised over family relations and inheritance.[9] Yet their jurisdiction in property matters was by no means meager, and out of it came a substantial body of law. The church had enormous wealth, acquired through gifts and taxes as well as through its own agricultural, manufacturing, and commercial enterprises. Indeed, it is said to have owned between one-fourth and one-third of the land of western Europe. It is hardly surprising that not only the church's legal scholars but also church courts and church legislators had a great deal to say about rights and duties pertaining to the possession, use, and disposition of such wealth. In addition, canon law had something to say about rights and duties pertaining to secular property as well.

To be sure, the canon law of property was influenced by contemporary secular law to a much greater extent than was the canon law of family relations. For one thing, it was never suggested that property—even ecclesiastical property—had a sacramental character. Material resources of the church were always treated as part of its "temporal" power. Moreover, in the context of feudal land tenure, ecclesiastical property rights were often closely interconnected with secular property rights. For example, a parish might "hold" its land and building "of" a bishopric or an abbey (ownership of parish churches by monasteries was very widespread throughout Europe from the twelfth century on), and the bishopric or abbey might "hold" the same land "of" a baron. Disputes over ground rent owed by the parish to the bishopric or abbey would usually be within the jurisdiction of ecclesiastical courts and would be settled by canon law, whereas disputes over feudal dues and services owed by the bishopric or abbey to the baron would normally be within the jurisdiction of secular courts and would be settled by secular law — although jurisdiction in the latter case might be a matter of contest between the ecclesiastical and the secular courts. The church was both inside and outside the contemporary feudal economic order. Its property law was necessarily partly feudal in nature. Similarly, the church was both inside and outside the contemporary urban economic order that prevailed in the thousands of free cities and towns that emerged in Europe in the eleventh, twelfth, and thirteenth centuries, so that its property law was necessarily partly urban in nature. Yet the canon law of property relations was also partly nonfeudal and nonurban; that is, it was based partly on specifically ecclesiastical considerations and on the principles of canon law as a whole. The canonists of the time not only systematized the law of property for the first time; they also introduced some wholly new concepts and rules of property law — concepts and rules that had a profound and lasting effect on the Western legal tradition.

Most church lands and buildings in the period from the late eleventh to the fifteenth centuries were held by a tenure known in English as "free alms" (in Norman French, *frankalmoign*; in Latin, *libera elemosina*). Typically, a donor (or several donors jointly) would make a gift to God and to a named ecclesiastical corporation, its officers and members: for example, "to God and to St. Wilfred of Dumfries Abbey and the Abbot Duncan and the monks of St. Wilfred." If the purpose was to build a church, or a hospital, or an educational institution, the gift might include not only land but also resources for construction and maintenance of the building and for carrying on its operations in the future. But the donor of land would often retain rights in it for himself and his heirs. In particular, he would often retain the right to "present" a new priest to the church to be built on the land, whenever the priestly office was vacant: such a right of patronage (*advocatio*, "advowson") was valuable property — it gave power to nominate someone (perhaps a relative) to what might be a lucrative office. The donor might also retain for himself and his heirs the right to ground rent, feudal dues, military service, and other rights that inhered in tenure of the land in question. Sometimes, however, a donor might wish to give to a charitable cause not only tenure of a parcel of land but also all the rights that were attached to the tenure of the land. In such a case, consent to and concession of such rights might have to be obtained from the donor's superiors in the feudal hierarchy. Church land thus freed from all feudal obligations was quite different from the heavily burdened feudal property characteristic of contemporary secular landholding. In fact, a large part of land held in free alms came to be so emancipated.

Ecclesiastical property presented a sharp contrast with feudal property not only by virtue of its emancipation, in many instances, from feudal obligations but also by virtue of its corporate ecclesiastical character; that is, it was always the property of an ecclesiastical corporation, never of an individual person. Moreover, it was always committed to the purposes of the corporation. It was what in German is called *Zweckvermögen* ("property for a purpose"). According to canon law, it was required to be used for the purposes for which it was acquired; in that sense, it was impressed with a trust. The officers of the ecclesiastical corporation which owned the property—whether it was an abbey (monastic house) or a bishopric (diocese) or a parish or a university or a hospital or, for that matter, an archbishopric or the papacy itself—were trustees, required by canon law to use the property conscientiously for the benefit of those for whose benefit it was acquired.

To speak of ecclesiastical property in the twelfth century as a "trust" is to take some liberties with a word which came to have specific meanings in English law four centuries later. Yet the English concept of the trust was derived historically from the concept of the "use," which was known and used throughout Europe from the twelfth century on, and which was developed in England in the chancellor's court in the fourteenth and fifteenth centuries. Land and other property were given to certain persons "for the use" of individual churches, monasteries, or other ecclesiastical bodies. This practice became very widespread with the founding of the various Franciscan orders in the thirteenth century, since they were forbidden by their own rule to possess property in excess of their daily needs. The person to whom the property was transferred "owned" it, but he was required by canon law—and eventually, in England, by the chancellor's court as well—to administer it for the benefit of those for whose "use" it had been given.

The "use" (like the later English "trust") presupposed three parties: a donor, a donee, and a beneficiary. The donee took the gift as a trustee for the beneficiary. Normally, however, property given to an ecclesiastical corporation was owned by the corporation; *it* was the donee. Nevertheless, it was also a beneficiary. If its officers had power to possess, use, and dispose of the corporation's property, they were required to exercise such power as its "trustees." That is still the rule of English company law as well as of American corporation law. It was, and is, also the rule of the canon law of the Roman Catholic Church.

The canonists also developed a legal device called a "foundation" or "corporation of goods" (*universitas bonorum*), as contrasted with "corporation of persons" (*universitas personarum*). This had been wholly missing from the older Roman or Germanic law. Although it has no exact parallel in later English secular law, it was received into the secular legal systems of other European countries. (In German it is called a *Stiftung*, in French a *fondation*.) It consisted of a personification of the purposes to which property, money, land, and incorporeal rights had been dedicated. Thus an ecclesiastical benefice itself — the property rights and duties connected with a clerical office, the income from economic activities adhering to the office, and all other perquisites of it — was treated as a legal person, with power through its officers to conduct its own economic and legal affairs as a single entity. A hospital or poorhouse or educational institution, or a bishopric or abbey, could be viewed not only as a corporation of persons but also as a corporation of goods.

In addition to developing the modern concepts of corporate ownership, trust, and foundations, the canonists also developed modern concepts of possessory remedies. In particular, they developed in the twelfth century a legal action for the recovery of possession of land, goods, and incorporeal rights, whereby a prior possessor who had been violently or fraudulently dispossessed could recover against a present possessor merely by proof of the wrongful dispossession and without the necessity of proving a better title.

Possessory remedies were needed because of the widespread practice of violent taking and retaking of land by rival claimants. The church was directly affected when two persons claimed the same bishopric or abbey and the person in possession was ousted by armed supporters of his opponent. The disputants might be ecclesiastics — bishops or abbots themselves — or they might be secular lords claiming the right of presentation of bishops or abbots. The forcible ejection of the possessor was called *spoliatio* ("spoliation" or "despoiling"). In dealing with this problem, church councils as well as patriarchs, popes, and others at various times prior to the twelfth century had occasionally decreed that the prior possessor was entitled to be restored to possession before the question of the ultimate rights of the parties could be decided.

In Causae II and III of his *Decretum* (called originally *The Concordance of Discordant Canons*), Gratian dealt with the question of spoliation in the context of two fairly complex cases, each involving a bishop who had been forcibly dispossessed because of alleged crimes. Two important parts of the analysis are the answers to Quaestio 2 of Causa II and Quaestio 1 of Causa III. Both are quite short.

The first is headed, "That one who has been despoiled cannot be brought to trial is established by many authorities." Three popes are then quoted to the effect that "before suit everything must be restored to the one who possessed it." A letter of Bishop Eusebius to the monks of Alexandria and Egypt is quoted: "We find in your letters that certain bishops in your countries have been accused by their own flock . . . and some have been despoiled of their things and some have been expelled from their sees. You know that they cannot be called before either a provincial or a general synod . . . [or] judged anywhere else before all that has been taken away from them is wholly returned to their power, according to the laws." Two other papal letters are then quoted to a similar effect.

Quaestio 1 of Causa III is headed, "Whether restitution shall be made to anyone whomsoever who has been despoiled." Once again, Gratian quotes from two papal epistles stating that bishops who have been despoiled or expelled should have everything wholly restored (*redinte-granda*, "reintegrated") before crimes are charged against them. In one papal epistle it is stated: "nor may any among their superiors or their subordinates bring any charges against them so long as they are deprived of their churches, things, or powers."[10]

Gratian then drew from these two papal epistles, which had been written with reference to specific cases, a rule of very great breadth. Anyone is entitled to a judicial decree of restitution of everything that has been taken from him, including incorporeal rights and powers, whether it has been taken by force or by fraud; and further, the remedy lies not only against the initial wrongdoer but also against third persons.

The jurists who "glossed' Gratian's *Decretum* in the last half of the twelfth and the first half of the thirteenth centuries seized on the breadth of this rule. The Ordinary Gloss, that is, the accepted interpretation, written by Johannes Teutonicus in 1215, annotated Causa II, Quaestio 2, by stating: "The difference between this quaestio and quaestio 1 of Causa III is that here the restitution is prayed by means of an *exceptio* [that is, an affirmative defense to a criminal accusation], while there it is prayed by means of an action [that is, an independent cause of action]." The gloss of John Faventinus said: "Causa III, quaestio 1: Note that what is said about the despoiled bishops is generally understood to extend to all ecclesiastics." (In fact, Gratian extended it to all persons.) And Huguccio wrote: "Causa III, quaestio 1, c. 3: If anybody has been despoiled of his things with violence, or by threats, or with fraud by his adversary, or by any deceit, he must be restored."[11]

Gratian's rule was called the *canon redintegranda* ("rule of restitution"). Shortly after Gratian, the canonists created a new action called *condictio ex canone redintegranda*, which was later called *actio redintegranda* and still later *actio spolii* ("action of spoliation").[12] The actio spolii was available for any kind of spoliation (including spoliation by fraud); it could be used to recover possession of incorporeal rights as well as of movable and immovable things; it was available against third persons, including persons not in possession of things claimed; and the plaintiff was not required to show title to the land or goods or rights which he claimed. Finally, the action was available even to one who was himself wrongfully in possession. To take the most extreme case, if A forcibly dispossessed B, and then in retaliation B forcibly dispossessed A, A would be entitled to a judicial decree restoring him to possession. The principle was that a person out of possession who could prove that he had been forcibly or fraudulently dispossessed should have a preliminary judicial remedy of restitution before anything else concerning the matter was considered, and he was not to be benefited by taking the law into his own hands.

The protection of possession was of utmost importance in a feudal society in which what today is called ownership was characteristically divided among several persons. The feudal tenant held his land of his superior lord, who might also hold it of the king: the lord might lawfully enter the land for certain purposes, and he might have rights in certain products of the land; the tenant did not own the land, yet he needed legal protection against interference with his possessory rights by strangers. The canonists' analysis of the right of one who had been despoiled to be restored to what he had had, without proof of anything more than the "spoliation," was therefore of general significance.

One of the main forces behind the growth of royal law in twelfth- and thirteenth-century Europe was the need for a stronger central authority to keep peace among the barons. In this connection, too, the canonists' rule discountenancing self-help, even on the part of one who had the better right, had much to commend it.

The Roman law of Justinian's texts, by contrast, offered very little help in solving the twin problems of protection of possession and discouragement of self-help. The matter is dealt with only briefly in the Code, the Digest, and the Institutes.

In the Code, three examples are given of an interdict issued by praetors in the reigns of the Emperors Diocletian and Maximian and the Caesars.[13] (An interdict was an order given directly to the parties, stating the rule of law governing the case which they had brought to the praetor.) The interdict in question was called the interdict *unde vi* ("Whence by force"). In Justinian's three examples it is adapted to three different factual situations. In the first, the praetor states: "A person lawfully in possession has the right to use a moderate degree of force to repel any violence exerted for the purpose of depriving him of possession, if he holds it under a title which is not defective." This seems to refer solely to the right of defense of property against an attack in progress, a matter which for the canonists was wholly outside the scope of the problems which gave rise to the canon redintegranda and the actio spolii. Note also that ownership is protected by this rule but not mere possession. The second example of the interdict unde vi follows immediately after the first: "It is a positive rule of law that, by the employment of the interdict, those who have been forcibly ejected from property can have it restored to them if the available year has not expired, and that the heirs shall be liable for the amount which in the meantime has come into their hands." Again, this seems to have little bearing on the problem of self-help. In addition, there is no indication whether or not the plaintiff must prove his title in order to recover possession. The third example adds little or nothing to the second.

The Digest is somewhat more elaborate. In a passage entitled "Concerning the Interdict Vi et Armata," there are two relevant passages, one from Ulpian, the other from Pomponius. Ulpian quotes a slightly different version of the interdict from those given in the Code: "The Praetor says: 'If you or your slaves have forcibly deprived anyone of property which he had at that time, I will grant an action, only for a year; but after the year has elapsed, I will grant one with reference to what has come into the hands of him who dispossessed the complainant by force.'" Ulpian then comments: "This interdict was established for the benefit of a person who has been ejected by force; as it is perfectly just to come to his relief under such circumstances. This interdict was devised to enable him to recover possession." One is still left in uncertainty with respect to the defense of ownership, which in Roman law was sharply distinguished from possession. Can the true owner use force to dispossess one who occupies under a claim of ownership which is faulty? Ulpian does not say. He does, however, limit the scope of the interdict very substantially by stating: "This interdict does not have reference to all kinds of violence, but only to such as issued against persons who are deprived of possession. It only relates to atrocious violence, and where the parties are deprived of the possession of soil; as, for instance, to a tract of land, or a building, but to nothing else . . ." Pomponius adds a brief remark: "If, however, you are ejected by armed force, you will be entitled to recover the land, even if you originally obtained possession of it either by violence, or clandestinely, or under a precarious title." Note that the true owner may have obtained possession by violence or clandestinely or under a precarious title.[14]

Finally, in the Institutes there is a passage concerning the interdict unde vi which follows very closely a passage in the Institutes of the great Roman jurist Gaius, who lived in the second half of the second century A.D., and which clears up some matters but leaves others in even worse confusion. First it is stated that the interdict (applicable only to land and buildings) gives a remedy even though the person who was forcibly ejected himself possessed, as against the ejector, "by force, or secretly, or at will" (*vi, clam, precario*). Then it is stated that "if a person has taken possession of a thing by force, and it is his own property, he is deprived of ownership of it . . . " It is not clear, however, whose property it becomes. Finally, the passage makes reference to the Lex Julia relating to private or public violence, and states that one who forcibly deprives another of his possession is liable for private violence if it was done without arms, but for public violence if he expelled the other from possession by arms. "By the term arms we understand not only shields, swords, and helmets, but also sticks and stones."[15]

A comparison of the treatment of the remedy against wrongful dispossession in Justinian's texts and in Gratian's *Decretum* is most illuminating. In some ways, the papal epistles play a role for Gratian analogous to that which the praetor's interdicts play for Ulpian, Pomponius, and Gaius. However, the quoted comments of the Roman jurists stick much more closely to the language of the interdicts. They tend to bind themselves to the terms of the authoritative rule rather than to extrapolate from them, although they may add to the cases covered by them. They generally follow the distinctions stated or implied in the rule. Thus if the interdict says "land," the Roman jurist in commenting on it tends to say that it means "land, not goods." With Gratian, however, the tendency is to look for the principle underlying the authoritative rule. If land, why not goods as well? and if land and goods, why not rights? The authorities say "bishop"; Gratian adds abbot or any priest and, ultimately, anyone at all, since the principle is to him the same. Thus Gratian concludes his analysis of spoliation with a comprehensive principle, applicable to a wide variety of situations, while the Roman texts yield only a set of discrete rules, rather narrowly conceived and difficult to rationalize.

It was the genius of the Romanist legal science of the twelfth and thirteenth centuries to extract from Roman texts such as those quoted here a coherent doctrine relating to the rights of persons wrongfully dispossessed of their property. The Romanists did so by applying to the interdicts *unde vi* and *vi et armata* and to the comments of Ulpian and Pomponius and Gaius the same kind of logic that Gratian applied to the decisions of the early popes and that later canonist glossators applied to Gratian's work. Under the influence of both canonist and Romanist legal science the various secular rulers of Europe enacted their own laws providing that even the rightful owner is not entitled to drive out the possessor by force or fraud, and that the possessor whose position rests on a prior wrongful dispossession is to give up the possession even though he might ultimately, in another action, regain the property if it is his.

Whatever policies may have motivated the secular authorities, the canonists' canon redintegranda and actio spolii were designed not primarily to protect possession as such but to punish self-help and bad faith. This is apparent from another innovation of the canonists, namely, the modification of the doctrine of Roman law that permitted a possessor to acquire title to land by a sufficient lapse of time, provided only that he came into possession lawfully. One who purchased land in good faith, for example, but later discovered that his seller had not had title to it, could ultimately acquire absolute ownership "by prescription." For the canonists, however, if the possessor knew that the land was not rightfully his, and if he knew to whom it rightfully belonged, then it was bad faith, and a sin, for him to retain possession of it. In the twelfth century, shortly after Gratian's treatise appeared, an anonymous author classified such retention as theft, and thereafter Pope Innocent III decreed that he who claimed by prescription must not at any time have been aware that the object belonged to another. This provision of canon law conflicted sharply with the secular law in most parts of Europe. It nevertheless represents a basic structural element in the system of the canon law of property.

The Canon Law of Contracts

A developed body of contract law was needed by the church in the twelfth century, if only to regulate the myriads of economic transactions between ecclesiastical corporations.[16] In addition, the ecclesiastical courts sought and obtained a large measure of jurisdiction over economic contracts between laymen, where the parties included in their agreement a "pledge of faith"—and for that, too, it was important that the canon law of contracts should command respect. Moreover, the canon law of marriage contained important elements of contract law.

In contract law, more even than in property law, the canonists were able to incorporate a great many of the concepts and rules that were being developed contemporaneously by the glossators out of the rediscovered texts of Justinian. The reasons for that were twofold: first, the older Roman law (especially the ius gentium) had achieved a very high level of sophistication in the field of contracts, and much of its vocabulary in that field, as well as many of its solutions to individual questions, could be applied in the twelfth century to the newly burgeoning commercial life of western Europe; second, the twelfth-century glossators of the Roman law were particularly sophisticated in their reconstruction and transformation of the older Roman law of contracts, in part just because of the demands placed upon them in that respect by the rapid economic changes of their time.

In particular, the older Roman law provided names for various ways of forming contracts and for various types of contracts that fell within those forms. Thus Gaius had written that certain types of contracts were formed by following a prescribed verbal formula, others by formal entry in certain account books, a third type by delivery of the object covered by the contract, and a fourth type by informally expressed consent. In the third class, contracts formed by delivery, he listed the loan of money or fungible goods for consumption, the loan of an object to be returned in specie, the deposit (to be returned on demand), and the pledge (to secure performance of some obligation). In the fourth class, contracts formed by informally expressed consent, he listed sale, lease, partnership, and mandate (a form of agency). Later Roman jurists added several other classes of contracts; the most important was the innominate ("unnamed") contract, of which there were four types: a gift for a gift (*do ut des*), a gift for an act (*do ut facias*), an act for a gift (*facio ut des*), and an act for an act (*facio ut facias*). Innominate contracts were actionable only after one party had performed his promise.

In addition to an elaborate classification of classes and types of contract, the Justinian texts included hundreds of scattered rules—opinions of jurists, holdings in decided cases, decrees of emperors, and so forth —concerning their operation. Nowhere, however, did they contain a systematic explanation of the reasons for the classification or for the rules.

In attempting to construct such an explanation, the glossators of the late eleventh and twelfth centuries seized on an obscure passage in the Digest which states that even an innominate contract gives rise to an obligation if there is a basis (*causa*), though otherwise it does not, and that "therefore a naked agreement does not give rise to an action."[17] The writer may have meant only that innominate contracts do not give rise to an action until one party has performed. "The glossators," as James Gordley has put it, "took him to mean a great deal more. The word they picked out and turned into a general principle was 'naked'; to produce an action, an agreement must be 'clothed.' *Causa* was then defined as the presence of 'clothing.' Accursius defines *causa* as 'something given or done which clothes an agreement.' "[18] Thus the word causa was used by the glossators as a generic term for the various reasons why various types of contracts were (or should be) legally binding. The word itself had many shades of meaning: basis, reason, purpose, cause, and others. Gordley points out that by distinguishing between different kinds of causa, such as, on the one hand, the purpose for which the contract was entered into, to which they applied the Aristotelian term "final cause" (*causa finalis*), and on the other hand, the motivation which stimulated the parties to contract, to which they applied the term "impelling cause" (*causa impulsiva*), the glossators found a language for determining the validity of contracts in controversial cases. It was not, however, until two centuries later, after the translation of Aristotle's *Metaphysics* and *Ethics* and after the systematic application of Aristotelian philosophy to Christian theology by Thomas Aquinas, that the postglossators—especially the fourteenth-century Italian jurists Bartolus and Baldus—were able to go further and to construct not merely a synthesis of the Roman law of contract but what today might be called a general theory of contract. They did so by starting from Aristotelian concepts of distributive and commutative justice and by using Aristotelian categories of substance and accidents as well as authentic Aristotelian definitions of final cause, formal cause, material cause, and efficient cause.[19]

The theory of contract which was developed by the postglossators in the fourteenth century was built, however, not only on the foundations of the Romanist legal science of the twelfth- and thirteenth-century glossators—as viewed through Aristotelian concepts, categories, and definitions—but also on the foundations of the legal science, and, above all, the legal *system*, of the twelfth- and thirteenth-century canonists. What the canonist added to Romanist legal science was, first, the principle that promises are in themselves binding, as a matter of conscience, regardless of whether or not they are "clothed"; and second, that the causa which forms the basis of a contract, and which—if it is a proper causa—gives it validity, is to be defined in terms of the preceding moral obligation of the parties which justifies their having entered into the particular contract.

The canonists started from the principle of penitential discipline that every promise is binding, regardless of its form: *pacta sunt servanda* ("agreements must be kept"). Therefore it is not a defense to an action on a contract that the contract was not in writing or not made under oath. An oath and a promise without an oath are equal in the sight of God, they said; not to fulfill the obligations of a pact is equivalent to a lie.

Yet it did not follow that all promises are binding. Only agreements supported by a proper causa—in the sense of justification—were considered legally binding. "There was *causa* if the promisor had in view a definite result, either some definite legal act or something more comprehensive such as peace. And in order that morality might be safeguarded, it was not only necessary that the promisor should have an object but that this object should be reasonable and equitable."[20]

In contract law, "reason" and "equity," for the twelfth-century canonists and Romanists alike, required a balancing of gains and losses on both sides. In every contract the things or services exchanged should have an equal value. This was called the principle of "just price." The phrase itself, *pretium iustum*, was taken from a passage in the Digest which provided that where the seller of an estate (*fundus*) had received less than half the "just price" he might sue the buyer, who would, however, retain the choice of the manner of discharging the obligation (presumably either by paying the balance or by rescinding the contract).[21] This rule (which on the face of it looks like a remedy for an unpaid seller) first reappeared in western Europe in the *Brachylogus*, a textbook on Roman law of the early twelfth century, where, characteristically, it was broadened to apply to any contract of sale.[22] The canonists applied the same rule.[23] By further elaboration, the doctrine of just price was developed as an overriding principle for testing the validity of any contract.

The problem, of course, was to determine what is just. Both the Romanists and the canonists started with the principle that normally the just price is the common estimate, that is, the market price.[24] It was not considered to be a fixed price: it varied according to diversity of time and place. Where, as in the case of land, it may be difficult to establish a market price, the just price might be determined by consideration of the income from it or by examining sales made of places existing nearby or, if all else failed, by asking the opinion of men who have special acquaintance with local prices.

The Romanists treated a deviation from the just price as a

misrepresentation or a mistake of fact; that is, they assumed that if a buyer paid more than the market price, or a seller took less, it was because he did not know what the market price was, and they devised various remedies for the victim, depending on whether or not the misinformation had been deliberately conveyed by the other party. They also applied the rule that was used by the canonists in cases of marriage contracted under a mistake of fact, namely, that if the person who was so mistaken would have entered into the contract even if he or she had known the true circumstances, then the mistake was not material and would not render the contract void.

The canonists were also concerned, however, with another aspect of a sale at other than the just price, namely, the excess profit derived by one of the parties. Profit making in itself—contrary to what has been said by many modern writers—was not condemned by the canon law of the twelfth century. To buy cheap and sell dear was considered to be proper in many types of situations. If one's property had increased in value since the time it was first purchased, there was nothing wrong with selling it at an increased price. If a craftsman improved an object by his art, he was entitled to charge more for it than he had paid. But even when there was no improvement, as when a merchant bought goods for the purpose of reselling them at a profit, the canonists said that this profit was entirely proper, provided that the motive was not greed but the desire to maintain himself and his dependents.[25] What was condemned by the canon law was "shameful" profit (*turpe lucrum*, "filthy lucre"), and this was identified with avaricious business practices. These, in turn, were defined partly by whether they deviated from normal business practices. Thus for the canonists the doctrine of the just price became, in essence, both a rule of unconscionability, directed against oppressive transactions, and a rule of unfair competition, directed against breach of market norms.

As such, it paralleled another doctrine of the canon law, the prohibition against usury. Usury was denounced in the Old and New Testaments and had been denounced in the church from early times.[26] However, the definition of usury was never entirely clear and it kept changing. Sometimes it seemed to refer to any profit derived from the lending of money, no matter what the purpose or form. In agrarian societies, where tillers of the soil must survive hungry periods prior to the harvesting and sale of crops, those who engage in lending money at interest are apt to be both needed and hated, both wanted and condemned. In western Europe in the ninth, tenth, and early eleventh centuries (before the great revival of commerce), when borrowing was almost always for consumption rather than for production or investment, the church had proclaimed many blanket prohibitions against the sin of usury. In the late eleventh and early twelfth centuries, however, the economic situation began to change drastically. Henceforth money was needed also for financing fairly large-scale economic enterprises. It was also needed for financing fairly large-scale military enterprises of the church itself. At the same time, as John Noonan has pointed out, "many churches and monasteries were heavily endowed and under a constant pressure to find suitable investments for their funds. The monasteries were, indeed, the chief lenders to the nobles departing on the Crusades. The purchase of annuities by churches and pious institutions was on a very large scale . . . The papacy itself often had large idle sums on deposit in banks."[27]

Under these circumstances, the canon lawyers began to systematize for the first time the law of usury. They started with the broad, general concept of an earlier time — the sin of usury consists in lending money for profit. Gratian defined it as "whatever is demanded beyond the principal," and stated that the usurer, like the thief, was bound to restore what he has taken in excess of the loan.[28] Moreover, canon law in the twelfth century extended the doctrine of usury to the sale of goods on credit where the price charged is higher than that charged for a cash sale. At the same time, however, a large number of different types of financing operations and credit devices — for profit — were declared to be nonusurious. Where the borrower was an enemy, a vassal, or an unjust possessor, interest might be charged. Where interest was compensation for a loss incurred through lending, it might be charged; also an agreement was valid that the borrower would pay a financial penalty if he failed to return the loan at the agreed time. In addition, a lender holding a pledge might deduct from its revenues his expenses in caring for it. Eventually, in the latter part of the thirteenth century, it was held that a higher price might be charged for a credit sale than for a cash sale where the lender, as a result of making the loan, suffers a loss or is deprived of a profit that he would otherwise have made. Indeed, the canonists first used the Roman word "interest" (*interesse*) to mean a lawful charge for the loan of money, as distinguished from the sin of usury.

In addition, canon law recognized the validity of a wide variety of commercial contracts that began to flourish in the late eleventh and twelfth centuries, under which risk money was advanced for the sake of a profit. These included joint ventures in the form of a partnership, the so-called *census* (which was an obligation to pay an annual return from income-producing property), and the sale of debts by a creditor to a third party at a discount. Finally, the Roman "deposit" was transformed into a loan of money for investment, with an optional rate of interest.

The canon law of usury thus developed as a system of exceptions to the prohibition against usury. Like the doctrine of the just price, the doctrine of usury was a flexible rule both against unconscionability and against unfair competition. John Gilchrist is unquestionably right in his judgment that the principles of the canon law provided an important foundation for the rapid expansion of commercial and financial activities in western Europe in the twelfth century.[29] Through enforcement of formless contracts ("a man's word is his bond"), through the concept of preceding moral obligation (*causa*) as the key to determining what contracts are valid, through doctrines of unconscionability and unfair competition in the form of unjust price and usury, the canonists were able, with the help of Romanist legal science, to create a subsystem of contract law within the system of canon law as a whole.

Procedure

The canonists borrowed much both from the old Roman texts and from the contemporary Germanic custom. Yet they gave a new twist to both (if only by combining them), and the resulting ensemble was much different from either.

This appears nowhere more strikingly than in the procedure of the ecclesiastical courts.[30] (1) In contrast to both the older Roman and the Germanic systems of procedure, canonical procedure was written. A civil or criminal action could only be commenced by a written complaint or accusation containing a short statement of the facts. The defendant was supposed to reply in writing to the points set forth by the plaintiff or accuser. By the early thirteenth century a written record of the proceedings was required. The judgment had to be in writing, although the judge did not have to give his reasons in writing. Parties examined witnesses and each other on written interrogatories. (2) Testimony, whether written or oral, was required to be under oath, with heavy penalties for perjury. The oath itself was a Germanic institution, but the canonists were the first to use it systematically as a testimonial device in the modern sense. In contrast to the Germanic system of compurgation (oath-helping), in which a party by oath "purged" himself of charges and others supported him by swearing the same oath, the canonists required a party or witness to swear an oath in advance to answer truthfully any proper questions that might be put to him. (3) Canonical procedure permitted the parties to be represented by counsel, who argued the law before the judge on the basis of the facts disclosed by the evidence. Earlier, both in the classical Roman law and in Germanic law, one who acted for another had assumed the rights and duties of the other; he was a substitute rather than a representative. The concept of legal representation was first introduced by the canonists, and was closely linked with both theological concepts and ecclesiastical concerns. (4) The canonists also invented the concept of a dual system of procedure, one solemn and formal, the other simple and equitable. The simple procedure was available for certain types of civil cases, including those involving poor or oppressed persons and those for which an ordinary legal remedy was not available. It dispensed with legal counsel as well as with written pleadings and written interrogatories. (5) Finally, in criminal proceedings the canon law, in contrast to both the Roman and the Germanic systems, developed a science of judicial investigation of the facts of the case, whereby the judge was required to interrogate the parties and the witnesses according to principles of reason and conscience. One of these principles was that the judge must be convinced, in his own mind, of the judgment he rendered. The system of procedure was said to be designed "to inform the conscience of the judge" — a phrase later used in the equitable procedure of the English chancery. A second principle was that the judge must put himself in the position of the person before the court, in order to discern what that person knew and to elicit from him, by subtle questioning, "that which the sinner himself perhaps does not know, or because of shame will wish to hide."[31]

The emphasis on judicial investigation was associated not only with a more rational procedure for eliciting proof but also with the development of concepts of probable truth and of principles of relevancy and materiality. Rules were elaborated to prevent the introduction of superfluous evidence (matters already ascertained), impertinent evidence (matters having no effect on the case), obscure and uncertain evidence (matters from which no clear inferences can be drawn), excessively general evidence (matters from which obscurity arises), and evidence contrary to nature (matters which it is impossible to believe).[32]

The more modern, more rational, more systematized procedure of the canon law of the twelfth century offered a striking contrast to the more primitive, formalistic, and plastic legal institutions that had prevailed in Germanic judicial proceedings in the earlier centuries. Indeed, the principles of reason and conscience were proclaimed by the ecclesiastical jurists as weapons against the formalism and magic of Germanic law. The most dramatic example of this was the decree of the Fourth Lateran Council in 1215 prohibiting priests to participate in ordeals. This law effectively ended the use of ordeals throughout Western Christendom, thereby forcing the secular authorities to adopt new trial procedures in criminal cases. In most countries the secular courts adopted procedures similar to those in use in the ecclesiastical courts. In England the royal courts replaced the ordeals with the sworn inquest, later called the jury, which had been in use in the English royal courts in various types of civil cases for over fifty years, but which had not before been used in criminal cases; in the fourteenth and fifteenth centuries, however, the English chancellors adopted many features of ecclesiastical procedure in cases that were brought before them (later called suits in equity).[33]

Yet despite its sophistication, and despite its emphasis on reason and conscience, the canon law also contained its own elements of magic. These were evident throughout, but most strikingly in the solemn ("ordinary") as contrasted with the summary ("plain") procedure. Above all, the emphasis on writing was so exaggerated as to strongly suggest a magical element. As Mauro Cappelletti has said, "Procedural acts not reduced to writing were null and void . . . The judge was required to base his decision exclusively upon the written record."[34] Eventually, in the most formal types of ordinary procedure, the judge did not himself examine the parties and the witnesses but only studied the written record of their examination drawn up by subordinate court officials. This, of course, defeated the original purpose of judicial investigation, which was to enable the judge to form an "inner conviction" of the truth of matters in dispute.

Coupled with the sanctity or magic of the writing was the elaboration of a set of formal rules for evaluating evidence, which existed alongside the rational rules of relevancy and materiality. Two oracular or auricular witnesses were required to establish a fact (although judicial notice could be taken of notorious facts). The testimony of a woman counted only one-half and had to be supplemented by the testimony of at least one man. The testimony of a nobleman counted more than that of a commoner, that of a priest more than that of a layman, that of a Christian more than that of a Jew. The artificial weighing of evidence—full proof, half proof, one-fourth proof, even one-eighth proof—assumed increased importance as the judge became removed from the examination of witnesses and had nothing else to go on but the written record.

The rigors of proof, both formal and rational, were such as to make it often very difficult to establish grounds for conviction in criminal cases.[35] It was this fact, more than any other, that eventually led to the widespread use of torture to extract evidence, and especially to extract that "queen of proofs," a confession. In cases where the state of mind of the accused was at issue—heresy cases were a prime example—there was no one more qualified to testify concerning his state of mind than the accused himself, and no more effective way to secure his admission of a criminal state of mind than the use of physical force.

In civil cases not only the rigors of proof but also, and more especially, the complexities of taking evidence by written interrogatories, without participation of the judge, led inevitably to the widespread use of dilatory tactics by the lawyers. This, in turn, was counteracted by the establishment of a series of compulsory stages, with separate rulings by the judge at each stage. However, the system could not resist the pressure to allow appeals to be taken from the separate rulings, and then to require such appeals to be taken at the risk of waiver of the right to object to the rulings at a later stage. It is not surprising that some cases went on for years and even decades.

These vices in the Romanist-canonical procedure were more characteristic of its use in the secular courts than in the ecclesiastical courts, where the judge's participation was more extensive and judicial discretion was given more scope. They were also more characteristic of its later development than of its use in the twelfth and early thirteenth centuries. It is likely that the increased reliance on written proofs, on formal rules of measuring evidence, and on confessions in criminal cases all reflected a decline in respect for oaths, which itself, paradoxically, may have reflected the increased emphasis upon rationality in the law.

The Systematic Character of Canon Law

In the late eleventh, twelfth, and early thirteenth centuries there emerged—indeed, there was consciously created, though not all at once but only gradually, and not out of whole cloth but rather by reconstituting and restructuring preexisting disparate elements—a system of canon law, a jus canonicum (as it came to be called in the mid-twelfth century), a corpus juris canonici (as it came to be called in the thirteenth century). Breaking it down into corporation law, criminal law, marriage law, law of inheritance, property law, contract law, and procedure has given it a greater appearance of coherence than the canonists themselves gave it at the time: they wrote treatises on procedure, but they did not generally analyze individual subsystems of substantive law; that style of analysis only came into vogue many centuries later. Yet the subsystems were there to be analyzed.

The analytical integration of canon law, that is, its explicit logical systematization, proceeded from a belief that underlying the multiplicity of legal rules and procedures was a set of basic legal principles, and that it was the task of jurists to identify those principles and to help shape the law so that it would conform to them. The jurists thought in principles. Out of the principles they built systems, which, like the theologians, they elaborated in books called *summae,* meaning both "highest" and "total."

It was believed, further, that the underlying legal principles had not only a logical aspect, being subject to reason, but also a moral aspect, being subject to conscience. Therefore, not only an analytical or logical systematization was required, which would strive for consistency in the law, but also a moral systematization, which would strive for equity. In addition, the principles underlying the law were believed to have what today would be called a political aspect: they were, on the one hand, the principles already implicit in the law, but they were also, on the other hand, a program, a standard by which to judge and correct and, if necessary, to eliminate particular existing laws. They were supposed to be realized in practice. Thus in addition to the logical element of reason and the moral element of conscience in the systematization of canon law, there was also the political element of reformation, or development, or growth.

The logical, moral, and political aspects of basic legal principles were summarized in the concept of natural law. This was a substantially different concept from that held by the Greeks and the Romans. The earlier natural law had been defined as the right of every man — as it was put in the first title of Justinian's Digest — to receive what was his due; natural law was justice, equity, what was right; it was an ideal law, the law not of the state but of nature itself, to which the law of the state might or might not conform. It lacked the programmatic character of the natural law of the later European Romanists and canonists. For the canonists, natural law was primarily a standard to be held up to secular rulers by the church, and secondarily a standard by which to interpret and shape the law of the church as well. Natural law was not an ideal law standing outside the existing legal systems but rather the morality of the law itself standing within the existing legal systems. It was a kind of constitutional principle, or *Grundgesetz*, a "due process clause." It was because of the programmatic or political character of the law, represented particularly by that part of it that was called natural law, that thousands of young men went annually to the universities to study law — as in the United States today — in order to prepare themselves for political careers. These were among the most intelligent and ambitious young men of Europe. They were taught the positive law and the techniques of applying it, but they were also taught the natural law, the law that was to be. The glosses had a political function.

What is called here the political aspect of the canon law, its principle of conscious development, of growth, of reform, was manifested concretely in the stream of legislation which proceeded from the papacy, and from church councils called by the papacy, from the late eleventh century on. It was manifested also in the continuity of legal scholarship, as canons, glosses, decretals, and other sources were collected and treatises were written. Finally, and perhaps most important, it was manifested in the continuity of the legal profession, as successive generations of lawyers were trained in the universities and went out into the ecclesiastical and secular chanceries and courts to practice what they had been taught.

The combination of logical, moral, and political elements contributed to a systematization that was quite different from a merely doctrinal or dogmatic analysis of legal rules, however complex and however coherent. The canon law as a system was more than rules; it was a process, a dialectical process of adapting rules to new situations. This was inevitable if only because of the limits imposed upon its jurisdiction, and the consequent competition which it faced from the secular legal systems that coexisted with it.

7 | Becket versus Henry II: The Competition of Concurrent Jurisdictions

THE NORMAN CONQUEST of England was undertaken in 1066—nine years before the *Dictatus* of Pope Gregory VII—partly in the name of reforming the English church by freeing it from local and feudal pressures and centralizing ecclesiastical authority in the hands of the king. William the Conqueror had a commission from Pope Alexander II in this endeavor, which was seen as being in the spirit of the Cluniac Reform. In a famous decree of 1067, William asserted that the king (rather than local lords) has the power to determine whether or not a pope should be acknowledged by the church in Normandy and England; that the king makes canon law through church synods; and that the king has a veto power over ecclesiastical penalties imposed on his barons and officials.

Eight years later, however, Pope Gregory VII was saying that he the pope, and not emperors or kings, was the head of the church; that the pope alone has the power to depose bishops—and, indeed, emperors and kings as well; and that the pope, and not kings or emperors, determines whether actions taken by church synods may be considered canonical.

William and his two successors (his sons William II, 1087-1100, and Henry I, 1100-1135) successfully opposed papal claims to supremacy over the church in their dominions, although Henry I made some substantial compromises in the Concordat of Bec. In the reign of Stephen (1135-1154), however, which English historians have called "the anarchy of Stephen" because of the civil disorders that characterized it, the papal party in England made important gains in prestige and power.[1] New monastic orders, loyal to the pope, were founded; they received strong popular support, especially because they provided relief and welfare to the victims of civil strife. At a time when civil justice was often in abeyance, church synods continued to meet and law was administered in episcopal courts. The canon law attracted adherents among both clergy and laity: Gratian's treatise of 1140 was soon being studied and dis-

cussed by educated Englishmen, who must have been impressed by its
intellectual superiority over the almost entirely unwritten secular law,
with its formalistic procedures of ordeals, trial by battle, and compurgation.[2] In a time of troubles, the church of Rome was the main pillar of
order and justice, and when peace ultimately came in 1154 and a new
dynasty was placed on the throne, it was partly as a result of the mediation of the political struggle by supporters of papal supremacy.

Nevertheless, the new king, Henry II (1154-1189), reasserted royal
supremacy over the church. In 1162 he appointed as Archbishop of
Canterbury his close friend Thomas Becket, who already occupied the
chancellorship, which was the highest office in the realm next to the
kingship. Henry expected Thomas to continue as chancellor while he
was archbishop, thus more effectively to carry out the policy of resistance
to papal claims. Becket, however, resigned the chancellorship and, as
archbishop, became an ardent supporter of the church's independence
from royal control. When Henry issued the Constitutions of Clarendon
in 1164, restoring much of the king's power over the church, Thomas denounced the new legislation as a usurpation. For six years a bitter
political struggle continued between the two men, in which leading ecclesiastical and secular figures from many parts of Europe were
involved. Finally in 1170, in response to Henry's words, "Will no one rid
me of this pestilential priest," four of the king's men murdered the archbishop in his cathedral at Canterbury. That act, however, so shocked
England, and indeed the whole of Christendom, that Henry did penance
by walking barefoot to Canterbury (true, he only walked from the out-
skirts of the town), and—more important—in 1172 he submitted to a
papal legate on the heights of Avranches and before its cathedral publicly renounced those portions of the Constitutions of Clarendon that
were "offensive."

The Constitutions of Clarendon

The constitutions—that is, decrees or enactments—which were issued
at Clarendon in 1164 purported to be a record of sixteen "customs, liberties, and privileges" of Henry II's grandfather (Henry I), acknowledged
by the leading clergy and nobles. The first of these (article 1) provided
that all disputes over the right of patronage of church offices—called advowson—were to be decided in the king's court, though the dispute arose
between a laymen and a cleric or even between two clerics. The
significance of attributing this custom to Henry I is that in Stephen's
reign such disputes had often been tried in ecclesiastical courts. Another
provision (article 9) established royal jurisdiction over (and jury trial of)
the question whether or not particular land was church property
(*frankalmoign*, "free alms"). For this custom, too, ancient authority was
better than more recent, for under Stephen the church courts had

asserted their own supremacy in determining their jurisdiction over church property. Other provisions prohibited archbishops, bishops, and other clergy from departing the kingdom without permission of the king (article 4); provided for appeals from the archbishop's court to the court of the king (article 8); imposed procedural safeguards on accusations of laymen in ecclesiastical courts (article 6); prohibited excommunication of a tenant-in-chief of the king (one who held land directly of him, as contrasted with a subtenant), or of an officer of the king's household, without the king's permission (article 7); reiterated the settlement reached in 1107 at Bec to the effect that elections of bishops and other beneficed clergy "ought to take place in the lord king's chapel with the assent of the clergy of the realm . . . And the clerk elected shall then no longer do homage and fealty to the lord king . . . before he is consecrated" (article 12); gave jurisdiction to the king's court for "pleas of debt due under pledge of faith" (article 15); and prohibited the ordaining of sons of villeins without the consent of the lord on whose land they had been born (article 16).

Of these nine provisions (articles 1, 4, 6, 7, 8, 9, 12, 15, 16), all except the one on investiture (article 12) were in violation of the prevailing canon law of the church.[3]

It was the third article of the constitutions that ultimately became the most notorious. It provided, in effect, that any cleric accused of a felony (including homicide, arson, robbery, rape, mayhem, and certain other serious crimes) should be sent by the king's court to the ecclesiastical court for trial and, if convicted there, should be brought back to the king's court to be sentenced. This meant, in practice, to be executed or mutilated by exoculation or by the cutting off of hands or legs. A royal officer should attend the proceedings in the ecclesiastical court "to see how the case is there tried."

Historians of English law have analyzed the titanic conflict between Henry and Becket largely in terms of their respective positions in regard to article 3. In fact, however, other provisions of the constitutions were more significant. Article 8 would have made the king, rather than the pope, the supreme arbiter of canon law in England.

Historians have also placed much emphasis upon the psychological aspects of the conflict. It is usually said that the tragic end could have been avoided if either of the chief protagonists had been less stubborn. Indeed, each vacillated between insistence on extreme demands and poorly timed offers of compromise. One commentator argues that at a certain point Henry was "apparently" prepared to "jettison" the Constitutions of Clarendon and to "concede almost all for which Becket was fighting."[4] If that were so, then the failure to settle the dispute might indeed be blamed solely on Becket's personality. This suggests, further, that his martyrdom (as one of his slayers argued in T.S. Eliot's play,

Murder in the Cathedral) was really his own fault, a kind of suicide. (A contemporary historian calls Becket "an unreconstructed Gregorian intent upon martyrdom.")[5] Yet, even assuming that Henry was willing to renounce the constitutions as a document, the question remains whether he would have renounced his ambition to control the church in his territories. In fact, Henry did *not* respond to the death of Becket as though the archbishop had brought it upon himself. Of course, Henry's response may be explained at least in part by the enormous revulsion caused by the assassination. Yet that very revulsion, as well as the subsequent political and historical reverberations of Becket's death, make a purely psychological interpretation of the conflict seem inadequate. The two men represented not just themselves but two great competing forces in Western history, the ecclesiastical and the secular.

There remains the question—important for one's understanding of the Western legal tradition—who was right? Almost a century ago, Maitland argued that Henry was right, because the customs he asserted were in fact those practiced by his grandfather, Henry I. Maitland took one of Becket's arguments, "Christ said, not 'I am the custom,' but 'I am the truth,' " as a tacit admission that Henry was acting lawfully. In fact, the same argument was made by Tertullian (about 155-220 A.D.), and was used by Pope Gregory VII in answering Emperor Henry IV a century before; Gratian had repeated it only a generation before, as a basis for overturning unreasonable customs. Becket's argument was in effect a reference to historical precedent within the church and to the authority of ecclesiastical law. However, even assuming that (secular) custom has a higher legal force than (ecclesiastical) truth, Maitland's contention omits the possibility that the customs of Henry I were changed during the so-called anarchy of Stephen. On this point Maitland only states: "For legal purposes Stephen's reign is to be ignored . . . because it was a time of war and of 'unlaw.' Sixty years later this doctrine still prevails; a litigant cannot rely on what happened in Stephen's reign, for it was not a time of peace."[6]

It is characteristic of English legal historians to treat a revolution as a mere interregnum: they have done the same with the Puritan Revolution under Cromwell. If, however, the reign of Stephen was the period when the Papal Revolution finally asserted itself in England, should not Henry II's claim to return to the customs of his grandfather be considered as counterrevolutionary? From this point of view, Becket was fighting for a cause that had already been won. In the matter of royal supremacy over the church, Henry was, on the one hand, at least a generation too late, and on the other hand, three and one-half centuries too early.[7]

The particular balance to be struck between the two powers, there being no question of simple supremacy of one over the other, remained always in question; and here the unique circumstances of Becket's martyrdom made a difference.

Benefit of Clergy and Double Jeopardy

Was Becket right in considering article 3 of the Constitutions of Clarendon to be a violation of the principle against double jeopardy? "God does not punish twice for the same offense" (*ne bis in idem*). These words used by Becket go back to a mistranslated Biblical text (Nahum 1:9) and were sometimes applied in the twelfth century by canonists as authority for excluding double jeopardy in the ecclesiastical courts. Becket seems to have been the first to apply the phrase to justify the privilege of the clergy to be punished — for certain offenses — solely in the ecclesiastical forum.[8] Yet total clerical immunity from secular jurisdiction was never claimed. It is true that in both the Byzantine and Frankish empires, bishops — though not those below them — were generally to be tried and sentenced only by their clerical peers.[9] At that earlier time, however, no sharp distinction existed between clerical and secular courts; clergy sat in both. In any event, in England as elsewhere, it was quite common before the twelfth century for clerics who had been condemned and deposed or otherwise disciplined in ecclesiastical proceedings to be turned over to local or feudal or royal courts to be tried and punished for the same act. It was only with the establishment of the new system of ecclesiastical jurisdiction in the late eleventh and early twelfth centuries that benefit of clergy became a crucial issue.

The arguments against Becket's position have been forcefully stated by Maitland. Becket's doctrine that the state must not punish the criminous clerk for that crime for which he has already been deposed or degraded "had neither been tolerated by the state nor consecrated by the Church." The canonists did not support the rule urged by Becket, and it was not law elsewhere in Europe; had it been followed, Maitland pointed out, "no deposed or degraded clerk would ever have been handed over to the lay power [to be executed] as a heretic or a forger of papal bulls." Further, Maitland contended that at the time of the Becket controversy, trial in the church courts in criminal cases "was already becoming little better than a farce." At that time, ecclesiastical procedure in cases of felonies was by compurgation. "Bishop Jocelin of Salisbury," Maitland stated, "cleared himself of complicity in the murder of Becket with four or five oath-helpers. Hubert Walter, sitting as archbishop, forbade that more compurgators than the canonical twelve should be demanded." Furthermore, even if the clerk failed in his purgation and was convicted, the ecclesiastical punishments were relatively mild: the bishop "could degrade the clerk from his orders, and, as an additional punishment, relegate him to a monastery or keep him in prison for life. A whipping might be inflicted . . . This then was the punishment due to felonious clerks; we fear that but few of them suffered it." Benefit of clergy was "an invidious and mischievous immunity."[10]

Maitland's argument, which has been adopted by George Greenaway, W.L. Warren, and others, proves too much. Was the ecclesiastical trial more farcical than trial by battle or by ordeal in the secular courts? Were the sanctions of the royal courts — hanging or mutilation — a more fitting punishment for a first offense than confinement in a monastery or prison? Moreover, Maitland omits the most subtle of the ecclesiastical penalties: the bishop could order that penance be done — on pain of excommunication — in the form of reimbursement of the victim or his family, charitable works, and other good deeds. Further, the penalty of excommunication itself could be very severe, since in its extreme form it was in effect an outlawry from the church, involving virtual ostracism.

Greenaway states that the principle of double jeopardy was not violated by the Constitutions of Clarendon, since Henry was not proposing a second trial but only a sentence.[11] This is a strong point, but by no means answers all the questions. What is it that makes double jeopardy abhorrent? Is it merely the fact of two trials, or may it not also be the fact of condemnation by two jurisdictions? Moreover, can the second tribunal impose a sentence without, in fact, some sort of trial, or at least some characterization of the offense? What might be burglary in the king's courts, punishable by death, might be a minor offense in the ecclesiastical courts if motivated, for example, by need and followed by voluntary surrender and return of the stolen goods.

Contemporary legal systems have no difficulty in permitting prosecution of a man for embezzlement even though he has already been discharged by his employer for the offense, since the discharge is viewed not as an official condemnation but as an act of a private organization within the state. Was this, then, the issue for Becket: whether the church was an organization within the state — or the state an organization within the church?[12]

Ecclesiastical Jurisdiction in England

The conflict between Becket and Henry was essentially a conflict over the scope of ecclesiastical jurisdiction; it was thus a paradigm of the Papal Revolution, which established throughout the West two types of competing political-legal authority, the spiritual and the secular. One effect of this dualism was to enhance the political-legal authority of kings in the secular sphere. Another effect was to create tensions at the boundaries of royal and papal jurisdictions. These tensions were resolved in different ways in different kingdoms. Their resolution in England was strongly influenced by the circumstances of Becket's martyrdom.

In twelfth-century England, as in Europe generally, the ecclesiastical courts claimed jurisdiction (though they did not always get it) over: (1) all civil and criminal cases involving clerics, including all cases involving church property; (2) all matrimonial cases; (3) all testamentary cases; (4) certain criminal cases, such as heresy, sacrilege, sorcery, usury, defamation, fornication, homosexuality, adultery, injury to religious places, and assault against a cleric; and (5) contract, property, and other civil cases, where there was a breach of a pledge of faith (called "perjury," that is, violation of an oath). As far as the canon law was concerned, any case involving any of these matters could be instituted by filing a complaint in the court of the appropriate archdeacon or bishop, and an appeal could be taken by the losing party to the court of the appropriate archbishop and thence to the court of the pope in Rome. In fact, in the thirteenth century more cases heard on appeal by the papal court in Rome came from England than from any other country. The pope also exercised a universal *original* jurisdiction: the plaintiff could impetrate (procure) a writ from the papal curia nominating papal delegates to try any case locally. This, indeed, was quite common in cases involving considerable sums of money as well as in cases in which the parties resided in different archbishoprics, since no major country in the West contained only one ecclesiastical jurisdiction. (A decision of the Archbishop of York, for example, could not be appealed to the court of the Archbishop of Canterbury.)

At the same time, the church's jurisdictional claims were challenged — and often successfully challenged — by the secular courts. As Maitland has put it:

> Never in England, nor perhaps in any other country, did the state surrender to the ecclesiastical tribunals the whole of that illimitable tract which was demanded for them by the more reckless of their partisans. Everywhere we see strife and then compromise, and then strife again, and at latest after the end of the thirteenth century the state usually gets the better in every combat. The attempt to draw an unwavering line between "spiritual" and "temporal" affairs is hopeless. Such it will always be if so-called "spiritual courts" are to exercise any power within this world of time. So ragged, so unscientific was the frontier which at any given moment and in any given country divided the territory of secular from the territory of ecclesiastical law that ground could be lost and won by insensible degrees . . . We have only to consider the incurable vagueness of such phrases as "testamentary causes" and "matrimonial causes," and we shall understand how easily one small annexation might follow another without any pitched battle, any shout of triumph or wail of defeat. The rulers of the church, therefore, had to tolerate much that they could not approve, or at any rate much that they could not approve in the name of the church. They could give and take without any sacrifice of first principles. No doubt there were principles for which they would have professed a willingness to

die after the fashion of St. Thomas; but they were not called upon to shed
their blood for every jot and tittle of a complex and insatiable
jurisprudence. Popes, and popes who were no weaklings, had taught them
by precept and example that when we are dealing with temporal power we
may temporize.[13]

Here, then, was a highly uncomfortable situation: two sets of
courts—one ecclesiastical, the other royal—both of which claimed
jurisdiction over the same cases. How were these rival claims to be
resolved? On the one hand, the king was a Christian and hence a subject
of the pope; one would have thought that the pope, or his subordinate,
the Archbishop of Canterbury, would only have had to admonish an
English king that unless he yielded to Holy Church's jurisdictional
demands he would be damned in hell. On the other hand, the church
itself was the author of the concept of dual authority, two swords, the ecclesiastical and the secular, the spiritual and the temporal. Yet by the
church's own definitions, much of what the ecclesiastical courts claimed
for their jurisdiction was secular. As Maitland indicates, such phrases as
"matrimonial causes" covered not only intimate spiritual questions of
family relations but also questions of property relations that often had
much to do with the economic and political order for which the crown
was responsible.

And then—apart from concept and theory—there were questions of
power. The church, lacking armies of its own, was dependent upon the
secular arm for enforcement of its wishes against recalcitrants; in addition, popes and archbishops were generally not named to office without
secular support. But the church had a powerful, though unarmed,
political corps, the clergy, who could enforce some very potent spiritual
sanctions, including excommunication and interdict.

Excommunication meant deprivation of the right to receive the
sacraments (including last rites and, consequently, a Christian burial)
and, in extreme cases, expulsion from the church altogether, under
anathema (a virtual ostracism). Interdict was a partial or total suspension of public services and sacraments; it could extend to one or more
persons or to a whole locality or kingdom. In 1208 Pope Innocent III
placed all England under interdict and excommunicated King John,
threatening to depose him and give his crown to Philip Augustus of
France. The reason was John's refusal to accept the pope's nominee as
Archbishop of Canterbury. England groaned under the interdict.
Churches remained closed for years. King John counterattacked by putting his own men in clerical offices, but he ultimately submitted; in fact
he gave England to the pope and received it back as a fief, swearing an
oath of vassalage and agreeing to send a yearly tribute to Rome. In 1215
King John, in the very first provision of Magna Carta, declared *quod ec-*

clesia Anglicana libera sit — "that the English Church be free" — which meant, of course, free under the papacy from control by kings or barons.

Given, then, acute rivalry between powers armed with both theoretical and practical weapons, a resolution by legal means must have been greatly desired — especially since both sides had a very high appreciation of the role of law in resolving conflict, and moreover, the particular conflict was itself a legal one, over jurisdiction.

With respect to clergy charged with serious crimes (felonies) the issue in England seemed to have been settled following Becket's martyrdom: secular jurisdiction even to punish, let alone to try, was excluded. Nevertheless, the king's courts eventually adopted the procedural device of trying the person before inquiring about his clerical status, and only then, if he was convicted, could he plead benefit of clergy and be remitted to the ecclesiastical court. Moreover, the issue of the secular liability of clergy for crimes less than felonies, and for civil offenses, was apparently not raised by Becket; in any event, there remained secular jurisdiction over the clergy in such matters in England. In France, on the contrary, the clergy were immune from secular prosecution for minor crimes, but not for the most serious ones, such as premeditated homicide, mutilation, highway robbery, and recidivism ("incorrigibility"), and not for "royal cases," which included treason and other crimes touching the prince or the dignity of his officers as well as crimes of public safety, such as holding forbidden assemblies and teaching idolatry, atheism, and other prohibited doctrines. Such "royal cases" were in the secular jurisdiction whether the crime had been committed by a cleric or by a layman.

As for other matters dealt with in the Constitutions of Clarendon, Henry II renounced those provisions which were "offensive" to the papacy, but it was not specified which of them fell into that category. In fact, serious struggles took place in the thirteenth century between the crown and the clergy before the boundaries between the two jurisdictions were more or less settled.

With respect to purely ecclesiastical matters, the jurisdiction asserted by Henry II in the Constitutions of Clarendon was never asserted again until the English Reformation of the sixteenth century. Prior to Henry VIII, the king did not obtain appellate jurisdiction over decisions of the court of the archbishop (article 8). Also the clergy insisted on their right to depart the realm without the king's permission (article 4), though he often restrained them in fact. The king retained the right to be consulted before excommunication of his officers (article 7), but here the pope had the upper hand and could excommunicate the king himself.

With respect to matrimonial and testamentary causes — matters not touched on in the Constitutions of Clarendon — the ecclesiastical courts in England had an almost exclusive jurisdiction. However, "real property" could not be left by will, and in the thirteenth century the king's courts asserted exclusive jurisdiction over all realty.

With respect to disputes between clerks concerning presentation to churches (article 1) and disputes between laymen over debts due under a pledge of faith (article 15), both the ecclesiastical courts and the royal courts asserted their respective jurisdictions. In both of these types of disputes the ecclesiastical courts exercised a very considerable voluntary jurisdiction.

A comparison of the boundaries between ecclesiastical and secular jurisdiction in England and in France reveals that the church held a less privileged positon in France than in England. (1) With respect to matrimonial causes, the secular jurists in France distinguished between the civil marriage contract and the marriage sacrament; disputes over the former were for the secular courts to resolve (for example, disputes over whether both spouses had freely consented to the marriage). (2) Testamentary causes in France were subject to the concurrent jurisdiction of the ecclesiastical and secular courts in the twelfth and thirteenth centuries and thereafter were in the exclusive jurisdiction of the secular courts. (3) With respect to clerical benefices in France in the fourteenth and fifteenth centuries, a distinction was made between possessory rights, which were for the king's court to determine, and ownership rights, which were in the ecclesiastical jurisdiction. In England the royal courts considered advowsons (rights of presentation) to be a species of real property and thus within their exclusive jurisdiction, but the church courts sometimes successfully challenged this view. (4) In England, but not in France, recovery of tithes, church dues, and taxes for improvement of churches and churchyards were in the sole jurisdiction of the ecclesiastical courts, as were the administration of pious gifts and revenues given to prelates or religious houses — that is, until the English chancellor extended his concurrent jurisdiction in the fourteenth and fifteenth centuries to include transfers made "to the use of" another. (5) Only in matters of breach of promises made under oath or pledge of faith (perjury), did French ecclesiastical jurisdiction surpass the English; in France these matters were apparently not claimed by the secular authority. Finally, (6) the criminal jurisdiction of the French royal courts over "ideological" crimes was considerably larger than that of the English royal courts.

Writs of Prohibition

The scope of the conflict between royal and ecclesiastical courts in England was defined by the legal device of the writ of prohibition. This was an order issued by the chancellor in the king's name, forbidding an ecclesiastical court to take further cognizance of a particular case on the ground that the church's competence to judge the matter at issue had been put in question by the defendant in the case. The ecclesiastical court was then either to drop the case or else to consult with the king's justices. If after consultation the king's justices determined that the case was properly before the ecclesiastical court, they would authorize it—by a "writ of consultation"—to proceed notwithstanding the previous prohibition. If the ecclesiastical court persisted in hearing a case despite a prohibition, or despite an unfavorable outcome on consultation, the king's court would issue a writ of attachment instructing the sheriff to bring the ecclesiastical judges before the king or his justices "to show why they hold a plea in court christian . . . against our prohibition."

A royal prohibition could be a powerful weapon, and it was occasionally used with great effect to restrain the ecclesiastical courts. For the most part, however, it was complex and unwieldy, relatively difficult to obtain, and relatively easy to circumvent.

It was the defendant in the ecclesiastical court who had to take the initiative. If both parties consented to ecclesiastical jurisdiction, the royal court would not intervene. This surely amounted to an enormous royal concession in the struggle between the two systems of courts.[14] It meant that almost all disputes between clerics were effectively removed from secular jurisdiction. It also meant that laymen who had contracted to exclude secular jurisdiction were barred from obtaining a writ of prohibition, though the royal courts read such contractual stipulations strictly.[15]

To obtain a writ of prohibition, the defendant in the ecclesiastical action had to allege that he had been cited to appear before such and such ecclesiastical judges as defendant in a plea that a certain party (giving his name) had sued against him concerning a particular type of matter that fell within the jursdiction of the royal courts. Typical matters were disputes over real property other than church sites, churchyards, and cemeteries ("lay fee"); disputes over the right of patronage to ecclesiastical offices (advowson); disputes over chattels and debts except those derived from marriage or testament, those which belonged to the church such as tithes and offerings, and goods seized from a cleric; disputes over trespasses by clerics; and defamatory statements made in connection with cases in the king's courts.

In general, the royal courts would grant a writ of prohibition on the mere allegation of the defendant in the ecclesiastical case, provided the allegation was sufficient on its face. However, if it turned out later that the matter in dispute was of a different nature from that alleged in the writ of prohibition, the prohibition would not be enforced and, indeed, the defendant could be fined by the royal justices for making a false claim.

The defendant had to serve the writ both on the ecclesiastical judges and on the plaintiff. They were then to appear before the king's justices to defend the ecclesiastical jurisdiction. The purpose of the writ, as G.B. Flahiff points out, was "to publicize and make prevail two important claims of the king: first that he alone and his court have jurisdiction in the matters named in the various writs of prohibition—lay fee, advowson, lay chattels, etc.; secondly, that the royal authority alone has the right to determine what jurisdiction is competent in doubtful cases."[16] The question concerned the competence of a court to determine its own competence.

However, the ecclesiastical courts also claimed a similar competence. In 1147 Pope Eugene III ordered that "bishops, abbots, archbishops, and other prelates of churches shall not submit ecclesiastical transactions to the judgment of laymen, nor shall they cease to administer ecclesiastical justice because of the prohibition of laymen."[17] English church councils issued similar decrees, stating further that the king had no right to take umbrage at ecclesiastical judges who were but doing their duty in continuing to hear spiritual pleas, even contrary to a prohibition.

The ecclesiastical court did not lack practical resources to resist prohibitions. First, canon law—in contrast to the English royal law of the time—permitted the court to hear witnesses and proceed to judgment in the defendant's absence, even in personal actions. Second, the defendant who failed to appear after three citations was subject to excommunication. And third: "The spiritual authorities may go yet farther. Not content with excommunication and pronouncing sentence against the defendant, they may sometimes institute a new suit against him and cite him to answer for the canonical offense of having caused an ecclesiastical action to be unjustly prohibited by the secular power."[18] Of course, the new suit was also subject to a writ of prohibition, if the defendant wished to go further with the matter.

Excommunication for suing out a writ of prohibition raised the question of whether the secular power would cooperate in enforcing the excommunication. In normal cases of excommunication, if the excommunicate did not seek absolution within forty days, the bishop could inform the king thereof and the king would order the sheriff to arrest the sinner and keep him in custody until he was willing to be reconciled. Also, excommunicates could not sue in the king's court. Flahiff gives some amusing examples of subterfuges used by ecclesiastical judges to procure secular aid in enforcing excommunications imposed for seeking a writ of prohibition,[19] but in general the royal authorities would not honor an excommunication directed against their own rightful jurisdiction.

In England, conflicts between the church and the crown over writs of prohibition were to some extent resolved in 1286 in the royal statute, or writ, *Circumspecte Agatis*. The king, who previously had sought unsuccessfully to limit the property jurisdiction of ecclesiastical courts over laymen to matrimonial and testamentary cases, finally admitted the right of these courts to impose monetary penalties for fornication, adultery, and other mortal sins; require parishioners to contribute to the upkeep of their church and cemetery; hear suits by the rector of a church against his parishioners for the payment of various customary church taxes (mortuaries, oblations, tithes); hear suits by one rector against another for tithes, provided these did not exceed one-quarter of the value of the church, which would have brought into question the right of patronage (advowson); and award damages in cases of violence against clerics, defamation, and breach of pledge of faith, provided correction of sin was also involved. Moreover, in cases of defamation or violence against a cleric, it was provided that if one who was sentenced to bodily punishment by an ecclesiastical court wished to have the penalty commuted to a money payment, the court could accede to this wish without being subject to a royal prohibition.

In France, the place of the writ of prohibition was taken by the *appel comme d'abus*. It permitted direct recourse not only by aggrieved parties but by any person, lay or ecclesiastic, to the secular courts, and in later times to the king, to prevent "abuse" of ecclesiastical jurisdiction. It seems to have been considerably more effective in limiting that jurisdiction than its English counterpart.

The jurisdiction of ecclesiastical courts was one of the principal objects of attack during each of the great European national revolutions — the Protestant Reformation in Germany in the sixteenth century, the English Revolution of the seventeenth century, the French Revolution of the eighteenth century, and the Russian Revolution of the twentieth century. In most Lutheran and Calvinist countries, church courts were replaced in the sixteenth century by consistories or synods, whose jurisdiction was generally confined to discipline of ministers and other church officials; and the state took over most of the former ecclesiastical jurisdiction over the laity in criminal and civil matters. In England, on the contrary, the Reformation merely placed papal authority in the hands of the king, who continued to maintain (and even broaden) the former ecclesiastical jurisdiction. However, in the seventeenth century the Puritan Revolution and the Restoration transferred many civil and criminal matters from the church courts to the common law courts (as well as chancery). Nevertheless, it was not until the nineteenth century — in the wake of the massive secularization introduced by the French Revolution — that England, by a series of statutes, reduced the ecclesiastical jurisdiction of the Anglican Church to discipline of clergy, discipline of laity for certain types of sexual offenses, and various minor matters pertaining to worship services. In Roman Catholic countries as well, the nineteenth century saw the gradual implementation of a law of the French Revolution (September 1790), which had proclaimed the suppression of all ecclesiastical jurisdictions. Except in Spain and Portugal, the jurisdiction of Roman Catholic ecclesiastical courts over the laity became entirely a matter of conscience, and their decisions had no temporal legal consequences. In practice, these courts generally confined their jurisdiction over laymen to questions of marriage, betrothal, and legitimacy of children.

Historians will no doubt continue to differ in their interpretation of the conflict between Becket and Henry. Perhaps a new insight may be gained, however, by viewing it as part of the Papal Revolution and the formation of the Western legal tradition.

From this point of view the most significant fact about the conflict was the extraordinary tension between ecclesiastical and royal authority, and the eventual resolution of that tension by legal compromise.

In asserting ecclesiastical jurisdiction over spiritual causes, the papal party in the twelfth century defined "spiritual" to include contracts between laymen in which there was a pledge of faith, crimes committed by clerics, and many other matters that secular authorities inevitaby considered to be essentially secular. Similarly, in asserting royal jurisdiction over secular causes, the royal parties of various countries defined "secular" to include disputes between bishops concerning the right to present clerics to lucrative ecclesiastical offices, appeals from decisions of archbishops' courts, and other matters that ecclesiastical authorities inevitably considered to be essentially spiritual. Both sides came to agree that there should be two distinct jurisdictions, one ecclesiastical, the other royal. They could not agree, however, on the boundaries between them. At best they could only agree that those boundaries should be fixed not by force but by law.

Both Henry and Becket attached great importance to the legal definition of the boundaries between their respective jurisdictions. Both started with the expectation — by then almost universally shared — that a legal solution could be found to the question of ecclesiastical versus secular control over matters in which both had strong conflicting interests. The resort to force by Henry's men was an affront to that expectation; it resulted in an almost universal revulsion, which in turn compelled the English crown to renounce its most extreme claims.

To be sure, time was on the side of the expansion of the secular jurisdiction at the expense of the ecclesiastical, in England as elsewhere in Europe. However, such shifts in the balance of power had to be carried out in the context of legal competition and compromise.

The competition between the ecclesiastical and the secular courts had a lasting effect upon the Western legal tradition. Plural jurisdictions and plural legal systems became a hallmark of Western legality. When Blackstone wrote that eighteenth-century English law consisted of natural law, divine law, international law, ecclesiastical law, Roman law, law merchant, local customs, common law, statute law, and equity, there still remained several different kinds of courts administering those various kinds of law—ecclesiastical courts, university courts, admiralty courts, common law courts, and courts of equity—although Parliament and the common law courts had by then achieved supremacy. Even in the United States today there remains a certain competition between federal courts and state courts, and, within each, a competition between federal law and state law. Important distinctions are also recognized between international law and national law, as well as between common law and equity. Even when these bodies of law are applied by the same courts, the opportunity to appeal to one law against another enhances freedom.

Underlying the competition of ecclesiastical and royal courts from the twelfth to the sixteenth centuries was the limitation on the jurisdiction of each: neither pope nor king could command the total allegiance of any subject. Becket died for the principle that royal jurisdiction was not unlimited (which the king did not deny) and that it was not for the secular authority alone to decide where its boundaries should be fixed (his assassins did deny that). For three and one-half centuries tens of thousands of pilgrims from all over Europe traveled annually to Canterbury to celebrate the integrity of this man in standing up for his convictions against the king.

When the church eventually became, in the secular mind, an association within the state, as contrasted with an association beyond and against the state, then the plural jurisdictions in each country of the West were swallowed up by the one national jurisdiction, and the plural legal systems were absorbed more and more by the one national legal system. Yet something is left of Becket's heritage today. There is in most countries of the West not only a residual conflict of jurisdictions and of laws but also a constitutional limitation upon the power of the state to control spiritual values. Becket's stand against the assertion of royal authority over the clergy is reproduced in contemporary resistance to legal control over belief and morality. There are still restrictions upon the power of legislatures and courts to interfere in purely religious affairs and to punish purely moral activities. There are still difficulties in defining the legal boundaries of these affairs and activities. There is still the belief—or was, until recently—that if the legal boundaries set by the state conflict with a higher law, then there is a right—and a duty—to violate them.

PART II

The Formation

of

Secular Legal Systems

8 | The Concept of Secular Law

THE PAPAL REVOLUTION brought into being, for the first time, a separate, autonomous ecclesiastical state and a separate, autonomous body of ecclesiastical law, the canon law of the church. By the same action it brought into being, for the first time, political entities without ecclesiastical functions and nonecclesiastical legal orders. The papal party gave the names "temporal" (time-bound) and "secular" (worldly) to these other political entities and their law.

The reduction of the sacral quality of secular government was linked to the concept of the nonecclesiastical polities and their legal orders as being many and diverse, rather than one. The new canon law was one, even as the new ecclesiastical polity was one; but the secular law was manifold, corresponding to the various types of secular polities: imperial, royal, feudal, manorial, mercantile, urban. These new types of polities required new types of law, if only because their religious functions, their "spiritual" aspects, had fallen into the hands of a separate and independent organization which existed universally and whose head was in Rome.

The use of the word spiritual to characterize the law of the church was intended to signify a dimension of sanctity which was lacking in the time-bound or worldly law of the nonecclesiastical realms. Nevertheless, the secular order, including secular law, was no longer considered to be *fundamentally* chaotic or aimless. It was unredeemed; but it was redeemable. It was capable of being regenerated. Like ecclesiastical law, secular law was considered to be a reflection, however imperfect, of natural law and, ultimately, of divine law. It was subject to reason and conscience. It was rooted in divine revelation. Indeed, the very division between the ecclesiastical and the secular presupposed the mission of the church to reform the world, and consequently the mission of all Christians (but especially those in holy orders) to help make imperfect secular law conform to its ultimate purpose of justice and truth.

Secular law was supposed to emulate the canon law. All the various secular legal systems—feudal, manorial, mercantile, urban, royal—adapted to their own uses many basic ideas and techniques of the canon law, if only because the canon law was more highly developed and was available for imitation. This was inevitable, since in the twelfth and thirteenth centuries most lawyers, judges, and other professional advisers and officers of secular legal institutions were clerics and either had been trained in canon law or were generally familiar with its basic features. At the same time, the secular authorities resisted the encroachments of the ecclesiastical authorities upon the secular jurisdiction; and for that reason, too, they sought to achieve for secular law the cohesion and sophistication of the canon law.

Developing partly in emulation of and partly in rivalry with the canon law, each of the various types of secular law eventually came to be treated—though in widely varying degrees—as a legal system, that is, as an integrated and organically developing body of legal institutions and concepts. Yet in comparison with the canon law, the new secular legal systems were much less directly connected with the major political and intellectual events and movements of the time and much more directly connected with diffuse social and economic changes. Feudal law and manorial law, to a somewhat lesser extent mercantile and urban law, and to a still lesser extent royal law were more rooted in custom, and therefore emerged more gradually, than the canon law of the church. The development of the class consciousness of the feudal nobility, and the legalization of its relations with the peasantry, proceeded much more slowly and invisibly than the development of the class consciousness of the clergy and the legalization of its relations with the secular authorities. In addition, the emergence of such "institutions" as commercial markets and urban self-government differed in character from the emergence of such "institutions" as universities and ecclesiastical courts. The differences had to do in part with the kinds and numbers of people who were directly affected. Secular law emerged "on the ground." It was less programmatic. Partly for that reason its growth was much less clearly marked. By the time university-trained jurists began to "summarize" feudal law or urban law or royal law, it was already there.

Indeed, the first systems of secular law did not *need* to be portrayed in textbooks or taught in university courses in order to be accepted as integrated, ongoing, autonomous bodies of law. Scholarly books on the various branches of secular law helped, to be sure, and they were forthcoming, although not in anything like the quantity and quality of the legal literature produced by the canonists and Romanists. Also, problems that arose in the various types of secular law often found their way into university law courses, although none of those types of law ever at-tained the dignity of being taught as an independent subject in the university curriculum. By contrast, legal scholarship was indispensable to the creation of the modern system of canon law; without textbooks and courses it was unimaginable, since an articulated theory was a necessary part of its subject matter and an academically trained profession was essential to its practice.

Thus the concept of secular law, as it developed in the late eleventh and twelfth centuries, was a concept of various emerging legal systems, each limited in scope to particular types of temporal affairs, growing out of custom, imperfect, yet divinely guided and subject to correction in the light of reason and conscience.

The Emergence of New Theories of Secular Government and Secular Law

It is the thesis of this chapter that modern Western political science, including modern Western theories of the state and of law, are rooted in the struggle between the opposing forces of the Papal Revolution. This runs counter to the conventional view—still held, despite the contrary evidence of specialized scholarly literature on the events of the eleventh and twelfth centuries—that modern Western political science originated, in the first instance, in classical Greek thought, especially that of Plato and Aristotle, and in the second instance, in the revival of classical Greek thought during the so-called Renaissance, that is, in the fifteenth and sixteenth centuries, when (it is said) secular states first came into being.

Between ancient times and the fifteenth century, according to the conventional view, political thought was dominated by Stoic and patristic theory, as modified by medieval theology; and both Stoic-patristic political theory and medieval theology are thought to be too much concerned with Christian doctrine to qualify as "modern." To be sure, in the late thirteenth century, especially with the first Latin translation of Aristotle's *Politics* (1260), there were some foreshadowings (it is said) of modern political science, although political thought remained basically theological and "scholastic." Only in the next century were there a few writers who are counted as important precursors of modern ideas and methods of analyzing politics. In particular, Marsilius of Padua (about 1275-1342) stressed the principle of popular consent as the basis of all legitimate government, whether secular or ecclesiastical, and from that drew the conclusion that the secular ruler could be supreme over the church (the papacy being merely an executive ecclesiastical office established by the community). The first really modern political thinker, however, is usually said to have been Niccolò Machiavelli (1469–1527), who is often given the credit not only for inventing the word "state" to refer to the secular polity but also for founding the modern science of politics based on empirical observation and rational analysis of political institutions.

It is the conventional view that no systematic theory, or science, of the state could have been developed before the late fifteenth or sixteenth century, because prior to that time there existed no fully developed state, in the modern sense, although some individual attributes of statehood may have appeared in the late thirteenth and fourteenth centuries. It is further argued that the very concept of the state, in the modern sense, is alien to the "Middle Ages" since it is contrary to the existence of papal supremacy or claims of supremacy over the whole of Christendom, contrary to the feudal system of decentralized political power, and contrary to the Christian idea that the king should be under God and the natural law.

It has been shown here, however, that the first state in the West was that which was established *in the church* by the papacy in the late eleventh and the twelfth centuries. This, of course, will not satisfy the objection that—for some reason not fully articulated—the discussion should be limited to secular states. But even if this limitation is accepted, it is not difficult to find examples of modern European secular states that were first formed at the height of papal power, at the height of the feudal regime, and at the height of belief in the supremacy of divine and natural law. The Norman Kingdom of Sicily under the rule of Roger II (1112-1154), England under Henry II (1154-1189), France under Philip Augustus (1180-1223), Flanders under Count Philip (1169-1191), and Swabia and Bavaria in the time of Frederick Barbarossa (1152-1190), would qualify, as would many independent city-states which had elaborate systems of secular law and government as early as the middle of the twelfth century—cities such as Genoa, Pisa, Freiburg, Cologne, Ghent, Bruges, and dozens of others. Each of these was a state in the sense of a unified, independent, territorial polity under the authority of a sovereign ruler empowered to raise armies and fight wars as well as to make and enforce laws. Furthermore, during the twelfth and thirteenth centuries theories of secular government and secular law were developed by political and legal thinkers to explain and justify the existence of those states.

John of Salisbury, Founder of Western Political Science

The first Western treatise on government that went beyond Stoic and patristic models was the *Policraticus* of John of Salisbury, written in 1159,[1] which created an immediate sensation throughout Europe. Its significance can best be shown by comparing it with an earlier work, perhaps the last important pre-Western (that is, premodern) treatise on government, the so-called *Norman Anonymous* of 1100.[2]

Written at the height of the Papal Revolution, the *Norman Anonymous* presented the case for sacral kingship and against the claims of the papal party. The author contended that both Christ's kingship and his priesthood are transferred directly to kings through the sacrament of coronation. As vicar of Christ, the king is himself divine and is also the priest of his people. Indeed, he can perform sacraments; after his coronation—in accordance with Byzantine, Frankish, and Anglo-Saxon tradition—the emperor or king would go inside the sanctuary and present the bread and wine for his own communion.[3] The king is also the propitiator and savior of his people; therefore he can forgive sins.

According to the *Norman Anonymous*, Christ's priesthood is also transferred to all bishops, through St. Peter. The author criticized papal usurpation of the right of bishops to control monasteries within their own dioceses. Rome's uniqueness, he argued, consists merely in her ancient political and military power; St. Peter bestowed no more distinction on Rome than on Jerusalem and Antioch. The legalism of the canonists was also criticized: canon law, it was said, must always be interpreted in the spirit of the New Testament. Clerical marriage was defended: not all priests are called to celibacy. The high role of the laity in the church was defended. The sacrament of baptism was said to be fundamental to all others, including the eucharist. In all these matters the *Norman Anonymous* represented the ancien régime, the prerevolutionary order which dated from Carolingian times and before.

The style of the argument is of special interest. The *Norman Anonymous* was not a sober evaluation of the pros and cons of alternative positions; it was, instead, an impassioned plea of a dogmatic and prophetic character. It rested its major conclusion—the Christ-centered quality of kingship—not on practical experience but on scriptural symbolism, not on a logic of ends and means but on liturgy, not on legal justifications and analogies but on ecclesiastical tradition.

To a considerable extent, the stylistic qualities and the mode of analysis found in the *Norman Anonymous* were well suited to the basic political-ecclesiastical position to which the author adhered. Yet one may also find similar stylistic and methodological characteristics in many of the polemical writings of the papal party during the late eleventh and early twelfth centuries. It was only with the end of the great struggle, and after great compromises had been made by both sides, that there emerged a new style and a new mode of analysis and eventually a new science of the nature of government. The beginnings of the science are to be found in the writings of the jurists—the canonists and the Romanists—of the late eleventh and early twelfth centuries. The first systematic treatise, however, was John of Salisbury's *Policraticus*, which built on the earlier juristic writings but went beyond them.

The *Policraticus* was not, of course, written in the style of present-day

Western scholarship or even in the style of a John Locke or a Thomas Hobbes. Hobbes, who denounced scholasticism generally, would have had little patience with the discursive character of John of Salisbury's analysis, its apparent flitting from one subject to another, its abundant use of Biblical examples, its moralizing tendencies, and above all, its apparent inconsistencies. Many different theories of government were espoused, sometimes almost in passing. Moreover, the dominant theory of recent centuries of Western politics — that (in John Dickinson's words) "the community can organize itself for the accomplishment of its common purposes by developing institutions for pooling the ideas and harmonizing the ends of its members" — was completely lacking.[4]

Nevertheless, the *Policraticus* "discloses still in combination a number of separate strains of thought whose later dissociation was to form the main currents of opposing doctrine for many succeeding centuries."[5] Prior to the Reformation these strains of thought continued to remain largely in combination; thereafter they came apart, and it was this dissociation that most distinguished post-Reformation from pre-Reformation political thought. Thus Salisbury's derivation of the ruler's title directly from God foreshadowed the sixteenth-century theory of the divine right of kings, while his patriarchal theory of monarchy foreshadowed the seventeenth-century conception of personal absolutism; in his conception of a higher law binding the ruler he foreshadowed the doctrine of judicial supremacy advanced by Sir Edward Coke; his doctrine that insofar as men are free from sin and can live by grace alone they need no government anticipated (as Dickinson notes) the Christian communism of radical sects of the Protestant Reformation as well as modern doctrines of philosophic anarchism. So in the *Policraticus* Salisbury "discloses the more or less confused mass of contradictory ideas in which [later political theories] were originally embedded, and which served to limit and correct them."[6] In that sense the book may seem at first reading to be eclectic and syncretistic — a fascinating hodgepodge. But on closer study it becomes apparent that it was not Salisbury's ideas that were confused; it was the political conditions of his time which were complex and contradictory, and it was his virtue to portray the complex structure of those political conditions and to rationalize their contradictions. That is what makes *Policraticus* a scientific work and not merely a utopian or programmatic work. In contrast to classical political thought, which saw various types of political authority (monarchy, aristocracy, democracy) as mutually exclusive alternatives, Western political thought — starting with John of Salisbury — saw them as coexisting in combination with one another.

For over a century *Policraticus* was considered throughout the West to be the most authoritative work on the nature of government. Its supremacy was not challenged until Thomas Aquinas, relying on Aristotle's *Politics*, published his book *On Kingship* (*De Regimine Principum*).[7] Even then, however, it was recognized that Aquinas built not only on Aristotle but also on John of Salisbury.

Although the *Politics* was not available in the West when Salisbury wrote, the *Policraticus* has a strong Aristotelian dimension, due in part to the author's thorough grounding in those writings of Aristotle which had been translated (some of them very recently).[8] There were also non-Aristotelian dimensions. Stoic and patristic influences were strong, reinforced by references to natural law, justice, equity, and reason from the lawbooks of Justinian. In addition, the *Policraticus* derived much from the Old and New Testaments, as well as from the history of the church and of the Roman Empire, including both its Byzantine and its Frankish-German counterparts. Yet none of these sources and influences were decisive; what was decisive was the way all of them were put together, and that way was characteristic of Western thought after the Papal Revolution.

This last point needs elaboration in view of the tendency of historians to explain the new by its origins in the past—and thereby to explain everything about it except its newness. Some say that medieval political thought, including that of John of Salisbury, was basically in the tradition of the Stoics and the church fathers, supplemented by the Roman lawyers; that Aristotle had little or no influence until the writings of Aquinas; and that even thereafter Aristotelianism was not taken very seriously in *political* theory.[9] Others say, per contra, that all medieval thought, including political thought, is the history of the translation of Aristotle and that John of Salisbury's political theory was essentially an application of Aristotelian logic to the political realities of his time.[10] Still others claim that the theory of government expressed in the *Policraticus* is essentially Platonic.[11] Finally, it is stated that the *Policraticus* was simply a further development in a long tradition of Christian writings on the relation of the secular power to the church, that it merely applied to new circumstances the "two swords" doctrine of Pope Gelasius I, who in the fifth century had charged Emperor Anastasius to confine himself to the exercise of royal power and to leave the exercise of sacred authority to the priesthood.[12]

Yet it is also said that John of Salisbury's *Policraticus* was something new—that it "contains the first political theory which breaks with the conceptions of the early middle ages and leads onwards to an era in which discussion of the rights and duties of princes takes the place of the old theory of the two swords."[13]

What was new in the *Policraticus*, in the first place, was the author's effort to put together in a comprehensive way theories, texts, and examples from the most diverse and contradictory sources—Plato, Aristotle, Cicero, Seneca, Vergil, Ovid, the Old Testament, the New Testament, the church fathers, the Roman lawyers of Justinian's texts as glossed by John of Salisbury's own contemporaries, the canon lawyers, and others—and to attempt to synthesize them. All were, in one sense, authoritative; but in another sense each was subject to criticism in the light of the others. This was the first application to politics of the method (later called "scholastic") which had already been applied—much more rigorously—to Roman law by Irnerius and his successors, to theology by Abelard (under whom John of Salisbury had studied), and to canon law by Gratian (with whose *Decretum* John of Salisbury was familiar).

In the second place, in addition to the effort to synthesize, John found a method of actually achieving synthesis through the use of concepts which combined contradictory norms by abstracting their common qualities. Perhaps the most important example of this was his use of the Latin word *princeps* ("the prince") to refer not to a particular ruler or a particular office but to any ruler, that is, to rulers in general. In classical and postclassical Roman writings, princeps had been used to signify the Roman emperor. Not any ruler, not even more than one ruler, but only the holder of the office of emperor was the prince. In later centuries the title was usurped by the Frankish emperor, and still later by other kings, and eventually by the papacy, but it was always used to refer to one person or one office alone; in other words, princeps meant the supreme ruler, or office of the supreme ruler, of a particular polity. That is why, in the struggle between the papacy and the emperor, it was important for each side to appropriate the title princeps and the texts of Roman law that went with it. Moreover, the polity of the princeps—prior to the Papal Revolution—was not considered to be territorial in character but rather, as Gerhart Ladner has put it, functional;[14] that is, his powers and duties were examined in terms of the relation of a lord to his vassals, or a master to his servants, or a priest to his flock—or of Christ to his followers—without regard to the character of the polity as a community of people attached to a given territory, a given country. John of Salisbury, in contrast, set out to analyze the general subject of political and legal relationships between a ruler and his subjects in a territorial system. The prince could be emperor or king or duke or count or some other ruler. The prince's subjects formed a *res publica* (a "republic" or "commonwealth") in the territory which he ruled. Thus in the *Policraticus* the term prince meant something very similar to, though not identical with, what writers in later centuries called the state. It meant "a form of public power . . . constituting the supreme political authority within a certain defined territory."[15] Indeed, in the *Policraticus* the prince is expressly defined as "the public power."[16] What it did not mean, in contrast to what the state came to mean in the sixteenth century, was "a form of public power *separate from the ruler and the ruled.*"[17] In the *Policraticus*, princeps was a general concept, but it had not yet become an abstract concept: the prince as public power was still seen as the "head" whose task was to maintain the "state" (*status*) of the res publica, which was seen as the "body." The significant linguistic change in the sixteenth century was to identify that "state of the commonwealth," which hitherto the ruler had had the duty to direct and to serve, with the supreme political authority, the form of public power itself.[18]

Having converted the term prince into a general concept, John of Salisbury was able to develop a theory of government based on a distinction between two general types of princes which were contradictory to each other, although each was a species of the same genus. Princes of the first type ruled according to law, equity, and the "principle of the common welfare." Princes of the second type ruled by force, serving only their own wicked ends; they were "tyrants . . . [by whom] the laws are brought to nought and the people are reduced to slavery."[19]

A similar distinction between a law-abiding king and a tyrant may be found in the writings of the church fathers and in ancient Greek political thought. But John of Salisbury's theory was far more complex than the earlier theories, since it accepted — and drew conclusions from — both the unity and the contradictory nature of the two types of rulership. Like the law-abiding king, the tyrant holds his power from God, since "all power is from the Lord God." "[When the ruler's] will is turned to cruelty against his subjects . . . it is the dispensation of God for His good pleasure to punish or chasten them . . . for good men thus regard power as worthy of veneration even when it comes as a plague upon the elect."[20] The tyrant's laws must be obeyed. Even if they are evil laws, God's will is nevertheless accomplished through them. God "uses our evil for His own good purposes. Therefore, even the rule of a tyrant, too, is good, although nothing is worse than tyranny."[21]

But this more or less traditional argument gradually shifted. An evil ruler, it was said, can no more escape the judgment of God than an evil people; if his people are patient, and if they turn from their own wickedness, God will at last free them from the oppressor. The history of oppression shows that evil rulers are usually punished. But more than that, if the tyrant commands a subject to act contrary to his faith, the subject must disobey. "Some things are . . . so detestable that no command will possibly justify them or render them permissible."[22] For example, if a military commander commands a soldier to deny God, or to commit adultery, the soldier must refuse.[23] More generally, "if [the prince] resists and opposes the divine commandments, and wishes to make me share in his war against God, then with unrestrained voice I must answer back that God must be preferred before any man on earth".[24]

Thus the reader is confronted with two contradictory norms: the tyrant's laws must be obeyed, for the tyrant rules by God's will; yet the tyrant's laws must be disobeyed when they conflict with God's laws. At first the second norm appears as an exception to the first, only applicable in the case of the most evil commands. Yet the very tyranny itself may conflict with God's laws. The contradictions are carried further and further. Ultimately, the reader is confronted with the startling conclusion that a person may have a right and even a duty not only to disobey a tyrant but even to kill him — the famous right and duty of tyrannicide, which John of Salisbury was the first Western writer to elaborate as a doctrine and to defend with reasoned arguments. He starts with passive resistance: "If princes have departed little by little from the true way, even so it is not well to overthrow them utterly at once, but rather to rebuke injustice with patient reproof until finally it becomes obvious that they are stiff-necked in evil-doing".[25] In the last analysis, however, every person is under a duty to enforce the law by killing a tyrant who has put himself outside the law:

> To kill a tyrant is not merely lawful, but right and just. For whosoever takes up the sword deserves to perish by the sword. And he is understood to take up the sword who usurps it by his own temerity and who does not receive the power of using it from God. Therefore the law rightly takes arms against him who disarms the laws, and the public power rages in fury against him who strives to bring to nought the public force. And while there are many acts which amount to lèse majesté, none is a graver crime than that which is against the body of Justice herself. Tyranny therefore is not merely a public crime, but, if there could be such a thing, a crime more than public. And if in the crime of lèse majesté all men are admitted to be prosecutors, how much more should this be true in the case of the crime of subverting the laws which should rule even over emperors? Truly no one will avenge a public enemy, but rather whoever does not seek to bring him to punishment commits an offence against himself and the whole body of the earthly commonwealth.[26]

John's acceptance of the fundamental unity of two contradictory norms — government by law and government by force, both of which were attributed to divine will — served as a foundation for later theories of Western political science. The complexity and modernity of such theories were enhanced by the fact that the contradictory norms which John postulated corresponded to the contradictory political realities of his age. Yet he never specifically identified those contemporary realities, nor did he ever refer to them. Despite — or more likely, because of — the fact that he was intimately acquainted with the leading figures of his time, including popes and antipopes, kings and tyrants, John avoided naming names and left his readers to apply his analysis to contemporary heroes and villains. No doubt it would have been politically risky for him to have done otherwise. It also would have been a distraction from his main purpose, which was to explore the basic theoretical dilemmas of power and justice which confronted the newly emerging secular states. But how was it possible to analyze political and constitutional norms realistically without giving actual cases?

This question was resolved in the *Policraticus* in a manner characteristic of the new scientific method of the twelfth century. A great many actual cases were put, but they were drawn from ancient Greek and Roman history, from the Old Testament, from the history of the Roman Empire, and so forth. The problems that determined the selection of these cases were not, however, the problems that had vexed ancient Greeks and Romans, Hebrews, or other predecessors of John and his contemporaries. They were the underlying political problems of the twelfth century, which were being debated in the universities, in the papal curia, and in the centers of political and cultural life in England, Normandy, southern Italy, Lombardy, Saxony, Swabia, France, Flanders, Hungary, Poland, Spain, and elsewhere in Europe. To be sure, the numerous cases—the fact situations which were analyzed, often at some length—were found in the literary record of earlier civilizations. But this was by no means so unsatisfactory as it may at first seem. An empirical-inductive quality was introduced, a concern with actual experience, a casuistry, even though the cases were clothed in biblical, Graeco-Roman, or other costumes from older times. The result was a book which was not the portrayal of a utopia or ideal republic, on the one hand, and not a chronicle of decaying times, on the other, though it contained some elements of both. The mixture of empirical-inductive and ethical-normative qualities constituted, in fact, a third innovation of style and method introduced by the *Policraticus*.

One example of the way in which the ethical-normative method and the empirical-inductive method were combined in the *Policraticus* is the treatment of the fundamental problem of the selection of a new prince when a throne becomes vacant. Generally speaking, tribal, feudal, and imperial tradition had all emphasized two basic principles of succession: heredity and election. The ideal solution was for the leading men to elect the oldest son of the dead ruler. However, when the oldest son did not command sufficient support among the leading men, there was trouble. Some might favor another son or a brother or cousin or another relative. The closer his relationship to the dead king by blood or marriage, the easier it was for a candidate to gain support from those who had the power to elect, unless there was an uprising against the entire dynasty.

Prior to the Papal Revolution, the role of ecclesiastical leaders in the choice of a successor was not apt to be essentially different from the role of lay magnates. Bishops and other leading churchmen were themselves imperial and royal councillors, feudal lords, and even clan or dynastic figures. With the centralization of clerical control in the hands of the papacy, however, and with the separation of the ecclesiastical from the secular authority, the church began to play a distinct and independent role in influencing royal elections. Thus an additional complicating factor was added to the great uncertainty which often surrounded the succession.

In 1159, when John of Salisbury wrote the *Policraticus*, a new dynasty had recently been founded in Norman England by a powerful monarch who was most anxious to secure the succession for his descendants. (In 1170 Henry II had his oldest son, Henry, crowned in advance, and in 1172 he had him crowned again, with his wife.) John was thoroughly familiar with similar tendencies to strengthen the hereditary principle in other states, including Norman Sicily (southern Italy) and Capetian France. He was also aware of the problems connected with the election of the emperor: a system had been developing, especially since 1125, whereby the imperial succession was determined principally by vote of a certain number of the princes of the various (mostly German) duchies; eventually the number of "electors" was fixed at seven, including three archbishops, those of Mainz, Cologne, and Trier. However, the election was usually strongly influenced in favor of the reigning imperial dynasty; in fact, the imperial crown tended to descend to the eldest son or to some other close relative of the deceased emperor.

In the twelfth century and thereafter, the lawyers—Romanists and canonists alike—had a great deal to say about these matters. They tended to analyze them in terms of a wide variety of fairly narrow topics, such as the rules of hereditary succession through male and female lines, the question of the source of power to elect a king or emperor, the validity of election procedures, and the effect of papal excommunication on the legitimacy of the ruler. Such questions were discussed by the jurists in the light of various authoritative texts and legal doctrines, in the light of customs and decrees, and in the light of actual historical cases.[27]

The *Policraticus* did not go deeply into the legal aspects of the question of royal succession; instead, it sought to establish a theoretical resolution of the conflict between the principle of heredity and the principle of election, and to justify ecclesiastical intervention. The "cases" selected for illustration or support were not drawn from the history of Europe. There was a discussion of the selection of Joshua to succeed Moses: "Moses called together the whole synagogue to the end that he might be chosen in the presence of the people, so that afterwards no man might remain to cloud his title." On the other hand, it was God Himself who told Moses to name Joshua the ruler. John commented: "Here is plainly no acclamation by the people, no argument or title founded upon ties of blood, no consideration accorded to family relationship."[28] Then another story from the Bible was mentioned: the daughters of Salphaat came before Moses to claim their father's inheritance. Their petition "was a just one, for a man's inheritance of lands and estates is to be left to his relatives, and so far as possible, his public office likewise. But governance of the people is to be handed over to him whom God has chosen, to wit such a man as has in him the spirit of God . . . [and who has] walked in the judgments of the Lord."[29]

Thus John of Salisbury concluded that to become a prince one must be chosen by God—which meant that one must have the approval of the ecclesiastical authority. Since the prince is subject to God, he is subject also to the priesthood, "who represent God upon earth."[30] He is a "minister of the priestly power," which has handed over to him the temporal sword, "the sword of blood," which the priesthood itself is too pure to wield directly.[31]

It was not denied that heredity is an important factor in the succession to princely power: "It is not right," John stated, "to pass over, in favor of new men, the blood of princes, who are entitled by the divine promise and the right of family to be succeeded by their own children."[32] Election is also an important factor: John cited a famous passage in Justinian's Digest which refers to the transfer of power to the emperor by the Roman people, and argued that the prince is therefore "representative" or "vicar" of the people.[33] Yet he rejected each of these principles as an absolute. Heredity creates a presumptive claim to the throne, which must be confirmed by election, but the priesthood—that is, the papacy—has a decisive voice when it is in the overriding interest of the church to exercise it. The theory on which this is based is that royal title is derived from God *either* through heredity *or* through election *or* through such other means as God in a given instance chooses to apply.[34]

This example illustrates the synthesis of opposites which was characteristic of scholastic thought in the twelfth century. More specifically, it exemplifies the combining of ethical-normative reasoning with empirical-inductive reasoning. The ethical-normative aspect is obvious: first, the prince should follow the judgments of God and should attempt to obey the divine commandments; second, if the pope, who is charged with supreme responsibility for interpreting the divine will, determines that a candidate for the throne is a heretic or schismatic or otherwise an enemy of the church, such a candidate will not be qualified despite any claims he may have by virtue of heredity or election. The empirical and inductive aspect is less obvious, but it is there. In the first place, the entire exposition is concerned with the realities that determined succession to European thrones in the twelfth century and afterwards: heredity, election, and papal intervention.[35] In the second place, John's recourse to the Bible and to Greek and Roman literature for concrete examples gave the *Policraticus* a broad empirical basis from which to draw conclusions. Contemporary European cases were too close to home to be analyzed objectively in terms of political theory; they could only be analyzed objectively in terms of *legal* theory, because there the terms of analysis were narrower and were ultimately limited by textual authorities. Contemporary cases were also too complicated; that is, too much was known about them, and hence they were much more difficult to simplify. Examples from antiquity were, for John of Salisbury and his contemporaries, rather like the examples from other cultures used by modern political theorists. They provided a kind of universal anthropological context.

Closely connected with (1) the effort to synthesize opposite norms, (2) by use of general concepts, (3) which corresponded to empirical realities, was a fourth innovation of the scholastic method, which John of Salisbury was the first to apply to the study of secular political institutions. That was the effort to grasp the entire subject matter under consideration as a single whole, an integrated system, and characteristically, to portray the whole in organic terms, as a body.

The *Policraticus* introduced into European thought, for the first time, an organic theory of the secular political order: it was the first European work to elaborate the metaphor that every principality, that is, every territorial polity headed by a ruler, is a body. The prince is compared with the head, the senate with the heart, the judges and provincial rulers with the eyes, ears, and tongue, the soldiers with the hands, the tillers of the soil with the feet. The analogy is carried so far as to liken the financial officers and keepers of the king's treasure to the stomach and intestines, "which, if they become congested through excessive avidity, and retain too tenaciously their accumulations, generate innumerable and incurable diseases, so that through their ailment the whole body is threatened with destruction."[36] Similar metaphors may be found in ancient Greek political thought, and John of Salisbury was familiar with at least Plutarch's use of them and drew on it; nevertheless, the organic metaphor in the *Policraticus* had distinctive features. One is reminded of modern systems theory, with its concepts of flows, subordination, and hierarchy, feedback, controller, and program.

The organic metaphor implies that government, that is, political rule, is natural to man. It is not something which is necessarily imposed on society by force, nor does it originate in a compact or convention. These two alternatives — the coercive theory and the contractual theory — had been elaborated by the Stoics and the church fathers, and had dominated Western political thought prior to the eleventh and twelfth centuries.[37] Both rested on an essentially static view of human nature. Stoic and patristic thought postulated that originally man had lived in a state of virtue, either in paradise or else, in Israel, under the patriarchs, Moses, and the judges. Through his inherent sinfulness, however, man had forfeited rule by charity or higher law. Positive regulation had been forcibly imposed upon him by coercive monarchical government; or else civil strife had induced him to consent willingly, by a kind of social contract, to monarchical government. Whether introduced by force or by compact, political controls were viewed as a response to man's wickedness rather than to his fundamental desire to live in peace and harmony.

The organic concept of political rule and the concept of its naturalness, which are found in the *Policraticus*, are more akin to Aristotelian thought than to Stoic or patristic thought. Although Aristotle's *Politics* was not available to John of Salisbury, he shared with Aristotle the view that the political community is subject to the law of nature, which is reason, and that nature or reason requires the king to rule according to justice and equity. This view is explicit in the *Policraticus*; it is also implicit in the metaphor of the "body politic."

The metaphor of the body politic also supported a territorial view of the political community. This, too was congenial to classical Greek concepts of organic unity and of a natural division of labor between rulers and ruled. Such concepts became more relevant as Western society moved rapidly from tribal, local, feudal, and sacral-imperial modes of ordering to large, consolidated territorial polities with fairly strong central governments.

Yet it is a mistake to suppose that Aristotelian and other ancient Greek concepts meant the same thing to John of Salisbury and his contemporaries as they had meant to the ancient Greeks. The very premise of Aristotle's political theory, expressed in the first paragraph of the *Politics* — namely, that the highest end of human life is the common good of the political community[38] — was acceptable to medieval Christian thought only by a series of reinterpretations which would have seemed very strange to Aristotle. In the *Policraticus* it is taken for granted that the political community is subordinate to the salvation of human souls under the judgment of God. Aristotle's "nature" is understood by John of Salisbury to be an instrument of divine will. Aristotle's "reason" is taken by John to be a mode of proving divine revelation. It is only with considerable difficulty, and only at a rather high level of abstraction, that such views can be reconciled with Aristotelian thought. A little more than a century after John, Thomas Aquinas labored to show that secular naturalism and religious naturalism — insofar as they are both concerned with *human* nature, and especially with man's *moral* and *rational* nature — do lead to similar conclusions from different starting points. But the difference in starting points can never be obliterated, and it always returns to haunt the argument.

Another aspect of John of Salisbury's theory was not only difficult to reconcile with Greek thought but was wholly repugnant to it: that God manifests himself in two opposing communities at the same time and place, and that every Christian lives in both — the community ruled by the temporal authority and the community ruled by the priesthood. These are two distinct political communities. Yet the temporal community—the prince and all his subjects—are also members of the ecclesiastical community, the church, and are under its authority. Moreover, the church, while it has the quality of a spiritual community which is not of this world, also has a political dimension: it, too, is a body ruled by a head, a prince (namely, the pope), and in pursuing its spiritual interests it inevitably becomes involved in temporal, that is, secular, affairs.

Thus the classical Greek metaphor of the body politic and the Aristotelian concept of the source of government in nature and reason were used by John of Salisbury in a historical context that was completely non-Greek and non-Aristotelian. The political community, which for Aristotle meant the entire social life of the people of a given place, was split into two bodies, the body of the church and the body of the secular polity, whether a kingdom, duchy, city, or empire. Indeed, Western thinkers could only conceive of the secular community as a body after the Papal Revolution had divided the West into ecclesiastical and secular polities.[39] Before then, the political community, headed by sacral emperors and kings, was wholly mixed up with the church; neither one was a body in the Greek sense, and both together, as the Christian community, were called a body in another mystical sense—namely, the spiritual body of Christ. Thus for St. Augustine priests and bishops lived in the same two cities—the heavenly and the earthly—like other saints and sinners, and neither city was an organic political entity. It was only with the division of Western Christendom into an ecclesiastical polity and a secular polity in the late eleventh and twelfth centuries that the Greek organic theory became applicable to Western politics for the first time—but to only half of it, the secular half.

In fact, the circumstances to which Greek modes of thought were applied by John of Salisbury and other writers of his time were so different from the circumstances in which those modes of thought had originated that it is astonishing that John and the others were able to apply them at all. John was concerned to explain—and influence—a situation which Aristotle would have found completely strange: the coexistence of a number of kingdoms, principalities, feudal territories, cities, and other autonomous secular polities within a centralized ecclesiastical state. It was John's genius to construct a theory—partly out of Aristotelian, partly out of Stoic, and partly out of other (Roman, Hebraic, patristic, Byzantine, Frankish) elements—which interpreted that situation in both normative and empirical terms.

Theories of the Roman and Canon Lawyers

John of Salisbury was strongly influenced by the writings of the Roman and canon lawyers of his time, who were also engaged in the same herculean effort to formulate a theory of government and law which, on the one hand, would correspond to the realities of their age, but which, on the other hand, would set limits upon the arbitrary exercise of power by rulers. The lawyers, however, worked more closely than John with authoritative texts and tended to focus more closely on issues capable of practical resolution.

The Romanists took as their field of study the classical and postclassical Roman law contained in the rediscovered works of Justinian, enriched by new concepts derived from canon law and from the newly emerging systems of feudal, urban, and royal law, as well as from theology and philosophy. The Roman texts themselves reveal little political or legal theory of any kind. What little there is consists of scattered references to reason, justice, or equity, and to the powers of the emperor and of subordinate magistrates. Occasionally, very broad principles are discussed very briefly, such as the principle that "justice is the giving to each his due," or that "what pleases the prince has the force of law." More frequently such broad references are connected with specific rules of law; for example, Gaius is quoted as saying that natural reason makes it lawful for every man to defend himself against an aggressive attack. It remained for the twelfth- and thirteenth-century students of these texts—the glossators—to put them together in such a way as to yield a system of general concepts concerning the location, character, and limits of political power.

The canon lawyers of the time engaged in the very same task, but they were less restricted in their sources of authority. Although they did not hesitate to use the Justinian texts, for theoretical matters they tended to look first in other places: the many canons issued by church councils in the twelfth and thirteenth centuries, the abundant legislative and judicial materials which proceeded from the papal curia at the time, the *jus antiquum* systematized by Gratian, the writings of Abelard, Peter Lombard, and other contemporary theologians, the writings of the church fathers, and the Old and New Testaments. The canonists could be just as technical as the Romanists, and the Romanists just as philosophical as the canonists; but on the whole the canonists tended to paint with a broader brush than the Romanists. Also, in analyzing the relations of the ecclesiastical and secular powers the canonists tended to support the ecclesiastical claims more consistently than did the Romanists, though there was rarely unanimity in either group on any controversial question.

An excellent example of the application of Roman law to political theory is the way in which the greatest Romanist of the time, Azo (1150–1230), developed the Roman law texts concerning *iurisdictio* and *imperium* into a concept of sovereignty.[40]

The Digest states, "*Jurisdictio* is a very broad office: for it is able to give possession of goods and to transfer possession, to appoint guardians for orphans who do not have them, to assign judges to litigants." This is the closest the Roman law of Justinian came to a definition of *jurisdictio*. Other texts give examples of conditions under which it exists, and some indication of why it exists under those conditions. It is stated, for example, that one who judges a dispute between parties has iurisdictio only if he heads some tribunal or holds another jurisdiction. In other words, the agreement of private parties does not create iurisdictio. In another provision it is stated that one who has iurisdictio ought not to exercise it over his family or his companions. Still another text provides that a proconsul has *plenissima iurisdictio* ("the fullest jurisdiction") and consequently has in his province *maius imperium* ("greatest dominion"), suited to all purposes and exceeded only by that of the emperor.[41]

Imperium ("dominion") also remains undefined in the lawbooks of Justinian. Examples of its exercise are given, in which it appears that sometimes imperium and iurisdictio may be used interchangeably and that sometimes they are to be distinguished from each other. Imperium is said to be of three kinds: (1) *maius imperium* ("greatest dominion"), the holder of which can give a final judgment in any matter over which he has iurisdictio; (2) *merum imperium* ("pure dominion"), an example of which is the power to impose the death sentence in cases of capital crimes; and (3) *mixtum imperium* ("mixed dominion"), an example of which is the dominion that is involved in jurisdiction in civil cases. All iurisdictio is said to involve at least moderate compulsion. Capital criminal jurisdiction is in one place equated with dominion.[42]

Confronted with this rather chaotic picture, Azo, citing his great predecessor Irnerius (1060–1125), the founder of Romanist legal scholarship, started by noting that the relevant provisions of the Digest fail to define iurisdictio and only give examples of it. He then offered a definition which would embrace all the examples: iurisdictio, he said, is the publicly established power and duty to pronounce judgment and establish justice. He derived his definition in part from the etymology of the work: *ditio* (*dictio*), he stated, means power (*potestas*) (that is, the power of utterance), and *ius, iuris* means right, "which is to say that *iurisdictio* is legitimate power."[43]

Then Azo proceeded to classify in four ways the various uses of iurisdictio in Roman law. Here he played a trick with the sources—a trick that seems wholly justified if it is assumed that the sources lay a foundation for the development of a system of general concepts and, more particularly, for a theory of political power. The trick was to classify imperium as a species of iurisdictio. Thus Azo's first division of iurisdictio is that of *plenissima* ("fullest") jurisdiction, which is in the prince alone, and *minus plena* ("less full") jurisdiction, which is in the remaining magistrates; however, some magistrates have plenissima jurisdiction with respect to other magistrates inferior to them. Azo's second division is that of voluntary and contentious jurisdiction. His third division separates general jurisdiction ("ordinary" jurisdiction) from special jurisdiction, such as that of a legate entrusted with a single type of cause. Finally, Azo listed, as a fourth division of jurisdiction, pure and mixed imperium.

John Perrin has said that "the significance of this [classification] cannot be overemphasized . . . *Iurisdictio* is not that which belongs to both *merum* and *mixtum imperium*. But rather these elements of command, these grades of *imperium*, are divisions of *iurisdictio*. *Iurisdictio*, in essence, contains them."[44] The immediate significance of the classification is threefold.

First, "pure dominion," which is the power of the sword, the power of bodily punishment, the power to take life, is limited, in Azo's theory, to those who have jurisdiction, defined as the legitimate power to pronounce judgment and establish justice. (Azo also extended pure dominion to criminal procedure generally, including examination of suspects, arguing that pure refers to any cause in which there are no monetary claims.)

Second, it is implicit in Azo's classification that the ruler's right and power to legislate, which at a later time came to be considered the essence of sovereignty, is viewed as an aspect of his right and power to adjudicate. Indeed, the subordination of the power of the sword to the power of adjudication suggests a concept of sovereignty in which even the ruler's right and power to make war is derived from his right and power to render judgment and do justice.

Third, since the power of the sword is a species of jurisdiction, it is not necessarily true that it can only be exercised by the magistrate with the fullest jurisdiction, namely the emperor. Azo argued that it can also be exercised by magistrates with less full jurisdiction. In other words, Azo distinguished the power of the emperor from that of other rulers not on the basis of imperium but on the basis of plenissima and minus plena iurisdictio. The emperor has the greatest dominion and the fullest jurisdiction, but other magistrates may have pure dominion, including the power of the sword, and less full jurisdiction.

Involved in Azo's analysis is a recognition that the jurisdiction and dominion—the sovereignty, as a later generation would say—of kings, princes, heads of municipal governments, and other magistrates are not derived from the jurisdiction and dominion of the emperor. They have their own jurisdiction and dominion, which is less in quantity, so to speak, than his, but nevertheless independent of his. This is reflected analytically in the classification of various kinds of imperium as comprising one of four divisions within the genus iurisdictio, separate from the division plenissima and minus plena.

Behind this new legal classification stood, of course, a more fundamental conception of the source of sovereignty. Azo stated that all rulers have imperium because they have iurisdictio, the right to establish law in their respective states. But what was the source of that lawmaking right? Azo answered that the source was in the corpus, the universitas, the communitas. Jurisdiction did not descend downward from the emperor but upward from the corporate community.

The Rule of Law

The idea of the secular state, which was implicit in the Papal Revolution from its inception, and the reality of the secular state, which emerged out of the historical struggle between ecclesiastical and secular forces that constituted the Papal Revolution, were in essence the idea and the reality of a state ruled by law, a "law state" (*Rechtsstaat*).[45] This meant, first, that the respective heads of each body, the ecclesiastical and the secular, would introduce and maintain their own legal systems, that is, would regularly enact laws, establish judicial systems, organize government departments, and, in general, rule *by* law. Second, it meant that the respective heads of each body would be bound by the law which they themselves had enacted; they could change it lawfully, but until they did so they must obey it — they must rule *under* law. (This was implicit in the subordination of the sovereign's legislative power to his judicial power.) It meant, third, that each jurisdiction would also be bound by the law of other jurisdictions insofar as that law was itself lawful; each state existed within a system of plural jurisdictions. This last meaning undergirded the other two meanings. If the church was to have inviolable legal rights, the state had to accept those rights as a lawful limitation upon its own supremacy. Similarly, the rights of the state constituted a lawful limitation upon the supremacy of the church. The two powers could only coexist peacefully through a shared recognition of the rule of law, its supremacy over each.

The difficulties of the concept of the supremacy of law over the state are, and were then, abundantly apparent. How can a prince have imperium (or as one would say today, how can a state have sovereignty) if his (or its) legitimate power is subordinate to the will of other sovereign rulers? That is a "contradiction" of the finest scholastic sort. Even more important, how can one speak of the rule, or supremacy, of law within a given polity when no one has been authorized to challenge the chief officer of the polity, whether the pope within the church or the king within the kingdom?

Gratian and his successors said that the pope should be deposed if he breaks the law, but there was no one higher than the pope either to say authoritatively that he broke the law or to depose him. Similarly, royal jurists such as Bracton said that the king has a duty to obey the law, that the king is "under God and the law," that it is not the king that makes law but the law that makes the king; yet they also said that no judge may dispute the king's acts, that no writ can run against the king, that the king "ought" to obey his own laws but that he cannot be legally required to do so.[46]

Nevertheless, the *Saxon Mirror* (*Sachsenspiegel*), written in the early thirteenth century about the time of Bracton, stated that "a man must resist his king and his judge if he does wrong, and must hinder him in every wrong, even if he be his relative or feudal lord. And he does not thereby break his fealty."[47] Likewise a famous legal formula of Aragon stated that subjects will obey a king only so long as he performs his duties, "and if not, not."[48]

The right and duty to disobey the divinely appointed king-autocrat when he violates fundamental law was based on the belief that that fundamental law was itself divinely instituted. Popes and kings made laws, but they did so as deputies of God; not they themselves but "God is the source of all law."

Thus the concept of the rule of law was supported by the prevailing religious ideology. It was also supported by the prevailing political and economic weakness of rulers and by the pluralism of authorities and jurisdictions. Finally, the concept of the rule of law was supported by the high level of legal consciousness and legal sophistication that came to prevail throughout the West in the twelfth and thirteenth centuries. It was well understood that the preservation of legality required not merely abstract precepts of justice, equity, conscience, and reason but also specific principles and rules such as those embodied in the English Magna Carta of 1215 and the Hungarian Golden Bull of 1222. In many types of documents such as these, including the charters of liberties given to towns and cities by kings and feudal lords, various civil, political, economic, and social rights were specified.

In Magna Carta the barons and the church exacted from the crown the commitment that no scutage or aid beyond the three recognized feudal aids would be levied by the king without the consent of the "general council of our realm" (that is, the king's tenants-in-chief), that "common pleas . . . shall be held in some fixed place," that "no man shall be put on trial upon an accusation unsupported by credible witnesses," that "no free man shall be taken or imprisoned or disseised or outlawed or exiled or in any way destroyed . . . except by the lawful judgment of his peers or the law of the land," that "to no one will we sell, to no one will we refuse or delay, right or justice," that "merchants shall have safe conduct in and out of England except in times of war and the merchants are of the enemy, in which case they and their goods will be safe if our merchants are treated the same way," that "all can freely leave and enter England except in time of war and except those who have been outlawed and people who are at war with us," that "only those who know the law shall be appointed as justiciars, constables, sheriffs, or bailiffs," and other such commitments.[49]

Similarly, in the Golden Bull, King Andrew II of Hungary accepted specific limitations on the power of the crown in favor of "higher and lower nobles" (that is, free men), committing himself and his successors to hold a court at a fixed time and place every year, not to "seize any noble, nor destroy him out of favor to any powerful person, unless he shall first have been summoned and convicted according to law," to "collect no tax and exact no money payments nor visit uninvited the estates, houses, or villages of nobles," to confer no offices on foreigners who come into the kingdom "without the consent of the council," to degrade, dismiss, and require restitution from "any lord-lieutenant who shall not conduct himself in accordance with the dignity of his office or shall despoil the people under his authority." Further, hereditary lord-lieutenancies shall not be granted, new money shall not be issued at shorter intervals than twelve months, and if any one has been legally condemned, no protection of powerful persons shall avail to protect him from the consequences. The Golden Bull ends with the words: "We also ordain that if We or any of Our Successors shall at any time contravene the terms of this statute, the bishops and the higher and lower nobles of Our realm, one and all, both present and future, shall by virtue thereof have the uncontrolled right in perpetuity of resistance both by word and deed without thereby incurring any charge of treason."[50]

Many centuries later, the concept of the rule of law came to be identified with the separation of the legislative, administrative, and judicial powers.[51] The later concept shared two features with the earlier concept. First, power was divided, although in the earlier period the "checks and balances" had been provided chiefly by concurrent polities within the same territory rather than by concurrent branches of the same polity. Second, law was derived from, and rooted in, a reality that transcended the existing structure of political power. In the later period, that transcendent reality was found in human rights, democratic values, and other related beliefs. In the earlier period it had been found in divine and natural justice.

9 | Feudal Law

THE TERM "FEUDALISM" was only invented in the eighteenth century. Prior to that time—ever since the twelfth century, in fact—people had spoken and written not of feudalism or of "feudal society" but of "feudal law,"referring primarily to the system of rights and obligations associated with lord-vassal relationships and dependent land tenures. During the eighteenth-century Enlightenment, however, the entire social order in which such lord-vassal relationships and land tenures had once existed was for the first time called feudal society, and the chief characteristics of that society were defined as a privileged nobility and a subject peasantry. This definition was broad enough to include many aspects of eighteenth-century European society, as well.

Eventually, the term feudalism came to be associated with an older phrase, dating from the time of the Reformation: "the Middle Ages." Feudalism was said to be that type of society which had existed in the West during the Middle Ages; more than that, it was said to be a type of society that had existed in non-Western cultures as well, during the "medieval" period of their history. This usage conceals an ethnocentric assumption that certain characteristics of Western social and economic history may also be taken to define the social-economic order of other societies. Moreover, many historians of the nineteenth and twentieth centuries, by neglecting the belief system, the relations between ecclesiastical and secular authorities, and above all, the legal institutions and concepts that accompanied the feudal economies of the West, have given a distorted view of the dynamics of so-called feudalism, both in the West and elsewhere. Marxist historians, in particular, who treat the mode and relations of production as the infrastructure or base of feudal society, and the politics, ideology, and law as a superstructure, have failed to show why Western feudalism produced a fundamentally different kind of superstructure from that produced by, say, Japanese or Russian feudalism.

At the same time, many other historians who reject the Marxian categories of base and superstructure have also failed to show in any systematic way the interaction between the political, ideological, and legal institutions and concepts of the West, on the one hand, and such social and economic institutions as dependent land tenure, lord-vassal relations, and serfdom, on the other. But if the former are not merely the reflection and instrument of the latter, as Marx claimed, then what *are* the relations between the two? Can it be shown that, contrary to Marxist theory, "consciousness" determined "being"? Or, if these categories themselves are wrong, what categories should replace them?

The relationships between social and economic factors on one side and political and ideological factors on the other side can be clarified by proceeding from the basis of four methodological postulates.

First, legal institutions should be seen to overlap the dividing line between social-economic factors and political-ideological factors. Law must be treated as an essential part of both the material structure of Western society ("mode and relations of production") and its spiritual life ("political and social consciousness") — as both "base" and "superstructure."

Second, an analysis should be made, not of feudal*ism* but of the different kinds of law that regulated social and economic relations in the period under consideration. This analysis must include not only *feudal law* in the technical sense of that phrase, that is, the law regulating feudal tenures (fiefs) and lord-vassal relations (fealty), but also *manorial law*, the law regulating lord-peasant relations and agricultural production and manorial life generally. The juxtaposition of feudal law and manorial law should help to overcome the objections of those social and economic historians who rightly charge certain political and legal historians with having neglected a principal feature of feudalism, the existence of a subject peasantry bound to the land. The countercharge of excessive breadth (and consequent vagueness) may be avoided by adhering to the important technical distinction between the two types of regulation: the regulation of fiefs and fealty, on the one hand, and the regulation of manorial relations, on the other. These were two distinct branches of law, just as corporation law and labor law are two distinct branches of law in the West today, although sociologically and historically they are closely interrelated.

Third, a dynamic element is added to the study of Western feudalism by examining the changes that took place in feudal and manorial law from the time of the Papal Revolution. For the tremendous convulsion of Europe which accompanied the so-called Gregorian Reform and Investiture Struggle could not have left legal regulation of the mode and relations of production unaffected, and indeed this periodization of Western feudalism is supported by leading social and economic historians.[1] Marc Bloch divides feudalism into the "first feudal age," from the eighth to the mid-eleventh century, and the "second feudal age," from the mid-eleventh to the fifteenth century. "There were," he writes "in a word, two successive feudal ages, very different from one another in their essential character." Similarly, Georges Duby considers the eleventh century to be the critical period in the emergence of Western feudalism, and he calls the years from 1070 to 1180 "the century of great progress," in which feudalism as a system was established throughout Europe.

Fourth, it should be recognized that prior to the mid-eleventh century lord-vassal relations and land tenure, on the one hand, and lord-peasant relations and manorial life, on the other, were not subjected to systematic legal regulation; that although they were legally regulated by custom (including customary law), feudal and manorial custom were largely inchoate and diffused in general social and economic custom; and that a most important aspect of the crucial changes that took place in the eleventh and twelfth centuries was that both feudal law and manorial law were disembedded and substantially systematized. If the late Russian historian George Vernadsky was correct in saying that Russian feudalism was "feudalism without feudal law," it can also be said that Western feudalism before the eleventh century was "feudalism without feudal law." Of course, that is an exaggeration: there was some feudal law (and some manorial law) in both Russia and the Frankish Empire, but it was largely diffuse and unsystematized. In the century between 1050 and 1150 feudalism in the West became legalized, in the sense that feudal law and manorial law were for the first time conceived as integrated bodies of law, with a life of their own, by which all aspects of feudal and manorial relations were consciously governed.

Feudal Custom in the West Prior to the Eleventh Century

Before the great upheavals of the late eleventh and early twelfth centuries, the peoples of Europe were organized politically in a loose, complex, and overlapping structure of (1) local units, (2) lordship units, (3) tribal (clan) units, (4) large territorial units such as duchies or principalities, which might include a number of tribes (clans), and (5) kingdoms, of which the Frankish kingdom, from the year 800, was also called an empire. The kingdoms were conceived not as territorial units but primarily as the community of the Christian people under a king (emperor), who was considered to be Christ's deputy and supreme head of the church as well as of the nobility, the clans, and the army. The church itself was not conceived as a political unit but primarily as a spiritual community led ultimately by the king or emperor and intermediately by bishops, of whom the Bishop of Rome was by tradition the most important.

Within this general classification, there were very wide differences from locality to locality, lordship unit to lordship unit, tribal unit to tribal unit, and so on. The economy of Europe before the eleventh century was largely local and agrarian. There was very little intercommunication; apart from monks and some others of the clergy and a small number of merchants, and except for military campaigns, only the higher nobility and kings traveled. There were practically no permanent representatives of the central authorities in the localities. Efforts to place them there were generally frustrated. Not only power but also culture was widely dispersed. The customs of one place might differ substantially from the customs of another place fifty miles away.

Nevertheless, the political organization of the peoples of Europe in the period from the sixth to the eleventh centuries reveals a common pattern of development.

The smallest local political units were generally called *villae* ("villages," or "vills"); these were grouped into *centenarii* ("hundreds"), which were grouped, in turn, into *comitatus* ("counties"). These local units first came into being when the wandering tribes from western Asia, having swallowed up what was left of the Roman Empire in the West, finally settled down in the fourth, fifth, and sixth centuries.

The second type of unit, lordship units, came into being soon thereafter. Their number increased as settlers "commended themselves" to leading personages among them and promised to render services in return for food and clothing as well as for protection against enemies. The person who commended himself became "the man" of the lord. He might live in the lord's household, or the lord might provide him with land to work for himself.

Lordship units also came into being when leading personages, and especially clan chiefs and kings, granted a benefice (*beneficium*, "benefit"), that is, land or other property, or an office or other privileges, to be held in return for services. The term "benefice," which at first connoted that the tenant was to receive the grant on relatively easy terms, was eventually confined chiefly to grants to a church; in the late eighth and ninth centuries it was largely replaced by the Germanic term *feod*. *Feod*, which was rendered *feudum* in Latin (hence the English word "feudalism" and the French word *féodalité*), originally meant cattle (as the German cognate *Vieh* still means "cow"); then it came to signify valuable moveable goods (compare the English word "chattels," derived from "cattle"); and finally it came to mean a form of land tenure, rendered "fief" or "fee" in Norman English. (Thus to speak of a lawyer's or doctor's "fee" is to perpetuate the concept of a grant of a form of tenure that carries the obligation to render services.)

In the nineteenth century, many historians traced the remote origins of the first kind of lordship unit, formed by commendation, to the *Gefolgschaft* ("following") of the Germanic tribes, which was a band of trusted soldiers surrounding the war chief. Others traced the remote origins of the second kind of lordship unit, formed by grant of a fief, to the *patrocinium* ("patronage estate") of the late Roman Empire, which was land allocated by the patron to his *clientes*, who held it with a certain degree of immunity from state authority. Debates over the Germanic as against the Roman origins of "feudalism" were conducted with extraordinary passion because important nineteenth-century political interests were at stake. The Germanists were the nationalists and the romantics. The Romanists were the cosmopolitans and the individualists. Both sides believed in a unilinear legal evolution from earliest times. And both repressed the memory of the Papal Revolution.

Today it is generally accepted that neither the Gefolgschaft nor the patrocinium survived even the Frankish period, much less the Papal Revolution. In the late eighth and ninth centuries, commendation and the granting of a fief were often merged. Moreover, in the ninth century the fief, with its obligations of service, often descended to the heirs of the tenant—then usually called by the Celtic term "vassal"—upon the renewal of their oaths of commendation.

The oaths were part of a solemn rite. The vassal, bareheaded and unarmed, went down on his knees, placed his hands together and put them (pointing upwards) between the hands of the lord, and acknowledged himself to be the lord's "man" (*homme, homo*). By the tenth century it had become a widespread practice for the two then to kiss each other on the mouth. By this ritual of homage the vassal became the lord's "man of mouth and hands." But with the linking of commendation and land tenure, a second part was added to the ceremony, namely, a religious oath of fidelity ("fealty") by the vassal. Laying his hand on the Bible or on relics, the vassal pledged his faith (*fides, fidelitas*) to his lord. Often the lord would then perform a symbolic investiture of the vassal, handing over some object, such as a flag or a cross or a key, to symbolize infeudation, that is, the granting of a fief. In time every vassal swore fealty.

The linking of vassalage with fiefs through the oath of fealty became characteristic of Frankish feudal custom, though there were wide variations in that custom, both in time and in space. The Frankish kings carried this "feudo-vassalitic" (as modern historians call it) custom to all parts of their domains, including northern Italy (down to Rome), Spain, Hungary, and Poland. Only Scandinavia, Friesland, and a part of the Netherlands that borders on the North Sea remained immune. In England, feudal custom developed along different but parallel lines: the institutions of vassalage and fiefs were known, but in a less systematized form and without the same linkage between the two. However, the Norsemen, who had settled in the western part of the Frankish Empire in the early 900s and had absorbed Frankish feudal custom, carried it with them to England in 1066 and to Sicily and southern Italy in the 1070s and 1080s. The Crusaders carried it to Palestine in 1099. eventually founding there the Norman Kingdom of Jerusalem, whose Assizes of Jerusalem created a model system of serfdom, knighthood, lordship, and fiefs.[2]

Feudal lordship units and local political units (vills, hundreds, counties) could and often did exist side by side. The vill, the hundred, and the county each had its own governing body, which was a court (in England, "moot") consisting of an assembly of free men. Each assembly met at regular intervals to transact the public affairs of the vill, hundred, or county. This included (but was by no means confined to) the resolution of what would today be called criminal and civil disputes. Each lordship unit, which in the tenth century very often took the form of a manor, had its own court, consisting of the periodic assembly of all freemen and serfs of the manor, but not the slaves. The manorial court also resolved criminal and civil disputes.

In the western parts of the Frankish Empire, but not in the eastern and southern parts (especially not in Germany and Italy), local government was absorbed to a considerable extent by feudal manors in the tenth and eleventh centuries. In England, hundred government and county (shire) government continued to predominate — although manorial government also existed — until the Norman Conquest, when a majority of the hundred courts were absorbed into the feudal manors allocated by the Conqueror and when the county courts became, to a large extent, instruments of royal authority.

Above the level of the manor and the hundred or county, government in the period prior to the late eleventh century was greatly hampered by difficulties of communication. The lords of lords — clan chiefs, dukes, princes, and other leading nobility — were victims not only of the local character of the economy but also of the sparseness of settlement in Europe from the sixth to the early eleventh centuries, which was accentuated by a generally stationary or declining population throughout the period. The Roman cities had virtually disappeared; there were only a small number of important towns, and hardly any of them had more than a few thousand inhabitants. Travel was difficult; twenty to twenty-five miles a day was the normal rate of speed for a nobleman moving with his entourage from one vassal's estate to another. Such visits were necessary for the nobleman, not merely to supervise the administration of his estates but also to support himself and his household. Food had to be consumed on the spot; to transport it to a central location would have been too expensive. For the same reason, durable goods had to be procured on the spot and carried with one or left on deposit, so to speak. Such merchants as existed were chiefly peddlers, *pieds poudreux* ("men of dusty feet"), since there were generally not enough customers assembled in one place to justify selling through local representatives.

Kings and emperors also lived by travelling. In the course of the year 1033, for example, Emperor Conrad II journeyed from Burgundy to the Polish frontier, thence back again across Europe to Champagne, and eventually to his native Saxony—a distance of some 1500 miles as the crow flies![3]

The empire, as well as those kingdoms (like the Anglo-Saxon kingdom) that were outside the empire, had virtually no central administration, virtually no centrally administered fiscal system, virtually no central judiciary, virtually no representatives whatsoever in the localities; emperors and kings carried their government, for the most part, with them, in their imperial or royal households, as they "rode circuit" through their domains.

The story of the peripatetic emperor or king, always on the move, and of peripatetic dukes, earls, princes, and other high noble lords, most of them on the move most of the time, with an immobilized agricultural population living in sparsely settled villages and manors, almost completes the foundation for an analysis of the transformation of feudal custom into a system of feudal law in the eleventh and twelfth centuries. What is missing is the military aspect, which in some ways was the most important.

In fact, throughout the entire period prior to the eleventh century, war was the dominant daily concern of emperors, kings, and nobility. Constantly attacking the periphery of Europe, and always ready to swoop into the central parts, were the Norsemen, the Saracens, the Magyars.[4] Within Europe itself there were continual wars among the clans. The Carolingian kings sought, with some success, to induce the leaders of the various clan and territorial units to send foot soldiers to form a "popular," that is, an imperial army. Similarly, the Anglo-Saxon kings relied on a general levy (*fyrd*). However, these were not standing armies but rather reserves available for a common emergency. In time, the vast majority of people came more and more to think of themselves as peasants rather than as soldiers. They resisted conscription, and eventually they were supported in this by the church; the Cluniac Reform of the tenth and eleventh centuries proclaimed the Peace of God, whereby clergy and peasantry were to be exempted from military attack. The other side of the coin was the fact that the peasantry increasingly diminished in military value as the foot soldier gave way to the heavily armed horseman.

Various explanations have been given for the fateful emergence of the armed horseman in Frankish military history. The example of the Arab enemy in the eighth-century wars in Spain and southern France was one factor. The importation of the stirrup and the horseshoe from Eurasian tribes in the East also seems to have played an important role. There were undoubtedly other causes of a social nature. In any event, the consequences for feudal custom were momentous. It was extremely expensive to produce an armed horseman, not to mention a horse capable of carrying him. Since hitherto almost all soldiers had had to furnish their own equipment, it took a very wealthy man to provide himself with heavy armor plus a fighting horse, and it also took a man with leisure to undergo the necessary training in the use of them. In the year 1000 the price of a knight's armor alone would buy a good piece of farm land.[5]

Very gradually, in the eighth, ninth, and tenth centuries, a warrior class of armed horsemen, called knights (*milites* in Latin; *chevaliers* in French, from *cheval*, "horse"; *Ritter*, "riders," in German), emerged in the Frankish Empire, whose sole occupation was to serve their lords in battle. The peasants gradually came to be used only rarely for combat — chiefly for defense in emergencies — although they were often required to deliver provisions to the knights and food for the horses. In the tenth century the warrior knights were generally supported by their lords in the two-story wooden castles that came to be built on hills, surrounded by moats, for defense against marauders — and as bastions for marauding.

Thus in many parts of Europe, though not everywhere, the knight came to have a virtual monopoly of the military art. At the same time, by the practice of vassalage he was incorporated into (1) the system of land tenure and (2) the system of government. This manifested itself in various ways. The knight, having pledged fealty to a lord, might be invested with a fief, in which case he himself became a lord; if the fief included a manor and serfs, the knight was both landlord and governor. More often, the knight served in the household of his lord, keeping himself in readiness for combat. He might fight for his lord directly, or his lord might send him to his own superior lord in fulfillment of the feudal obligation of service which attached to his fief. A fief which carried the obligation to provide upkeep of one knightly family was called a knight's fee. A fief which carried the obligation to provide a superior lord with one or more knights was said to be held in knight's service. As the military significance of armed cavalry increased during the tenth and eleventh centuries, more and more land throughout Europe came to be held in knight's service.

In economic terms, it has been calculated that in the eleventh century one knightly household was worth about fifteen to thirty peasant families: that is, it took that number of peasants on the lord's estate to produce the wealth necessary to procure a horse and armor and to support a professional warrior and his family. Thus it was not accidental that the spread of knighthood across Europe was accompanied by the spread of manorial estates in which the labor force consisted largely of a peasantry bound economically, and in many places legally, to the land.

The Emergence of a System of Feudal Law

In the period from 1000 to 1200 A.D., and chieflly between 1050 and 1150, feudal arrangements in Europe underwent substantial changes, which may be classified under the following headings: (1) objectivity; (2) universality; (3) reciprocity of rights of lords and vassals; (4) participatory adjudications; (5) integration; and (6) growth.

Objectivity and Universality

In this period feudal arrangements which had previously been relatively arbitrary and loose in their signification and diverse and discriminatory in their local operation became substantially more objective and precise and substantially more uniform and general.[6]

For example, starting in the latter part of the ninth century, especially in France and Italy, the heir of a vassal often succeeded to the vassal's position upon his death. Nevertheless, only in a very loose sense may one speak of the "heritability" of fiefs at that time. Then, however, the *usage* (pattern of behavior) developed that upon a vassal's death a new investiture would be granted by the lord to the vassal's heir if he was willing to do homage; and next, this usage became internalized as a *norm* of behavior, so that it was considered to be a violation of a customary norm (norm of customary law) for the lord to withhold such investiture from the heir. Yet the norm of customary law did not exist in all places or under all circumstances. Indeed, throughout the ninth and tenth centuries European feudal custom (including both patterns of behavior and norms of behavior, both custom as usage and customary law) was extremely diverse. By no means all homage was accompanied by investiture with a fief, and by no means all fiefs were bestowed upon "men of mouth and hands." Many fiefs were still granted in return for payments in kind and not services, under arrangements that were terminable at the will of the grantor. This was also a period when knighthood was only beginning to become of great military importance, and when consequently the emerging class of knights were pressing for recognition — and for land.

In the eleventh and twelfth centuries, however, both the military situation and the legal situation were more favorable to the knightly class and hence to the vassals upon whom lords relied to furnish knights for military service. Therefore the vassal was able to insist on the right of his heir to inherit his interest in the fief. Indeed, in the late twelfth century in England and Normandy this right came to be vindicated in the royal and ducal courts, respectively, by a special writ called "mort d'ancestor," under which the heir was awarded possession and the lord who wrongfully entered was a trespasser.[7] Also, in most places the custom of primogeniture was established, whereby the oldest son inherited the entire fief, which was thus preserved against dismemberment — although parts of the fief ("appanages") might be set aside to compensate younger sons.

Thus in the eleventh and twelfth centuries the heritability of the fief became an objective and universal norm, relatively precise in its signification and more or less uniform throughout Europe.[8] A similar development took place with respect to other norms of feudal customary law, such as the alienability of the fief by the vassal, the commutation of various personal feudal obligations into money payments, and suit of court.

RECIPROCITY OF RIGHTS OF LORDS AND VASSALS

In the same period, and chiefly between 1050 and 1150, various forms of personal subjection of vassals to lords became transformed into property obligations, and at the same time various forms of direct economic domination by lords became commuted into taxes, leaving vassals with substantially more personal freedom and economic autonomy.

Personal subjection of vassals in the ninth and tenth centuries had taken the form of the right of the lord to require the vassal to perform military service, the right of the lord in certain cases to marry (or marry off) the vassal's daughter, the right of the lord to the personal assistance of the vassal in the event of need, and various other such lordly rights. In the eleventh and twelfth centuries, the duty of military service was generally commuted into money payments (in England and Normandy, "scutage"), the right of marriage was generally commuted into a one-time tax on the marriage of a vassal's daughter, and the right to personal assistance was also generally commuted into various taxes ("aids").

Economic domination had previously taken the form, in many places, of the power of the lord to enter the fief and supervise its administration and take its products, the absence of any right on the part of the vassal to alienate the fief, and the power of the lord to have it back on the death of the vassal. In the eleventh and twelfth centuries these powers of the lord were subjected to stringent legal limitations. The concept of "seisin" was developed in the eleventh century to characterize possessory rights of persons who "held" land or goods without owning them; one who was "seised" could not be forcibly ousted by anyone, nor could his chattels be lawfully taken from him against his will — even by his lord. Also, the development of the heritability of the fief by the vassal's heirs was accompanied by the development of its alienability by the vassal. Such alienation sometimes took the form of subinfeudation, that is, the enfeoffment of a subvassal. In the event of transfer of a fief to an heir or transfer by subinfeudation or other form of alienation, a tax was to be paid to the lord.

These legal developments in the direction of reification of rights obviously fostered the increased economic autonomy of the vassal. More and more his obligations to the lord were expressed in terms of payments, whether in kind or in money, instead of in terms of personal services as before. More and more he managed the fief without the lord's strict personal oversight.

The increasing legal protection of vassals is not to be interpreted, however, as the victory of one economic class over another. Except for the king, who was liege lord of all, every lord was also someone else's vassal; and as the result of subinfeudation every vassal who held a fief was also someone else's lord, except at the lowest rung of the ladder where the lord of the manor ruled not over vassals but over serfs and other peasants.

As Marc Bloch writes: "In a society in which so many individuals were at one and the same time commended men and masters, there was a reluctance to admit that if one of them, as a vassal, had secured some advantage for himself, he could, as a lord, refuse it to those who were bound to his person by a similar form of dependence. From the old Carolingian capitulary to the Great Charter, the classic foundation of English liberties, this sort of equality in privilege, descending smoothly from top to bottom of the scale, was to remain one of the most fertile sources of feudal custom."[9] Bloch's reference to the Carolingian period seems to contradict the emphasis that has been placed here on the changes that occurred in the eleventh and twelfth centuries; but only two pages later, Bloch makes the crucial distinction: "As early as the Carolingian age, custom favored the claims of descendants [of vassals to inherit] . . . During the second feudal age [that is, after the mid-eleventh century], which was everywhere marked by a sort of legal awakening, it became law."[10]

These developments in the direction of increased personal freedom and economic autonomy of vassals were especially manifested in the legalization of the element of reciprocity in the lord-vassal relationship. Of course, a certain degree of reciprocity was always present in the relationship; to become "the man" of a lord always required an acceptance by the lord of a lifelong relationship involving not only the man's loyalty but also the lord's loyalty, and when this was joined with enfeoffment of the vassal a reciprocal landlord-tenant relationship was also established. Yet the practice of reciprocity in these loose forms, and even the acceptance of a binding customary norm of reciprocity, was a far cry from the full-fledged contractual reciprocity that began to be associated with the lord-vassal bond in the eleventh century.

The phrase "contractual reciprocity" is subject to a qualification: the feudal contract (whether of homage or of fealty without homage) was a contract to enter into a status. In that sense it was like a marriage contract, to which in fact it was compared by the twelfth century jurists. In contrast to commercial contracts, for example, virtually all the rights and obligations of the lord-vassal contract were fixed by (customary) law and could not be altered by the will of the parties. The contractual aspect was the consent to the relationship; the legal content of the relationship, however, was ascribed. In addition, the contract of homage could not be dissolved by mutual consent because it was founded on sacred vows of lifelong commitment. On the contrary, the contract of fealty could be dissolved by mutual consent, and both the contract of fealty and the contract of homage could be dissolved by one party upon breach of its fundamental obligations by the other.

It is sometimes suggested by writers on feudalism that the homage of the vassal was reciprocated by the grant of a fief. That suggestion confuses homage and fealty. The reciprocity in homage consisted of the fact that the vassal became the lord's man in return for the lord's becoming the vassal's lord; this was the lifelong relationship, sealed by a kiss, the equivalent — almost — of a marriage.[11] The vassal's pledge of faith (fealty) to the lord was another matter. That was reciprocated by the lord's pledge of faith to the vassal. In addition, the lord often invested the vassal with a fief. The vassal's pledge of fealty included the duty to manage the fief faithfully. The lord's pledge of fealty included the duty not to overstep the legal limitations upon his powers as well as the duty to assist the vassal in various specific ways. The vassal could owe homage and fealty to more than one lord, just as he could hold different fiefs of different lords. A system of *ligantia* developed in the mid-eleventh century in France and elsewhere, under which a vassal reserved his obligations to one or more "liege lords." In England from the twelfth century on, the king was always a liege lord and at enfeoffment the vassal was required to say: "save my fealty due to the king." As fiefs became heritable and alienable, within broad legal limits, vassalage was once again separated from homage and became subject to its own rules of reciprocity.

Of critical importance from a theoretical standpoint, and not without substantial practical importance in unusual situations, was the right of either the vassal or the lord to dissolve a contract of homage or of fealty upon sufficient provocation. If one party violated his obligations and thereby caused the other party serious injury, the latter had the right to dissolve the relationship by a solemn gesture of defiance, called *diffidatio* ("withdrawal of faith"). In the first systematic treatise on English law, written in 1187 and attributed to Glanvill, it was stated that a vassal owed his lord no more than a lord owed his vassal, reverence alone excepted, and that if the lord broke faith the vassal was released from his obligation to serve. The diffidatio is a key to the legal character of the feudal relationship in the West from the eleventh century on. Moreover, as Friedrich Heer has written, the diffidatio "marked a cardinal point in the political, social, and legal development of Europe. The whole idea of a right of resistance is inherent in this notion of a contract between the governor and the governed, between the higher and the lower."[12]

PARTICIPATORY JUSTICE

It was a basic principle of justice throughout the West that every lord had the right to hold court, that is, to preside over his vassals — or over his tenants, whether or not they were vassals — in court proceedings. This principle was an expression of the merger of military-economic and political relations: the military-economic enterprise of administering a fief was at the same time the political enterprise of governing the community of people who were attached to the fief. And government took the form, chiefly, of exercising jurisdiction through proceedings of a broadly judicial character.

One way to view the emergence of feudal courts in the tenth and eleventh centuries is to emphasize the breakdown of centralized royal authority during the ninth century, accompanied by royal grants of immunity to great landowners. This view must be qualified, however, by the recognition that centralized royal authority had never been firmly established even in Charlemagne's empire. To be sure, Charlemagne and his successors had tried to provide in each district of their domain a permanent group of "law-finders" (*scabini*), centrally appointed, who were to decide cases under the presidency of the centrally appointed governor of the district (*Graf*, or count). Yet these lay tribunals, which usually consisted of prominent local landowners, could hardly be controlled from the center. Moreover, local justice continued to be administered to a very considerable extent by popular assemblies. It was these popular assemblies, as well as such scabini courts as continued to exist, that were largely replaced by feudal courts in the tenth and eleventh centuries in the Frankish Empire. Similarly, in England after the Norman Conquest it was the local popular assemblies — the hundred courts and the shire courts — that were replaced by feudal courts, though to a lesser extent than in France.

Thus the tradition of group adjudication was strong, while the tradition of professional adjudication by legally trained officials hardly existed, prior to the late eleventh century. The dominant concept of the judicial process was "suit of court": the lord presided, either in person or through his steward, but the judging was done by the "suitors," that is, the vassals or tenants. A person charged with an offense or an obligation was entitled to be judged by his fellows — his equals (*pares*, "peers"). This phrase — the right of a person to be tried "by judgment of his peers" (*per iudicium parium*) — was made famous in England by its inclusion in Magna Carta in 1215; it may be found, however, in similar documents issued in other countries of Europe. Thus a constitution promulgated by Emperor Conrad II in 1037 declared that no vassal should be deprived of an imperial or ecclesiastical fief "except in accordance with the law of our predecessors and the judgment of his peers."[13]

Feudal courts were not merely agencies of dispute resolution or law enforcement in the narrow sense; they were assemblies for consultation and deliberation on all matters of common concern. Thus seignorial courts might be asked to fix the amount of aids to be paid by vassals to support a military campaign, or to declare rules concerning the use of common fields or forests, or to consent to the enfeoffment of a new tenant or the expulsion of a defaulting tenant. At the same time, seignorial courts might exercise what in France was called *haute justice* ("high justice"): that is, they might decide cases of capital offenses, such as murder, robbery, and other felonies. Eventually, first in the Norman kingdoms of Sicily and England and subsequently in Normandy and France and elsewhere, the king's (or duke's) courts acquired a large share of the jurisdiction over haute justice — also called "pleas of the sword". Even in England, however , some great lords retained such jurisdiction, and in France and Germany a great many lords continued to exercise high justice up to the sixteenth century. Everywhere seignorial courts continued to have jurisdiction over petty crimes and certain types of civil actions (*basse justice*, "low justice"), as well as general jurisdiction over rights in land held of the lord whose court it was. (English seignorial courts also retained for some centuries capital jurisdiction over "hand-having thieves," that is, thieves caught in the act.)

Either the lord himself or his steward presided over the feudal court, and the suitors gave judgment. In communal and civil cases, proof was generally by compurgation or battle or, prior to its abolition in 1215, ordeal. In addition, juries were often appointed to decide disputed matters. Procedure was oral and informal. These were characteristics of seignorial justice throughout Western Europe.

A striking feature of seignorial justice was the jurisdiction of the seignorial court over claims by a lord against a vassal. The lord used his court to sue his tenants for defaults in paying feudal dues, for trespasses on the lord's domain, and for other breaches of obligation. Maitland writes: "As to the objection that the lord is both judge and party, that fails, for the lord is not judge; the defendant has the judgment of his peers."[14] Of course, the lord could make life difficult for those who voted against him. However, the vassal could appeal from a decision of the court of his immediate lord to the court of that lord's superior. This right of appeal was articulated in specific legal terms. For example, the French jurist Philippe de Beaumanoir, writing at the end of the thirteenth century but describing a legal regime — that of the county of Beauvaisis — that had existed for more than a hundred years, listed the following grounds upon which a knight could appeal from a judgment of the court of his lord to the next higher seignorial court: (1) the denial of justice, (2) false judgment, (3) lack of jurisdiction, (4) authorization to appeal granted by writ of the count or of the king, (5) direct concern in the case on the part of the count, as when the knight claimed that he had recently been unjustly disseised of his freehold land.[15] In addition, although the vassal could not sue his lord in the lord's own court, he could, if the lord refused a demand for justice, go to the court of the lord's lord.

The vassal's right of recourse to a higher seignorial court to enforce a claim against his immediate lord, though not often exercised, is a dramatic illustration of the importance both of the feudal court system and of the principle of reciprocity of rights between lords and vassals. Feudal law gave the West its first secular experience of mutuality of legal obligation between persons of superior and inferior rank.[16] Indeed, the entire feudal hierarchy was viewed as an integrated legal structure; the upper classes, from knights to barons to counts to dukes and earls and even kings, were considered to be subject to common legal standards. This was, in part, a manifestation of the ideal of legality. It was also, in part, a reflection of the actual experience of subinfeudation, in which the lord of one vassal was himself vassal to another lord. Both the ideal of legality and the practice of subinfeudation helped to maintain a common upper-class consciousness, in sharp contrast to the feudal structures of many non-Western cultures, in which there were sharp divisions within the aristocracy, especially between the higher nobility and the gentry. Such divisions also characterized Western society in later stages of its own development. But in the formative era of the Western legal tradition, under feudal law, the knightly class could claim a fundamental *legal* equality with all those who were politically, economically, and socially above it in the feudal hierarchy.

Mutuality of feudal legal obligation, equalization of feudal privilege, and the hierarchy of feudal jurisdictions were buttressed by a high degree of litigiousness on the part of the feudal aristocracy. This was linked with chivalry itself. "Litigation was second only to feuding and warfare as a form of conflict favored by the baronage," writes Heer. Indeed, as he points out, "trial by battle and trial by law were both forms of single combat. 'God and my right': let God determine the issue, in the duel and in the ordeal."[17] The litigiousness of the upper classes, like the concept of reciprocity of rights between lords and vassals, not only constituted a structural element in the system of feudal law but also marked an important contribution of feudal law to the development of Western legal consciousness, which is distinguished from the legal consciousness of many non-Western cultures by its strong attachment to formal adjudication of rights as a mode of dispute resolution.

INTEGRATION

The phrase "integration of feudal law" refers to that development of Western legal consciousness which made it both possible and necessary to interpret the various rights and obligations associated with lord-vassal relations as constituting an integrated whole. It came to be understood that the concepts and institutions of homage and fealty, ligantia, the so-called feudal incidents (military service or scutage, reliefs, aids, marriage, wardship, and others), the heritability and alienability of the fief, the rules of escheat, diffidatio, suit of court, and other related concepts and institutions all formed a distinct and entire legal system.

Although the system remained for the most part a system of customary law rather than enacted law, it eventually acquired written sources as well. In the eleventh and twelfth centuries numerous charters, issued to confirm the enfeoffment of vassals by lords, recorded specific feudal customs.[18] Urban statutes, such as the charter of Pisa of 1142, did the same. The *Usages* of Barcelona, written in 1068, was largely a restatement of feudal law. In time, feudal customs, both unwritten and written, came to be analyzed by learned jurists, who sought to define their underlying principles. Thus at some time between 1095 and 1130 Umberto de Orto, a Milanese consul, wrote a book entitled *Consuetudines Feudorum* (*Customs of Fiefs*), later called the *Libri Feudorum* (*Books of Fiefs*), which was an attempt to set forth systematically the feudal law. This book was used as a text at Bologna, where it was glossed and expanded, and its final version of 1220 was added to Justinian's Novels. It restated both customary feudal law and particular enactments of the emperors Lothar II, Frederick I, and Henry VI. Thus it purported to analyze not only Lombard feudal law but a more universal customary law, different from canon law, different also from royal or urban or mercantile law, yet common to the West and applicable to feudal relations generally. Umberto and the jurists who followed him considered, in David Herlihy's words, "that the customary law of the fief was logically consistent and entirely amenable to scientific investigation . . . [They] assumed that the aggregate of feudal customs was more than a formless mass of regional idiosyncrasies; rather, the customs shared common principles and therefore did constitute a true legal system. But the jurists fully recognized that these customs still constituted only one part of the total body of laws by which society was governed."[19]

The law of feudal land tenures merged with the growing body of royal (or ducal) law in Sicily, England, Normandy, France, the German duchies, Flanders, Spain, and elsewhere. In 1187 Glanvill's treatise on the laws and customs of England systematized most of the fundamental principles of feudal law in England under the categories of the royal judicial writs that had been issued in the preceding decades. About 1200 a Norman book of customs, the *Très ancien coutumier de Normandie*, contained a very similar body of feudal law applicable to Normandy. About 1221 there appeared the *Sachsenspiegel* (*Mirror of the Saxons*), written by the German knight Eike von Repgau; it contained two parts, one on the Saxon *Landrecht*, or common law; the other on the Saxon *Lehnrecht*, or feudal law. (The *Sachsenspiegel* was the first lawbook written in German. It was preceded by a Latin edition, now lost.)[20]

In addition, the three greatest Western monarchs of the last part of the twelfth century—Henry II of England and Normandy (1154-1189), Philip Augustus of France (1180-1223), and Frederick Barbarossa of Germany (1152-1190)—issued important laws regulating various feudal questions.

In the thirteenth and fourteenth centuries, treatises on feudal law were written by leading Romanists. Many books appeared that reported local customs—in Denmark, Jutland, Normandy, Vermandois, Orléans, Anjou, and elsewhere. The great summa of English law attributed to Bracton, written in the first half of the thirteenth century, contained a very detailed analysis of feudal law; and in 1283 this was followed in France by the famous *Customs of Beauvaisis* by Beaumanoir.

Marc Bloch contrasts the place of feudal law in the legal structures of France, Germany, and England after the year 1200. In France the law of fiefs and of vassalage was woven into the whole legal fabric, so that it was impossible to distinguish between feudal and nonfeudal law. In Germany, feudal law was treated as a separate system whose rules were applicable only to certain estates or certain persons and were administered by special courts; not only at the manorial level or in the towns but also among the upper classes of the countryside many types of legal relations were governed by *Landrecht* (*lex terrae*, "law of the land") and not by *Lehnrecht* ("feudal law"). England was like France in that there was no separate body of feudal law erected out of the custom of the feudal classes; Landrecht and Lehnrecht were merged. However, as in Germany, a considerable part of the English common law—that relating to rights in land—could be identified as feudal law, even though it was administered by royal courts and was technically part of the common law.[21] Bloch's analysis can be seen as a qualification and clarification of the thesis presented here concerning the systematization of feudal law in the eleventh and twelfth centuries. This systematization did not result in the creation of a body of law which operated independently of other bodies of law. Instead, all the secular legal systems—feudal, manorial, mercantile, urban, and royal (common)—overlapped one another. This was true even in Germany despite the division between the law of the land and feudal law. Nevertheless, each body of law had its own character, its own logic: even though feudal and nonfeudal legal norms were interwoven in the French books of customary law and in Bracton's analysis of the law applicable in the English royal courts, feudal law still had its own coherent principles.

One of the most important integrating elements of feudal law was its combination of political and economic rights—the right of government and the right of use and disposition of land. The legal term used to express this combination was the Latin word *dominium*, which meant, on the one hand, something like lordship and, on the other hand, something like ownership. "Lordship" is the right word if it is understood to include jurisdiction, that is, the right to hold court and declare law. "Fief and justice—it is all one," said Beaumanoir.[22] "Ownership" is also the right word if it is not restricted to the meaning it originally had when it was first used in the seventeenth century. Then it referred to an absolute, undivided, exclusive right over the thing owned. Feudal dominium, in contrast, was usually limited, divided, and shared in a variety of ways. A person could have certain rights in land valid against his lord, and the lord could have certain rights in the same land valid against *his* lord, as well as other rights valid against that lord's lord, who might be the king. The conflicting rights inhered in the land itself, which was conceived as a kind of legal entity: thus one parcel of land might be considered "servient" to another in the sense that services might be required to be transferred from it to the "dominant" parcel. Land, in fact, was not "owned" by anyone; it was "held" by superiors in a ladder of "tenures" leading to the king or other supreme lord. ("Tenure," derived from the Latin word *tenere*, "to hold," itself means "a holding.")

The concept of divided property, or multiple bearers of rights in the same land, is not a uniquely Western idea. The Western system of feudal property *was* unique, however, in its conception of the interrelationships of the various competing rights. A knight, for example, might have dominium over a parcel of land solely for his life, with such dominium to revert, at his death, to the lord who had granted him such a "life estate." Or the land might have been granted to the knight "and the heirs of his body," in which case the heirs, upon birth, might have a certain kind of "future interest" in the land. Or the grant might be to Knight A for life and, on his death, to his brother, Knight B, if B survived A, but if B predeceased A then, on A's death, to his cousin, Knight C. This would create other kinds of "future interests" in the land for B and C. Such gifts of land (or of other property) designed to revert to the donor on the death of the donee, and the creation of various kinds of contingent interests in land to take effect at a future time, did not derive from either Roman law or Germanic law. The very idea of measuring property rights by their duration in time was largely an invention of the late eleventh and twelfth centuries in the West. This idea persisted long after the decline of feudalism; indeed, it has persisted in English and American land law to this day. What is involved is not merely a set of techniques for effectuating the devolution of property on death but also the inclusion of various persons, born and unborn, in the rights of possession, use, disposition, and control of property. The conscious entailment of future generations in the property regime was a characteristic example of the time sense of the Western legal tradition in the formative era of its development.

Together with the measurement of property interests ("estates") in land by their duration in time, and the allocation of such estates for future enjoyment ("future interests"), the distinctive legal concept of seisin, which spread through Europe in the late eleventh and twelfth centuries, made an enduring contribution to Western legal values as well as to Western legal institutions, concepts, and rules. Seisin has already been mentioned in connection with the development of the legal autonomy of vassals — a vassal "seised" of the land had a right of action against anyone who "disseised" him, even his lord — and also in connection with the canon law of property, especially the law of spoliation. From the point of view of the development of the Western legal tradition as a whole, the importance of the concept of seisin lay in its interweaving of legal and factual elements. It did not mean simply — or even necessarily — factual occupation or physical control of the land; in this it differed from the older Roman concept of possession. Thus one could remain seised of land while one was away on a crusade or pilgrimage. Yet seisin did not mean simply — or even necessarily — a right of ownership. Thus the heir or grantee who had not yet entered upon the land did not yet have seisin of it. Seisin was, in effect, a legal right to continue in a factual situation, which right was derived from previously having been in that factual situation.[23] It was a right of possession independent both of ownership and of contract — a concept unknown either to Germanic law or to the older Roman law. This idea of "possessory right" — not possession but right of possession — has persisted in all Western legal systems to this day. It is particularly strong in English and American law.

The concept of seisin was a product partly of the feudal concept of divided ownership and partly of the canonist concept of due process of law, with its antipathy to force and self-help. A person seised of land, goods, or rights could not be ousted by force even by the true owners. This, too, not only formed a structural element of feudal law but also made an important and enduring contribution to Western legal consciousness.

Finally, feudal law was characterized by its conception of tort, or legal wrong, as a breach of a relationship. From an early time, it had been a rule of customary feudal law that if a vassal "broke faith" with his lord, the fief reverted ("escheated") to the lord, just as it escheated on the vassal's death or, at a later period, when there were no heirs. The Norman word for such a breach of faith was "felony." In England after the Norman Conquest the most serious crimes came to be called felonies because they were considered to be breaches of the fealty owed by all people to the king as guardian of the peace of the realm. (The felon's land escheated to his lord, however, and only his chattels to the crown.) Apart from felonies, other criminal and civil wrongs — in England called "trespasses" (Norman French for the Latin *transgressiones*, "sins") — were also conceived generally as breaches of relationships: for example, relationships between landlords and tenants, between masters and servants, between bailors and bailees of goods.

GROWTH

Once feudal law became systematized in the eleventh and twelfth centuries, it developed rapidly. The specificity of its norms increased; the uniformity of its principles gradually swallowed up local differences; the reification of rights and obligations increasingly overcame the personal aspects of the lord's domination of the vassal and also gave the vassal more and more economic autonomy in managing the fief; reciprocity of rights and obligations became more and more important, as did adjudication of disputes; and the degree of integration increased. In other words, all these characteristic features of feudal law became also tendencies of feudal law, characteristics of its autonomous growth in time.

Thus feudal law shared with the new canon law of the late eleventh and twelfth centuries many of the basic qualities of legality that marked the Western legal tradition in its formative era. It was an autonomous legal system in the distinctive Western sense, characterized, on the one hand, by a conscious integration of legal values, legal institutions, and legal concepts and rules and, on the other hand, by a conscious tendency and capacity to develop in time, to grow over generations and centuries. The new feudal legal system was also characterized by a strong emphasis on the generality and objectivity of rights and obligations, on the autonomy of persons as holders of rights and obligations, on reciprocity of rights and obligations among persons of unequal social and economic status, and on wide participation of holders of rights and obligations in the proceedings in which such rights and obligations were declared. In these respects, too, feudal law resembled canon law.

Yet once this has been said, it must immediately be added that in comparison with canon law feudal law was much less systematic, much less integrated on the conscious level, much less professional, much less scientific. It was largely customary law and as such was treated more critically and more skeptically than the laws enacted by popes and kings, not to mention the learned law of Gratian's *Decretum* and glosses on Justinian's Digest. Moreover, feudal law was secular law, the law of a world still in slow and painful process of being redeemed. It was not the spiritual law of the church. True, canon law was also subject to interpretation in the light of reason and conscience, but feudal law was much more open to correction, and even repudiation, when it was found to work injustice.

Finally, canon law, in contrast to feudal law, was considered to be a complete system of law, governing every kind of legal question that might arise. Technically, of course, canon law covered only those questions that were within the ecclesiastical jurisdiction; but in fact that jurisdiction was limited only by the concept of sin, which, in turn, was defined partly in terms of the interests of the church. Thus even the rights and duties of a king toward his barons might fall within the jurisdiction of the church—as, for example, in the case of King John of England at Runnymede in 1215. Feudal law, on the other hand, was much more narrowly conceived. It was the law of fiefs, the law of lord-vassal relations. It was not only secular law, as contrasted with the spiritual law of the church, but it was only one among several competing systems of secular law.

10 | Manorial Law

LIKE THE FEUDAL LAW of lord-vassal relations and dependent land tenure, so the manorial law of lord-peasant relations and agricultural production came to form a legal system. Of course, the two systems were closely related to each other. Both were also related (though much less closely) to the systems of mercantile law, urban law, and royal (common) law which developed contemporaneously — just as all these secular law systems were closely related to the system of canon law. All were integral parts of an overarching structural process, the Western legal tradition.

The manorial economy did not become predominant in Europe until the eleventh century. In the preceding era, after the Germanic tribes had settled down in western Europe, no one type of agricultural economic relations had prevailed. On the one hand, within the tribal and village structure there were large numbers of peasant family households that were free, in the sense that they were not tilling the soil of a superior (except sometimes as hired laborers) and were not bound in personal service to a superior. On the other hand, slavery also abounded in European agriculture of that period. Many of these slaves were either descendants of persons captured in battle and reduced to slavery by the Germanic tribes, or they had themselves been captured in the more or less continual warfare that was waged in Europe prior to the eleventh century. Others were descendants of persons who had been slaves in the late Roman Empire. In addition, there seems to have been an upsurge of slavery in Europe in the eighth, ninth, and tenth centuries when many Slavs were captured and enslaved by the Frankish armies in the East; indeed, the Western word "slave" (in German, *Sklave*) derives from this historical experience. (The name "Frank," in contrast, came to mean "free.") Many slaves served in their masters' households, but most worked in the fields.

With the emergence of lordship units, and especially with the linkage of vassalage and fiefs in the eighth, ninth, and tenth centuries, a third class of peasant—neither free nor slave—became increasingly important. These peasants, often called serfs, were distinguished by several characteristics: (1) unlike slaves, they were not owned by a master and could not be bought and sold; (2) unlike slaves, they could contract legal marriages; (3) unlike most slaves, they provided their own food and clothing; (4) unlike most slaves, they had certain rights in house and land and goods; (5) unlike free peasants, they were bound to the land—that is, they could not leave without the lord's permission and they went with the land when it was transferred; (6) unlike most free peasants, they were required to perform heavy labor services on the lord's demesne; (7) unlike most free peasants, they were required to pay the lord various dues in kind and in money for the land which they held; and (8) unlike most free peasants, they were severely restricted in their rights of use and disposition of the land, and their property remained with the lord upon their death.

In some respects, the serfs were like another class which had survived from the late Empire, the *coloni*, who were not slaves but who performed labor services on the lord's demesne. There were also other kinds of peasants in varying degrees of dependency.

In the eighth, ninth, and tenth centuries, peasants of all kinds—free peasants, slaves, coloni, and others—were involuntarily or voluntarily or semivoluntarily drawn, in increasing numbers, into the estates of the lords as serfs. The *mansi* (landholdings) of the serfs were divided from the *mansus indominicatus*, or dominant estate ("demesne") of the lord. Yet the serfs performed labor services and other duties on the lord's demesne, and the lord exercised economic, fiscal, police, and judicial rights over the serfs on the tenements held by them. In addition to the serfs, many freemen also lived on the manors as tenants—in effect, subjects—of their lords. It is doubtful whether the number of serfs in Europe ever exceeded one-half to two-thirds of the total peasant population.[1] At the same time, however, there were many degrees of freedom among free peasants.

From the point of view of its internal relations, the fief took the form of an autonomous community, and in most parts of Europe it was given the name "manor" (*manerium*).[2] One important characteristic of the manor, viewed as an autonomous community, was the exalted position of the lord of the manor and the menial position of the serfs. Another important characteristic was the economic and political interdependence of all members of the manor, including the lord's household, the serfs, and the intermediate classes of knights, manorial officials, and other freemen (including free peasants) who lived there. A certain tension existed between these two characteristics.

With regard to the menial position of the serfs, Philippe de Beaumanoir wrote in the thirteenth century that of "the third estate of men," that is, of "such as are not free," "some are so subject to their lord that he may take all they have, alive or dead, and imprison them, whenever he pleases, being accountable to none but God." Beaumanoir contrasted this position of some of the serfs with that of the others, who in his time were the vast majority.[3] Prior to the eleventh century, however, his statement would have applied to almost all serfs. In the earlier period, manorial custom, even more than the feudal custom of that time, had substantially lacked objectivity and universality (as defined in chapter 9) and was therefore subject to far greater arbitrariness and abuse than at a later period; it also substantially lacked the other qualities of the later Western systems of law—reciprocity of legal relations between superior and inferior, participatory adjudication, systematic integrity, and organic growth.

Nevertheless, the interdependence between the peasants and the lord of the manor tended to overcome, to some extent, the hardships of their legal insecurity. Typically, the lord was not an absentee landlord or a mere tax collector, as in many non-Western lordship regimes. Instead, he lived on the estate and supervised its management. Even when he managed his manor (or manors) through an agent (or agents), he was entirely dependent on its economic profitability for the satisfaction of his own military and economic obligations to his superior lord (whether it was the king or an intermediate lord). Equally important, he was the political ruler of the entire manorial community, responsible for maintaining order within it, for protecting it against outside attack, and for appointing officials to administer it and preside over its assemblies. Once again, these aspects of manorial life were far more loosely ordered and far more subject to local and individual eccentricities in the period prior to the eleventh century than in the period thereafter.

Just as feudal custom was transformed into a system of feudal law in the eleventh and twelfth centuries, and especially between 1050 and 1150, so manorial custom was transformed into a system of manorial law in roughly the same period. As in the case of feudal law, so in the case of manorial law there was in that period a substantial increase in the objectivity and universality of its norms. An element of reciprocity also developed in the legal relations between peasants and lord, although it was less apparent than in feudal law since homage and fealty were absent from lord-peasant relations, and there was no concept of a lord-peasant contract to enter into a lifelong relationship; nevertheless, the peasants brought group pressure to bear upon lords in order to exact more favorable conditions of labor, which had the force of concessions reciprocally granted on condition of loyalty. In addition, manorial law was administered by an assembly of members of the manor, including the serfs, who participated in adjudication of disputes under the presidency of the lord's official, the steward. Finally, manorial law in the eleventh and twelfth centuries, like feudal law though to a lesser extent, acquired the quality of an integrated system of concepts and procedures as well as the quality of a developing system with the capacity for incremental growth over generations and centuries.

In contrast with feudal law, however, the emergence of a new system of manorial law in the eleventh and twelfth centuries was directly connected with economic class struggle. Whereas feudal law chiefly regulated relations among persons belonging to a single economic class, the feudal aristocracy, manorial law chiefly regulated relations between rich and poor, rulers and ruled, "management" and "labor." This does not mean that manorial law was simply imposed on the peasants; on the contrary, they were not without substantial leverage to protect their class interests. Especially in the eleventh and twelfth centuries, improvements in economic conditions made it economically feasible for them to insist on substantial improvements in their conditions of servitude. However, the development of a new body of law to secure those improvements was dependent not only on changes in economic conditions but also on changes in legal conditions. New legal concepts and institutions, and new attitudes toward law, had emerged or were emerging, to which both lords and peasants resorted in the effort to resolve the conflicts between their economic interests.

A crucial aspect of the enormous growth in prosperity that occurred during the late eleventh and early twelfth centuries was the final cessation of military attacks from the north, east, and south. Indeed, by the end of the eleventh century the West had achieved sufficient economic strength to launch its own military invasion of the Middle East (the First Crusade, 1095-1099). Another aspect of the growth of prosperity was the movement for land reclamation and colonization: in the eleventh and twelfth centuries, Europeans cleared forests and encroached on waste lands, drained marshes, and reclaimed land from the sea — in England, Germany, Flanders, and elsewhere. Many migrated to Slav and Magyar lands. These activities were connected with population growth: after centuries of either stable or declining population, the population of France leaped from approximately seven million to over twenty million between the mid-eleventh and early fourteenth centuries, and the population of England from approximately two million to approximately three and one-half million in the same period. In addition, there were substantial technological improvements which resulted in a substantial increase of agricultural production in the eleventh century and thereafter; commerce grew; new cities and towns sprang up all over western Europe.

These factors substantially strengthened the economic position of the peasants. It might be thought that the increase of population would have lessened the value of their individual labor, but any such tendency was counteracted by the economic factors which had helped to produce the increase: the availability of land, the possibility of movement to the expanding cities and towns, and the beginnings of a money economy. There was, in fact, a great shortage of labor for the work to be done. Moreover, the increase of population contributed to the rise of peasant class consciousness, which was itself an important factor in the struggle for better working and living conditions.

The church, too, in carrying out the Papal Revolution, pursued policies that were favorable to the peasants. It offered serfs an opportunity for emancipation through entry into holy orders.[4] In launching the First Crusade, it offered them an opportunity for emancipation through enlistment in the Holy War.[5] In addition, the church, which was by far the largest proprietor in Europe, holding perhaps one-fourth or more of all the land, often attracted peasants from other estates by offering more favorable conditions of life and work. Escape to church manors, whether legal or illegal, encouraged escape to other more congenial manors as well, or to the cities, thereby putting pressure on lords to yield to peasant grievances.

In addition, the church generally emancipated the slaves on its own domains and thereby, as well as through other means, contributed to the virtual elimination of peasant slavery throughout most of Europe in the eleventh, twelfth, and thirteenth centuries. (Household slavery survived in some places.) This had the secondary effect of relieving serfs from the pressure of competition from an even more downtrodden class. Here again, economic and ideological factors were joined. Christian leaders had previously accepted slavery as a fact of life, while teaching that slaves should be treated with humanity and that the freeing of a slave was a pious and meritorious act. As a result of the Papal Revolution the church for the first time gave a systematic legal formulation of its views on slavery. It took the position that slavery itself was not illegal but that it was a sin for a Christian to hold a Christian as a slave.[6] In England, for example, almost 10 percent of the population recorded in Domesday Book just after the Norman Conquest were slaves. These were mostly herdsmen and ploughmen. In the succeeding two or three generations most of them were given small holdings as serfs, and slavery in England virtually disappeared.[7]

European serfs in the eleventh and twelfth centuries were for the first time in a strong enough position to take the risk of illegal escape from their lords to other lords who offered better working conditions. The age of widespread peasant rebellions and large-scale manumissions of serfs in France, Germany, and England did not come until the late thirteenth and fourteenth centuries. In Italy, however, and occasionally in France, Germany, and England, there were spasmodic peasant rebellions and grants of peasant charters of liberties in the twelfth and early thirteenth centuries. Apart from these more dramatic events, between about 1050 and 1250 the economic position of the serf gradually improved and, even more to the point, his basic legal rights were gradually established. In fact, it was in the name of the basic legal rights of serfs that rebellions and manumissions took place.

The transformation of manorial custom into a system of manorial law in the eleventh and twelfth centuries may best be considered in terms of the six categories that have already been used in describing the transformation of feudal custom into a system of feudal law: (1) objectivity, (2) universality, (3) reciprocity, (4) participatory adjudication, (5) integration, and (6) growth.

Objectivity and Universality

In the earlier centuries the services and other obligations of serfs and other peasants were of the most varied kind, with relatively few limitations imposed by norms of customary law. The most important labor services included plowing on the lord's demesne (which might involve the duty of the peasant to provide the seed), week work (that is, a duty to work a number of days per week on the lord's demesne), boon work (extra services, theoretically voluntary, usually associated with haymaking and harvesting), carrying services (carrying supplies to and from the lord's household), felling of timber, carrying of manure, and repairing of roads. The lord was free to assign other tasks as well.

In addition to labor services, there were various financial and other obligations. The so-called headtax (*capitagium*; in French, *chevage*), though only a small fee, was an important symbol of the peasant's inferior status. A customary fixed farm rent, or *cens*, was generally charged as well. The lord also imposed various regular and occasional taxes under the generic name "tallage" (from the French *taille*, a cut or notch in a piece of wood, made to record payment of the tax). Upon the death of a serf, the lord was to be given his best beast and other goods (*heriot*). There were a host of other charges, burdens, and obligations, which varied widely in their incidence from place to place and from time to time, but which were always a reminder of servility. A serf could not marry without the lord's permission; and he could not voluntarily depart the manor. If he died without heirs, the land which he occupied reverted to the lord.

In the eleventh and twelfth centuries these various types of services and obligations became subject to substantially more precise regulation. It came to be widely accepted that definite limits should be set to the kinds of services that the lord could require and also to the amounts of services of each kind. For example, week work was limited to a maximum number of days' work per week or commuted to a monetary payment. Also such limits came to be established on a general basis, that is, not merely for individual manors or individual localities but for all manors within a given region or even a given country, and in some cases for all manors within (Western) Christendom as a whole. Thus the requirement that a serf receive the lord's permission in order to marry was commuted everywhere to the payment of a tax (*forismaritagium*) when the serf married outside the lord's domain, and of a composition (*mercheta mulierum*, "marketing of women") when he married within the lord's domain; and Pope Hadrian IV, himself of humble birth, declared that the marriage of a serf, with or without his lord's consent, was valid and indissoluble.

The commutation of services and other obligations of peasants into fixed money payments in the eleventh and twelfth centuries, which was a widespread phenomenon throughout Europe, reflected not only the percolation of money into the manorial economy but also the tendencies of manorial law in that period toward objectivity and universality. Nevertheless, manorial law did not achieve nearly so high a degree of objectivity or universality as feudal law, mercantile law, urban law, and royal law, not to mention canon law. One reason may have been the sharpness of class conflict on the manor; yet domination by the lord could have taken the form of imposition of his will through objective and universal norms of law. A more plausible reason is that by its very nature manorial life required informal, intimate, and diffuse regulation rather than a set of precise, specific, generally applicable, and nondiscriminatory norms. The manor was in many ways like a small clan or village, or a large household. What is surprising, therefore, is not the extent to which manorial law responded to the will and interests of the head of the household — the lord and his immediate entourage — but rather the fact that it acquired any objectivity and generality whatsoever. The lord or his agent (bailiff, reeve, "mayor") was present, with his servants, to exercise his will, by law or by other means. The peasants, however, needed to legalize their relationships with the lord, if only to curb the arbitrary exercise of his power. The strengthening of manorial law was thus an index of the balance of power between the sharply conflicting interests of the lord and his immediate entourage, on the one hand, and those of the peasant households of the manor taken as a whole, on the other. It was also an index of the extent to which the manorial system received its character from the larger social, economic, and political context of the time, a context in which legality played a central role.

Reciprocity of Rights of Lords and Peasants

By the twelfth century, all peasants in Western Christendom, including serfs, had legally protected rights. Among these were the right to hold land of their lords on certain terms and conditions and the right to receive his protection and patronage. Also, all peasants had customary rights to use the communal village lands, including pastures, meadows, and forests. In addition, in most parts of Europe many peasants continued to have virtual rights of ownership in free peasant land (alod or alodium), which had survived from earlier times.

The right, even of a serf, to hold land of a lord was of great importance. The manor was divided into two parts: the lord's demesne, managed by his stewards and worked by his peasants, and the peasants' own holdings, which they worked on those days when they were not required to work on the lord's demesne. As Perry Anderson has pointed out, this "dual agrarian statute within the manor" was one of the "structural specificities of Western feudalism"; and it had the important economic consequence that it left a "margin for the results of improved productivity to accrue to the direct producer."[8] More than that, it gave a legal foundation to the peasants' inclination to distinguish their own economic interests from those of their lords—and to pursue them.

In addition to rights of land tenure, peasants also had rights with respect to the rent, taxes, services, and other obligations due their lords. As a general rule, these obligations could not be increased; they were considered to have been fixed by custom. Disputes over their character and extent were supposed to be resolved by law. In contrast to the lord-vassal relationship, reciprocity of rights and duties of lords and peasants (including serfs) was not achieved through individual pledges of faith or other forms of contractual arrangement; nevertheless, it was understood that the loyalty of the peasants was given reciprocally for the willingness of the lord to abide by concessions previously granted by him or his predecessors, to grant new concessions when required, and in general to deal justly with them.

When peasants' rights were infringed by their lords, those who were freemen could sometimes carry their grievances over the heads of the immediate manorial lord to his feudal superior or to royal authority. Rodney Hilton tells of a dispute that raged for thirty-five years (from 1272 to 1307) between free tenants and a lord in Staffordshire, England. Because the land had formerly been part of the royal demesne, the tenants appealed to the crown, relying on custom from the time of Henry II, a century earlier. They claimed that they were obliged only to pay a fixed rent of five shillings a year plus certain tallages, while the lord claimed that they owed a large variety of labor services, taxes in kind, a heavy death duty (heriot), "merchet" on the marriage of a daughter and "leywrite" if she was found to be unchaste, as well as other obligations.[9]

The legal remedies of serfs were more limited, in that they were not entitled, as a matter of right, to resort to any court except that of the manorial lord. Yet they were not without protection in the manorial court. Moreover, they had still other means of exerting pressure upon their lord in order to maintain and advance favorable conditions of labor. They could make collective demands upon him, including the demand that he emancipate them; such manumission became more and more frequent, although the peasant often had to pay a high price for it. Also, the peasants could sometimes back up their demands by a strike. As a last resort, they could run away to another manor.

A dramatic early example of such group pressure was the desertion en masse of the inhabitants of the Île de Ré in France in the twelfth century, owing to their lord's severity. The lord was thereby induced to make substantial concessions in order to retain any labor force at all. To combat such pressures, lords often resorted to mutual assistance agreements to capture fugitive serfs. Perhaps equally often, however, they competed with one another to entice serfs away from neighboring domains.[10]

An even more remarkable example of reciprocity achieved through class conflict and its resolution is that of charters of liberties granted by Italian city communes to serfs as early as the twelfth century, after peasant uprisings. Such charters contained not only guarantees of fixed rents and services but also safeguards against imprisonment without due process of law.

Eventually, the disloyalty of the serfs came to be a retaliation against the unwillingness — or inability — of the lord to grant concessions or to abide by concessions previously granted. This was an informal, unofficial analogue to the vassal's right of *diffidatio*. In the fourteenth and fifteenth centuries, flights of peasants from the manors assumed catastrophic proportions.[11] As a result, laws were passed imposing imprisonment, branding on the forehead, and other severe penalties for abandoning feudal service. It was forbidden by English law in the fifteenth century for persons attached to a manor to learn a handicraft or for any man holding land of less than twenty pounds' annual value to apprentice his son to a trade. However, these measures were futile; the manorial system was defeated in England, as in many other parts of Europe, by the peasants' desertion of the manor.[12] The earlier reciprocity had broken down.

Participatory Adjudication

Within a manor, as in other political units of the West during the formative era of the Western legal tradition, formal government was closely associated with adjudication: that is, legislative and executive activities were to a considerable extent merged with judicial activities and were conducted by an institution called a court. The use of the word "court" rather than "legislature" or "executive" for this institution did not signify that the making and enforcement of laws were not regarded as important functions of government. In fact, the manorial courts, like the papal court and the royal, seignorial, urban, and mercantile courts, had wide legislative and executive powers within their respective jurisdictions. Perry Anderson is correct in stating that "justice was the *central* modality of political power," but he is incorrect in supposing that this was necessitated by the "parcellization of sovereignty" under feudalism, which "excluded any 'executive' at all, in the modern sense of a permanent administrative apparatus of the State for the enforcement of the law," and also left "no room for an orthodox 'legislature' of the later type either, since the feudal order possessed no general concept of political innovation by the creation of *new* laws."[13] In fact, a centralized state apparatus existed in the church, which was nevertheless governed by the papal curia; and the church, both through the papal curia and through church councils, did innovate by creating new laws. There were parallel developments in royal government. Indeed, the manorial courts themselves not only heard and decided disputes but also enforced law through a developed administrative apparatus and from time to time made new laws as well. The difference between twelfth-century and twentieth-century conceptions of government does not lie in the absence then, and the presence now, of the legislative and executive functions, but rather, first, in the fusion then and the separation now of those functions, and second, in the subsumption then of the legislative and executive under the adjudicative. Then, lawmaking itself was regarded as a process of deliberation and discovery. Laws were considered to be either true or false, either just or unjust, and therefore the making and administering of them were not sharply distinguished from their application in cases of dispute.

Manorial justice was the prerogative of the lord of the manor, just as royal justice was the prerogative of the king and ecclesiastical justice the prerogative of the pope. "Each baron is sovereign in his barony," wrote Beaumanoir, while "the king is sovereign everywhere and by his law [*droit,* "right"] guards his realm."[14] Beaumanoir also wrote: "Every lord has all justices — high and low — in his fief . . . Fief and justice — it is all one."[15] This was, to be sure, an exaggeration, applicable only to great lords. Most lords of manors had only "low" justice. Yet the justice of the lord of the manor authorized him to exercise a wide variety of powers over the staff of manorial officers who in effect constituted his household, and over the peasants who constituted the basic population of the manor. At the same time, the justice of the lord of the manor was a substantial restriction upon the arbitrary exercise of the lord's power and a substantial means of maintaining the reciprocity of rights of lords and peasants.

The steward of the manor, who commonly served as the lord's deputy in all matters affecting manorial government, usually presided over the manorial court. Other manorial officials — the reeve (who acted as general overseer), the hayward (who watched over the lord's crops), the woodward (who guarded his woods), the rent collector, and various others—also participated in the proceedings of the manorial court, often as prosecutors of persons who had offended against the lord's prerogatives.

The court itself consisted of all the members of the manor, from the lord and his steward down to the lowliest serf. All were judges. They were called "suitors," and were said to "pay suit of court"; indeed, it was an obligation to attend court and to judge, and, as part of the obligation, a fee had to be paid to the lord. Little is known about the methods of voting in the manorial court; the extant reports of manorial cases occasionally show a division of opinion, but generally the decision is presented as that of the court as a whole. No distinction was made between freemen and serfs either with respect to the right and duty to judge or with respect to the procedure applied to them when they were parties to disputes.

A high degree of cooperation among all members of the manor was required for manorial justice to work. But such cooperation was required also by the whole system of agriculture in Europe during the late eleventh and twelfth centuries. Here many historians, in concentrating on the inequality of status and of privilege between lords and peasants, have neglected other aspects of the mode and relations of production that were equally important. Under the open-field system, the arable land was usually divided into long, narrow strips, which were widely scattered among the various peasant families. In order to make rational use of animals for plowing adjacent strips belonging to different tenants, and in order to time the sowing and harvesting so as to avoid conflict, it was necessary for the peasants to agree on work methods. Also, the common ownership of pasture, meadows, and woodland required agreement concerning their utilization. In addition, the system of crop rotation allowed for arable land to be converted periodically into pasture, to be grazed over and fertilized by all the animals of the manor.[16] Thus the open-field system itself required a very high degree of cooperation among all members of the manor. As Hilton writes, the fact that the village (or the manor) was often called a "community" and the members "neighbors" was "not a matter of sentiment but of fact. Open-field cultivation meant that one man's injury was everybody's, even the lord's." Hilton cites a case in which seven persons were accused of failing to keep up their fences, with the result that the corn (wheat) of the abbot and of "other neighbors" had been damaged. "These were the fences which every tenant who had parcels on the perimeter of the open fields had to keep up when the corn was growing, to prevent the animals getting in, not merely to his own corn, but, since the fields were open, into the corn of all who had parcels in that field."[17]

The rules and procedures for maintaining cooperation in these and other matters were considered to constitute the custom of the manor. If plow oxen were damaged, if arable land was not fertilized, if a person failed to help in bringing in the harvest, then the custom of the manor might be invoked against the offender in the manorial court. Similarly, if one person struck or defamed another, or failed to pay for goods which he had bought, or broke his promise to build a shed for another, or slandered another, the victim could complain in the manorial court.[18]

Thus the very complexity of communal serf-regulation of the manorial economy gave rise to a large variety of types of civil and criminal matters to be settled by manorial justice. In addition, fines were imposed for violation of the lord's rights — as by trespassing on his land, stealing his crops, of failing to perform labor services or pay taxes due to him.

All these matters were decided by the manorial court, by vote of all the suitors. One may suppose that the power of the lord and his officials was such as to influence the outcome in his favor. Yet cases are reported in which his interests were not protected. For example, it happened sometimes that peasants would successfully sue for land which the lord had rented to others. In one case the lord of the manor had sought to deprive a serf of certain land on the ground that the serf's holdings exceeded that to which he was entitled; the serf argued that he and other tenants in a comparable situation "for all time theretofore were accustomed to hold several tenements without fine or license or complaint," and that he was "prepared to verify this by the homage [that is, by all the tenants of the manor] or other lawful means as may be necessary." The report of this case concludes: "The matter is put in respite until there can be a fuller consultation etc."[19] In addition to cases in which the lord's property rights were directly involved, there were many cases in which the manorial court, whether by judgment of the whole community of tenants or by judgment of an inquest or jury, gave remedies against the lord's bailiff and other officials.[20]

The manorial court not only gave judgment in disputed matters and imposed fines for offenses but also issued regulations and rules for administering the manorial economy. In the eleventh and twelfth centuries these regulations and rules were apparently unwritten; in England no written records of them have been found prior to the second quarter of the thirteenth century. From that time on, however, there are abundant records of "by-laws" and "ordinances," which regulated the use of common fields and pasture, the gathering of grain and other crops (including gleaning by paupers), the keeping of fences and gates, the tethering of horses and beasts, the seasonal transition from one type of land use to another, and other matters affecting the communal economy. These regulations were issued periodically by all members of the manor collectively acting as suitors to the manorial court. Characteristically such regulations were introduced by the phrase: "Ordered by the assent of the whole homage," or "Ordered by all the tenants both free and servile," or "Ordered by the lord and the tenants." Strong emphasis was laid on protection of the property rights of the lord; but the main emphasis was on the organization of the work of the manor, and this included protection of the rights of all tenants, serf as well as free, against unwarranted interference by others.[21]

Integration and Growth

Although there were many interrelated features of manorial law which helped to give it the character of an integrated system of rules and procedures, yet it lacked the high degree of logical coherence and the consciously principled character of canon law, and certainly of the Roman law taught in the universities. Manorial law, indeed, was customary law, that is, it was largely unwritten (or more precisely, unenacted). Even compared with feudal law, however, which was also largely customary law, manorial law was much less consciously integrated, much more particularistic and diffuse. This was reflected in the absence of contemporary scholarly writings on manorial law. It appears that few professional jurists were concerned with its development.

The relative lack of sophistication of manorial law was also connected with the fact that it took part of its character from the other systems of law which impinged on it. When the manorial court decided cases of slander, for example, it was usually applying — perhaps in a very crude and unlearned manner — the canon law; when it decided cases of assault or theft or trespass to land or to chattels, it was usually imitating the tort law and criminal law of the locality or dukedom or principality in which it was situated; when it laid down rules concerning rights and duties attached to peasant land holding it borrowed many concepts from feudal (that is, lord-vassal) law. In addition, the procedure of manorial courts was strongly influenced by the local law. In short, one would not expect to find in the manorial courts innovations in branches of law that were being developed concurrently by other legal systems.

Yet there were certain distinctive elements of manorial law that did receive conscious legal formulation in terms of principles and concepts. In the eleventh and twelfth centuries the legal concept of serfdom was formulated for the first time. Serfs were called *glebae adscriptae* ("[persons] attached to the soil"). This meant that they could not leave except under certain conditions. It also meant that they could not be evicted — again, except under certain conditions. Perry Anderson has written that the first use of the term glebae adscriptae in the eleventh and twelfth centuries reflected a characteristic "lag" in the "juridical codification of economic and social relationships" that had been in existence for centuries.[22] But the new legal term actually changed the preexisting situation, if only by giving it a new legal character. Henceforth the bondage of serfs was legally defined, which meant that serfdom became a matter of rights and duties and not merely a matter of habit and will and bargaining power. On the one hand, the lord had a right to many things that had previously been subject to challenge. On the other hand, the serf's duties, legally classified in terms of specific labor services, rents in kind, and customary dues, became fixed and could not legally be increased or varied by the lord.

Moreover, the serf was given the possibility of buying off his bondage; he could become a free man through the legal process of manumission. This typically involved a symbolic ceremony or written charter granted on condition of immediate payment of a sum of money or of a perpetual commitment, binding upon heirs, to pay certain charges or perform certain services.

This is not to say that the serf did not remain poor and oppressed. It is only to say that he had acquired rights under a system of law. He was henceforth a person, a member of the manorial community, part of "the whole homage."[23] He coexisted on the manor with free peasants, with other freemen holding under various forms of tenure involving only honorable services, with manorial officials, knights, the lord of the manor and his household — all being members of a community divided according to status but united as suitors in the manorial court, that is, as citizens of the manor. This unity was the foundation of manorial law. It was linked with the very mode of production, the open-field system of agriculture.

The unity of the manor was reflected in the capacity of its inhabitants, sometimes collectively and sometimes individually, to lease the manor from the lord and to dispose of it at their will. Between the late eleventh and the fourteenth and fifteenth centuries such leases became more and more common. They were a way out for lords who were being increasingly pressured by peasant demands, peasant uprisings, and peasant desertions.

The legal definitions of peasant obligation also had important economic consequences, since they contributed to the tendency to substitute fixed cash payments for labor services and rents in kind. Since a similar tendency to commute services into monetary obligations characterized feudal legal relations between vassals and lords, the lord of the manor had an interest in collecting from his tenants a sufficient cash income to enable him to meet his obligations to his superior lord. As early as the thirteenth century in many if not most parts of Europe, manors came to be considered income-producing enterprises, and persons were appointed to manage them, with the duty to collect and pay over the required income, called *firma* or *feorm*, from which is derived the word "farm." In addition "farmers" responsible for fixed returns were often replaced by professional managers who were expected to maximize manorial cash profits and to render annual accounts. Thus the gradual conversion of peasants into lessees (or alternatively, hired laborers) was connected with the gradual transformation of the manor itself from a community into a business; and these two processes were linked with the increasing reification of both feudal (lord-vassal) rights and obligations and manorial (lord-peasant) rights and obligations.

These developments did not, of course, take place uniformly throughout Europe, although everywhere there was a general process of absorption of the manor by the peasants. In France and western Germany, however, the nobility succeeded in maintaining quasi-manorial domination over all classes living within their private jurisdictions, whether or not they were tenants. This was accomplished chiefly through numerous small taxes and services (*banalités*, *corvées*, and others), no one of which, taken alone, was excessively onerous, but all of which, taken together, were extremely oppressive. These included: payments for crushing grapes at the lord's wine press, baking bread in the lord's oven, and grinding corn at the lord's mill, over all of which the landlords maintained a monopoly; labor services in repairing roads, constructing bridges, and the like; and tolls on roads, fairs, and markets, fines for transfers of land and goods, and other assorted aids and taxes.

Despite these and many other variations in different regions and different countries, manorial law underwent the same general pattern of development throughout the West during the period from the eleventh to the fifteenth centuries. This remarkable fact bears witness to the Western concept of manorial law as an integrated body of concepts and procedures. It also bears witness to the related concept of manorial law as a system capable of incremental growth. As in feudal law, so in manorial law the characteristics attributed to the system became tendencies of the system, and the tendencies were self-fulfilling. Growth, once believed in, became inevitable. Manorial legal concepts and institutions had a certain life of their own, which was just as "basic" and just as much a part of the infrastructure as the economics of production and distribution of goods. Even so, it is striking that despite extreme diversity of local conditions manorial law underwent the same general movements from stage to stage virtually everywhere in western Europe.

Perhaps the most significant stage in this development was the widespread emancipation of the serfs in the thirteenth, fourteenth, and fifteenth centuries, which must be seen in part as a culmination of the greater legalization of lord-peasant relations introduced in the late eleventh and twelfth centuries. Here manorial law was in tension with feudal law, for under feudal law, emancipation of a serf by his lord could only be accomplished with the consent of the lord's superior; without that consent, a serf whose lord had emancipated him simply escheated to the superior, and the lord who had granted the emancipation was estopped from claiming him again.[24] Thus for a serf to buy his freedom required that he pay off both his immediate lord and all superiors in the feudal chain. Nevertheless, in the long run both the economic and the legal circumstances favored emancipation. In many places the resistance of superior lords to the freeing of serfs was counteracted by a strong movement for collective emancipation. In Italy the initiative came from urban communes, whose motive was partly to increase the number of free taxpayers and partly to attract workers from the countryside; as early as 1256-57, Bologna enfranchised all serfs within its jurisdiction. In France the initiative came from the crown itself, whose motive was partly to derive revenue from redemption payments and partly to appease peasant unrest and forestall the peasant revolts that were endemic in France as well as in England, Italy, Spain, and elsewhere. Thus in 1290 and again after 1310 French kings offered freedom to serfs on various crown lands—for a price. By 1450 serfdom had been abolished in almost all of the western parts of Europe, though not in the central and eastern parts.

It would be a profound mistake to discount the moral and legal aspects of enfranchisement, for it was not only the economic hardships of serfdom which caused European peasants to rebel in the thirteenth, fourteenth, and fifteenth centuries but also the gross injustices of their servitude. In the era after the Papal Revolution, which was fought in the name of the freedom of the church, and especially of the clergy, it is not surprising that demands for freedom were raised by other polities and other classes as well. One revolutionary cry for freedom in the twelfth and thirteenth centuries was for freedom of the cities. Concurrently came the cry for freedom of the peasantry, which grew much louder in the fourteenth century; and in that connection freedom was said to be the natural condition of all men. Thus in declaring the enfranchisement of the serfs of Bologna in 1256-57, the city authorities declared that serfdom was a consequence of the fall of man, that man's natural conditon was freedom. Similarly, in proclaiming the enfranchisement of serfs on certain crown lands in 1315 and 1318, the kings Louis X and Philip the Long of France declared, in language that would be echoed in succeeding centuries:

> As according to the law of nature everyone should be born free, but by certain usages and customs of great age preserved in our kingdom . . . and also perhaps because of the misdeeds of their predecessors, many persons of our common people have fallen into the bonds of servitude and into various conditions, which much displeased us, considering that our kingdom is called the Kingdom of the Franks . . . we have ordered . . . that these servitudes shall be brought to freedom and to those who by birth or long standing or recently through marriage or residence have fallen into servile condition, or could so fall, freedom shall be given on good and convenient terms.[25]

Even if one assumes that the French kings were hypocrites, they were nevertheless appealing to ideals and values that were widely shared. The peasants, surely, would have agreed that serfdom was against the law of nature, that by the law of nature "everyone should be born free," and that freedom was man's natural condition. The peasants also hoped, no doubt, that the abolition of serfdom would lead to a better economic life; but even if that hope proved ill-founded, emancipation was required. It was required by the moral order of the universe.

This conviction was not, however, simply a product of a theory of natural law. It was much more the product of historical experience, and especially the experience of the development of manorial law during the late eleventh, twelfth, and early thirteenth centuries. The grant of legal personality to serfs within the manor, that is, the recognition of them as "citizens" of the manorial community, with the duty and right of suit of court, was itself an implicit challenge to serfdom long before any movement arose to abolish it. The challenge was nurtured, in turn, by the belief in and the experience of the integrity and growth of legal systems, including the system of manorial law. The belief in and experience of the *integrity* of manorial law required that serfs be treated on an equal basis with free peasants. The belief in and experience of the *growth* of manorial law required that in the course of time such equality be given full legal expression.

Thus it was the consciousness of the injustice of serfdom in a legal sense, its fundamental illegality, coupled with the belief in the capacity to correct that injustice by law, that changed the mere fact of the economic exploitation of serfs into a social and political cause in which members of all classes could eventually unite.

11 | Mercantile Law

AS WITH FEUDAL and manorial law, so with mercantile law the crucial period of change was the late eleventh and twelfth centuries. It was then that the basic concepts and institutions of modern Western mercantile law — *lex mercatoria* ("the law merchant") — were formed, and, even more important, it was then that mercantile law in the West first came to be viewed as an integrated, developing system, a *body* of law.

The changes in mercantile law were even more striking than the changes in feudal and manorial law: informal, customary feudal and manorial relations had been widespread in the ninth and tenth centuries, although they had not then been given systematic legal expression, whereas, since the decline of the western Roman Empire, commercial relations had existed only on a very limited scale. To be sure, trade had never entirely died out. Some agricultural products continued to be sold by traveling merchants, who also bought and sold small luxuries and local handicrafts. Fairs and markets also existed, though they were not widespread, and some towns, especially seaports, survived from Roman times. Nevertheless, the Frankish Empire, in contrast to the Roman Empire, was not a Mediterranean civilization with abundant maritime trade, but a land-centered economy, hemmed in — in Henri Pirenne's phrase, "bottled up" — on all sides by Norsemen, Arabs, Magyars, and Slavs. Also, unlike the Roman Empire, the Western economy between the sixth and the tenth centuries was based not on thousands of cities but on perhaps a hundred thousand agrarian villages and manors. In the year 1000 only about two dozen towns of western Europe had more than a few thousand inhabitants, and probably only Venice and London had more than ten thousand. (Constantinople, in contrast, had a population of hundreds of thousands, possibly even a million.)

Then in the eleventh and twelfth centuries there occurred a rapid expansion of agricultural production and a dramatic increase in the size and number of cities. At the same time there emerged a new class of professional merchants, who carried on large-scale commercial transactions both in the countryside and in the cities. It was primarily to meet the needs of the new merchant class that a new body of mercantile law was developed.

Although the flourishing of commerce and the development of mercantile law were closely connected with the rise of cities and the development of urban law, they also had an important nonurban aspect. Expanded trade in the countryside was initially a result of the "agricultural revolution" rather than of the "urban revolution"; indeed, the growth of agriculture was itself a precondition for the growth of the cities. This fact has importance for social and economic theory, because it refutes that school of thought which postulates that agricultural relations are, in themselves, inevitably static and that commercial development can only be introduced into an agricultural society from the outside. It also has importance for social and economic historiography, because it refutes that school of thought which postulates that in the West a "capitalist age" succeeded a "feudal age" in time. In fact, in the eleventh and twelfth centuries extensive commerce coexisted with the manorial mode of production and with feudal social and political relations. The newly emerging system of mercantile law—which was capitalist law par excellence—was contemporaneous with the Western systems of feudal and manorial law.

Even apart from these theoretical and historiographical implications, the development of Western commercial law in the eleventh and twelfth centuries should be seen in the context of trade in the countryside, and not only in the context of trade in the cities. English merchants, for example, living in the countryside, bought wool from the manors and sold it to Flemish merchants, who distributed it to spinners and weavers in the countryside of Flanders to be worked up in their households; the Flemish merchants, in turn, sold cloth from Flanders at international fairs in England. This kind of trade, which played a very significant role in the economy of northern Europe from the eleventh to the fifteenth centuries, was governed by a general body of European law, the law merchant, which also governed intercity trade and overseas trade—for example, the sale of glass from Cologne to Paris, the sale of leather goods or wrought iron from Florence to Bari, the sale of Oriental spices or Moroccan grain by a joint venture of Genoese merchants to merchants of London. The law merchant governed not only the sale, in the strict sense, but also other aspects of commercial transactions, including transportation, insurance, and financing.[1]

The rise of a merchant class was a necessary precondition for the development of the new mercantile law. Prior to the eleventh century, the merchant had been a relatively isolated figure in western Europe. There had been occasional Jewish, Syrian, and Greek merchants traveling by land and sea between East and West. The native western European merchants had been largely itinerant peddlers ("foot-men"), who went from town to town, village to village, manor to manor. Trade had also been carried on by nonprofessionals: manors or monasteries or villages (for example, fishing villages) would send out representatives to various parts of Europe to sell their goods.

The transformation of agriculture in the eleventh and twelfth centuries created both the opportunity and the need for the rapid expansion of the merchant class. There were large agricultural surpluses to be traded. At the same time there was a large increase in population from which traders could be drawn. However, the development of feudal and manorial law made it illegal for feudal lords or members of the manor to engage in part-time trade; being a lord or a peasant—or a steward or other manorial official—had become a full-time, permanent calling, a status. Yet there also existed the legal or illegal possibility of large-scale exodus of peasants from the manors. Many ex-peasants became merchant peddlers, and many more went into the emerging cities to become either artisans or merchants. In addition, sons of the lesser nobility began to leave the countryside and enter the cities to take up manufacture or commerce. In Italy and some other parts of Europe, even the upper nobility sometimes shifted from agricultural production to commerce, especially large-scale trade and finance.

It is difficult to determine the exact scale of the migration from the countryside to the cities of Europe. It is even more difficult to determine the exact scale of the growth of the merchant class, both in and outside of cities. One may estimate, however, that whereas in the year 1050, out of a total population of about twenty million, some hundreds of thousands of people in western Europe lived in some hundreds of towns (few of which had more than a few thousand inhabitants), by the year 1200, out of a total population of about forty million, some millions of people lived in some thousands of towns and cities (many of which had populations of over twenty thousand, and some had populations of over one hundred thousand). In short, the total population doubled, roughly, and the urban population increased from perhaps 1 percent to perhaps 10 percent of the total. With respect to the numbers of merchants, it may be estimated that whereas in the year 1050 the merchant class of western Europe was numbered in the thousands, by the year 1200 it was numbered in the hundreds of thousands.[2]

In speaking of the social and economic background of the development of the new system of mercantile law, there is a danger of concentrating on technological and demographic factors and of neglecting the political and religious factors which also played an important part in what has been called "the commercial revolution."[3] The political and religious factors were, of course, closely interrelated with the technological and demographic factors as well as with one another. The Crusades and the colonization movement—which constituted the foreign military and economic programs of the Papal Revolution—fostered long-distance trade, both overseas and overland. The papacy also sought to extend its authority eastward both overseas and overland. At the same time, the new theology of the papal party emphasized the mission of the church to reform and redeem secular activities.

There is also a danger of viewing the law always as a consequence of social and economic change and never as a constituent part of such change, and in that sense a cause of it. In fact, the new jurisprudence of the late eleventh and twelfth centuries provided a framework for institutionalizing and systematizing commercial relations in accordance with new concepts of order and justice. Without such new legal devices as negotiable bills of exchange and limited liability partnerships, without the reform of the antiquated commercial customs of the past, without mercantile courts and mercantile legislation, other social and economic pressures for change would have found no outlet. Thus the commercial revolution helped to produce commercial law, but commercial law also helped to produce the commercial revolution. Indeed, what occurred was a revolutionary transformation not only of commerce but of the whole society; in that total transformation commercial law, like feudal law and manorial law, had its origins and from it, like them, it took its character.

Religion and the Rise of Capitalism

Although many historians have shown that Western commercial capitalism originated not in the sixteenth and seventeenth centuries, as is commonly supposed, but in the eleventh and twelfth centuries—in the heyday of the manorial mode of production and of feudal class relations—nevertheless many of the same historians have continued to perpetuate the view that Christian teaching prior to the Reformation remained fundamentally opposed to the profit motive. Thus the great French social and economic historian Henri Pirenne wrote that "in vigour and relative rapidity of its development [commercial capitalism in the twelfth century] may, without exaggeration, be compared with the industrial revolution of the nineteenth century"; yet in the same paragraph he remarked that "the attitude of the Church . . . towards commerce [was] not merely passive but actively hostile."[4] On another page Pirenne quoted as characteristic of the later Middle Ages the statement: "The merchant is rarely or ever able to please God."[5] Ecclesiastical prohibitions against speculation and lending at interest (usury) and the doctrine of the just price have been cited by Pirenne and others to illustrate the alleged opposition of the church to the rise of capitalism.

One is thus presented with a striking paradox: the *spiritus capitalisticus* (as Pirenne called it) is said to have originated at a time when the prevailing system of beliefs placed primary emphasis on the mystical and ascetic sides of life and on rewards and punishments in the hereafter. Moreover, the prevailing system of beliefs was backed up by the entire moral and legal authority of an all-powerful ecclesiastical hierarchy—and yet in fact commerce flourished.

Various explanations have been given which might resolve this paradox. First, it has been said that the church's insistence on an anticommercial moral philosophy was a reflection of its own economic position as a great feudal landowner and its own identification with a conservative agricultural civilization.[6] Second, it has been said (without always noticing the contradiction) that the church did not seriously try to put into practice its doctrine of the sinfulness of the profit motive but on the contrary introduced a whole range of exceptions or else simply winked at violations. This enabled the church to benefit from its own commercial activity, and it also justified many of the practices of the merchant class.

These and similar explanations have left open the question of how it was possible to create an economic system whose fundamental premises contradicted the prevailing ideology, and how it was possible to maintain for over four hundred years the dominance of an ideology whose fundamental premises conflicted with the economic system. Still another way of putting the matter is to ask how it was possible for two conflicting economic systems—feudalism and capitalism—to coexist in a society whose leadership was dedicated to the perpetuation of a single, internally consistent system of beliefs.

These questions, however, arise from a view of the relation of Christian doctrine to the development of commercial capitalism which is based on a distortion not only of Roman Catholic thought in the period from the late eleventh to the fifteenth centuries but also of Protestant thought in the sixteenth and seventeenth centuries. It is wrongly supposed that Roman Catholic thought was fundamentally otherworldly and ascetic; in fact, in the late eleventh and the twelfth centuries Roman Catholic theology broke away from the predominantly otherworldly, ascetic ideal which had prevailed earlier and which still prevails in much of Eastern Orthodoxy. It is also wrongly implied that the "Protestant ethic" of Luther or Calvin was more worldly, more rationalistic, more individualistic, and therefore more compatible with capitalist enterprise than were Roman Catholic moral teachings. This misconception deserves a separate examination; it should be noted, however, that writers, like Max Weber and R.H. Tawney, who have stressed the interconnection of capitalism and Protestantism, have also assumed that capitalism and feudalism were contradictory to each other, that capitalism succeeded feudalism in time, and that capitalism in the West originated in the sixteenth century.[7]

If the opposite is true—namely, that in the eleventh and twelfth centuries (and for some time thereafter) capitalism and feudalism were essentially compatible with each other, and indeed utterly depended on each other—then the way is opened to reexamine the economic morality taught by the Western Church from a different point of view. What may appear as hypocrisy to one who believes in the fundamental antagonism of feudal-agrarian and capitalist-commercial values may appear as a legitimate compromise to one who believes in their fundamental reconcilability.

The Western Church of the late eleventh and twelfth centuries—in contrast to the Eastern Church, and also in contrast to the entire church both in the East and in the West, prior to the Papal Revolution—believed in the possibility of reconciling commercial activity with a Christian life, just as it believed in the possibility of reconciling agrarian activity with a Christian life. Its moral attitude toward wealthy merchants was not essentially different from its moral attitude toward wealthy landlords. It continued to teach the words of St. Paul, that "the love of money is the root of all evil," (1 Tim. 6:10) and that "those who are rich in this world's goods" should be instructed "not to be proud and not to fix their hopes on so uncertain a thing as money," and further, that such rich persons should be told "to grow rich in noble actions, to be ready to give away and to share" (1 Tim. 6:17, 18).[8] The monastic life, in which not only wealth but all the values of "this world" were renounced, continued to be considered closest to the kingdom of heaven. But except for a few voices, the Western Church of the late eleventh and twelfth centuries not only did not denounce money or riches as such, but indeed encouraged the pursuit of money or riches provided that such pursuit was carried on for certain ends and according to certain principles. The secular activities of those engaged in commercial enterprise were to be organized in ways that would redeem them from the sin of avarice. The merchants were to form guilds that would have religious functions and would maintain standards of morality in commercial transactions. This was consistent with the church's new emphasis on incarnation, and on the embodiment of the spiritual in the secular. Thus the church-state set an example for the city-state, and church law set an example for city law and for commercial law. Legitimate trade based on good faith was distinguished from illegitimate trade based on avarice, and trade based on the satisfaction of legitimate needs was distinguished from trade based on mere self-interest or on fraud; legitimate interest charges were distinguished from usury; the just price was distinguished from the unjust price.[9]

Pirenne rightly pointed to the problem of the "deracination" of the new city dwellers of the twelfth century.[10] They had left the highly structured, deeply rooted life of the village and the manor to enter the looser and more superficial relations of manufacture and commerce. Pirenne ignored, however, the steps that were taken to meet that problem through the formation of close-knit artisan and merchant guilds and the establishment of a relatively tight moral and legal framework for urban society generally.

From the point of view of the Christian social theory which prevailed in the formative period of Western commercial institutions, the economic activities of merchants, like other secular activities, were no longer to be considered as necessarily "a danger to salvation"; on the contrary, they were considered to be a path to salvation, if carried on according to the principles laid down by the church. These principles were spelled out in the canon law. From the church's point of view, the law developed by the merchants to regulate their own interrelationships, the lex mercatoria, was supposed to reflect, not contradict, the canon law. The merchants did not always agree with that. They did not disagree, however, that the salvation of their souls depended on the conformity of their practices to a system of law based on the will of God as manifested in reason and conscience.

Thus the social and economic activity of merchants was not left outside the reach of moral issues. A social and economic morality was developed which purported to guide the souls of merchants toward salvation. And that morality was embodied in law. Law was a bridge between mercantile activity and the salvation of the soul.

The New System of Commercial Law

To say that the basic concepts and institutions of modern Western commercial law were formed in the period of the late eleventh and twelfth centuries does not ignore the debt which the creators of those concepts and institutions owed to the Roman law as it was reflected in the newly discovered texts of Justinian. The Roman texts contained a highly sophisticated set of rules for forming contracts of various types, including loan of money, loan of goods, pledge, sale, lease, partnership, and mandate (a form of agency). These rules, however, were not consciously conceptualized; they were classified but not explicitly interrelated with one another and not analyzed in terms of general principles. Moreover, no conscious distinction was made between commercial contracts and noncommercial contracts; all were treated as civil contracts.

The old Roman jurists had also recognized that many contracts were governed not by the civil law but by customary law, including the *jus gentium*. Indeed, it was the jus gentium, the (customary) "law of nations," applicable to those who were not Roman citizens, that governed most types of commercial transactions within the Roman Empire, especially those involving carriage of goods over long distances.

Included in the customary law of commerce of the Roman Empire was the Sea Law of Rhodes, usually thought to date from about 300 B.C., as well as the customs of maritime trade that had been developed subsequently by eastern Mediterranean traders. Some of the rules of the Roman customary law of commerce, as well as some of the rules of Roman civil law, had survived in the West from the fifth to the eleventh centuries, independently of the texts of Justinian; they are to be found, for example, in Lombard law as well as in customs of the merchants of Venice, which remained as a flourishing trading center throughout the period.

Nevertheless, neither the newly rediscovered Roman civil law nor the barely surviving Roman customary law, including the jus gentium, was adequate to meet the kinds of domestic and international commercial problems that arose in western Europe in the late eleventh and twelfth centuries.

It is conceivable that the learned Romanists in the European universities of the late eleventh, twelfth, and thirteenth centuries could have created a new body of mercantile law out of the Roman texts, just as they created a new body of civil law out of those texts. It is also conceivable that the canon lawyers at the same universities, together with their colleagues in the papal and episcopal chanceries, could have done the same, especially in view of the fact that ecclesiastical corporations engaged heavily in commercial activities. It is characteristic of the time, however, that the initial development of mercantile law was left largely, though not entirely, to the merchants themselves, who organized international fairs and markets, formed mercantile courts, and established mercantile offices in the new urban communities that were springing up throughout western Europe.

Occasionally, rules of mercantile law developed by merchants were collected and circulated. One of the earliest examples was a collection of maritime laws adopted about the time of the First Crusade (1095) by the Republic of Amalfi on the Italian coast of the Tyrrhenian Sea; known as the Amalfitan Table, its authority came to be acknowledged by all the city republics of Italy. About 1150 a compilation of maritime judgments by the court of Oléron, an island off the French Atlantic coast, was adopted by the seaport towns of the Atlantic Ocean and the North Sea, including those of England. The Laws of Wisby, a port on the island of Gotland in the Baltic Sea, were adopted about 1350; they were similar to and possibly derived from the Laws (or Rolls) of Oléron, and they gained wide authority in surrounding Baltic countries. About the same time the Consolato del Mare, a collection of customs of the sea observed in the Consular Court of Barcelona, based partly on the earlier collections and partly on statutes and compilations of the Italian cities, came to be accepted as governing law in the commercial centers of the Mediterranean. All these collections dealt exclusively with maritime law, including contracts of carriage of goods by sea.

At the same time a large body of law was created that governed overland trade. Markets and fairs had existed since the seventh or eighth century, but on a relatively small scale and without a highly developed legal character. From the eleventh and twelfth centuries on, however, great international fairs were held regularly in scores of cities and towns throughout Europe. International markets were also common, especially in seaport towns, These fairs and markets were complex organizations, and with the growth of legal systems, both ecclesiastical and secular, there developed the concept of a special law merchant, which included not only the customary law of fairs and markets but also maritime customs relating to trade and, finally, the commercial laws of the cities and towns themselves. The Italian cities took the lead in collecting systematically and enacting the customary rules by which commercial activity was governed.

The law merchant, then, governed a special class of people (merchants) in special places (fairs, markets, and seaports); and it also governed mercantile relations in cities and towns. It was distinct from ecclesiastical, feudal, manorial, urban, and royal law, although it had especially close connections with urban law and ecclesiastical law.

The law merchant shared with the other major legal systems of the time the qualities of objectivity, universality, reciprocity, participatory adjudication, integration, and growth. These six qualities not only show its close links with the Western legal tradition as a whole but also provide an index to its own specific characteristics.

OBJECTIVITY

As in the case of feudal law and manorial law, so in the case of mercantile law, during the period from 1000 to 1200, and chiefly between 1050 and 1150, rights and obligations became substantially more objective and less arbitrary, more precise and less loose. There was a movement away from mere custom in the sense of usage (patterns of behavior) to a more carefully defined customary law (norms of behavior). The specificity of the norms of mercantile law increased as they were increasingly reduced to writing—partly in the form of commercial legislation but primarily in the form of written commercial instruments of a more or less stereotyped character. In addition, the objectivity of the new system was reflected in a greatly increased emphasis on impartial adjudication of commercial disputes and the emergence of new forms of mercantile courts.

Universality

In the late eleventh century and thereafter, rights and obligations under mercantile law became substantially more uniform and less diverse, more general and less discriminatory in their local application. This was due partly to the cosmopolitan, transnational character of much of the commerce in that period. Great international fairs were held at regular intervals at designated places throughout Europe or at permanent market towns and cities to which merchants came from many countries. Transnational trading associations established permanent representatives at the leading commercial centers of Europe. Transnational trade often predominated over local trade and provided an important model for commercial transactions generally.

The universal character of the law merchant, both in its formative period and thereafter, has been stressed by all who have written about it. In 1473 the Chancellor of England declared that alien merchants who came before him for relief would have their suits determined "by the law of nature in chancery . . . which is called by some the law merchant, which is the law universal of the world."[11] In the first English book (1622) on the law merchant, *Consuetudo vel Lex Mercatoria, or the Ancient Law Merchant*, the author, Gerard Malynes, stated: "I have entitled the book according to the ancient name of Lex Mercatoria . . . because it is customary law approved by the authority of all kingdoms and commonweals, and not a law established by the sovereignty of any prince."[12] And Blackstone wrote in the mid-eighteenth century: "The affairs of commerce are regulated by the law of their own called the Law Merchant or Lex Mercatoria, which all nations agree in and take notice of, and it is particularly held to be part of the law of England which decides the causes of merchants by the general rules which obtain in all commercial matters relating to domestic trade, as for instance, in the drawing, the acceptance, and the transfer of Bills of Exchange."[13]

In twelfth-century Europe the transnational character of the law merchant was an important protection against the disabilities of aliens under local law as well as against other vagaries of local laws and customs. In England the Statute of Westminster of 1275 declared: "It is ordained that in any city, borough town, fair or market, a foreign person who is of this realm shall not be distrained for any debt for which he is not debtor or pledge." However, not all other countries eliminated distraint of foreigners for the debts of a fellow citizen; in northern Italy a long series of treaties among the cities "was slowly and fitfully securing for the Italians this same protection."[14] The movement toward uniformity in this and other respects was a gradual process. The customs even of the international fairs were not always the same. On the whole, however, the differences among countries and localities in the law and custom applicable to mercantile transactions were differences of detail. As William Mitchell has put it, "Each country, it may almost be said each town, had its own variety of Law Merchant, yet all were but varieties of the same species. Everywhere the leading principles and the most important rules were the same, or tended to become the same."[15]

It was not only discriminatory treatment under local law that "merchant strangers" had to fear, but also the violence of pirates and robbers en route and the rapacity of local taxing authorities. To protect against the dangers of travel, maritime commerce was carried on largely by coastal convoys, and on land a merchant traveled armed and usually in the company of others, often in caravans. There was no way, however, in which merchants could protect themselves against tolls, which on the Rhine, for example, were so numerous and heavy as to earn the characterization *furiosa Teutonicorum insania* ("Teutonic madness").[16] A French reform of 1431 still left about 130 tolls on the Loire and its tributaries.[17]

The fact that the foreigner was often without rights under local law as well as without protection by local rulers made the universality of the merchant's own law a matter of urgent necessity. In time, the universal law merchant came to be safeguarded also by the increasingly powerful central political authorities. One of the earliest examples of this is to be found in Magna Carta (1215), which provided: "All merchants shall have safe conduct to go and come out of and into England, and to stay in and travel through England by land and water for purposes of buying and selling, free of legal tolls, in accordance with ancient and just customs."[18] Such protection eventually extended — in England as elsewhere — to cooperation by the public authorities in the enforcement of the process of mercantile courts. Thus in 1292 a London merchant named Lucas was alleged to have left the fair of Lynn by stealth without paying thirty-one pounds for goods he had bought from a German merchant and to have failed to appear to answer charges in the court of the fair according to the law merchant, "wherefore no merchant stranger after that deed wished to make any sale to citizens of London before they were paid in full . . . calling them false debtors." Lucas fled from Lynn to St. Botolph, then to Lincoln, then to Hull, and finally to London, the German pursuing him all the way. At the instance of London merchants, who feared for their reputation, Lucas was put in the Tower of London, and eventually his case was reviewed on habeas corpus by the King's Council.[19]

Secular rulers also helped to secure the universal character of mercantile law by treaties with each other. From at least the twelfth century on, Italian cities entered into bilateral treaties in which each side agreed that citizens of the other side would have freedom to settle within its borders, to own property there, to carry on industry and trade, to worship, and to have access to courts.[20] These treaties often established impartial tribunals of merchants to decide commercial disputes between citizens of the two treaty partners speedily and in accordance with mercantile custom and, in the absence of a custom governing the matter, according to "good conscience."[21] Also, in the twelfth century a treaty between King Henry II of England and the city of Cologne assured the citizens of Cologne of treatment no less favorable than English merchants received — perhaps the oldest surviving example of the "national treatment" clause and a precursor of the most-favored-nation clause in modern commercial treaties.[22]

RECIPROCITY OF RIGHTS

The principle of reciprocity of rights was at the heart of the new system of mercantile law that emerged in the late eleventh and twelfth centuries. Of course, reciprocity itself, in the sense of mutual give-and-take, has been at the heart of all commerce, in all civilizations, insofar as all commerce involves the exchange of burdens or benefits on the part of those engaged in commercial transactions. The seller parts with the goods and the buyer parts with his money; the lender advances funds and the borrower binds himself to repay what was advanced plus an additional sum; the carrier undertakes to transport the goods and the seller or the buyer undertakes to pay the freight. Each makes a sacrifice, and both expect to be better off as a result. Yet the principle of reciprocity of rights, as it has been understood in the West since the late eleventh and early twelfth centuries, involves something more than mere exchange: it involves, ideally, the element of *equality* of burdens or benefits as between the parties to the transaction — the element, that is, of fairness of the exchange. This, in turn, has two aspects, one procedural, the other substantive. Procedurally, the exchange must be entered into fairly, that is, without duress or fraud or other abuse of the will or knowledge of either party. Substantively, even an exchange which is entered into willingly and knowingly must not impose on either side costs that are excessively disproportionate to the benefits to be obtained; nor may such an exchange be unduly disadvantageous to third parties or to society generally.

Both the procedural and the substantive aspects of reciprocity of rights are implied in the very term "rights" as it has been understood in the West since the late eleventh century. Rights are necessarily viewed as part of a whole legal system. They derive their character from the purposes of that system. Those purposes include some protection, at least, against some kinds of unfairness in commercial exchanges.

The principle of procedural reciprocity was highly developed in the jurisprudence that accompanied the Papal Revolution. The canon law, in particular, stressed principles of equity in contract formation. As a pledge of faith gave the ecclesiastical courts jurisdiction over contracts, so good faith (*bona fides*) was itself a necessary test of the sanctity of the contractual undertaking. In canon law, concepts of fraud, duress, and mistake were fashioned into a complex theory which, on the one hand, supported the freedom of the parties to make binding promises but, on the other hand, protected them against sharp practices. Above all, the formalism of oaths, which had dominated the Germanic folklaw, was subjected to correcting influences. In contrast both to Germanic law and to the preexisting Roman law, the new canon law, supported by the new Romanist legal science, not only enforced informal oral agreements but also refused to enforce the most formal agreements (under oath or in writing under seal) if entered into as a result of deception or even of a misunderstanding for which the promisor was not responsible. These principles were taken over, with some modifications, by the new system of mercantile law. They reflected the principle of procedural reciprocity of rights in contract formation.

The principle of substantive reciprocity of rights, though less highly developed, was reflected in the canonists' doctrines of usury and the just price.[23] Many subtle qualifications were introduced into these doctrines in order to accommodate them to commercial needs. Lawful interest was permitted. A lawful profit was not unjust. Nevertheless, the merchants often resisted the attempts of the canonists to regulate mercantile practices, and especially their assertion of ecclesiastical jurisdiction in mercantile cases. A late example, but one that is also characteristic of the period between the late eleventh century and the early thirteenth, is a decree issued in 1369 by the Doge and Council of Aldermen of the city of Genoa imposing a substantial fine on any person who had recourse to an ecclesiastical or other court on the ground that a commercial contract which he had entered into, such as a contract of insurance or exchange of currency, was usurious or against canon law or otherwise illegal.[24]

The conflict between merchants and ecclesiastics over the applicability of canon law to commercial contracts did not reflect any fundamental difference of opinion concerning the subordination of freedom of contract to moral considerations. The merchants did not believe in the right of the individual to enrich himself at will. Although they did not think that commercial activity should be bound to the moral standards of monastic life, they did not deny that it was subject to the principle of the just price, the law of usury, and other similar protections against oppressive or immoral agreements. Nor did they contest the supremacy of the church in matters of morals. Yet they insisted on their own relative autonomy in matters of commercial law; and in theory, at least, the church did not deny them that autonomy. Therefore their formulations might differ from ecclesiastical formulations, just as their jurisdiction might differ from ecclesiastical jurisdiction — and each of the different formulations might be valid, just as each of the jurisdictions might be valid. This was the scholastic dialectic in action. The mercantile community had its own law, the lex mercatoria, just as the church had its own law, the jus canonicum. The merchants were, of course, members of the church and hence subject to the canon law, but they were also members of the mercantile community and hence subject to the law merchant. When the two bodies of law conflicted, it might not be clear which of the two should prevail. Both might be right. Only time could mediate the conflict.

Thus procedural and substantive reciprocity of rights, invoked by both merchants and ecclesiastics, must be seen not as an abstract principle but as a principle enunciated and implemented within specific communities. The merchants constituted a self-governing community, divided into religious brotherhoods, guilds, and other associations. From that historical fact are derived all the characteristics of the new system of mercantile law — its objectivity, universality, reciprocity of rights, participatory adjudication, integration, and growth.

Participatory Adjudication: Commercial Courts

Commercial courts included courts of markets and fairs, courts of merchant guilds, and urban courts. Although guild and urban courts were not concerned exclusively with commercial matters, their commercial jurisdiction was sufficiently extensive to warrant their being treated as commercial courts.

Market and fair courts, like seignorial and manorial courts, were nonprofessional community tribunals; the judges were elected by the merchants of market or fair from among their numbers. Guild courts were also nonprofessional tribunals, usually consisting simply of the head of the guild or his representative, but often he chose two or three merchant members of the guild to sit as assessors in mercantile cases. Occasionally, a professional jurist would sit with the merchant assessors. Professional notaries often acted as clerks to take care of legal formalities.[25] Urban mercantile courts, too, often consisted of merchants elected by their fellows. A law of Milan of 1154 authorized the election of "consuls of merchants" to sit on commercial cases, and this system of merchant consular courts spread to many Italian cites. It permitted foreign merchants to choose judges from among their own fellow citizens. The courts of the merchant consuls in the city republics of northern Italy gradually extended their jurisdiction over all mercantile cases within the city. Other European cities adopted the Italian institution of the merchant consul or else developed similar institutions for adjudication of commercial cases by merchant judges. In some countries, royal authority was asserted over merchant guilds and over town markets and fairs, but even then the law merchant continued, in general, to be administered by merchant judges.

Various other types of commercial courts developed in the course of time in various parts of the West. In England, Wales, and Ireland, so-called courts of the staple were established in the fourteen towns through which the flourishing English trade in certain "staple" products — chiefly wool, leather, and lead — was channeled. Italian, Flemish, and German merchants and bankers handled much of this business. The English offered protection to "merchant strangers" in the staple towns, and under the Statute of the Staple of 1353 the merchants of each staple town, as well as their servants and the members of their households, were to be "ruled by the law merchant [in] all things touching the staple, and not by the common law of the land, nor by the usage of cities, boroughs, or other towns." They were subject to the jurisdiction of the staple court, whose presiding officer was to be the mayor of the town, elected for a one-year term "by the commonalty of merchants, as well of strangers as of denizens." Thus foreign merchants participated in the elections of the mayors of English towns! The mayor was required to have "knowledge of the law merchant" and to judge according to it. Trials involving both a merchant stranger and an Englishman required a mixed jury composed half of foreigners and half of English subjects. Appeals could be taken to the chancellor and the king's council.[26]

Another type of commercial court was the local maritime court in seaport towns, with jurisdiction over both commercial and maritime causes involving carriage of goods by sea. These courts — called admiralty courts — would sit on the seashore "from tide to tide."

In all types of commercial courts the procedure was marked by speed and informality. Time limits were narrow: in the fair courts justice was to be done while the merchants' feet were still dusty, in the maritime courts it was to be done "from tide to tide," in guild and town courts "from day to day." Often appeals were forbidden. Not only were professional lawyers generally excluded but also technical legal argumentation was frowned upon. The court was to be "ruled by equity . . . whereby every man will be received to tell his facts . . . and to say the best he can" in his defense. A typical statute of a merchant guild provided that commercial cases "are to be decided *ex aequo et bono*; it is not meet to dispute on the subtleties of the law."[27] These procedural characteristics sharply distinguished commercial law from the formalistic procedure of urban and royal courts and also from the written procedure of the canon law in ordinary cases.

The procedure of the commercial courts was, however, related to the summary (as contrasted with the ordinary) procedure in ecclesiastical courts. Summary procedure in special types of cases, including commercial cases, was authorized by a papal bull of 1306, the Decretal "Saepe Contingit" (from the opening words, "It often happens"). The bull referred to the pope's practice of sometimes referring cases to (ecclesiastical) judges with the instruction that the procedure "be simple and

plain and without the formal arguments and solemn rules of the ordinary procedure." To explain these words, the bull stated that the judge
in such a case need not require a written complaint, that he should not
require the usual type of pleading, that he might proceed even in time of
vacations, that he should cut off dilatory exceptions, and that he should
reject unnecessary appeals that caused delay as well as the "shouting" of
advocates, prosecutors, parties, and superfluous witnesses. In such
cases, the bull stated, the judge "shall interrogate the parties, either at
their instance or on his own initiative wherever equity so requires."[28]
This decretal found its way into later Italian statutes establishing mercantile courts; it also influenced German, French, and English commercial and maritime courts, including the English chancellor's court in its
equity jurisdiction.

In England, the speed of merchant justice was stressed by Bracton,
who wrote that there were certain classes of people "who ought to have
swift justice, such as merchants, to whom justice is given in the Court
Pepoudrous" (the "piepowder" or "dusty feet" courts of fairs and
markets).[29]

The principle of speedy, informal, and equitable procedure in the
commercial courts was, of course, a response to mercantile needs. That
response could only be made, however, because of the communal, or
participatory, character of commercial adjudication. Like the other
characteristics of mercantile law—its objectivity, universality,
reciprocity of rights, integration, growth—the communal character of
commercial adjudication (that is, the participation of merchants in the
resolution of mercantile disputes) may be viewed as a principle of
abstract justice, a legal ideal. From that point of view it may be
evaluated negatively as well as positively, for while it contributed to the
equitable solution of individual commercial cases it also helped to in-
sulate commercial law from ecclesiastical, royal, and even urban control
and to preserve mercantile privileges. But the system of participatory
adjudication of commercial cases must also be viewed in historical terms
as an aspect of the relative autonomy of the mercantile class and of its
law in the formative era of the Western legal tradition—an autonomy
relative to the overarching unity of Western law, with its interaction of
spiritual and secular authorities and, within the secular, of feudal,
manorial, commercial, urban, and royal legal systems.

THE INTEGRATION OF MERCANTILE LAW

Western mercantile law acquired in the late eleventh, twelfth, and
early thirteenth centuries the character of an integrated system of principles, concepts, rules, and procedures. The various rights and obligations associated with commercial relations came to be consciously interpreted as constituent parts of a whole body of law, the lex mercatoria.
Many diverse commercial legal institutions created at that time, such as

negotiable instruments, secured credit, and joint ventures, together with many older legal institutions that were then refashioned, were all seen as forming a distinct and coherent system.

The following distinctive characteristics of Western mercantile law were introduced during these centuries:

the sharp separation of the law of movables (chattels) from the law of immovables (land and fixtures attached to land);

recognition of rights in the good-faith purchaser of movables superior to those of the true owner; [30]

replacement of the older requirement of delivery of goods in order to transfer ownership by the device of symbolic delivery, that is, transfer of ownership (and of risk of loss or damage) by transfer of transportation documents or other documents;

the creation of a right of possession of movables independent of ownership; [31]

recognition of the validity of informal oral agreements for the purchase and sale of movables;

limitation of claims for breach of warranty, on the one hand, and development of the doctrine of implied warranties of fitness and of merchantability (*marchandise loyale et marchande*), on the other hand;

the introduction of an objective measure of damages for nondelivery of goods, based on the difference between the contract price and the market price, together with the introduction of fixed monetary penalties for breach of some types of contracts;

the development of commercial documents such as bills of exchange and promissory notes and their transformation into so-called abstract contracts, in which the document was not merely evidence of an underlying contract but itself embodied, or was, the contract and could be sued on independently;

the invention of the concept of negotiability of bills of exchange and promissory notes, whereby the good faith transferee was entitled to be paid by the drawer or maker even if the latter had certain defenses (such as the defense of fraud) against the original payee;

the invention of the mortgage of movables (chattel mortgage), the unpaid seller's lien, and other security interests in goods;

the development of a bankruptcy law which took into account the existence of a sophisticated system of commercial credit;

the development of the bill of lading and other transportation documents;

the expansion of the ancient Graeco-Roman sea loan and the invention of the bottomry loan, secured by a lien on the freight or by shares in the ship itself, as means of financing and insuring a merchant's overseas sales; [32]

the replacement of the more individualistic Graeco-Roman concept

of partnership (*societas*) by a more collectivistic concept in which there
was joint ownership, the property was at the disposition of the partnership as a unit, and the rights and obligations of one partner survived the death of the other;

the development of the joint venture (*commenda*) as a kind of joint-
stock company, with the liability of each investor limited to the
amount of his investment;

the invention of trademarks and patents;

the floating of public loans secured by bonds and other securities;

the development of deposit banking; [33]

Thus a great many if not most of the structural elements of the
modern system of commercial law were formed in this period. Implicit
in them were certain basic legal principles which were shared by all the
legal systems of the time and which were adapted to the special needs of
the mercantile community. These included the principle of good faith,
which was manifested particularly in the creation of new credit devices,
and the principle of corporate personality, which was manifested particularly in the creation of new forms of business associations.

Credit devices. As payment in kind became exceptional in the twelfth
century, there was a proliferation of new types of commercial contracts
involving the use of credit. Indeed, payment in cash was itself a kind of
credit transaction because there was no sovereign state to guarantee the
value of money and many different kinds of coins were in circulation.

The chief forms of credit extended by sellers to buyers were promissory notes and bills of exchange. Either the buyer signed a document
addressed to the seller, promising to pay him a certain sum of money
either at a certain time in the future or upon presentation of the document; or else he issued a draft (bill of exchange) on a third person ("To
X, pay Y for my account . . . "), which was also payable either on a certain date or on presentation. Commercial instruments had been used by
the Arabs in Mediterranean trade between the eighth and tenth centuries, but they were apparently not then treated as "abstract contracts,"
that is, as obligations independent of the contractual relations that gave
rise to them. When they became common in the West in the late
eleventh and twelfth centuries, they not only acquired the character of
independent obligations, like money itself, but they also acquired
another characteristic of money, namely, negotiability. The maker of
the note (or drawer of the bill) made the instrument payable to the payee
"or to his order."[34] This meant that any person to whom the payee
transferred the instrument (whether by endorsement or otherwise) had
an unconditional right to be paid by the maker (or drawer), even if the
latter had a valid defense (such as the defense of fraud) against the
original payee — provided only that the transferee had taken the instru-

ment in good faith and without knowledge of the fraud or other defense. It was anticipated that the instrument would pass from hand to hand. Similarly, a bill of exchange made payable to the payee "or bearer" was valid in the hands of any innocent holder.

Neither the concept nor the practice of negotiability of credit instruments was known to the older Roman law or to the Germanic law, nor was it a developed concept or practice among the Muslims and other traders of the Mediterranean between the eighth and tenth centuries. Its invention by Western merchants of the late eleventh and twelfth centuries was, of course, a response to the emergence at that time of a developed market for goods. Yet to produce the response, more than the economic stimulus was needed. There had to be a reservoir of credit itself, for without credit, that is, without confidence in the future of the community of persons that constituted the market, there could not have been either credit instruments or the extra credit embodied in their negotiability. Credit, of course, means belief or faith or trust in someone or something. A system of transferring a debtor's future obligation from one creditor to another could not have been developed and maintained if there had not been a strong belief or faith or trust in both the integrity and the duration of the community to which all creditors and debtors belonged. Indeed, it was only such a belief in the future of the mercantile community that made it possible to measure the value of immediate payment against the value of payment at a later date.

As Robert S. Lopez has written, "Unstinting credit was the great lubricant of the Commercial Revolution. It was altogether a novel phenomenon . . . the Graeco-Roman economy was well supplied with cash of all kinds but ill-suited for commercial credit on a larger scale, and . . . the economy of the barbarian age was deficient both in cash and in credit; it never got far off the ground. The take-off of the following period was fueled not by a massive input of cash, but by a closer collaboration of people using credit. It did not occur in Germany, where new silver mines began their activity between the tenth and the twelfth century, but in Italy, where the gulf between agrarian capitalists and merchants was narrowed down [and where] credit enabled a small investment of hard cash to go to work simultaneously at more than one place."[35]

Credit flourished in many forms in this period, not only in Italy but throughout western Europe. In addition to the extension of credit by sellers to buyers through negotiable instruments and other devices, buyers also extended credit to sellers through various types of contracts for the purchase of goods to be delivered in the future, to be purchased by the seller and resold, and the like. Once again, such contracts presupposed the existence not only of a developed market but also of a belief in the future of the community that made up the market and a concept of time as a factor to be valued in commercial transactions.

The extension of credit by the seller to the buyer, or by a third party (for example, a banker) to the buyer, was much more common than the extension of credit by the buyer to the seller, and as a result devices were sought to protect the lender against default. The most important such device was the mortgage of movables (chattel mortgage), under which the party that extended the credit retained a security interest in the goods so that they could not be resold or otherwise disposed of until he was paid, and if he was not paid he could take possession of the goods and resell them to satisfy the debt. Neither Roman law nor Germanic law had had such a sophisticated security device. Once again, the existence of a cohesive mercantile community with a developed body of mercantile law was essential to the effectiveness of such a mortgage of movables, for there was a danger that the same goods would be fraudulently pledged to more than one lender. This danger was met in many of the European cities by the development of a system of registration of chattel mortgages with public officials, so that potential lenders could discover any preexisting encumbrances.[36]

Essential to the developed system of commercial credit which was created in the West in the late eleventh and twelfth centuries was a law of bankruptcy which, on the one hand, took security interests into account in protecting creditors and, on the other hand, was not ruinous to debtors. The Germanic law had been especially harsh on the defaulting debtor; his creditors took everything he had and could even come to live in his house, exploit his servants, and consume his crops. The Roman law of Justinian, on the other hand, had been very humane to the defaulting debtor but had left the creditors poorly protected. The bankruptcy law of the West from the twelfth century on struck a balance between these two extremes. It permitted limitation of the liability of debtors and at the same time gave preferences to secured creditors. In Levin Goldschmidt's words, the bankruptcy law of this period "forms an original and extremely influential stage of European legal development."[37]

Types of business associations: joint ventures. A new type of business arrangement, the *commenda*, came to be used in Italy, England, and elsewhere in Europe in the late eleventh century, by which capital was mobilized for long-distance trade overseas and, less frequently, overland. The earliest forerunner of the commenda may have been a Muslim commercial practice which found its way into Byzantium, including the seaports of southern Italy, in the eighth to tenth centuries. In northern Italy and beyond the Alps, the commenda probably started in the eleventh century as a loan contract, but it soon developed into a partnership agreement for a single venture, usually a round-trip voyage to the Middle East, Africa, or Spain. One partner, called the *stans,* supplied the capital but stayed at home; the other partner, called the *trac-*

tator, did the traveling. In return for making the difficult and perilous voyage, the traveling partner usually received one-fourth of the profits, while the partner who risked his money received the remaining three-fourths. As Lopez remarks, "This arrangement may seem unfair, but in the twelfth and thirteenth centuries life was cheap and capital scarce."[38]

A variation of the commenda was the *societas maris* ("sea partnership"), in which the tractator supplied one-third of the capital and the stans two-thirds, and the two shared the profits equally.

Lopez points out that the stans was not necessarily a sleeping partner. He might be "an older merchant who no longer went overseas, but who was still actively engaged in business and sometimes undertook the sale of the goods brought back by his partner." Moreover, the tractator of one commenda was often the stans of another reciprocal commenda, so that the two types were not two antagonistic groups of investing and traveling partners, or of exploiters and exploited. On the other hand, there were "numerous cases in which the investing partners were widows and orphans, priests and nuns, public officials and notaries, artisans or other persons without business experience."[39]

The commenda and the societas maris had the great advantage that the liability of partners was limited to the amount of their initial investment. In this respect it was like the modern joint-stock company. Also, investors could reduce their risks by dividing their money among several different commendae rather than putting it all in one venture. But the commenda differed from the modern business corporation in that it was generally a short-term arrangement which was dissolved at the completion of the particular voyage for which it had been established.

Long-term overland ventures were often arranged, in the late eleventh, twelfth, and early thirteenth centuries, under a different form of partnership, called a *compagnia*. This was originally an association of members of the same family who worked together to increase their family wealth. Such "companions" often became involved in trade. Eventually they were joined by outsiders and became a business unit, a "company." In contrast to the commenda, the compagnia did not have limited liability; each partner was fully liable to third parties for the debts of the company. Also, the compagnia usually carried on diverse trading activities over a period of many years. It was often sufficiently large and lasting and flexible to establish branches in various cities.

The short duration of the commenda and the unlimited liability of the compagnia were both subject to some modification by special clauses inserted in the respective contracts by which they were formed. There were also other types of contracts available for forming other kinds of business associations.[40] However, the commenda and the compagnia were the chief models.

Both the general principle of good faith, which underlay all the legal systems of the Western legal tradition in its formative era, and the special manifestation of that principle in the credit devices of the new system of commercial law, were reflected in the commenda, the compagnia, and various other forms of commercial partnership in which the partners pooled resources and shared profits and losses. These business associations depended on each partner's confidence that the other partners' promises would be kept. In addition, however, there was another basic legal principle manifested in the developing law of business associations, namely, the principle of the collective personality of the members of the association. Though formed solely on the basis of agreement, the partnership constituted a legal person which could own property, enter into contracts, and sue and be sued. The partners were empowered to act jointly in behalf of the partnership, and they were jointly liable for the debts of the partnership. In addition, however, each partner acting alone could bind the partnership, and each was also severally liable for its debts. Together they constituted a corporation, in the sense that a bishopric or a parish was a corporation and that a university or a guild was a corporation; that is, they constituted a self-governing body, a community, whose personality was both transcendent and immanent, that is, both distinct from and linked with the persons of its members.

The form of business partnership of the twelfth century that was most like that of the modern business corporation, namely, the commenda, was created for a short term and for a specific purpose. It was a "secular" association in the full meaning of that word: it was wholly a creature of time. Yet even the commenda was a community; the partners were not mere agents, for under the emerging system of commercial law an agent, unlike a partner, could not bind an undisclosed principal in loans and bailments (though he could in sales and hirings).[41]

Thus it appears, once again, that the integrity of the new system of mercantile law, that is, the structural coherence of its principles, concepts, rules, and procedures, derived primarily from the integrity and structural coherence of the mercantile community whose law it was.

The Growth of Mercantile Law

The integration of mercantile law, its structural unity, was closely connected with its organic growth. It was conceived as a developing system. Its development was quite rapid, not only in its formative period but also thereafter, in the thirteenth, fourteenth, and fifteenth centuries. As in the case of canon law, feudal law, manorial law, and other contemporary legal systems, the objectivity of mercantile law, the specificity of its norms, and the precision of its concepts increased over time; its universality and generality, its uniformity, increasingly prevailed over local differences; reciprocity of rights became increasingly important as contractual opportunities expanded; adjudication of commercial disputes became increasingly regularized; and the degree of integration of commercial law increased. In other words, as in the case of the other legal systems that formed the Western legal tradition, the characteristic features of commercial law became also tendencies of its organic growth in time.

The conscious development of the system of commercial law was greatly facilitated by the existence of institutions responsible for its development. The rulers of Europe, especially the ruling authorities in the various leading commercial cities, helped to develop the system of mercantile law by codifying the commercial customs. Examples are the *Customs of Genoa* of 1056, the *Constitutum Usus* of Pisa of 1161, and the *Book of Customs* of Milan of 1216. Growth was facilitated also by the keeping of records of mercantile court decisions, including courts of the fairs as well as city courts and maritime courts.

In addition, the creation of an elaborate system of notaries in the late eleventh and twelfth centuries made it inevitable that commercial custom would be consciously adapted to new conditions. The notaries not only registered commercial documents but also drew up contracts and other notarial instruments. These notarial instruments were regarded as having the force of contractual obligations. Thus a notary would prepare a promissory note or a bill of exchange or other order of payment, and these would then have legally binding force. Indeed, the notarial contract of exchange seems to have been the progenitor of the bill of exchange, and the notarized promise to pay was probably the progenitor of the promissory note. In northern Europe, where notarial instruments were not so widely used as in southern Europe, records certified by municipal and guild authorities, such as the Guildhall of London, enjoyed a similar authority.

In addition to notarial records, bank ledgers and cartularies of ships also had legal force, and even merchants' accounts were admissible in evidence. Thus there was a vast system of recording commercial operations, and while this undoubtedly exerted some restraint upon change it also channeled change and gave it continuity and direction.

Whatever the factors were that made for growth, there can be no doubt that growth took place. The development of the sea loan and the invention of the bottomry loan were used as indirect means of insuring overseas shipments in the twelfth century; in the fourteenth century the first documents of marine insurance made their appearance, and by the fifteenth century marine insurance was a thriving business.[42] Again, in the twelfth and thirteenth centuries merchant bankers issued letters for their customers assuring prospective creditors that the banker would honor obligations that the customer incurred; in the fourteenth and fifteenth centuries such letters developed into commercial letters of credit in which the banker assured particular sellers that he would pay for particular goods the customer wished to purchase.[43] In the twelfth century the capacity to enter into commercial contracts was extended to former peasants and to the feudal nobility; thereafter it was gradually extended to others, including women and minors. These were not merely changes but developments, and not merely automatic developments but conscious adaptations of preexisting legal institutions and ideas to new situations — a conscious expansion of their range of application to meet new needs.[44]

Thus there took place throughout the system of mercantile law a process of differentiation, which had the appearance of an unfolding of the past into the future, an autonomous growth over centuries. There was an illusion, at least, not only of the basic unity of the body of law which the merchants made to govern their activities, but also of the continuous cooperation of successive generations of merchants in making that body of law live and grow.

12 | Urban Law

SOME THOUSANDS of new cities and towns came into existence in the late eleventh and the twelfth centuries — in northern Italy, Flanders, France, Normandy, England, the German duchies, Castile and Aragon, and other parts of Europe. Indeed, the new cities and towns emerged before these larger territories themselves became integrated political units, and in some respects the urban communities had more in common with one another than they had with the respective countries in which they were situated. For however diverse their character, they all had a common consciousness of themselves as urban communities and they all had similar legal institutions: they were all governed by a system of urban law.

These were not, of course, the first cities in world history. Yet there had never before been anything quite like them. In the period from the first century B.C. to the fourth and fifth centuries A.D., the Roman Empire had been made up of thousands of cities, but they had served chiefly as centers for administrative control by the Roman imperial authority and had been governed by imperial officers. The cities of ancient Greece, on the contrary, had been self-contained, independent city-states. In contrast to both Greece and Rome, the cities and towns that emerged in Europe in the eleventh and twelfth centuries were neither administrative centers of a central authority nor self-contained republics. They were something in-between.

After the Western Roman Empire was finally demolished by Germanic invaders in the fifth century, almost all the Roman cities in the West rapidly declined, and by the ninth century they had virtually disappeared. This was true even in northern Italy. But in southern Italy, which remained largely Byzantine with a strong Arab influence, Naples, Salerno, Bari, Syracuse, Palermo, and other Roman cities survived. In addition, some important early seaport towns outside of southern Italy remained, such as Venice and Durazzo on the Adriatic and a few ports on the Mediterranean coast of what later became France and Spain. Some inland commercial centers such as Cologne, Milan, and London also continued to exist, but they became essentially trading settlements, the commercial quarters of fortified places.

With rare exceptions, including the city of Rome itself, there was no political continuity between the former Roman cities and the modern European cities that ultimately emerged, often on or near the Roman sites, in the eleventh and twelfth centuries. There was, to be sure, a continuity of ecclesiastical authority in those cities that were seats of bishoprics (headquarters of episcopal dioceses), but even they had declined from great metropolitan centers to small towns, largely integrated with the countryside. Although such episcopal seats continued to bear the name of *civitas* ("city"), all other towns were called by various names signifying either fortification (*bourg,* borough, *borgo,* or *burgus;* also *castellum, castrum, opidum, urbs, municipium*) or else, more rarely, commercial center (*portus,* port, or *wik*). In the year 1000 there were few settlements west of Venice or north of Palermo with more than several thousand inhabitants. (See map 1.)

It was not, however, their small size or their small number which most sharply differentiated the cities and towns—henceforth these two designations will be used more or less interchangeably—of western Europe in the year 1000 from the modern cities and towns that emerged in the following two centuries, but rather their relatively indistinct social and economic character, on the one hand, and their relatively indistinct political and legal character, on the other. Socially and economically, towns before 1000 consisted mostly of people who lived by cultivating the soil. There were also merchants living in trading settlements in the towns—usually just outside the walls of the castle or other fortification—as well as knights and nobles living on the castle grounds, but these classes generally were a minority of the town population, while artisans and craftsmen were only a small fraction. For the most part, a town was simply a large village, with some mercantile and military families among its inhabitants. Politically and legally, also, the town did not form an independent unit, nor did its residents have a special status or special privileges distinguishing them from their neighbors in the countryside. Unless it happened to coincide territorially with a hundred, a manor, a bishopric, an abbey, or some other political unit, a town had no administrative or judicial organization of its own. In terms of legal status, its residents were not citizens but knights, free peasants, serfs, slaves, clergy, merchants. If they held land, it was according to the same system of land tenure that prevailed outside the town. As Henri Pirenne has emphasized, the towns that existed in Europe before the eleventh century lacked the two fundamental attributes of a modern Western city: a middle-class population and a municipal organization. Pirenne states that in the year 1000 there were *no* cities in Western Europe, if by "city" is meant either a locality whose population lives not by cultivating the soil but by commerce (he should have added "and industry"), or a community which is a legal entity and which possesses laws and institutions peculiar to itself.[1]

Causes of the Rise of the Modern City

Several types of factors contributed to the rise of the modern city: economic, social, political, religious, and legal.

ECONOMIC FACTORS

Pirenne attributed the emergence of the modern European city in the eleventh and twelfth centuries primarily to the revival of commerce. He stressed the fact that in the eleventh century the marketplace, which usually existed in the *faubourg* ("suburb") of the castle or episcopal palace or abbey, began to swallow up the principal area. It was this suburb that became the core of the new city or town. Pirenne also traced the founding of thousands of new towns throughout Europe in the eleventh and twelfth centuries primarily to pressures exerted by the new merchant class. Later scholars have properly criticized this explanation for neglecting the fact that producers, not merchants, composed the overwhelming majority (probably four-fifths) of the inhabitants of most cities and towns of that time, and that these producers—chiefly artisans and craftsmen—came largely from the surplus agrarian population created by the rapid increase in agricultural productivity in the eleventh century. The increased prosperity of the countryside was also an essential precondition for supplying the cities with food and raw materials and for the marketing of the cities' products. Thus the economic causes of the emergence of modern cities must be traced not only to the expansion of commerce and the rise of a merchant class but also to the expansion of agriculture and to the rise of a class of artisans and craftsmen and other industrial producers.[2] The cities provided a new mode of production, as well as a new mode of distribution.

SOCIAL FACTORS

Closely related to the economic causes of urbanization were broader social causes. The eleventh and twelfth centuries were an age of great outward and upward social mobility. The exodus of serfs, free peasants, and lesser nobility from the manors was part of a more general pulsation and expansion of life, a quickening of the tempo, a search for new opportunities. These social factors were also causes, and not only effects, of what Robert Lopez has called "the commercial revolution"—but what might also be called "the industrial revolution"—of the eleventh and twelfth centuries. In Lopez's words, there was a "continuous creation of new opportunities . . . to climb from one class to another . . . Apprentices became masters, successful craftsmen became entrepreneurs, new men made fortunes in commerce and money-lending . . . Expansion was also stimulated by constant immigration from the country . . . Entire villages gradually lost to nearby towns all their inhabitants, peasants and landowners."[3] Although in most of the cities of Europe social and economic as well as political power eventually became more and more highly concentrated in the hands of a relatively small group of wealthy merchants, the original conception of the city as a place of opportunity to move upward in the social-economic hierarchy had a lasting influence on its character. It is significant that in the northern European cities of the eleventh and twelfth centuries and thereafter, and in some of the Mediterranean cities as well, slavery hardly existed, in contrast to the situation in the cities of ancient Greece and imperial Rome and in the European settlements before 1000.

POLITICAL FACTORS

Emperors, kings, dukes, and lesser (seignorial) rulers, as well as popes and bishops, were often able to increase both their military protection and their wealth by chartering towns which would be open to immigrants from the countryside — principally peasants and lesser nobility.

Such towns were often more efficient militarily than castles, since the citizens were generally given the right and duty to bear arms. The peasants for centuries had had no such military right or duty (although they could be called up under special circumstances), and knights had had to be paid to perform military service. Citizens, to be sure, had to be supplied with arms, but they were subject to universal military service in defense of the city. In many places where the popular militia of the tribes and villages of the Germanic age had disappeared and the feudal levies were precarious, the twelfth-century feudal monarchs, dukes, counts, and other great lords relied heavily upon urban military obligation for defense of their territories. Thus the English Assize of Arms of 1181 provided that "all townsmen and all communes of free men" were to bear certain kinds of arms[4] — thereby making all citizens soldiers and all cities military units.

In addition to giving military support, the new cities and towns substantially increased the economic resources of territorial rulers by providing tolls and market taxes and rents as well as industrial goods. In this connection the right of many cities and towns to coin money — and the obligation of citizens to pay for their land in money — represented a significant shift away from a largely barter economy. The royal and feudal rulers of Europe stood to benefit from this shift equally with the new commerical and industrial classes.

Of course, such political incentives for rulers to found cities and towns had existed in earlier centuries, at least potentially; but in the eleventh and twelfth centuries political conditions became more favorable for their realization. The invasions of Europe had ceased. Kinship, village, and manorial associations were being supplemented by larger territorial associations: kingdoms, principalities, duchies. The rulers of these territories were strong enough politically to tolerate, and to turn their attention to, a new type of political entity in their domains; and peasants and lesser nobility were available to move there.

Undoubtedly, social and economic and political factors all worked together to stimulate the emergence of new cities and towns, and without the presence of those factors it is hard to imagine that perhaps 5,000 new cities and towns would have emerged, as they did, all over western Europe during the same centuries — starting in the eleventh, peaking in the twelfth, and continuing in the thirteenth, fourteenth, and fifteenth.

Yet there were also social and economic and political factors working in the opposite direction. Feudal lords, including bishops and abbots, often had a strong economic interest in preventing the departure of their peasants; also they were not disposed to yield political power to the new urban complexes. Similarly, emperors, kings, and other rulers who granted charters to cities and towns had a strong interest in inserting clauses in those charters which would secure their own continued control over the citizens. Often the cities had to fight for independence and often they lost. Moreover, one cannot assume that most peasants and lesser nobility were keen to leave the manors and the villages; to do so was to risk the loss of traditional ties and values for the sake of something new and unknown.

Here one confronts the limitations of conventional social theory in explaining historical change. It is not enough to show that basic social, economic, and political conditions were favorable to the change that eventually took place. Conditions alone do not produce change, any more than soil and seed alone produce crops. Moreover, conditions that are favorable to change may be favorable also to stability. Even the Marxian theory of dialectical materialism only postulates that "ultimately" the forces of change will triumph, leaving open the crucial questions of time and circumstance. Surely, however, one cannot know *why* a great historical change occurred without first knowing *when* and *how* it occurred.

RELIGIOUS AND LEGAL FACTORS

If one examines more closely the timing and the circumstances of the emergence of modern cities and towns in Europe, if one asks what brought urbanization about precisely in the late eleventh and twelfth centuries and not before, if one wishes to explain the *process* by which the urban movement developed and was brought to fulfillment — then one must take into account two factors often neglected by social, economic, and political historians: the religious factor and the legal factor.

The new cities and towns of the eleventh and twelfth centuries were religious associations in the sense that each was held together by religious values and rituals, including religious oaths. Many of them were sworn communes (*conjurationes,* "conspiracies"), and of these a considerable number had been founded by insurrectionary organizations. Those that were formed initially by merchants were often governed by a merchant guild, which was itself a religious association, dedicated to charitable and other religious works as well as to regulation of business activities. Those that were established by imperial, royal, ducal, or episcopal (or other ecclesiastical) initiative were also conceived as brotherhoods and were held together by oaths.

To stress the religious character of the cities and towns is not to say that they were ecclesiastical associations. They were wholly separate from the church, and in that sense they were the first secular states of Europe. Nevertheless, they derived much of their spirit and character from the church. Indeed, it would have been astonishing if it had been otherwise, since they emerged during the era of the Papal Revolution.

The new European cities and towns of the eleventh and twelfth centuries were also legal associations, in the sense that each was held together by a common urban legal consciousness and by distinctive urban legal institutions. In fact, it was by a legal act, usually the granting of a charter, that most of the European cities and towns came into being; they did not simply emerge but were *founded.* Moreover, the charter would almost invariably establish the basic "liberties" of citizens, usually including substantial rights of self-government. Of course, the legal character of the new European cities and towns was closely associated with their religious character. The charters were confirmed by religious oaths, and the oaths, which were renewed with successive installations of officers, included, above all, vows to uphold the municipal laws.

The importance of both religious and legal factors in the emergence of the western European cities may be judged by contrasting the development of cities in the contemporary Islamic civilization of the Middle East. There, despite similar economic and political factors (flourishing commerce, small-scale industry, a middle class, strong central territorial rulers), and despite the head start furnished by the physical survival of many of the cities of the Roman Empire, urban culture was weak.[5] Both economically and politically, the Islamic cities lacked corporate unity and an independent character; they were essentially large villages, more or less integrated with the countryside. The crucial difference, in comparison with the West, was that, on the one hand, Islamic cities and towns were never sworn communes and never consisted of religious guilds or brotherhoods and, on the other hand, they were never incorporated and never given charters of rights and liberties. In contrast to Western culture from the time of the Papal Revolution, Islam lacked both the zeal to reform and redeem secular society and the concept that competing plural polities and legal systems can serve as instruments of such reform and redemption.

The rise of the European city in the late eleventh and the twelfth centuries was due at least as much to the contemporaneous transformation of religious and legal consciousness, associated with the Papal Revolution, as to the commercial-industrial and political-military transformations (which were also associated with the Papal Revolution). What made urbanization possible then and not before, and there and not elsewhere, were new religious and legal concepts and institutions and practices—and new religious and legal passions and acts—concerning communes and other kinds of fraternal associations, collective oaths, corporate personality, charters of liberties, rational and objective judicial procedures, equality of rights, participation in lawmaking, representative government, and statehood itself. These concerns, in turn, were related to structural characteristics of the Western legal tradition that were shared not only by urban law but also by the other contemporaneously emerging legal systems.

Without urban legal consciousness and a system of urban law, it is hard to imagine European cities and towns coming into existence at all. But even if they had—that is, even if large, densely populated centers of commerce and industry could somehow have been formed in the West without a foundation in urban law—perhaps they would have been, like the ancient Roman cities, merely administrative and military outposts of some central authority (or authorities), or else, like Islamic cities, merely large villages, without their own independent character as cities, without an autonomous, integrated urban community life, or perhaps like something else; but they would not have been cities in the modern Western sense. They would not have had the self-conscious corporate unity and the capacity for organic development that have given the Western city its unique character.

The Origins of the Cities and Towns of Western Europe

In the early decades of the fourteenth century—before the Black Death of 1348–50 wiped out at least one-third and possibly more than one-half of the urban population—there were perhaps six million western Europeans living in cities and towns, out of a total population of about sixty million. Though it is impossible to obtain exact statistics for this period of history, nevertheless there is sufficient evidence to support an educated guess that in the late twelfth century there were about four million city-dwellers out of a total population of about forty million. In the early fourteenth century, four cities—Venice, Florence, Palermo, and Paris—are thought by some specialists to have had a population of over 100,000 each, and five others—Milan, Genoa, Barcelona, Cologne, and London—a population of about 50,000 each. A larger group of towns, including Bologna, Padua, Ghent, Bruges, Strasbourg, Nuremberg, Lübeck, and Hamburg, are thought by some specialists to have had between 20,000 and 40,000 inhabitants, and a still larger group, including York, Bristol, Ypres, Antwerp, Augsburg, Frankfurt, Zürich, Basel, and others, between 6,000 and 20,000.[6] Other estimates are higher: some experts would credit Milan and Venice with about 200,000 each, and Genoa and Naples (along with Florence, Palermo, and Paris) with about 100,000 each.[7] Still another writer has assigned to Paris about 100,000 at the end of the twelfth century and about 240,000 at the end of the thirteenth.[8] Then, of course, at the other end of the spectrum there were thousands of towns of under 6,000 inhabitants, many of them with only a few hundred. (See map 3.)

These cities and towns, highly diverse in size, emerged and developed in highly diverse ways and for highly diverse reasons. Yet there were certain common patterns that made them all cities or towns, just as there are certain common patterns that make the diverse nation-states of the twentieth century all nation-states.

The best way to discover those common patterns is to describe the origin and early development of various kinds of cities and towns in various parts of Europe, starting in France and moving on to Normandy, Flanders, the German duchies, England, and finally Italy.

PICARDY (FRANCE): CAMBRAI, BEAUVAIS, LAON

Cambrai, the site of a former Roman city called Camaracum in Picardy (in the far north of what is now France), had been invaded by Magyars and Normans. By the tenth century it had become a small episcopal civitas with a stockaded merchants' quarter (faubourg) outside its walls. By 1070 the suburban merchants had grown sufficiently prosperous and strong to require that their quarter be walled with stone.

In 1075, shortly after Pope Gregory VII had declared the political and legal unity of the church and its independence from the empire, the population of Cambrai, led by a papalist priest and wealthy merchants, rose up against the authority of the emperor and his bishop and "swore a commune." This revolt was quickly put down. However, two years later, when a new bishop left the diocese to receive imperial investiture, a second revolt succeeded. Under the leadership, once again, of a Gregorian priest and the wealthiest merchants, the citizens swore oaths of fidelity to the commune and pledged themselves to defend it against a restoration of episcopal authority. In 1106, however, the emperor intervened to repress the commune once again. Only after the end of the Investiture Struggle (1122) did Cambrai receive a modern charter of liberties, the oldest extant copy of which is dated 1184.[9]

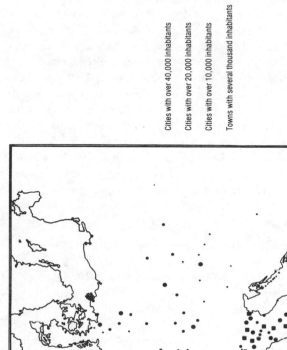

Map 3. Cities and towns of Western Europe circa 1250.

Other episcopal towns of Picardy in the north of France followed the example of Cambrai in rising up against imperial authority in the late eleventh and early twelfth centuries and establishing sworn communes. As in the case of Cambrai, the bishops, whose power had originally derived from the emperor, were often (though not always) against the communes, while the papal party often supported them.[10] This was true not only in northern France but also in the Netherlands and northern Italy, where urban revolts similar to those of Cambrai took place.

Beauvais—also in Picardy— is of particular interest because in the twelfth century it received a charter providing for strong powers of self-government and extensive privileges of citizens (bourgeois). A sworn commune had been instituted in Beauvais in the last years of the eleventh century, after four decades of sharp conflict between the bourgeois and a succession of bishops. Eventually, King Louis VI (1108–1137) issued a charter recognizing the authority of the commune, which was confirmed in 1144 by Louis VII and (with some additions) in 1182 by Philip Augustus. The seventeen articles of the charter included the following provisions:

> all men within the walls of the city and in the suburb shall swear the commune;
>
> each shall aid the other in the manner he thinks to be right;
>
> if any man who has sworn the commune suffers a violation of rights, and a claim comes before the peers of the commune (in French, *pairs*, literally "equals," referring to leading citizens generally), they shall do justice against the person or property of the offender, unless he makes amends according to their judgment; and if the offender flees, the peers of the commune shall join in obtaining satisfaction from his property or person or from those to whom he has fled;
>
> similarly, if a merchant comes to Beauvais to the market and someone within the city violates his rights, and a claim comes before the peers, they shall grant the merchant satisfaction;
>
> no one who has violated the rights of a man of the commune shall be admitted to the city unless he makes amends according to the judgment of the peers; this rule may be waived, by advice of the peers, in the case of persons whom the Bishop of Beauvais has brought into the city;
>
> no man of the commune shall extend credit to its enemies and no man shall speak with them except by permission of the peers;
>
> the peers of the commune shall swear that they shall judge justly, and all others shall swear that they will observe and enforce the judgment of the peers.[11]

Other provisions dealt with regulation of mills, collection of debts (no person was to be taken as security for a debt), communal protection of food, equal measures of cloth, and restrictions on various feudal labor services still owed to the bishop.

The charter did not specify the form of government of the commune but only provided that its peers were to render judgment and to secure the life and property of the members. Indeed, the charter added nothing to what had been established at least one or two decades before, except that its final provision stated that "we [the king] do concede and confirm the justice and judgment which the peers shall do." In short, the charter was a recognition of a fait accompli: the uprising—at the height of the Papal Revolution—of the bourgeois of Beauvais, the formation by them of a sworn commune, and the restriction of the political and economic power of the bishop, who had previously been not only the chief ecclesiastic but also the chief feudal lord of the place, wholly involved in local and interfamily politics.[12] Although the charter itself was laconic in the extreme, it clearly implied that seignorial rights in the town of Beauvais were to be severely restricted.

The provision that "all men" were to swear the commune and be subject to its jurisdiction was not intended to include clergy or nobles, whether or not they lived within the walls. In fact, the new urban communities of Europe were in competition with clerical and feudal authorities. In the background, helping to regulate this competition, were the central royal and papal authorities.

Beauvais was somewhat unusual, though by no means unique, in that the episcopal authority and the feudal authority were united in the person of the bishop. The feudal court of the Bishop of Beauvais, which was attended by the entire nobility ("freemen") subordinate to his feudal lordship, maintained a substantial secular criminal and civil jurisdiction over the town. On the whole, however, these and other feudal prerogatives of the bishop declined in the course of the twelfth and thirteenth centuries, partly because the French crown gave considerable support to the towns in their struggle against feudal control. The bishop's ecclesiastical jurisdiction was another matter: here, the efforts of the communal authorities to reduce the immunities of the clergy from communal jurisdiction were largely unsuccessful—partly because in that contest not only the papacy but also the crown was generally on the side of the church. An ordinance of Philip Augustus in 1210 forbade magistrates of French towns to arrest clerks unless they seized them in the commission of the offense, and even then they were to be turned over to the ecclesiastical court, which alone had power to judge them in most types of cases. Finally, to the royal authority itself the commune had to yield "high justice," that is, jurisdiction over capital offenses, as well as some appellate jurisdiction in cases of "middle" and "low" justice.

Nevertheless, despite these limitations at the hands of the feudal, episcopal, and royal authorities, there remained a substantial autonomous jurisdiction of the commune over its own members and a substantial body of autonomous and distinctive communal law.[13]

Many of the new communes of both northern and southern France, as well as of many other parts of Europe, called themselves "communes for peace" (*communia pro pace*). Among these was Laon, located not far from Beauvais and Cambrai, where Louis·VI in 1128 proclaimed an Institutio Pacis, recognizing the city as an "asylum of peace and safety for all, whether free or unfree."[14] Here, too, the immediate political issue was the conflict between the bishop and the citizens, which was partly a conflict within the church concerning the nature of episcopal authority and the competing royal and papal claims to episcopal allegiance, and partly a conflict between feudal and urban economic and social interests and values. The suppression of an earlier commune had been followed by a long period of disorder. Indeed, in 1112 the bishop had been killed. The Institutio Pacis was an attempted compromise, in the spirit of the recent Concordat of Worms (1122) by which the Investiture Struggle as a whole had finally been compromised. The superior feudal jurisdiction of the Bishop of Laon was recognized, and he continued to appoint local judges (*échevins*); but the mayor and "jurors" (*jurati, jurés*, or oath takers, equivalent to the peers of Beauvais and other communes) also had jurisdiction to enforce the customs of the city and to supply justice when the bishop's justice failed. Serfs who came to the town from outside were to be given freedom, and serfs of local lords were to be relieved of many obligations; *mainmorte* and *formariage* were abolished, and *taille* was reduced to a fixed payment and restricted to certain persons.

In Picardy as elsewhere in Europe, time was on the side of urban self-government. Where episcopal appointees remained, as in Laon, they became municipal magistrates, and by the end of the twelfth century they were generally elected by the jurors. Everywhere a small group of men, nominated by the leading citizens and elected by the whole people, constituted the magistracy.

FRANCE: LORRIS, MONTAUBAN

The very extensive liberties granted by Louis VI to the episcopal cities of Picardy may be contrasted with what Carl Stephenson calls the "elementary liberties" granted by the same monarch to scores of towns situated on the royal demesne centered in the area of Paris and adjacent regions. One such town, Lorris, near Orléans, received from Louis VI a famous grant which served as a model for many similar places. It fixed a maximum rent for house and land, eliminated *taille* and various other taxes, reduced military obligations to one day's service within the immediate vicinity, eliminated *corvées* except that men who owned horses and carts had to carry the king's wine once a year to Orléans, limited fines and punishments, and restricted tolls, customs, and other dues. It provided that any person who lived peaceably in the town for a year and a day was henceforth free and could not be claimed by a previous master. Citizens could sell their possessions and go elsewhere. They could not be tried outside the town, and various rules of procedure were declared for trials within the town. There was to be no obligatory granting of credit, except that the king and queen were to be given two weeks' time to pay for their food.

Stephenson comments: "Lorris was a very small town, with distinctly second-rate liberties. It had no self-government; all political powers were reserved to the king and his ministers. And yet the privileged condition of its inhabitants was clearly marked . . . the man of Lorris . . . was economically and legally free. He was far removed from the arbitrary regime of domainal exploitation. His tenure and status were typically bourgeois . . . The normal holding was not a field but a building plot. The privileges of the residents were essentially such as were everywhere demanded as a minimum by commercial settlers. It was for this reason that the customs of Lorris proved so remarkably popular during the ensuing centuries."[15]

If the liberties of Lorris were more "elementary" than those of Beauvais, it was undoubtedly because Lorris was on the royal demesne while Beauvais was on the lands of one of Louis' vassals. Not only kings but also dukes, counts, and other territorial rulers had strong incentives to encourage settlements in towns on their lands, to which artisans, craftsmen, and merchants would be attracted and from which money rents could be derived. At the same time, however, the territorial ruler was reluctant to give up his political control over the towns. The nature and extent of the liberties that were granted depended on a delicate balance of forces and interests. A good example is the charter of liberties granted in 1144 to Montauban, in southern France, by Count Alphonse of Toulouse. The count had offered, as a site for a new settlement, a section of his own land adjacent to the older town of Montauriol, which had experienced chronic trouble between the townsmen and the head of the abbey alongside whose walls Montauriol was built. Wishing to draw people from Montauriol, the count not only granted liberties similar to those previously given by Louis VI to Lorris, but in addition agreed to consult on various matters with "townsmen of the better sort." Probably it was with the help of such townsmen that the new town was organized and financed. By the end of the century Montauban was being administered by its own elected officials.[16]

NORMANDY: VERNEUIL

In the eleventh and twelfth centuries the towns of Normandy were not very different from French towns with respect to their liberties, government, and laws. The classic example of a Norman city charter is that granted to Verneuil by Henry I, Duke of Normandy and King of England from 1100 to 1135. The charter provided that each citizen (bourgeois) was to receive three acres of land and garden, for which he was to pay twelve *deniers* annually, no matter how many houses he put up. He was also to pay an initial fee of seven deniers to become a citizen, plus an annual sum of four deniers toward upkeep of the watch. These were small amounts. He owed no military duty unless the king personally commanded the army. He could not be ordered on royal business except for the king's own service. He could not be required to extend credit even for the benefit of the king himself. He was to be free of all customs duties on imports for three years, and from certain customs duties, such as on food and clothing to satisfy personal needs, permanently. The king could tax sales in the local market, including sales of livestock, wine, salt, grain, fish, leather, and cloth. Milling, baking, brewing, and wine-making were to be open to citizens on payment of specified sums. Justice was to remain in the hands of the *prévot*, but trials were to be held in the town except when pleas were taken to the king in person. In Stephenson's words, "Elaborate articles limit[ed] the fines and punishments that [could] be inflicted in certain cases, prescribe[d] methods for the collection of debts, restrict[ed] appeals to combat, and [made] provision for the dozen other judicial matters considered important by an urban population."[17]

In the course of time, the liberties of Verneuil were extended to various other Norman cities.

FLANDERS: SAINT-OMER, BRUGES, GHENT

By the mid-twelfth century Flanders had become the foremost industrial region of Europe, primarily by virtue of its textile industry, and Bruges and Ghent were the most flourishing commercial cities north of Genoa and Milan. Although the Count of Flanders was a vassal of the King of France, he ruled Flanders quite independently of the king throughout the eleventh, twelfth, and thirteenth centuries. At the same time, the cities of Flanders, although politically subordinate to a strong ruler, achieved considerable independence — more, in fact, than their French counterparts. Some of the Flemish cities started as revolutionary communes, but most of them appear to have achieved communal status peacefully with the encouragement of the count, who granted charters liberally but was careful to preserve in them certain rights of his own.

The charter of Saint-Omer, granted by Count William Clito in 1127, served as a model for later charters given to other Flemish cities. It stated that William, on the petition of the citizens (burghers), confirmed the laws and customs of Saint-Omer and the independence of the commune which they had sworn. All citizens were guaranteed peace and justice according to the right judgment of their échevins, who "shall enjoy whatever liberty is best enjoyed by échevins throughout the land of Flanders." The échevins were to judge disputes arising in the town

proper (the "forum"); however, the count's prévôt and the clergy also retained jurisdiction over certain types of disputes.[18] The charter confirmed the citizens' ancient pasture rights and their ancient exemption
from military service, except for service to defend the county of Flanders. They were also to be free of various feudal taxes and services:
chevage, avouéries, unjust exactions by the castle garrison, scot, and
taille.[19] In addition, the charter recognized the merchant guild of the
town. Members of the guild were declared to be exempted from various
tolls, and the count promised to secure for them, if he could, similar
liberties in Normandy, England, and Boulogne. Finally, Count William
gave the townsmen, for the benefit of their merchant guild, his mint of
Saint-Omer, worth annually thirty livres. This meant that Saint-Omer
was to make its own coins; it would derive profit from minting, and taxes
to be paid to the count would not have to be paid with coins acquired
elsewhere.[20]

The charter of Saint-Omer did not purport to give the citizens formal
independence from the territorial ruler. The count retained jurisdiction
over the town, and échevins were to be named by him from among the
citizens and to act as his judges. In fact, however, the échevins were at
first appointed for life, which gave them a certain independence, and
later, when they came to be selected annually, they were chosen by the
citizens according to a system of election.

Bruges and Ghent, like Saint-Omer, each had a sworn commune, a
board of échevins, and a merchant guild.[21] They were, of course, much
larger than Saint-Omer, being among the fifteen or twenty leading cities
of Europe. Count Philip (1169–1191) granted charters, called "keure," to
Bruges and other Flemish cities, establishing the legal basis for limited
self-government and for the rights and liberties of their citizens.

GERMANY: COLOGNE, FREIBURG, LUBECK, MAGDEBURG

The flourishing Roman city of Cologne (Colonia) on the lower Rhine
declined precipitously after its conquest by the Franks in the fifth century. Some commercial and industrial activity remained, and the presence of a bishopric and a cathedral provided an element of continuity.
But Cologne ceased to be a city in the Roman sense, and it was not yet a
city in the modern European sense. The river harbor was allowed to become a marsh; the production of glassware was transferred to the countryside; the size of the population declined to that of a large village; the
government, which was chiefly in the hands of the archbishop, was integrated into that of the surrounding region, Lothringen (Lorraine).[22]

In 953 Emperor Otto III appointed his younger brother Bruno to be
Duke of Lothringen and Archbishop of Cologne. Bruno enclosed the
merchants' suburban *wik* within the city's fortifications. He and his successors in the late tenth and early eleventh centuries established markets,

tolls, and a mint. By 1074 the merchants and artisans were sufficiently strong and united to rise up against the archbishop, who nevertheless was able to mobilize troops from outside to suppress the revolt. In 1106, however, another uprising confirmed the establishment of an independent municipal government and a system of urban law, which, indeed, was referred to frequently in the twelfth century as *jus coloniensis* ("Cologne law") and occasionally as *jus civilis* ("law of the city").

The Archbishop of Cologne remained an important figure in the life of the city, and he continued to be the ruler of the entire Duchy of Lothringen and usually also of Westphalia. Nevertheless, his political and governmental role within the city was greatly reduced in the twelfth century, when it was supplemented and to a certain extent replaced by a system of government by elected officials acting within various patrician bodies.

Cologne was unique in being organized into self-governing, secular parish communities (*Sondergemeinden*), sometimes called communes, twelve in number, each of which normally had two magistrates elected (probably annually) by the members of the parish community. Past, present, and candidate magistrates formed a fraternity or guild (*Amtleutegenossenschaft,* "fellowship of officials"), which played an important part in urban affairs. One could become a member of the parish community by acquiring heritable property in the parish, registering it, and paying a fee. Members were obliged to help and defend a fellow member against anyone who might make a charge against him. Claims and defenses concerning property within the parish were to be made in the civil court of the parish, with right of appeal to the full assembly of the guild of parish magistrates. Minor crimes and offenses against the parish community were to be tried in the criminal court of the parish, with accusations brought by a committee of the guild of parish magistrates selected to investigate allegations of crimes or offenses. If a parish member refused to respond to accusations made against him in the parish court, he was to be expelled from the community. Anyone who attempted to break the regulations of the community was to suffer eternal punishment in the company of the devil and his angels.

Among the most important functions of the parish was the registration of land transfers and mortgages. An early entry in one of the parish registers describes the procedure whereby Heinrich Longus purchased a house from a certain Gottfried. The act of purchase and sale was performed "before the citizens and the parish magistrates and before the judges and rectors." Then Heinrich paid the citizens and judges the customary fees for witnessing the transaction and for its registration. Anyone who doubted the fact of the registration was specifically instructed to consult the register (*Schrein*) of the judges, where he would discover the truth. Finally, Heinrich appeared at the city hall and transferred to Gottfried's son and heir three marks in the presence of the city assessors (*scabini, Schoeffen*), thus securing himself and his heirs against any claims by the heirs of the seller.

The city assessors' tasks, however, included much more than witnessing transactions and keeping registers of them. Chiefly, the assessors sat as lay judges, either in the high court (*Hochgericht*) as a body, together with a presiding professional judge, or else, in minor cases, individually. In the high court they heard cases in first instance as well as civil and criminal appeals from the parish magistrates' courts. They declared the law and gave judgment, which the professional judge executed. Literally, they "found" the judgment; they were said to represent the accumulated knowledge of the customary law. When one assessor sat alone on a case, he submitted the decision to the other assessors for their consent.

There were approximately twenty-five assessors actively serving at any one time. However, past assessors and candidate assessors were also included among the "brothers" (*fratres scabinorum*), who, like the parish magistrates, constituted a guild. Although they swore an oath of loyalty to the archibishop, they were also bound by oath to declare the law and find judgment impartially and truly. The reports of their cases include decisions against the interests of the archbishop as well as decisions against the interests of the merchants of Cologne. Thus in a number of twelfth-century cases in which the archbishop, acting through his chamberlain, claimed that various members of various parish communities were members of the archbishop's household (*familia*) and hence subject to certain taxes collected by the chamberlain, the assessors decided against the chamberlain. And in 1103, according to the earliest surviving document mentioning the assessors, in a case brought by the merchants of Liège and Huy against the merchants of Cologne to enforce privileges granted by the former Archbishop of Cologne, the assessors decided in favor of the foreign merchants.

In addition to their judicial functions the assessors exercised many of the powers of a city council, and in that context they were often called not only assessors (*scabini*) but also elders (*senatores*). Records of Cologne in the twelfth century show the scabini or senatores planning and approving the expansion of the city walls, making gifts of city land for charitable purposes, administering town property (such as the meat- and fish-sellers' stands, which belonged to the town rather than to a guild), and even on three occasions making treaties with other cities granting various rights to their merchants — without the confirmation of the archbishop.

In addition to the parish magistrates and the scabini or senatores, a third guild ruled Cologne, the *Richerzeche*, which literally meant "tavern of the rich." Two members of the Richerzeche were annually elected to be *Bürgermeister* ("mayors"), one of whom had to be a scabinus; and the

Richerzeche itself consisted of past, present, and candidate mayors. Its principal task was to regulate craft guilds and markets as well as terms of trade (including the prices) of agricultural products, wine, and beer. The Richerzeche (or Bürgermeister) held a court at the three main marketplaces in order to police the observance of its ordinances. The Richerzeche also heard appeals from decisions of the civil courts of the parish magistrates.

The municipal government of Cologne was thoroughly patrician in the twelfth century. The only check on patrician authority came from the archbishop, who appointed two chief officials: one, called the *Burggraf* ("city count"), presided over the assessors in judicial proceedings of the high court and was, in addition, the military head of the city and had authority over public streets and places; the other, called the *Stadtvogt* ("town prefect"), presided over certain general sessions of the high court. In fact, the authority of these two officials, and of the archbishop himself, became subordinate to that of the guilds of assessors, mayors, and parish magistrates. The archbishop's authority gradually revived in the course of the thirteenth century, but by then the law of Cologne had acquired a character of its own that in some respects, though not all, transcended the structure of political power.

Scholars have debated the origin of municipal government in Cologne: whether its primary source was a peace movement, a revolutionary commune, a territorial community, or the merchant guild. It could have been any one of these, or a combination of them, without affecting the larger question of the relation of Cologne municipal government and municipal law to the great transformation of Europe that occurred at the very time when Cologne was establishing its political and legal identity. The separation of the city from the archdiocese and the duchy that surrounded it, the establishment of its own secular urban institutions, and above all, the establishment of its own political and legal history—that is, historical consciousness, or sense of organic development and growth—were made possible by the fact that the church itself had declared the dualism of ecclesiastical and secular authorities and had supported the pluralism of secular authorities, and, further, by the fact that the idea of the gradual reformation of the world through law had become a leading concept and a governing motive in both the ecclesiastical and the secular spheres. These revolutionary changes in people's minds and hearts were an essential part of the revolutionary changes in political, economic, and social life that took place throughout Europe in the late eleventh and the twelfth centuries. The founding of self-governing cities and of a new type of law, urban law, was an important expression of these changes—in Cologne as elsewhere.

Cologne was an exception to the usual method of forming towns in the

German duchies—the issuance of charters by emperors and princes. Sometimes such charters were given by the emperor to appease rebellious townsmen; thus the people of Worms formed a *conjuratio* against their bishop in 1073 and were granted liberties by Emperor Henry IV. Mainz followed suit in 1077. Other charters were granted by princes. One of the earliest examples of such a charter was that issued to Freiburg in 1120 by Duke Conrad of Zähringen, who established a so-called forum (town) on wasteland adjoining one of his castles. The forum consisted originally of merchants invited from neighboring regions. The very name Freiburg ("free town") revealed its character. The freedom of its inhabitants lay in their exemption from the ordinary law of the countryside and their subjection to the special law of trading communities. The charter provided that each citizen (*burger*) was to have a plot of land fifty by one hundred feet, for which he was to pay only one shilling in annual rent; the duke was to guarantee peace and protection to all settlers; they were to hold their lands by hereditary right, with the privilege of free sale and devise; they were to be exempt from all forced entertainment, all tolls throughout the duchy, and all taille or aid except for a lawful military expedition; they were to share free use of pasture, forest, and river; they were to be subject only to the law of merchants, particularly the law enjoyed by the merchants of Cologne; and the duke was not to appoint any chief magistrate or priest who had not been elected by the merchants. The merchants and the ducal officials swore to preserve and defend this settlement, and the duke pledged himself to the same engagement by means of a solemn handclasp. Soon a group of elected *conjuratores fori* ("selectmen") were associated with the chief magistrate in the government; in the thirteenth century they began to be called consuls.[23]

The example of Freiburg, like that of Saint-Omer, tends to support the thesis of Pirenne, which is shared by Stephenson, that merchants played the leading role in the formation of cities. However, even in those cities, and in others that were similarly formed, the merchants were soon required to share their power with other classes or elites—with craft guilds, with nobility (including bishops), and often with princes, kings, and emperors.

Lübeck, a Baltic port, was founded in 1143 by Count Adolf II of Holstein, who invited residents of Westphalia, Flanders, and Frisia to settle there. In 1158 the town was taken over by Henry the Lion, the Welf Duke of Saxony, who established a mint and tolls and gave the townspeople special privileges, including a form of government borrowed from the town of Soest. (Henry also founded Munich and Braunschweig.) In 1181 Emperor Frederick Barbarossa seized Lübeck and later gave it a charter of liberties, including certain rights of self-government and exemption of merchants from all tolls throughout the Duchy of Saxony. By the mid-fourteenth century Lübeck had become the wealthiest city in the north.[24]

Perhaps the most dramatic illustration of the birth and growth of a system of urban law within the Western legal tradition is the process by which the laws of more than a dozen major German cities were formally received in the hundreds of new cities that were founded between the twelfth and fourteenth centuries. For example, the laws of Lübeck were received in forty-three cities, those of Frankfurt in forty-nine, of Hamburg in four, of Freiburg in nineteen, of Munich in thirteen, of Bremen in two, of Braunschweig in three. Most important, however, was the dissemination of the laws of Magdeburg, a city on the river Elbe, to over eighty new cities.[25] The Magdeburger Recht became the predominant basis of written law for central and eastern Europe.

It was not, however, the original Magdeburger Recht, or Lübecker Recht, or Frankfurter Recht that each new city within the particular "legal circle" (*Rechtskreis*) received, but rather the laws of the "mother city" as they existed at the time of the reception. Typically, the lord of the new "daughter city" would grant it, say, the Magdeburger Recht, and then the city authorities would send to Magdeburg, whose leading judicial officers, the assessors or Schoeffen, would prepare a new edition of the then prevailing Magdeburg laws, or of those parts of them that were requested—dealing, for example, with the city government, the administration of justice, the guilds, and civil and criminal law. Some cities sent several times for updated laws. Also, the courts of the daughter city would frequently submit individual cases to the assessors of the mother city, and would receive declarations of the rules applicable to the particular fact situations. Thus one can see reflected in the laws and decisions of the younger cities the organic growth of the original Magdeburger Recht or Lübecker Recht or other "mother law" (*Mutterrecht*).[26]

Magdeburg had for centuries been a center for trade with the Slavs. In 968 it became an archbishopric. Later it served as an important military base for attacks upon the Slavs. It was not until the early 1100s, however, that Magdeburg developed its own continuous governmental and legal institutions and its own civic consciousness. In 1129 there was an armed uprising of the citizenry against the archbishop, which he successfully suppressed; in that year also the phrase *maiores civitates* ("leading citizens") first appeared in a Magdeburg document. In the 1160s references appeared to the "assessors and judges of the city of Magdeburg." Also in this period the guilds played an important role; in 1183 their status was confirmed. In the same year reference to the assessors' court first appeared. Finally in 1188 Archbishop Wichmann reformed the city's government, retaining the hereditary ruler (Burggraf) and hereditary deputy ruler (*Schultheiss*), but establishing in addition a twelve-man council consisting of eleven life-tenured assessors and the Schultheiss. The archbishop, who ruled the entire archdiocese, retained ultimate control over the city, although it kept its autonomy in the administration of justice, taxation, and related matters. The "bench" of assessors (*Schoeffenbank*) filled vacancies in its own number by appointments from among the leading families.

In connection with his reform of 1188, Archbishop Wichmann promulgated the first recorded legislation of Magdeburg, a document consisting of nine articles. These did not purport to be the whole Magdeburg law; they seem to have been, rather, a resolution of some major disputed questions, based perhaps on prior judicial decisions. For example, traditional procedural technicalities were eliminated from oath-taking in certain types of cases. The liability of a father for the wounding or killing of a person by his son was eliminated, provided the father could prove by the testimony of six worthy men that he had not been present or, if present, had not participated in the crime. The same rule was extended to persons other than the father. One provision dealt with the time within which a claim must be made in case of spoliation, wounding, or killing within or outside the city. Another article allowed persons absent on pilgrimage or pressing business to delay bringing an action in the court of the Burggraf or the Schultheiss. Article 7 provided that in a suit between a citizen and a stranger, justice should be done without delay and the case decided on the same day that it was moved. Article 8 gave general jurisdiction over all kinds of cases, both of citizens and strangers, to the court of assessors, with the proviso that if the assessors were absent, justice was to be done by the Burggraf or Schultheiss. Finally, article 9 provided, "in order that city law may not suffer harm," that anyone who disrupted the assembly of citizens by shouting or inordinate or foolish speech should be "punished severely by the citizens, so that no other will dare to do such."[27]

These nine articles of 1188 were, as far as is known, the first written collection of rules of the Magdeburg law; they presupposed the existence of a large body of unwritten rules. Indeed, Magdeburg customary law had already been formally adopted by some other cities and towns in the middle 1100s. The growth of Magdeburg law in the subsequent century and a half can be traced by examining the sets of rules sent by the Magdeburg assessors to Breslau in 1261 and to Görlitz in 1304.

The Breslau law contained 64 articles and the Görlitz law 140 articles. In the Görlitz law, certain fields, such as the sale of goods, ownership, and inheritance, were treated in far greater detail than in the Breslau law. The provisions on criminal law and evidence were also much more detailed. Moreover, the Magdeburg Schoeffen had not simply sent the 64 Breslau articles to Görlitz in their original form, with other articles appended or inserted; rather, they had consciously rationalized and changed the earlier collection. Separate articles of the earlier law had sometimes been combined into a more comprehensive article. Some articles that were out of place had been rearranged. Still other articles had been expanded. Thus Article 8 of the Görlitz law begins by repeating Article 11 of the Breslau law, which dealt with the punishment applicable to a person caught after the victim of a wounding had raised the hue and cry; but then Article 8 goes on to state that more drastic measures may be taken if the injury was by a knife and the culprit was caught in the act.[28] This is an example of the enlargement of the original article in the light of experience.

Most of the 140 articles of the Görlitz law of 1304 were taken either from the Breslau law (as supplemented) or from the *Sachsenspiegel*, a body of legal rules drawn up about 1221 by a Saxon jurist, which came to form an important part of what might be called in a loose sense the common law of Germany. (Ten of the original 64 Breslau articles were also drawn from the *Sachsenspiegel*.) Twenty-five of the Görlitz articles were wholly new: six of these were interspersed throughout the law and nineteen were added at the end.

The 64 articles of the original Breslau laws of 1261 were themselves supplemented by an additional 24 articles received from Magdeburg in 1283 and by another 23 articles received in 1295. These supplementary provisions seem to have been, for the most part, clarifications of earlier provisions.

Thus the law that spread from Madgeburg to Breslau and Görlitz, as well as to more than eighty other cities of Brandenburg, Silesia, Bohemia, Poland, and other parts of central and eastern Europe, underwent a conscious evolution, an organic development or growth. Its chief formal source was the "sayings" (*Sprüche*) of the Magdeburg assessors (Schoeffen) that is, their rulings in cases brought to them for decision; these *Schoeffensprüche*, however, were not isolated ad hoc decisions but an integral part of a body of customary law, which were remembered, written down, and later collected and transmitted as codices.

The conscious growth of the law was closely connected with its systematic, or unified, character. The Breslau law was finally edited in the mid-fourteenth century as a systematic body of law in five books, containing a table of 465 articles.[29] The first book dealt principally with the election and installation of city councillors, the rights and duties of councillors, and the publicity and validity of their acts. The second book dealt with the judicial organization and procedure, including that of the assessors and other judges, the selection of assessors and other judges, their remuneration, the time and place of their sessions, the jurisdiction of the various courts (especially in criminal matters and inheritance), requirements concerning court fees, distraint, settlements, arbitration, duels, representation in court by another, and many other procedural matters. The third book dealt with types of complaints: woundings and homicides, which were remediable by civil action; other violations of rights, including embezzlement, perjury, usury, fraud, counterfeiting; debts, including the liability of heirs for the debts of the decedent; payments for services; and various other types of actions. Various kinds of proof required to support various kinds of actions were specified. Money obligations were also provided for, including pledge, mortgage, and sworn debts; and the remedies included levying against property, arrest of a debtor who had fled, and ultimately, outlawry. The fourth book contained family laws, including a substantial portion of the law relating to rights of family members in the hereditary property of the family (*Erbgut*). The first part of the fourth book dealt with dowry, with marriage and inheritance contracts, and with the rights of the head of the household, the wife, and the children to dispose of various kinds of family property. The second part dealt with inheritance law and with guardianship. The fifth book, containing 23 articles, seems to have been an unfinished collection of important miscellaneous rules of law and decisions that did not fit under the rubrics of the first four books.

The "systematic assessors' law of Breslau-Magdeburg" (as this body of law of the mid-fourteenth century came to be called) was not only much more detailed but also much more comprehensive — much more systematic — than the Görlitz law of 1304, which, in turn, had been more detailed, more comprehensive, and more systematic than the first Breslau law of 1261. All three were derived from the continually developing system of law within Magdeburg itself. Incidentally, the Breslau and Görlitz versions of Magdeburg law, like daughter laws of other mother cities, were themselves transmitted to other new cities and towns, which thus became "granddaughter" cities of Magdeburg. Indeed, Breslau law became the mother law of the entire kingdom of Bohemia.

The Magdeburg law made a fundamental distinction between law in the large sense, Recht, which was understood as the general framework of law ("right"), and law in the more specific sense of an enacted rule or particular usage, which was called *Willekor* (from the German words for "will" and "choose"). Recht contained the general principles or rights that are given by the nature of social life itself and ultimately by divine providence; it was a mixture of customary law and natural law. Willekor was either an enactment or decree of the civil authorities or a local usage accepted by them; sometimes it was called *buyrkor* ("civil law"), which meant literally either "the choice of the city" or "the choice of the citizens." Both the Breslau law of 1261 and that of a century later started with the same provision: "according to *Willekor*" the Magdeburg Recht was to apply in Breslau. In another section of the later law — a section not contained in the earlier law—the possibility of a conflict between Recht and buyrkor was recognized. This section provided that the city council (*Rat*) had power to decide questions raised by any person to whom the councillors gave the right to speak in the city assembly, and this provision, it was stated, the (Magdeburg) assessors "proclaim as a civil law (*buyrkor*) and not as [a matter of] right (*Recht*)."

Yet it was the Recht that gave the councillors many of their powers to make positive law. For example, to the Recht were attributed the powers of the councillors to regulate weights and measures, to regulate the sale of food and other goods, to set prices, and to establish the penalties applicable to those who violated their regulations. The modern German word for a specific statute, *Gesetz*, did not appear in the Magdeburg law, but the verb *gesetzt* was used to refer to the activity of the city authorities in "setting" regulations. For example, the city council was given power to punish the selling of goods at prices higher than those set (gesetzt) according to the decree (Willekor) of the city authorities.

Of importance also was the emphasis of the Magdeburg law, as reflected in its Breslau versions, on property law and commercial law. It was provided that a person could pledge his retail shop, his butcher shop, or other business premises as security for a debt. One who held such a place of business was "deemed to be a holder of heritable property or a propertied man." He could sell it or devise it by will. In addition, merchants (as well as pilgrims) could not be sued when they were away from the town. Of particular interest were the provisions concerning the heir's liability for the debts of the decedent: these were said to be contrary to the law stated by Gratian. Thus Magdeburg urban law differed both from feudal law and from canon law.

ENGLAND: LONDON, IPSWICH

In Anglo-Saxon England, as elsewhere in western Europe, the emergence of the modern city was a phenomenon of the late eleventh and early twelfth centuries. Prior to that time the Anglo-Saxon town (borough), as Stephenson states, "was not a community of privileged citizens. Its inhabitants enjoyed no uniform burgess franchise; they held their properties by no systems of burgage tenure; they had no self-government. The typical borough of 1066 was essentially what it had been a century earlier—a military and official centre. The men who lived inside the walls [were] principally members of the agrarian aristocracy [and] their dependents. Except for the fact that the borough might be administrative headquarters for a larger district, its judicial organization was that of a rural hundred."[30]

In the last third of the eleventh century, however—after the Norman conquest—English towns grew substantially in population, and their character began to change. As in other parts of Europe, the commercial quarters (the markets) often swallowed up the adjacent fortified places. The expanding agricultural population migrated in substantial numbers to the boroughs. That remarkable survey of the English economy called Domesday Book, compiled in 1086, describes 46 boroughs: of these only York had as many as 10,000 inhabitants (unaccountably, London and Winchester are not described), Norwich and Lincoln had over 5,000, and Oxford, Thetford, and Ipswich about 4,000; 21 other boroughs had a population of from 1,000 to 3,000; and the remaining 16 had fewer than 1,000 people, including some boroughs that had hundreds or only scores of inhabitants. In the early 1100s the number and size of the boroughs increased dramatically, and by the end of the twelfth century several hundred of them had substantial populations.[31] Still more important, almost all of them had charters of liberties, a distinctive form of government, and their own legal systems. In Stephenson's words, "From the time of Henry I [1100–1135] the borough . . . appears as a town . . . Burgage was more than a tenure [that is, more than the right to alienate or devise town land]. It was a civil and legal status, a mode of life dependent on membership in a community."[32] During the twelfth century, the military and fiscal boroughs of Anglo-Saxon times — essentially royal fortifications, largely undifferentiated politically from the countryside — became "free" associations with their own law, their own government, their own common consciousness.

The history of London illustrates this development. Although Roman legions had occupied the town from the first to the fifth centuries A.D., little that was Roman survived the Anglo-Saxon invasions except for the remains of roads and buildings and the great stone wall. With the introduction of Christianity in the seventh century, a bishop was installed in London (officially entitling it to be called a "city"). The Venerable Bede, who died in 735, described London as a meeting place of many people coming by land and sea. It was mentioned next in Anglo-Saxon sources over a century later, in connection with King Alfred's wars against the Danes. Archaeological remains indicate that it was a substantial city in the tenth and eleventh centuries, after Venice the largest in Europe, with over 10,000 inhabitants. At the time of the Norman Conquest more than twenty moneyers were minting simultaneously. Folkmoots, which all citizens were expected to attend, met three times a year. Dealings took place between English and foreign traders. Nevertheless, London had no charter and few "liberties" in the twelfth-century sense. Like other Anglo-Saxon cities and towns, it was a military and official center, with substantial trade, but not a self-governing "community of privileged citizens."

Almost immediately after the Conquest, William granted London a charter, and in the next two generations the rights of London citizens and of London as a city expanded dramatically. In the early twelfth century, the two ruling "reeves" (sheriffs), previously appointed by the king, were elected from among the citizens, and this right of election was granted in perpetuity by a charter issued by Henry I in 1129. At that time London was referred to as a "commune," and it was headed by a mayor. The king agreed to lower the annual tax to be paid by the city (called the "ferm" or "farm") from five hundred to three hundred pounds. The city exercised its jurisdiction through a folkmoot of the entire citizenry meeting three times a year and through a smaller court called a husting. The twenty-four aldermen who managed the city's affairs took an oath to exercise their duties "by the law of the lord king which belongs to them in the city of London, saving the liberty of the city." Citizens had the right to sell their land on account of poverty, in defiance of heirs. Imprisonment as a form of attachment for claims of debt was available only when suitable pledges could not be found. Foreign merchants' rights were to be protected. Each alderman was charged with the duty of assuring that everyone in his ward had weapons and a horse for purposes of defense. The wages of carpenters, masons, tilers, plasterers, and ditchers were fixed. Thatched and reed roofs were forbidden, fire watches were established, and every house was required to maintain a tub of water in front of it for emergency use.[33]

The charter of London issued by Henry I (1129) provided "that the citizens . . . shall appoint from among themselves as justice whomsoever they choose to look after the pleas of my crown and the pleadings which arise in connection with them. No other shall be [royal] justice over the same men of London. And the citizens shall not plead outside the walls of the city in respect of any plea; and they shall be quit of scot and of Danegeld and the murder-fine. Nor shall any of them be compelled to offer trial by battle." It provided further that "no one be billeted within the walls of the city, either of my household, or by the force of anyone else. And let all the men of London and their property be quit and free from toll and passage and lastage and from all other customs throughout all England and at the seaports."[34] These liberties and privileges of the citizens of London were expanded by the charters of Henry II.

The charter of London served as a model for Norwich, Lincoln, Northampton, and other cities. Similarly, the charter that was granted to York by Henry II served as a model for Wallingford, Andover, Salisbury, Wilton, and Portsmouth; and some of the charters granted to these towns served, in turn, as models for the later chartered towns.[35]

The town of Ipswich (about seventy miles northeast of London), which in 1086 had about 4,000 inhabitants, is of special interest because its original charter has survived, as well as a document describing in detail the procedure by which its municipal government was first organized.

The charter was issued on May 25, 1200, by King John, granting to the citizens (burgesses) of Ipswich exemption from toll, stallage (payments for stalls in markets and fairs), lastage (payments at markets and fairs for buying and selling by measure), passage (payments by out-of-town merchants at markets and fairs), pontage (tolls for maintenance of bridges), "and all other customs throughout our whole land and in seaports." The citizens were also to be exempt from all lawsuits outside of Ipswich except those involving foreign tenures and those concerning royal officers. In addition, the town was granted the right to have a merchant guild and a guild hall (hansa). No one was to be billeted, or to take anything by force, within the town. In all cases involving lands or tenures within the town, "justice shall be done them according to the ancient custom of the borough of Ipswich and of our free boroughs," and all cases concerning debts incurred or pledges made in Ipswich were to be tried in Ipswich. No citizen was to be adjudged to pay a fine except "according to the law of our free boroughs." The charter further provided that the burgesses "by common counsel of the town shall elect two of the more lawful and discreet men of the town and shall present them to our chief justice at our Exchequer and they shall keep the office of provost of the aforesaid borough of Ipswich well and faithfully; and they shall not be removed so long as they conduct themselves well in that office [*quamdiu se in baillia illa bene gesserint*] except by the common counsel of the aforesaid burgesses." In addition, four "more lawful and more discreet" men were to be elected "by the common counsel of the aforesaid burgesses" to keep the pleas of the Crown and other matters affecting the crown "and to see that the borough reeves justly and lawfully treat the poor as well as the rich."[36]

A little over a month after the charter was granted, on Thursday, June 29, 1200, the whole community of the town assembled in the churchyard of St. Mary at the Tower.[37] They proceeded to elect, with one voice, two bailiffs, who were sworn to keep the office of provost, and four coroners, who were sworn to keep the pleas of the crown and to handle other matters affecting the crown in the town "and to see to it that the aforesaid bailiffs justly and lawfully treat the poor as well as the rich." On the same day it was ordered "by the common counsel of the town" that there should also be twelve sworn capital portmen (*capitales portmenni,* literally, "chief townsmen"), "just as there are in other free boroughs England," with "full power to govern and uphold the said borough and all its liberties, and to render the judgments of the town, and to ordain and do in the said borough all things necessary for the status and honor of the town." The following Sunday was appointed for the election of the twelve.

On Sunday, July 2, the bailiffs and the coroners, with the assent of the community, appointed four men of each parish of the borough, and they elected the twelve capital portmen. (Understandably, the two bailiffs and four coroners were among those elected.) After they were sworn faithfully to govern the borough and maintain its liberties, and justly to render the judgments of its courts, "without respect to any person," all the townsmen stretched forth their hands toward the "Book" (the Gospels) and with one voice solemnly swore to obey and assist, with their bodies and their goods, the bailiffs, coroners, and every one of the twelve capital portmen in safeguarding the borough, its new charter, its liberties and customs, in all places against all persons, the royal power excepted, "according to their ability, so far as they ought justly and rationally to do." On the same day the new charter was placed in charge of two tried and lawful men, who were sworn faithfully to preserve it and to produce it at the request of the community.

On Thursday, July 13, the bailiffs, coroners, and other capital portmen assembled and ordained that, in future, the customs of the town should be collected by the bailiffs and four tried and lawful men of the borough; that the right and customary farm should be paid annually at the king's exchequer; that there should be two beadles to make attachments and to execute the commands of the bailiffs, coroners, and capital portmen; that one of the beadles should be keeper of prisoners arrested by order of the bailiffs; that a common seal should be made for use in important matters touching the community of the borough, and that it should be placed in the charge of three or four tried and lawful men of the borough.

It was also ordained that the new charter be sent to the full county courts of Suffolk and Norfolk, to be openly read, so that the liberties contained therein would be publicly known and proclaimed in the individual localities of each county.

On Sunday, September 10, the whole community assembled once more to hear all the new ordinances, that is, the ones that had been made on July 13. After hearing them publicly read, the whole community consented to them with one voice. They then elected two bailiffs for the next year and four men to help them collect the customs of the town, as well as two beadles.

On Thursday, October 12, another full assembly was called. The common seal was shown and three men were elected to keep it. They were also to have custody of the charter.

On the same day five of the capital portmen were elected to govern the merchant guild—one alderman and four associates. They swore that they would govern the guild well and faithfully, and all the articles relating to it, and that they would treat all guild brothers well and lawfully. "Afterwards the alderman and his four colleagues, in the presence of the people of the town, stated that all who are of the freedom of the town shall come before the alderman and his colleagues on a certain day, when and where to be hereafter made known to them, to constitute a gild and to give their initiation fee (*hansa*) to the gild." The report continues as follows:

"On the same day the aforesaid bailiffs, coroners, and other portmen and the whole community discussed by what means and in what way they could better maintain the aforesaid merchant gild and all that pertains to it. The bailiffs, coroners, and other portmen and the whole community with one voice consented and ordered that the alderman who had just been elected and all aldermen to be elected thereafter ought to have and to exercise for the profit of the gild the purchase and sale of all the following merchandise, namely . . . [various kind of stones] and mortars and pavingstones of marble. And that from year to year the alderman ought on his oath to give a right and just account before the bailiffs and coroners of the aforesaid town concerning all profit and increment which he gained in the previous year and which he acquired by reason of the purchase and sale of all the abovementioned merchandise. And beyond that, by unanimous assent and consent they consented that no inhabitants of the aforesaid town nor any other person, native or foreign, within the aforesaid town or within its liberties and precincts, shall have or ought to exercise the purchase or sale of the aforesaid merchandise except only the alderman of the aforesaid gild for the use and profit of that gild. And this under penalty of forefeiture of all the said merchandise thus bought or sold."

On the same day "the whole community" granted to the twelve capital portmen the meadow of Odenholm for the keeping and feeding of their horses, in return for the labor which they were to do for the community. And it was further ordered and agreed to by the whole community that the laws and free customs of the town be placed in a certain roll, to be called "the Domesday," which was to remain in the custody of the bailiffs "so that they will be able to know and to recognize how they ought to act in their office." Also all the statutes of the merchant guild were to be entered in another roll, "as is done elsewhere in cities and boroughs where there is a merchant gild," and this roll the alderman should always have near him, "so that he will know how to operate in his office."[38]

In general, English cities and towns did not achieve the same degree of independence from royal or princely control that was achieved by cities and towns in many other parts of Europe. Formal grants of self-government to the English boroughs were infrequent. Some charters granted citizens the right to elect borough officials: thus London in 1131 was granted the right to elect its sheriffs and a justiciar, and a century later it received the right to elect a mayor; Northampton in 1189 gained the right to elect reeves and later coroners; and other cities gradually gained similar rights. Nevertheless, the crown kept ultimate control over urban political life, including urban justice and urban finance.

Yet despite ultimate control by the crown, the everyday rights, privileges, liberties, and immunities of the English burgesses in the late eleventh, the twelfth, and the early thirteenth centuries did not differ essentially from those of burghers in other parts of Europe. The burgess was a freeman; a serf who migrated to the borough acquired that freedom in England, as in Europe generally, by residence of a year and a day. Citizenship in the town carried the right to bear arms, exemption from feudal and manorial dues and services, free hereditary tenure of land with the right to buy and sell it, the right to trial in the borough court with freedom from trial by ordeal or by battle, and restrictions upon the power of the crown to tax and to fine.[39] Moreover, although the crown would not relinquish its formal power to govern the borough, it did recognize the rights of merchant and artisan guilds to govern the professional lives of their members; and in fact borough officials in England, as in Europe generally, viewed public works, made arrests, issued proclamations, arrayed troops, imposed local taxes, and themselves collected the annual tax owed to the crown.

The Italian Cities

Nowhere, in the century between 1050 and 1150, did cities flourish so abundantly as in Italy. Hundreds of Italian urban centers were formed in that period as independent, self-governing communities. They were often called communes (*communia*), often corporations (*universitates*), and often other names, such as "communities" (*communitates*). This movement was further accelerated in the following century, especially after the Peace of Constance (1183), which has been called "the Magna Carta of communal liberties."

Prior to the eleventh century, however, one cannot speak of the Italian cities—with the possible exception of Rome—in terms of their own organic development. As cities of the Roman empire they had been branches of imperial power, whose fate was wholly determined by that of the empire. Milan provides a good example.[40] In the third and fourth centuries A.D. it was the main administrative center of the Western Empire. Thus it was in Milan that Constantine in 313 proclaimed Christianity to be the imperial religion. Yet Milan hardly had a history of its own—except possibly an ecclesiastical history during the century after St. Ambrose, the Bishop of Milan from 374 to 397, had made that bishopric a stronghold of the fight against Arianism.

In the latter half of the fifth century, Milan and the rest of northern Italy were overrun first by the Huns under Attila, then by the Heruli under Odoacer, and finally by the Goths under Theodoric. In 539 the city was virtually destroyed by Uraia the Goth. Thirty years later it was conquered by the Germanic Lombards (*Langobardi*, "long beards"). Like the earlier invaders, the Lombards made Pavia their capital, and Milan declined. The incorporation of Lombardy into the Frankish Empire by Charlemagne in 774 may have improved the fortunes of Milan somewhat. But not until a century later, after the disintegration of the Carolingian Empire, did the first signs of Milan's civic independence appear. The counts of Milan, originally Carolingian royal officials, lost their authority, and the archbishops began to exert control over both secular and ecclesiastical matters. In the early tenth century, the pressure of Magyar invasions was substantial, and refugees poured into Milan; but at the end of that century the tide turned. Increased agricultural prosperity in the country-side brought an expansion of Milan's commerce and industry, and the archbishops succeeded in extending the city's political and diocesan boundaries as far as the Swiss Alps. Between 1037 and 1039 Archbishop Aribert led the self-styled "Plebeians" of Milan—members of the semi-religious guilds—to oppose successfully the privileges granted to the lesser nobility by Emperor Conrad II. All this is important as chronicle, and also as the history of the Lombards and of the Frankish Empire, but it hardly forms the basis of a serious history of the city of Milan.

Moreover, in speaking of "the city of Milan," one must recall that, like virtually all European towns of the late tenth and early eleventh centuries, Milan was essentially a large village. The fortified area, where the archbishop's household was located, together with the shops and residences of the merchants and artisans in the "suburb," probably did not contain more than one or two thousand souls; more important, these did not constitute an independent political or economic unit but were an integral part of the larger territory in which the town was situated. Politically, the entire territory, including the town, was ruled by the archbishop and the nobility; there was no separate town government. Economically, the families of the merchants and artisans generally went out daily to work in the fields outside the town.

The modern history of Milan—that is, the organic development of the modern city—began in 1057 when a popular movement, led by militant advocates of papal reform, attacked the aristocratic higher clergy led by an imperialist bishop and ultimately drove them out. Thereafter the constitution of Milan underwent a radical change. A sworn commune was established. By 1094 at the latest, communal magistrates, called consuls, were elected for a fixed term by a regular assembly of all the citizens.

Together with the other cities of Lombardy, Milan was geographically in the center of the conflict between the imperial and papal authorities. The formation of self-governing sworn communes by the Lombard cities was often directed against their bishops, who were appointees of the emperor. Eventually fourteen of these cities formed the Lombard League, which successfully fought against the emperor, Frederick I. In

1180 these fourteen cities—Verona, Venice, Vicenza, Bergamo, Treviso, Ferrara, Brescia, Cremona, Milan, Lodi, Piacenza, Parma, Modena, and Bologna—wrote to the pope: "We were first to bear the emperor's attack so that he might not destroy Italy and suppress the liberty of the Church. We refused, for the honor and liberty of Italy and for the dignity of the Church, to receive or listen to the emperor."[41] This is one of the first uses of the name "Italy" to refer to a political entity, namely, the archipelago of free cities that stretched from Lake Como halfway down the peninsula to the Papal States.

The emperor also favored the formation of sworn urban communes when they were directed against the pope or his supporters. Thus in the early 1080s, at the height of his struggle with Pope Gregory VII, Emperor Henry IV gave charters of liberty and self-government to the Tuscan cities of Lucca and Pisa in order to help them win their freedom from Gregory's friend and supporter, the Countess Matilda.

The system of communal self-government by consuls (as they were usually called), elected for fixed terms by popular assemblies, was introduced in the late eleventh and early twelfth centuries in a great many of the towns of northern Italy. There are records of such consuls in Pisa in 1084, Asti in 1093, Arezzo in 1098, Genoa in 1099, Pavia in 1105, Bologna in 1123, Siena in 1125, Brescia in 1127, Florence in 1138.[42] The mass meetings of citizens to elect consuls were variously called *commune*, *colloquium*, *parlamento*, and (most often) *arengo*. The arengo legislated, declared peace or war, and ratified treaties in addition to electing consuls.

The number of consuls varied from city to city, and it could vary within a single city from year to year. In Milan there were eighteen consuls in 1117, twenty-three in 1130, four in 1138, eight in 1140, and six in 1141. In most cities there were usually between four and twelve consuls. They administered the commune, led it in war, adjudicated disputes among its members. In time, special "consuls of justice" were appointed to be judges in many cities.

The most striking constitutional innovation made by the Italian towns in the late eleventh and early twelfth centuries was the introduction of limited terms of political office. The consuls were usually elected for a year. This principle, which spread to most of the other European countries, represented a fundamental change in the concept of government in the West, for hitherto in Europe all political leaders, whether ecclesiastical or secular (royal, ducal, baronial) had ruled for life. The temporary character of urban political office became even more prominent in the last decades of the twelfth century when the system of plural consuls in Italy gradually gave way to that of a single ruler, usually called a *podestà* (*potestas*, "power"). The podestà was the military leader, the chief administrative officer, and the chief judge of the commune, but his term of office was often limited to six months and he could not be reelected.

The podestà is found in Pisa in about 1169, in Perugia in 1177, in Milan in 1186, in Piacenza in 1188, in Florence in 1193, in Siena in 1199. In the early thirteenth century the podestà system became almost universal in northern Italy. "Soon it became normal to select the *podestà* from another town (not usually a neighboring one) to ensure his neutrality in local disputes. He came with his own household [and] took an oath on arrival to serve the commune loyally . . . The *podestà* was a noble, and he needed a legal training. His office became a recognized profession, in which able men specialized, traveling on from one post to the next."[43] He was, in effect, a professional "city manager," and at the end of his term of office his performance would be carefully reviewed by a special commission appointed for the purpose.

By limiting the ruler's term of office to a fixed period of months or years, the Italian communes emphasized the "temporal" character of secular rule. The governors of the new European cities, in contrast to those of the ancient Greek or Roman cities, were not responsible for religious matters—matters of cult or faith; those were left to the church, which the Papal Revolution had separated from what later was to be called "the state." In fact, the new municipal governments of Europe were the first purely secular political bodies, the first modern secular states. Their function was to keep the peace and to do justice in the legal sense. The word podestà is significant in this connection, for it clearly marks off political from spiritual functions—"power" from "authority."[44]

Because the podestà's term of office was so short, it was necessary to allocate long-term political functions to other political bodies. Most commonly, the arengos (parliaments) were succeeded by "great councils," which, however, were also usually too big to govern effectively. (In Milan the great council had 800 members.) At the same time there developed smaller "secret" councils, or "councils of trust" (*consiglio della credenza*), often limited to 24 (or even 16) members, but occasionally numbering as many as 100. In addition, ad hoc commissions were often created to exercise special powers in military, financial, or constitutional matters. The podestà was required to consult the councils of the citizens on all important matters. In theory, at least, the councils alone had the power to make new laws.

The Italian cities took the lead not only in creating new forms of government but also in systematizing and reforming the laws. The earliest systematization of urban law in Italy took the form of collections of rules sworn to by the consuls upon assuming their duties and collections of rules sworn to by the people in response. The oaths were called *brevia* ("writs"). The consular brevia specified the detailed rules which the consuls were obligated to follow in the exercise of their functions. The popular brevia specified the basic rules which the citizens were obligated to follow in dealing with the municipal government. Public officials other than consuls were also required, upon taking office, to swear oaths specifying the rules they were to follow. As the Italian legal historian Francesco Calasso has written: "Clearly this network of oaths constituted an ensemble of legal norms that regulated the constitutional and administrative life of the commune."[45]

Calasso states further that the subsequent centralization of power in the podestà "brought about a consolidation of the various oaths in a single corpus of rules, separated by rubrics, which the *podestà* swore to observe and to enforce."[46] This marked the second stage in the systematization of urban law in Italy. It was often fused with the writing down of the customs of the commune. The third stage was the codification of the resolutions of the legislative organ of the commune, the popular assembly or the grand council. These decisions were usually called statutes (*statuta*); sometimes, by analogy to the laws of the Roman Republic, they were called *leges*. In some cities there was a fusion of customary law and statutory law; in others there was not. In Pisa, for example, there were two codes, one consisting of rules of customary law, called *constitutum usus*, and one consisting of the resolutions of the assembly, called *constitutum legis*; there were also two tribunals, each judging on the basis of one of the two codes.[47]

The politicians and jurists of the Italian cities, like the ecclesiastical politicians and jurists, were concerned to systematize and synthesize legal materials coming from different sources, to eliminate contradictions and fill in gaps. For this purpose special officers and special commissions were appointed. In some cities, such as Parma and Pistoia, the practice developed of shutting up the codifiers in a building until they had completed their work, in order to prevent outside influence. In other cities the opposite practice developed; the persons charged with codification were actually encouraged to avail themselves of the opinions and suggestions of the people.

Guilds and Guild Law

Just as the urban commune often started as a sworn "conspiracy for peace," so within the commune the guilds were sworn brotherhoods whose members were bound by their oaths to protect and serve one another. The guild system of the eleventh- and twelfth-century towns may have derived ultimately from the early Germanic guild, which had been a military and religious brotherhood "in which the dead entered the living by a kind of demonic possession."[48] The later guilds also owed much to the Peace of God movement of the tenth and eleventh centuries, which operated in part through sworn brotherhoods, often called "peace guilds." These served as mutual protective associations and as volunteer law enforcement agencies. With the rise of cities in the last decades of the eleventh century, merchant guilds, social guilds, craft guilds, and other guilds of a secular nature became widespread; yet these, too, retained strong religious features, generally taking it upon themselves to provide for the spiritual, and not only the material, aspects of their members' lives. Thus the guild would typically seek to maintain high moral standards, punishing its members for blasphemy, gambling, usury, and the like. It would hold religious ceremonies for its own patron saint as well as that of the town. Guild statutes often began by enumerating the alms the guild would give and the works of mercy it would perform. The celebration of feast days was an important part of the life of the guild.

The guilds, where they existed — some towns, notably Paris, had no guilds — were also lawmaking bodies. Each of the various guilds of merchants and artisans within a city or town had its own ordinances. The ordinances varied in content, depending on the type of guild, whether merchant, artisan, professional, bankers', seamen's, or other type; if artisan, whether of producers of wool, silk, leather, silver, or some other product; if professional, whether of judges, notaries, doctors, or some other profession. Within these classifications there were numerous forms of association, reflected in the large variety of names given to what is translated here simply as guild: *ars, universitas, corporatio, misterium, schola, colleguim, paraticum, curia, ordo, matricola, fraglia,* and, for the merchant guild, *hansa* or *mercandancia.* Nevertheless, the ordinances of all the dozens of guilds that might exist within a city had many features in common, and these common features existed throughout the West. Thus all guilds were fraternal associations (in which incidentally, women were normally included, for those trades in which they engaged), imposing obligations on their members to help their fellow members who were sick or disabled or poor or in legal trouble, to provide for burial of the dead and for offerings for their souls, as well as to found schools for the children of their members, to build chapels, produce religious dramas, and provide occasions for hospitality and conviviality. The members periodically swore oaths of fraternity and pledged never to abandon the guild but to observe its statutes faithfully.[49]

The guilds were also monopolistic economic associations whose ordinances regulated such matters as conditions of apprenticeship and membership, calendars of workdays and holidays, standards of quality of work, minimum prices, distances between shops, conditions of selling so as to limit competition within the guild and to equalize sales, prohibitions against selling on credit except within the guild, restrictions upon imports, restrictions upon immigration, and other protectionist measures. Since slavery had been virtually abolished in the cities, labor was based on contract; however, the terms of labor contracts were tightly regulated by guild and urban customs and ordinances on the basis of types of jobs (*officia*). To strike was a grave crime.[50]

The form of government of the guild was typically modeled after the form of government of the city or town. At its head were usually two or more representatives, often called consuls, elected annually or sometimes semi-annually, usually without participation of the city officers. There was usually a general assembly of the guild with deliberative powers, as well as a small council to back up the consuls or other chief executives. The officers of the guild often formed an arbitration tribunal before which the members were expected to appear before carrying their disputes into the courts.

Lawyers (notaries) often played an important role not only in serving individual companies within the guilds, drawing up deeds and contracts and (as advocates) acting as representatives in judicial and other adversary proceedings, but also in helping directly to govern the guilds as well as the municipal government. Notaries would often accompany municipal officers (merchant consuls, podestas, mayors, Bürgermeister) when they went out to decide disputes. They would draw up official documents, compose local statutes, arrange elections, write letters to neighboring cities or lords, and interpret municipal charters. From early stages of the development of cities as autonomous polities, lawyers played an important role in their administration.

In many cities of Europe the leaders of the guilds became the magistrates of the communes. A law of Milan of 1154 authorized the appointment of "consuls of merchants" to perform judicial functions, among others; the courts of the merchant consuls in the cities of northern Italy gradually extended their jurisdiction over all mercantile cases within the city. Other European cities adopted the Italian institution of the merchant consul, or else they developed similar institutions. In England, Wales, and Ireland, the mayors of the fourteen staple towns were elected "by the commonalty of merchants" for a one-year term; like the Italian merchant consuls, English mayors performed not only executive functions but also judicial functions, according to the universal law merchant. Thus mercantile law and urban law overlapped each other, in England as elsewhere in the West.

The Main Characteristics of Urban Law

The three systems of secular law that were considered earlier — feudal, manorial, and mercantile law — were analyzed under the headings of objectivity, universality, reciprocity, participatory adjudication, integration, and growth. In considering urban law, it seems preferable to use a slightly different classification. This system of law will be analyzed in terms of its communitarian character, its secular character, its constitutional character, its capacity for growth, and its integrity as a system.

COMMUNITARIAN CHARACTER

Of primary importance in the system of urban law was its communitarian character. Urban law was the law of a close-knit, integrated community — one that was often called, in fact, a "commune." The community, in turn, was based on a *covenant*, either express or implied. Many cities and towns were founded by a solemn collective oath, or series of oaths, made by the entire citizenry to adhere to a charter that had been publicly read aloud to them. The charter was, in one sense, a social contract; it must, indeed, have been one of the principal historical sources from which the modern contract theory of government emerged. The urban charters were not, of course, contracts in the modern sense of a bargained exchange between two parties whereby each agrees to perform discrete acts during a given period of time. Acceptance of the urban charter was rather an avowal of consent to a permanent relationship. Like the feudal contract of vassalage or the marriage contract, it was an agreement to enter into a status, that is, into a relationship whose terms were fixed by law and could not be altered by the will of the parties. In the case of the founding of a city or town, however, the status that was formed was that of a corporation (universitas), under the prevailing Romano-canonical theory that a corporation is a body of people sharing common legal functions and acting as a legal entity. In one sense, therefore, the promulgation and acceptance of the urban charter was not a contract at all but a kind of sacrament; it both symbolized and effectuated the formation of the community and the establishment of the community's law.

The communitarian character of urban law took the form not only of a covenantal relationship but also of a *participatory* relationship among the members. This participatory relationship was reflected in legal requirements of mutual aid among citizens and mutual protection against strangers and enemies; provisions for exercise of the "common counsel" of the citizenry in consenting to new laws; provisions for common consent to the elections of officials; a system of formal adjudication by fellow citizens ("peers") of the person who claimed vindication of his rights or against whom a claim for vindication of rights had been made by another; a system of informal arbitration of civil disputes, lightly supervised by town authorities; strict regulation of economic activities through guilds of artisans and merchants; and many other provisions for popular participation in the life of the community.

Just as the covenantal aspect of the community should not be understood in terms of contemporary concepts of contract, so its participatory aspect should not be understood in terms of contemporary concepts of democracy. The urban community of the twelfth century was usually governed by a relatively small group of particians. More basically, it was not founded on individuals as such but on subordinate communities—it was a "community of communities." French social historians have given the name *société des ordres* ("society of orders") and German social historians have given the name *Ständestaat* ("state of estates") to this type of social structure, which they have mistakenly identified solely with the "postfeudal" and "predemocratic" Europe of the sixteenth to eighteenth centuries. In twelfth-century European cities and towns as well, the "order" or "estate" of which one was a member—or, to put it more simply, one's class (in the non-Marxian sense of that word)—formed an important basis of rights and duties. Thus urban law, while recognizing a certain legal equality of all citizens, rich and poor alike, *as citizens*, nevertheless did not generally permit the poor to participate in the election of leaders. Further, it recognized the separate legal orders of the various artisans and merchant guilds, with their glaring inequalities of masters and apprentices. It also assigned separate kinds of rights and duties to various classes of noncitizens, including nobility, clergy, students, Jews, and others. Just as the urban community was part of a large community of communities, a *communitas communitarum*, comprising the whole of Western Christendom, so it itself constituted a little community of communities. The individual had no legal existence except as a member of one or more subcommunities within the whole, and his individual freedom consisted primarily in his mobility, that is, his capacity to move from one subcommunity to another or to resort to one in defense against another. In the case of some—Jews, for example—that mobility was extremely limited, although it was not nonexistent; Jews could and often did resort to the crown or the papacy, for example, against measures of oppression taken against them by city governments.

Thus the communitarian character of urban law was itself structured in covenantal, participatory, and class dimensions.

SECULAR CHARACTER

In addition to its communitarian character, urban law had a secular character. In contrast to Greek and Roman cities of antiquity and of the imperial period, Western cities and towns did not have responsibility for maintaining the religious cult. Religious worship and religious belief were not part of urban jurisdiction but were under the separate jurisdiction of the church, which everywhere in the West was subordinate to the Bishop of Rome. The law relating to religious observances and doctrine within the city or town was not urban law (or imperial law) but the canon law of the Roman Church.

This did not mean that the urban community was indifferent to religious faith. On the contrary, all the cities and towns of western Europe were actively Christian. They were filled with churches and sanctuaries to saints. They considered themselves to be divinely instituted. "It is to Jesus Christ that we owe the development of the laws and advantages of our city," states the concord by which the citizens of Marseilles established a peace with the citizens of Nice in 1219. "It is God alone, Himself, who governs our city."[52] Their mission, however, *as cities*, was defined as secular, or temporal, rather than sacred or eternal; it was, primarily, to control violence and to regulate political and economic relations — that is, to keep peace and to do justice.

The fact that the city considered itself to be a secular polity and did not claim to apply ecclesiastical law or to perform sacred rites or propagate religious doctrine, but left those tasks to the church, was an essential part of its character as a city in the Western sense. This was not only a negative thing; it also had the positive significance of establishing the independent value of worldly, or temporal, goals. Not only were the new city governments independent of direct ecclesiastical authority in the institutional sense, but their tasks of maintaining peace and justice were independent of the tasks of the church in maintaining the Christian faith. And those independent tasks of maintaining peace and justice were themselves taken to be, though temporal, nevertheless ordained by God, worthy of unstinted devotion, and an important part of God's plan of salvation for mankind. This was "the secular city," but in a much more optimistic sense than that of St. Augustine, though in a much less optimistic sense than that of many twentieth-century secularists.[53]

The secular character of urban law was reflected in the fact that every city had its own variation of urban law and, further, that urban law was only one of several varieties of secular law, including royal law, feudal law, manorial law, and mercantile law. The coexistence of various types of secular law was inherent in its secular character. No one system of secular law claimed to embrace the whole of the secular jurisdiction. Each was a particular local system, governing one part of the life of those subject to its jurisdiction. This, too, distinguishes the law of the European cities of the eleventh and twelfth centuries and thereafter from the law of the cities of ancient Greece and imperial Rome. The Greek city was the sole polity to which its citizens owed allegiance, and its law was the sole law by which they were bound. The Roman city did not have a law of its own; the Roman citizen was governed solely by the Roman law, the noncitizen solely by the jus gentium, the law of nations. The unique feature of the law of Western Christendom was that the individual person lived under a plurality of legal systems, each of which governed one of the overlapping subcommunities of which he was a member.

Constitutional Character

The third major feature of the system of urban law was its constitutional character. The word "constitutionalism" was invented in the late eighteenth or early nineteenth century to refer chiefly to the American doctrine of the supremacy of the written constitution over enacted laws. Yet the reality of modern constitutionalism, in the full sense of the word, was present first in the urban law systems of western Europe in the eleventh and twelfth centuries. On the one hand, European cities of those centuries were modern states—just as the church of that period was a modern state—in the sense that they had full legislative, executive, and judicial power and authority, including the power and authority to impose taxes, coin money, establish weights and measures, raise armies, conclude alliances, and make war. On the other hand, the state power and authority of cities, like that of the church, was subject to various constitutional restraints. The constitutional character of urban law manifested itself in five important ways.

1. Urban law was founded, in a great many instances, on written charters, and these were charters both of governmental organization and of civil rights and liberties. They were, in effect, the first modern written constitutions. Even when there was no written charter, the city or town was considered to have a fundamental law which established its governmental organization and the basic rights and liberties of its citizens.

2. The system of governmental organization which was established by the charters—or without charters—was similar in some significant ways to contemporary systems of constitutional government: the urban governments were limited in their powers; they were often divided into executive, legislative, and judicial branches, which exercised certain restraints upon one another; there were periodic elections of officers; in many places judges were to serve out their terms of office on good behavior or until recalled by the citizens; the laws were published and collections of laws were issued.

3. The civil rights granted by urban law characteristically included a rational trial procedure, with judgment by peers rather than proof by ordeal or trial by combat. There were to be no arbitrary arrests and no imprisonment without legal process. Body attachment for debt was prohibited. Types of punishment were limited. In theory, rich and poor were to be judged alike. Citizens had the right to bear arms. They had the right to vote. Immigrants were to be granted the same rights as citizens after residence for a year and a day. Merchant strangers were to have rights equal to those of merchant citizens.

4. Civil liberties characteristically included exemption from many feudal services and taxes, and the strict limitation of many others. In addition, they often included restrictions upon royal prerogatives: the king, for example, would agree to accept a fixed tax to be paid by the city or town and would be forbidden to impose forced loans. Above all, the principle was generally established that citizens' obligations would be

specified in advance, and that they could retain everything they acquired that was not subject to such specific obligations.

5. The constitutional law of civil rights and liberties included rights and liberties connected with popular participation in urban government. This, in turn, was connected with the constitutional theory, never fully accepted but never fully rejected, that political power was ultimately vested in the whole body of citizens.

Although the forms of government of European cities were quite diverse in nature, there were certain common patterns. A very large proportion of newly founded cities and towns were governed by popular assemblies of all the citizens, whose consent was required for election of officials and for introduction of new laws. In the course of the twelfth and thirteenth centuries, however, there was a strong tendency throughout Europe for the popular assembly to be replaced by a council. Some Italian cities had two councils, a great council and a small council. At first, urban councils were usually elected for a term of several years. Later, co-optation replaced election. An aristocrat form of government superseded the democratic form, although the larger public assemblies sometimes remained in the background with the power to exercise a veto or at least to disapprove any changes in the basic laws.

At first, executive officers were elected for short terms. In many places, however, there was a strong tendency toward concentration of executive power. In some Italian cities the term of office of the podestà was extended from six months or a year to longer terms, and finally, in some places, the office was granted for life. In other cities, an oligarchy of great merchants came to dominate the executive. Thus in twelfth-century Venice, the Doge and the Little Council, consisting of six councillors, had full executive power, while the Doge and a Collegio, consisting of 26 heads of departments, initiated legislation in the 120-member Senate of the 480-member Great Council. However, in the thirteenth century the Doge and Little Council as well as the Collegio became puppets of the *Grandi* (the "great ones"), and the term *popolo* ("the people"), which had once referred to the sworn association of all citizens, came to refer (in Venice and many other places) to a people excluded from the government and often hostile to it.

Popular participation in urban government in the late eleventh and twelfth centuries extended also to the judiciary. Certain townspeople — called Schoeffen in Germany, échevins in the Netherlands and northern France, consules in Italy — were chosen or elected to act as popular judges. In Venice a Council of Forty, or Tribunal, was selected from the Great Council to conduct judicial business. In other places, however, the judges were professional jurists.

In England, even though the communal movement was weaker and the boroughs more dependent on the crown and less democratic in form of government than was the case in Italy, Germany, Flanders, and parts of France, borough officials were often elected. The citizens of London acquired the right to elect their sheriffs as well as a justiciar in 1131, and their mayor in 1231.

CAPACITY FOR GROWTH

The fourth characteristic of the system of urban law was its capacity for growth, that is, its tendency not merely to change but also consciously to develop continuously and organically. This capacity and tendency were reflected in the occasional collection and systematization of the customs of the city or town together with the oaths of the various offices. It was also reflected in the regular enactment and periodic systematization of ordinances and laws by the governing bodies of the city or town as well as by the various guilds within it. In addition to such indigenous sources of conscious growth, urban law often benefited from the inspiration of Roman law and of the canon law. Some cities expressly "adopted" Roman law. This was always, however, the ideal, dynamic Roman law of the universities, rather than a set of unchangeable rules. Roman law was viewed as a reservoir from which legal ideas and principles could be drawn to meet new needs; hence it, too, was an element in the conscious growth of the law.

INTEGRITY AS A SYSTEM

The capacity of urban law for growth and its tendency toward growth were connected with its character as a legal system, which was also partly inspired by the systematic character of both Roman law and canon law. Especially in the Italian cities, but to a lesser degree elsewhere as well, urban law was considered to be based, in the first instance, on custom (*mos, consuetudo, usus*), and in the second place, on rules enacted by rule-making authorities, which were in turn divided into ordinances (*statuta*) of guilds and other associations and laws (*leges*) of the city legislative authority or of the king or emperor. Statuta and leges had the quality of being written, which gave them a special significance. Nevertheless, the writing down of the customs by order of public authority did not necessarily deprive them of their quality as customary law. In urban law as in canon law and the other legal systems of the time, in cases of internal conflict among the sources of law, custom yielded to statute and statute to lex. Guild statutes were subject to frequent examination and approval by urban authorities, which often imposed on guilds the duty to revise their statutes periodically.

Other characteristics of urban law were connected with specific features of social and economic relations within the city or town. Thus it was characteristic of urban law that the citizen or townsman could legally acquire land and buildings by a form of tenure called burgage tenure, or town tenure. In sharp contrast to clan and feudal tenures, town tenure included the right to devise the property by will, to sell it, to mortgage it, to lease it, and, in general, to have rights similar to what in the eighteenth century came to be called "ownership" (*propriété*, *Eigentum*). However, the restrictions upon private use of land and buildings were much greater in the late eleventh and twelfth centuries than in the late eighteenth and nineteenth centuries, since urban economic activities in the earlier period were usually strictly regulated by customary law, on the one hand, and by guild rules, on the other.

The City as a Historical Community

In recent decades American sociologists have paid increased attention to the history of the city, partly as a result of the translation into English of Max Weber's writings on the city.[54] Weber mastered the secondary literature on the history of the Western city that had accumulated in the late nineteenth and early twentieth centuries, and he synthesized it and integrated it with his own general theory of society. Yet Weber's influence has not been wholly benign. He failed to correct some major errors concerning urban history that had been made by his predecessors, and his general theory of society suffers from serious defects that are especially harmful when applied to urban communities.

Above all, Weber's theory of the city, although cast in historical terms, fails even to mention, much less to explain, the most striking and distinctive characteristic of the Western city, namely, its historical consciousness—that is, its consciousness of its own historical development, its belief in its own movement from past to future, its sense of its own ongoing, developing character. Weber's theory makes an important contribution in that it addresses the structural unity of the Western city as a community at a given moment, namely the moment of its historical origin in the "late Middle Ages"; but a serious weakness of the theory is its failure to address the dynamics of the development of the Western city —its failure to notice that the Western city, in contrast to Roman, Islamic, and Oriental cities, believed in the organic growth of its political and economic and social institutions over generations and centuries.

Weber wrote that although the rudiments of the Western type of city may be found occasionally in other cultures, principally in the Near East, "an urban 'community' in the full meaning of the word appears only in the Occident." "To constitute a full urban community," he stated, "a settlement had to represent a relative predominance of trade-commercial relations, with the settlement as a whole displaying the following features: (1) a fortification, (2) a market, (3) a court of its own and at least a partially autonomous law, (4) a related form of association, and (5) at least partial autonomy and autocephaly, thus also an administration by authorities in the election of whom the burghers participated." Such a peculiar system of forces, according to Weber, could only appear under special conditions and at a particular time, namely, in medieval Europe.[55]

The constituent elements attributed by Weber to the "full urban community" of the Occident reflect its structural integration, but they do not account for its dynamic character, its development in time. They do not explain why or how the twelfth-century city developed into the city of the sixteenth and twentieth centuries, many of whose characteristics are identical to, or at least continuous with, those of the twelfth-century city, but others of which are substantially different in degree if not in kind. A typical twentieth-century city has the following characteristics: (1) it is a corporation, endowed with legal personality, with capacity to sue and be sued, hold property, make contracts, purchase goods and services, employ labor, borrow money; (2) it is a political entity, usually governed by a mayor or city manager together with an elected council, which may employ officials, levy taxes, exercise the right of eminent domain, and perform other governmental acts and functions; (3) it is an economic unit, which usually purveys or controls the purveyance of water, gas, electricity, and transportation, and regulates the construction and use of housing and the location of economic enterprises; (4) it is an agency for the promotion of social welfare, including education, health protection, poor relief, and public recreation.[56] Like their twentieth-century progeny, the cities of twelfth-century Europe were also corporate, political, economic, and social entities; however, the range of their activities in each of these roles was much more limited than that of a present-day city. Much of what a city does today was done then, within the city, by guilds and by the church, as well as by the extended family. Also the city today is much more integrated in, and much more representative of, the modern national state, an entity which was only beginning to come into existence in the twelfth century. Yet despite these differences, the present-day city developed, by a process of organic growth, out of the cities and towns that were created, or recreated, in the period of the Papal Revolution; and that process of growth was part of its character as an urban community.

The process of growth of the Western city cannot be explained without reference to its historical self-awareness, its sense of its own historical continuity and development, its consciousness of its own ongoing character as a community, its own movement from the past into the future. Historically, this was connected, first, with the religious dimension of the Papal Revolution, and especially with the mission of the church gradually to reform and redeem the secular order. It was connected, second, with the political dimension of the Papal Revolution and especially with the belief in the coexistence of plural autonomous secular polities; it was this belief that made it both possible and urgent for citizens to form urban communes independent of royal, feudal, and even ecclesiastical authority—something that would have been unthinkable before the papacy desacralized kingship. It was connected, third, with the legal dimension of the Papal Revolution, and especially with the belief that the reformation and redemption of the secular order had to take place by the continual progressive development of legal institutions and periodic revision of laws in order to overcome the forces of disorder and injustice.

Strangely enough, Weber in a later chapter contradicted his own earlier statement of what constitutes the uniqueness of the medieval Western city. Without noticing the discrepancy, he attributed all five characteristics of a "full urban community"—which at first he had said "appears only in the Occident"—to the Asiatic and oriental city also. The latter, too, he stated, was a fortress and a market. It, too, contained farms held in socage (that is, in nonfeudal tenure), with land alienable without restriction, or hereditary in an unencumbered way, or obligated only with a fixed land rent. It, too, had its own "autonomous constitution," which presumably meant its own form of association and at least partial autonomy and autocephaly.[57] In all these respects, the differences between the medieval occidental city and its Asiatic counterparts were differences—Weber stated—only in degree. What "absolutely" distinguished the Western city, he finally concluded, was the personal legal condition, that is, the *freedom*, of the citizen.[58] Serfs emigrating to the cities had a common interest, he stated, in avoiding the imposition of military or other services by their erstwhile lords. "The urbanites therefore usurped the right to violate lordly law. This was the major revolutionary innovation of medieval occidental cities in contrast to all others."[59] Weber went on to say that the "cutting of status connections with the rural nobility" had been connected with the formation of municipal corporations—legally autonomous communes. "Similar preliminary stages of the constitution of a polis or commune may have appeared repeatedly in Asia and Africa," he added. (Note the cautionary words "preliminary" and "may".) "However, nothing is known [in Asia or Africa] of a legal status of citizenship."[60]

Thus Weber eventually recognized that there was something about Western law that was of critical importance in the rise of the Western city. Also, it appears, there was something critically important about Western religion as well—which Weber also dealt with only obliquely. He pointed out that in the Asiatic cultures, including China and India, it was impossible to bring all the inhabitants of a city together into a homogeneous status group. "Foremost among the reasons for the peculiar freedom of urbanites in the Mediterranean city, in contrast to the Asiatic," he wrote, "is the absence of magical and animistic caste and sib constraints. The social formations preventing fusion of urban dwellers into a homogeneous group vary. In China it was the exogamous and endophratric sib; in India . . . it has been the endogamous caste."[61] Here Weber turned to Fustel de Coulanges's work to show that the ancient Greek and Roman cities did create a religious foundation of citizenship by substituting the city cult meal for the cult meal of the family. Yet Weber offered no explanation of the relationship of the religious factor to the legal and political factor; more particularly, he did not confront the fact that ancient Greek and Roman cities rested on slavery and lacked that "peculiar freedom of urbanites" which was characteristic not of "the Mediterranean city" as such but of the western European city of the late eleventh century and thereafter. Thus Weber stopped short of saying that the emergence of urban liberties in the West was part of a revolutionary *religious* change, in which, on the one hand, the ecclesiastical polity declared its independence from all secular polities, and, on the other, the very concept of secular polities was for the first time created and secular polities were said to be reformable and redeemable.

Why did Weber underestimate the role played by law and religion in the origin and development of the Western city? And why did he miss entirely the role of Western historical consciousness, that is, the Western belief in the organic growth of religious and legal institutions over generations and centuries?

Karl Marx had attributed changes in social consciousness, including religious and legal consciousness, to changes in technologies for meeting economic needs (the mode of production), and in the class struggle to control those technologies (relations of production). Weber, for his part, believed that in addition to the material economic forces that determine social consciousness there are also material political forces—in other words, that the drive for political power is an independent objective force and not (as Marx had thought) merely a reflection of the drive for economic power. For Weber, therefore, the rise of the Western city in the late eleventh and early twelfth centuries was due not merely to the development of a new mode of production (artisan and craft industry), which drew the serfs from the manor in opposition to their feudal lords, but also to the development of new political relationships. Weber could see that the nobility, too, had political reasons to favor the creation and development of cities. But Weber, like Marx, believed that consciousness, and especially legal and religious consciousness, were essentially instruments of domination. More specifically, Weber, like Marx, believed that the idea of creating cities, the growth of communal consciousness within cities, and the development of urban legal and religious institutions which on the one hand manifested urban consciousness and on the other hand maintained the economic and political power of the ruling classes—that all these constituted a nonmaterial (spiritual, ideological) "superstructure" built on a material (economic and political) "base."

Western legal institutions cannot, however, be explained satisfactorily either as mere superstructure or as mere ideology; indeed, any interpretation of Western history that is built on a distinction between a material base and an ideological superstructure cannot account satisfactorily for the Western legal tradition. This does not mean, however, that values, ideas, beliefs, concepts, and other forms of social consciousness come first, so to speak, and that they "cause" changes in economic and political life — or, for that matter, in legal institutions. Legal institutions in the West are to be explained *neither* in idealistic terms, solely as manifestations of preexisting concepts, *nor* in materialistic terms, solely as instruments for exercising economic or political power. They can only be satisfactorily explained in terms that encompass and go beyond both idealism and materialism.

Conventional social theory errs in supposing that historical change is caused by changes in basic social, economic, and political conditions alone. There is, in fact, no such thing as social, economic, and political conditions (or forces) alone; they are always part of a context of perception and feeling. Nor are there values, ideas, beliefs — alone; as a social matter, they are always interconnected with "material interests." Power is also an idea; justice is also a force. Neither *causes* the other, in the physical-science sense of that word.

To understand *why* a great historical change occurred, one must go beyond the interrelationships between ideas and material conditions to the times and cirumstances themselves, not only to recount them but also to show their historical significance, their meaning for the past and the future. Such legal institutions as the corporate character of the city, the alienability of urban property, and the liberties of the citizen are to be understood partly as manifestations of ideas and values and partly as instruments of economic and political power, but they are also to be understood as significant historical events and as parts of significant sequences of historical events. They were not merely "manifestations" and "instruments"; they *happened*; and knowing when and how they happened, and as part of what larger happenings they happened, helps one to understand *why* they happened. Indeed, the legal institutions of the Western city cannot be explained satisfactorily in any other way. In addition to the objective materialist "why" and the subjective idealist "why" there is a historical "why" — a "why" that adds to the outer and inner dimensions of the inquiry both a past and a future dimension.

13 | Royal Law: Sicily, England, Normandy, France

THE PAPAL REVOLUTION gave birth to a new conception of kingship in Western Christendom. The king was no longer the supreme head of the church. The era of "sacral kingship" gradually came to an end. In matters denominated as "spiritual," the bishop of Rome was supreme—not only over kings but also over the most important sovereign of all, the emperor. For the first time emperor and kings were conceived to be "secular" rulers, whose principal tasks were, first, to keep the peace within their respective kingdoms, that is, to control violence, and second, to do justice, that is, to govern in the political and economic spheres. Even in these matters, moreover, the church played an important role.

The reduction of royal authority in ecclesiastical matters was compensated, however, by a very large increase in royal authority in relation to other secular polities—tribal, local, feudal, and urban. In Joseph Strayer's words, "The Gregorian concept of the Church almost demanded the invention of the concept of the State."[1] The very division into spiritual and secular polities led to the ascendancy of a territorial concept of kingship, in which the king was no longer primarily chief warrior of the clan (or federation of clans) and chief baron in the feudal hierarchy. Before, he had governed directly his "wise men" and tenants-in-chief and only indirectly, through them, local leaders, subvassals, and their subjects. Henceforth he governed directly—through his officials—the whole people, or at least all freemen, of the territory over which he was sovereign. This, too, was a gradual process, taking several generations in the case of the Norman rulers of southern Italy, England, and Normandy, and another several generations in the case of France and the German lands.

The new conception of kingship involved the recognition for the first time, in the twelfth and thirteenth centuries, of the lawmaking role of the king. For the first time the kings of Europe began to enact laws regularly, and to justify their legislation not merely as the writing down of ancient customs or as an extraordinary means of dealing with emergencies but as a normal exercise of royal functions, an essential part of a king's responsibility to keep the peace and to do justice. Royal lawmaking became distinct from royal administration, finance, military activities and politics in general.

Also, the conduct of royal government became professionalized and departmentalized—in that sense, bureaucratized. Lawmaking was carried on through the medium of a new professional body, usually called the "king's council," which was smaller than and quite different from the older tribal consultative assemblies and the feudal great councils. Similarly, the traditional royal function of judging was professionalized. Central royal courts broke off from the king's council. The very name "king's court" (*curia regis*) was transferred from the royal household as a whole to royal officials acting professionally in a legislative or an administrative or a judicial capacity. The king's household officials became the heads of departments—the secretary became the head of the chancery, the financial officer became the head of the treasury, and the like.[2]

The new legal concept of kingship owed much to the new legal concept of papal authority that had been proclaimed initially in 1075 by Pope Gregory VII in his Dictates of the Pope. Just as the pope was head of a corporate church, governed by a body of law to which he contributed by his legislation and his judicial decisions, so the kings sought to unify their respective kingdoms through a body of law, to which they contributed by their legislation and their judicial decisions. And like the popes, the kings legislated and adjudicated by means of professionally trained officials specially assigned to those tasks.

It is sometimes said that the new conception of the king as lawmaker arose as a result of the discovery of the Roman law texts of Justinian in the last years of the eleventh century and the subsequent development of the new science of Roman law in the European universities. The grains of truth in this thesis are, first, that the supporters of the royal lawmaking authority did turn to the Roman texts to find justification for that authority, and second, that the kings did find in the vocabulary of the Roman law many of the terms for their own legislation. However, the supporters of papal lawmaking authority and urban lawmaking authority did the same. The "argument from Roman law," as it has been called, was chiefly just that—an argument, a justification, not a motivation or a cause. That the motivation and the cause of the development of royal lawmaking authority cannot be substantially attributed to the discovery of Roman law is apparent from the fact that the royal lawmaking authority was most prominent in England, Normandy, and the Norman Kingdom of Sicily, where the revival of Roman law was weaker than, say, in France, while in northern Italy, where the revival of Roman law was strongest, the lawmaking authority of the emperor remained rudimentary and kingship did not exist at all.

The coupling of the territorial and the legal concepts of kingship gave birth to a system of royal law within each of the kingdoms of Europe. Kings established central law courts with jurisdiction—over certain types of cases—throughout the territories over which they reigned, and they issued laws to be applied in those courts. In addition to applying the laws issued by the kings, the royal courts also applied legal principles and concepts and rules which were considered to be binding throughout the land—"the law of the land" (*lex terrae*)—and which were derived from custom, from reason, and from conscience, in accordance with the new legal science. This legal science was informed by the new Roman law of the universities and by the new canon law of the church.

In the various kingdoms of Europe the common law of the king and of the king's courts gradually replaced most of the disparate features of tribal, local, and regional law within the territory. In England, for example, it replaced the law of Wessex, the law of Mercia, and the Danelaw, into which English law was still divided at the beginning of the twelfth century. In Sicily, the laws of the Greeks, the Arabs, the Lombards, and the Normans were subordinated to a common law by Roger II, who ruled from 1112 to 1154. Roger was the first of the great lawmaking kings of the twelfth century. He was followed in the second half of the twelfth century by Henry II of England (1154-1189), Frederick Barbarossa of Germany (1152-1190), Philip Augustus of France (1180-1223), and Count Philip of Flanders (1169-1190), and in the thirteenth century by Frederick II of Sicily and Germany (1208-1250), by Henry III (1216-1272) and Edward I (1272-1307) of England, by Louis IX of France (1226-1270), and by Ferdinand III (1217-1252) and Alfonso X (1252-1284) of Castile and Léon. In contrast to legislators of a much later time, these kings legislated primarily through the establishment of procedures and remedies to be applied in the royal courts; nevertheless, the list of important legislative acts promulgated by European monarchs in the twelfth and thirteenth centuries is impressive (see figure 2).

Prior to the late eleventh and early twelfth centuries, kingdoms had been unified—to the extent that they were unified at all—not by a body of common law administered by royal officials but by the person of the king himself and the belief in his sacred character and thaumaturgic powers. This fact was dramatically illustrated by the peripatetic character of kingship in that earlier time: kings had continually to ride circuit throughout their kingdoms in order to quell uprisings and do justice. The great lords who were their vassals in the countryside governed not as their delegates or officials but as autonomous rulers.

There were, of course, exceptions—one thinks of Charlemagne—but in general the emperors and kings of the Germanic era represented chiefly the spiritual unity—in current terminology, the ideological unity—of their subjects, on the one hand, and, on the other hand, their military unity in resisting the heathen invaders from north, east, and south; economically, politically, and, above all, legally, there was hardly any unity at all. It was this situation that changed dramatically in the late eleventh and early twelfth centuries. Supreme guardianship over ecclesiastical unity became the prerogative of the papacy, while the kingship in many parts of Europe acquired vastly increased secular power—including economic and political and legal power—vis-à-vis the smaller secular polities. The German historian Heinrich Mitteis was right in saying that "the twelfth century had not yet arrived at an abstract conception of the [secular] state as a corporate entity or 'legal person.' " He was also right in saying that "the Investiture Contest gave rise to a broader concept of the function and competence of the state." But he was not quite right in saying that "belief in the sacred character and thaumaturgic powers of kingship, as inherited from the pagan past and preserved by the early medieval Church, survived the Investiture Contest."[3] This statement may be correct if the twelfth century is compared with a later time—say, the fourteenth century and thereafter. It is not correct when the comparison is between the twelfth century and the centuries prior to the Investiture Contest. One need only recall the contrast between John of Salisbury's *Policraticus* and the *Norman Anonymous*. Mitteis himself added that "it is true that twelfth-century rulers tended to adopt an increasingly secular attitude toward politics," and that the concept of a secular state was reflected in the fact that "the officers of the royal household—especially in France and England—tended to become a close council of specialized permanent administrators."[4] It was more than that, however. The ruler himself became a constitutional figure, a legally defined officeholder, whose *imperium*—as Azo said—was limited, at least theoretically, by his *iurisdictio*, his legitimate authority. The power of the king was constitutionally limited also by the subject's right of resistance to a king's wrongful commands, extending even to the right and duty to kill a king tyrant (*rex tyrannus*).

Of course, these constitutional rights of the subject were largely theoretical, in the sense that individual subjects were usually much too weak to assert them. Yet there were substantial practical limitations on royal power, imposed partly by practical difficulties of communication, which fostered delay, argument, and token obedience, and partly by the various communities to which the individual subjects belonged—the feudal nobility, the townsmen, the merchants, the clergy, and also the local and regional and clan communities that continued to command the loyalty of their members. In later centuries these various communities eventually demanded representation in assemblies ("parliaments") that advised and sometimes opposed monarchs, and entirely apart from political representation, the various classes constituted "estates" or "orders" with which kings had always to reckon. Even where a theory of tyranny was asserted, as in the Norman Kingdom of Sicily, such practical limitations on royal power were substantial. One writer has correctly described the politics of Sicily—at the height of royal despotism—in terms of a "dynamic tension between monarchy and classes of privilege that was productive of continuing renegotiation of the relationship between crown and community."[5] This description applies even more aptly to other secular territorial monarchies of that time.

To summarize, in most parts of Western Christendom there emerged in the late eleventh, twelfth, and thirteenth centuries a new type of political community, the secular territorial kingdom, which had nine significant characteristics:

1. The king was no longer the supreme spiritual leader in his domain but was instead a secular (or temporal) ruler, subordinate in spiritual matters to the Church of Rome, headed by the pope.

2. The king was no longer merely first among his leading wise men and warriors and chief lord over his vassals, but instead had authority to rule directly all subjects within his territorial domain.

3. As temporal ruler of all his subjects, the king's principal tasks were to keep the peace and to do justice, which in practice meant, chiefly, to control violence and to regulate relationships arising from landholding.

4. These and other tasks the king performed through bodies of professional royal officials, including professional royal judges, and through staffs of professional royal servants, and not only by ruling (as before) through an autonomous feudal nobility whose authority derived from their own hereditary positions.

5. The king also asserted for the first time the right and duty to legislate, that is, to enact new laws more or less frequently as the need for them arose.

6. Like the ecclesiastical state headed by the Bishop of Rome, and like the city-states headed by mayors and consuls and other officials, so the royal state, with the aid of professional adjudication and legislation, developed its own body of law.

7. In political and legal *theory*, the power of the king was limited by constitutional restraints, including restraints upon his jurisdiction as well as upon the exercise of power within his jurisdiction, and these limitations went as far as to confer upon his subjects the theoretical right and duty to resist wrongful commands and even to use force against a king tyrant.

8. In political and legal *practice*, the power of the king was limited by the power of the various communities that lived within the kingdom, in-

cluding one class — the clergy — whose power transcended the territorial boundaries of the kingdom. The power of the mercantile class, too, had an international dimension.

9. Kings constituted an international professional elite. They were very often interrelated by blood, and it was somewhat unusual for a king to be married to anyone but a member of the royal family of another European kingdom. Such intermarriage within the network of royal families certainly strengthened the kings' common consciousness of what kingship meant in practice and in theory. Each watched the others, if only as potential sources of marital alliances. More than that, each derived his character as a king partly from the recognition of his legitimacy by the others. This was the first stage in the development of the modern European system of states, in which each state took its character as a state from its participation in the system of states and from the body of international law, produced by that system, which defined state sovereignty.

These general characteristics of the new type of kingship that emerged in western Europe in the late eleventh, the twelfth, and the early thirteenth centuries were manifested in many different ways in the various Western kingdoms: Sicily (including southern Italy), England, Normandy, France, the German duchies, Flanders, the northern Spanish kingdoms, Denmark, and Hungary. The list itself suggests that there were a great variety of species within the genus.

The Norman Kingdom of Sicily

In the early decades of the eleventh century, Norman knights began going from Normandy to Italy, singly and in small groups, to serve as mercenary soldiers and otherwise to make their fortunes. Among them were eleven sons of a petty Norman baron named Tancred de Hauteville. Tancred's sons led an ever increasing number of other Norman countrymen, together with local mercenaries, in successful military raids on Apulia, Calabria, and Capua. By the 1050s they had established themselves as rulers of large parts of the southern Italian peninsula and were getting ready to attack Sicily.

For centuries Italy south of Rome had been chiefly under the rule either of Byzantium or of Islamic caliphates, or of both, and the population was predominantly Greek and Arab but also Latin, and, to a lesser extent, Jewish. In addition, some places were under Lombard rule. That was the situation when the Normans came on the scene. However, in the 1050s the papacy, which was preparing to cast off the shackles of imperial domination, and was even dreaming of leading a crusade against Islam for recovery of the Holy Sepulchre, also turned its eyes to southern Italy. In 1053 Pope Leo IX made the serious blunder of leading an army of more than a thousand Swabian, Lombard, and other mercenaries into battle against the Normans, thinking finally to stop these brigands and marauders. The papal troops were slaughtered at Civitate, east of Naples.[6]

Thereafter the papacy took a different tack: it sought to enlist the Norman leaders as allies in the impending struggle against the emperor. In 1059 at a synod held at Melfi in Apulia, Pope Nicholas II received two of Tancred's sons, Robert Guiscard (Robert the Crafty) and his brother Richard, as his own vassals—Richard as Prince of Capua and Robert as "Duke of Apulia and Calabria, by the Grace of God and of St. Peter; and, with their help in the future, Duke of Sicily." In return for this papal legitimation of their kingdom-building ambitions, Robert and Richard swore to protect the person and status of Pope Nicholas, to defend the freedom of papal elections that had been first proclaimed several months earlier at Rome, and "to support the Holy Roman Church everywhere and against all men in holding and acquiring the possession of St. Peter." Strengthened—or at least comforted—by papal support, Robert Guiscard's younger brother Roger de Hauteville took a leading role in the wars against the Moslems for the conquest of Sicily in the 1060s, and in 1072 Robert Guiscard and Roger together captured Palermo, then the largest city in Christendom except for Constantinople. Robert Guiscard named himself King of Sicily and gave most of the kingdom to Roger as a feudal fief.

Roger, who took upon himself the title Great Count of Sicily, which he held until his death in 1105, was technically not a king, though he is usually referred to as Roger I; and Robert Guiscard (who died in 1085) was a king only by his own designation. They both had strong ambitions, however, to play the kind of role which was attributed to kingship in the eleventh century and which is described in the *Norman Anonymous* of 1100: the role of vicar of Christ, chief priest and chief ruler, divinely endowed with unlimited sacral as well as political authority. Forty years before the papacy summoned the whole of Western Christendom to a crusade for the liberation of Palestine, Robert Guiscard and Roger viewed their military campaigns as Holy Wars. Embarking on battles against Moslem forces, they exhorted their followers to fight as soldiers of the army of Christ. In describing Robert Guiscard's preparations to invade Sicily, his chronicler quotes him as saying, "My desire is to deliver Catholics and Christians from the Saracens and to be an instrument of God's vengeance." During the ensuing campaigns he is represented as urging his followers to go into battle fortified by the sacrament. "Let them trust in God rather than in numbers, and rely on the Holy Spirit who will give their righteous cause the victory."[7] This was Robert's and Roger's crusade, not the pope's, though they were glad to have the papal blessing of it.

In addition to leading their followers in Holy Wars against the heathen Saracens, and incidentally against the Christian Greeks as well, Robert Guiscard and Roger also exercised supreme authority over the church within their domains. They reorganized the established bishoprics within the conquered countries and formed new ones, and they appointed their own bishops—Norman prelates or prelates with Norman sympathies. "In the course of my conquest of Sicily," said Roger, "I have established the Sicilian bishoprics."[8] He and Robert Guiscard were ardent churchmen. Both were concerned with strengthening the canon law, and they created separate ecclesiastical jurisdictions for trial of clerics. But it was *their* church and *their* canon law. They remained supreme heads of the ecclesiastical jurisdiction within their respective domains.

For this, too, they were able to secure papal support. The pope "might denounce lay investiture in unmeasured terms, but he normally confirmed without effective protest the episcopal arrangements which had been made in Sicily by that 'champion of the Christian faith the warrior Roger,' 'a man excellent in counsel and valiant in war.' "[9] Indeed, in 1098 Pope Urban II by papal bull actually conferred upon Count Roger and his successors the hereditary powers of a papal legate in Calabria and Sicily. This notorious bull (which was not revoked until 1867, shortly before the unification of Italy) gave assurance that no papal legate would enter Roger's dominions without his consent.

Why was the papacy—at the height of the Papal Revolution—willing to sacrifice, for the sake of an alliance with the Norman rulers of Sicily, the basic principle for which the revolution was being fought, namely, the freedom of the church?

First, the papacy needed the support of the Norman military power to defend the city of Rome against the emperor; and in fact, in 1084 when Henry IV, after a long siege, entered Rome, Robert Guiscard moved against him with a large force of Calabrian and Saracen mercenaries and forced him to withdraw.

Second, the papacy needed an alliance with the Norman Kingdom of Sicily in order to legitimate its struggle for the political independence of the church, and especially in order to legitimate its revolt against political domination of the papacy by the emperor. In 1059, when the Easter Council at Rome proclaimed freedom of papal elections, the papacy was, from a political point of view, still an integral part of the empire. It lacked the capacity to have independent political relations with any other body. The existence of the Norman polity gave the papacy an opportunity to establish political relations with another power, independently of the emperor or of anyone else. The fact that Robert Guiscard and his brothers were wholly outside the empire enhanced the significance of this assertion of an independent papal power to conduct foreign relations. Thus the alliance with the Normans of the south marked an important step in the emergence of the papacy as a state in the modern sense.

The papacy, however, paid a heavy price for taking this step. The Norman rulers of southern Italy were ruthless tyrants, and they and their followers not only dominated the church in their domains but also displayed a sadistic cruelty that was wholly incongrous with their passionate belief in Christianity. For example, in 1084, three days after Robert Guiscard and his troops had liberated Rome from Emperor Henry IV, they proceeded, because of an uprising, to burn, ransack, and destroy the city, to rob, rape, and murder, and to send many leading citizens into slavery. Pope Gregory VII fled in desolation from his capital—ravaged not by his imperial enemies but by his Norman allies and liberators.

To turn to the other side of the coin, why were the Norman rulers willing to risk, for the sake of an alliance with the papacy, a possible challenge to their absolutist theories of power and their conception of the sacral kingship? Why, indeed, for the sake of that alliance, were they willing to fight the emperor even though at the time they had no other reason to do so and were quite preoccupied with the Arabs and Greeks in the south?

First, Robert Guiscard and Roger needed the blessing of the papacy to make them kings. Otherwise they had power but not authority. In the case of the Germanic kings, authority had rested traditionally on heredity or election. The theory of the papal party added a third source of royal authority: consecration by authority of the pope. The Norman chiefs had no hereditary claim to rule southern Italy. They did, in fact, arrange to be "elected" by their followers and "consecrated" by their own prelates, but everyone saw through this device. Only the Bishop of Rome could legitimate their power and their conquests and thus make them permanent—just as only they could legitimate his political independence from the emperor and thus make it permanent.[10] By recognizing each other's legitimacy, the pope and the Norman ruler of Sicily established the first two modern states in Europe, the one an ecclesiastical state, the other a secular state.

Second, under the papal party, the Roman Church gave a new mission to the kings and the kingdoms of Europe, a mission which coincided particularly with the interests of the Norman rulers of the south and in which those rulers ardently believed. In part, the mission was geopolitical—to unite the West against the Saracen world, to turn the West militarily and politically and economically to the south and east. In part the mission was national—to inspire secular rulers to organize their respective territorial polities and to establish peace among warring tribes and among warring feudal lords. In part the mission was legal—to establish justice, and to reform the world by law. The Normans of southern Italy enthusiastically embraced these goals of the papal party. They were delighted to lead armies in crusades against the Saracens (and Greeks), and eventually to establish peace and trade among the polyglot peoples of their own and neighboring kingdoms. Also they were, like their fellow Normans in Normandy and in England, great administrators and lawyers; they came to share the papacy's faith in the reforming and redeeming power of legal institutions.

Their ties with Rome helped the Normans to create in southern Italy not only a legitimate state power but also a brilliant civilization — indeed, the wealthiest and most powerful state and the greatest center of art, science, and technology in the West in the mid-twelfth century. Under Roger II (1112-1154), its capital, Palermo, was the largest and most cosmopolitan city in the West. Its commercial fleet was the greatest in Europe. It was the granary for North Africa and the largest supplier of silks and silk fabrics to the European continent. It was foremost in astronomy, geography, and other sciences, drawing heavily on the intellectual resources of the Moslem world and, through it, on those of the East, including possibly China. Its medical school at the University of Salerno was the best in Europe. Literature and learning at the royal court at Palermo combined the best of the Latin, Arabic, and Greek traditions. French poetry and Arabic poetry were read, and Plato, Euclid, and Ptolemy were translated into Latin. The palaces and cathedrals of twelfth-century Sicily, combining the Norman Romanesque style of architecture with Byzantine mosaic art, remain among the greatest artistic treasures of Europe.

Yet the Normans, too, eventually paid a heavy price for their alliance with the papacy. The tensions between their belief in the Roman Church and their total domination of the clergy within their own domain, between their belief in legality and their own tyrannical power, between their passionate Christian faith and their own barbaric cruelties, as well as the tensions among the Western, Byzantine, and Moslem, the Norman, Greek, and Arab components of their culture, led them into their self-destruction. That self-destruction came after Roger II's grandson, Emperor Frederick II — who was also the grandson of Emperor Frederick Barbarossa — used his mighty power to restore imperial authority over the church and to include under his domination not only southern Italy and, nominally, the German territories, which he ruled by heredity, but also the Italian cities of the north. Indeed, Frederick, who was perhaps the most brilliant and the most powerful monarch in the history of Europe after Charlemagne and prior to Napoleon, did not stop with Italy but led a crusade in defiance of papal excommunication and crowned himself King of Jerusalem. When he died in 1250, his son Manfred continued his policy of subduing the northern Italian cities, until Pope Urban IV found a champion in Charles of Anjou, to whom the pope offered the crown of Sicily if he would eliminate Manfred. This Charles finally did, in 1266. However, Charles, too, succumbed to overweening ambition, arrogance, and cruelty. His downfall came on the island of Sicily, which he had subjected to despotic rule by Frenchmen. The Sicilian population rose in 1282 and massacred the French oppressors. Called the Sicilian Vespers, this uprising resulted eventually in the expulsion of the French from the island of Sicily and their confinement to Calabria and Apulia, henceforth called the Kingdom of Naples. Sicily itself was henceforth ruled by Aragon. Both parts of what was called later "the two Sicilies" were devastated and demoralized by the wars that led to their separation, and neither fully recovered.

THE NORMAN STATE

If the Norman Kingdom of Sicily, which was the leading kingdom of Europe in the twelfth century, had had a future comparable to that of the Norman Kingdom of England, the political and legal institutions that were created in twelfth-century Sicily would be as much studied and as widely known today as those of twelfth-century England. For the Kingdom of Sicily constituted the first modern territorial state in the West, with the first modern Western system of royal law.

The Normans of Sicily showed the same administrative genius as that shown by their fellow countrymen in Normandy and England. Characteristically, they did not attempt to abolish the preexisting political and legal institutions of the conquered peoples but rather sought to exploit those institutions to the maximum extent possible within the framework of a new political-administrative-legal structure that was both more centralized and more decentralized.

A similar willingness to preserve the old and adapt it to the new had characterized those Norsemen who, in 911, first settled permanently in the Frankish empire, in what came to be called Normandy: they respected and assimilated and adapted to new conditions the more advanced customs of the vanquished Franks. Their descendants who occupied England a century and a half later were also concerned to preserve, where feasible, the political and legal institutions of the Anglo-Saxons. So in southern Italy the Norman rulers adapted to their own use various features of the preexisting political and legal culture, while at the same time transforming that culture into a new type of state and a new type of law.

In southern Italy the Normans found an advanced, though decaying, polity, itself a mixture of many elements. It was organized partly under a Moslem governor at Palermo, called an "emir," who ruled autocratically through a number of governmental departments. The Norman rulers — starting with Robert Guiscard — retained the office of governor at Palermo, and even the title "emir," rendered in Latin as *amiratus* (from which the modern naval title "admiral" is derived); moreover, most of the persons who held this office in the first century of Norman rule were of Greek or Arab origin. The amiratus, like his predecessors, ruled through governmental departments, and these, too, were staffed with officials trained in the earlier administrative theory and practice — chiefly Byzantine in Apulia, chiefly Arab in Sicily. The Normans added, however, a system of civil service examinations, open to persons of various classes; this innovation may have been inspired by the Chinese example as reported by Arab or Jewish travelers.[11]

In addition to exploiting existing institutions, the Normans created new central offices connected closely with the royal court. One was the chancery, probably modeled after the papal chancery. Its head, at first called protonotary and later chancellor, had the power of the royal seal and was responsible for issuing, in the name of the king, mandates, diplomas, decrees, and writs of various kinds. Roger II's chancellor, Guarin, was the king's alter ego, who ruled the kingdom when the king was away fighting wars.

Another new central office was the treasury, at first called the *dogana*, which handled royal accounts and administered a sophisticated system of taxation. The treasury owed something of its character to the preexisting Arab financial office of the *diwan* and to the Arabic system of reckoning. It probably also owed much to the highly developed structure of financial administration and taxation created in the late eleventh and early twelfth centuries in the papal curia.

Still another new official body created by the Normans was a professional royal court, with jurisdiction over the most serious crimes as well as over civil disputes between freemen involving breach of the peace and property rights in freehold land. In 1136 Roger II appointed a "justiciar" to hear cases and to head the royal system of justice. Itinerant justices were sent out from the royal court to hold assizes in the provinces. In time, the itinerant justices became permanently settled, and the high court in Palermo was reserved for the most important cases. By the end of the twelfth century the courts of feudal lords and of the cities were brought into direct subordination to the king's courts, which had a monopoly over what were variously called "pleas of the crown," "pleas of the sword," "blood jurisdiction," and "high justice." This had no parallel in Byzantine or Moslem practice.

The Normans in twelfth-century Sicily also created the institution of royal bailiffs, called *baiuli*, who were similar both in name and in function to the bailiffs (*ballivi*) of the Duchy of Normandy. They were, at first, executive officers of the crown, delegated to carry out royal orders. Later they acquired broader administrative and quasi-judicial powers. They had tenure of office. In the thirteenth century, under Frederick II, they became salaried, removable officials.

Through such sophisticated governmental institutions, the Norman kings of Sicily strengthened their links with the people as a whole and thus their control over the feudal and urban aristocracy. The king was not merely overlord of his tenants-in-chief; he ruled all the people in his territory directly—though not in all respects. If his vassals sought to exercise their feudal right of resistance against him, he could call on the entire population to support him militarily and could invoke not merely feudal but royal penal sanctions, including destruction of castles, money fines, incarceration, and outlawry.[12]

The centralized control of the Sicilian monarchy over the feudal nobility is reflected in the system of military service, and particularly in the issuance of a written register of fixed duties of knight's service. The *Catalogus Baronum*, issued by Roger II, fixed the number of mounted knights to be provided to the king by each baron. This was the minimum number, however, and in case of need the crown could claim the military services of the entire nation. Provision seems to have been made also for money commutation of knight's service.[13] The Sicilian *Catalogue of Barons* very likely served as a model for the English and Norman inquests of knight's service of 1166 and 1172, respectively, and for the record of fees (*scripta de feodis*) of King Philip Augustus of France.

Another example of central control by the Sicilian monarchy over the feudal aristocracy was the practice of reserving liege loyalty to the king in every mutual oath of fealty sworn by a vassal and his lord. Still another example was the maintenance of the royal power of consent to the marriage of a vassal or subvassal—a power which for the most part was exercised indirectly as a tax measure but which on occasion could be exercised directly as a political measure. Both these examples have parallels in twelfth-century England, where a similar royal control was also exercised over the feudal aristocracy through a chancery, an exchequer, itinerant royal justices, sheriffs, knight's service, and the reserve power of a military conscription of the whole people (*fyrd*).

In sharp contrast to England, however, as well as to the other countries of Europe, the Norman kings of southern Italy were not considered to be subject to law (and in that sense prototypes, at least, of constitutional monarchs), but on the contrary were considered to be autocrats and even tyrants. Here Byzantine and Arabic models may also have made a contribution. Ruling the church, like the Byzantine emperors, the Norman kings were the chief priests of their kingdom. A mosaic in the twelfth-century church of the Martorana in Palermo shows King Roger II receiving his crown directly from Christ, without mediation by pope or archbishop, and a similar mosaic in the cathedral at Monreale shows his son William II also receiving his crown directly from Christ. Moreover, there were no free cities in the Norman Kingdom of Sicily; that is, cities were governed by appointees of the crown, and although there were urban privileges they were always subordinate to the royal will. Finally, the king was not chief baron in the feudal hierarchy but directly lord of all subvassals and, indeed, of all inhabitants of his territory. In all these respects he was an autocrat (a "self-ruler"), with no limitations on his jurisdiction.

He was, in addition, a tyrant, in the sense that there was no legal restraint, in theory or in practice, upon his power to act arbitrarily and despotically. His authority was absolute, in the technical sense of that term; that is, he was "absolved" from the law. The Norman kings of southern Italy generally preferred to rule by law, and to a considerable extent they were compelled to rule by law in order to control their subjects, but they themselves were considered to be above the law. In fact, they did not hesitate to engage in barbaric cruelties not only against those who opposed them but also against those who did not oppose them. They were pleased to inspire even in their supporters not only awe but also terror.

The experience of the Norman Kingdom of Sicily challenges the conventional view that modern Western concepts of legality originated in compromises between the needs and policies of strong monarchies, on the one hand, and the traditions and interests of preexisting feudal and local political communities, on the other. The history of Sicily shows, on the contrary, that it was possible for a highly developed system of royal law, which penetrated the country from top to bottom, to coexist with the despotic power of the ruler. There are striking similarities between the systems of royal law in England and in Sicily in the twelfth century: in both, the monarchy established links with the nation as a whole, and, by constructing a central legal system that reached down to all the people, succeeded in confining the special interests of the feudal aristocracy. Yet in England, as Mitteis has said, "the royal law always found its limit in the legal sense of the community."[14] In southern Italy there had never been a strong tradition of tribal (clan) and regional customary law such as had existed in Germanic and Frankish Europe. Perhaps the weakness of the legal sense of the community led its rulers to excesses; perhaps their claim of unlimited authority weakened still further that legal sense. A simpler though not unrelated explanation is that in England, as in all other countries of the West *except* Sicily, the Church of Rome was strong enough to limit substantially both the power and the authority of the monarchy.

THE PERSONALITY OF ROGER II

In attempting to discover the causes of legal development, one is aware that individual personalities may play a significant role, especially in times of rapid legal change, and yet it is usually very difficult to assess that role with any high degree of assurance. Do the times create the man, or the man the times? Roger II was clearly the right man at the right time. Born in December 1095, Roger was nine years old when his father, the Great Count Roger I, died in 1105. His mother, Adelaide, a north Italian, the Great Count's third wife, ruled as regent, relying principally on Sicilian ministers of Greek or Arab extraction. In 1112 Roger, at sixteen and a half, was thought to be mature enough to rule in his own name. Brought up in the predominantly Arab city of Palermo, surrounded by Moslem and Greek tutors, secretaries, and officials, he had been educated in the most advanced geography, mathematics, and science of his time, in Byzantine as well as Norman art and music, and in the poetry and philosophy of both the East and the West.

Both during the regency and in the first decades of his own reign there were frequent baronial revolts. Roger was a determined and successful but unenthusiastic warrior. He had not been trained in feudal virtues and values. He had been trained, rather, for absolute power of the kind wielded formerly by the Roman emperors of Byzantium and contemporaneously by the Sultan of Egypt. According to the chroniclers of his time, Roger craved power and glory, but preferred to gain and maintain them less by war than by diplomacy and intrigue. He is described as intelligent, devious, patient, sometimes ferocious, sometimes generous, combining enlightened tolerance with terrible cruelty. In avenging himself against rebellious barons he did not hesitate to raze cities and destroy every man, woman, and child left in them. Yet he much preferred science and philosophy, music and art, the display and ostentation of court life, the pleasures of his harem.

Was there something in Roger's personality that drew him to law? One may speculate that he saw in law both a key to power and glory and a peaceful means of controlling his polyglot kingdom. No doubt also his ambition to be like the Eastern Roman emperors led him to emulate them in lawmaking as well. In addition, he had other examples before him—the example of the papacy, which was at that very time promoting the rapid development of a new body of canon law, and the much earlier example of the Lombard kingdom, which before its disintegration had had a written "code" of customary law, the *Liber Papiensis*.[15] Some features of Roman law and of Lombard law survived in Roger's kingdom, and of course canon law was applicable there—at least theoretically—as it was throughout Europe. Moreover, the very weakness of canon law, Lombard law, Roman law, and the other kinds of law in southern Italy—above all, the very absence of a strong tradition of folklaw—added to the challenge to create a new system of royal law.

These reasons for creating such a system existed apart from Roger II's personality. It required, to be sure, a ruler of intelligence, ambition, power, and similar virtues, to respond to the need. Yet Roger contributed something more than the carrying out of a preexisting historical mission. He added a new element, which is easier to recount than to characterize. He carved out of the legal universe a separate jurisdiction, that of the King of Sicily in matters of high justice, and then he defined that jurisdiction by a set of interlocking principles and rules that created a unified and developing body of law. He set forth a series of interrelated principles establishing and justifying royal jurisdiction of a certain type. No one had ever done that before.

Roger's achievement, which was embodied in the Assizes of Ariano (1140), was closely related to his personality and character, and especially to the combination of his Norman, Byzantine, and possibly Arab qualities. Max Hoffman has rightly called Roger the "first modern Prince," who "founded the first absolute monarchy of Western Europe."[16] But he did more than that. He founded the first modern system of royal law. He united a polyglot people of the most diverse character, who previously had had only the weakest tradition of law, under a unified, developing body of legal rules and procedures applicable in the king's courts. His legislation was not the whole law applicable to his subjects, and not even the whole royal law; but that substantial part of the royal law which it did cover, it covered systematically and in a principled way. It did not attempt to reduce the entire complexity and disorder of life to a system or a set of principles, but rather it carved out of that complexity and disorder a particular area, or jurisdiction, to which an intelligent and coherent order could be brought, thereby making the surrounding chaos more tolerable.

THE NORMAN LEGAL SYSTEM

That the Norman kings of southern Italy used law to effectuate their rule imposed certain practical limits upon their power as well as upon their authority.

In contrast to the Germanic kings of an earlier time, who were judges but not legislators, the Norman rulers of the twelfth century and thereafter considered it part of the office of the king to make new laws. Roger II declared that the king is a "maker of laws" (*conditor legum*). Indeed, Roger promulgated the first modern code of royal law in the history of the West, the Assizes of Ariano. This is called a modern code and the first of its kind in the West because it did not purport to be merely a collection of rules and principles but instead was a systematic presentation of what were thought to be basic features of the legal system. Moreover, it was presented as positive law, enacted by the king as legislator. It drew, to be sure, on customary law, natural law, and divine law, and it fused many diverse features of the Byzantine, Moslem, Lombard, Norman, and Romano-canonical legal traditions, but it recast those sources in the form of a new and comprehensive legislative act.

The Assizes of Ariano consist of a preamble and forty-four separate, numbered articles, many of them comprising several paragraphs. The text purports to be written by the king himself; there is no mention in it of the assembly of dignitaries at Ariano at which the Assizes were adopted. The preamble states that "since God in his mercy has . . . restored peace [and] reformed the integrity of the kingdom . . . we [the king] are compelled also to reform the paths of justice and piety where we see it being wretchedly distorted." "This is not from pride, as though we claim by our vigils to be more just or more moderate than our predecessors in issuing laws and interpreting them, but because . . . piety itself has instructed us, saying: 'Be merciful even as your father is merciful.' " Of special importance here are two points: the laws are issued in order to reform the paths of justice and piety, and it is the role of the king to issue laws and to interpret them.

Article 1 (technically the articles are referred to as "Assizes") is entitled "Concerning the interpretation of laws." It provides: "We command that the laws newly promulgated by our majesty be observed by all generally, softening too great strictness by the sentiment of piety, stiffening flexibility by a certain restraint, clarifying what is obscure." Thus the text is understood necessarily to contain ambiguities and to be subject to interpretation.

Article 2 is entitled "Concerning the privilege of holy churches," and it affirms that the king will protect churches and keep them inviolate. Of interest is the fact that throughout the Assizes "church" is always in the plural and, in addition, no mention is made of any ecclesiastical independence from the crown or of any subordination of the clergy to papal authority. Rights of the churches are spelled out in articles 5 through 16, dealing with such matters as the sale of holy relics, right to sanctuary, royal jurisdiction over cases of violation of churches, privileges of bishops not to testify except in certain matters and of priests not to swear oaths, prohibition of illegal conventicles (house worship), prohibition of purchase and sale of clerical offices, and similar matters.

Articles 17 through 21 deal with high crimes against the crown, including the crime of disputing the king's judgments, conspiracies against him, forgery of royal documents, and counterfeiting of money. Article 22 deals with the inquisitional procedure to be used in cases of "falsehood," which are then defined in article 22 through 26 to include issuance of false documents, bearing of false witness, interference with the making of wills, taking of public funds by public officers and judges, and negligent or intentional loss or taking of public goods.

Article 27 concerns family law (celebration of marriage), and articles 28 through 33 deal with sex offenses (adultery, prostitution, pandering, rape). Article 34 provides for composition in cases of insult; this alone is treated as a matter to be settled privately. Under article 35 injuries are punishable according to the status of the person injured. Article 36 provides that physicians may not practice without being licensed by the king. (In fact, a system of examinations was introduced for doctors, the first example of such a system in Europe.) Articles 38 to 43 deal with kidnapping (selling into slavery), killing in self-defense, nonresponsibility of infants and insane persons, homicide by a thief in the night, arson, causing a crime to be committed (which was not itself made punishable), and poisoning. The last article (44) makes a judge punishable for fraudulently or negligently rendering a false judgment.[17]

Max Hofmann has contrasted the "structured" character of the Assizes of Ariano with the "casuistic" character of the older Lombard *Liber Papiensis*. The latter was much longer, with about one thousand items, and purported to cover the whole law. However, in Hofmann's words, it "tries to regulate every fact situation separately and rarely sets forth principles." It is disjointed and "full of gaps and contradictions." In contrast, the Assizes of Ariano do not purport to cover the whole law. Nevertheless, "none of its provisions are thinkable except in relationship to the others . . . Moreover . . . in the areas covered by it it is sufficiently complete; the gaps can be filled by purpose-oriented (*Zweckentsprechende*) interpretation of the laws that are given."

Hofmann adds: "Precisely this necessity of interpreting the laws before applying them strengthened the influence of the state power, since the interpretation could not simply be carried out by everyone, but rather was in principle the right of the king."[18] "Justice [became] a public concern, [to be] handled by specially trained officials."[19]

Roger II's laws clearly established royal supremacy over the church, over the feudal nobility, over the city communes, and over the people generally. The prosecution of heretics was entrusted to the monarchy in its own right and not as executor of a decision of the ecclesiastical authorities. The king severely limited the jurisdiction of feudal courts. None of the cities succeeded in constituting itself a free town; all of them were headed by officials appointed by the king. The entire population was subjected directly to the royal authority, and it was made punishable as treason, *laesio maiestatis*, to conspire not only against the king but also against any of his leading men.

Royal supremacy did not, however, exclude the rights of subordinates vis-à-vis each other, and even (within limits) vis-à-vis the crown. With respect to the church, the Norman kings generally accepted the jurisdiction of ecclesiastical courts, operating under canon law, in most types of cases involving clerics, as well as in cases of spiritual offenses of lay persons, family matters, wills, and any dispute which both parties agreed to submit to ecclesiastical jurisdiction. The ecclesiastical courts were, to be sure, themselves under the king as hereditary papal legate. Normally, however, the king would follow papal decisions and interpretations of the law, and if he did not, his decision might be reversed by the pope. The Norman kings, for all their Caesaropapist policies, did not deny—in theory—the supremacy of the papacy in spiritual matters. Even Emperor Frederick II, in a famous letter to the teachers and students of the University of Bologna, in which he asserted that the emperor is God's vicar on earth in all temporal matters, reaffirmed that the pope is God's vicar on earth in all spiritual matters.[20] Thus the dualism of church and state had important constitutional and legal consequences in the Kingdom of Sicily, as it did throughout the West, although in Sicily the scales were weighted much more heavily in favor of the state than they were elsewhere.

In addition to legal limitations on royal power and authority imposed by the dual jurisdiction of ecclesiastical and temporal courts, there were also legal limitations imposed by the dual jurisdiction, within the temporal sphere, of feudal and royal courts. The king severely limited the feudal jurisdiction, particularly by withdrawing into royal courts cases of serious crimes committed by lay persons, as well as many types of disputes involving freehold land. Nevertheless, for lesser crimes and for many types of civil matters each feudal lord had his own court, to which his tenants paid suit. This meant that a great part of local government—outside the cities—was in the hands of feudal lords, ruling chiefly by manorial law.

In addition, lord-vassal relations were governed by feudal law, which also exercised a restraining influence on royal absolutism. In the eleventh century, the Norman rulers in southern Italy had parceled out the conquered lands to their Norman countrymen as fiefs, dispossessing prior landholders and creating a new aristocracy. The most important of the new landholders held their estates directly from the king as tenants-in-chief and were charged with the duty of providing a specified number of mounted knights for military service. Subinfeudation was permitted, but subtenants were required either to provide the military service of others or else to serve themselves. The contractual aspects of these relationships were strongly emphasized. The amount of service owed by tenants to lords was supposed to be clearly specified in advance of the grant of a fief. Careful distinctions were drawn between various types of feudal obligations. Seignorial courts had competence to resolve lord-vassal disputes. The royal court itself might meet as a feudal court, with the chief tenants attending as suitors. In all this, Norman Sicily followed a pattern remarkably similiar to that followed by the Norman rulers in England and Normandy. The Sicilian monarch dominated his tenants-in-chief—and also their subtenants—to a greater extent than his English counterpart; nevertheless, the feudal system in the Kingdom of Sicily (especially in Apulia, where central authority had been established much more slowly and there was a multiplicity of small fiefs), like the feudal system in England and Normandy, as well as in France, Germany, and elsewhere in western Europe, combined centralized and decentralized elements, holding them together through legal institutions and legal processes.

The judicial authority of the king was exercised immediately by his own "great court" (*magna curia*), consisting of himself and the principal officers of his household together with various lay and ecclesiastical dignitaries. However, professional judges also existed from an early time, inherited from the Byzantine government. Roger II made use of local professional judges ("justiciars") in the cities and also introduced professional judges into the royal *curia*. Professionals came to play a predominant role, and after 1168 the exclusive role, in the king's central court.[21] Roger II also introduced professional justiciars at the provincial level; in the 1140s such justiciars, many of them bishops and archbishops, were stationed in all the major subdivisions of the kingdom. "Evidently a group of justices was assigned to a particular region for a series of years."[22] They had jurisdiction over major crimes, which included robbery, housebreaking, assaults on the highway, rape, homicide, ordeals, criminal slander, and arson. (Lesser offenses were tried by lesser royal officials, the bailiffs.) In addition, the competence of the provincial justiciars included civil disputes over lands or villeins and complaints concerning the exactions or royal officers. (The bailiffs had cognizance of civil cases that did not relate to feudal tenures.)

Charles Haskins states that "no difference can be discerned between the matters which were brought before the *magna curia* and those submitted to the provincial justices, so that it seems probable that these were simply two forms of the same royal jurisdiction; but the complaint would seem to have been lodged in the first instance with the *magna curia*, and the justices regularly act by virtue of a royal writ."[23]

The procedure of the various royal courts (central, provincial, local, and urban) in twelfth-century Norman Italy differed in different types of cases. It also showed traces of many different traditions, including Norman, Lombard, Byzantine, and Arab. Under Lombard influence, local laymen were used as wise men to advise the judge in certain types of cases. The Germanic ordeals of fire and water and compurgation by twelve oath helpers were also used, as well as the Norman trial by combat. However, under the influence of the new Romano-canonical procedure of the twelfth century, and of the new scholastic legal science, Roger II also introduced an inquisitional procedure, in which the judge interrogated witnesses (including witnesses not presented by the parties) and examined written evidence. Article 22 of the Assizes of Ariano prescribed that "a diligent inquisition should examine arguments, witnesses, written evidence, and other indicators of truth," and that the udge should respect not only the evidence presented by the prosecutor but also "should be in the middle between each person, so that he will only render judgment according to all competent evidence carefully sought out." This is a very early example of the introduction of a system of rational proof in the royal courts of Europe. In Carolingian times, to be sure, proof by inquest, or inquisition, had been used, but in a much more primitive form and for proof of facts in a much narrower circle of cases, and only in the court of the king himself or the courts of ecclesiastical or noble dignitaries specially designated. The Assizes of Ariano, by contrast, provided for a much more elaborate procedure which was extended to a substantial variety of cases in all the courts that had jurisdiction over them; moreover, the procedure was used not only at the stage of trial to prove the elements of the offense but also, in criminal cases, at the stage of indictment, to discover the probable offender.[24]

The Growth of Royal Law in Norman Italy

In the century and a half, roughly, from the accession of King Roger II in 1112 to the death of his grandson Frederick in 1250, the rulers of southern Italy remained among the most powerful, the wealthiest, and culturally the most sophisticated of the secular rulers of western Europe. Their success in these respects was due in considerable part to the genius of their governmental and legal institutions. It was, to be sure, an autocratic genius: the king remained above the law, not only in practice but even in theory. There was in Norman Sicily no doctrine similar to that which was later called in England "the rule of law," and in Germany the *Rechtsstaat*. There was, however, a strong belief in rule *by* law. Moreover, the law by which the autocrat ruled was believed to have the function of maintaining not only order but also justice; and further, it was conceived as a continually developing system, one that grew over time. Roger's successors built on the foundations that he had laid, periodically issuing new laws to meet new circumstances, while maintaining the basic principles of the system as a whole.

Frederick, who inherited the throne of Sicily in 1197 at the age of three and began to rule in 1208 at the age of fourteen, completed the process of centralization and bureaucratization of state authority that his maternal grandfather, Roger, had begun. (His paternal grandfather was Emperor Frederick Barbarossa and his father was Emperor Henry VI; he himself was crowned Emperor Frederick II in 1220.) Among Frederick II's reforms was the confiscation of all the castles of his southern Italian kingdom, both on the island of Sicily and on the mainland, and their transformation from private fortresses and residences into government forts operated by a department of defense and occupied by small garrisons.[25] He converted all the government officials into a royal civil service, and paid their salaries as well as other costs of royal government out of customs duties, taxes, and royal monopolies. He founded the University of Naples for the express purpose of training government officials. He enacted comprehensive legislation and expanded the scope of the judicial power to apply it.

Frederick II was called by his European contemporaries *immutator mundi* ("transformer of the world") and *stupor mundi* ("wonder of the world"). He was indeed a man of extraordinary dynamism and stupendous abilities, probably one of the most talented persons who ever lived. In addition to being an outstanding military leader, statesman, and lawgiver, he was a skilled scientist, especially in the fields of mathematics, anatomy, and zoology; he was also a speculative thinker, an architect, a poet who wrote love songs in vernacular Italian two generations before Dante, and the author of what is said to be the most authoritative book on falconry ever written, *The Art of Falconry*. He spoke not only Italian but also French, German, Arabic, Latin, and Greek. These civilized qualities were combined, however, with an utter ruthlessness and barbarism which he practiced not only against his enemies but also against innocent people, sometimes only for the sake of satisfying his scientific curiosity. Frederick's ruthlessness was manifested also in his lust for power and his belief in his own destiny to be the absolute ruler of Christendom.

To one degree or another, many of these conflicting qualities are reflected in his codification of the law of the Kingdom of Sicily, promulgated in 1231, which he called the Augustan Laws (*leges augustales*, or *constitutiones augustales*). In modern times it has usually been called the *Liber Augustalis* (Augustan Book) and sometimes the *Constitutions of Melfi*.

The *Liber Augustalis* is a far more comprehensive and systematic codification than the Assizes of Ariano. It contains 253 articles (called "titles") and runs to some 150 pages in a modern printed translation.[26] It is divided into a preamble and three "books," of which the first is devoted primarily to questions of public order, including substantive criminal law, administration of justice, and pretrial civil procedure, the second primarily to civil and criminal procedure, and the third primarily to substantive civil law, including royal and feudal property law, and to miscellaneous offenses. The whole was intended to be "a mirror of perfection for all who look therein, the envy of every prince, the model of every kingdom."[27] Yet it was also intended to be—and was—rooted in the historical circumstances of the Sicilian kingdom and designed to meet its practical needs of government.

The Western concept of law as an organically developing system is reflected in the fact that the *Liber Augustalis* included sixty-two articles expressly attributed to Frederick's chief predecessors on the Sicilian throne—Roger II, William I, and William II. Moreover, it was later supplemented by new enactments of Frederick II, which were added under the heading "Novels."

An example of the way in which the *Liber Augustalis* built on the foundation of earlier legislation is found in two of its provisions concerning the legal status of women. The first is a law attributed to King Roger, which states: "We settle the equity of the laws for women who have been injured because of the weakness of their sex by ordering that they should be aided by us as well as by our officials to the best of their ability as is decent and necessary" (bk. 2, title 41). This is followed by a much longer law of Emperor Frederick, which starts with the words, "In order to clarify the obscurity of the law that the divine King Roger, our grandfather, promulgated about the restitution of legal status for women, we order . . . " The new law then distinguishes between injury to women through the negligence or fraud of their guardians or attorneys and losses suffered by women who were adequately represented and which were not due to their weakness as women. It also lists specific types of cases in which women should be protected against the consequences of illegal acts committed by them "through ignorance of the law" or "through ignorance on account of the weakness of their sex" (bk. 1, title 44).

Another example of continuity and development is the reproduction of a very brief law of King Roger forbidding nobles, both secular and ecclesiastical, to alienate or diminish royal property or royal rights (bk. 3, title 1), followed by a law of Frederick that begins, "In order to amplify the constitution issued by our grandfather, King Roger, of divine memory, about the forbidden diminution of fiefs and feudal property, we order that all alienations and contracts of any king that diminish or alter fiefs or feudal property should have no validity at all unless they are confirmed by the special license of our highness." Frederick's law goes on to say that all oaths or penalties inserted in such contracts should have no validity, and that judgments handed down by anyone other than a justiciar, based on compromise or negotiations in such matters, should be invalid. However, an exception is provided for barons and knights to settle on inheritances, provided that rents and services owed by ancient custom are not diminished (bk. 3, title 5).

A third example of the growth of law reflected in the *Liber Augustalis* has to do with the licensing of physicians. A law of King Roger provided that no one might become a physician without examination by royal officials and judges, "so that subjects in our kingdom may not be experimented on by inexperienced physicians" (bk. 3, title 44). To this Frederick added the requirement that the prospective physician be "approved in a convened public examination by the Masters of [the University of] Salerno," and, in addition, that he present certificates of trustworthiness and sufficient knowledge both from the masters and from persons appointed by the king, and that he obtain a "license for healing" from the king or, in his absence, from the person ruling in the king's place. The penalty for violation of this law was confiscation of goods and a year in jail.

In addition to reflecting the Western concept of law as a growing body, a developing system, of principles, rules, procedures, and institutions, the *Liber Augustalis* also reflected the Western concept of law as a complex unity based on synthesis and reconciliation of opposing elements. It was drafted by men trained in the scholastic legal science of Bologna. The text itself refers to the fact that the laws which it contains were "compiled by Master Petrus della Vigna of Capua, judge of our great court," who is known to have studied at Bologna and to have been a protégé of Archbishop Jacopo of Capua, himself a teacher at Bologna. Many of the legal terms and legal doctrines are derived from the Justinian texts as glossed and commented on by contemporary legal scholarship. "Still it would be a serious mistake"—as James M. Powell has said—"to regard the *Liber Augustalis* as merely an adaptation of Justinianic law. As a matter of fact, the manner of compilation suggests that this was not the case at all. The approach was one of seeking the law from the *viri antiquores* of the kingdom as well as from the practices of the court. As the constitutions make clear, it was the task of the compilers to find the common law of the kingdom and to transform it into a royal law." "But," Powell adds, "if no such law existed for the whole kingdom, and it did not, then the task was to create one."[28]

The text itself uses the phrase "common law" to refer to both Roman law and Lombard law. In addition, as Powell emphasizes, the traditions of Norman law and of the canon law provided sources on which the compiler of the *Liber Augustalis* drew. Above all, however, he was "moved by the spirit of scholasticism that informed the intellectual life of the age to resolve differences within the existing legal tradition of the *regno* and to distill his legal knowledge and that of his associates, probably practical men of the courts, into a unified body of law . . . the active force in shaping the corpus sprang from the practical political needs and the internal social conflict faced by the Sicilian monarchy."[29]

A major political need of the Sicilian monarchy was to give legal expression to the vast increase in royal power that had taken place by 1231. The *Liber Augustalis* departs from the spirit and theory of the Papal Revolution in presenting the king as a person of unlimited authority. The preamble states that "princes of nations" are "judges of life and death for mankind" and "executors in some way of Divine Providence," who have the power to "decide . . . how each man should have fortune, estate, and status." It also states that princes "render account" to God—the implication is, directly to God—for their defense of Holy Church. Elsewhere Frederick stated: "As God the father is manifested through Christ, so is justice manifested through the emperor. As Christ, has founded his church, so the emperor has founded his empire."[30] The church, in this concept, insofar as it is a visible, institutional church, is within the empire, and all temporal power of the church is subordinate to the emperor. Frederick not only defied the temporal power of the papacy but fought it with force of arms. In 1228 he launched his own crusade, against papal orders, and after capturing Jerusalem he returned to defeat a papal army that had invaded his southern Italian kingdom in his absence. He also fought the papal authority in the northern Italian cities over which he was emperor. In 1245 Pope Innocent IV formally declared him to be "rejected by God," deposed from imperial authority, and outlawed.

Nevertheless, despite the assertion of absolute royal authority, Frederick's legislation recognized the continued autonomy of feudal law and ecclesiastical law, though not of urban law.

With regard to feudal law, the *Liber Augustalis* provided: "So that due honor may be completely preserved for . . . counts, barons, and other knightly men, we reserve their judgments to their peers." Counts and barons were to judge "according to our sacred decrees or in their lack according to the approved customs of the kingdom" (bk. 1, title 47). Higher penalties were imposed for offenses against nobles by nonnobles, and greater weight was given to the oath of a noble in suits for debt (bk. 1, title 101.) In addition, dower rights of wives were protected against superiors in the feudal hierarchy (bk.3, title 16). Aids could be exacted from vassals for the ransom of their lord, for the knighting of their lord's sons, at the marriage of his daughters and sisters, and also when he bought land for service to the king or for his army (bk. 3, title 20). A lord was authorized to disseise a vassal who was unwilling to give a pledge for him or make account for him in legal proceedings, or who committed a felony against him, his children, or his wife; and "in the contrary case, if a lord is not willing to give a pledge for his vassal who has been accused in a criminal matter in court that does not concern the royal majesty, or if he beats him without cause, or if he commits adultery with his wife, or if he violates his daughter against her will, the lord will lose his homage and the aforesaid man will belong directly to our court" (bk. 3, title 19).

With regard to the church, the *Liber Augustalis* retained the law enacted by King William II providing for a broad benefit of clergy. It provided that "if any cleric of our entire kingdom should be charged for something done openly for which a person ought to be tried and condemned, he should be judged not by us or by our court, but by the church and in the court of the church . . . Also, he should be condemned according to the canons and the ecclesiastical law, unless someone has charged him with treason or another major crime of this kind that belongs . . . in our court" (bk. 1, title 45). Civil suits against clerics involving church land held by them were likewise triable only in ecclesiastical courts; however, suits against clerics involving land not held of the church were to be tried in the court of him of whom the land was held (bk. 1, title 68).

Another law of King William II concerning the clergy that was retained in the *Liber Augustalis* provided that only those villeins were forbidden to become clerics who were in personal servitude, but that "if any who owe service by reason of a holding or a benefice desire to become clerics, they may do so even without the permission of their lords, after they have resigned what they hold from the lords into their hands" (bk. 3, title 3).

Urban law is referred to in the *Liber Augustalis* in only a few places, and then chiefly in negative terms. Towns (communes) that create podestàs, consuls, or other officials, by authority of some custom or by election of the people, shall "suffer perpetual desolation, and all the men of that city should be held as perpetual forced laborers . . . [and] anyone who has received any of the aforesaid offices should be punished by death" (bk. 1, title 50). Also privileges previously granted to Messina, Naples, Aversa, Salerno, and other cities, and customs observed in such places, by which city residents were permitted to avoid the jurisdiction of the central or regional royal courts, were declared invalid and void (bk. 1, title 106). In addition, any commune that was sued had to respond or be punishable by fine for contumacy (bk. 1, title 107).

In prohibiting the establishment of autonomous municipal government, the *Liber Augustalis* stated: "We desire that everywhere through the kingdom there should be only those officials established by our majesty or by our command: master justiciars, justiciars, chamberlains, bailiffs, and judges" (bk. 1, title 50). Of this list, all were judges except for the chamberlain, but he also, though he was primarily a financial officer, had some judicial duties. In fact, the establishment of a central royal government was closely connected in Norman Sicily, as elsewhere in Europe in the twelfth and thirteenth centuries, with the expansion of the judicial office as well as with the rationalization of the central financial machinery. Here Frederick was building on what Roger had begun and what intervening rulers had continued.

Book 1 of the *Liber Augustalis*, which is concerned primarily with public order, starts (title 1) with a denunciation of heresy, which it classifies as a "public crime" comparable to treason. For some reason treason is not the subject of a special article; it is only referred to as being even "more horrible [than heresy] because it is recognized that someone has attempted injury to the divine majesty." The comparison is carried further in title 4, which makes it a crime "comparable to sacrilege" to "dispute about the . . . decisions, deeds, constitutions, [and] plans [of the king], and whether he whom the king has chosen is worthy." (This was a law of King Roger, carried over by his successors.)

The other crimes dealt with in book 1 are crimes of violence and crimes against or by royal officials. There is a strong emphasis upon recourse to courts on the part of victims, instead of self-help. A right of self-defense is granted, but it must be exercised immediately and the defense must be proportionate to the attack. Also, one may kill a nocturnal intruder provided at the same time one raises a "clamor" against him. Otherwise the right of self-defense, "granted by the law of nations," is to be exercised by prosecution in court, either by the victim or by public authority.

It is forbidden to carry sharp weapons (of which a list is given) or to wear a coat of mail, except that officials may carry such weapons to and from the king's court and knights and townsmen may carry swords when they ride on business outside the locality where they live. Striking a person with a prohibited weapon is punished by loss of a hand. Murder is punished by death by the sword when the murderer is a knight or higher, and by hanging when the murderer is of lower status than a knight. Infancy and insanity are defenses. Violent disseisin of land and other immovables incurs a fine of one-half the value of the property; of movables, four times their value. The disseised person has an action against the innocent transferee of the property.

Persons who have suffered losses by stealth or fraud or force are entitled to restitution of their losses; if the perpetrators cannot be found, "or if, as so often happens, they are hidden by the inhabitants of the area," restitution is to be made by "men of the same area where the crime was committed." This law was intended partly to protect Jews and Saracens, "against whom we believe that the persecution of the Christians is too great at present." Torture, it is said, may be used as an exceptional measure to extract information concerning the concealment of the perpetrators of such crimes (bk. 1, title 27). (This is the only place in the *Liber Augustalis* where torture is mentioned.)

Embezzlement of public monies by royal officials or judges is made punishable by death; neglect, loss, or diminution of public goods by an official is punishable by lesser penalties "at the discretion of the royal clemency" (bk. 1, title 36, law of King Roger).

The following important features of the Sicilian system of administration of justice were reflected in Book 1 of the *Liber Augustalis*.

1. Justiciars were given jurisdiction over robberies, grand theft, destruction of houses, intentional insults, arson, the cutting down of fruit trees and vines, attacks on women, duels, crimes of treason, sharp weapons, "and generally all crimes for which the person convicted might suffer the penalty of death or mutilation." They also had jurisdiction of civil cases where there was a denial of justice by chamberlains and bailiffs or by feudal lords. However, certain of the most important of these criminal and civil cases were reserved to the court of the king himself (title 44).

2. Judges were to receive a salary from the court of the king and were to take nothing at all from litigants during the proceedings "save once for food and drink for themselves or for another." However, after decision or settlement of the case the judges were to receive one-thirtieth of the amount involved in the case or of the estimated value of the property involved, from both the litigants. There were also circumstances under which instead of one-thirtieth, or in addition to one-thirtieth, they were to receive one one-hundredth or one-sixtieth (title 73).

3. Only persons examined by judges of the king's court and approved by the king were permitted to plead as advocates in that court. Also, advocates were required to be examined and approved by regional justiciars (title 83).

4. Justiciars were required to swear an oath "that, with God and justice before their eyes, they will do justice without fraud to every plaintiff and will have care to expedite litigants as quickly as possible" (title 46). Chamberlains and bailiffs were required to swear much more detailed oaths (title 62).

5. Lawyers (*advocati*) in all courts were required, before being admitted and every year thereafter, to swear the following oath to their office, before the justiciars: "They will have care to aid the parties whose defense they accept with all trust and truth and without any subterfuge. They will not instruct them about the facts of the case. They will make no allegations counter to their true knowledge, and they will not take irremediable cases. If they do perhaps take cases that are distorted by the lies of one party, which at the beginning appear to them just and in the course of the judgment or of fact or law appear to them unjust, they will cease their defense immediately . . . They will also swear not to seek an increase in fees during the course of the judgment and not to enter into agreements concerning the party in the litigation." Any violation of this oath was punishable by a fine of "three pounds of the purest gold" (title 84).

Book 1 concludes with a series of provisions on commencement of court proceedings, especially in civil cases. Every trial, civil or criminal, was to begin with a writ, called a letter of summons, issued to the defendant or the accused by the justiciar or bailiff. "These letters should contain clearly before whom and by whom and for what matter, as well as the kind of litigation being brought, and the period should be expressed in which the person summoned should appear in court in person if it is a criminal action, or in person or through a representative if a civil complaint has been brought. There should be one . . . peremptory summons and the limit of thirty days at most . . . If the person cited is living outside the kingdom, the summons should contain a period of sixty days" (title 97). If the whereabouts of the defendant were unknown or he would not allow access to himself, the summons could be served at the house where his wife or close relatives resided. "But if the house is not opened for the one desiring to serve the summons, we order that the summons should be placed at the threshold of the house in the presence of [a public person or two or three] witnesses" (title 98). Then follow several provisions on penalties for contumacy and contempt of established time limits.

The problems that were faced in the provisions on commencement of proceedings were among the most critical for new systems of royal justice in the twelfth and thirteenth centuries: how to bring a reluctant person into court, how to give him adequate notice of the charges made against him, how much leeway to allow two parties who were seeking to avail themselves of the official process of adjudication. What is particularly striking about the solutions provided by the *Liber Augustalis* of 1231 is their modernity. Frederick went far beyond what was achieved in other countries of Europe in his age. For example, in relation to peremptory summons, in England it took centuries to solve the problem of excuses ("essoins") for not responding to a civil action. In relation to a letter of summons stating "for what matter" the "kind of litigation" was brought, in England and America it took until the nineteenth and twentieth centuries to overcome the burden of stereotyped "forms of action." In relation to service of process by delivery at the threshold of the residence, one is reminded of the artful process server of a contemporary megalopolis who skillfully tosses the summons so that it lands at the feet of the unwilling defendant who may be ensconced behind some barrier.

Interrogation of witnesses and examination of written and other evidence constituted the sole mode of proof in civil cases; trial by combat and by ordeal were abolished for such cases. The novelty of the interrogatory, or inquisitional, mode of trial apparently raised some problems, for a special provision was introduced to discourage persons "who often disturb the proceedings of trials by their tumultuous cries." "We order that in the future litigants and any others present at trials should observe the peace of justice with reverence for the magistrate who is declaring the laws. They should not dare to assert their rights or to ask for something before they obtain permission from the one in charge of the trial . . . If a co-advocate or the principal party remembers some point of law or fact while the advocate is speaking, he should take pains to whisper what he is asserting in his ear . . . But if anyone who has been warned three times over a period of time by the bailiff or the judge and he will not be silent . . . he should pay one augustalis to our court if he is a peasant. If he is a townsman, he should pay two. If he is a knight, four; a baron, eight; a count, sixteen. All our officials should know that if they dismiss this penalty out of favor for someone, we will, without doubt, except it in full from their own goods." "Respect for justice requires silence" (title 32).

As Book 1 ends with contumacy in civil cases, so Book 2 starts with contumacy in criminal cases. It goes on to the process of indictment, which was apparently by inquiry on the part of the master justiciar of the king's great court or the justiciars of the regional courts; such inquiry was made when persons were accused or suspected. It was facilitated by preservation in the archives of the king's court of the names of those who had been banned or exiled or were otherwise notorious, and of their sons (title 5). Deception or fraud in legal transactions, called calumny, was a punishable offense; "judges . . . should . . . condemn accusers or denouncers whom they catch in open calumny to the same penalty as the nature of the crime of their opponent required should be imposed on the accused if they had proved their accusation" (title 14).

Once issue was joined in a civil or criminal case, the plaintiff or accuser "should either offer in person or through his advocate or should propose in writing on the same day or at most on the following day everything that proves or supports his evidence . . . The defendant . . . should at the same time . . . propose all de facto competent defenses in person or . . . in writing . . . or through his advocate" (title 24). The litigants were then to be interrogated by the judge, who could, in his discretion, require a person who was being interrogated "to take on the sacred obligation of the oath, depending either on the rank of the person or the nature of the case or whether he has a suspicion that someone is lying" (title 31).

Trial by ordeal was entirely abolished (title 31). Trial by combat was abolished except for a very few cases (title 32), notably traitors, murderers by stealth, and poisoners (title 33). The number of witnesses required to prove a criminal accusation against a count depended on their class—two counts, four barons, eight knights, sixteen townsmen; against a baron—two barons, four knights, eight townsmen; and so on (title 33).

Book 2 ends with a provision entitled, "How evidence should be produced in appeals." The first words are, "We desire to make an end to the disagreements of lawyers." The gist of the provision is that evidence may not be introduced on appeal unless it is new evidence that the appellant was unable to present on trial.

Book 3 is concerned at the outset with the relation between royal property and feudal property. Needless to say, the royal restrictions on feudal property were substantial. Frederick forbade any count, baron, or knight, or any other who held a barony or fief as a chief tenant of the crown, to marry without royal permission, or to marry off any female or any son with movable or immovable property, "notwithstanding the contrary custom which is said to have been observed in some parts of the kingdom" (title 23). He also decreed that "when a count or baron has gone the way of all flesh, their sons or grandsons may not dare to receive oaths from the men [that is, from the decedent's vassals] unless they have first, as is the custom, obtained the license and mandate of our excellency for receiving these oaths"—under penalty of confiscation of the countship or barony and fief with all remaining movables and immovables (title 24).

The last fifty or so provisions of Book 3 of the *Liber Augustalis* deal with a variety of matters, many of which are of great interest.

1. To preserve the healthfulness of the air, it was provided that no one should be permitted to soak flax or hemp in water within a mile of any city or near a castle, that burials of the dead which were not contained in urns should be at a certain depth, that cadavers and filth should be thrown a quarter of a mile out of the district or into the sea or river (title 48).

2. Artisans were required to produce products fit for the use to which they were to be put, butchers and fishmongers were prohibited from selling adulterated meat or fish, tavern keepers and wine sellers were forbidden to sell watered wine as pure, and no one was permitted to work gold or silver that contained less than a certain amount of pure gold or pure silver per pound. In addition, a procedure for exposing such frauds was established, and graduated penalties for repeated offenses were set up, starting with a fine for the first offense (or a beating if the artisan or merchant was too poor to pay), loss of a hand for the second, and "death on the forks" for the third, with the same penalties for officials who because of influence or bribery failed to expose the frauds (title 49).

3. A uniform system of weights and measures was established for merchants throughout the kingdom (titles 50, 51).

4. Penalties against merchants selling corrupt and forbidden merchandise or selling at false measures and weights were doubled when foreigners were deceived by them (title 52).

5. Persons who dispensed love potions or harmful foods or who made illicit exorcisms were punishable by death, if people died or lost their minds as a result; but if the recipients were not harmed, the perpetrators were nevertheless punished by confiscation of goods and confinement in jail for a year. Frederick added: "Although it may seem frivolous to those knowing the truth and the nature of things . . . that the minds of men should be influenced by food or drink to loves or hates unless the guilty suspicion of the recipient induces these feelings, nevertheless we are not willing to leave unpunished the rash presumption by which they have at least desired to injure another, even if they cannot" (title 73).

England

In 911 Rollo (Rolf) the Norseman and his followers ceased their raids on the Frankish coast and, with the blessing of the emperor, settled down in the region of the lower Seine. Within a century the Normans, having assimilated Frankish institutions, including Frankish law and the Frankish language, began to show a genius for military exploits as well as for political alliances and the art of government. In 1047 the eighteen-year-old William, Duke of Normandy, a direct descendant of Rollo, started on a military and political career that made him one of the two or three most powerful rulers of Europe. The first years were occupied with repelling internal and external enemies, including the Count of Anjou and the King of France. During this time William was comforted by support from the English king, Edward the Confessor, who in 1051, being childless, apparently named him as his heir. On Edward's death in 1066, William, who by then had consolidated his power in Normandy and had added the counties of Brittany and Maine to his dominions, landed on the English coast with some seven thousand men, including about one thousand trained horsemen (many with their mounts), and defeated the rival claimant to the throne, Harold, son of Godwin.

The Norman conquest of England was not unrelated to the contemporaneous Norman conquest of southern Italy. In the first place, the Normans had a strong sense of common nationality. Wherever they were, they never forgot that they were Normans. Duke William is said to have encouraged his troops at the Battle of Hastings by reminding them of the exploits of their compatriots in Apulia, Calabria, and Sicily. More important, perhaps, was their sense of common mission. Both in England and in Italy the Normans came as crusaders, bearers of the true faith, self-styled "soldiers of Christ." William, like Robert Guiscard and the Great Count Roger, was a partisan of the Cluniac Reform and therefore an opponent of clerical marriages, purchase and sale of church offices, and baronial domination of the priesthood. By the same token, they were partisans of the sacral kingship—the chief priesthood of the emperor or king, his headship of the church within his domain. This did not, at first, bring them into confrontation with the papacy; on the contrary, it brought them into alliance with the papacy, which had supported the Cluniac Reform and was only beginning to turn it in a new direction, toward freedom of the clergy from "secular" control. The papacy in the 1060s and 1070s welcomed the reforming zeal of the Norman rulers—and exploited their political support in the impending struggle against the emperor. Just as Pope Nicholas II blessed in advance the conquests of Richard and Robert Guiscard in 1059, so Pope Alexander II in 1066 gave his blessing in advance to William's conquest of England, which he called a crusade to reform the corrupt English churches.[31]

A few years later Pope Gregory VII hoped to persuade the Norman rulers both of England and of southern Italy to accept the claims to supremacy that he made in the *Dictatus Papae* of 1075. This they politely refused to do, however, and he was not in a position to press them very hard. They remained in complete control of the clergy within their respective kingdoms. William the Conqueror—like Robert Guiscard and Roger—made his own appointments to the episcopate, without consulting Rome in advance He replaced all except two bishops of England with appointees of Norman birth or training. (His Archbishop of Canterbury, the great Lanfranc, was Italian by birth, as was Lanfranc's famous successor, Anselm, but both had for decades held important posts in Normandy before being brought to England by William I and his son William II, respectively.) Also, William the Conqueror did not hesitate to enact ecclesiastical laws binding upon the church in England and Normandy.

Thus the Caesaropapist inclinations of the Norman kings of England were not essentially different from those of the Norman kings of southern Italy. William II (William Rufus) of England—Normandy went to his brother Robert on the Conqueror's death—who reigned from 1087 to 1100, ruthlessly violated the rights of the church, and would have been excommunicated by the pope in 1098 had he not had Anselm's support. Yet even the tyrannical William II never sought to be appointed papal legate, while Count Roger not only sought such an appointment but obtained it for himself and his successors in perpetuity.[32] The Norman rulers of England and Normandy, though they thoroughly dominated the church in their domains during the first two generations after the Conquest, had to reckon with the fact that, in contrast to Sicily, the population of England and Normandy contained many supporters of the papal party, and that some concessions by the king to the "freedom of the church" were necessary in order for him to retain the support of prominent Norman leaders as well as of the Anglo-Saxons, who constituted not only the vast majority of the English lower classes but some elements of the upper classes as well.

This division concerning the permissible limits of royal control over the church in England and Normandy was important for the future. It contributed to the virtual breakdown of civil authority during the reign of the Conqueror's grandson, Stephen (1135-1154), and it led finally to the fateful controversy between Stephen's successor, Henry II (1154-1189), and Archbishop Becket.

No doubt the sociocultural as well as the political differences between England and Normandy, on the one hand, and southern Italy on the other hand, including the historical background of Greek, Byzantine, and Islamic settlement in southern Italy, help to explain the differences in the situation of the church in the two countries and, in particular, the failure of the Sicilian church to rise against the tyrannical rule of Count Roger I (died 1105), King Roger II (died 1154), and their successors.

Nevertheless, the legal situation of the church in England and in Normandy, in the period immediately after 1066, bore a certain similarity to that of the church in the Norman Kingdom of Sicily. William, like Roger, appointed the bishops in his domain and controlled them. In a decree of 1067 he declared that the King of England and Duke of Normandy had the power to determine whether a pope should be acknowledged by the church in England and Normandy, that no ecclesiastical council held in his kingdom could make canon law without his consent, and that the king had a veto power over ecclesiastical penalties imposed on his barons and officials.[33] William separated the ecclesiastical and secular courts; in 1072 he ordered that spiritual pleas should henceforth be tried by bishops and archdeacons in their own courts "in accordance with the canons and episcopal laws."[34] This separation, which was also introduced in Sicily by Roger I, strengthened the church courts against local influences but not against the king, who retained his supreme authority within the church courts themselves. Both the Conqueror and his son William Rufus defied the efforts of Pope Gregory VII and his successors to assert papal supremacy over the English and Norman clergy. William Rufus showed his contempt by allowing the archbishopric of Canterbury to remain vacant for four years after the death of Lanfranc so that the crown might collect its revenues.

When William Rufus's brother, Henry I, ascended the English throne in 1100, however, the position of the papacy was strong enough to secure from King Henry substantial compromises with respect to the appointment of clergy. In return, Henry had papal support for his reconquest of Normandy from his brother Robert. The Concordat of Bec (Normandy), made in 1107, anticipated the Concordat of Worms of 1122 in transferring from the king to the pope the authority to invest bishops and abbots with the insignia of their offices, the ring and the staff, uttering the words "Receive the church!" Like the emperor in 1122, King Henry I agreed to the free election of bishops and abbots by the church in Normandy and England but retained the right to be present at such elections and thus, in effect, to intervene when elections were disputed. Moreover, as later in Germany, the bishops and abbots in England and Normandy were not to be consecrated by the church until the king had invested them, by scepter, with the "regalia," receiving from them in return homage and fealty.[35]

These royal concessions with regard to the naming of bishops and abbots did not—at the time—substantially affect the other powers that Henry I exercised over the church in England and in Normandy. It was only during the so-called anarchy of Stephen that the papal party in England and Normandy made important gains in prestige and power, and only in the subsequent reign of Henry II—and especially after the martyrdom of Becket—that the church in England and Normandy achieved a substantial measure of freedom from royal and ducal domination. It was not, of course, as substantial a measure as the papal party would have liked; but it was a greater independence than the church obtained in most other countries of Europe in the twelfth and thirteenth centuries, and, of course, far greater than in Sicily.[36]

Paradoxically, the freedom of the church in England and Normandy nourished the growth of royal governmental and legal institutions. This was due in part to the theory of the dualism of the ecclesiastical and secular authorities, according to which secular rulers were responsible for keeping the peace and doing justice in their respective realms. It was also due in part to royal competition with, and emulation of, the ecclesiastical state. It is therefore not accidental that England and Normandy, the European polity in the late twelfth and early thirteenth centuries where the church was most free of royal control and most subject to papal authority, was also a polity where the system of royal government and royal law was very highly developed—almost as highly developed as in Sicily. It was, in fact, under Henry II that the foundations were laid for the modern English system of royal law (the English common law) as it existed and developed until at least the sixteenth and seventeenth centuries.

THE PERSONALITY OF HENRY II

Like his fellow Norman, King Roger of Sicily, Henry Plantagenet had great personal qualities to match the great challenge of his time, including qualities especially adapted to the development of a strong system of royal law.[37]

Though Henry was only twenty-one years old when he became King of England, he had already had a highly successful political and military career. His father was Geoffrey, Count of Anjou; his mother was the Empress Matilda, granddaughter of William the Conqueror and daughter of Henry I, King of England and Duke of Normandy. At his father's early death in 1151, Henry succeeded to Anjou and Maine and, through his mother, to Normandy. The next year he married Eleanor of Aquitaine, divorced wife of King Louis VII of France, and thereby acquired not only Aquitaine but also Poitou. In 1153 he invaded England and compelled his cousin Stephen to adopt him as his heir. In 1154 Stephen conveniently died and left Henry the English throne.

Henry II was a man of enormous energy. He was known for his physical exploits. The contemporaneous chronicler Walter Map wrote that "he was always on the move, travelling in unbearably long stages . . . a great connoisseur of hounds and hawks, and most greedy of that vain sport: perpetually wakeful and at work. When troubled by erotic dreams he would curse his body which neither toil nor abstinence could avail to tame or reduce. From that time we used to ascribe his exertions, not to fickleness, but to fear of growing too fat."[38] He was also hungry for political power, both abroad and at home. He led his feudal armies throughout England and Normandy and into Ireland and parts of France, down to the Pyrenees, continually acquiring new vassals, razing castles illegally held, collecting revenues due him as supreme feudal lord.

It is not known how he came by his great interest in law, but there are many accounts indicating that he was more than a layman in legal matters. It is told that he arose early every morning to review current cases with his clerks; that he was ready to intervene in the cases heard by his justices and was quite capable of giving his vice-chancellor a lesson in conveyancing; that he circuited his kingdom at a wearing pace to hear cases in the provinces. Map reports that Henry told the following story: "Once after I had heard a concise and just judgment given against a rich man in favour of a poor one, I said to Lord Ranulf [Glanvill], the Justiciar: 'Although the poor man's judgment might have been put off by many quirks, he had obtained it by a happy and quick decision.' 'Certainly,' said Ranulf, 'we decide causes here much quicker than your bishops do in their churches.' 'True,' said I, 'but if your king were as far off from you as the pope is from the bishops, I think you would be quite as slow as they.'"[39]

Henry was by no means so popular with everyone as he was with Map. The introduction of a system of royal law into England was in part a means of enriching royal coffers as well as royal power at the expense not only of barons and ecclesiastics but also of the general population. Henry's detractor, Radulfus Niger, said that the king let no year pass without molesting the country with new laws. One of his least popular acts was the revived enforcement of the harsh forest laws, which was attributed to his desire to protect his own sporting pleasure.

Finally, there is the question of Henry's conception of his role as a lawmaker. No doubt he did not consider that he was innovating but rather that he was protecting the heritage of the past against new challenges. Yet, like Pope Gregory VII a century earlier, Henry knew that in preserving the past he was altering it fundamentally. Many legal devices that previously had been exceptional or occasional became normal and regular. Preexisting legal institutions were revalued and rearranged to make a new ensemble. As a distinguished English legal historian has put it, there was a "leap forward." The wheel was set in motion "which generated the English common law."[40] However different Henry II's conception of history may have been from conceptions that prevail today, he undoubtedly knew that what he was doing was important and, indeed, epoch-making.

THE ENGLISH STATE

When Henry II came to the throne in 1154, England was divided politically, as it had been since before the Norman Conquest, into local units and feudal units. Local units were villages (called vills), groups of villages (called hundreds), counties (shires), and towns. Each hundred and each shire was governed by an assembly of all the people, or all the free men, which was called the hundred court or the shire court. The feudal units were the manors, each headed by its feudal lord. After the Norman Conquest, something like half of the hundred courts were taken over by the feudal lords and became, in effect, manorial courts.

Lords of the manor were themselves subject to, and tenants of, higher lords, in whose "seignorial courts" they could be judged; and the highest lords in turn were subject to, and tenants of, the chief lord—the king. William the Conqueror had, in effect, leased all the land of England to his tenants-in-chief on condition that they provide him with an army of about five thousand mounted knights; they, in turn, had leased much of their land to subtenants, on condition that each provide a certain number of such knights. Each knight was to serve for forty days a year, at his own expense. The duty to furnish knights went with the land, which was therefore said to be held in knight's service. The tenure, or "fee" (feod, feud, fief), could not be split up in such a way as to deprive the superior lord of his knight's service and other feudal "dues" ("incidents of tenure").[41]

Another dimension was added to the feudal system, however, by the very complex concept of the kingship. During the period from 1066 to 1154, the king's court (*curia regis*) was not only a feudal assembly of the king's tenants-in-chief; it also contained a group of royal officials who administered the affairs of the crown throughout the realm. The king appointed a so-called justiciar or other official to represent him in all matters and to act as regent in his absence, which was frequent—indeed, most of the Anglo-Norman kings spent much more time in Normandy than in England. The chancellor, subordinate to the justiciar, was in charge of the king's secretarial staff. Barons of the exchequer were appointed to help transact the king's financial and legal business. And since the king's business included maintaining peace in the realm, and seeing that justice was done, administrative devices were developed for settling disputes not merely between the king and his tenants but among the king's subjects generally. As in Anglo-Saxon times, the king delegated local magnates to preside over the shire courts (shire reeves, or sheriffs). He also issued to local magnates executive orders, in the form of sealed writs, usually commanding that some wrong which had come to his attention be corrected.

Prior to the reign of Henry II, however, these institutions—the exchequer, the chancery, the judiciary, and others—were in an embryonic stage. William the Conqueror and his successors had substantially increased the central authority of the Crown, which reached vertically through vassals and subvassals down into the villages and manors, but the system of royal government and royal law still rested essentially on their own personal household control and on feudal loyalties. With the possible exception of the exchequer, there was no autonomous system of government departments such as existed in Roger II's Italian kingdom—no permanent administrative, judicial, and legislative bodies that could operate by their own independent authority to regulate feudal and local problems. The king's justice could reach down to any man in certain types of cases of flagrant denial of justice as well as in certain types of cases affecting crown property, treason, and several other matters; but it was extraordinary justice, not regular professional justice administered by permanent courts.

With regard to adjudication of disputes, prior to the reign of Henry II there was no professional judiciary to hear the cases with which the executive writs dealt. In the first decades of the twelfth century, to be sure, Henry I had sent out perhaps a half-dozen justiciars to travel to various places in the realm and to do justice, and it may well be that some of them, at least, had had some professional legal training in the emerging canon law and possibly had even studied Roman law at Bologna. However, their task as justiciars was to handle not only judicial matters but also any other matters of government in which the king might be interested. They were sent out irregularly as representatives of the king for general administrative purposes, including the hearing and resolving of disputes. Moreover, most criminal and civil matters were within local or feudal, and not royal, jurisdiction; the crown stepped in when its own interests were directly involved or when there was a "denial of justice," that is, when a party appealed to the king for mercy because local or feudal justice had broken down.

The absence of a regular, permanent, professional royal judiciary was associated with the absence of the concept of the kingship as a regular legislative agency. Kings did occasionally issue laws, usually with the consent of the bishops, barons, and other leading men. But the entire legislation of the first four Anglo-Norman kings from 1066 to 1154 could probably be summarized in one page. Only a few laws are known to have been issued by William the Conqueror; no laws whatever have survived from the reign of his son William Rufus; from the thirty-five year reign of Henry I there survive references to only five laws; the nineteen-year reign of Stephen has left no traces of royal legislation. Clearly, English kings prior to Henry II did not consider it to be one of their responsibilities regularly to enact new laws.

The upheavals of Stephen's reign left no doubt that the Anglo-

Norman kingship lacked the legal institutions needed to keep peace in England in the long run. The country was torn by violent disorders, and especially by private warfare over rights in land. Into this turbulent situation there came the struggle for the independence of the clergy — under the pope — from the secular authorities. Prior to Stephen, three strong kings had been able to subdue these forces of division. Now a weaker king found himself helpless to control the situation. But it was not only his personal weakness that disabled Stephen. It was also a defect in the Anglo-Norman system of government, under which the king or his chief lieutenant had to march continually through the land with his armies in order to keep peace among his tenants and subtenants and to offer such protection as he could and would to the local population against oppression by their feudal lords.

It was out of this general background, and at the height of civil disorder, that Henry II came to the throne, not only determined to replace anarchy and violence by law and order but also willing to do so through political and legal institutions and concepts that had only been foreshadowed by his predecessors in England and Normandy. To be sure, Henry and his advisers relied on those foreshadowings. In the traditional spirit of Norman administration, they retained the old customs to the maximum extent possible in light of new needs and new policies. Henry's father, Geoffrey of Anjou, though not a Norman, had educated his son in that spirit, telling him expressly that he should not try to transplant the customs of Anjou and Normandy to England or the customs of England to Anjou and Normandy.[42] Henry sought to use preexisting Anglo-Saxon and Anglo-Norman institutions wherever he could do so to advantage. Nevertheless, the hallmark of Henry's reign was institutional innovation, not continuity with the past.

Moreover, although Henry's innovations had roots in the past, those roots are to be found not only in the Anglo-Saxon or Anglo-Norman experience (the ruling elite in England was very largely Norman and the languages of the court were Norman French and Latin) but also in the experience of other contemporary polities. The new governmental and legal institutions and concepts that were introduced in England in the latter half of the twelfth century bore a distinct family resemblance to those that had been introduced during the previous two generations in the Roman church-state and in the Norman state in southern Italy, as well as to those that were to be introduced in later generations in France, and elsewhere in Europe. They also bore a general resemblance in important respects to the governmental and legal institutions and concepts that had emerged during the late eleventh and early twelfth centuries in the free cities and towns of the West, including those in England.

This is not to say that Henry II "copied" anything from elsewhere. Great statesmen rarely if ever copy other people's laws. It is only to say that what Henry did—taken in its broad outline—was not uniquely "English," or even uniquely Norman, but was part of a general historical development in twelfth-century Europe. It was uniquely Western, in the sense that it was part of the founding of the Western legal tradition and of the Western type of state. Henry was well aware of the new concepts and forms of government and law that had developed in the church and in the Norman Kingdom of Sicily as well as in the new cities and towns of Europe. Although he did not copy them, there can be little doubt that he found them suggestive for his own purposes.

Henry transformed the system of public administration in England and Normandy by greatly increasing the functions and powers of permanent, professional, central governmental departments. Of these the most important were the treasury (exchequer), which administered taxation and finance, the high court (court of common pleas), which administered justice, and the chancery, which directed and coordinated the work of the other departments. This was roughly similar to what King Roger II had done in Sicily some decades earlier, which was similar, in turn, to what the papacy had done in Rome, probably in the wake of the First Crusade (1095).

The handling of finances in England and Normandy through the exchequer was clearly related to Sicilian experience.[43] The main financial problems confronting the crown in England and Normandy were essentially the same as those that confronted the crown in Sicily: to establish a general system of taxation suitable to a centralized feudal polity (that is, one characterized by subinfeudation, with reservation of allegiance of subvassals to the monarch), together with appropriate methods of auditing returns furnished by feudal and other taxpayers to Crown officials in the localities. That there was Sicilian influence on English practice is highly probable, if only because of the striking example of Thomas Brown, who served as a baron of the dogano in Palermo for some decades between 1130 and 1154 and then, having fallen out of favor after the death of Roger II, went to England where he served as a baron of the exchequer for several more decades between 1154 and 1190.[44] There may also have been important influences in the other direction, since English barons of the exchequer heard crown fiscal cases in the localities as early as the reign of Henry I.

The creation of a central royal bench of judges in England also paralleled developments in southern Italy. In both places, the process started with the occasional sending out of justices from the king's household to hear cases in the localities as well as to handle other royal matters. In England, despite the exceptional example of the exchequer, the professionalization and systematization of this practice was accomplished only under Henry II. Then for the first time the judicial functions of the itinerant justices became clearly distinguishable from

their economic and administrative functions (which, however, they continued to exercise). Moreover, Henry II instituted for the first time a
regular set of tours for a fixed set of justices. In 1176 six groups of three
justices each were sent out to tour the country and hear all cases brought
under the king's writ, provided they did not exceed a certain jurisdictional amount (half a knight's fee). The number of these "justices in eyre"
ultimately rose to twenty. (Eyre, pronounced "air," is the English
translation of the Latin *iter*, or journey, which is the root of "itinerant.")
In 1175, Henry had appointed three men to be judges in his own personal household court; and finally, in 1178, he appointed five persons
"from his household" (*de sua familia*), two clergy and three laymen, to "remain [in his court] to hear the people's complaints."[45] By 1180 this new
bench, later called the Court of Common Pleas, was residing permanently at Westminster. The king continued also to judge in person as
he traveled; in the early thirteenth century the task of judging before the
king was allocated to professional judges, called the Court of King's
Bench. (In time, the Court of King's Bench restricted its jurisdiction to
felonies and to cases affecting the royal person, while other civil
disputes—"common pleas"—were decided by the Court of Common
Pleas.) These two courts plus the Exchequer were the first permanent,
central, professional royal courts of civil and criminal jurisdiction in
England, and the second (after the Sicilian) in Europe. They
represented an institutionalization of the royal function of adjudication—a function which previous kings had for the most part exercised
only in special instances, "for great men and great causes."[46]

The exchequer and the court of common pleas were two pillars of the
new English state. They were supported by a third, the chancery, which
(again, like its counterparts in Sicily and in Rome) had the power of the
royal (in Rome, papal) seal. That meant that the chancellor could issue
orders in the name of the king. His role was to direct and coordinate,
through such orders, the work of all the other departments of government. Through writs and other kinds of formal documents, the chancery
could not only initiate proceedings in the exchequer and the king's court
but could also deal directly with barons, bishops, and other persons who
participated in the government of the country at lower levels.

The critical importance of the chancery in the development of the
state—in England as elsewhere in Europe—was due to its combination
of professional expertise with overall direction and coordination of the
business of government. The chancery operated through a staff of expert
clerks who, in Strayer's words, "developed and preserved regular administrative routines and carefully worded, consistent formulae for their
letters."[47] Government was, in this sense, "bureaucratized." Nevertheless—and this has not been sufficiently emphasized—it was the mission of this new secretariat to save government from a narrow depart-

mentalism. None of the new bureaus of government, not even the judiciary, was to be free to go its own way without control by a superdepartment, the government itself, acting through its secretariat.

Yet this secretariat was *not* the king, that is, not the whole kingship. It was the very nature of the chancery to identify the business of *government* as a distinct activity, separate from the person of the king and, by the same token, separate also from those aspects of crown business that were most closely identified with his person, especially the military and diplomatic aspects. Prior to the reign of Henry II, the English king (and Norman duke) had to be continually on the move within his territories, not only to maintain military and political control over his vassals but also to keep his government functioning. After the time of Henry II, the king-duke did not have to be present in order for his government to function. Richard the Lion Hearted, who succeeded Henry II, was absent from England for virtually the entire ten years of his reign, first on crusade and then in captivity, yet government in England went on as usual. It was headed, to be sure, not by the chancellor but by another official, called the justiciar (for six of the ten years the justiciar was Hubert Walter, who was also Archbishop of Canterbury and papal legate), but the chancery furnished the main administrative staff of the justiciar. In later times it was often the chancellor who ruled in the king's absence. More important, it was the chancellor who, when the king was present, carried out most of the royal function of directing and coordinating public administration.

The emerging concept of the state depended on the existence of an agency such as the chancery that would define public administration, the business of government, as something less than politics as a whole (represented by the person of the ruler) and as something more than the aggregate of individual government offices—an agency, therefore, that would have sufficient acumen to understand and respond to overall policy and at the same time sufficient expertise to control the various specialized departments. Here again is an example of the scholastic dialectic in action. The papal chancery, as Strayer has said, "was far in advance and served to some extent as a model for others, but by the time of Henry II . . . the English chancery was not far behind . . . By the thirteenth century almost every European government had an effective chancery."[48]

ENGLISH ROYAL LAW ("THE COMMON LAW")

Henry II revolutionized the system of law in England primarily by imposing royal jurisdiction, and royal law, upon criminal and civil matters that had previously been under local and feudal jurisdiction and local and feudal law. He succeeded in this endeavor not only by creating a royal judiciary that operated under the control of a royal chancery but also by providing a more rational type of law and by enlisting community participation in administering it.

Henry's five major reforms of procedural and substantive law were closely interrelated. (1) The old executive writs were "judicialized." Instead of requiring the defendant or a local official to execute the king's order in behalf of a complainant, the new writs required the defendant to appear before an impartial tribunal to answer the complaint. (2) Community participation was enlisted, in the form of a sworn inquest of neighbors, to decide disputed facts in civil cases arising from disputes over freehold land. (3) Community participation was also enlisted, in the form of a sworn inquest of neighbors, to present to the king's justices for trial all persons suspected of serious breach of the peace amounting to a felony. (4) Through the new judicial writs, forms of action in the king's court were developed that categorized various types of wrongs in terms of the legal remedies available to redress them. (5) The burning question of peaceful protection of rights in land was resolved by the development of the legal doctrine of seisin, a concept similar to but not the same as the Roman concept of possession; disseisin, by force or by fraud, of land held by military or other freehold tenure was brought under the royal jurisdiction, and a body of law concerning it was gradually created.

The judicialization of the writs. The word "writ," which simply means a writing, is an English translation of the Latin word *breve*, meaning "something short" and, by extension, "a letter." Short written orders and notices, called writs, had been issued by popes, kings, and other rulers for centuries. Under William the Conqueror and his successors, one of the chief means of royal administration was the issuance of royal writs commanding earls, barons, bishops, abbots, sheriffs, and others to undo some wrong that had come to the king's attention: to "restore the manor of M. to John of Styles," to "render quickly to the abbot, your lord, whatever you justly owe him in rent," to allow someone the right to use common land, to release certain cattle taken as a pledge.

These executive writs were enormously varied in character, each being designed to solve an individual case in which the king had undertaken to intervene. Often they were based on ex parte allegations: "We see the king order some measure on allegations which someone 'instilled into his ear' or 'made him believe'"; sometimes "the king had to retract a measure because it had appeared that the plaintiff had been lying — and probably . . . paying well to support his lie."[49] The practice also developed of addressing royal writs to sheriffs and other local officials ordering them to "do full right" in a particular matter. These, too, "left a great margin of decision to the executive officer . . . and therefore left the door wide open to arbitrary behaviour on the part of many a local tyrant."[50]

Occasionally, especially in cases involving ecclesiastical claims, Henry

II's predecessors issued writs ordering a bishop or other lord to settle a case, or a sheriff to convene the hundred to decide a dispute. But normally the royal writ did not lead to an adjudication. Prior to the time of Henry II, the English kings had not imitated the writ system which had developed in the ecclesiastical courts in the early part of the twelfth century, whereby a plaintiff obtained a writ from the papal chancery in Rome authorizing the trial of his claim in a bishop's court or by a tribunal of papal legates. (More such papal writs initiated litigation in ecclesiastical courts in England than in any other country of Europe.)

Henry II transformed the royal writ from the command, "Do such and such," to, "Summon an inquest to be before my justices to determine the matter in dispute — and have there this writ." The writ, in other words, was designed (unless the defendant yielded) to lead to a judicial proceeding. The plaintiff would go to Westminster to the king's chancellor to state his claim; the chancellor would issue a writ to the sheriff in the locality in which the trial was to take place; the writ would order the sheriff to initiate one of the various types of proceedings to settle the matter in the court of the king's justices.

Two examples will illustrate the difference between the older "executive writ" and the newer "judicial writ" (sometimes called "returnable writ," since it had to be brought into court).

The executive writ is from the period 1087-1091:

> William, king of the English, to R[anulf], brother of Ilger, greeting. I command and order you to let abbot Herbert have the half hide of land of Sawtry which Ailwin the reeve has held and which Walter de Beaumais now holds by force, as I have ordered by my writ. And see that I hear no further complaint thereof for default of right on £ 10 forfeiture. Witness: Ranulf, the king's chaplain.[51]

The judicial writ is taken from the treatise on English law attributed to Glanvill, written between 1187 and 1189:

> The king to the sheriff, greeting. N. has complained to me that R. unjustly and without a judgment has disseised him of his free tenement in such-and-such a vill since my last voyage to Normandy. Therefore I command you that, if N. gives you security for prosecuting his claim, you are to see that the chattels which were taken from the tenement are restored to it, and that the tenement and the chattels remain in peace until the Sunday after Easter. And meanwhile you are to see that the tenement is viewed by twelve free and lawful men of the neighborhood, and their names endorsed on this writ. And summon them by good summoners to be before me or my justices on the Sunday after Easter, ready to make this recognition. And summon R., or his bailiff if he himself cannot be found, on the security of gage and reliable sureties, to be there then to hear the recogni-

tion. And have there the summoners, and this writ and the names of the sureties. Witness, etc.[52]

The judicial writ accomplishes three things: (1) it sets forth a narrow factual test for determining which of two parties has the right to immediate possession of certain land, leaving for another time the more complicated question of who has the right of ownership; (2) it submits the question of fact to a sworn inquest (jury) of neighbors; (3) it establishes royal jurisdiction over the issuance of the writ and over the proceedings of the jury.

The jury of trial. From the eighth century on, Frankish emperors and kings had occasionally summoned inquests of neighbors to answer questions put by itinerant royal officers—chiefly questions concerning customary royal rights in the locality and violations of royal commands. The Normans had taken over from the Franks the occasional use of inquests. Shortly after the Norman Conquest, William I conducted a mammoth inquest of England, neighborhood by neighborhood, requiring public disclosure of all landholdings and tax assessments, the whole census being recorded as the Domesday Book (1085-1086).

Apart from the Frankish and Norman sworn inquest conducted by royal officials, the occasional practice of submitting disputes to a group of neighbors for decision was also a feature of Germanic local law. In addition, church courts in the twelfth century occasionally put questions of guilt or innocence to groups of twelve; and Henry II's father, Geoffrey of Anjou, had made trial by inquest available for important civil cases in Anjou and Normandy. The idea, then, of summoning a group of people—twelve was considered an appropriate number and perhaps even a magic number—to give information under oath in a solemn proceeding, and even to give judgment in a case, was by no means new (though it was not very widely practiced) when Henry came to the English throne.

What Henry did that was new was to combine the use of the inquest with his new "judicialized" writ system, and thus to make trial by inquest available, as a regular matter, to the whole public in certain types of civil cases within the royal jurisdiction. Article 9 of the Constitutions of Clarendon of 1164 authorized the use of an inquest ("recognition") to determine whether (*utrum*) particular land was held by ecclesiastical or lay tenure (the "assize utrum"). In 1166 another royal assembly, probably also held at Clarendon, provided for trial by inquest in cases of claims for restitution of land based on the allegation that the plaintiff had been in possession and had been recently dispossessed by the defendant. The enactment was called an assize—the assize of novel disseisin —although the word "assize," meaning "session," originally referred to a solemn assembly. (Eventually an inquest itself—that is, the jurors sworn to answer a question put to them — came to be called an assize; finally, justices presiding at inquest were called "justices of assize," and ultimately sessions of courts on circuit were called "the assizes.")

Gradually, other questions came to be considered appropriate for jury determination. In 1176 it was enacted that the question of who was entitled to possession at the time of the death of a landholder should be decided by an inquest (the assize of mort d'ancestor). Later, the assize of last presentation (darrein presentment) was invented to determine which of two parties had last exercised the right to present a person to a church benefice when it fell vacant. In 1179 the inquest was allowed as an option for the defendant under the "writ of right" — a writ which raised the issue of full right, and not just prior possession — as an alternative to trial by battle. Thus the procedure for establishing "right" (in the sense akin to ownership) was assimilated with the procedure for establishing seisin under the so-called possessory assizes, namely, novel disseisin, mort d'ancestor, and darrein presentment.

Four important points should be noted here. First, the regular use of a small group of neighbors to decide cases before royal judges first emerged, in English law, in civil cases, and only two generations later was it taken into criminal law. Second, the inquest did not hear evidence, but answered a question or questions of fact on the basis of what it knew prior to the trial. Third, because the jurors, who were neighbors and had had advance notice of the questions that would be put to them when the justices visited, were able to give answers without a time-consuming process of interrogation of witnesses at trial, it was possible for a few justices — twenty-five in all, counting both the court of common pleas and the justices in eyre — to handle all the judicial business of the entire country. Fourth, the decision of cases by jury verdicts of the local population, under the direction of royal justices, was a politically palatable alternative — perhaps the only politically palatable alternative — to the decision of cases by local and feudal assemblies, whose procedures were more primitive and whose authority was too limited to control the kinds of interfeudal disputes that were causing the most trouble.

The jury of accusation. Neither Anglo-Saxon law nor Frankish law nor Norman law had distinguished between civil and criminal cases. Prosecution of what are today called crimes was generally at the hands of the victim or his near relatives. Trial, whether for breach of the peace or to determine property or other rights, was by ordeal or compurgation; the Normans added battle. In Anglo-Saxon times, the guilty party had to compensate the victim or his relatives, but the Normans changed that in cases of felony: if the defendant lost, he was immediately hanged or mutilated (usually by exoculation), his land escheated to his feudal lord, and his chattels were forfeited to the king. The very concept of felony seems to have been introduced into England by the Normans. The term originally referred to a breach of faith between man and lord. Thus not only kinsmen but also a lord or vassal was entitled to bring a prosecution, called an "appeal of felony." (The word "appeal" in this phrase had no such connotations as it has today.)

One obvious disadvantage of the appeal of felony as a means of controlling violence was that it took a high degree of public spirit to initiate proceedings. The "appellor" got nothing if he won, and indeed was fined if he lost. The primary motivation for bringing an appeal of felony was to avenge one's kindred or the feudal relation, or else to induce the other party to make a monetary settlement. If trial was by battle, the risks were enormous: the parties fought from morning to night to the death or until one cried craven—warriors with swords, the lower classes with heavy clubs and, if they broke, with tooth and nail. If trial was by ordeal, the outcome was speculative: judging from contemporary accounts, most people seem to have been acquitted. Also there were obvious pitfalls in trial by compurgation ("wager of law"): much depended on who had the benefit of proof.

The king, charged with responsibility for keeping the peace, and, in the person of Henry II, determined to subdue violence in the land, could not effectively compel people to bring appeals of felony. One resource for controlling crime which his predecessors had left him was the frankpledge system, under which the royally appointed sheriffs could examine frankpledge groups for unreported crimes and could impose fines; but this did not get rid of murderers, rapists, robbers, private marauders, and others who were plundering the countryside. In addition, Henry's grandfather, Henry I, had required the presentation of felons to itinerant justices by representatives of hundreds and shires, but this was an intermittent practice.

It should be remembered that the king had no police force, and clearly it would have been impossible for him to create one. He had all he could do to raise an army of reservist knights subject to forty days of military duty per year. Even if he could have paid a police force, he could not have controlled it. He would have had to convert the barons into a civil service, as the pope had converted the bishops into a kind of civil service; but the king had no such relationship to the barons as the pope had to the bishops—he did not have the power to appoint them, depose them, or transfer them.

The solution which Henry adopted to control crime was once again the use of sworn inquests—in this case, to report felonies to the itinerant justices. The Assize of Clarendon of 1166 provided that sworn inquests should present to the justices in eyre, when they arrived, all persons suspected of murder, theft, robbery, or of receiving men who committed those offenses, as well as all persons suspected of counterfeiting or arson.

All such suspects were then to be tried forthwith by the ordeal of cold water. This was a regularization and systematization of the previous intermittent and less well defined practices of Henry I as well as of still earlier Anglo-Saxon Frankish kings. In the past, however, persons presented by their neighbors had been able to clear themselves by compurgation (oath helpers), whereas henceforth they had to be tried by ordeal before royal justices.[53]

It should be noted, first, that the justices had available to them records kept by local officials, which they checked before impaneling juries; then they questioned the juries with respect to the various matters so recorded which had arisen since their last visit. Second, if the jurors—large numbers of them being assembled at each visitation, twelve from each hundred, four from each vill—concealed a crime or made a foolish presentment, they were fined by the justices. Third, appeals of felony were not abolished, but if for some reason an appeal of felony failed because of a technicality (and the technicalities were many), the justices only had to ask the assembled jurors whether they suspected the defendant, and if the answer was affirmative he would be sent to the water. Hundreds of cases could be disposed of in a few days by a single judge (or bench of three). In John P. Dawson's words, the device of the presenting jury "was extraordinarily efficient—a great invention." On the other hand, as Dawson also points out, "it was hardly a safeguard of local liberties."[54] Fines for nonpresentment or faulty presentment were extremely numerous and very heavy. As in the frankpledge system, the idea was to compel people to inform on one another.

It is noteworthy that Henry II did not extend *trial* by jury, as contrasted with *accusation* by jury, to criminal cases. That only came later, after the abolition of ordeals by the Fourth Lateran Council in 1215.[55] Nor did he abolish appeals of felony. However, persons presented by sworn inquests could only be tried by the ordeal of cold water; unlike persons privately accused by appeal of felony, they could not be tried by the ordeal of fire (hot irons or hot water), wager of battle, or wager of law (compurgation).

The forms of action. In considering the legal revolution which Henry II effected, it must continually be borne in mind that prior to his reign royal jurisdiction had been extraordinary jurisdiction—in both the technical and the nontechnical sense of the word "extraordinary." Apart from ecclesiastical and urban courts, *general* jurisdiction over *ordinary* legal matters had been confined to local and feudal courts, which were not professional courts but assemblies of neighbors and of members of the manor. What Henry II did was not to abolish local and feudal jurisdiction, but rather to create a *concurrent* royal jurisdiction in ordinary cases involving particular types of claims—and they were fairly numerous—which had a direct bearing upon peace. Thus in the Assize of Clarendon of 1166, Henry listed those particular felonies that were serious enough to justify his direct intervention. Similarly, in property matters he identified, through the writs which he made available to petitioners, what particular types of claims were remediable in the royal courts. Property claims could still be brought in feudal courts. Criminal and civil cases could still be tried in church courts. But for the first time a whole series of particular types of cases could also be tried, as a matter of right, by the king's justices.

The key to royal jurisdiction was the type of claim involved—the type of felony to be reported to the justices in eyre by the neighborhood juries or the type of writ granted by the king's chancery to one who sought redress of civil wrongs. In other words, the king did not say that he was prepared to give a judicial remedy to anyone who was wrongfully injured, regardless of the cause. Instead he said that he was prepared to give particular judicial remedies in particular classes of cases. The classification of wrongs actionable in the royal courts in terms of the remedies such courts would grant was the characteristic feature of royal justice, which gave the English common law its peculiar style.

The available alternative was the style of the canon law, which set forth broad theories of legal liability. The bishops' courts would hear any cases in which sin was alleged, and sin was broken down by categories synthesized from Roman law—breach of contract, injuries to person or property, the withholding of property belonging to another, fraud, and so forth. Henry II was familiar, at least in a general way, with the canon law as it was being practiced in the church courts, and with the Roman law as it was being taught in the universities. Perhaps he would have liked to establish a royal jurisdiction as all-embracing as that of the church. What he did in fact was to declare, at least by 1164, that if a dispute arose as to whether a particular parcel of land had or had not been given to the church, the claimant could go to the king's chancellor for a writ, which would direct the sheriff to assemble a certain number of men from the neighborhood to tell the king's justices whether or not the land had been given to the church; and to declare in 1166 that if a person claimed that he had been seised of freehold land and had been disseised, the chancellor would issue a writ directing the sheriff to assemble a certain number of men from the neighborhood to tell the king's justices whether or not the plaintiff had been seised at a certain time and whether or not the defendant had ousted him; and to say at other times that other types of claims were remediable in the royal courts by writs directing that particular types of questions should be put to inquests summoned by royal justices.

The writ, in short, defined the theory of the plaintiff's case and established the procedure whereby it was to be decided. Its effect, however, extended far beyond the individual case. It was taken for granted that similar writs should be granted in similar cases. As aggrieved persons brought new kinds of complaints to the king's chancery, the chancellor invented new kinds of writs, on the stated principle that "where there is a wrong, there is a remedy." The multiplication of stereotyped writs amounted to a substantial legislative activity, clothed in the forms of the judicial process. Thus in the late twelfth century, in addition to remedies for breach of rights of ownership and possession (writs of right, novel disseisin, mort d'ancestor, and darrein present-ment), the chancellor also granted writs of debt for money which the plaintiff claimed as his property, writs of detinue for chattels which the plaintiff claimed as his property, writs of gage for return of land pledged as security for a debt that had been repaid, writs of replevin for recovery of chattels pledged for an obligation that had been fulfilled, writs of cove-nant for breach of a sealed instrument. In the thirteenth century many other types of writs were created, the most important of which were various writs of trespass (*transgressio*, "wrong"), such as trespass for forci-ble entry onto land, trespass for forcible taking of chattels, and trespass for assault and battery to the person. From the trespass writs there ultimately developed much of the modern English and American law of torts and contracts.[56]

By the year 1300 there were hundreds of different writs, each of which, in effect, was both an assertion of policy (to protect certain in-terests against infringement) and an assertion of royal jurisdiction. The original basis for these two assertions, namely, to protect the peace of the king against the use of force and arms, had by that time given way to much more complex considerations. What had started as a response to the challenge of anarchy and violence and to the competition of local, feudal, and ecclesiastical courts had become the heart of an entire struc-ture of government.

The doctrine of seisin. The violent struggles over rights in land were not only a contest for wealth but also, and more significantly, a contest for political power, since the right to land carried with it the government of the community that lived on the land and worked it and also carried with it political relationships with superior feudal authorities. To establish a system for resolving such complex economic-political struggles peacefully, Henry II needed more than new techniques of adjudication through professional courts, judicial writs, royal inquests, and forms of action; he also needed a new substantive test of landholding—one which would cut through the complexity of the economic and political interests involved. He found that test in the concept of seisin.

The classical and postclassical Roman law had distinguished sharply between ownership and possession. Speaking very generally, ownership, in Roman law, was treated as a unitary concept: one either had owner-ship or one did not; and if one had it, one had full rights of possession, use, and disposition. This concept—even when taken together with various qualifications of it—was inadequate to describe feudal land-holding, in which each parcel was subject to the rights of superiors and inferiors in the feudal hierarchy. It was hard to say that a lord "owned" land which was granted to him on condition that services be rendered and which would be repossessed by his superior lord upon his death until his heir paid a "relief." It is of the essence of feudal law—or at least of Western feudal law—that there are divided interests in land, not absolute, indivisible ownership.

The classical and postclassical Roman conception of possession was also inadequate to meet the problems of feudal land tenures. Under Roman law, possession divorced from ownership received only a limited protection: if a nonowner in possession of land was ejected by armed force (*vi et armata*) he had a right to be restored, provided the defendant was not himself the owner. Thus the question of ownership lurked in the background even in that case. Also in the case of dispossession not by force but by fraud, the nonowner had an action, but it did not lie against a subsequent holder. Finally, possession in classical and postclassical Roman law was identified with factual occupation and control of tangibles, that is, land and goods: one could not "possess" incorporeal rights such as the right to services or the right to money obligation ("choses in action"), and one could not have a right of possession distinct from the rest of the bundle of rights called by the unitary name "ownership."

The church had for a long time grappled with the problem of possession in a context quite different from that presupposed by the classical Roman doctrines. Disputes had frequently arisen between persons claiming the same bishopric or abbey. Where one of the claimants ousted the other by force, church councils and popes had decreed that the prior possessor was entitled to be restored to possession before the question of who was the rightful claimant could be decided. In this connection it must be stressed that a bishopric or abbey was a new type of legal entity, a foundation, which was not land or goods, but which involved very extensive rights in land and goods and also rights to offices and services as well as other incorporeal rights.

Gratian, in his treatise of 1140, collected the various early decrees on this question and drew out of them a much broader principle than had previously been recognized. Quoting the decrees which dealt with "spoliation" (ejectment) as an affirmative defense in proceedings against bishops and abbots, Gratian then put a concrete case, and analyzed the case in terms of "questions." His first question was, "Whether restitution shall be made to anyone whomsoever who had been despoiled." His answer was in the affirmative. In elaborating it, he declared that anyone (and not only a bishop or abbot) was entitled to restitution of all that had been taken from him, including rights and powers as well as land and goods, whether by force or fraud, and that the remedy lay not only against the initial wrongdoer but also against subsequent holders. Gratian's rule was called the *canon redintegranda* ("rule of restitution"); later glosses interpreted the canon redintegranda as implying not only an affirmative defense but also an independent action, the *actio spolii*, or "action of spoliation."[57]

Henry II and his lawyers did for English law what Gratian and his successors did for canon law. They developed an action against the dispossessor wholly independent of ownership, an action to which even the defendant's own ownership was no defense. Thus a vassal was protected against a forcible ouster by his own lord. At the same time Henry and his lawyers made this action available for the recovery not only of land but also of chattels and incorporeal rights, and for the recovery of them not only against the dispossessor by force but also against the dispossessor by fraud and against subsequent holders. The plaintiff had only to prove prior possession and a wrongful dispossession. This was the assize of novel disseisin enacted in 1166; it had parallels in the laws of every country of Western Europe.

The broadening of possession to include possession of rights and not only of land and goods, and the broadening of the remedy for dispossession to include restitution even by the true owner, involved a subtle but important transformation of the very concept of possession. A new word was found for this transformed concept, not only in England but all over western Europe: seisin (in Latin, *saisina*). Seisin was more than factual occupation or control; it was a *right* to occupy and control, a right to "hold" land, chattels, or incorporeal rights: one could be seised of an office or of a liberty, or of a right of patronage, or of feudal services of various kinds. The scope of the right was defined in part by the remedies available to enforce it, namely, the "possessory" remedies, one of which, novel disseisin, in effect converted the property question into a tort question. That seisin meant more than physical occupation and control is evident from the fact that a plaintiff who went on pilgrimage could, by the writ of novel disseisin, recover his seisin against one who wrongfully occupied his land while he was away. This was called seisin *animo* ("mental seisin") as contrasted with seisin *corpore* ("physical seisin").

In Roman law there was no equivalent to the European concept of seisin. The nearest parallel was possession, which in Roman law was merely a fact, or an act, and in itself, with rare exceptions, generated no rights. In Roman law, the source of rights in land and goods, including the right to possess them, was ownership; without ownership, or rights derived from ownership (as in the case of a lease), possession was at best neutral, at worst illegal. In Europe, however, both in ecclesiastical and in feudal property relations, ownership was typically divided—often among many parties. The Europeans developed the concept of seisin to meet the needs of the lawful possessor who did not derive his right of possession from ownership. In one form or another, the action of novel disseisin — in England, in Normandy, in Sicily, in France, in the German duchies, and elsewhere — gave the lawful possessor, and also one who had a right to possession, a right to be reseised as against one who had unjustly disseised him.

The assize of novel disseisin, which Bracton, writing some ninety years later, said was "excogitated and contrived after many night watches," was one of Henry II's great devices for wresting jurisdiction over disputes in land from the baronial courts. "The ownership of land may be a matter for the feudal courts: the king himself will protect by royal writ and inquest of neighbours every seisin of a free tenement."[58]

Henry went further. He decreed that where a person brought suit in feudal court to challenge another's seisin on the ground of ownership, the defendant could remove the case to the king's court to be tried by an inquest of twelve "recognitors," thereby escaping the feudal trial by battle as well as the more solemn and more elaborate inquest called "the grand assize," which was used to try the question of ownership as contrasted with the question of seisin.

Through these and other decrees, Henry II established the principle that no man need answer for his free tenement without royal writ. Through the possessory assizes, the question of seisin could be brought into the king's court by the plaintiff; through the grand assize, the question of right could be brought into the king's court by the defendant whose seisin was alleged to be defective. In the words of a distinguished French historian of English law, "Henry II used the distinction between seisin and right [of ownership] — a romano-canonical distinction — to wrest power from the barons."[59]

Thus a substantial part of property law and tort law which had previously been a matter of local custom became a matter of royal law, just as a substantial part of local criminal law became "royalized" through the device of the accusing jury. It is this historical expansion of royal jurisdiction in the reign of Henry II that marks the origin of the English common law — although the phrase "English common law" is itself of later origin. Indeed, in the twelfth and thirteenth centuries, the phrase "common law" (*jus commune*) was primarily a concept of canon law: it was that part of the canon law (the major part) which was applicable in ecclesiastical courts throughout Christendom, as contrasted with local canonical custom (called *lex terrae*, "law of the land"), which was applicable locally. The Roman law was also called *jus commune*, since it was viewed as a body of theoretical principles and rules valid everywhere. Yet the absence of the phrase in English law and its subsequent importation from the canon law, or possibly from the Roman law, or from both, does not obscure but rather illuminates the critical point: that Henry II created the English common law by legislation establishing judicial remedies in the royal courts.

THE SCIENCE OF THE ENGLISH COMMON LAW

It is more than coincidence that the revolution in legal technique and legal practice which was effected under Henry II was accomplished by the writing of the first systematic treatise on the English common law, Glanvill's *Treatise on the Laws and Customs of the Kingdom of England* (*Tractatus de Legibus et Consuetudinibus Regni Angliae*). This book summarized, in effect, Henry's law reforms.

The treatise—which is usually dated about 1187, nearly a decade after the publication of another important (but much less systematic) English law book, *The Dialogue of the Exchequer*—evidently was written not by Glanvill, who was justiciar in the reign of both Stephen and Henry II, but very likely by his nephew, Hubert Walter, who in 1170 succeeded Thomas Becket as Archbishop of Canterbury and who ruled England from 1193 to 1198 while Richard I was on crusade. The likelihood that the author of Glanvill was a leading ecclesiastic—Hubert Walter was not only archbishop but also a papal legate—would support the view that English law in its formative period was heavily influenced by ecclesiastical legal ideas.

At the same time, there is nothing in the book about canon law. The ecclesiastical author confines himself chiefly to a summary of English royal law—law as distinct from administration, and royal as distinct from local, feudal, and ecclesiastical. This is a fact not only of legal but also of high political significance. In the opening words of the treatise the writer states:

> Not only must royal power be furnished with arms against rebels and nations which rise up against the king and the realm, but it is also fitting that it should be adorned with laws for the governance of subject and peaceful peoples; so that in time of both peace and war our glorious king may so successfully perform his office that, crushing the pride of the unbridled and ungovernable with the right hand of strength and tempering justice for the humble and meek with the rod of equity, he may both be always victorious in wars with his enemies and also show himself continually impartial in dealing with his subjects.[60]

Thus "Glanvill" ranked the king's laws with his armies as a basis of his authority. Thereby he legitimated royal power.

Further, Henry II's laws were reproduced in the treatise and were termed "royal benefits granted to the people by the goodness of the king

acting on the advice of his magnates." Thus the king's legislative power
was justified and his enactments were given permanence as part of the
"laws and customs of England."

In that connection the very writing was a matter of importance. That
royal law was set forth in writing gave it a certain dignity, perhaps even
a sanctity. The writing also gave the law a certain fixity, a certain stability. In addition, it laid a foundation for further elaboration and hence for
organic change. Bracton's treatise, written during the next seventy
years, built on Glanvill.

Finally, Glanvill's treatise focused on procedure, and especially on the
writs. He was not nearly as scholarly or as philosophical as Gratian. A
little political theory appeared at the beginning, but soon the author
devoted his energy to reproducing various types of writs, with only occasional arguments explaining their virtues. Why was this so? At least part
of the answer is that the king's legal authority stemmed from his command of a procedure for resolving conflicts which was more highly
developed, more sophisticated, more rational than that available in local
and feudal courts. The king was not yet in a position to legislate many
substantive norms of the law of contract, property, tort, or crime, let
alone matters like family law and inheritance which were in the exclusive
competence of the church. But the king had—for the first
time—established a central court of professional judges to hear cases
throughout the land, cases commenced by writs issued by his chancellor.
By focusing primarily on the writs, Glanvill's book made history, for the
writs themselves, by defining particular types of remedies for particular
types of wrongs, created what the English historian J.E.A. Jolliffe has
called "a revolution in legal science."[61]

The emphasis on procedure is of significance not only as an expression
of royal power but also as a limitation on royal power. The king had
greatly extended his jurisdiction as against that of both feudal and ecclesiastical courts; but the conditions of his assertion of royal jurisdiction
were expressly stated and they would therefore serve as limitations. The
categorization of types of remedies, as well as the statement of the procedures for invoking them, defined the royal jurisdiction. Thus, to quote
Jolliffe again, the "growth of definition" as means of confining power,
which was applied both to ecclesiastical and feudal power, was also applicable to royal power.

No assertion of absolute royal power, or of royal omnicompetence,
such as is found in the legislation of King Roger II of Sicily, is to be
found either in the legislation of Henry II or in the treatise attributed to
Glanvill. On the contrary, Glanvill, by defining royal jurisdiction in
terms of writs, limited that jurisdiction. In Maitland's words, the rule of
writs is the rule of law. The king, to be sure, could not be prevented
from usurping power beyond the limits which he set for himself; for him

to do so, however, would be to weaken public confidence in the legality on which his legitimacy rested and therefore to increase the likelihood that he would have to resort to the inefficiency of force in order to maintain his power. This is implicit in Glanvill's analysis of the dual character of royal power: its need for military arms to subdue rebels and foreign enemies and its need for just laws to govern peaceful subjects. Two generations later Glanvill's concept was carried much further in Bracton's *Treatise on the Laws and Customs of England.* Bracton also started by saying, "To rule well a king requires two things, arms and laws." He went on, however, to say that the very power of the king was derived from law — it was *lex* that made him *rex* — and that when he ruled only by force of arms, he ceased to be king.

Normandy

The Duchy of Normandy furnishes a key to the unity of Western civilization in the late eleventh and early twelfth centuries.

By the time the Normans conquered England, the Norman dukes had already established the first large-scale, centralized, territorial polity on the European continent. Throughout the huge duchy — approximately as big as all the Anglo-Saxon polities put together and several times as big as the territories ruled by the King of France — no lord could build or maintain a castle without the duke's permission. Each lord owed military service to the duke. The duke not only had a monopoly of coinage within his realm, but a network of ducal officials, called *vicomtes* ("vice-counts," or "viscounts" — "sheriffs" in English), controlled local government, commanded local military contingents, guarded castles, collected revenues, and held court. In addition, the duke was ruler of the churches within his territory; he had power to appoint bishops and abbots and to preside over provincial synods. He was the sacral ruler, the vicar of Christ, as described in the *Norman Anonymous* of the early 1100s.[62]

The history — and especially the legal history — of the Duchy of Normandy, like that of the Norman Kingdom of Sicily, has not been emphasized by modern historians because the duchy itself ceased to be an independent polity during the thirteenth century. In an age of nationalist historiography, those countries that eventually "didn't make it" either have been forgotten — like Norman Sicily — or have been treated as part of some other country's history — in Normandy's case, that of France, which eventually conquered it, or else of England, which it had previously conquered.

Nevertheless, Norman legal institutions had an important influence on both English law and French law. Moreover, the interaction that took place between Norman and English legal institutions and between Norman and French legal institutions testifies to the essential unity of the basic legal concepts, values, and processes of the European peoples.

After settling in Normandy in 911, the Norse rulers, starting with Duke Rollo, assimilated the governmental institutions of the Franks and established themselves as first-rate administrators. Among the Frankish legal processes that the Normans adopted was the inquest, consisting of an examination of the local population, under oath, by centrally appointed officials. The questions put by the official inquisitors might require the respondents to give economic or other data, to present suspected criminals, or to state whether the charges made against suspects were true. Soon after the conquest of England, the Norman rulers introduced inquests of various kinds into English practice, the most famous being the Domesday tax census of 1086. The Normans also introduced into England their own earlier practice of sending special justices to hold local courts, and they established a new system of central agencies of finance in both polities.

In the last third of the twelfth century legal institutions were fundamentally transformed not only in England but also in Normandy. In both countries there was a maturing of the system of itinerant justices, judicial writs, presenting and adjudicating inquests, and possessory assizes. In both a division was made between royal (ducal) "high" justice and feudal and local "low" justice. In both a civil case in the royal (ducal) courts was initiated by a letter (writ) from the king's chancery. According to Charles Haskins (the leading comparatist of Norman and English law in the twelfth century), the movement was largely from Normandy to England, rather than from England to Normandy. The writ of right seems to have developed simultaneously in Normandy and England during the reign of Henry I. However, Normandy was the source of the possessory writs of Henry II, and of the sworn inquest (petty jury) called to answer the questions contained in them.[63]

Haskins also attributes the origin of the English exchequer under Henry I partly to the experience of Normandy, although he is unable to state whether the English or the Norman exchequer came first. Also, Henry II introduced similar systems of judges and of bailiffs in both countries at more or less the same time. The timing was not of critical importance, however. As Haskins writes, "If the English military inquest of 1166 preceded the Norman returns of 1172, the Assize of Arms and the ordinance for the Saladin tithe were first promulgated for the king's Continental dominions. The order of these measures may have been a matter of chance, for to a man of Henry's temperament it mattered little where an experiment was first tried, but it was impossible to administer a great empire upon his system without using the experience gained in one region for the advantage of another."[64]

A remarkable textbook of Norman law in Normandy, written about 1200 A.D. and called the *Très ancien coutumier de Normandie* (*Very Old Customary Law Manual of Normandy*), describes a system of law remarkably similar to the law described a decade earlier in Glanvill's *On the Laws and Customs of England*.[65] If one had been a lawyer in England in the year 1190 or 1200, one could easily have moved to Normandy to practice there, without having to acquire a great deal of new learning. Thomas Brown, who was a baron of the Sicilian exchequer for two or three decades and then a baron of the English exchequer for another two or three decades, could have moved to the exchequer of the Duchy of Normandy without encountering any great surprises; similarly, a Norman judge could have moved from the court of Palermo to that of Westminster or Caen without substantial retraining.

Chapter 7 of the *Très ancien coutumier de Normandie* describes the jury to be summoned to decide disputes over seisin as a jury of twelve freemen of the vicinage unrelated to either party. Chapter 73 gives an example of a writ of novel disseisin that is virtually identical with the writ authorized by the English Assize of Clarendon in 1166: "King or his seneschal to the sheriff of such and such place, greeting. Command H. that he reseise without delay R. of his tenement . . . of which he was seised at [a certain time] . . . of which he was later disseised wrongfully and without judgment."

A few years after the writing of the *Très ancien coutumier*, the Duchy of Normandy was conquered by King Philip II of France and incorporated within the French empire that he established. In the following two decades, Philip adopted some of the basic institutions of Norman law for the royal law of France, including important features of the Norman administrative and judicial system. Thus the Duchy of Normandy, by its direct influence on both England and France, played a major part in the formation of the Western legal tradition.

France

The *Song of Roland*, written about the time of the First Crusade (1099), stirred the patriotism of Frenchmen — *Franci* — by its portrayal of their heroism and piety and by its references to *la douce France*. Yet at that time France as a political entity hardly existed. The King of France was master of less than a twentieth of the territory inhabited by Burgundians, Picards, Normans, Bretons, Gascons, Provençals, and a score of other major clans ("stems") that composed the slowly emerging nation of Franci. What the king ruled was the Île de France, the region surrounding the episcopal cities of Paris and Orléans, consisting largely of the patrimonial royal domain. The rest of what France later became was divided into duchies, counties, and lordships of various kinds, many of which were, in theory, held in feudal tenure of the king, but all of which were, in fact, quite independent. Among the half-dozen dukes were those of Normandy, Aquitaine, Britanny, and Burgundy; among the score of counts were those of Flanders, Anjou, Toulouse, Blois,

Manche, Barcelona; some of these—for example, the Duke of Normandy and the Count of Flanders—commanded considerably more power, wealth, and territory than the King of France.

More than a hundred years earlier, in 987, the last Carolingian king of the Western Franks, Louis V, had died and been succeeded by Hugh Capet. (The title of "emperor" had already passed to Eastern Frankish rulers.) The Capetian dynasty had been unable to do much more than maintain control over its vassals in the royal domain. In the 1100s it began to do better. Louis VI (1108–1137) and Louis VII (1137–1180) introduced more sophisticated governmental and legal institutions. They also increased their territory by judicious marriages, although the most judicious of these, Louis VII's marriage to Eleanor of Aquitaine, ended—after fifteen years—in divorce, and Eleanor took her rich dowry of Aquitaine and Guyenne with her to another "Frenchman," Henry Plantagenet, Duke of Normandy, Count of Anjou and Maine, soon to become King Henry II of England.

The first great king of France, and the founder of the French state and of French royal law, was Philip II (1180–1223), whom later generations called Philip Augustus. By marital alliances and by conquest, and especially by his victory at Bouvines in 1214 over King John of England, Emperor Otto IV, and Count Ferrand of Flanders, Philip created, in effect, a French empire. In addition to the royal domain, that is, *Francia* proper, which had grown to include (besides the Île de France) Champagne, Blois, Burgundy, Nevers, and the fiefs of the northeast extending to the English Channel, Philip's jurisdiction also included all or part of the duchies and counties of Normandy, Aquitaine, Brittany, Anjou, and Toulouse, which had been won chiefly from King Richard (1189-1199) and King John (1199-1216) of England. It was Philip's achievement to establish an integrated political and legal structure encompassing both the territories that belonged to him as his royal patrimony and the territories that he acquired by military or political means. Philip II did for France what Henry II had done a generation earlier for England and what Roger II had done two generations earlier for southern Italy.

Philip's "empire," like the "empires" of King Henry II of England and King Roger II of Sicily, constituted a federal state. In each of the three there was a kingdom (France, England, Sicily) together with diverse duchies and counties and lordships that technically were not part of the kingdom. In each of the three, the various constituent polities—kingdom, duchies, counties, lordships—retained a certain degree of autonomy. Each of the constituent polities had its own governor, whether the king himself, a hereditary vassal of the king, or an official appointed by him. Each had its own customary law. Yet the king also governed and enacted laws applicable to all the diverse polities within his realm, and the king's courts had jurisdiction over certain types of cases arising in any of them.

France, to be sure, was much less unified than either England or Sicily—much less, even, than the entire territory ruled by Henry II or the entire territory ruled by Roger II. This is to be explained by several interrelated factors. France was much bigger; it had perhaps four or five times the population of either England or southern Italy. It started the process of unification later. It lacked the strong tradition of kingship and the strong legal sense of the Anglo-Saxons, on the one hand, and the great administrative talent of the Normans, on the other. Perhaps its kings also lacked the utter ruthlessness of the Norman rulers, their lust for violence. Finally, the form of feudal economic system that prevailed in France also favored political dismemberment—though what was cause and what was effect is here, as elsewhere, difficult to say.

Nevertheless, starting in the last two decades of the twelfth century and the first two decades of the thirteenth, there took place in France a rapid development of governmental and legal institutions parallel to that which had previously taken place in England and in Sicily.

THE PERSONALITY OF PHILIP AUGUSTUS

Philip II, the only child of Louis VII, was raised from birth to be a king.[66] He succeeded his father in 1180, at the age of fifteen. In the first few years of his reign he foiled the plots of the nobles against him, particularly those of the house of Champagne, to which his mother belonged. His marriage in 1180 to the daughter of Count Baldwin V of Hainault and niece of Count Philip of Flanders turned the tables on the plotters. By diplomatic and military prowess Philip established himself as his own master despite his youth. Already he had shown qualities that were indispensable to all successful rulers of that period.

The first decade of his reign was dominated by shifting political alliances with and against Philip of Flanders and Henry II of England. The second decade saw an alliance with the German emperor (first Frederick Barbarossa, then Henry VI) against Richard I of England, which was followed in the early 1200s by Philip's conquest of most of the French parts of the English king's domain—Normandy, Maine, Touraine, Poitou, and Anjou. The great military skill and power of Philip reached its culmination in the Battle of Bouvines (1214), where the French forces routed those of Flanders, Germany, and England.

Philip's ability as a politician and warrior were matched by his ability as an administrator and lawmaker. He surrounded himself with persons trained in law, who gave him counsel and acted as his agents. Impressed with the organizing genius of the Normans in Normandy, England, and Sicily, he adopted for all his territories—especially after the conquest of

Normandy in 1203-1204—various institutions resembling those of the Anglo-Norman itinerant justices and sheriffs. Increasingly he commuted feudal services to money payments in order to pay mercenary troops. He asserted strong rights of overlordship over the barons. He played off clergy, feudal lords, and town authorities against one another, favoring especially the towns, to which he granted considerable self-government, and the great merchants, to whom he granted trading privileges and monopolies.

In all these abilities, interests, and policies, Philip resembled the other great royal lawmakers of his time, especially Roger II of Sicily, Henry II of England, Frederick Barbarossa of Germany, and Philip of Flanders. He also resembled them in personal traits: according to contemporaries he had great physical strength, was a lover of good cheer, wine, and women, and was an indefatigable hunter and swordsman. He was generous to his friends and harsh to his enemies, combining a hot temper with a cold reserve to control it. He was a devout Roman Catholic. Though he withdrew from the Third Crusade because he fell out with Richard II of England, he undertook the repression of the Albigensian heretics with full ruthlessness. He was willing and eager to borrow, adapt, experiment, and innovate in order to achieve his goals. What Heinrich Mitteis calls "imperturbable self-assurance and resourcefulness" were the hallmarks of his character, as they were hallmarks of other great monarchs of the twelfth and early thirteenth centuries.

His belief in law as an instrument of power was matched by his belief in law as an instrument of justice. He told his son Louis before his death that he should "maintain justice for low and high and poor and rich."[67]

THE FRENCH STATE

Philip Augustus inherited a royal court (*curia regis*) that was essentially feudal in spirit and tradition.[68] It consisted of hereditary magnates and royal vassals, both ecclesiastical and lay, as well as royal household officials mostly chosen from the baronage. It met when summoned by the king. It exercised a mixture of advisory, judicial, and legislative functions. In the reigns of Louis VI and Louis VII, the Abbot Suger of St. Denis, a cleric of humble origin, had exercised, as the chief adviser of the king, an important influence in increasing the power of the royal household officials and diminishing the power of hereditary magnates and royal vassals. It was this tendency that Philip Augustus carried forward. Under him the financial and judicial functions of the curia regis were separated from it and the royal chancery became a coordinating agency for those and other governmental departments. In these respects, Philip did—or began doing—for government in France what Henry II had done for government in England and Normandy, what Roger II had done for government in Sicily, Calabria, and Apulia, and what popes since the end of the eleventh century had done for the government of the church. What Philip began was brought to fruition by his son Louis VIII (1223-1226) and especially by his grandson Louis IX (1226-1270).

The establishment of central governmental institutions in France could not take place until royal governmental authority could be exercised locally, through royal delegates, in the territory under the king's jurisdiction. Such a combination of central and local governmental institutions, based on the principle of delegated authority, was an essential ingredient in the formation of the Western type of state. A second essential ingredient, related to the first, was a system of law by which the royal delegates could be guided — and bound. It was the earlier inability of the French crown to establish such a law-guided, law-bound, delegated authority in the localities that had prevented the formation of the French state until the time of Philip Augustus. Prior to that time, not only French dukes and counts but lesser barons as well would not allow royal officers to enter their dominions. Moreover, the French kings could not make effective use of local village and county institutions, as English kings could, because the tradition of local self-government was less developed in the Frankish than in the Anglo-Saxon kingdom and was therefore more vulnerable to takeover by the feudal barons.

What the French kings had done, under these circumstances, was to govern their own domain through local persons, called provosts (*prévôts*), who lived on the royal lands as managers and governors, collecting revenues, arresting and judging lawbreakers, summoning knights and the like. They usually paid the crown a rent ("forfeit") for the rights and powers they exercised, which were called a "farm" (*ferme*) and were held as a fief, often hereditary. Occasionally the king would send inspectors to check on the provosts. This system was not dissimilar to that which prevailed in England in the eleventh and early twelfth centuries.

Philip II increased the number of inspections and raised the authority and prestige of the inspectors, to the point of creating a new type of official called (as in Normandy under Henry II) a bailiff (*bailli*).

The creation of the new institution of bailiffs was suggested to Philip and his advisers by the Anglo-Norman bailli or sheriff of Henry II's reign. Philip consciously adapted and changed the institution by entrusting to the bailiffs some of the administrative duties of Anglo-Norman sheriffs and some of the judicial duties of Anglo-Norman itinerant justices. Like the Anglo-Norman sheriff, the French bailiff could represent the king in many kinds of matters; he received instructions from the king, supervised his finances, and reported to him. Like the Anglo-Norman itinerant justices, the French bailiffs were delegated from the king's court to hear pleas of the crown (*cas royaux*) and, in general, to uphold the rights and prerogatives of the king. By a royal ordinance of 1190, the bailiffs were instructed to hold assizes once a month, at which they were to hear claims (*clamores*), with the counsel of four trustworthy men (*legales homines,* "law men") of the locality. In time, each bailiff was assigned a fixed bailiwick which he administered for the crown and in which he sat as a royal judge. Also, after 1226 there appeared in some parts of France a similar office, that of the seneschal, who differed from the bailiff chiefly in being somewhat more independent of the crown. Bailiffs and seneschals were normally recruited from the lesser nobility of the royal household; normally they were trained in law; always they were salaried officials, servants of the crown as well as of intermediate dukes and counts.

The provost continued to administer his district, executing the king's orders and doing justice in his name. He also held court with the counsel of local residents. Appeals were taken from the courts of the provosts of a bailiwick to the court of the bailiff. The more important types of cases were reserved for judgment by the court of the bailiff in first instance. The bailiff would hold assizes periodically in the principal towns of his bailiwick with the assistance of the local provost and of "law men" or the local "council of notables" or, in some areas, lay judges (*hommes jugeans*). The profits from these cases — the substantial fees required from litigants and the taxes imposed on communities in connection with adjudication — went to the crown and to intermediate lords.

The introduction of the system of bailiffs was a precondition for the development of a central, professional, royal judicial body. Prior to the accession of Philip II relatively few law cases had been decided by the court of the king; from 1137 to 1180, there were apparently only eighty-five all told, or less than two a year on the average.[69] These were chiefly cases in which claims of denial of justice or false judgment were brought against a great feudal lord, or cases of dispute between an ecclesiastical lord and an urban commune to which he had granted a charter of liberties. The king usually presided in person. The judges were great lords and officers of the crown invited to participate by the king. There was, as yet, no central royal court of professionals, with responsibility for applying and shaping a system of royal law.

The emergence of such a court took place in the thirteenth century. At first, periodic judicial sessions of the curia regis, called *parlements* (meaning "discussions" or "deliberations") were held several times a year. Eventually, after about 1250, the Parlement of Paris sat as a permanent judicial body, with full-time professional judges presiding regularly over civil and criminal cases, sometimes in first instance but mostly on appeal from courts of bailiffs or, less frequently, from courts of dukes, counts, and other lords. The king participated in person only very rarely and finally not at all. The Parlement of Paris survived as the supreme royal court of France until the French Revolution.

The creation of a central royal court of justice was, as in the case of

Sicily and England and also in the case of the Roman Church, characteristic of the early development of the modern Western type of state. It represented both the combination and the separation of political power (*imperium*) and legal justice (*jurisdictio*) — their political combination in the office of kingship and their legal separation in the offices of king's council and king's court. France was slower than England and Sicily to centralize royal justice in a single professional court, just as it had been slower to create a system of decentralized royal judges. Eventually, however, the establishment of a system of distinct, permanent, royal courts was essential to the new state structure, one of whose characteristic features was its heavy reliance on adjudication as a means of social, economic, and political regulation.

Royal administration of justice between particular parties signified, in turn, the existence of a body of royal law to be applied, and it was further understood that this body of law was subject to be replenished and changed from time to time by the king. In contrast to their predecessors, Philip Augustus and his successors were legislators, in the sense that they were recognized — and they recognized themselves — as having the right and duty regularly to enact new laws. Increasingly in the thirteenth century, the French kings issued statutes (*établissements*) and ordinances (*ordonnances*) expressly changing the preexisting law. Many of these new royal laws had to do with the new system of administration of justice. Perhaps the most famous example is Louis IX's ordinance of 1258 outlawing trial by combat and converting the Parlement of Paris into an appellate court. Other laws extended the royal coinage to the entire realm, enforced more rigorous control over the towns, and, in general, increased the efficiency of royal government. It was sometimes stated in such royal laws that they were issued "for the common welfare of all," or "for the common profit of the realm." This reflected the canonists' justification of the lawmaking power of the king, expressed in Thomas Aquinas's famous definition of a law as "a prescription for the common good promulgated by one who has charge of the community."[70]

THE FRENCH SYSTEM OF ROYAL JUSTICE

Legal historians often treat the development of the French system of royal justice as having been almost a century behind that of England. They point out that in England there was a central royal court in the 1170s, whereas it was not until the 1250s that a central royal court, the Parlement of Paris, was established in France. This, however, is comparing apples and oranges. The Parlement of Paris was primarily an appellate court; it heard appeals from cases decided in first instance either by subordinate royal courts of provosts and bailiffs or by subordinate courts of dukes, counts, or other lords. The English royal judges, by contrast, whether on circuit or at Westminster, normally heard cases in first instance, initiated by original writ. One should therefore compare the twelfth-century English royal jurisdiction with the twelfth-century ducal and county jurisdiction in the individual French duchies and counties—Burgundy, Maine, Toulouse—as well as with the king's jurisdiction in the royal domain. (For France, the term "county" refers to the polity governed by a count, not to the English type of county, or "shire.") One should also compare the English royal jurisdiction with the French system of royal judges—bailiffs—established by Philip II in 1190; the main difference was that the bailiffs were neither itinerant nor centrally located but operated in separate districts, having a dual allegiance to the king and to the duke or count of the region. Louis IX's Parlement of Paris, on the other hand, did something the English central royal court did not do: it regularly heard appeals. This difference is neglected by those who treat the English development as "precocious" or the French as "backward."

If one compares centralized justice in England with centralized justice not in France as a whole but in a large French duchy, one finds marked similarities between the two during the twelfth century. A striking example is that of Normandy, since in the twelfth century the trial of important civil cases in Normandy by ducal judges was essentially similar to the trial of important civil cases in England by royal judges, the Norman duke being identical with the English king. At that time, there was no system of appeals from decisions in such cases, either in Normandy or in England. A century later, when King Louis IX of France was ruler of Normandy, cases tried in the central ducal court of Normandy were, for the first time, subject to appeal—to the new central royal court in Paris.

In establishing a hierarchical system of courts, with a regular procedure for appeals from courts of provosts to courts of bailiffs and from courts of bailiffs, as well as from courts of dukes or counts or other lords, to the central royal court in Paris, the French state was considerably "ahead" of the English state, not "behind" it.

Of course it would have been quite incongruous for the English kings to have attempted to fashion a system of appeals, since under the procedure of the English royal courts such appeals would have had to be taken from verdicts of inquests consisting of yes-or-no answers, based on the jurors' previously acquired knowledge, to questions of fact—or of a mixture of fact and law—put by royal justices. The nearest the English law came to instituting such appeals was the procedure of attaint, applicable in civil cases only, under which a "grand assize" of twenty-four persons was summoned to review a prior jury verdict; if it was found to be false, the aggrieved party was given back all that he had lost by reason of the unjust verdict, and the original jurors forfeited their goods, were themselves imprisoned, their wives and children thrust out of doors, their homes razed, their trees extirpated, and their meadows plowed up.

The French system of civil and criminal trial procedure was at first—that is, in the twelfth and early thirteenth centuries—not so different from the English. Not in central royal courts, to be sure, but in central ducal and county courts, and in local royal courts of provosts and bailiffs, judges presided over tribunals of laymen. The decision of the court was rendered not by the officer who presided but by the lay "suitors." This division of the tribunal into a presiding officer and suitors went back in time—just as the English jury did—to the Frankish inquest. Reliance upon the people of the countryside to participate in the trial of cases was enhanced by the legislation of Philip Augustus establishing the bailiffs' courts. The institution of "inquest by the people" (*enquête par turbe*) was also devised to determine local customs: twelve men were summoned to state the customs, and their unanimous opinion was expressed by their spokesman.

The French system underwent dramatic changes in the latter part of the thirteenth century and thereafter. As John P. Dawson has shown, the French procedure grew more learned and more complex.[71] Professionally trained lawyers appeared not only at the appellate level but also in courts of provosts and bailiffs as well as of dukes and counts and even of lesser lords. Eventually, in the fourteenth and fifteenth centuries, not only the Parlement of Paris but also the judges in lower courts, even at trial, followed a written procedure similar to that of the canon law: the parties exchanged written statements of claims and defenses; there were written interrogatories and sworn testimony of witnesses, taken in secret; the court's decision was expressed in written findings and a reasoned opinion. Parties challenged each other's questions. The rulings of examiners were recorded. Formalities abounded. Appeals based on alleged errors in the voluminous records were taken from lower courts to higher courts, and ultimately to the Parlement of Paris. As Dawson puts it, the lay membership of the lower courts gradually drifted away, "discouraged and confused by an increasingly complex procedure."[72] The official element predominated over the popular element, although the *enquête par turbe* survived.

From the perspective of later developments, one may plausibly argue that the early adaptation by the French kings of the procedure of the canon law, and their creation of a hierarchical system of appeals culminating in the central royal court in Paris, had deleterious effects upon the subsequent history of French law, and that the early adaptation by the English kings of the inquest system of the Frankish tradition had beneficial effects upon the subsequent history of English law. From the perspective of the twelfth and thirteenth centuries, however, the French system of courts and court procedure had considerable advantages over the contemporary English system, advantages in terms both of justice for litigants and of royal ordering of the society.

In terms of justice for litigants, the French procedure, like the procedure of the ecclesiastical courts, was designed to permit all the facts and all the issues of the case to be exposed, whereas the English procedure was designed to reduce the facts and issues to the narrowest possible point or points. The English system of pleadings and jury verdict—a verdict rendered without a trial—was well adapted only to certain types of cases. It was this defect, more than anything else, that required the English chancellor to establish an equity jurisdiction in the late fourteenth and fifteenth centuries in order to protect the poor and helpless, to enforce relations of trust and confidence, and to give injunctive and other forms of specific relief (as contrasted with the "common law" remedy of money damages). The English chancellor, who was almost invariably a high ecclesiastic, followed the canon law procedure—which was also the French royal procedure—of summoning witnesses by subpoena and interrogating them under oath.

In terms of the ordering of society, it is true that the French system of royal law could not be so effective in France as the English system of royal law was in England, partly because the French king had four or five times as many people to control, and they were divided into many more rival political units. A more sensible question to consider is whether the system of royal law developed under the French kings in the twelfth and thirteenth centuries was well adapted to the maximizing of their control over disorder, or whether they would have been better advised to develop a system of royal law more like that of England. Philip Augustus did model his system of bailiffs partly on the English sheriffs and itinerant justices, but under Louis IX the development of the appellate jurisdiction of the Parlement of Paris, and of the complex and sophisticated written procedure that went with it, eventually reduced the role of popular participation and created a special class of learned jurists who in the course of time became more and more removed from the population and more and more corrupt. But once again, one must not judge what was done under Louis IX by what happened under Louis XIV. In respect to the twelfth and thirteenth centuries, it seems fair to conclude that the system of royal law which prevailed in France—as compared with that which prevailed in England—was a remarkably effective instrument for royal ordering of the economic and social life of the country, and that if it was less effective in repressing crime, that was probably due to the fact that criminal jurisdiction was more decentralized in France than in England—more under the control of dukes, counts, and other lords, and of urban communes—which was not necessarily a bad thing.

The effectiveness of French royal law in the thirteenth century rested on its subtle combination of local custom with legal learning, and its sophisticated procedure for applying legal learning to local custom. The application of legal procedure and legal learning to local custom created a body of French customary law that operated as a powerful unifying and educative force.

"Local custom" refers to the diverse customs of the various localities, towns, and lordships, and of the counties, feudal domains, duchies, and other polities of which France was composed. There were relatively few customs of France as a whole, although there were some — for example, central customs relating to the descent of the crown, as well as common local customs such as that restricting the power of a husband to dispose of a wife's property during their married life. Also, despite the increased number of *établissements* and *ordonnances*, there was not a great deal of substantive statutory law of France as a whole; French statutory law was mostly procedural. However, the fact that cases in the royal courts of France were most often decided on the basis of local custom did not mean that the royal courts played no role in shaping that custom. On the contrary, the royal courts, including the Parlement of Paris, and on occasion the king himself, exercised the authority to reject all customs that were "bad" and to accept only those that were "reasonable." This carried with it the authority to interpret customs so as to make them conform to reason. Thus one can speak of a common *customary law* of France as a whole, consisting of the diverse customs that prevailed in diverse places as interpreted and shaped by the royal courts.

To say that France was governed by a common customary law is not to deny that a great many of the lawyers and judges of France were trained in Roman law. Nor is it to deny that in certain parts of France, notably in the south, Roman law had survived to a certain extent from pre-Merovingian times. But these were two different kinds of Roman law. The first kind — the Roman law in which the lawyers and judges were trained — was the law of the texts of Justinian as reorganized and rethought and revalued by the learned jurists in the universities (including, in France, the University of Montpellier founded in the twelfth century and the University of Orléans founded in the thirteenth). The Roman law of the universities was an ideal law, not an enacted code or statute or some other form of positive law. It was a body of legal concepts and principles through which the prevailing rules of customary law and enacted law could be screened and interpreted. The second kind of Roman law — that which survived, particularly in southern France, from pre-Merovingian times — consisted of scattered Roman legal terms and rules and procedures that had remained in the popular consciousness over the centuries, some of which had entered into successive Germanic codifications (such as the Visigothic and the Lombard) and into decrees and other acts of rulers. This "vulgar Roman law," as it is often called, had itself become customary law. The learned Roman law, on the contrary, was not so much law in the sense of binding rules as it was law in the sense of legal reasoning.

The learned Roman law was particularly helpful in determining which customs were "reasonable" and which were "bad." The canon law of the church also gave important guidance in this regard. It was the canon law that first taught the necessity of distinguishing reasonable from unreasonable customs. Indeed, the canon law also taught the necessity of distinguishing between what was acceptable and what was unacceptable in Roman law itself. Canonist principles of interpretation of custom were generally superimposed on Roman law rules and concepts.

In the French royal courts in the thirteenth century, custom could be proved in any of a variety of ways, according to the judge's discretion. The judge could state that he had personal knowledge of a custom since he had himself applied it in a previous analogous case, called a "precedent."[73] He could consult the lay counselors who assisted him in his court. He could call in a group of people who would know the custom — a group of clerics to state the custom of a parish or an abbey, a group of citizens to state the custom of a town, a group of sailors to state the custom of a port. Finally, under the procedure of the *enquête par turbe*, the judge could call twelve knowledgeable men and ask them to report, through a spokesman, concerning the existence of a particular custom or customs.

In the thirteenth century the king himself at times intervened as a representative of the "common weal of all" (*bien commun de tous*) to preside over a discussion among experts concerning contested customs and to declare or write down his finding. In the words of the thirteenth-century French jurist Philippe de Beaumanoir, "the king should keep and cause to be kept the customs of his realm."[74] An unreasonable custom was to be "overthrown." At the same time, however, the king could confer "privileges" on certain persons or groups, derogating from customs and dispensing with them on the basis of equity, that is, as an exception. Thus the king accorded privileges "against the general custom" to certain churches, certain towns, certain guilds, crusaders, and others.

Finally, if the custom was unsatisfactory not merely as applied to a particular person or group, for whom an equitable exception should be made, but more generally, so that it needed to be changed, the king could enact a new statute or ordinance revising the custom. Sir Henry Maine's theory that in the history of law there is a movement from equity to legislation finds support in the medieval French practice, which itself was derived from the theory of the canonists, authorizing the change of custom by equity and the generalization of equity by statute.[75]

In fact, however, there were in France relatively few new statutes or ordinances changing old customs, nor were there a great many privileges granting exceptions to old customs. For the most part, customs considered unsatisfactory by the royal courts either were rejected as "bad" or else were reinterpreted to make them "reasonable." In effect, a rule of reason and of conscience was itself built into the customary law.

Thus thirteenth-century French royal law was, on the one hand, far more learned than English royal law, in the sense that there were a far greater number of learned judges and lawyers in the French system;[76] yet it was less influenced by royal statutes. On the other hand, it was more diversified, in that there was not a substantial body of uniform customs applicable throughout France; yet there was a large body of "common law" in the sense of a common body of procedures and standards applied by the royal courts to the diverse customs of the multiplicity of polities which made up the French kingdom.

French Royal Civil and Criminal Law

Although the law that was applied in the French royal courts in the twelfth and thirteenth centuries was largely customary law, with wide variations from place to place, there were also important common features. Indeed, although the *customs* were highly diverse in their details, the customary *law*, that is, the manner in which the customs were conceptualized and the underlying principles by which they were interpreted, was remarkably uniform.

The following description of customary law applied in the French royal courts is based largely on the great work by Beaumanoir entitled *Books of the Customs and Usages of Beauvaisians*, written about 1283.[77] The author was bailiff of Clermont in Beauvais. Previously he had been bailiff in Vermandois, Touraine, and Senlis, and a seneschal in Poitou and Saintonge. His lord, the Count of Clermont, was a son of Louis IX and a brother of King Philip III. Beaumanoir had studied at the university and was thoroughly trained in Roman and canon law. He was also familiar with the case law of the Parlement of Paris. In addition to being a well-trained jurist, he was a perceptive and sensitive thinker. His book, although written in a concise style, was meant to be thorough. In a modern edition it runs to more than a thousand pages. Despite its relatively late date, and its concentration on chiefly one region of France, it is a useful source of information on the main characteristics of the law that was applied in royal courts throughout France in the twelfth and thirteenth centuries. Beaumanoir also analyzed, although in less detail, the jurisdiction and procedure of other courts in Beauvais — the court of the count, the ecclesiastical courts, the courts of local feudal lords, the courts of the towns, mercantile courts, and courts of arbitration (to which he devoted an entire chapter). All these courts exercised a concurrent jurisdiction. All of them applied "the customs and usages of the Beauvaisians."

The procedures in the royal courts were more or less uniform throughout France, at least after 1190, when Philip Augustus established the system of bailiffs' courts. The bailiff, to be sure, was a servant of the lord of the duchy or county in which he served. Yet he was ultimately subordinate to the crown, and after 1250 his decisions were reviewable in the king's central court, the Parlement of Paris. As Beaumanoir states, "each baron is sovereign in his barony, [but] the king is sovereign over all."[78] The procedure of the bailiff's court in Clermont, described by Beaumanoir, is similar to the procedure in bailiffs' courts in other parts of France as described in other contemporary sources.

In bailiffs' courts generally, and presumably also in provosts' courts subordinate to them, civil suits were commenced by a summons served orally by the plaintiff or his agents on the defendant, either in person or at his domicile or by notice (through neighbors). The summons was required to state in general terms the nature of the complaint. If it was too general, however, or vague, the defendant could plead excuse or delay. The court might require such pleading to be sworn. At trial the plaintiff was required to state in detail his complaint (*demande*), and the defendant was entitled to state his defense (*barre*). Beaumanoir compares and contrasts this procedure with that of the ecclesiastical courts: there the plaintiff's *libellus* and the defendant's *exceptiones*, he says, are in writing, and in Latin, whereas in the bailiff's court they are oral and in French; in addition, in the ecclesiastical courts there may be further pleadings—replications, triplications, quadruplications—whereas in the bailiff's court the issue must be joined by the demande and the barre.

The parties could be represented in court by others, called *procureurs*— relatives or friends or other agents to whom a power of attorney was given. They could also be represented—in another sense of that word—by advocates, who undertook to advise them and to present their case. By the time of Beaumanoir advocates constituted an "office," or profession, whose conduct was regulated by royal ordinance.[79]

Beaumanoir lists and discusses eight kinds of proof: (1) by oaths, (2) by written documents, (3) by judicial duel (which was still admitted in exceptional cases), (4) by witnesses, (5) by court record, (6) by admission of the opposing party, (7) by judicial notice, and (8) by presumptions. Of these, witness proof was the most modern at the time and the most important for the future. Many kinds of witnesses could be disqualified or their testimony restricted, including clerics and monks, women, lepers, minors and aliens, persons convicted of crime or false witness, bastards, serfs, and Jews. Members of the family or household of a party were disqualified from testifying for him. Procureurs and advocates could not testify concerning what they had learned while acting as agents or advisers. Witnesses testified orally under oath in answer to questions put by the parties and by the judge.[80]

Thus the trial procedure in bailiff's courts, unlike that of the canon law in civil cases, was oral, not written. But a written record was made, for the purpose of making possible an appeal to a higher instance, namely, to the Parlement of Paris.

Serious criminal cases, involving so-called high justice, were tried in the courts of lords, including the court of the chief lord, that is, the duke or count. However, serious criminal cases could also be tried in the court of the provost or the bailiff, when the king had jurisdiction by virtue of the nature of the crime or the tenure or condition of servitude of the accused. Jurisdiction was obtained through an accusation, whether by an aggrieved person or witness or another. Apparently there was nothing in the French courts comparable to the community presentment of felons through a grand jury to itinerant royal justices, such as existed in England. Thus although French law, in contrast to the older Frankish and Germanic law, distinguished between civil and criminal cases, it continued to use an accusatory procedure in criminal cases similar to the "demande" procedure in civil cases.

The chief types of cases heard in the bailiff's court, according to Beaumanoir, were disputes over the right to chattels, inheritances, contracts, gifts, guardianship of a minor, interference with seisin, and crimes against the person. However, many other types of legal problems, legal relationships, and legal transactions are also dealt with by Beaumanoir, including various aspects of the law of family relationships (dowry, infants, minors, illegitimate children), inheritance, wills, gifts, associations (mercantile ventures, companies, cooperatives, communes), transport, weights and measures, and labor services.

French royal law, like the English and the Sicilian royal law, shared with feudal law the sharp distinction between land and chattels, as well as the sharp distinction between seisin and ownership ("full right"). These distinctions rested upon the fact that in feudal law rights in land brought with them powers of government. The additional fact that Roman law, too, distinguished sharply between "movables" and "immovables," and between "possession" and "dominion," was convenient for the lawyers, since it made it possible for them to apply Roman terminology to the feudal realities. This was somewhat illusory, however, since the Roman distinction between movables and immovables was not the same as the distinction between chattels and land, nor was Roman possession the same as Western feudal seisin. The Western jurists were not overly troubled by this; they simply converted the Roman law to their own use.

In France, Beaumanoir comments, the bailiff's court—which is to say, the court of the king in the county or duchy or other lordship—was especially concerned with seisin and interference with seisin. This characteristic did not distinguish French royal law from the royal law of other kingdoms in Europe in the twelfth and thirteenth centuries. In all places where there were relatively strong central rulers, they wrested jurisdiction from feudal lords by asserting jurisdiction over tortious disseisins. Belatedly in 1277, the French king issued a statute asserting jurisdiction over "novel disseisin," but in fact the crown had long exercised such jurisdiction concurrently with dukes and counts.

Beaumanoir's analysis of seisin was highly sophisticated, relying heavily on the learning of the canonists in this area of the law. He distinguished among various forms of complaint for disseisin by force, disseisin by fraud and by other tortious acts not involving force, and interference with rights of seisin short of actual disseisin.[81] French law, like English law and canon law, also protected seisin of chattels as well as of land, and in addition seisin of rights; further, it protected seisin even when unaccompanied by factual possession, as when a person was considered to remain seised of his land and of his rights of government associated therewith, even when he was away on crusade.

In contrast to the English royal courts, the French bailiffs took jurisdiction over contracts as such and not merely over sealed covenants. Beaumanoir bases this jurisdiction on the moral principle—declared by the canonists—that contracts must be kept, *pacta sunt servanda*. "All contracts must be kept," Beaumanoir writes "and therefore it is written, 'A contract prevails over a law,' except those contracts made for bad purposes [as, for example,] if one contracts with another to kill a man for 100 livres."[82] Beaumanoir then goes on to recite other principles of contract law that were generally accepted by contemporary Romano-canonical legal science: that the contract must not have been procured by force or constraint, that the object of the contract must not be impossible or immoral or illegal, that gambling debts and usurious contracts are unenforceable, that certain defenses may be expressly waived in the contract (for example, a seller may waive any right to complain that he has obtained less than half the value of his property). What is interesting here is that these doctrines of Romano-canonical legal science had become part of the customary law of Beauvais—and of the other regions of France—applied in the royal courts.

Criminal law formed a substantial part of French customary law as practiced both in the royal courts and in the courts of dukes, counts, and lesser lords. Beaumanoir's longest chapter (114 separate articles) is devoted to crimes.[83] These he divides into: (1) those punishable by death, together with confiscation of the criminal's goods by the lord on whose property they were situated; (2) those punishable by fine, confiscation of goods, and long imprisonment; and (3) those punishable by fine only. The first group includes murder, treason, violent homicide, rape, arson, robbery, heresy, counterfeiting, escape from prison, poisoning, and attempted suicide. Normally death was imposed by dragging and hanging; however, heretics were burned to death and counterfeiters were boiled before being hanged. An example of a crime punishable by long imprisonment — one of those in the second group — is perjury ("false witness"); the term of imprisonment was fixed at the discretion of the judge. The third group includes cuts and wounds, disobedience to orders of a lord, trespass, and the like. Peasants paid smaller fines; nobles paid larger fines.

Conspiracies against the common good are another example of the crimes classified by Beaumanoir as punishable by long imprisonment. These include conspiracies among merchants or artisans to increase their prices, accompanied by threats against those who would not join them. Such conspiracies were under the jurisdiction of the lord within whose competence it was to fix prices. Also included among unlawful conspiracies are those with the political goal of insurgency. Beaumanoir states that the lord who apprehends such a conspiracy should condemn the participants to long terms of imprisonment and the confiscation of their property, and should sentence the organizers to be hanged. He recalls the formation of a league of the principal cities of Lombardy against the Emperor of Rome (it was the Lombard League organized against Frederick Barbarossa in 1167): having been prepared for five years, the revolt broke out everywhere on the same day, the emperor's officers were massacred, and the conspirators "established in their cities such laws and customs as they pleased."

When a person was caught in the act of committing a crime and arrested, the lord of the place where the crime was committed had jurisdiction to try the case. If the criminal was arrested later, after the crime had been committed, the lord of the place of his domicile had jurisdiction. If the crime infringed the rights of the count or the duke or the king, then jurisdiction belonged to the one whose rights were thus infringed. Thus the murder of a royal officer or treason to the crown was tried in the king's court. In contrast to England, however, there was not in France a general or exclusive royal jurisdiction over serious crimes ("felonies"), just as there was not a general or exclusive royal jurisdiction over serious civil offenses ("trespasses"). French royal criminal jurisdiction was somewhat analogous to that of the federal government of the United States — it was a jurisdiction over "federal crimes," many of which could also be prosecuted as "state crimes" by the various polities that made up the kingdom of France.

FRENCH AND ENGLISH ROYAL LAW COMPARED

In the late thirteenth and fourteenth centuries, especially after the Parlement of Paris began to flourish and the English bar became established in London, the law of the king's courts in France began to diverge more and more sharply from the law of the king's courts in

England. Eventually, after another century or so, the two systems acquired many of the contrasting features that have continued to characterize them in the twentieth century. The French system came to rely heavily on written procedure, the English on oral procedure; the French relied on hundreds of highly trained professional judges, the English on lay jurors and lay justices of the peace and only a very few professional judges; the French on judicial interrogation of parties and witnesses under oath, the English on accusation and denial by the opposing parties with resolution by the jury. With regard to substantive law, French royal law was more systematic, more learned, more Roman, more codified, while English royal law was more particularistic, more practical, more Germanic, more oriented to case law. French royal law covered more ground: civil obligations, including contracts, delicts, and unjust enrichment; property; corporations; trusts; crimes; public law; the law of nations. English royal law was restricted to the forms of action: writ of right, assize of novel disseisin, debt and detinue, covenant, the trespass actions, the common law felonies, the prerogative writs — yet it also entrusted to the chancellor's court in the fourteenth and fifteenth centuries a highly flexible and inchoate body of remedies and doctrines that eventually came to be called equity.

These later contrasts should not be allowed to obscure the fact that in the twelfth and early thirteenth centuries, when the English and the French kings first fashioned their respective systems of royal law, these two systems had a great deal in common. Even later they had much more in common than a nationalistic legal historiography will admit: to a Chinese the differences might still seem minimal compared to the similarities. But in their formative era, each combined in itself many of the contrasting features that later distinguished each from the other. The English had a written summons stating the theory of the plaintiff's action, while the French had an oral summons as well as an oral trial procedure. The English relied on professional narrators and pleaders and judges at the stage of the pleadings, while the French relied on lay judges — suitors, jurors, and others — to render the verdict. The interrogation of parties and witnesses under oath was only one method of proof in the French royal courts; among the other methods, some had counterparts in the English system. It is true that the English practice of requiring the jury to determine the facts in advance and to render a unanimous verdict without any trial whatever was unique. However, the French *enquête par turbe* presupposed that the jury knew, without hearing evidence, the customs of the locality, and its unanimous report on the existence or nonexistence of a custom undoubtedly had an effect, in some types of cases, similar to that of the English jury verdict.

There were other similarities. In both France and England, as in Sicily, the central justice of the king (or duke) competed successfully with the justice of a multiplicity of feudal lords. The king continued, as in earlier times, to offer recourse against a denial of justice or a false judgment in the court of a lord. To that extraordinary recourse was added, in the latter part of the twelfth century, first in England and then in France, a royal jurisdiction in first instance for a fairly wide range of cases, chiefly those involving violent breaches of the peace and disputes over seisin of freehold land. Moreover, in both countries royal justice was more rational, more professional, and more objective than feudal justice.

Royal justice was more rational in that it excluded, in most cases, trial by judicial duel and by compurgation.

It was more professional in that it was administered by professionally trained judges.

It was more objective in two respects. First, the judges owed an allegiance to the law, and to God, which was considered to be even higher than their allegiance to the king, let alone their allegiance to feudal lords of lesser station. As Bracton's great line states, government is not under man but under God and the law: it is law that makes the king. Similarly, Beaumanoir states that the judge's duty of obedience to his lord does not excuse him from obedience to God, and that the judge is not bound even by a direct commandment of his lord if to perform it would cause him to "lose his soul." In such a case, Beaumanoir says, the judge must leave the service of his lord rather than carry out an order that would violate his duty to God.[84] Such statements reflected the oath, taken by French royal judges in the twelfth and thirteenth centuries upon entry into office, "to respect the good customs of the country."[85] Yet even in learned treatises these statements were not made without risk in an age when kings and lords chopped off heads with impunity.

Second, the objectivity of judicial decisions in the royal courts was strengthened by the emphasis on the need for consistency in application of the law. In both the French and the English royal courts the principle was maintained that like cases should be decided alike. This was not a doctrine of precedent in the technical sense; that came much later, with the systematic reporting of cases and the development of the distinction between the "holding" of a case, which was binding in future similar cases, and "dictum" (or "obiter dictum"), which consisted of reasons given by the court that were not necessary to the decision and therefore not binding in future similar cases. In the twelfth century, and indeed until the sixteenth and seventeenth centuries, there was no such doctrine of precedent; moreover, reasoning "by example" was considered a less convincing method of reasoning than reasoning from principle. Yet the inferring of principles from analogous cases was a predominant mode of legal reasoning in the twelfth century as in the twentieth. Both Bracton in thirteenth-century England and Beaumanoir in thirteenth-century

France based their respective treatises on thousands of cases with which each had become familiar through a lifetime of judicial experience.[86]

This intense interest in cases was linked with the moral principle of equality before the law—that principle which underlies the maxim, "like cases should be decided alike." Thus Beaumanoir states that where a (similar) case has been judged before, "even if the judgment was made for different persons," it should not be presented to the suitors of the court for judgment but should be decided directly by the bailiff on the basis of precedent, "since one should not render diverse judgments in the same case."[87]

The striking similarities between the thirteenth-century treatises of Beaumanoir and Bracton have been overshadowed, in the minds of many commentators, by their differences. The same is true of the striking similarities between the twelfth-century treatise of Glanvill and the books of customary law that appeared in Normandy and France shortly after Glanvill. The two English treatises, one is told, contain the first scholarly statements of the common law of England (although the phrase "common law" does not appear in them); that is, they are centered on the rules applicable in the central royal courts at Westminster—the rules which constitute, as the titles of both books indicate, "the laws and customs of the Kingdom of England." In contrast, Beaumanoir's *Customs and Usages of Beauvaisians* and the earlier French and Norman "custumals" (*coutumiers*) are said to be centered on local customs, which differ widely from place to place. Yet the customs of Beauvais, as conceived and organized and rationalized and applied by the royal courts, were quite similar *in general* to the customs of the other regions of France, as sifted by the royal courts. Periods of prescription differed, excuses for nonappearance differed, required formalities for transfer of land differed, and many other things differed; nevertheless, the permissible limits of differences in detail were set by the royal courts in the localities and, indeed, in the time of Beaumanoir, by a supreme court in Paris. In addition, there were some uniform customs throughout France, and these were expressly referred to as "the common law." Above all, the general principles were the same.

Moreover, the common law of England is usually said to be itself a customary law. It is not easy to know what this means. The English common law is usually traced back to the Assize of Clarendon and other twelfth-century royal enactments; these constitute enacted law, which is the opposite of customary law. What is meant, no doubt, is that the royal enactments established procedures in the royal courts for the enforcement of rules and principles and standards and concepts that took their meaning from custom and usage. The rules and principles and standards and concepts to be enforced—the definitions of felonies, the concepts of seisin and disseisin—were derived from informal, unwritten, unenacted norms and patterns of behavior. These norms and patterns of behavior existed in the minds of people, in the consciousness of the community. Of course, in that general sense all law rests ultimately on custom and usage.

If one were to specify more precisely the meaning of the phrase "customary law," one would no doubt find that it means something different when applied to the law followed in the royal courts of England from what it means when applied to the law followed in the royal courts in France. Yet it must also mean something similar. There are many illustrations of such similarity. For example, in both England and France the legal concept of seisin was rooted in customary law; in both countries royal courts took jurisdiction over cases of novel disseisin (nouvelle disseisine); in both countries the king used the customary concept of seisin, as embodied in the enacted law of novel disseisin, to wrest from feudal lords jurisdiction over disputes concerning rights in freehold land. There were differences, of course. But the similarities testify to the overlapping of customary law and royal law in both kingdoms.[88]

14 | Royal Law: Germany, Spain, Flanders, Hungary, Denmark

Germany

In speaking of the origins and early development of royal law in Germany, one is confronted by the fact that there was no king of Germany in the sense that there was a king of Sicily or a king of England or a king of France. There were dukes, kings, and other princes of the individual autonomous territories (*Länder*, "lands") that made up the empire. Each Land was, in effect, a kingdom in itself. Included were the five major German duchies of Saxony, Swabia, Bavaria, Franconia, and Lothringen, plus others such as Friesland and Thuringen; the Lombard cities of northern Italy; the Frankish kingdom of Burgundy; the Slavic kingdom of Bohemia; a number of border "marches" (including the Ostmark, which in 1156 was elevated to the status of Duchy of Austria); and various other polities. In the year 1075 a duchy such as Saxony or Bavaria was roughly comparable in size and wealth and power to the Kingdom of France (as it then was) or the Duchy of Normandy or the Kingdom of England. The king of the whole German empire ruled his own Land in addition to being chief of the imperial federation.

Hence royal law in Germany may be taken to refer either to the law of the empire as such (imperial law) or to the law of any one of the duchies or other principalities that constituted the empire (princely law). In fact, during the twelfth and thirteenth centuries imperial law, which had previously been quite rudimentary, took root and blossomed temporarily, although it did not match the development of royal law in Sicily, England, or France, while princely law not only took root and blossomed but continued thereafter to flourish rather as the royal law of Sicily, England, France, and other parts of Europe flourished.

IMPERIAL LAW

The empire, founded by Charlemagne (768-814), had been from the beginning a universal idea superimposed on a diverse multitude of tribal, local and lordship units. It was not a territorial entity but was the sphere of authority — the *imperium* — of the person of the emperor, who represented the religious unity of Western Christendom and its military resistance to Norse, Arab, Slavic, and Magyar attacks. Charlemagne himself had instituted some central controls of a legislative, administrative, and judicial nature, but they were weak. Imperial legal institutions were scattered sparsely throughout the empire and did not take deep root. Charlemagne's empire has rightly been called a "frail giant." After his death it quickly became fragmented and was divided among his heirs, the title "emperor" descending to the leaders of the eastern Franks, who inhabited what many centuries later came to be called Germany.

For two hundred years the "German" empire continued to be called the Empire of the Franks, or the Christian Empire, but only rarely the Roman Empire. Then in the early eleventh century the practice was instituted of giving to the heir selected to be the future emperor the title "King of the Romans" instead of "King of the Franks"; after the emperor's death, that son would normally proceed to Rome to be crowned by the pope as "Emperor of the Romans." This symbolized, above all, the Frankish emperor's claim to the theocratic authority of the Roman emperor Constantine and his successors as head of the church. In the twelfth century, the empire itself came to be called, for the first time, the Roman Empire; by then, however, papal supremacy over the church had been established, and the word "Roman" in the title of the empire symbolized its political and legal unity and authority in the secular sphere. (Only in the thirteenth century did it come to be called the Holy Roman Empire and, finally, in the fifteenth century, the Holy Roman Empire of the German Nation.)

To appreciate the rudimentary character of imperial law prior to the Papal Revolution, one must recall that the empire had no capital city, no bureaucracy, no professional judiciary, not even an established fiscal authority. The emperor governed through his household, which moved with him continually throughout the empire. The chancellor was the emperor's secretary. The chamberlain was in charge of the emperor's household budget. Royal advisers were not permanent officials but were chosen ad hoc, from case to case. As Heinrich Mitteis has said, "The empire was only in full strength at the particular place where the king was staying; only through frequent appearances in the various parts of his empire was he able to be respected. That required a superhuman personal achievement and consumed the powers of the rulers prematurely: their early death was not a mere regrettable accident but the consequence of the grinding system of government."[1]

This does not mean that there was no imperial law other than household law. There was, above all, the imperial prerogative of judging: wherever the emperor was, he held court, applying customary local or tribal or feudal law and also dispensing a universal justice and mercy in his capacity as vicar of Christ and supreme head of the *imperium christianum*. The emperor had the right to "evoke" (*jus evocandi*) a case from any tribunal, whether local, feudal, territorial, or ecclesiastical. Even more important, he had the power to pronounce the "ban" of the empire, which required accused persons to submit to imperial "high justice" or else be outlawed. The power of the imperial ban was also vested in the office of the count (in Latin, *comes*; in German, *Graf*); counts survived from Carolingian times, when they had been appointed by the emperor to perform judicial and administrative functions in his name in the localities (counties, *Grafschaften*). However, in the course of the succeeding centuries the central imperial character of the office diminished greatly and in most places it became largely hereditary and local.

In addition, the emperor exercised a substantial influence upon the development of ecclesiastical law, which was itself at that time (as in Roman times) considered to be one of the principal branches of imperial law. Prior to the Papal Revolution, of course, the emperors appointed abbots and bishops (including the Bishop of Rome), called and presided over church synods, and even occasionally promulgated ecclesiastical canons of both a theological and a legal character.

The weakness of imperial law on the secular side was reflected in the rule that the emperor had no power to tax his subjects but had to raise his revenues from his own estates, which were scattered throughout the empire. There were also severe limitations on his right to acquire new land by escheat. In the eleventh century the emperors succeeded in raising up a class of imperial servants (called *ministeriales*) by gifts of land; these were appointed to manage imperial estates and also, being armed and mounted, to serve as part of the imperial army. However, when lands escheated to the emperor from his vassals (princes and other nobles) because of lack of heirs, he was required by the imperial feudal law to convey them to other vassals. This so-called *Leihezwang* ("compulsory enfeoffment") sharply distinguished imperial feudal law from the feudal law of the duchies and other principalities of the empire as well as from that of France, England, Sicily, and the other emerging secular powers of Western Christendom.

The Papal Revolution significantly altered the nature of the imperial office, and with it the scope and character of imperial law. On the one hand, the emperor's constitutional role within the church was greatly reduced: he became a mere layman, albeit a powerful one since bishops and abbots, though no longer invested by him with their ecclesiastical powers, remained his feudal vassals. His constitutional position vis-à-vis the rulers of the various constituent territories of the empire was also changed. The princes, in fact, had taken a decisive role in bringing about the final settlement of the investiture controversy; in the deliberations that led to the Concordat of Worms in 1122 they had appeared, in Mitteis's words, "as guarantors of imperial rights,"[2] mediating between the emperor and the papal legates. Many new princely houses of the twelfth and thirteenth centuries first became prominent during the civil wars that marked the course of the Papal Revolution, including the Hohenstaufen, the Wittelsbach, and the Wettin families. By the mid-twelfth century, again in Mitteis's words, the empire "no longer consisted of tribal territories (*Stammesländer*) but of territories of a new type, ruled by dukes who were supposed to participate in the government of the empire."[3]

Indeed, the emperor became wholly dependent on the dukes and other princes of the empire for his election. In 1077 the princes held a diet (*Reichstag*) in Forchheim at which they passed a resolution, approved by Pope Gregory VII, requiring election of the emperor by them; and in 1125 at a diet in Mainz this principle was applied for the first time when the heir of the deceased Emperor Henry V, Duke of Swabia, was rejected by a committee of princes, who instead elected Lothar, Duke of Saxony. In 1138, after Lothar's death, the princes again passed over the emperor's heir and elected Lothar's rival, Conrad of Swabia; and in 1152 they passed over Conrad's son in favor of his nephew Frederick (Frederick Barbarossa). By the end of the twelfth century it had become established that emperors were to be elected by an electoral college of princes, in which the archbishops of Mainz, Cologne, and Trier and the Count Palatine of the Rhineland had a preferred place.

In addition, the emperor was supposed to summon the "princes of the realm" whenever decisions of fundamental importance were to be made. The old empire had consisted of the imperial household and tribal duchies (*Stammesherzogtümer*, "stem-duchies"); the new empire consisted of the emperor's own territorial Land (Swabia or Saxony or whatever) plus the other Länder ruled by the imperial princes (*Reichsfürsten*), which gradually lost most of their character as stem-duchies and became primarily territorial polities.[4]

The new empire developed new political and legal institutions. The secularization of imperial power impelled the emperor to develop a civil service that relied much less on ecclesiastical personnel and that was concerned much less with ecclesiastical affairs. Secular concerns, especially the maintenance of peace and justice, which by the very terms of the Papal Revolution remained within the emperor's supreme jurisdiction, acquired increased importance. The very division of Western Christendom into an "ecclesiastical" sphere and a "secular" sphere, and the legal demarcation of the boundaries between them, along with the heavy emphasis on the legal character of the ecclesiastical sphere under the papacy, made it inevitable that there would be a responsive emphasis on the legal character of the secular sphere under the emperor. The emperor found new forms for strengthening his government and for controlling violence. These new forms reflected a shift toward statecraft in the modern sense, though not to the same extent as in Sicily, England, and France.

The emperor retained and regularized his position as supreme judge in the empire. He heard appeals against judgments of courts of princes and noblemen as well as of city courts. The procedure followed in such cases was the traditional Germanic procedure of group judgment, with the emperor sitting as presiding officer and the judges, drawn usually from among his courtiers, declaring their verdict. In cases involving feudal law (*Lehnrecht*), the judges had to be drawn from peers — class equals — of the defendant, and in cases involving local law (*Landrecht*), from fellow nationals (*Stammesgenossen*) of the defendant. These two types of procedure were dramatically illustrated in the famous proceedings instituted against Henry the Lion, Duke of Bavaria and Saxony, in 1179-80. Henry, charged by his enemies with various crimes, including treason against the emperor, was tried for violation of the Landrecht by a court composed of Swabian doomsmen (since he was of Swabian origin), and was sentenced by them for contumacy in failing to appear. He was also charged by the emperor, Frederick Barbarossa, with violation of his feudal obligations to Frederick as his overlord, and was tried according to the Lehnrecht by his peers, the princes of the empire. The sentence for contumacy was outlawry, which, however, was not permanent, and after a few years of exile in England Henry was allowed to return to his castle at Braunschweig and to recover part of his allodial possessions. The sentence for violation of his feudal obligations was more severe — permanent confiscation of his fiefs, including the duchies of Bavaria and Saxony; these escheated to the emperor, who, under the rule of compulsory enfeoffment, bestowed Bavaria on the house of Wittelsbach and divided Saxony between two other principalities, thus ending the territorial power of the Welf family to which Henry belonged.[5]

The emperor also had the right to summon the nobility, including the great princely tenants-in-chief both secular and ecclesiastical, the knighthood, and eventually representatives of the imperial cities, to participate in occasional deliberative assemblies. These "imperial days," or "diets" (from the Latin *dies*, "day"; in German, *Tag, Reichstag*), which became regularized in the thirteenth century, were an analogue of the contemporary English parliaments. They were means whereby kings could secure the assent of the ecclesiastical, feudal, and urban magnates — the "estates" — to royal laws, in return for which the assemblies might wring concessions from the supreme ruler. Mitteis states that in contrast to the English parliaments of the thirteenth, fourteenth, and fifteenth centuries, the German diets did not purport to represent the kingdom as a whole (the *communitas regni*), but rather each prince thought in terms of his own principality or, at most, his own class.[6] At the same time, the German emperor had less power over the Reichstag than the English king had over the parliament. In both cases, the periodic assemblies of notables symbolized a political structure in which power is divided among various estates or orders: higher nobility, lesser nobility, clergy, merchants, artisans. The institution of the diet, or parliament, was an expression of the interrelationship of monarch and estates; it constituted a characteristic feature of Western constitutional law in its formative era.

In addition, the emperors of the twelfth and thirteenth centuries greatly improved the administration of their own imperial landed estates, from which they derived most of their revenues, through expanding and strengthening the system of ministeriales. These became more like imperial civil servants and less like feudal vassals. Lacking, however, was the structure of departments—especially treasury, judiciary, and chancery—that characterized state-building in the other great kingdoms of Europe in the twelfth century, including some of the German principalities, as well as in the Roman Church. There was an imperial chancery, to be sure, but it embraced the entire staff of imperial household officers and did not serve as a separate coordinating department. As Mitteis has said, the empire failed, in comparison both with the German territories and with England, France, and Sicily, to create a modern royal bureaucracy. The imperial chancery was backward, "Germany had nothing remotely equivalent to England's financial administration," and there was no professional imperial central judiciary.[7]

Yet it would be a mistake to suppose that the German emperors of the late eleventh, the twelfth, and the early thirteenth centuries did not participate effectively in the law-creating enterprise that swept over Western Christendom in the wake of the Papal Revolution. They did so chiefly through legislative measures, often promulgated at imperial diets, usually under the title of a "peace statute" (*constitutio pacis*), but also called a "land peace" or "territorial peace" (*pax terrae, Landfriede*). These purported to contain new laws, declared by the emperor, and constituted the first example of German imperial legislation in the modern sense. Many scholars have discounted the importance of the peace statutes as legislation on the ground that the imperial authority was itself ineffectual, lacking adequate judicial and administrative machinery to enforce these laws. It is true, of course, that imperial power was relatively weak even in the late twelfth century when it was at its height, and that thereafter it deteriorated rapidly and almost disintegrated. Nevertheless, various imperial peace statutes enacted after 1150 contained much new law that was, in fact, enforced at the imperial level; and more important, they contained much new law that penetrated the territorial law of the duchies and other principalities as well as the law of the cities.

The emperor who, more than any other, was responsible for these imperial peace statutes was Frederick Barbarossa (1152-1190).

The personality and vision of Frederick Barbarossa. In 1152 when Frederick, at the age of twenty-eight, was elected "King of the Romans" at an assembly of German princes and bishops, Roger II (1112-1154) was still on the throne of Sicily and Henry II (1154-1189) would soon become King of England and Duke of Normandy; later in Frederick's reign, Philip Augustus (1180-1223) became King of France. These men were all builders of centralizing territorial states. They all shared many personal characteristics that were essential to the assertion of strong political and legal authority over the diverse villages, towns, and cities, the diverse clans, the diverse principalities, and the diverse estates, including the clergy, that constituted their respective realms. As a personality Frederick may be compared especially to Henry II. It is revealing that in 1165 the two discussed combining forces in a crusade at some future time—a plan that did not materialize.

Like Henry, Frederick was a man of apparently inexhaustible energy and vitality. Having no fixed abode, he ruled from the saddle, so to speak, moving constantly from castle to castle and from city to city during his reign of thirty-eight years. As Henry had to travel continually to repress actual or potential threats to his authority throughout England, Ireland, Scotland, Wales, Normandy, Anjou, Aquitaine, Poitou, and other parts of his "empire," so Frederick had to do the same throughout Burgundy, northern Italy, and the many territories of Germany. To be a successful ruler in the twelfth century required a strong physical constitution. More than that, it required a tenacity of purpose, almost a ferocity of will. Rulers who lacked those qualities were overpowered and their territories were swallowed up.

Frederick's purpose was not merely conquest, although without conquest none of his other purposes could have been accomplished. It was primarily the construction of a well-ordered state based on law. That purpose was not unconnected with conquest, of course, since it was much more efficient to rule by law than by force: where one's judges were obeyed it was not necessary to be present with one's armies. Law was also closely connected with revenue: litigants paid high fees into the coffers of the emerging territorial rulers of Europe. Yet law was also an end in itself: the keeping of peace and the doing of justice were the two main justifications of royal authority, the two main sources of its legitimacy, and, beyond that, the two main criteria of the monarch's "success," as one would say today, or "salvation," as they said in the twelfth century. The twelfth-century European kings, and especially the emperor, were, to be sure, no longer the sacral rulers that their tenth-

and eleventh-century forbears had been, but they nevertheless still ruled "by the grace of God" and, more than that, they claimed to have (and were recognized by others as having) important religious characteristics and functions. Frederick himself died in Asia Minor while on a crusade.

The accounts of Frederick's contemporaries give the impression of a man of great personal power, striking in appearance, with a fine physique and red beard, eloquent in speech, highly intelligent, moderate in his appetites and emotions, pious and respectful toward the church, a man who in general preferred to work within the traditional restraints that his society imposed on him—but who also was capable of great anger and of violent excesses of cruelty that horrify the modern reader although they apparently shocked only a few of his contemporaries. His reputation for moderation was also belied by his enormously imaginative and bold policies, and especially by his dream of subjecting the northern Italian cities to the imperial authority. The total, systematic destruction of Milan by his army in 1162 was hardly an example of moderation.

Frederick's election to the German throne was the result of a compromise between the Staufen and Welf families, both of which had hereditary and political claims to rule. On his father's side Frederick was a nephew of Emperor Conrad III (1137-1152), a Staufen, while on his mother's side he was a nephew of Welf VI and a cousin of Henry the Lion. His mission was to provide stability in Germany after a period of great disorder—which he did. Although almost nothing is known of his childhood or education, it may be assumed that he was probably not raised to be a king; nevertheless, the rapidity with which he seized the reins of government revealed a remarkable vocation for ruling. His fame as an arbiter spread rapidly and many resorted to him to seek justice. Within months of his election he issued his first peace statute asserting royal jurisdiction over violent crimes and disputes over seisin, and in the following year he concluded a treaty with the papacy providing for his coronation as emperor and regulating various matters of foreign policy. In 1155 he was crowned Emperor in Rome in a ceremony that was carefully controlled by him to symbolize his independence of papal political power.

Frederick very early recognized that law could play an important role in maintaining his authority—not only vis-à-vis the papacy but also vis-à-vis the territorial rulers of Germany, the cities of Germany (Frederick himself founded many of them), the cities of Lombardy, and the feudal lords of his own domains. During his first journey to Rome, in 1155, to be crowned Emperor, he met with the professors ("doctors") of the law school in Bologna, where tens of thousands of students had already been trained for governmental posts throughout Europe. A few years later, in 1158, Frederick relied on the greatest of the Bolognese jurists—"the four doctors," Martinus, Bulgarus, Jacobus, and Hugo—to draft important legislation for the Diet of Roncaglia.

Frederick's concern with law was not disinterested. He thought of law both as an instrument for maintaining the stability of his vast empire and as an instrument for strengthening his own power as emperor. He sought, therefore, to maintain the various customs of the various territories and at the same time to introduce new legislation that would enhance the central authority. Connected especially with the first goal—the maintenance of stability—were the various peace statutes that he promulgated. Connected especially with the second goal—the increase of imperial power and authority—were various other statutes that he promulgated, concerning royal powers (called *regalia*), royal control over subordinate government officials, and taxes, as well as feudal law generally.

Frederick's enlistment of the four doctors gives some important clues to his attitude toward law. He asked them to present to him a list of all the rights to be accorded to the emperor under the ancient laws of Lombardy as they had existed prior to the rise of independent cities. They replied cautiously that they could not give such a list without full consultation with the judges from all the cities. Frederick then formed a commission consisting of two judges from each of the major cities. The result was the promulgation at Roncaglia of a statute ("definition") of imperial powers which listed: (1) jurisdiction over and income from public ways, navigable rivers, ports, and tolls, as well as fish ponds and saltworks; from coinage; from exchange of money; from fines and amends, from ownerless property, and from lawful exactions from unworthy persons; from goods of persons who had entered into incestuous marriages or who had been condemned and outlawed or who had committed high treason; from services by manual labor, with teams or with carts or boats; from contributions for royal military expeditions; and from treasure trove; (2) the power to appoint magistrates to exercise justice; and (3) the maintenance of palaces in certain cities. Another statute adopted at Roncaglia in 1158 stated simply, "All jurisdiction and all judicial power belong to the prince, and all judges must accept office from the prince and must swear an oath as required by law." A third statute provided that the prince might have palaces and courts in any places he pleased. A fourth and last statute provided for specific head taxes and specific ground taxes.

Although the four statutes referred to Roman law, and although there were further traces of Roman law in the other legislation promulgated at Roncaglia, in fact the idea of listing specific royal or imperial powers was entirely alien to the law of Justinian as it had been understood before the late eleventh century; it was the Papal Revolution that gave birth to the very word "regalia".[8] Moreover, the gist of the Roncaglia statutes — namely, the emperor's right to income from certain commercial, judicial, and other activities or situations, and his right to "jurisdiction and judicial power," that is, to high justice (*bannus*) — was entirely Germanic and Frankish in origin and, again, received a great impetus from the Papal Revolution. Frederick showed himself to be a man of his own time and his own culture in using some of the language of Roman law in order to legitimize his assertion of imperial powers.[9]

Perhaps the most extraordinary aspect of Frederick's policy at Roncaglia was its futility. The empire was not in a condition to become a strong, centralized territorial state; it was too big, too diverse, too disorganized, and it lacked the necessary bureaucracy. Yet Frederick attempted to make it strong and centralized: partly by military action, which proved ineffective for that purpose; partly by attempting to transform his corps of unfree administrators, the ministeriales, from vassals into imperial servants, which also proved ineffective for the larger purpose;[10] and partly by legislation. The Roncaglia laws on taxation provide a good example of misguided faith in the power of legislation. Lacking an effective financial administration, Frederick could collect virtually none of the taxes he proclaimed.

Yet Frederick was far from being a failure. The imperial power did, in fact, increase substantially under his aegis and did acquire some of the characteristics of territorial statehood as he envisioned it. In addition, there were other, even more important aspects of his vision that were realized much more fully. Frederick was deeply concerned with the future not only of the empire in the narrow sense but also of the German territories that constituted its core. He envisioned and fostered the development of the political and legal identity and integrity of those constituent German territories. It was one of his main goals to keep peace among them. And in those policies he succeeded. Indeed, many of the provisions of his imperial law, especially of the peace statutes, passed over into the emerging German territorial legal systems. This is the other side of German political and legal development in the twelfth and thirteenth centuries: the principalities became modern states, or prototypes of modern states, surpassing the empire in this respect.

Here, too, the personality and vision of Barbarossa played an important part. Early in his reign he established Austria, Würzburg, and Burgundy as separate autonomous polities bound to the emperor only by loose feudal ties. Later he established a new dynasty in Bavaria and encouraged that duchy, too, to develop its own political and legal institutions. He also fostered the autonomy of the German cities.

Finally, in 1180 Frederick linked the principalities with the empire in a new constitutional relationship by creating an "order" of imperial princes (*Reichsfürstenstand*). The leading princes and bishops were constituted as a body of temporal and spiritual tenants-in-chief of the emperor; they were strengthened in their relations with him by their corporate unity, and at the same time they were strengthened individually in their relations with their own subjects by virtue of being the sole tenants of the emperor in their respective territories and thus the suzerain lords of their own vassals. The princes became princes *of* their territories rather than, as before, princes *in* their territories.[11]

A striking example of the emperor's interest in maintaining princely authority within the principalities of the empire was his creation of the Duchy of Austria in 1156. Frederick raised the status of Austria from that of a subordinate border territory of Bavaria (the *Ostmark*, or Eastern Marches) to that of an autonomous duchy, with the heritability of ducal authority in both the male and the female lines. The duke was only required to attend diets in Bavaria and to render military service in neighboring lands—otherwise he was freed from obligation to the empire. Most important, the charter finally establishing the duchy, the Privilegium Minus of 1160, provided that no one could exercise the right of justice in the duchy without the permission of the duke. Thus the ruler was to have ultimate control over the courts within his territory on the sole basis that he was the ruler of that territory, without regard to his position as feudal overlord or clan chief. Similarly, in 1168 the emperor issued a "Diploma" creating the Duchy of Würzburg, whereby the Bishop of Würzburg, as duke, received "all jurisdiction and full power of doing justice" in matters previously within the competence of local lords acting under a traditional imperial grant of authority. No competing jurisdictions could henceforth be exercised within the new duchy. To a certain extent this confirmed the preexisting powers of the Bishop of Würzburg, but it also added imperial recognition of the title and the theory of ducal power. That theory rested, above all, on the postulate that the authority to rule—sovereignty, as it would later be called—was grounded in control over adjudication. This postulate was at the heart of the Western legal tradition in its formative era.

In laying the foundations of a new order in the German territories and in the empire, Frederick Barbarossa was guided not only by a political vision but also by a religious vision. His aim was the *reformatio totius orbis*—"the reformation of the whole world."[12] His uncle, biographer, and close adviser, Bishop Otto of Freising, had written a universal history in which he had portrayed the reformation of Pope Gregory VII as the beginning of a new historical stage, leading eventually to the triumph of the crusading ideal, on the one hand, and the monastic, contemplative ideal, on the other. This twin triumph would be carried out by the last emperor, after whom the Day of Judgment would arrive, then the Antichrist, and ultimately the posthistorical age of eternity. As Peter Munz has said, "We cannot avoid the conclusion that Frederick, well acquainted with the ancient prophecy, was confirmed in his belief that he was to be the last emperor."[13] It was a vision of this character which underlay Frederick's desire to undertake a new crusade to liberate Jerusalem and the Holy Sepulchre from the infidels; such liberation was an essential part of the apocalyptic drama. It was a vision of this character which also underlay Frederick's strong sense of the importance both of peace through law and of justice through law; the emperor's mission to secure peace and to do justice was the sign of his appointment by God to fulfill the divine plan of salvation, and in the new age introduced by Pope Gregory VII, law was the chief instrument for peace and justice that was available to secular rulers. Finally, there was the practical necessity of settling the affairs of the empire in order to have the time, the energy, and the resources to go on a crusade:

> All through his life, Frederick had realized that the ultimate and most formidable task of the emperor of Christendom was to protect the church and defend the holy places in Palestine against the infidels. His belief in this ultimately trans-political end of empire had provided him with the detachment necessary to scrap one political plan after another and to view each of his political enterprises as a mere experiment, a means to an end. When, towards the end of 1187, he realized the extreme urgency of a new crusade, he must have considered himself fortunate that the latest experiment had succeeded sufficiently for him seriously to entertain the thought of a departure to the Holy Land. Given his age and his knowledge of the physical hardships that awaited him at the best of times, he cannot have had any great illusions as to the likelihood of returning to Europe alive. But his departure was not an afterthought indulged in when he happened to have nothing better to do. It was the crowning act of his reign, an act which he had planned all along, and for the sake of which he had undertaken experiment after experiment. And now that, finally, one of these experiments had proved comparatively successful, he was free to turn his mind to the real task that lay ahead.[14]

The imperial peace statutes (*Landfrieden*). The prominent use of the term "peace" in comprehensive statutes issued by emperors and dukes in the twelfth and thirteenth centuries (*constitutio pacis, pax terrae, Landfriede*) linked those statutes with the Peace of God movement which had been sponsored by the church since the latter part of the tenth century. The first German proclamations of a Peace of God were in the bishopric of Lüttich in 1082, the archbishopric of Cologne in 1083, the province of Saxony in 1084, and at Mainz for the empire as a whole in 1085. Like the earlier Peace of God proclamations in southern France, Normandy, and elsewhere, each of the German proclamations was limited to certain times, places, and groups of people. They did not purport to make new law but rather to reinforce the preexisting law by exacting from the entire local population an oath to observe the peace and by imposing addi-

tional ecclesiastical sanctions, especially excommunication, for violations.

The first secular peace statute (*Landfriede*, "peace of the land") issued
by an emperor appeared in 1103. Before that, there had been two
secular peace statutes issued by dukes together with the magnates of the
duchy—in Swabia in 1093 and in Bavaria in 1094—as well as one issued
by a provincial assembly in Alsace, also in 1094. The 1103 imperial
statute was followed by at least seventeen additional imperial peace
statutes, in 1119, 1121, 1125 (two), 1135, 1147, 1152, 1158, 1179, 1186,
1207, 1208, 1221, 1223, 1224, 1234, and 1235. At least eight additional
territorial peace statutes were issued in that period in Swabia, Bavaria,
Saxony, Brixen, Hennegau, and Alsace, in 1104, 1127, 1152, 1156,
1171, 1200, 1229, and 1233.[15]

The imperial peace statutes of the twelfth and thirteenth centuries
drew from the earlier Peace of God movement not only the word
"peace," with its many connotations, but also, at first, the practice of exacting oaths from the population to adhere to the peace. They differed
from the earlier movement, however, in many important respects. They
were intended to bind all people within the respective jurisdictions of the
rulers who promulgated them, without limit of time. Also the idea of a
voluntary sworn peace disappeared; instead of asking their subjects to
consent to renounce various forms of violence, rulers demanded that
they obey a series of new laws which systematized and reformed the
preexisting legal order. In addition, the scope and content of the peace
statutes were gradually extended; they came to be concerned not only
with the prevention of violence and of blood feuds and duels but also
with the preservation of public order generally, including some matters
of an economic and administrative nature. In that connection their sanctions were extended to include a much greater variety of criminal
penalties and also some civil and administrative sanctions and remedies.
In short, the imperial peace statutes of the twelfth and thirteenth centuries gradually developed into comprehensive legislative acts in the
modern sense.

This process of transformation is revealed by comparing two very
early peace statutes—the Bavarian statute of 1094 and the first imperial
peace statute of 1103—with the imperial peace statutes promulgated by
Frederick Barbarossa between 1152 and 1186, and then by comparing
the Barbarossa statutes with the one promulgated by his grandson
Frederick II at Mainz in 1235.

The Bavarian peace statute of 1094 had been adopted at the initiative
of the duke, but in order to take effect it needed to be sworn to by the
Bavarian magnates assembled at a diet (*Landtag*);[16] it also needed the
oaths of the people. It contained seven very short articles. The first
stated that the duke had sworn peace to all churches, clergy, and mer-

chants ("except those who sell horses outside our kingdom"), and also to those who "swear, have sworn, or will swear to us this peace," and that "we will maintain this oath from now until Easter and after that for two years." The second article, which was also confirmed by an oath, required that anyone who committed a theft of things worth one shilling "shall be punished and shall pay double". Article 3 provided that if anyone broke the peace by stealing things worth five shillings, or raped a virgin, he should lose his eyes or a foot or hand. Article 4 provided that if one raped a virgin and was besieged in a castle, the castle should be destroyed and the fugitive captured. Article 5 provided that if oath takers pursued a peacebreaker, or if "our army" went somewhere to enforce the peace, they should take only what they and their horses needed and should leave all else undisturbed. Article 6 provided that on every such journey hay, grass, and uncut wood for construction might be taken at will. Finally, in article 7 the duke reserved to the jurisdiction of his own officials disputes concerning allodial lands and fiefs (benefices).

The first imperial secular peace statute, issued at Mainz in 1103, was roughly similar in style, scope, and content to the 1094 Bavarian peace statute.[17] It also required the oaths of the magnates and of the people. It was to last for four years. It forbade the invading or burning of another's house, seizure of a person for money, wounding, beating, and killing, and declared them punishable by loss of eyes or of a hand. It repeated in a modified form some of the provisions of the Bavarian peace concerning theft. In addition it forbade pursuing one's enemy into the house of another.

The imperial peace statutes promulgated by Frederick Barbarossa a half-century later differed from these two early statutes in at least eight respects.

1. There was no mention in them of the magnates of the realm, except as addressees. His first peace statute, issued in 1152, began: "Frederick, by the grace of God emperor of the Romans and ever august, *to* the bishops, dukes, counts, margraves, and officials who receive this document."[18]

2. The meaning of the word "peace" had changed; it no longer meant something that came into being by being sworn to, a kind of social nonaggression compact, but rather something that existed independently of the consent of magnates or people. The peace of the land was, in effect, the king's peace. No time limit was set for it. There was no mention of oaths.

3. Sophisticated legal concepts appeared for the first time. Such words as *leges* and *jus*, which had been absent from the 1103 imperial peace statute as well as from all the territorial statutes, were stressed. "We wish to preserve to all persons their right (*jus*)," Frederick stated in the preamble to the 1152 statute.

4. The earlier peace statutes had said nothing specific about means of enforcement of their provisions, except that they were to be sworn to, whereas Frederick's peace statutes emphasized repeatedly the procedures for administering them. Thus article 2 of the 1152 statute provided that movable property of contumacious peacebreakers was to be seized by the judge (*Richter*) and divided by him in favor of the people, while their hereditary property was to be seized by the count (*Graf*) and under certain circumstances was to escheat to the king; article 4 provided that certain fines for minor offenses were to be collected and distributed by the judge; article 6 provided that the count was to pursue the peacebreaker to the lord's castle. Other articles defined the procedures to be followed in trials by the judge and the count, respectively.[19]

5. The scope and content of the 1152 peace statute went far beyond anything envisioned in the earlier statutes. While control of violence remained an important motif, other kinds of ordering were also included. Thus article 11 provided that the count in each locality was to choose seven men of good repute to set grain prices for the year. Article 17 stated that one who improperly performed his duties as lay patron of a monastic foundation or as administrator of a benefice, and who was warned by his lord but nevertheless persevered in his waywardness and was ousted by a judicial proceeding, and who thereafter attempted to regain his advowson or benefice, was to be treated as a peacebreaker. These provisions represented new law. Other important innovations were limitations on the use of the duel, the establishment of a system of financial security for money fines and seized land, and the establishment of royal jurisdiction over clergy who broke the peace and over servants of a lord who engaged in a feud.

6. Innovations were also introduced to increase the emperor's economic and judicial power. It was provided that allodial fiefs confiscated from offenders were to be converted into fiefs of the empire. This was especially important in view of the requirement of compulsory enfeoffment of feudal land that escheated to the crown because of absence of heirs. It was also provided that possessory disputes between two vassals of the same lord were to be dealt with in the emperor's court by means of a sworn inquest, although baronial courts retained jurisdiction over the rarer cases where the issue was not seisin but ownership. "Thus," as Mitteis has said, "like Henry II of England, Frederick Barbarossa attempted to establish possessory assizes under royal auspices, which had the effect of restricting baronial justice."[20]

7. In contrast to the earlier statutes, the 1152 peace statute defined the procedures to be applied in various types of proceedings. In the court of the count, if two men disputed over a fief, and one claimed to have been enfeoffed, the count was to receive the testimony of the feoffor (article 8).

But if several men disputed over a fief and various enfeoffors were named, the court of the judge was to question under oath two persons of good reputation who lived in the province of the litigants, in order to determine which of them had possessed the fief without force (article 9). Article 10 set forth the different types of proof needed when men of different estates were accused of peacebreaking; if a knight accused a peasant, the peasant could prove his innocence through divine or human judgment (that is, by ordeal or oath helpers), or else by seven suitable witnesses chosen by the judge; if a knight accused a knight and challenged him to a duel, the person challenged could avoid the duel by proving that he and his parents were of legitimate knightly heritage.

8. Finally, the 1152 peace statute, though equally concise in style, is approximately seven times longer than the Bavarian peace statute of 1094, and probably almost seven times longer than the imperial peace statute of 1103.

It seems highly probable that the 1152 peace statute of Frederick I was influenced by his knowledge, or the knowledge of his advisers, of the Sicilian legislation of Roger II, or at least by the common education and experience of Frederick's and Roger's advisers. Indeed, exiles from Sicily were at the court of Frederick. In any event, similarities may be found between the treatment of felony in Frederick's peace statute and in an 1129 peace statute of Roger, and between the law applicable to knights in the 1152 peace statute and in Roger's 1140 Assizes of Ariano.

Six years later, in 1158, at the Diet of Roncaglia, Frederick promulgated another peace statute as well as three other related pieces of legislation.

The Roncaglia peace statute, which contained only eleven articles, began as before, "Frederick, by the grace of God emperor of the Romans and ever august," but this time it was addressed to "all the subjects of his empire." It started with the words, "By this decreed law, which is to prevail in perpetuity, we order . . . " All subjects of the empire, it continued, were to observe true and perpetual peace among themselves. All persons from eighteen to sixty years of age were to bind themselves by oath to keep the peace, and such oath was to be renewed every five years (article 1). This was a return, in form, to the oath procedure of the past, but the substance had changed since the oath was no longer voluntary even in theory and the peace to be kept was a preexisting legal order that had no limit in time. A violater was therefore punishable even if he had not sworn the oath.

Article 2 contained a general prohibition of self-help. It provided: "If anyone believes that he has a right against anyone in any cause or transaction, he shall resort to the judicial power and through it he shall pursue his appropriate right." Article 3 imposed heavy financial penalties on "anyone who by a rash reckless act presumes to violate the aforesaid peace." Thus "the peace" consisted in the enforcement of rights by "the judicial power" and not by violence.

Article 4 stated in broad terms a general legal prohibition against major crimes: "Violation of rights and theft shall be legally punished. Homicide and mutilation and any other wrong shall be legally vindicated."

Article 5 made judges and other magistrates appointed by the emperor or his subordinates liable to compensate losses suffered by anyone as a result of their neglect to do justice and their failure to vindicate legally a violated peace. Additional penalties could also be imposed in grievous cases, and those magistrates who could not pay because of poverty were to suffer corporal beating and to be exiled for five years to a place fifty miles from their residence.[21]

It is noteworthy that these and the remaining provisions of the Roncaglia peace statute do not, in general, repeat the provisions of the 1152 peace statute but instead presuppose their continuance in force while adding to them. In this, too, they have the character of legislation, in the modern sense, rather than that of a general recapitulation of customary law.

In addition to the peace statute several other legislative acts were promulgated at the Diet of Roncaglia, including a statute concerning the mutual rights and obligations of lords and vassals and another statute concerning the rights and obligations of scholars. The statute on feudal obligations forbade vassals to alienate fiefs without the consent of their lords, recited various circumstances in which a vassal could be ousted by his lord, and dealt with problems created by subinfeudation. One article of this statute begins with the words: "We firmly establish both in Italy and in Germany . . . " ("Italy"—*Italia*—refers to the cities that formed the Lombard League; "Germany"—*Alemannia*—refers to Swabia, Bavaria, Saxony, and the other German Länder.) The last article (article 10) states: "We also order that in every oath of fealty the emperor shall be excepted by name." The Roncaglian statute on scholars goes even further to make clear that it is intended to be legislation and not merely a restatement of customary law, for it concludes with the instruction: "We order that this law [*lex*] be inserted among the imperial decrees under the title '*Ne fillius pro patre, etc.*' " This was a reference to a Roman imperial decree excluding the liability of a son for the debts of his father. Similarly, Emperor Frederick's *lex* excluded the liability of traveling scholars for the debts of their countrymen.[22] Barbarossa's instruction was obeyed by contemporary jurists who inserted the 1158 statute in the appropriate place in their manuscripts of Justinian's lawbooks.

The legislative process that was reflected in Frederick I's statutes of 1152 and 1158, as well as in his statute on arson, issued in 1186,[23] reached a high point in the Mainz peace statute promulgated by his grandson, the Emperor Frederick II, in 1235.[24] This was, of course, the same Frederick II whose other grandfather, King Roger II, had promulgated the Assizes of Ariano in 1140, and who himself in 1231, as King of Sicily, had promulgated the *Liber Augustalis*. In governing his vast empire, Frederick II concentrated on attempting to subdue the cities of northern Italy and largely neglected his German territories; indeed, by the end of his reign in 1250 the empire as a whole was divided and weakened beyond recovery. The peace statute issued at Mainz in 1235 was a deliberate use of law reform as a means of reviving imperial unity in Germany, but it did not succeed in that respect and therefore did not have very great significance for the future development of imperial law as such. It did, however, have very great significance for the development of the law of the various principalities and other territories within the empire, as well as for the development of the law of the various cities, whether imperial, princely, or independent.

In the preamble to the 1235 peace statute Frederick II declared that "since those who dwell throughout all Germany now live, in their lawsuits and private transactions, according to age-old customs and unwritten law, and because some important reforms contributing to the general state and tranquillity of the empire have not yet been specially introduced, and when a case is considered that concerns some part of this the judgment is determined more by arbitrary opinion than by established law . . . therefore, with the advice and consent of the beloved ecclesiastical and secular princes in solemn assembly at Mainz, we have caused to be promulgated certain decrees." There followed twenty-nine articles, which in a modern edition occupy some five hundred printed lines.

The first article stated that the liberties and rights of the churches should be liberally fostered, and it commanded that no one should "unjustly resist" ecclesiastical jurisdiction. Article 2 ordered that patrons of all churches should protect them diligently and should be reasonable in administering their property, "so that no serious complaints concerning this may come to us." Article 3 dealt with breach of a promise made by two people to keep peace, sealed by a handshake; such a breach was to be tried before a judge and proved by oaths of two witnesses.

Article 4 stated that the office of judge should be filled by persons worthy of it, "since one who examines the charges of others should excel in his manner of life." It provided further that princes and others who held court directly or indirectly of the emperor should decide cases "by just judgment according to the reasonable custom of the lands," and "whoever does not do so we will punish severely, as is just." Article 5 continued this theme: "Magistrates and rights are established for this, that no one may be the avenger of his own grief, since where the authority of law ceases, arbitrary cruelty abounds. Therefore we establish [*statuimus*—*the* word from which *statuta*, "statute," is derived] that no one . . . shall avenge himself before bringing his complaint before his judge and pursuing it according to law to a definitive judgment; except that for the protection of his body or goods he may immediately repel force by force, which is called *nothwere* [in modern German, *Notwehr*, 'necessary defense']."

Article 6 provided that if one had brought a complaint before the judge but the law had not been followed (presumably because the defendant had not obeyed the order of the court), the complainant had the right to "defy" his enemy, that is, publicly challenge him to a duel. However, he must do this in the proper way or else he was to be declared without honor and without right.

Articles 7 to 10 dealt with tolls and other obstructions to travel. All tolls imposed in travelers by land or water without the permission of the emperor were declared to be abolished. Protection of foreigners against such tolls was emphasized.

Articles 11-13 prohibited certain violations of imperial law (counterfeiting of coinage), feudal law (sale of safe conducts by persons who did not "hold of the empire, by feudal law, a right of safe-conduct") and urban law (asserting the rights of a citizen while living outside the city, or asserting the protection of a feudal lord while living within the city).

Article 14 stated that no one had the right to take another as security without permission of the judge, and that whoever did so should be punished as a robber.

Articles 15-21 dealt with offenses of sons against fathers, particularly patricide and the ousting of a father from his land.

Articles 22-27 dealt with punishments, especially outlawry. Outlawed persons were to be prosecuted as for a "public crime" and were not to be allowed the option of composition or penance. Thus a sharp distinction was made between crime and tort or sin. An outlaw of the emperor was subject to be declared without honor and without right. The same penalty was applicable to high treason, perfidy, and "homicide, which is called *mord*." Those who harbored an outlaw were subject to the same penalty as that imposed on the outlawed person, and a city that "collectively and knowingly" harbored an outlaw was subject to severe penalties, including the destruction of its walls. Also, the receiver of stolen goods and the harborer of a thief were equally punishable with the thief—as under "the civil laws" (a reference to the Roman law of Justinian as interpreted by contemporary Western scholars). However, for a first offense the receiver or harborer was to be required to pay double the amount stolen, and only for a second offense was he to be punished as a robber or a thief.

Article 28 provided that a justiciar should be appointed to preside over the imperial court in place of the emperor when the emperor could not preside personally. He should be "a man of proved trust and of honest opinion . . . of free condition, who shall remain in such office during good behavior for at least one year." The justiciar was to conduct the court every day except Sundays and major holidays, "doing right to all complainants, except princes and other noble persons, in cases that touch their persons, right, honor, fiefs, property, or inheritance, except the greatest cases, whose investigation and judgment we reserve to our own highness." The power to outlaw or absolve from outlawry remained with the emperor.

The justiciar was to "swear that he will accept no matter for judgment because of love or hate, favor or reward, fear or grace, and that he will not judge on any other basis than what he knows or believes to be just according to his conscience, in good faith without fraud or wrong." The justiciar was to receive the fees that were paid for absolution of outlaws, "which are popularly called *Gewette*," "so that he will judge with greater willingness and will not receive gifts from anyone."

Finally, under article 29 the justiciar was to have a special notary to receive and keep writs containing complaints, to make records of judicial proceedings, to keep records of outlawry and absolutions from outlawry, to write down all judgments in major cases in the imperial court, especially when they took the form of contradictory judgments, which were popularly called *gesamint urteil* — in modern German, *Gesamturteil*, or "collective judgment," that is, one which arises by collecting the votes of the judges — "so that in the future in similar cases the ambiguity will be removed and the land according to whose custom the judgment was rendered will be expressly named." The notary was to be a layman, so that he could write down judgments of blood, which clerics were forbidden to do, and further, so that he could be punished appropriately if he was delinquent in his office. The notary was to swear an oath that he would "behave faithfully and legally in office," and would "write and do nothing against right and obligation, according to conscience, in good faith, without any wrong or fraud."[25]

The Mainz peace statute of 1235 was intended primarily for the German parts of Frederick II's empire; it was, in fact, the first imperial law to be issued in both Latin and German. It was meant to be German law. Yet its author was the same King of Sicily, Duke of Apulia, and Count of Calabria who four years earlier had promulgated the comprehensive Sicilian law code called the *Liber Augustalis*, which greatly overshadowed the new German statute not only in length but also in sophistication. How could the same ruler have produced such different pieces of legislation at more or less the same time?

There are, to be sure, some signs of common authorship. Both documents are presented as royal legislation. Both are directed against private vengeance, self-help, and violence generally. Both emphasize adjudication as the primary means of keeping public order. Both have the same vision of a society governed by law. The Mainz provision for an imperial justiciar and a notary to assist him is derived directly from Sicilian experience. Both statutes contain many similar basic legal concepts and institutions. Certain substantive rules of law, such as the right to kill in necessary defense of person or property, are the same in both.[26]

Yet the differences are more striking. The Mainz statute provides only the barest framework of rules, a selection of those few that were presumably the most important from the emperor's standpoint; the *Augustalis* is a comprehensive code. In dealing with crimes, for example, the Mainz statute specifies only a few, and its provisions on punishment are confined chiefly to outlawry, whereas the Augustalis specifies a great many crimes and makes applicable to them a variety of punishments. Moreover, the *Augustalis* deals with a host of noncriminal matters that are not even suggested in the Mainz statute. Why did not Frederick simply present to the solemn assembly at Mainz in 1235 the magnificent code of laws that he had promulgated at Palermo in 1231?

The answer, though simple, is revealing: each of the two pieces of legislation was intended to serve the function of expanding, rationalizing, and systematizing the legal order that existed within the polity for which it was designed. Each built on existing foundations. These were not castles in the air. The royal legal order that existed in the Norman kingdom of Sicily in the early thirteenth century was quite different from the legal order that existed in the German parts of the empire. Sicily—southern Italy—had had a sophisticated royal law for ninety years; it had effective, centralized judicial and administrative and financial institutions. In the German parts of the empire, by contrast, imperial institutions were weak. For almost forty years there had been almost no effective imperial government in the north. There was not even a central imperial judiciary; the emperor himself judged in person as he traveled from place to place—and in those years he rarely traveled north of Rome. From a political point of view, the Mainz peace statute may be viewed as the last gasp of imperial power in the German territories.[27]

Yet in some respects the Mainz peace statute was more innovative than the *Liber Augustalis*. The Sicilian code went back again and again to the legislation of "our grandfather Roger II" and of William I and II, whereas the Mainz statute studiously ignored "our grandfather Frederick I" and his 1152, 1158, and 1186 peace statutes. More significantly, the provision in the Mainz statute for an imperial justiciar and notary meant that for the first time imperial court decisions were to be collected and kept in a single place, so that a body of imperial legal norms could be established.[28] In fact, however, this did not come to pass for a very long time: after 1235 imperial power rapidly declined, and, indeed, almost all imperial activity disappeared. The new imperial justiciar did not sit at a fixed place or a fixed time. When the Habsburgs acquired the imperial title in the last decades of the thirteenth century, they confirmed the Mainz peace statute in 1281 and again, with some additions, in 1287, and once again in 1292. However, imperial law declined once more in the fourteenth and fifteenth centuries, and was revived only in 1495.

The Mainz peace statute, like the earlier imperial peace statutes, nevertheless survived as part of the "common law" of Germany. Technically, there was no "German law" in the twelfth and thirteenth centuries, but only the law of the empire, the law of the several territorial polities, and the law of the cities—just as there is, technically, no "American law" today, but only the federal law and the law of the several states. Yet in Germany there was a common body of legal institutions, concepts, principles, rules, which was universally accepted in the imperial and the territorial and the urban polities. Many parts of the Mainz peace statute and its predecessors found their way into that common body of German law.

The Mirror of Saxon Law (*Sachsenspiegel*). One important channel through which the earlier peace statutes became part of the German common law was a book written by a Saxon lawyer in the early thirteenth century (probably the 1220s) called the *Sachsenspiegel*. Its author, Eike von Repgau (c.1180–c.1235), was a well educated (though not university-trained) assessor of the knightly class, who first wrote the work in Latin and later translated it into German.

The *Sachsenspiegel* is a systematic collection of legal rules and principles. It is divided into two parts, one called *Landrecht*, "law of the land," and the other called *Lehnrecht*, "law of fiefs," or "feudal law." Each part is divided into some hundreds of numbered sections and subsections. In a modern edition the *Landrecht* takes up approximately 140 pages and the *Lehnrecht* approximately 100 pages. The subject matter is chiefly (1) the customary law of Saxony, for the first time written down and systematized, and (2) the royal law of the German king-emperor, both customary and enacted, applicable in Saxony and elsewhere. The author was predominantly concerned with certain aspects of civil law (especially property and inheritance), criminal law, the judicial system, constitutional law, and, in the second part, with lord-vassal relations. The law of the cities is omitted. The law merchant is omitted. There are some references to canon law, especially those parts of it that were applicable to papal jurisdiction, family law, and some other matters. There are virtually no references to Roman law. There are a few references to legal rules prevailing in other German territories, notably Swabia, where they differed from the Saxon; otherwise the author seems to have assumed that Saxon law corresponded in a general way to legal rules and principles common throughout the German territories.

The rules and principles are presented with very little conceptual analysis and with very few concrete illustrations. For example, it is provided that one who aids another to commit a crime is himself liable to punishment, but no definition of complicity is given and no effort is made to distinguish various forms of complicity. Similarly, several rules are stated concerning one who injures another in necessary defense, but the concept of necessary defense is not defined or analyzed. Indeed, the whole book is written in the style of a concise summary of rules, doctrines, principles, and precepts, some of them, to be sure, of considerable breadth.

The *Sachsenspiegel* contains many provisions relating to the constitutional law of the empire. Implicit in those provisions are three fundamental, interlocking concepts which are traceable directly to the Papal Revolution of the late eleventh and early twelfth centuries.

The first is the concept that the empire—indeed, society itself—is based on law. This is implicit in a statement which the author makes in the prologue: "God is himself law; therefore law is dear to him." The idea of the rule of law goes so far in the *Sachsenspiegel* as to include the express right of a person "to resist a lawless decision of his king and of his judge, and also to help another to do so if he is his relative or his lord."[29]

The second fundamental concept of the imperial constitution is that of the duality of the spiritual and secular polities—of church and empire as corporate political entities. This is implicit in the formulation of the "two swords" doctrine, which is stated in the very first article of the first book of the text: "God has left two swords on earth to protect Christendom. To the pope is given the spiritual sword, to the emperor the secular . . . What stands against the pope, what he is unable to compel by spiritual judgment, the emperor is to compel by secular judgment to be obedient to the pope. So the spiritual power should also help the secular judgment when it is in need." In a later article it is further provided that the church has ultimate jurisdiction over the emperor in matters of heresy (doctrine), divorce (family law), and security of the house of worship (church property).[30] Nevertheless, it is also provided that the church must enforce its will, ultimately, through the imperial power.[31]

The third concept, which interlocks with the first two to form the foundation of the constitutional law of the empire, is that of plural, interacting secular polities. This is expressed in many provisions concerning the respective territorial and imperial jurisdictions and concerning the application, in appropriate cases, of territorial law by courts exercising imperial jurisdiction.[32] It is also expressed in provisions concerning the election of the king by the princes and bishops of the territorial polities. Here the *Sachsenspiegel* built on Frederick Barbarossa's institution of the imperial order of princes. Indeed, the author went so far as to list and rank—for the first time—three ecclesiastical electors (the bishops of Trier, Mainz, and Cologne), and three lay electors (the Count Palatine of the Rhine, the Duke of Saxony, and the Margrave of Brandenburg). On the authority of the *Sachsenspiegel* these six continued to be the electors from that time forward.[33]

The constitutional law of the empire made it inevitable that many provisions of the imperial peace statutes, as well as of other imperial legislation, would pass over into the law of the territorial polities. One important vehicle for this reception of imperial law was the *Sachsenspiegel* itself. One of its articles expressly referred to "the old peace, which the imperial power confirmed for the land of Saxony with the assent of the nobility."[34] This was a reference to one of the early Peace of God compacts. In the tradition of those compacts, the *Sachsenspiegel* gave permanent protection to priests and clerics, women, Jews, churches and church property, cemeteries and hedges of villages, ploughs and mills, and the king's highways and waterways. Other articles adopted specific rules of criminal and civil law that had been promulgated in imperial peace statutes.[35] One such rule was that any person who killed or wounded a peacebreaker was not liable to make amends if he could prove that he had done so on the spot or in pursuit.[36]

Very early, the *Sachsenspiegel* was treated as though it was itself authoritative. Many of its provisions passed directly into city law and into the law of other territories. It was glossed by learned jurists. For centuries it was considered to be a subsidiary law, which could be used to supplement the prevailing city, territorial, or imperial law.[37] The fact that it was in German was of great significance, for it virtually created a common German legal language for all German-speaking parts of the empire.[38] Other "mirrors of the law" were written in imitation of it—the *Schwabenspiegel*, the *Deutschenspiegel*, the *Frankenspiegel*.[39]

THE LAW OF THE PRINCIPALITIES

The relative weakness of German imperial law in the twelfth and thirteenth centuries and thereafter, in comparison with the royal law of Sicily, England, and France, was balanced by the growing strength of the law of the individual German territorial duchies and other principalities that composed the empire in the north. While imperial financial and judicial institutions remained comparatively primitive, the central financial and judicial institutions of the various principalities underwent substantial development. While the growth of imperial officialdom fell behind that of royal officialdom in other countries, the growth of officialdom in the various principalities was impressive. While imperial power to enforce its legislation remained relatively backward by general European standards, the legislative power of the various principalities did not. The widespread view, based largely on the weakness of imperial institutions, that there was a general disintegration of government and law in Germany in the thirteenth century and thereafter is contradicted by the fact that in the principalities central institutions were being strengthened. In the various Länder the German tribes and clans ("stems") experienced a transformation of political and legal institutions, a systematization and rationalization of government and law, in the two centuries after the Papal Revolution, parallel to that experienced by the tribes and clans in the various kingdoms elsewhere in Western Christendom. In the words of one of the leading historians of this period, there was in Germany as elsewhere "a process of reconstruction which was so strong as to merit the name of a constitutional revolution."[40]

The rise of the territorial principalities in Germany, which began "dimly but discernibly" in the late eleventh and early twelfth centuries,[41] was given an extraordinary impetus in the middle and late twelfth century during the reign of Frederick I (Barbarossa). This was a direct consequence of the Papal Revolution. In his rivalry with and emulation of the papal power, and in his interaction with it and with other secular powers, the emperor needed peace and stability in his German territories. He needed to have the princes of the empire control their own subjects within their respective domains. Moreover, he had to depend not only on the secular princes but also on the ecclesiastical princes, who as bishops owed their appointment and their allegiance to the pope as well as the emperor. Frederick, in setting up the imperial order of princes, established direct control by them over the territories in which they were situated. Both the secular princes, who then numbered sixteen, and the ecclesiastical princes, who then numbered ninety, were to hold their territories of the emperor as his vassals, but they were to be supreme over the entire population within their respective territorial jurisdictions. The kingship, as Mitteis has put it, was cut off from the people by the nobility within each territory.[42] When Frederick established the Duchy of Austria as an independent power, he expressly declared that "no person great or small within the regime of his duchy shall presume to exercise any justice without the consent or permission of the duke."[43] As Geoffrey Barraclough says, the main point of this provision was the subjection of the various magnates of Austria to the authority of the duke.[44] Nevertheless, the emperor was also restricted. Frederick needed to subject the lesser nobility to control and he could not do it himself. His grandson Frederick II carried this principle to its conclusion in the Treaty with the Ecclesiastical Princes of 1220 and the Statute in Favor of the Princes of 1232, in which he guaranteed to the princes, both ecclesiastical and secular, their powers against all others within their territories. The emperor forbade anyone to interfere in various ways with the "territory or jurisdiction" of the princes and restricted the powers of imperial officers over such territorial rights as tolls and coinage.[45]

The princely power in the German territories manifested itself in governmental and legal institutions similar to those that had been developed first by the princely power of the papacy and later by the princely power of the secular kingdoms of Sicily, England, Normandy, and France: a treasury, a judiciary, a chancery, and other departments of government; civil and criminal and other branches of law; adjudication, legislation, and other institutional processes of legal development.

Of all the German principalities, the Duchy of Bavaria was the most powerful and the most advanced in governmental and legal institutions in the late twelfth and early thirteenth centuries. From 1154 to 1180 it was ruled by Frederick Barbarossa's cousin and rival, Henry the Lion, who also ruled Saxony; Henry played a major part in the transformation of Bavaria from a tribal and feudal polity to a territorial polity. This he did in considerable part by acquiring the judicial and other powers of the local lords who ruled over the counties of his territories.[46] Each count held the power of high justice (*Blutbann*, "blood justice") by grant from the emperor. The count was not, however, directly subordinate to the emperor or invested in his office by the emperor. He had his own hereditary free land (*allods*) and patronage of ecclesiastical benefices (churches and monasteries), as well as hereditary jurisdiction over the county. In the twelfth and thirteenth centuries the dukes of Bavaria (like the princes of other German territories) used a variety of devices to swallow up county jurisdiction. In case a count died without heirs, his property escheated to the duke. The duke sometimes acquired counties by inheritance, since his family had kin ties to the families of many counts. In addition, he sometimes purchased and sometimes received by gift the property — and with it the jurisdiction — of counts. Finally, if they were rebellious he would conquer them. In all these cases Henry the Lion's general practice, and that of his successors, was to appoint his unfree servants (ministeriales) to replace the free counts, not as counts but as prefects whom the dukes could remove at will. The dukes also appointed similar officials to govern towns and castles and to manage toll stations. When Henry founded Munich in 1157-58, he did not establish an autonomous city government but appointed ducal officials, including a ducal judge, to govern it.

Under Henry the Lion and his successors Bavaria was governed as a territorial polity rather than as an association of persons and groups whose main political allegiances were tribal and feudal.[47] In Saxony, Henry had created the first German territorial chancery, staffed with notaries, and he was the first German prince regularly to issue legal documents and to keep systematic records of legal transactions; in Bavaria, the chancery was created shortly after he was ousted and replaced by Otto von Wittelsbach. Moreover, both in Bavaria and Saxony Henry strengthened the ducal court, which came to exercise a substantial principal jurisdiction over disputes involving seisin of land. He also summoned representatives of the various estates to diets at which peace statutes and other laws were promulgated. In a legal document of one of his Bavarian monasteries Henry was called "the prince and the judge of the land."

The system of law and government founded by Henry the Lion was developed further by his successors in the thirteenth century. The office of deputy (*Viztum, vice-dominus*, "vice-lord"), which had been created under Henry the Lion, became institutionalized by the Wittelsbach dynasty in 1204. The deputy was in charge of financial matters and replaced the duke as president of the ducal court. Eventually Bavaria was divided into four parts, with a deputy in each. In addition it was divided into smaller departments (*Ämter*, "offices"), of which there were thirty-five by 1228; each department had two main officials, a curator in charge of administration and a judge with competence over both major and minor causes. The judges also had subordinate judges who sat in various districts of their respective departments. The deputy appointed and supervised the curators and judges of the departments. Meanwhile, the duke's traditional household officers — the marshal, the steward, the chamberlain, the cupbearer — became heads of bureaucratic organizations which extended throughout the duchy.

The new, more centralized system of administration was related to a new emphasis on ducal legislation. Five major peace statutes were enacted in Bavaria in 1244, 1256, 1281, 1293, and 1300, which expanded and reformed the customary law. The use of weapons was restricted; life, property, and honor were given greater protection; supplementary rules of inheritance and of commerce were enacted. Unlike most of the imperial legislation, the ducal statutes were directed not primarily to the higher nobility but to knights and to landowners generally, including peasants and citizens.[48] Moreover, they presupposed the existence of a developed officialdom to interpret and apply them.

Above all, the authority of the dukes of Bavaria, like that of the princes of the other German territories of the time, rested on their acquisition of judicial power. "More important than the possession and acquisition of *regalia* [financial and political perquisites] was the fact that within this whole system of power the dukes obtained the jurisdiction of the counts and of the patrons [of churches and monasteries]."[49] The royal prerogative to invest others with judicial authority, called in

German *Bannleihe*, passed from the emperor to the princes.[50] The dukes of Bavaria ruled their duchy primarily through the judges appointed by their deputies in the various departments.

The departmental judges had general jurisdiction over both high justice and low justice. Certain types of matters, however, were reserved to the ducal courts, chiefly because of their great importance or because of the very high status of the parties; the other types of matters remained in the village or other local courts, chiefly because of their minor importance or their local character.

The centralization of justice in Bavaria and the other German principalities in the twelfth and thirteenth centuries was accompanied by a rationalization of judicial procedure. Greater reliance was placed on presentation of evidence in court. Judges questioned witnesses. This was especially true of civil cases. In disputes over seisin of land the complainant could demand a "showing," at which both parties together viewed the land in dispute and each identified its appurtenances and boundaries in the presence of representatives of the community, who gave judgment in the matter. In another type of procedure, called *Kundschaft*, connoting exploration, search, or investigation, people of good repute and high calling who had knowledge of the matter in dispute were invited as official witnesses and were questioned under oath; in more important cases, twenty-one persons, chosen by the parties jointly, participated in the Kundschaft, and the agreement of seven, under oath, was required for a decision.[51] These new "inquest" procedures tended to replace the older procedures of compurgation and ordeal.

Ducal law in Bavaria also experienced a substantial change in the concept and purpose of criminal law during the twelfth and thirteenth centuries. Previously, crime and tort had not been sharply distinguished. High justice had been concerned principally with composition, that is, with imposing monetary settlements on wrongdoers in favor of their victims. "Blood justice" — usually involving hanging or mutilation — had been chiefly confined to cases in which the criminal had been caught in the act. In the twelfth century high justice in criminal matters became mainly blood justice, and composition was retained chiefly for cases in the lower courts. Thus there was a transition from the tribal system of criminal law to a state system, in which crimes were seen as offenses primarily against the public authority. This movement was also associated with a substantial increase in the types of crimes that were made punishable and in the severity of the punishments. The Bavarian peace statute of 1244 added to the types of homicide for which the death sentence was applicable: homicide committed at night, in open feud, in abduction of a married woman, and in rape of a virgin or of a woman of good repute. The peace statute of 1281 added others. Also, corporal punishment came to be applied to free men and not only to unfree.

Nighttime crimes were made equally punishable with cases of criminals caught in the act. A new distinction was made between "honorable" and "dishonorable" crimes; murder was honorable while theft was dishonorable, and those found guilty of dishonorable crimes were subjected to more painful forms of death while those who committed honorable crimes had the right of asylum and greater possibilities of commutation of the death sentence to composition.[52]

Finally, it is important to note that the system of adjudication was both very costly and very lucrative, and that it depended on the contemporaneous development of a more modern system of taxation than had existed in the earlier period—indeed, a more modern system than the imperial authority was able to develop at any time. The entire population of the duchy was taxed, free and unfree, secular and ecclesiastical; and the taxes were administered by a corps of ducal officials. Through the introduction of the system of universal taxation, "an immediate hierarchical relation was created between the prince of the land and the inhabitants of the land. The tax obligation was one of the most effective means for developing a state community. It made the existence and the sovereignty of the state palpable to every single person."[53] The amount of taxes to be paid was not determined unilaterally by the duke's chancery but was assessed by tax officials on the basis of the value of the property to be taxed. This required regular visits and inspections by tax officials. Sometimes the tax to be imposed on a village or castle or town was fixed in agreement with the inhabitants of the place.

Bavaria was, to be sure, one of the most advanced, if not the most advanced, of the German principalities. Yet it was not atypical. It was basically similar in its governmental and legal structure to Austria, Brandenburg, Braunschweig, Hesse, the Palatinate of the Rhine, ecclesiastical polities such as Wurzburg, Mainz, Trier, and various other principalities, both secular and ecclesiastical. These were not technically kingdoms (except for Bohemia and Burgundy), but they were ruled by princes who were monarchs in the same sense that the kings of Sicily, England, and France were monarchs; indeed the German territorial princes were in many ways more like those other kings than the German king-emperor himself, for they had more highly developed adjudicative, administrative, and legislative powers than he did. Especially after the decline of the empire in the thirteenth century, the type of monarchical rule that Emperor Frederick Barbarossa had sought to exercise came to be exercised in fact by the princes of the leading German territories.

Spain, Flanders, Hungary, Denmark

The development of royal (or princely) law in the period of the Papal Revolution and thereafter was not confined to the "great powers" of that time or of a later time; together with the systematization and expansion of feudal law, manorial law, mercantile law, and urban law, the systematization and expansion of royal law occurred throughout the West, wherever the Roman Catholic Church asserted its independence of the secular authority and wherever the kingship had the task of organizing peace and justice in the secular sphere. It is important, therefore, to avoid a nationalist interpretation of the development of royal law. That it was a Western phenomenon, and not merely a national phenomenon repeating itself in various countries, is illustrated by the fact that it occurred almost everywhere—on the geographical periphery of the West as well as at the geographical center.

Spain

In the seventh century the Moors conquered the entire Iberian peninsula and were only stopped, finally, in 732 by the Franks under Charles Martel, at Poitiers, less than two-hundred miles southwest of Paris. In the next few centuries a gradual Frankish Christian reconquest of the northern Spanish territories took place, resulting in the establishment of the independent kingdoms of Catalonia, Navarre, Aragon, Léon (Galicia), Castile, and eventually Portugal. In the eleventh and twelfth centuries these territories experienced the same revolutionary movement that swept over the rest of Christendom. In the field of law, the church came to be governed by the same basic principles and procedures of canon law in the Spanish territories as elsewhere. Also, feudal law, manorial law, and mercantile law became more systematized. New autonomous cities and towns were created, each with its own militia, its own government, its own law. The great seaport town of Barcelona, within the county of Barcelona but under the ultimate jurisdiction of the king of Aragon, was one of the leading cities of Europe. Where royal power asserted itself, especially in Castile, Catalonia, and Aragon, there arose systems of royal (or princely) law more or less comparable to those in Sicily, England, Normandy, France, and the German principalities.

Although there was no such thing as "Spain" at that time, certain historical events occurred in all the northern Iberian kingdoms. The first was the Moorish conquest and the Frankish reconquest. The second was the bare survival of the pre-Moorish Visigothic law, with some Roman elements, especially as reflected in a code issued by the Visigothic King Reckesvinth in the late seventh century, the Fuero Juzgo, or Book of Judgments, also known as the Lex barbara Visigothorum.[54] These common local historical factors were overshadowed, however, by the new legal science of the eleventh and twelfth centuries, connected with the revival of the study of Roman law and the development of a new modern system of canon law.

Catalonia and Aragon. Catalonia, ruled by the counts of Barcelona, came under the influence of the Peace of God movement in the early eleventh century (Synod of Elna, 1027).[55] An important part in this movement was played by Count Ramon Berenguer I (1053-1071), who also promulgated the Usages of Barcelona, a compilation of laws and customs from a wide variety of sources, Visigothic and Roman, secular and ecclesiastical, judicial and legislative. The Peace of God movement was followed in Catalonia in the twelfth century by an era of secular peace statutes, which appeared also in Aragon; these developed in a manner similar to that of the German peace statutes, the earlier ones being patterned after the Peace of God proclamations, the later ones taking a more legislative than contractual form and dealing with new areas of procedure, marriage, debt, and public crimes, and also, as in Germany, enlarging the role of royal officials. A statute on arson issued by Alfonso II in 1192 — by then the counts of Barcelona were also kings of Aragon — parallels Emperor Frederick Barbarossa's statute on arson of 1186.

In 1173 Roman law was formally recognized as subsidiary law in Catalonia. This was, of course, the learned Roman law of the universities, to which resort could be had in order to fill in the gaps in the prevailing Catalonian law.

In 1247 King Jaime I, who ruled Aragon for sixty-three years from 1213 to 1276, promulgated a code of laws for Aragon, the Libro de Huesca, which introduced a number of elements of canon and Roman law, especially with regard to succession, contracts, and evidence.[56] Drafted by the Bishop of Huesca, it was a systematic presentation of the law, divided into eight books, devoted chiefly to civil law, criminal law, and procedure. It was intended to be applied by the courts, including the king's court. It was subsequently augmented by Jaime's successors, just as the Usages of Barcelona were augmented by the successors of Count Ramon Berenguer I.

Castile and Léon. These two kingdoms were united during the first half of the twelfth and most of the thirteenth centuries. Their legal development came somewhat later than that of Catalonia and Aragon. It, too, grew originally out of the Peace of God movement, and it was greatly stimulated by the development of canon law and by the revived study of Roman law. The University of Salamanca, founded in the early 1200s, soon became an important center for the study of Roman and canon law.[57] In addition, the growth of royal law was greatly influenced by a succession of great kings: Ferdinand III (1217-1252), whose mother was a Swabian princess of outstanding intelligence and ability; his son Alfonso the Learned (1252-1284); and his great-grandson Alfonso XI (1311-1350). These kings promulgated important legislation and were responsible for issuing comprehensive legal texts, including the Fuero Real (1255) and the Siete Partidas (about 1265).[58] The latter was a systematic treatise, divided into seven parts, organized topically, and

containing over five-hundred articles. It was essentially a compendium
of Roman and canon law adapted somewhat to Castilian conditions.
However, it did not take deep root in actual life, and in general the
efforts of the great kings of the thirteenth and fourteenth centuries to
unify the law of Castile succumbed to the pressure of the localities to
keep their own customs.

FLANDERS

In the eleventh and twelfth centuries the counts of Flanders, whose
territory covered much of what is today Belgium and Holland and who
were kings in everything but name, took a full part in the revolutionary
transformation of Western law. The Peace of God movement appeared
in Flanders in the eleventh century, the most important peace
declarations being those of 1034 and 1099. The first secular peace statute
(Landfriede) was proclaimed in 1111 when, shortly before his death,
Count Robert II assembled his notables and had them swear the peace.
This document was of major importance for the future development
both of Flemish urban law and of Flemish common law ("law of the
land"). It was renewed by Robert's successors in 1111, 1119, 1138, and
frequently thereafter. It has been called "the foundation of most of the
provisions of the old Flemish law."[59]

It was Count Philip (1169-1191), however, whose reign coincided
with that of Henry II of England and of Emperor Frederick Barbarossa
and overlapped that of Philip Augustus of France, who may be said to
have founded the modern system of Flemish law. Philip has been called
"the first lawgiver of Flanders."[60] He legislated partly through peace
statutes. Also, he granted many cities, including Bruges, which was then
the leading commercial center of Europe, their own law, called *Keure*.
He centralized justice by maintaining a system of royal law-enforcement
officials, called bailiffs. In 1178 he issued a statute concerning the powers
of bailiffs which included a provision that the bailiff could seize any
wrongdoer who had not yet been presented before the assessors, and that
a penalty would be imposed on anyone who did not answer a bailiff's call
for assistance.[61]

Out of the dynastic struggles following Philip's death, Count Balduin
I of Henegau emerged to rule Flanders. In his own county he was
already renowned as a lawgiver: in 1200 he had issued two statutes for
Henegau, one on fiefs and one dealing with criminal law and procedure.
Henegau, unlike Flanders, also had a collection of customs, called the
coutume générale. When Balduin went to Flanders he took with him his
learned men to compose works on its law, its customs, and its history.

Although Flanders did not have strong rulers after Balduin, the activity of law-giving continued in the thirteenth century, and the
Flemish counts had some success in extending their administration into

the countryside and rationalizing their governmental and legal apparatus. The doctrine of *cas reserves* ("reserved cases") was developed as a device to remove various crimes from the traditional local and feudal jurisdictions to that of the counts. By the late thirteenth century the counts, on the advice of their professional jurists, were using arguments from Roman law to further their aims. However, their centralizing ambitions were eventually frustrated by corporate political entities of another type, which had their own law, a law granted by the counts—namely, the Flemish cities.

HUNGARY

The Hungarian kings had close connections with other European rulers and attempted to imitate them, but their successes always proved to be temporary, for the powers of the nobles, attached to their traditional ways, were too strong; the fact that the population was predominantly Magyar, not Germanic, also made a difference.[62] Then in the middle of the thirteenth century the Mongol invasion wiped out whatever progress had been made toward a centralized state. Still, even in Hungary on the periphery of Western civilization the inroads of the legal transformation can be traced.

In 1074, in the midst of civil war, King Geza appealed to Pope Gregory VII for aid. Gregory, attempting the same tactic that had proved successful in both Sicily and Croatia, promised that he would recognize Geza's claim in exchange for papal suzerainty. But Geza refused, and instead had himself crowned with a crown sent from Byzantium.

Geza's successors, Ladislas (1077-1095) and his son Koloman (1095-1114), were Hungary's first lawgivers. Ladislas issued three sets of laws that dealt with penal measures against pagans, the administration of royal justice, penalties for theft, protection of property, and other matters. Koloman, who married a daughter of Count Roger of Sicily, issued a legal reform in eighty-four articles, some of which mitigated the harshness of his father's laws. He did away with trial for sorcery, increased the number of courts, restrained judicial combats, set down jurisdictional limits and procedure, and sharply distinguished between ecclesiastical and lay discipline.

It was not until 1172 that there appeared another strong ruler interested in internal reform, Bela III (1172-1196). He married Margaret of Capet, daughter of Louis VII of France and widow of Henry the Younger, son of Henry II of England. During Bela's reign many Hungarian intellectuals went to Paris to study. They returned to staff new administrative organs modeled on Western examples, including a chancery.

However, Bela's successors were unable to carry on his centralizing policies. In 1222, in a reaction to the royal machinery, the nobles and small landholders forced King Andrew II to sign the Golden Bull, a document which, like the English Magna Carta of 1215 and the German Statute in Favor of Princes of 1232, relied on contemporary legal concepts to reduce royal power. Among its thirty-one provisions was one that made it illegal to imprison a noble until he had been properly tried and sentenced. Another forbade the chief royal judicial officer to hear cases involving life or property without the king's knowledge. Other provisions guaranteed the rights of small landholders and regulated other governmental abuses. The nobles' right of resistance against illegal acts of the king was also preserved. Partly as a result of the Golden Bull, royal law in Hungary remained weak in comparison with that of other Western countries in the early thirteenth century. And the Mongol invasion of 1241 left the whole country in devastation.

DENMARK

The development of royal law in Denmark was belated but impressive.[63] In the early thirteenth century King Canute II tried to issue taxes, collect fines, and, in general, assert royal authority, but he was overthrown and assassinated. However, in 1241 Valdemar II issued the Jutae Logh, or Jutland Law, the first official Scandinavian collection of laws;[64] it was preceded by two works by private individuals, the Scanian and Zealandic laws, also written during the reign of Valdemar II.

The Jutae Logh is divided into three books and contains a total of 242 chapters. There is a very rough division among property, civil, and criminal law. The sources of the law are mainly customary law, decrees of previous rulers, and the city law of Schleswig. No direct influences from Roman law are to be found, but the influence of canon law is apparent. The first sentences of the preamble state:

> By law shall the land be built. Were every man content with what is his and granted to other men the same right, no law would be needed. Were the land without law he would have the most who could take most; therefore law shall be made to meet the needs of all. It is the office of the king and chiefs who are in this country to guard the law and to do justice and to save whomsoever shall be put to duress such as widows and children without guardians and pilgrims and foreigners and poor men who are most often encroached upon.[65]

Among other "modern" features of the Jutland Law is the replacement of compurgation by trial by jury.

Other examples of Denmark's participation in the transformation of

Western law in this period are the creation of a chancery, of royal household officers, and of provincial officials. The sons of the nobles were often sent to Paris to study.[66]

It is likely that Danish influence contributed to the promulgation in 1275 of Norway's first law code, issued by a ruler with the wondrous name of King Magnus Lawmender.

Royal Law and Canon Law

The systems of royal law that developed in the various kingdoms and principalities of Europe in the twelfth and thirteenth centuries had many common features. At the same time, they all bore a structural resemblance to the system of canon law that prevailed throughout Western Christendom. In each kingdom or principality, royal law and canon law complemented each other in such a way that they may be said to have constituted integral parts of a single legal order.

1. Both canon law and royal law exercised a limited competence and limited jurisdiction. Canon law claimed competence to deal with criminal and civil causes arising out of sin and breach of faith; royal law claimed competence to deal with criminal and civil causes arising out of seisin of freehold land and breach of the king's peace. Canon law claimed jurisdiction over clerics and over church property as well as over laity charged with sin and breach of faith; royal law claimed jurisdiction over freeholders and felons as well as over matters directly pertaining to the crown and crown property. The competence and jurisdiction of the two types of legal system overlapped at certain points, and there were clashes between them. Yet for a long time they were able to coexist more or less peacefully.

2. Both canon law and royal law were grounded in the authority of external sources of law, to which they looked for objectivity and generality. Both found such sources in divine law and in natural law (reason and conscience). In addition, canon law looked to sacred texts, including the canons and decrees laid down by church councils, by popes, and by others in authority, whereas royal law looked generally to royal enactments (which, however, were on the whole much less elaborate than ecclesiastical legislation). Both systems also regarded custom as an important source of law, though royal law relied much more heavily on custom than did canon law. In judicial procedure, canon law relied on testimony obtained by interrogation under oath, as did many of the systems of royal law. English royal law, however, relied on the sworn recognition of neighbors, except that English parliaments in the thirteenth century, sitting as courts, and the chancellor's court in the fourteenth and fifteenth centuries, adapted the canonical procedure to their own uses. Also German royal (or ducal) courts relied on sworn declarations of prevailing customs by law speakers (*Schöffen*).

3. Both canon law and royal law were systematized. However, canon law was more highly systematized. It was even more systematized than the revived Roman law — its "handmaiden," which was not the positive law of any jurisdiction, though it was often called a "subsidiary law," and which, even where it was said to govern, was never the whole body of governing law.

Canon law (like Roman law) was a university discipline, a "science." Royal law was closer to customary law. Royal law was not so easily shaped into an intellectual structure. In England, where at first royal law developed primarily within the limits of the writ system, *analogy* played a major role in gradually expanding judicial remedies. By the same token, *generalization* and *synthesis* played a more limited role. Even in the fourteenth century, when the common law came to be studied and lectured on at the Inns of Court, heavy emphasis was placed on its technical aspects. To be sure, Glanvill wrote a fine book on English royal law in 1187, but it was basically a commentary on the writs, in the style of the canonists' monographs on canonical forms of complaint (*libelli*), and not a treatise (*tractatus*) or a summa. Bracton's great treatise in the next century was considerably more substantial and has been called a summa, but it fell into disuse after several generations and not much came along to supplement or replace it. In Sicily, Normandy, France, the German duchies, and elsewhere, as in England, royal law (or ducal law) was much less highly systematized than canon law. There were a few treatises, such as that of Beaumanoir and the *Sachsenspiegel*, summarizing French and German "common law" respectively, but there was no university training in such subjects except as they might be touched on in courses in Roman law and in discussions of custom as a source of law. Royal law, like other forms of secular law, did not need to be portrayed in textbooks and taught in university courses in order to be accepted as an integrated, ongoing, autonomous body of law, whereas legal scholarship was indispensable to the creation of the modern system of canon law.

Differences in the degree and character of the systematization of the two types of law are to be explained in part by differences in the conception of the spiritual and secular orders. The secular order was, by definition, more chaotic, more disorganized, more aimless than the spiritual (ecclesiastical) order. The secular order was more in need of reform and redemption. To be sure, secular law, in helping to fulfill that need, was subject to reason; it was intended to be scientific and systematic; it was to be tested by criteria of justice and truth. But it was closer to custom than canon law, and therefore closer to disorder and violence. At the same time it was more bound to formalities. For both reasons — its customary character and its formal character — it was more difficult to systematize.

Yet if one compares royal law in the year 1200 — in Sicily, in England, in France, in the German duchies, and elsewhere — with royal law in the year 1000 in the same countries, one is struck by the high degree of systematization that it had achieved, and by the extent to which it had been emancipated from custom and from formalism.

4. In addition to being governed by these three principles — competence and limited jurisdiction, reliance upon external sources of authority, and conscious systematization — both royal law and canon law were governed by the principle of conscious growth over generations. Both were assumed not only to be systems but also to be ongoing systems. In canon law this quality of ongoingness was expressed in the conscious continuity of legislation issued by church councils and popes as well as of judicial decisions handed down by the papal and other ecclesiastical courts. It was also expressed in the conscious continuity of teaching and scholarship. In the various systems of royal law, the principle of conscious growth, or ongoingness, was similarly expressed in the continuity of royal legislation and adjudication, as well as in the continuity of teaching and scholarship.

5. Finally, both royal law and canon law exemplified the belief that all law held within itself certain purposes, which were identified as justice; these built-in purposes were to guide the interpretation and application of legal rules and techniques. Thus neither royal law nor canon law was thought to be primarily a body of rules, although neither could function without rules, and in both it was accepted that the rules should form a body, in the sense of a coherent system. Each was regarded as primarily a process of making and interpreting and applying rules in such a way as to realize their built-in purposes of justice. Aristotle had defined equity as "the correction of the law where it is defective by reason of its universality." Equity is justice, he had said, but it is better than a certain kind of justice, namely, that kind "where it is necessary to speak universally, but impossible to do so correctly, [and] the law takes the most general case, though it is well aware of the incorrectness of it." In such instances "it is proper . . . to correct the defect, as the legislator would himself direct if he were then present, or as he would have legislated if he had been aware of the case."[67] This broad concept of equity was carried over into Stoic thought and into both Eastern and Western Christendom. It was manifested in the Roman law of Justinian through such equitable doctrines as those of good faith, unjust enrichment, and substantial justice. However, in reviving Aristotelian philosophy and Roman law, the church in the late eleventh and early twelfth centuries gave new moral and cultural content to the concept of equity. In particular, both canon law and royal law added to the earlier, more general concept of equity various specific requirements of Christian conscience: the protection of the poor and helpless (including widows and orphans), the en-

forcement of relations of trust and confidence (including gifts to be used for charitable purposes), and other requirements. In England, in the fourteenth and fifteenth centuries, when the two principal royal courts limited their competence in such matters, the king's chancellor, who was then almost invariably a high official of the Church of Rome, began to exercise an exceptional jurisdiction "for the sake of conscience" and "for the sake of equity." In other European systems of royal law, however, and in England in the twelfth and thirteenth centuries, "equity" was not considered to be separate from "law" but, on the contrary, an integral part of it. As in canon law, the equity of the royal courts was that aspect of law which gave it its capacity to adapt old rules to new ("exceptional") circumstances, in order to do justice.

Similar comparisons could be made between royal law and the other types of secular legal systems — feudal law, manorial law, urban law, and mercantile law. Royal law bore a relationship to those other secular legal systems analogous to the relationship that canon law bore to royal law: in comparison with them, royal law was more comprehensive, more sophisticated, more advanced, or at least would rapidly become so in the succeeding centuries. When the attack on the canon law of the church came in the sixteenth century, it was the law of kings and princes that played a leading role against it; manorial law had disappeared almost entirely, feudal law survived chiefly as a residue of the past, and urban and mercantile law had become increasingly subordinate to royal law.

Conclusion

T HE FIRST OF the great revolutions of Western history was the revolution against domination of the clergy by emperors, kings, and lords and for establishment of the Church of Rome as an independent, corporate, political and legal entity, under the papacy. The church, now viewed above all as the clergy, would work for the redemption of the laity and the reformation of the world, through law, in the direction of justice and peace. This was, however, only one side of the Papal Revolution. Another side of it was the enhancement of the secular political and legal authority of emperors, kings, and lords, as well as the creation of thousands of autonomous, self-governing cities. Still another side of it was the enormous expansion of economic activity, especially in agriculture, commerce, and crafts. Still another was the founding of the universities, and the development of the new sciences of theology and law. There were other sides as well. The Papal Revolution had, in short, the character of a total change. It envisioned not only a new heaven but also a new earth. The Investiture Struggle was only part of it. The Gregorian Reformation was only part of it.

The Papal Revolution had been in preparation for at least a generation. The first overt steps toward it were taken by the papal party in the 1050s and 1060s. In 1059 Pope Nicholas II, at the Synod of Rome, for the first time forbade lay investiture and established a procedure for election of popes by the cardinals, thereby taking the power to appoint the pope away from the emperor. In 1075 Pope Gregory VII threw down the gauntlet in his Dictates of the Pope. From 1076 to 1122 wars were fought in various parts of Europe between supporters and opponents of the papal authority and its program. Eventually, compromises were reached. Neither side was wholly victorious.

It was this total upheaval that gave birth to the Western legal tradition.

A system of law was necessary to the Western Church to maintain its new, visible, corporate legal unity under the papacy; the disembedding of canon law from theology and liturgy, and its systematization and rationalizing, were needed as a source of legitimacy and a means of control by the central ecclesiastical authorities and also as an effective symbol of the separate corporate identity of the clergy as a whole. The new *jus canonicum* was also essential to the maintenance of the church's new set of relations with the various secular authorities. Relatively autonomous and rational systems of law were needed by the various secular authorities as well, in order to enable them to legitimate and effectuate their newly developing central controls and to maintain themselves in the new competition of polities.

The need for legal systems was not merely a practical political one. It was also a moral and intellectual one. Law came to be seen as the very essence of faith. "God is himself law, and therefore law is dear to him," wrote the author of the *Sachsenspiegel*, the first German lawbook, about 1220. That was almost a century after the Concordat of Worms had settled the Investiture Struggle, but it was nevertheless a direct expression of the philosophy of the Papal Revolution. It was, indeed, a direct expression of the spirit of the Concordat of Worms. No one in the West would have said it before 1075; after 1122 it was, in one form or another, a commonplace. Law was seen as a way of fulfilling the mission of Western Christendom to begin to achieve the kingdom of God on earth.

The Papal Revolution gave birth to a new formulation of the doctrine of the two swords that had been introduced five centuries earlier by Pope Gregory I. The earlier formulation had been concerned with the relation between earthly and heavenly spheres of Christian living. For the theorists of the Papal Revolution, however, the main problem was the relation between the ecclesiastical and lay authorities in the earthly sphere itself. It was the church as a visible, corporate, political and legal entity that was to wield the spiritual sword; and that sword was to control not only life in the next world but also a large number of matters in this world as well, including administration of church property, activities of clerics, family relations, business morality, indeed, anything that could be brought under the heading of morals or belief.

For the first time the spiritual sword was embodied in a system and a science of law, the newly systematized and rationalized canon law of Gratian and of the great lawyer-popes of the twelfth and thirteenth centuries. The papacy developed also the governmental institutions and the bureaucratic apparatus needed to make this legal system work: a professional judiciary, a treasury, a chancery. This was the first modern Western system of government and law. It was eventually emulated by the secular polities that took form in the succeeding generations.

It may at first seem strange to attribute to the revolutionary events of the late eleventh and early twelfth centuries the subsequent development

Figure 2. Canon law, urban law, royal law, and feudal law, eleventh to thirteenth centuries.

	Canon law (including Roman law)	Urban law	Royal law: Sicily	Royal law: England and Normandy	Royal law: France	Royal law: Germany, Flanders, Hungary; Feudal law
1030						1037 Feudal statute of Emperor Conrad II
1040	1040 Truce of God introduced by Abbey of Cluny					
	1049 Pope Leo IX (1049–1054)					
1050	1054 Schism of Eastern and Western churches	1056 Customs of Genoa				
		1057 Commune established in Milan				
	1059 Synod of Rome: cardinals to elect pope; lay investiture prohibited		1059 Robert Guiscard invested by pope as Duke of Apulia and Calabria			
1060		1066 Charter granted to London		1066 William I (1066–1087); Norman conquest of England		1068 Usages of Barcelona
1070				1072 Decree separating secular and ecclesiastical courts		
	1073 Pope Gregory VII (1073–1085)	1073 Liberties granted to Worms				
		1074 Rebellion against Archbishop of Cologne				
	1075 *Dictates of the Pope*; Investiture Struggle (1075–1122)	1075 Commune sworn in Cambrai				
	1077 Emperor Henry IV at Canossa	1077 Liberties granted to Mainz				1077 Emperor Henry IV deposed Diet of Forchheim: election of emperor by princes Hungary: King Ladislas (1077–1095): three sets of royal laws
	1078 Anselm, *On the Existence of God*					
1080	1080 Discovery of Digest; Henry IV deposed by Pope Gregory	1080 Charters granted to Lucca and Pisa by Henry IV				1082 Peace of God in Lüttich
		1084 Consul elected for fixed term in Pisa	1085 Roger I, Count of Sicily (1085–1105)	1085–86 Domesday Book		1085 Peace of God in Empire
	1087 Law school founded at Bologna					1093 Peace statute in Swabia
1090	1095 Ivo of Chartres, *Decretum*	1095 Amalfitan Table				1095 Hungary: King Koloman (1095–1114); law reform in 84 articles

1096 First Crusade

1097 Anselm, *Why God Became Man*

1098 Cistercian order founded

1100

1100 Libri Feodorum

1103 Imperial peace statute

1100 Henry I (1100–1135) Origin of exchequer and of pipe rolls: government and administration of justice rationalized

1106 Independent municipal government and system of urban law established in Cologne

1107 Concordat of Bec, ending Investiture Struggle in England and Normandy

1107 Concordat of Bec, ending Investiture Struggle in England and Normandy

1108 Louis VI (1108–1137) and Louis VII (1137–1180). Royal domain expanded beyond Ile de France; more centralized governmental and legal institutions introduced

1110

1111 Flanders: first secular peace statute

1112 Roger II (1112–1154) Creation of chancery, treasury, professional royal court, itinerant justices, bailiffs, *catalogus baronum*

1115 Rolls of Oleron

1118 *Leges Henrici Primi*

1120

1120 Charter granted to Freiburg

1122 Peter Abelard, *Sic et Non* Concordat of Worms, ending Investiture Struggle in Empire

1122 Concordat of Worms

1125 Diet of Mainz: election of Lothar (1125–1138)

1127 Charter granted to Saint-Omer

1129 Unsuccessful rebellion against Bishop in Magdeburg London receives charter from Henry I confirming right of election of sheriffs

1130

1130 Death of Irnerius

1136 Justiciar established

1139 Peter Abelard, *Ethics* Second Lateran Council

Year	Canon law (including Roman law)	Urban law	Royal law: Sicily	Royal law: England and Normandy	Royal law: France	Royal law: Germany, Flanders, Hungary; Feudal law
1140	1140 Gratian, *Concordance of Discordant Canons*	1142 Charter of Pisa	1140 Assizes of Ariano			
	1147 Clerics ordered by Pope Eugene III not to participate in or submit to lay justice	1143 Lübeck founded by Count Adolf II of Holstein				
1150	1151 Peter Lombard, *Sentences*	1153 Lübeck granted privileges by Henry the Lion	1154 William I (1154–1166)	1150 Vacarius at Oxford		1152 Election of Frederick Barbarossa (1152–1190); imperial peace statute
				1154 Henry II (1154–1189)		1154 Henry the Lion, Duke of Bavaria and Saxony (1154–1180) Judicial power extended; administration rationalized; Munich founded
						1155 Frederick Barbarossa crowned in Rome, consults with "four doctors"
						1156 Creation of Duchy of Austria
						1158 Diet of Roncaglia
1160	1159 Pope Alexander III (1159–1181) John of Salisbury, *Policraticus*	1161 Constituta Legis et Usus of Pisa		1164 Constitutions of Clarendon		1160 Privilegium Minus for Austria
	1164 Constitutions of Clarendon of Henry II, regulating English church	1162 Destruction of Milan by Frederick Barbarossa	1166 William II (1166–1189) Royal laws established benefit of clergy and allowed all free men to enter clergy	1166 Assize of novel disseisin; inquest of knight's services		1162 Statute for county of Forcalquier in Provence
		1167 Lombard League established				1168 Creation of Würzburg
		1169 Podesta instituted in Milan				1169 Flanders: Count Philip (1169–1191); legislation through peace statutes
		1169–1191 Charters granted to Bruges and other Flemish cities during reign of Count Philip				
1170	1170 Death of Bulgarus, most renowned of the "four doctors" Murder of Becket			1170 Murder of Becket; repeal of offensive provisions of the Constitutions of Clarendon	1172 Inquest of knight's services	1172 Hungary: King Bela III (1172–1196); centralization and rationalization of administrative and legal structure
	1172 Henry II at Avranches Repeal of offensive provisions of Constitutions of Clarendon					

1179 Third Lateran Council

1180

1190 Huguccio, *Summa*

1190

1198 Pope Innocent III (1198–1216)

1200

1210

1215 Fourth Lateran Council: priests forbidden to take part in trials by ordeal; doctrine of transubstantiation officially proclaimed

---

1181 Lübeck seized by Frederick Barbarossa

1183 Peace of Constance, "Magna Carta of communal liberties"

1188 Magdeburg government reformed; first codification of Magdeburg law

1200 Charter granted to Ipswich by King John

1208- Frederick II (1208–1250) Creation of University of Naples and royal civil service; expansion of royal judicial power

1216 Book of Customs of Milan

1176 Justices in eyre: assize of mort d' ancestor

1178 Court of common pleas

1179 Inquest procedure under writ of right *Dialogue of the Exchequer*

1187 Glanvill, *Treatise on the Laws and Customs of the Kingdom of England*

1193 Hubert Walter appointed Archbishop of Canterbury and Justiciar

1199 King John (1199–1216)

1200 *Très ancien coutumier de Normandie*

1204 French completed conquest of Normandy

1209 John excommunicated by pope

1213 England made papal fief

1215 Magna Carta

1216 Henry III (1216–1272)

1219 Introduction of trial by inquest in criminal cases

1180 Philip II (Augustus) (1180–1223) French administrative structure rationalized; bailiffs and seneschals established; procedural uniformity established in royal courts

1214 Battle of Bouvines

1179–80 Trial of Henry the Lion Wittelsbach dynasty placed in Bavaria *Reichsfürstenstand* instituted

1185 Assise au Comte Geoffroy

1186 Statute on arson

1200 Charte Féodale for Hainaut

1204 Bavarian office of *Viztum*, followed by steps to rationalize and modernize bureaucracy and administration of justice

1212 Frederick II (1212–1250)

Year	Canon law (including Roman law)	Urban law	Royal law: Sicily	Royal law: England and Normandy	Royal law: France	Royal law: Germany, Flanders, Hungary, Feudal law
1220						1220 Treaty with the ecclesiastical Princes
						1221 Eike von Repgow: *Sachsenspiegel*
						1222 Hungary: Golden Bull
					1223 Louis VIII (1223–1226)	
					1226 Louis IX (1226–1270)	
1230			1231 *Liber Augustalis*			1232 Statute in Favor of Princes
	1234 Gregory IX. *Decretals*					1235 Mainz imperial peace statute
1240						1244 First of five major Bavarian peace statutes
1250	1250 *Glossa Ordinaria* of Accursius				1250 Parlement of Paris established as judicial body	
				1256 Bracton, *On the Laws and Customs of England*		
				1258 First parliament	1258 Statute outlawing trial by combat	
1260		1260 Magdeburg law received in Breslau				
1270						1274–5 Schwabenspiegel Deutschenspiegel
					1277 Statute of novel disseisin	
1280					1283 Beaumanoir. *Customs of Beauvais*	

of legal systems in the latter twelfth, thirteenth, and even later centuries. It might seem more logical to attribute the later developments to later events. Of course, without the later events there could not have been the later developments. Nevertheless, all the legal systems of Europe in the latter twelfth and thirteenth centuries manifested and embodied and carried to their conclusion principles that had been established in preceding generations. This is not to be understood in terms of a Hegelian progression of ideas; it is rather to be understood in terms of the dynamics of Western history, in which not only material and ideal factors but also, above all, great events themselves have exerted pressures for change in certain directions over a long period. To trace the growth of legal institutions in the late twelfth and thirteenth centuries back to the Papal Revolution of the late eleventh century, culminating in the Concordat of Worms, is no more strange than to trace the growth of racial equality in the United States in the late nineteenth and twentieth centuries back to the American Revolution of the late eighteenth century, culminating in the Civil War Amendments to the United States Constitution. Without a perspective of such duration it is impossible to understand either the periodic cataclysms of Western history or the great traditions that have succeeded those cataclysms and have served as bulwarks against their recurrence. Renewal is followed by continuity and growth, revolution by evolution.

That it takes several generations to make a revolution should not be surprising. Especially if one is concerned with the institutionalization of its goals, and with the necessary compromises that flow from the process of institutionalization, one must take into account long-term movements. In the case of the Papal Revolution, two of its major goals, rule *by* law and the rule *of* law—that rulers must seek to effectuate their policies systematically through legal institutions and that they are themselves to be bound by the legal institutions through which they govern—were quite new to Western society. If these principles were to be secure they had to be accepted and internalized as well as adapted and modified by the children and grandchildren of the people who first introduced them.

Most of the institutions, procedures, concepts, and rules of the Germanic folklaw disappeared in the centuries after the Papal Revolution. This did not happen all at once. The blood feud continued in many parts of Europe into the fifteenth century, despite the opposition of both canon law and royal law. Marriages of children continued to be arranged by their parents, especially among the nobility. Although Germanic procedures of compurgation were transformed into testimony under oath, nevertheless the measuring of the value of an oath according to the status of the witness showed traces of the old formalism. These are only a few examples of survivals. On the whole, however, the Germanic folklaw died out under the impact of the division of political authority into two parts, the ecclesiastical and the secular, the formation of the church-state and eventually of secular states, and the rationalization and systematization of church law and eventually of secular types of law.

Yet the integrated Germanic folk culture was a necessary foundation for the new program of rationalization and systematization of law. Western legalism was rooted in an earlier communitarianism. The Papal Revolution itself was only possible in a society already united as a *populus christianus*; the fight over who should control the church, and thus who should control "ideology" (as it would be called today), presupposed the existence of a common loyalty to the church and a common faith. The related question of who should control church wealth also presupposed the existence of a shared belief that that wealth should be used for religious purposes. The revolution shattered the unity that was the precondition for its occurrence. It erected and institutionalized new divisions of canon law and secular law and, within secular law, divisions of feudal, manorial, mercantile, urban, and royal law; within each of these divisions there were also divisions of reason and custom and command. The preexisting unity had been the unity of race, of soil, of class, of family, of faith. In fact, however, the various new, systematized, rationalized, ongoing, transcendent bodies of law were intended in part to preserve those old unities, although in very different forms from the ones that had previously prevailed.

The Germanic folklaw itself had been of one piece with the communitarian, essentially tribal society. Like Germanic myth, art, and language itself, the folklaw had been diffuse, embedded in custom, and thought to be more or less immutable. Christianity had introduced a dynamic element; it had cast doubt on the tribal values. But prior to the late eleventh century, despite some exceptions, Christianity had not been systematically reflected in the institutional life of the Germanic peoples; it was for the most part an otherworldly faith. The Papal Revolution, however, made Christianity into a political and legal program. The church became a state. Canon law became a specific means, first, of holding the church-state together, and second, of reforming the world. The other emerging law systems also sought to reform custom in accordance with reason and conscience. Yet this was not meant to destroy the old communities; on the contrary, it was intended to strengthen them.

To apply reason to custom, that is, to weed out the mass of unreasonable customs and to cultivate the reasonable ones into a system of law, was a bold program, to say the least. It was highly convenient, and not wholly accidental, that a manuscript of Justinian's Digest turned up in a library in Florence in the 1080s, and it was surely not accidental that very soon a university was founded at Bologna—the first European university—to study that manuscript. Henceforth the jurists had an entire dictionary, so to speak, in which to find legal terms, concepts, standards, and rules, a *ratio scripta*, as the Roman law was then called, by which to sift the customs. It was as though the Old Testament had suddenly been discovered for the first time by Christian theologians. The Western jurists applied a new dialectical method to the Roman texts, directed toward the reconciliation of contradictions. They were thus able to draw from these texts conceptual implications which the Romans themselves had never dreamed of—a theory of contract law, a concept of rights of possession, elaborate doctrines defining justifications for the use of force, and the like. The jurists thus gave the West its characteristic methods of analysis and synthesis of texts. They taught the West to synthesize cases into rules, rules into principles, principles into a system. Their method, which is still that of legal science in the United States today, was to determine what various particulars have in common. to see the whole as the interaction of the parts. This was the prototype of modern Western science, for it took the customs and the rules as data and adduced from the data the regularities—the "laws"—that explained them. Historically and sociologically, such a method was essential to the reconciliation of the contradictions among the conflicting legal systems—in the first instance, the reconciliation of canon law with secular law, and in the second instance, the reconciliation of the various secular legal systems with one another.

If the dialectical method of scholastic philosophy was essential to the structuring of law in the West, the theological doctrines that accompanied the use of that method were essential to its basic concepts, and especially its concept of crime and punishment. The theology of the Papal Revolution was a theology of judgment. God was, above all, a God of justice. Through his incarnation in Christ, and Christ's sacrifice of himself for mankind, the original sin of penitent Christians was forgiven, but actual sins must be atoned for either in this life or in purgatory. A price must be paid for the violation of the law. Upon payment of the price, the law was vindicated, and the erstwhile sinner could enter paradise. This theology underlay the church's establishment for the first time of an "external forum" for the trial of crimes, as contrasted with the "internal forum" of the confessional and the sacrament of penance. A set of principles of criminal law was developed which was similar to that which prevails in most Western countries today: that there must be an external criminal act, that it must be prohibited by law, that it must manifest a direct or an indirect intent, that it must have proximately caused the harm, that it must be vexatious to the community.

Underlying these principles, and underlying the canon law as a whole, was the belief in a God of justice who operates a lawful universe, punishing and rewarding according to principles of proportion, mercifully mitigated in exceptional cases. This theological belief corresponded to a political belief in the complex social unity called Christendom, in which the dialectic of interacting ecclesiastical and secular realms was regulated by a similar kind of justice-based-on-law and law-based-on-justice, with mercy playing an important role in exceptional cases.

The canon law, the first modern Western legal system, was conceived in the twelfth century as an integrated system of law moving forward in time. The church itself was conceived for the first time as a legal structure, a law-state, and it formed itself into a complex bureaucracy with a professional court, a professional treasury, and a chancery. The constitutional law of the church took the form of corporation law; it combined the Roman institutional (*Anstalt*) concept of the corporation with the Germanic fellowship (*Genossenschaft*) concept, adding to both the Christian concept of a group person, conceived in nominalist terms. From the canon law of corporations is derived the concept that the executive authority may not take certain actions without the "advice and consent" of a consultative body, and that such consultation rests on the principle that those who are directly affected by a decision should have the right to participate in making it. The canon law is also the source of modern distinctions between personal jurisdiction and subject-matter jurisdiction. In fact, limitations upon the competence and jurisdiction of the canon law are closely linked with constitutional standards for locating and limiting the church's sovereignty, for allocating governmental powers within it, and for determining basic rights and duties of members.

Systematization within the canon law took the form of the development of subsystems of law relating to marriage, wills, property, agreements, and delicts—based on the church's jurisdiction over sacraments, testaments, benefices, oaths, and sins, respectively. Each subsystem had its own structural features, and at the same time each shared the structural features of the system of canon law as a whole. Thus the canon law relating to marriage developed rules concerning nullity of marriages (based on fraud, duress, and mistake) that were similar to canon law rules concerning nullity of contracts generally and that were based on general principles that ran throughout the canon law. Restrictions imposed by secular authorities on devises of land led the canonists to develop a law of trusts which overlapped the law of succession and the law of property. In general, the canon law of wills, of contract, and of property was antifeudal, in the sense that the church favored freedom of testation, the enforceability of promises made without formalities, and full ownership of property. Also, contrary to what is sometimes supposed, the church strongly favored the charging of interest on loans—indeed, the canonists first applied the word "interest" to distinguish lawful charges for the use of money from unlawful charges ("usury").

That the definition of the jurisdiction of the church, and of the canon law, was a matter not merely of convenience but of principle, and of deep principle, for which men were ready to fight, bleed, and die, is illustrated by the martyrdom of Thomas Becket, who opposed King Henry II's effort to go back to certain limitations on ecclesiastical jurisdiction which Thomas considered to be offensive to the cause of freedom of the church under the papacy. In the Constitutions of Clarendon of 1164, the king had invoked the customs of his grandfather, Henry I, who had reigned until 1135. But the church had gained much ground during the so-called Anarchy of Stephen, from 1135 to 1154, before Henry II came to the throne. For six years Henry and Thomas struggled for a legal solution to their controversy; it was a legal conflict, over jurisdiction, and both sides had a very high appreciation of the role of law in resolving conflict of any kind. Eventually, Henry renounced the "offensive" provisions of the Constitutions of Clarendon, although it was never entirely clear which were the offensive provisions and which were not. The matter was ultimately settled — again, not quite satisfactorily — by the rivalry of the ecclesiastical and the secular courts. The secular courts would protect their jurisdiction by writs of prohibition, which, however, were difficult to apply and even more difficult to enforce. The ecclesiastical courts, if sufficiently provoked, could excommunicate the royal judges. If the pope himself was sufficiently provoked, as he was by the recalcitrance of King John, he could — and did — put the whole of England under interdict, thereby causing great distress. Mostly, the two jurisdictions cooperated with each other.

The Papal Revolution was like an atomic explosion that split Germanic Christendom into two parts: the church, viewed as an independent, visible, corporate, legal structure; and the secular order, viewed as divided among various polities. The church formed a single state structure, governed by a single system of law, the canon law. Being the church and constituting, therefore, the spiritual sphere, it was supposed to be as close as humankind could come, in this world, to the divinity. The canon law of the church was, to be sure, human law; yet it was supposed to be also a reflection of natural law and divine law. The secular order, however, was less perfect, more primitive, more earthbound. Its law was, therefore, more tied to irrational factors, to power, to superstition, to decadence. Yet it was capable of being regenerated; it was redeemable; it had positive significance. The church could help to make it conform more fully to natural law and ultimately to divine law. The canon law could serve as a model for the secular legal orders.

Each individual type of secular law was more or less limited to a particular type of temporal affairs: the feudal to the feudal, the urban to the urban, the royal to the royal, and so forth. This distinguished secular law from canon law, whose jurisdiction, though limited, extended to certain types of sins committed by anyone anywhere.

Secular law had the task of lifting up and transforming the secular relationships which it regulated. Feudal relationships were transformed by legal concepts of mutuality of obligations between lord and vassal. Manorial relationships were transformed by legal concepts of the subjection of the lord to the manorial customs of his predecessors. Mercantile relationships were transformed by legal concepts of credit, partnership, and joint venture. Urban relationships were transformed by legal concepts of the liberties of citizens and by the constitutional character of the sworn communes. Royal relationships of king and subject were transformed by legal concepts of the subordination of the king to law and the right and duty of the subject to disobey, and even to kill, a tyrant.

Thus the secular polity was considered to be subject to analysis and subject to regulation. A new political science was created, represented above all by the works of the great twelfth-century writer John of Salisbury, which analyzed the character of government, the responsibilities of rulers, the manner of choice of rulers, and the obligations of subjects toward them. Jurists, including both Romanists and canonists, also contributed to theories of sovereignty and constitutional limitations upon the powers of rulers.

Secular law, including feudal and manorial law, mercantile law, urban law, and royal law, was much more rooted in custom and consequently much less subject to revision by learned jurists than canon law. (Roman law was a different thing altogether: it was a learned law, taught in the universities, not the positive law of any jurisdiction, not generally subject to change — analogous in all these ways to legal history — yet at the same time an ideal law to which all positive law was supposed to conform, and a subsidiary law that could be used to fill gaps.) Nevertheless, secular law *was* changed, and radically changed, in the late eleventh and early twelfth centuries. It was changed by the decisions of secular rulers as well as by the influence of learned jurists. It was systematized, and it was reformed. The church consciously set out to bring about its reform.

In the period from about 1050 to about 1200 western Europe experienced the emergence of feudal law as a system. Feudal rights and obligations became more objective, less arbitrary, more precise. They became more universal, more general, and more uniform. Examples are the rights and obligations of heritability of fiefs, alienability of fiefs, and commutation of feudal obligations into money payments. In addition, there developed a greater reciprocity of rights of lords and vassals: the lord was to protect, assist, and support the vassal, while the vassal was to manage the fief. If the lord violated the faith of the vassal, the vassal was entitled to renounce the lord in the formal act of *diffidatio*. The vassal participated in administration of the lord's justice through suit of court. Thus feudal law gave the West its first secular experience of mutuality of legal obligation between persons of superior and inferior rank. Finally, feudal law acquired the character of a distinct and entire legal system, with integrating elements and with the capacity and tendency to develop over time. It was, to be sure, less systematic, less integrated on the conscious level, less professional or scientific than canon law; it remained largely customary law. Yet it moved in the pathway set by the canon law.

Lord-vassal relations were subject to a different legal regime from lord-peasant relations. The latter were characteristically encompassed in the custom of the manor. Typically, the Western lord of the manor was not an absentee landlord or mere tax collector, as in many non-Western feudal systems; he lived on the estate, supervised its management, and governed it as its political ruler. The peasants might be serfs or they might be free, but in either case they had certain rights under manorial law. For example, all peasants, including serfs, characteristically participated in the manorial court.

In contrast to feudal law, manorial law did not provide for contractual reciprocity between lord and peasant. However, group pressure was exerted by the peasants to exact more favorable conditions, which had the force of concessions reciprocally granted on condition of loyalty. This was reinforced by the legal right of the peasant, whether serf or free, to hold land. Also rent, taxes, and services were fixed by custom, and disputes over their extent and character were supposed to be resolved by manorial law. The manorial court, in which the peasants gave judgment together with the lord, decided criminal and civil cases, and cases have been reported in which decisions were granted to peasants against the lord. The peasant remained poor and oppressed; yet he acquired rights under a system of law. He was a person, a member of the manorial community, part of what was called "the whole homage." Indeed, in time his position improved as he found he could escape to the freedom of the city or to the monastery or school or to join in strikes or uprisings. In the fourteenth and fifteenth centuries the peasants began to absorb the manors, and the manorial system disappeared. Law had helped to pave the way for this development. The recognition of peasants, including serfs, as "citizens" of the manorial community was an implicit challenge to serfdom long before any movement arose to abolish it.

Feudal law and manorial law were destined to fade: manorial law to disappear altogether, and feudal law to remain as a fossil long after feudal economic and political relations had lost their vitality. Mercantile law, on the other hand, had a future. This body of law, too, was systematized in the late eleventh and early twelfth centuries as agricultural trade in the countryside and then overseas and intercity trade flourished. Thus capitalist mercantile law emerged as a twin brother of feudal and manorial law.

While the general population of Europe perhaps doubled in the period from 1050 to 1200, the urban population of Europe increased perhaps tenfold. Merchant guilds arose. Large numbers of traveling merchants participated in markets and fairs. A sophisticated body of legal institutions developed to handle mercantile transactions on a more or less uniform basis throughout the West.

Among the characteristic concepts and devices of mercantile law as it developed in the twelfth century were the concept of the good faith purchaser (whose rights in the goods might exceed those of the seller), symbolic delivery of goods through transfer of documents, implied warranties, the binding character of informal agreements, and joint ventures. Moreover, these characteristic features, which formed the structure of the integrated body of mercantile law, developed over time as customs were codified and interpreted. The notarized contract of exchange became the bill of exchange; the notarized promise to pay became the promissory note; sea loans and bottomry loans developed into a kind of insurance; bankers' letters became letters of credit. As in the case of canon law and (to a lesser degree) feudal law and manorial law, mercantile law gave the impression of the continuous cooperation of successive generations — in this case, of merchants — in making a body of law live and grow.

The thousands of new cities and towns of Europe also developed their own type of law, which also had the characteristics of objectivity, universality, reciprocity, participation, integration, and growth. Most of the old Roman cities had declined to villages and were refounded in the late eleventh, twelfth, and early thirteenth centuries. Typically, the new cities took form as covenanted, sworn communes, with charters of liberties granted by kings or feudal lords. They had a strong communitarian character, with obligations of mutual aid, mutual protection, common counsel, common consent to elections of officials, and participation in assemblies, in councils, and in adjudicatory procedures. They were usually exempt from feudal obligations. Here, too, are important sources of Western constitutionalism, especially in the area of civil rights and civil liberties of citizens.

Finally, a new type of royal law arose in the wake of the Papal Revolution. The king's spiritual authority over the church having been withdrawn, he henceforth governed as a secular ruler whose principal tasks were said to be the maintenance of peace and the establishment of justice in his realm. The Papal Revolution, by depriving emperors and kings of their sacral character and of their role as supreme rulers of the church, reduced them to the status of temporal monarchs. At the same time, however, it enhanced royal power by its support of a new territorial concept of kingship, which helped to transform clan chiefs and feudal overlords into supreme rulers of a given geographical area. Formerly, kings had for the most part governed their magnates, wise men, and tenants-in-chief directly, and only indirectly, through them, the local and tribal leaders, subvassals, and subjects generally. In the twelfth and thirteenth centuries, as territorial rulers, they came to govern all their subjects directly, through royal officers who were delegated to perform more or less specific roles, such as the royal judges and tax officials. These royal officers were guided and bound by royal law. Like the pope, the kings of Europe came to rule through delegates who were professionals, not subkings, and who formed permanent government departments, such as a chancery, a treasury, and a judiciary. Government became a distinct activity, something less than politics as a whole (kingship) but something more than an aggregate of individual government offices.

That the development of royal law in the twelfth and thirteenth centuries — including the "princely" law of duchies and other au-tonomous territories — was strongly influenced by, and indeed was part of, the Papal Revolution is shown by the striking parallels between the various systems of royal law, on the one hand, and the canon law of the church, on the other. As Gregory VII in 1075 declared for the first time the power of the pope alone "to make new laws" (*condere novas leges*), so thereafter in every kingdom of the West the monarch came to be a "maker of laws" (*conditor legum*, as he was called in Norman Sicily in the mid-twelfth century). The Assizes of Ariano, the peace statutes in Ger-many, the possessory assizes of the English kings, the French *ordonnances* and *établissements* all reflected the new belief in the power and duty of the monarch to legislate. Similarly, as the papal curia became a professional judicial body in the early twelfth century, so thereafter in the various kingdoms the *curia regis* was transformed from an assembly of notables to a court of law. Likewise, as the canon law became more structured and more scientific through the work of Gratian and his successors, so struc-tured systems of royal law were gradually created, which, like the canon law, developed organically through interpretation and legislation. Everywhere civil law became separated from criminal law. Everywhere rational methods of proof were introduced to supplement or replace the old methods of oath-helping and ordeals. Everywhere there developed similar basic legal concepts of jurisdiction, of high and low justice, of seisin.

"Bodies" of royal law began to be created in the various kingdoms of Europe. Legal writers emerged who saw in the systems of royal law — as earlier jurists had seen in the systems first of Roman law and then of canon law—an interlocking set of rules and institutions. Glanvill and Bracton in England, Eike von Repgau in Germany, Beaumanoir in France, and others "summarized" the laws of their respective territorial polities in substantial treatises. But before then, the laws themselves had been enacted with a view to their interrelationship. The Assizes of Ariano of King Roger II of Sicily, in 1140, in the very first article, announced the principle that ambiguities in the laws should and could be reconciled by interpretation. Interpretation, the drive for consistency and rationality, the "growth of definition," systematization, the view of law as a complex unity based on the synthesis of opposed elements—all these came to be accepted as important features of royal law, just as they had previously been accepted as important aspects of Roman and canon law from the time of Irnerius and Ivo, Azo and Gratian.

Presupposed in the concept of a body of law was the concept of its growth. Previously, in the periodic legislation of the Germanic rulers, each great "codification" had been conceived as a general recapitulation of customary law, superseding those that preceded it. After the eleventh century, new royal laws presupposed the continued existence of older ones, and, indeed, built on them. The law appeared to expand and develop, as one king added to the legislation of his predecessors. Perhaps the most striking examples of this are, first, the organic development of Sicilian legislation from the laws of Roger II (the Assizes of Ariano), to those of his sons, and to those of his grandson Frederick II (*Liber Augustalis*), and second, the series of possessory assizes and other writs issued by the English kings from the time of Henry II through the reigns of Richard, John, and Henry III.

The concept of the organic growth of law was associated with a principle of legality. It was taken for granted that kings ruled by law. "The land shall be built by law"—so begins the first Scandinavian law book. At the same time, rule *by* law was supported in theory, though by no means always in practice, by a widespread belief in the rule *of* law. This was the belief—expressed in the twelfth century by John of Salisbury and others, and in the thirteenth century by Eike von Repgau, Bracton, Beaumanoir, and others—that the king himself was bound by law and that the king's subjects might even have, in some circumstances, the right to disobey his command if it was unlawful.

This belief was rooted, first, in the theological conviction that the universe itself was subject to law.

Second, this belief was rooted in the duality of secular and spiritual authorities, which placed both practical and theoretical limitations upon the power of each. Every kingdom of Europe, including even Norman Sicily, experienced the tension between papal and royal authority. Even the most powerful secular rulers had to reckon continually with papal opinion, not only in their foreign affairs but also in their domestic policies, including the development of their legal systems. This was due in part to the fact that throughout the twelfth century, and to a lesser extent in the thirteenth (in other words, during the formative era of Western political and legal thought), the chief officers of kings were themselves high ecclesiastics, who owed part of their allegiance to Rome.

Third, the belief in the supremacy of law was rooted in the pluralism of secular authorities within each kingdom, and especially in the dialectical tensions among royal, feudal, and urban polities. This, too, was part of the totality of the Papal Revolution. The very division between secular and spiritual polities presupposed many secular authorities within one spiritual authority, which in turn presupposed an interaction among the secular. The pluralism of secular authorities within each kingdom was, of course, not only a concept but also an overriding political, economic, and social reality. The cities of Europe were built on the foundation of communal self-government and the liberties of citizens. Feudal authorities, too, continually resisted royal encroachment on their privileges. It would be many centuries before royal absolutism could become feasible in most parts of Europe. Nevertheless, the Sicilian example is strong evidence that tyranny was possible despite great economic, political, and social decentralization, and that the belief — elsewhere — in the supremacy of law was therefore not merely a reflection of material conditions but also played a positive role in maintaining those conditions.

Fourth, the belief in the supremacy of law was closely linked to the mutuality of obligations between superiors and inferiors in the feudal hierarchy and the acceptance of a dialectical interaction between central and local authorities as well as between official and popular agencies of government. The right of the vassal to "defy" his lord and the right of the peasant to rely on the customs of the manor were important factors in the development of a legal consciousness that could be invoked against arbitrary power.

The interaction between central and local authorities depended on the development of the concept and reality of delegated authority. In almost all parts of Europe there emerged in the twelfth century a royal officialdom at the local level — *baillis*, *Richter*, sheriffs, itinerant justices. They did not replace the local lords and other local authorities, but rather divided power with them. There also developed almost everywhere an interaction between royal judges and other royal officials, on the one hand, and people at the grass roots, on the other — juries, councils of notables, *Schoeffen*. The existence of various forms of popular participation in the administration of justice was an important and, in the long run, perhaps even a necessary factor both in the successful establishment of a system of royal law and in the maintenance of its supremacy over the arbitrary exercise of power by the king himself.

The individual parts of the story told in this book are well known to specialists in various fields of history and law. Yet the story as a whole is singularly unfamiliar and conflicts with conventional preconceptions in many ways. It contradicts the usual periodization of Western history. It treats the history of Western civilization as a whole rather than as a history of individual nations. It attributes modern characteristics to what is generally considered to be a premodern era. It denies the predominantly feudal character of what is usually called the age of feudalism, and treats feudal and manorial law as complementary rather than antagonistic to commercial law, urban law, and royal law. It traces the roots of the Western legal tradition to a violent separation of the ecclesiastical polity from secular authority and to the formation within the church of the first modern Western legal system. In these and other respects the narrative recounted here must contend with widely accepted assumptions, views, and theories concerning not only Western history but also the nature of history itself. These assumptions, views, and theories presuppose a quite different narrative—one that is in fact not supported by specialized historical research of the past two generations. It is necessary, therefore, in the concluding pages, to confront squarely some of the theoretical obstacles to a full understanding of the formation of the Western legal tradition and to state some of the theoretical implications of the story told in this book.

Most educated people still divide Western history into periods of Classical Antiquity, the decline and fall of the Roman Empire, the Middle Ages, and Modern Times (starting with the Renaissance and Reformation). They tend to view Modern Times in terms of the histories of the individual nations that make up Western civilization, and they tend to look upon the Middle Ages as a background out of which Modern Times emerged. The fact that the Renaissance and Reformation of the fifteenth and sixteenth centuries were directed against an earlier Renaissance and Reformation of the eleventh and twelfth centuries has only begun to reenter historical consciousness now that the West is experiencing the end not only of Modern Times but also of the entire millennium of which Modern Times forms one-half. It is finally beginning to be more widely recognized that the earlier Renaissance and Reformation constituted the first great turning point in the history of the West, and that it was the source not only of the Western legal tradition but of other major aspects of Western social thought and social action as well.

The fallacies of the conventional periodization of Western history are closely related to the exaggerated nationalism of the nineteenth century, when "scientific history" first began to be written. Indeed, the raison d'être of scientific history seemed to be, in many instances, the tracing of the growth of one's nation from tribal and feudal origins to contemporary glory and grandeur. Today nationalist historiography is giving way in many fields. In law, however, and especially in English and American law, nationalist historiography still reigns. The distinctive features of each national legal system within Western civilization are emphasized and their common features are minimized. Despite their common origins, each national legal system in the West is still hailed by its partisans for its unique qualities, which are said to correspond to the unique character and the unique history of the particular nation whose law it is. Comparative legal historians have only slightly counteracted this tendency by their traditional division of Western legal systems into the "Continental European" and the "Anglo-American." Lately, a third "family" has been added, that of the "socialist law" of the Soviet Union and Eastern Europe. The truth is, however, that these are all branches of the same family tree. All Western legal systems—the English, the French, the German, the Italian, the Polish, the Hungarian, and others (including, since the nineteenth century, the Russian)—have common historical roots, from which they derive not only a common terminology and common techniques but also common concepts, common principles, and common values.

In addition to nationalist fallacies, legal historiography has suffered also from religious fallacies, both Protestant and Roman Catholic, which have obscured the continuity between the Catholic Middle Ages and post-Reformation modern European history. To these have been added also the fallacies of the Enlightenment, which discovered a Renaissance contemporaneous with the Reformation, as well as the fallacies of Marxist theory, which discovered a Rise of Capitalism contemporaneous with the Renaissance and Reformation. The obscuring of the continuity between medieval and modern has also obscured the *discontinuity* between the periods before and after the Gregorian Reform of the Catholic Church in the late eleventh and early twelfth centuries. As a result, the background of the Western legal tradition in the communitarian folklaw of the Germanic, Celtic, and other peoples of Europe of the sixth to eleventh centuries has been largely forgotten.

The story of the formation of the Western legal tradition has also been obscured by the emergence, in the late eighteenth and early nineteenth centuries, of another kind of historiography, which was closely linked to the new science of sociology. This new historiography is sometimes called "social and economic history" and sometimes "social theory." Its pioneers included Montesquieu, Hegel, Saint-Simon, Comte, Tocqueville, and others. Its later masters were Karl Marx in the mid-nineteenth century and Max Weber in the late nineteenth and early twentieth centuries. These "social theorists," in contrast to the "scientific historians," sought to explain history in terms of the social and economic forces that were at work beneath the surface of political and ideological events. They were viewed by the scientific historians not as "real" historians but as "theorists"; however, they were theorizing primarily about a real history, namely, the history of the West.

The social theorists of the nineteenth and early twentieth centuries were especially concerned to explain the revolutions which had periodically interrupted the course of social evolution. Marx, in particular, had a comprehensive concept of revolution, which is followed in this study; he saw revolution as a total social, economic, political, legal, and ideological transformation, and, indeed, a transformation of man himself.[1] However, Marx's historical materialism led to over-simplified explanations of the causes of the great European revolutions and to a limited definition of social classes based on their relationship to the means of production. Thus he misconceived the Protestant Reformation and he missed the Papal Revolution entirely. Moreover, Marx extrapolated directly from the history of the European nations to the history of mankind, without sufficiently taking into account the importance of intermediate cultures such as the Western, the Islamic, the Chinese. As Robert Tucker notes, "For Marx the real social unit is the species, the human collectivity . . . all social revolutions are world revolutions."[2] Thus Marx unconsciously identified the history of the West with the history of the world. His famous statement, "Revolutions are the locomotives of history," which was true of the West, was not true of non-Western cultures when he made it; partly because he did make it, it has since become true of some non-Western cultures.

Notwithstanding their rebellion against conventional historiography, the social theorists simply accepted the prevailing periodization of Western history into a Middle Ages that had begun at some uncertain time in the past and a Modern Age that had commenced roughly in the sixteenth (or possibly seventeenth or eighteenth) century. To this they added, however, a premonition that the modern period of Western history was about to be superseded by a new age.

The social theorists gave a specific content to the social-economic formation of the Middle Ages. They called it the age of "feudalism." The Modern Age, in contrast, came to be viewed as an era of "individualism" or of "capitalism," depending on whether social values or economic values were considered primary. The social theorists sought to analyze these successive types of social order and to explain how and why they had come into being. They used an historical and comparative method in order to create a universal science of social evolution. Marx contended that every society tends to pass from an "Asiatic" or slave economy to feudalism, from feudalism to capitalism, and from capitalism to socialism. This progression was seen by him as an inevitable consequence of the dynamics of class struggle. The concept of feudalism was critical to this theory, which postulates that out of the conflict between a peasantry bound to the land and a feudal ruling class there arose, eventually, a new conflict between an industrial proletariat and a capitalist ruling class, and that out of that conflict there is destined to arise a socialist classless society.

Many non-Marxists have also attributed a universal character to feudalism, seeing it as a stage in the development of many cultures. The Japanese and Russian cultures, in particular, are seen as having experienced feudalism during the "medieval" period of their history. The cross-cultural study of feudalism has yielded interesting and valuable insights; yet it is deceptively cosmopolitan. Behind it lurks the ethnocentric question, "Which features of medieval Western societies are essential to a universal definition of feudalism?" Most social and economic historians have stressed four such features: a subject peasantry bound to the land (serfdom), a specialized military class (knighthood), a fragmented public authority in the hands of a nobility dispersed on landed estates (lordship), and a distribution of power and privileges among the nobility through a system of vassalage and dependent land tenure (fiefs). They have then looked for parallels in other cultures. This might be called a form of academic imperialism.

Omitted from most of the conventional definitions of feudalism is any reference to (1) the belief systems of people living under feudalism, (2) the relation between ecclesiastical and secular authorities in feudal systems, and (3) the types of legal theories and legal institutions that prevail in feudal societies. These omissions leave one without any guidance concerning the general significance of ideology, politics, and law under feudalism — although, at least in regard to Western feudalism, there is no doubt that all three played an extremely important part in the social order as a whole. Even if, as most historical materialists postulate, ideology, politics, and law in the Middle Ages are to be viewed as a superstructure built on the economic base of the feudal mode of production, the crucial question remains, "How and why did Western feudalism produce a very different kind of superstructure from that produced by Japanese or Russian feudalism?"

For Marx the essential elements of feudalism were, first, small-scale agriculture with dependent land tenure ("the petty mode of production"), and second, a subject peasantry bound to the land (serfdom). These made it possible for the feudal ruling class to take the surplus value of the peasants' labor. Other aspects of feudal land tenure as it existed in the West in its heyday, such as vassalage, knighthood, and fragmented public authority, were not, for Marx, defining features of feudalism. He saw feudalism, as he saw capitalism, in terms of its conflicts, not in terms of its cohesion. Moreover, Marx was not interested in the fact that money and commerce played an important part in the economy of the feudal age in the West, and that in the twelfth and thirteenth centuries a flourishing urban civilization, with thousands of cities, coexisted alongside the petty mode of production. Contemporary Marxists, at least, do not—they cannot—deny that this is so, but they generally do deny that it has any great significance. They continue to rely on Marx's postulate of an unremitting antagonism between more or less static, self-sufficient rural economies and commercially expanding urban economies, resulting eventually in the overthrow of the former ("feudalism") by the latter ("capitalism").

Unfortunately for this Marxian analysis, the "feudal mode of production"—that is, the manorial system—had broken down by the end of the fourteenth century, all over Europe, and the "capitalist" mode of production, as defined by Marx, only came into being in the eighteenth, or at the earliest the seventeenth century. This leaves a "transition" period of some three or four centuries during which a central state power developed, namely, the absolute monarchies of Europe. It was the function of the new national states, according to Marxist theory, to repress the peasantry, "since the local organs of feudal power no longer survived."[3] Thus it is argued that although the political system changed completely, the social-economic system remained the same. "The ruling class," says a leading Marxist historian, "remained the same, just as a republic, a constitutional monarchy, and a fascist dictatorship can all be forms of the rule of the bourgeoisie."[4] This view paints history with a very broad brush indeed!

Underlying the Marxian interpretation of feudalism is the postulate that political rule is essentially a means by which the dominant economic class maintains its dominance; therefore, the form which political rule takes, and especially the legal form, is only an instrument of such class dominance. As Marx's partner, Friedrich Engels, wrote, "The jurist imagines that he is operating with *a priori* principles, whereas they are really only economic reflexes."[5] Economics, and more particularly the economic interests of the ruling class, form the "material base" of every society, it is maintained; politics and law are only part of the "ideological superstructure" that is produced by, reflects, and preserves the base.

This scheme is thrown into confusion, however, by the fact that law under so-called feudalism not only supported the prevailing lord-peasant power structure but also challenged it; law was an instrument not only for enhancing but also for restricting the power of the feudal lords. The first professional jurists of the West—professors in the universities, judges, lawyers in the employ of popes and bishops or of emperors, kings, and the feudal nobility—raised the question when and how the will of a ruler, if contrary to law, might be thwarted. This was not merely a philosophical question. It was a question that was built into the very system of political power that was then being created, a system characterized by what would now be called "checks and balances," derived from the dualism and pluralism of political authorities within the same social and economic order.

The more sophisticated Marxist historians will concede the existence of a tradition of "legality" in the West, and of "the rule of law," but with few exceptions they will assert that it has no fundamental historical importance.[6] They will grant, for example, as Rodney Hilton does, that the emergence of politically and legally autonomous urban communities in western Europe in the twelfth and thirteenth centuries distinguished "European . . . from other feudalisms."[7] But it would be wrong, Hilton then adds, to attribute to communal independence the development of a new capitalist mode of production, or any substantial change in the class relations of lords and peasant. Therefore, he concludes, it has no *theoretical* importance. He would say the same about legality generally. Law, even politics, from his point of view, is part of the superstructure, part of the ideology, that is, it reflects but does not *determine* economic forces in society. Economic forces constitute basic reality ("being"); law, by definition, does not—it is only part of "consciousness." That dogma dominates the entire argument.

Still, if different feudalisms—as Hilton indicates—produce different legal systems, what was it that made feudal law in western Europe, for example, so different from feudal law in Russia or Japan? What was it that produced in the West the *feudal contract*, with its mutuality of rights and duties between lord and vassal; the *fief*, with its grant of tenure on condition of rendering services; the *manorial court*, in which the lord of the manor, the bailiff, and other officials, on the one hand, and the peasants, on the other hand, regulated their conflicting class interests? It must have been something other than feudalism as such, since feudalism existed elsewhere without producing these legal concepts and institutions.

But more than that, the economic system itself developed very differently in western Europe from the way it developed in Russia or Japan. Therefore, might not the differences in the *legal* systems of those three cultures have played an important part in producing changes in the *economic* systems, and not just the other way around? If so, then the model of base and superstructure becomes highly problematical. In fact, the development of law in the West under what is called feudalism, including constitutional law, property law, and the other parts of the legal system, was an essential precondition for the economic changes of the seventeenth to the nineteenth centuries which Marxists have identified with capitalism.

The historiography is basic to the theory: if the historiography is wrong, the theory falls with it. If the main features of modern Western law, the main legal concepts and institutions and processes, emerged in the late eleventh and twelfth centuries—the heyday of what social theorists, starting with the Enlightenment and the French Revolution, have called the era of feudalism—then that fact in itself is a substantial refutation of the usual materialist view both of law and of history.

To persons who are not historical materialists, this refutation may be uninteresting. However, more than historical materialism is at stake. The distinction between feudalism and capitalism has become important to modernists generally, and especially to those who see the Modern Age as the prelude to a new and very different future. In that context, the concept of feudalism is translated into the concept of "traditional societies," or "preindustrial societies," which are thought to be more or less static, more or less natural, while capitalism—and now socialism—are associated with dynamic societies characterized by "modernization" and "industrialization." In fact, this seems to be the way a great many educated people see the world today.

But in reality western Europe during the period from the late eleventh to the early sixteenth century was a traditional society that underwent rapid and dynamic expansion and development in the economic as well as in many other aspects of social life. This contradicts the view held not only by many Marxists and neo-Marxists but also by many social theorists of other schools. Thus the anti-Marxist economic historian W.W. Rostow has argued that contemporary traditional societies in Asia and Africa are, in themselves, incapable of substantial change, and that in order to change they require an "exogenous shock" or a "take-off" produced by a sharp upward shift in investment accompanied by the emergence of a new entrepreneurial elite.[8] This corresponds to the conventional (but mistaken) view that the feudal economy of medieval Europe remained static until it received an exogenous shock from the urban and commercial expansion of the sixteenth century. In fact, a great agricultural expansion occurred in the late eleventh and early twelfth centuries. Historians now speak of a "first feudal age" and a "second feudal age."[9] Further, in the fourteenth century vassalage declined, the manorial system died out, and leasehold and other forms of property relations were used to create what much later was called "agricultural capitalism."

The English economic historian Perry Anderson has attempted to explain, from a Marxist point of view, the fact that only in Europe did capitalism arise out of feudalism. He attributes that development to distinctive features of European feudalism that are often considered by other Marxists to have been part of the superstructure rather than of the economic base. Anderson argues that the distinction between superstructure and base is not applicable to feudalism. In precapitalist societies, he states, "the 'superstructures' of kinship, religion, law, or the state necessarily enter into the constitutive structure of the mode of production."[10]

The recognition of the integration of law and economy in feudal Europe seems, at first, to threaten the whole Marxian analysis. Perhaps, however, the Marxian distinction between base and superstructure can be saved by another means, namely, by limiting its applicability to times of breakdown in the social structure. Perhaps Marxists could agree that normally—in all societies—economic and legal institutions entirely overlap. For example, property (ownership) has normally both an economic and a legal aspect, which are inextricably interrelated. But at certain times the two aspects may split apart, and Marx may have had such times in mind when he distinguished property in an economic sense namely, economic power, from property in a legal sense, namely, economic right. Indeed, the clue to a proper understanding of Marx's social theory may be that he interpreted all history in light of a theory intended to be applicable chiefly to times of revolution.

This would also help to explain Marx's transfer of nineteenth-century ideas of causation, derived from the natural sciences, to historical developments. He searched for scientific laws of history analogous to the scientific laws of physics and chemistry. He found such laws in historical materialism—for example, the law that in every society the mode of production determines class relations between owners and nonowners of the means of production, which in turn determine the political development of the society. This monistic formula, which seems to be an extremely oversimplified method of explaining complex events in normal social life, served two important functions in Marxian thought: it explained the revolutionary origins of existing institutions and beliefs, and it provided a basis for a revolutionary attack upon them. Today, however, ideas of causation even in physics and chemistry are more complex, and in social history it has become less and less possible to speak of laws of causation at all. It is both more accurate and more useful to speak of the interaction of politics, economics, law, religion, art, ideas—without separating these inextricably interrelated aspects of social life into "cause" compartments and "effect" compartments. This is not to deny that some kinds of concerns and interests are more important, and more influential, than others. It is not necessary to retreat from a position of determinism to a position of relativism. The truth, however, seems to be that economic factors are of greater importance in some times and places, political factors in others, religious factors in others, legal factors in others, and so forth; and that of predominant importance in all times and places is the mode of interacton of these various factors.

From this point of view, the brilliant though often obscure writings on law by the great German social theorist Max Weber (1864-1920) represent a certain advance over classical Marxist thought. Weber rejected what he called the "evolutionary dogmatism of Marxism,"[11] especially its assertion that all societies tend to pass through successive stages of development from "Asiatic" or slave economies to feudalism, capitalism, and socialism. He also rejected Marxist historical materialism, with its postulate of economic determinism. "If we look at the causal lines," he said in 1910, "we see them run, at one time, from technical to economic and political matters, at another from political to religious and economic ones, etc. There is no resting point. In my opinion, the view of historical materialism, frequently espoused, that the economic is in some sense the ultimate point in the chain of causes is completely finished as a scientific proposition."[12]

Moreover, Weber, in contrast to Marx, stressed the unique character of modern Western society and the "universal significance and validity of its direction of development."[13] He attributed the uniqueness and the significance of modern Western society to unique factors that had already been present in the premodern, precapitalist, pre-Protestant period of European history. For Weber, Western feudalism, the medieval Western city, and other features of "traditional" (as contrasted with "rational") medieval Western society contained within themselves forces that were lacking in the traditional societies of other world cultures, forces which were ultimately capable of transforming the West.[14]

Thus Weber was able to perceive the unique character and unique importance of the early development of Western law, as well as its significance for later economic development. Only the Occident, he stated, had experienced a fully developed system of folk justice, a legal regulation of status groups under feudalism, constitutional controls over princely power by the estates, the replacement of a system of personal laws by "natural law," and the successive receptions of Roman law. "All these events . . . have only the remotest analogies elsewhere in the world," he wrote. "For this reason, the stage of decisively shaping law by trained legal specialists has not been fully reached anywhere outside the Occident."[15] The existence of highly developed, rational, legal institutions was, in Weber's view, a necessary precondition of the emergence of capitalism. "Economic conditions," he wrote, "have, as we have seen, everywhere played an important role [in the development of society], but they have nowhere been decisive alone and by themselves . . . To those who had interests in the commodity market, the rationalization and systematization of the law in general and . . . the increasing calculability of the functioning of the legal process in particular, constituted one of the most important conditions for the existence . . . of capitalistic enterprise, which cannot do without legal security."[16]

In rejecting—or at least severely qualifying—Marxist theories of economic determinism and of a universal pattern of social-economic evolution, and in emphasizing the unique character and the "universal significance and validity" of the history of the Occident, including the history of Western law, Weber's social theory reveals its indebtedness to the author's early training in law and more particularly in the history of European law. His first postgraduate degree was in law, and his first work was in the Berlin law courts. Then he returned to the university for another advanced degree in law, writing his dissertation on the commercial law affecting trading companies and artisan guilds in the Italian and other European cities of the twelfth to fifteenth centuries. Thereafter, at the age of thirty, he accepted a full professorship in economics at Freiburg University, and two years later he became a professor of sociology at Heidelberg University. Although he subsequently achieved fame as a sociologist, and especially as a sociologist of politics and religion, his sociological theories always drew heavily on legal history, and among his most important works was a book on the sociology of law.

Karl Marx, by contrast, although he too (sixty years before Weber) had taken his first degree in law, studying in Berlin under Germany's greatest jurist, Carl Friedrich von Savigny, rebelled not only against Savigny's historical approach to law but also against legal history and jurisprudence altogether.[17]

Weber's influence as a social theorist generally, and especially as a social theorist of law, derives chiefly from his classification of all societies into various types. Each type of society embraces a corresponding type of economy, type of political system, type of law, type of religion, type of art style, within the society. Thus Weber was able to present an integrated portrait of the structural elements of a given type of society and of their interactions. However, the various types of society are not intended to be actual historical types but rather "ideal types," that is, models or paradigms. They are not usually to be found in history in "pure" form, he stated. Yet they are also not intended to be merely intellectual constructs. They are intended to correspond to some degree, however roughly, to actual historical experience. For example, the ideal type of law characterized by "formal rationality" is one in which law appears as a logically consistent structure of abstract rules, in terms of which the operative facts of a given legal case or problem can be identified and the case or problem resolved. This type of law serves the needs of a capitalist economy, according to Weber, and is illustrated by many features of the actual legal systems of Western capitalist countries.

Nevertheless, said Weber, the law of England, the leading capitalist country of Europe in the nineteenth century, was not characterized by formal rationality but was instead an example partly of the "traditional" type of law (resting on an established belief in the sanctity of immemorial traditions) and partly of the "charismatic" type (resting on the exemplary character of individual persons, especially judges). Thus it seems that the distinction among the three ideal types of law, formally rational, traditional, and charismatic, is intended, on the one hand, to clarify essential features of actual legal systems; on the other hand, when it fails to correspond to historical reality, Weberians can fall back on its analytical or "heuristic" value. The fact that a given system may fall partly within one and partly within another ideal type is not disturbing to them.

The ambiguity of the concept of ideal types is thus manifested in the use of historical examples to confirm them, coupled with an unwillingness to allow the use of historical examples to refute them. Weber himself wavered between their use as descriptions of actual social systems and their use as mere analytical frameworks.

In addition to the three ideal types of law—the formally rational, the traditional, and the charismatic—Weber also postulated a fourth, the "substantively rational." In law, formal rationality signifies the formulation and application of abstract rules by a process of logical generalization and interpretation; its emphasis is on collecting and rationalizing by logical means all the legally valid rules and forming them into an internally consistent complex of legal propositions. Substantive rationality, by contrast, accords predominance not to logical consistency but to ethical considerations, utility, expediency, and public policy.[18] The same distinction between formal and substantive rationality was applied by Weber to economic action; the former refers to economic calculability, the latter to the economic fulfillment of ethical, political, utilitarian, egalitarian, hedonistic, or other such values or goals. However, substantive rationality in law or economic action does not correspond to any historical type of society (although Weber saw it emerging in "the anti-formalistic tendencies of modern legal development" and possibly in a future socialist society),[19] whereas formal rationality both in law and in economic action is said to be characteristic of social action generally in capitalist society since the sixteenth century.

Similarly, traditional law is said by Weber to be characteristic of traditional societies, and charismatic law of charismatic societies. He defines "traditional" as "determined by ingrained habituation." In law, at least, the term "traditional" seems to correspond to what is usually called "customary." In "traditional authority," legitimacy is based on "the sanctity of age-old rules and powers." "Obedience is owed not to enacted rules but to the person who occupies a position of authority by tradition or who has been chosen for it by the traditional master." Law is not openly created; innovations can be legitimized only by disguising them as reaffirmations of the past. Gerontocracy (rule by elders), patriarchalism, and patrimonialism are types of traditional domination. Ancient China, Egypt, and Islam provide examples. Feudal authority, according to Weber, has many characteristics of patrimonial, and hence traditional, authority, though "Occidental feudalism is a marginal case of patrimonialism."[20]

"Charismatic" is defined as determined by "devotion to the sanctity, heroism or exemplary character of an individual person, and of the normative patterns or order revealed or ordained by him." This is perhaps the least clearly conceived of Weber's types of authority. The word "charisma" means "the gift of grace," and it was used in the early Christian centuries to refer to the power of healing given to a Christian by the Holy Spirit. The great German legal historian Rudolph Sohm used the term "charismatic" to refer to the concept of sacramental grace which underlay the law of the church prior to the twelfth century. Weber took the term from Sohm and applied it to all individual personalities "endowed with supernatural, superhuman, or at least specifically exceptional powers or qualities." Weber included among these not only "saviors, heroes, and prophets" but also magicians, shamans, and demagogues, arguing that "value-free sociological analysis will treat all these on the same level."[21]

Weber stated that rational authority, especially that subspecies of rational which he called bureaucratic, is "bound to intellectually analyzable rules, while charismatic authority is specifically irrational in the sense of being foreign to all rules. Traditional authority is bound to the precedents handed down from the past and to this extent is also oriented to rules. Within the sphere of its claims, charismatic authority repudiates the past, and is in this sense a specifically revolutionary force."[22] It would seem, then, that there could be no such thing as charismatic *law*. However, Weber avoided that conclusion by postulating that although "in its pure form charismatic authority has a character specifically foreign to everyday routine structures," nevertheless, it can be transformed into such structures; it can be "routinized." Indeed, since it is inherently unstable, it must be so transformed if it is to survive, becoming "either traditionalized or rationalized or a combination of both."[23] Weber found examples of such "routinization of charisma" in ancient Roman society, Buddhist and Hindu societies, the Roman Catholic Church, German kinship and village society, and elsewhere. At one point he suggested that all types of authority and of law were originally charismatic: not only what is right in individual cases but also general norms for all future similar cases were revealed by charismatically qualified persons. "Such revelation of law . . . is the parent of all types of legal 'enactment,' " Weber wrote.[24] Moreover, "characteristics of the charismatic epoch of lawmaking and lawfinding have persisted to a considerable extent in many of the institutions of the period of rational enactment and application of the law . . . As late a writer as Blackstone called the English judge a sort of living oracle. . . . "[25]

Weber's concept of routinization of charisma introduces a dynamic element into what otherwise is an essentially static model. Another dynamic element is the transition from traditional to rational types of authority and law, in which the corps of legally trained specialists of the traditional society plays an important part in systematizing law to meet the needs of the new rational and bureaucratic society. It appears, however, that only the Occident has actually developed endogenously from a traditional to a rational, bureaucratic type of society, and Weber finds the sources of that development in the unique events of Western history rather than in any general tendency or "law of development" of traditional societies. Weber declares that "from a theoretical point of view, the general development of law and procedure may be viewed as passing through the following stages," and then he lists several stages, corresponding roughly to charismatic, traditional, and formal-rational types; however, he follows this immediately with the statement that "in historical reality the theoretically constructed stages . . . have not everywhere followed in the sequence which we have just outlined, even [in] the Occident."[26]

If one disregards Weber's sociology and his classifications, and considers only his description of specific features of Western legal institutions, one cannot help being impressed by the enormous amount of detailed information that he presents about the history of Western law during the eight centuries of its development. He confirms many of the root facts that form the foundation of the present study: that the Investiture Struggle of the late eleventh and early twelfth centuries laid the foundations for the separation of church and state, that the new canon law of the twelfth century was the first modern Western legal system, that the reciprocity of rights and duties of lord and vassal distinguished Western feudalism from that of other societies, that the Western city of the twelfth century and thereafter was unique in conferring constitutional rights upon its citizens. Yet Weber is prevented from drawing the right conclusions from these facts by his historiography, which postulates a sharp break in the sixteenth century between the Middle Ages and Modern Times, and between feudalism and capitalism. For Weber, as for Marx, Western law is bourgeois law, capitalist law, or in Weber's peculiar terminology, bureaucratic law, formally rational law.

If one applies Weber's classification of ideal types of law to the actual legal systems of the West as they emerged in the late eleventh and early twelfth centuries one is struck by the fact that in each of those legal systems all four of his ideal types were *combined*. The new canon law, the new urban law, the new feudal law, the new manorial law, the new mercantile law, the new royal law — all emphasized the importance of rules and of logical consistency in the application of rules; indeed, if one concentrates on the law taught in the universities, one sees the seeds of the conceptual jurisprudence of the nineteenth-century German Pandectists, which Weber took as the apotheosis of formal rational, bureaucratic law. They all emphasized also the importance of precedent and custom, which for Weber was the hallmark of traditional law. In addition, canon law and royal law, especially, had strong charismatic elements, looking to the pope or the king as the divinely appointed oracle of the law; and the other systems, too, preserved many links with the divine and often the magical. For example, all relied heavily on oaths. Finally, Weber's concept of substantive rationality was reflected in the emphasis on natural law and equity, in the sense of reason and conscience, which required rules to be interpreted in light of their purpose and which overrode "strict law" in exceptional cases, protecting the poor and helpless and enforcing relations of trust and confidence.

It is likely that such a combination of the logical, traditional, sacred, and purposive aspects of law was and is essential for an effective integration of law into an organic unity — a body of law that is conceived to have the capacity for continuous growth.

It is evident that Weber's classification of law into ideal types does not in itself provide an adequate basis for a social theory of law. It is useful as an introduction to an analysis of the similarities and differences among various historical legal orders, but it does not explain those similarities and differences. It does not answer the question "Why did charismatic law become traditionalized or rationalized in one society and not in another?" Moreover, it does not even mention, much less explain, the fact that the Western legal tradition is itself a combination of all four ideal types.

Weber's own explanation of the uniqueness of Western law, and of the differences among legal orders generally, came not from his theory of ideal types but from his theory of politics, and especially his theory that the primary motive force in political life is domination, and the primary means of domination is coercion. It was the "diversity of political power relationships," he wrote, that was primarily determinative of the important differences among legal orders. Even differences in the nature and function of legal specialists in diverse cultures, to which Weber rightly attributed great significance, were explained by him as "largely dependent upon political factors," by which he meant factors of political power.[27]

Thus Weber remains in the tradition of economic and political history to which Marx also belongs, but in contrast to Marx he traced the underlying causal factors in history—despite occasional disclaimers—to politics rather than to economics. By the same token, he attached more importance than Marx did to the role of ideas in history. For both of these reasons he also attached more importance to the role of law, in which political and intellectual elements are always combined. But ultimately Weber traced both ideas and law to politics, and politics itself to domination and coercion. Charisma, tradition, and rationality were, for Weber, primarily sources of legitimation of political authority, whereby coercion could be more effectively exerted.

In addition to Marxian and Weberian types of social theory a third, much less complex kind of sociohistorical analysis has been developed in the writings of anthropologists concerning the rise of "state-level societies" in various non-Western cultures—among the Incas of the Andes, the Mayas of Mesoamerica, within the Islamic civilizations of the Near East, and in ancient Egypt, India, and China. Many anthropologists have returned to nineteenth-century evolutionary concepts, stating that small egalitarian bands of single families developed into larger tribes based on groups of families, and that these in turn evolved into chiefdoms with ranked lineages and ultimately into stratified, differentiated, centralized states. The most important causes ("prime movers") of the transition from chiefdoms to states are said to have been new technologies of irrigation, warfare, population growth, and trade. In addition, two other factors, much less specific in nature, are sometimes stressed: increased "cooperation and competition" among differentiated groups in the society and the "integrative power" of great religions and art styles. A representative view is that no single cause has been operative, but that in general the environment and the economy have been decisive in producing a "hierarchical arrangement of the members and classes of society which [in turn] provides the actual integration in states." "The critical contribution of state religions and state art styles is to legitimate that hierarchy, to confirm the divine affiliation of those at the top by inducing religious experience." Cooperation and competition, including the institutional structures and processes of law, are viewed as wholly neutral: "they can as easily function to maintain homeostasis as to promote evolution."[28]

The key to the emergence of these state-level societies is said to be "stratification," that is, differentiation between rulers and ruled, and, among the ruled, between various groups and classes. With stratification came conflict, and out of that conflict came political centralization; the state, in turn, was supported by logical, systemic explanations of the universe, especially through science and theology, as well as by logical, systemic social control in the form of law.

Although the authors of these anthropological theories have paid little attention to early European history, they have tended to assume that the emergence of the state in the West, together with its systems of theology, science, and law, followed a course similar to that taken in other cultures. In fact, however, there are several important differences between the emergence of a state-level society in the West and its emergence in other cultures; and these differences resist explanation not only by the anthropologists' theories but also by the sociological theories of Marx and Weber.

The first difference is that it was not "the state" that first emerged in the West in the late eleventh century but rather the church in the form of a state. Moreover, although the church was centralized, and had a centralized and systematized law, it only claimed to govern half of life. The other half was governed by various secular authorities which coexisted with the church and with one another in the same territory. The political and legal institutions of the secular authorities gradually became centralized and systematized during the two or three centuries after the emergence of the centralized church and its centralized and systematized law. There was cooperation and competition — sometimes acute competition — between the state-level church and the state-level secular authorities, as well as among the state-level secular authorities themselves.

A second distinctive feature of Western society in the first principal stage of its development was that dialectical tensions existed in theology, science, and law, corresponding to the dialectical tension between the ecclesiastical and secular political authorities. The tensions between this world and the next, between reason and faith, and between human law and divine law threatened to tear Western Christendom apart; and ultimately, in the Protestant Reformation, they did.

Third, the society was held together, and its theology, science, and law were given their logical and systemic character, in part by a unique sense of development in time, of ongoingness, of evolution — coupled with a recollection of a great revolution in the past and a premonition of revolution in the future. The experience of a dialectical interaction between revolution and evolution, taking place over centuries, is a unique feature of Western history. The church looked back to the Gregorian Reformation and to the founding of the *jus novum* by Gratian, and it resisted new reformations such as those advocated by Wycliffe, Hus, and the proponents of the conciliar movement; city-states looked back to the issuance of their charters of liberties, which were periodically renewed, and resisted or welcomed political rebellions and reform movements from without and within; kingdoms were caught in a similar dialectic of legal evolution, slow or rapid, with fundamental revolutionary change and the Last Judgment in the background.

Neither anthropological theories of stratification nor sociological theories of economic determinism or of types of political domination can explain these distinctive features of the Western legal tradition. They do help to explain the need or desire for *some* kind of legal order, but not the need or desire for the distinctive kind of legal order, with its distinctive dynamics, that actually emerged in the West.

Yet the theories of Marx and Weber concerning law, its history, and its relation to economics and politics, as well as the anthropological theories of the rise of state-level societies, deserve consideration, partly because they have been widely accepted (though usually in watered-down versions) and partly because they suggest answers to important questions. One is challenged either to accept those answers or to find better ones. If law is not primarily an instrument of class domination, then what is it? If Western law in its formative era was not an ideological reflection of feudalism, then what was it? If contemporary Western law is not based on private property, freedom of contract, and other institutions of capitalism, on what is it based? If the characterization of the Western type of law as formal rational, and of the social order which it serves as bureaucratic, is not satisfactory, then what characterizations would be more appropriate? If law is not part of the ideological superstructure of a society, built on a material base, whether economic (Marx) or political (Weber), then is one driven back to an unacceptable Hegelianism, which views history in terms of the clash and synthesis of ideas? Must one believe that Western legal concepts and values simply sprang into being by an intellectual or spiritual effort and were themselves an initiating factor or driving force in the formation of Western economic and political systems?

Both Marxist and Weberian social theory serve as a valuable warning against the temptation to resort to a purely ideological, or idealist, explanation of the development of law and legal institutions. The social theorists are surely right in their belief that the emergence of sophisticated modern legal systems in the West is not to be explained simply as the result of a clash of ideas. It was caused in part, to be sure, by a political struggle of persons and groups with conflicting ideas; it was the result, in part, of a revolution. But the question for social theory is, "What caused the revolution?" If the revolution is only recounted in narrative form and not explained, there may be a hidden implication that it was in fact only what it appeared to be on the surface — a political and ideological struggle of elites (the papal party versus the imperial or royal party). Was not the revolution also directly related to what was happening among the mass of people living in villages, on manors, and in towns? If the questions of power at the top and of official ideology were, in fact, directly related to social and economic life at the bottom, then the new legal systems that came into being may be explained not only as part of political and intellectual history but also as part of social and economic history.

Even the Marxist classification of law as part of the ideological superstructure may lead to a treatment of legal history in terms merely of the unfolding of official legal policies and legal concepts rather than in terms also of regulation of the social and economic life of the whole society. Law is seen by many Marxists as separate from the economic base; property as a legal institution is seen as separate from property as an economic institution; and although tribute is paid to the basic Marxist postulate that law is a reflection of economic class interests, what is treated under that heading is not the way law actually functions in social and economic life but the way it expresses dominant social values or otherwise displays its ideological character.

An important corrective both to an idealist conception of law and to an elitist theory of political-legal change has been provided by those historians, sociologists, and anthropologists who have examined legal policies and concepts, and legal institutions generally, as they manifest themselves in social life at the base of the social pyramid, that is, among the great majority of the people of a society. In the era of the Papal Revolution that meant the mass of tribesmen and villagers, free peasants and serfs, artisans, traders, parish priests, monks — as contrasted with chiefs, princes, lords, bishops, abbots, lawyers, scholars. A study of the structure of the lower echelons of society at that time shows that there was a close relationship, and an interaction, between what was happening at the bottom of the social pyramid and what was happening at the top.

More particularly, the system of competition and cooperation among ecclesiastical and secular authorities which emerged from the Papal Revolution could not have been established unless there had developed in preceding centuries a grass-roots group pluralism, with intermediate groupings between the mass of peasants and the top layers of imperial and royal authority.[29] Similarly, the political unification of the Roman Catholic Church under papal authority could not have taken place unless there had developed in preceding centuries a grass-roots community of the faithful, a *populus christianus*, extending throughout Western Christendom. In addition, the systematization of law within the various communities, ecclesiastical and secular, was possible only because there had previously developed an unsystematized, informal structure of legal relations within those communities. Lord-vassal relations — knighthood, benefices — had come into existence. Lord-peasant relations had survived peasant revolts and had taken form in a manorial economy. Rodney Hilton reports that as early as the tenth century, villages in Normandy elected delegates from regional gatherings to a general peasants' assembly, and, in addition, that in this early period there grew up the practice of negotiation between the peasants and the village authorities over labor services, dues, fees, and rights.[30] From the bottom up, each echelon was able, on occasion, to demand rationality from its superior.[31] This occurred long before law became a university discipline, long before there were professional lawyers and judges, long before the various bodies of law became systematized.

Thus the Western legal tradition grew — in part — out of the structure of social and economic interrelationships within and among groups on the ground. Behavioral patterns of interrelationships acquired a normative dimension: usages were transformed into custom. Eventually custom was transformed into law. The last of these transformations — custom into law — is accounted for partly by the emergence of centralized political authorities, when a conscious restructuring at the top was needed to control and direct the slowly changing structure in the middle and at the bottom. Law, then, is custom transformed, and not merely the will or reason of the lawmaker. Law spreads upward from the bottom and not only downward from the top.

Social theory must therefore accept a broader concept of law than that which Marx and Weber adopted. Law is, as they believed, an instrument of domination, a means of effectuating the will of the lawmaker. But this theory of law, usually identified with the positivist school of jurisprudence, tells only part of the story. Law is also an expression of moral standards as understood by human reason. This view of law, which is associated with natural-law theory, is also partly true. Finally, law is an outgrowth of custom, a product of the historically rooted values and norms of the community. This third view, identified with the historical school of legal philosophy, can also claim — like each of the other two schools — one-third of the truth.

By combining all three perspectives it may be possible to give better answers than Marx and Weber gave to the questions that they posed. Law is, in part, an instrument of class rule and an ideological reflection of the ruling class's interests. In every legal system examples may be found to illustrate that. But that is not all. Law in the West has also been a protection against the arbitrary power of the ruling class, and much in it that is derived from reason and morals, as well as much in it that is derived from earlier periods of history, does not necessarily reflect the interests of the ruling class.

Similarly, to say that Western law prior to the sixteenth century was an ideological reflection of feudalism is to point to only one aspect of that law. Other aspects — for example, the law of commercial credits to finance the wool trade or the spice trade in the thirteenth and fourteenth centuries — were a reflection of capitalism. Much of the law of the guilds was socialist in nature. A large part of the canon law of crimes, with its strong emphasis on retribution in the sense of vindication of the law, seems equally appropriate to any social-economic system.

Likewise, it is a serious oversimplification to categorize modern Western legal systems as ideological reflections of capitalism. Much modern law is more feudal in character than capitalist. Much defies any characterization in socioeconomic terms. A more complex system of categorization and characterization is needed, which will draw not only on types of economic and political formations but also on philosophical, religious, and other kinds of criteria.

To the question whether law is to be viewed as part of the material base or as part of the ideological superstructure, the answer is once again that in the West law is both — which is to say that Western law shows that the dichotomy itself is wrong. Law is as much a part of the mode of production of a society as farmland or machinery; the farmland or machinery is nothing unless it operates, and law is an integral part of its operation. Crops are not sown and harvested without duties and rights of work and of exchange. Machinery is not produced, moved from the producer to the user, and used, and the costs and benefits of its use are not valued, without some kind of legal ordering of these activities. Such legal ordering is itself a form of capital. Marx distinguished property as economic power from property as legal right, making the former a cause and the latter an effect, but this distinction rarely occurs in social-economic reality; generally, these are two interlocking ways of referring to the same thing.

Yet this is not to say that law is *only* social-economic fact, or that legal right is *only* another way of saying economic power. Law is not only fact; it is also idea, or concept, and, in addition, it is a measure of value. It has, inevitably, an intellectual and a moral dimension. Unlike purely intellectual and moral standards, law is required to be practiced, but unlike purely material conditions it consists of ideas and values. Moreover, the ideas and values of law are supposed to have a certain degree of consistency with one another — and also with the nonlegal ideas and values of the community, that is, with its ideology as a whole.

The fact that law is, in its very nature, *both* material *and* ideological is connected with the fact that law *both* grows upward out of the structures and customs of the whole society *and* moves downward from the policies and values of the rulers of the society. Law helps to integrate the two. Thus theoretically at least, a conflict between social-economic conditions and political-moral ideology, which Marx saw as the primary cause of revolution, may be resolved by law. It was partly in order to avoid that — for him, unwelcome — theoretical result that Marx reduced law to ideology.

Finally, law in the West — ever since the Papal Revolution — has had a strong diachronic element, and more than that, a strong element of tradition. Tradition is more than historical continuity. A tradition is a blend of conscious and unconscious elements. In Octavio Paz's words, "It is a society's visible side—institutions, monuments, works, things,—but it is especially its submerged, invisible side: beliefs, desires, fears, repressions, dreams." Law is usually associated with the visible side, with works; but a study of the history of Western law, and especially its origins, reveals its rootedness in the deepest beliefs and emotions of a people. Without the fear of purgatory and the hope of the Last Judgment, the Western legal tradition could not have come into being.

It was also Octavio Paz who said, "Every time a society finds itself in crisis it instinctively turns its eyes towards its origins and looks there for a sign."[32]

Abbreviations

Notes

Acknowledgments

Index

Abbreviations

CLS	Canon Law Series
D.	Digest of Justinian
Decretum	Gratian, *Concordia Discordantium Canonum* (*Decretum*)
Just., C.	Codex of Justinian
Just., I.	Institutes of Justinian
Just., Nov.	Novels of Justinian
MGH	*Monumenta Germaniae Historica: Auctores Antiquissimi, Constitutiones et Acta Publica*
Migne, *PL*	J.-P. Migne, *Patrologia Latina*
TRHS	*Transactions of the Royal Historical Society*
ZSS (germ)	*Zeitschrift der Savigny-Stiftung für Rechtsgeschichte, germanistische Abteilung*
ZSS (rom)	*Zeitschrift der Savigny-Stiftung für Rechtsgeschichte, romanistische Abteilung*

Notes

Introduction

1. This movement is usually called the Gregorian Reform rather than Reformation; however, the word "Reform" is a translation of the original Latin term *reformatio*, which in other contexts is almost invariably translated "reformation."

2. Lon L. Fuller, *The Morality of Law*, 2nd ed. (New Haven, Conn., 1964), p. 106.

3. Robert A. Nisbet, *Social Change and History* (New York, 1969), p. 1. In this work Nisbet attacks the application of such metaphors to social change; however, he does not deal with their application to the consciousness or ideology of a society in which social change is believed by those experiencing it to have the character of growth or development. In a later work he accepts a milder metaphor. See his *History of the Idea of Progress* (New York, 1980).

4. Sir Frederick Pollock and Frederic William Maitland, *The History of English Law*, 2nd ed. (1898; reprint ed., Cambridge, 1968), II, 561.

5. "Trespass" was a remedy for harm caused "directly" by the defendant's tortious act; "trespass on the case" developed later as a remedy for harm caused "indirectly," including harm caused by negligent misconduct and negligent performance of an agreement. See generally, Albert K. Kiralfy, *The Action on the Case* (London, 1951).

6. In the early twentieth century, the German legal historian and sociologist Max Weber confirmed the fact that the West had developed a method of legal thought that cannot be found in any other civilization. See *Max Weber on Law in Economy and Society*, ed. Max Rheinstein (Cambridge, Mass., 1966), pp. 304–305. However, he identified that method by only one of its qualities, which he called "formal rationality." This was essentially the method of nineteenth-century jurists, especially in Germany (though not, according to Weber, in England), who were concerned to construct a logically consistent structure of abstract legal rules, in terms of which the operative facts of a given legal case or problem would be identified and the case or problem resolved. This method was called by its nineteenth-century opponents "conceptualism" (*Begriffsjurisprudenz*). Max Rheinstein suggests that Weber set out, in his *Sociology of Law*, to determine whether legal reasoning so conceived was a cause or an effect of the rise of capi-

talism. Rheinstein himself said that the method was characteristic of the European Civil Law—as contrasted with the English Common Law—"as it was developed from the twelfth century on in the universities first of Italy, then of France, Holland, and Germany." *Max Weber*, p. 1i. Yet one only has to read the legal literature of the twelfth and thirteenth centuries, whether of the Roman law (Civil Law) and canon law or of the royal law, feudal law, or urban law, whether in Italy or France or England or Sicily or elsewhere in western Europe, to know that conceptualism in the nineteenth-century sense played only a part, and not the major part, in the legal reasoning of that earlier time. A great emphasis was also placed, in all the legal systems of the time, on deriving rules and concepts from cases, which is rightly said by Rheinstein and others to be a primary method of reasoning in the English common-law tradition. The papal decretals, for example, which were a major source of canon law in the twelfth century and thereafter, were essentially the holdings in cases decided by the papal court. In addition, a variety of dialectical methods were developed for reconciling apparently conflicting authorities, including exposure of ambiguities and evaluation of the prestige of the authors. Above all, the integration of legal systems was accomplished by the idea, apparently invented by Gratian, of a hierarchy of the sources of law: in the very first lines of his *Concordance of Discordant Canons,* written about 1140, Gratian said that in case of conflict, custom should yield to enactment, enactment should yield to natural law, and natural law should yield to divine law. This meant that customs, which were by far the most widespread form in which law appeared at that time, were to be evaluated in terms of reason and if found to be unreasonable were to be rejected. This was hardly "formal rationality" or "logical formalism" in the Weberian sense. Yet it gave a basis for integration of the various legal systems into developing "bodies" of law—not merely of rules but also of principles and standards as well as procedures and decisions.

More generally, Weber's classification of all legal systems into three broad types—Rational, Traditional, and Charismatic—is suggestive from a philosophical standpoint, but misleading from a historical and sociological standpoint, since Western legal systems, and the Western legal tradition as a whole, combine all three types. It may be that such a combination is necessary for an effective integration of law into an organic unity—a "body" of law that is conceived to have the capacity for continuous growth.

These matters are discussed more fully in the concluding chapter of this book.

7. See C. K. Allen, *Law in the Making,* 7th ed. (Oxford, 1964), pp. 65–66.

8. F. W. Maitland, "Why the History of English Law is Not Written," in H. A. L. Fisher, ed., *Collected Legal Papers of Frederic William Maitland* (Cambridge, 1911), I, 488.

9. Cromwell's Great Seal of 1648–49 was engraved with the words, "The First Year of Freedome Restored," and subsequent seals were identified as issued in the second, third, etc., years of "freedome restored." See A. and B. Wyon, *The Great Seals* (London, 1887), p. 36, and discussion in Eugen Rosenstock-Huessy, *Out of Revolution: The Autobiography of Western Man* (New York, 1938), pp. 300, 761.

10. That the name Glorious Revolution had the connotation of a return of the wheel to an earlier position is apparent from the enormous efforts that were made to preserve continuity with the parliamentary measures that had been taken

since 1640. Because a parliament was not in session in November 1688 when William of Orange and his wife Mary were brought to England to replace James II, it was felt necessary to call a session of all those persons who had been members of the last parliament. Also a terrible fuss was made to produce a new Great Seal to replace the one that James had taken with him and petulantly thrown into the Thames during his getaway. Everything was to be as it had been at some time in the past, or it would not be a "revolution."

11. President John F. Kennedy, in his book *Strategy of Peace,* listed seven peaceful "revolutions" which "are rocking our nation and our world." They were the revolutions in population, on the farm, of technology and energy, in the standard of living, in weapons development, in the underdeveloped nations, and of nationalism. In 1964 an Ad Hoc Committee on the Triple Revolution presented a statement to President Johnson on the Cybernetic Revolution, the Weaponry Revolution, and the Human Rights Revolution. A great many other "revolutions" are listed in A. T. van Leeuwen, *Development through Revolution* (New York, 1970), chap. 2. As van Leeuwen says (p. 32), the lack of clarity in the use of the term "is a characteristic phenomenon in itself." Its transfer from the political sphere began with the coining of the term "industrial revolution" in 1884 by a British historian as an analogue to the French Revolution of 1789, for which a parallel event in British history needed to be invented. See Arnold Toynbee, *Lectures on the Industrial Revolution of the Eighteenth Century in England* (London, 1884). It may be that the profusion of applications of the words revolution and revolutionary since the end of World War II, extending even to the most ordinary consumer items ("revolution in hosiery," "revolution in deodorants"), is a similar linguistic reaction to the Communist revolutions of the twentieth century.

12. This is a major theme of his book *Out of Revolution* (New York, 1938).

13. Rosenstock-Huessy lists a seventh revolution, the Italian Revolution of the thirteenth century, consisting in the formation of the system of city-states in the north of Italy. See *Out of Revolution,* p. 562. I have treated the rise of free cities as part of the secular side of the Papal Revolution, not merely Italian but European in scope. Norman Cantor counts only four "world revolutions": the Papal Revolution, the Protestant Reformation, the French Revolution, and the Russian Revolution. He gives no explanation for omitting the English Revolution and the American Revolution. Apparently these two did not meet his definition of a world revolution as the "emergence of a new ideology which rejects the results of several centuries of development organized into the prevailing system and calls for a new right order in the world." Norman F. Cantor, *Medieval History: The Life and Death of a Civilization* (New York, 1968), p. 300. His account of the Papal Revolution supports the account given in this book.

14. Thomas S. Kuhn, *The Structure of Scientific Revolutions,* 2nd ed. (Chicago, 1970).

15. See Crane Brinton, *The Anatomy of Revolution,* rev. ed. (New York, 1965), p. 16: "We shall regard revolutions as a kind of fever . . . When the full symptoms disclose themselves . . . the fever of revolution has begun. This works up, not regularly but with advances and retreats, to a crisis, frequently accompanied by delirium . . . the Reign of Terror. After the crisis comes a period of convalescence, usually marked by a relapse or two. Finally the fever is over, and the patient is himself again, perhaps in some respects actually strengthened by the

experience . . . but certainly not wholly made over into a new man." Brinton applies this "conceptual scheme," as he calls it, to the English, the American, the French, and the Russian revolutions.

16. Marc Bloch, *Feudal Society,* trans. L. A. Manyon (London, 1961), p. 60. See Chapter 2 of this study, note 1, where numerous other distinguished historians are quoted to a similar effect.

17. Joseph R. Strayer, *On the Medieval Origins of the Modern State* (Princeton, N. J., 1970), p. 22.

18. Norman Cohn, *The Pursuit of the Millennium,* 2nd ed. (New York, 1972), p. 281.

19. Ibid., pp. 10–11, 285–286.

20. Norman O. Brown, *Love's Body* (New York, 1968), pp. 219, 220.

21. *Out of Revolution.*

22. Rosenstock-Huessy, *The Christian Future* (New York, 1946), p. 70.

23. Rudolph Sohm, *Weltliches und geistliches Recht* (Munich and Leipzig, 1914), p. 69. (All translations are my own unless otherwise indicated. H. J. B.)

24. See Gerrard Winstanley, *Platform of the Law of Freedom* (quoted in Rosenstock-Huessy, *Out of Revolution,* p. 291): "The spirit of the whole creation was about the reformation of the world." See also Thomas Case, sermon preached before the House of Commons in 1641: "Reformation must be universal. Reform all places, all persons and callings; reform the benches of judgment, the inferior magistrates . . . Reform the universities, reform the cities, reform the countries, reform inferior schools of learning, reform the Sabbath, reform the ordinances, the worship of God. Every plant which my heavenly father hath not planted shall be rooted up." Quoted in Michael Walzer, *The Revolution of the Saints: A Study in the Origins of Radical Politics* (Cambridge, Mass., 1965), pp. 10–11. The sixteenth-century Reformation was conceived as a reformation of the church; a century later the Puritans were seeking, in Milton's words, "the reforming of reformation itself," which meant, as Walzer shows (p. 12), radical political activity, that is, political progress as a religious goal.

25. See A. D. Lindsay, *The Modern Democratic State* (New York, 1962), pp. 117–118; David Little, *Religion, Order, and Law: A Study in Pre-Revolutionary England* (New York, 1969), p. 230.

26. Each of these four men was charged with civil disobedience. Each defended himself on the basis of a higher law of conscience as well as on grounds of fundamental legal principles derived from medieval English law (e.g., Magna Carta). The trials of Penn and Hampden are reported in *6 State Trials* 951 (1670) and *3 State Trials* 1 (1627) (the Five Knights' Case). An extract of the trial of Udall, together with background information, may be found in Daniel Neal, *The History of the Puritans* (Newburyport, Mass., 1816), pp. 492–501. The trial of Lilburne is discussed in Joseph Frank, *The Levellers: A History of the Writings of Three Seventeenth Century Social Democrats: John Lilburne, Richard Overton, and William Walwyn* (Cambridge, 1965), pp. 16–18.

27. The theory of social contract is generally traced to seventeenth-century philosophers such as John Locke and Thomas Hobbes. But a century earlier, Calvin had asked the entire people of Geneva to accept the confession of faith and to take an oath to obey the Ten Commandments, as well as to swear loyalty to the city. People were summoned in groups by the police to participate in the

covenant. See J. T. McNeill, *The History and Character of Calvinism* (New York, 1957), p. 142. See also Chapters 2 and 12 of this study, where the theory of social contract is traced to the Papal Revolution and the formation of cities as sworn communes.

28. See Roscoe Pound, *Jurisprudence* (St. Paul, Minn., 1959), III, 8–15.

29. The Moral Code of the Builder of Communism is part of the Program of the Communist Party of the Soviet Union adopted by the twenty-second Party Congress in 1961. It may be found in Dan N. Jacobs, ed., *The New Communist Manifesto and Related Documents,* 3rd rev. ed. (New York, 1965), p. 35.

30. See *The Laws and Liberties of Massachusetts* (Cambridge, Mass., 1929).

31. Grant Gilmore, *The Death of Contract* (Columbus, Ohio, 1974), pp. 87–94.

32. Roberto M. Unger, *Law in Modern Society* (New York, 1976), p. 194.

33. Ibid., p. 196.

34. Bloch, *Feudal Society* (Chicago, 1961), I, xvi.

35. Ibid., p. xvii.

36. Christopher Hill, "A Comment," in Rodney Hilton, ed., *The Transition from Feudalism to Capitalism* (London, 1976), p. 121.

1. The Background of the Western Legal Tradition

1. See H. R. Loyn, *Anglo-Saxon England and the Norman Conquest* (New York, 1962), p. 292. In this chapter the word "feudal" is used in a broad, nontechnical sense; the discussion of feudal law as it developed in the eleventh and twelfth centuries is reserved for later chapters.

2. Ernst Levy, *West Roman Vulgar Law* (Philadelphia, 1951), pp. 6–7. See also Fritz Schulz, *History of Roman Legal Science* (Oxford, 1948), p. 273.

3. Wolfgang Kunkel goes so far as to call the *Leges Visigothorum* "thin and crude as a work of legislation." Kunkel, *An Introduction to Roman Legal and Constitutional History* (Oxford, 1973), p. 162. Kunkel states that "even in Italy jurisprudence declined to the lowest level conceivable. Modern scholarship has tried in vain to prove the existence in Italy of a continuous Roman law tradition of some standing." Ibid., p. 181. See also P. O. King, *Law and Society in the Visigothic Kingdom* (Cambridge, 1972).

4. Terms, concepts, and rules of Roman vulgar law played a part in strengthening royal authority during the Carolingian period. However, the surviving Carolingian lawbooks do not reflect a legal culture comparable either to that of the classical Roman law or to that produced by the revolutionary events that took place three centuries later. See Rosamund McKitterick, "Some Carolingian Lawbooks and Their Functions," in *Authority and Power: Studies in Medieval Law and Government,* ed. Brian Tierney and Peter Linchan (Cambridge, 1980), pp. 13–28.

5. The Salic Law may be found in English translation in Ernest F. Henderson, ed., *Select Historical Documents of the Middle Ages* (London, 1912), pp. 176–189. Slightly earlier than the Salic Law came the compilation of the Lex Visigothorum by King Euric (reigned 466–484), which survives only in a fragmentary state. Other "laws of the barbarians" include: the Laws of Ethelbert, King of Kent, issued about 600; the Edictus Rothari of the Lombard King Rotharius, issued in 643; and the Lex Ribuaria (of the Ripuarian Franks), the Lex Alemanorum (of the Alemans), and the Lex Baiuvariorum (of the Bavarians), all issued in the

mid-eighth century. At the close of the eighth century, envoys of Charlemagne recorded the laws of the Frisians, the Thuringians, and the Saxons. These laws and others (Scottish, Welsh and Irish, Norwegian, Icelandic, and Russian) are discussed in A. S. Diamond, *Primitive Law Past and Present* (London, 1971).

6. Laws of Ethelbert, sec. 34–42, 50–55, 58–60, 65–66. The Laws of Ethelbert may be found in English translation in F. L. Attenborough, *The Laws of the Earliest English Kings* (New York, 1963), pp. 4–17.

7. See István Bóna, *The Dawn of the Dark Ages: The Gepids and the Lombards in the Carpathian Basin* (Budapest, 1976), pp. 80–81.

8. See Diamond, *Primitive Law,* pp. 228, 273. The relationship of primitive law to the so-called Archaic Law of the Indo-European peoples is discussed at the end of this chapter.

9. This analysis draws partly on James R. Gordley, "Anglo-Saxon Law," ms, 1970, Harvard Law School Library. The terms of the analysis are drawn from Anglo-Saxon law, which, however, are almost identical with the terms of the other Germanic legal orders of the time and are remarkably similar to the earliest legal orders of all the Indo-European societies.

10. Laws of Ethelbert, secs. 8, 15.

11. See Raoul Berger, "From Hostage to Contract," *Illinois Law Review,* 35 (1940), 154, 281.

12. Gordley, "Anglo-Saxon Law," p. 23.

13. Claude Lévi-Strauss, *The Elementary Structures of Kinship* (Boston, 1969), p. 482.

14. Peter Brown, "Society and the Supernatural: A Medieval Change," *Daedalus,* Spring 1975, p. 135.

15. Quoted in George W. Rightmire, *The Law of England at the Norman Conquest* (Columbus, Ohio, 1932), p. 37.

16. Ibid., p. 36.

17. Quoted in Sir Francis Palgrave, *The Rise and Progress of the English Commonwealth* (London, 1832), p. cxxxv.

18. Jakob Grimm, *Deutsche Rechtsalterthümer* (1828; 3rd ed., 1881), introduction. See also Grimm, "Von der Poesie im Recht," *Zeitschrift für Geschichtliche Rechtswissenschaft,* 2 (1816), 25–99.

19. Rudolph Huebner, *A History of Germanic Private Law,* trans. F. S. Philbrick (Boston, 1918), pp. 10–11.

20. Ibid., pp. 11–12.

21. Gordley, "Anglo-Saxon Law," p. 31.

22. "Maxims," p. 48, Cotton MSS, The British Library, London.

23. *Beowulf,* lines 2140–41. See also *The Icelandic Saga: The Story of Burnt Njal,* trans. Sir G. W. Dasent, new ed. with intro. by G. Turville-Petre (Edinburgh, 1957), in which the spirit of heroism and vengeance is exemplified in dramatic proceedings before the tribal judicial assembly (the *ting*). A similar outlook is found in the earliest German poetry, the *Icelandic Edda,* which is filled with stories of violence, vengeance, and desperate heroism. Franz Borkenau emphasizes that the Eddic poetry is dominated by a strong sense of guilt and personal responsibility, in contrast to the Siegfried saga of the later *Nibelungenlied,* in which guilt is generally denied and the killer may be the hero. Borkenau finds a parallel between the Eddic emphasis on incest and family murder, followed by retribution,

and the predominance (in his view) of incest ("in an astonishing variety of detail") and of murder (especially murder within the family), among the crimes made punishable by monastic penitentials of the seventh and eighth centuries and thereafter. See Franz Borkenau, "Primal Crime and Social Paranoia in the Dark Ages," *End and Beginning,* ed. Richard Lowenthal (New York, 1981), pp. 382–391. The penitentials are discussed later in this chapter.

24. Loyn, *Anglo-Saxon England,* p. 217.

25. Ibid., p. 300.

26. Claude Lévi-Strauss, *Structural Anthropology,* trans. C. Jacobson and B. Schoepf (New York, 1963), p. 132.

27. See Calvert Watkins, "Studies in Indo-European Legal Language, Institutions, and Mythology," in George Cardona, Henry M. Hoenigswald, and Alfred Seen, eds. *Indo-European and Indo-Europeans* (Philadelphia, 1970), p. 321. Watkins gives several examples of complex legal concepts which are common to Indo-European peoples, including one, noxal surrender, in which there is a common lexical item (*sarcire* in Latin and *sarnikzi* in Hittite) occupying the same position in the same legal structures of two societies which had no contact with each other during the period in which they used the same linguistic term. (It refers to the surrender or redemption of a slave or chattel which has caused harm to another.) Watkins emphasizes that the coincidence of a linguistic equation and an institutional similarity shows a common origin when mutual influence was impossible for chronological and geographical reasons. His example "proves that the institution of noxality in Indo-European society must be as old as the community of Latin and Hittite, which is to say at the present state of our knowledge that it belongs to the common Indo-European period" (ibid., p. 333).

Some of the common features of the Archaic Law of the Indo-European peoples are shared by contemporary primitive societies; nevertheless, modern anthropologists have on the whole avoided the study of early Indo-European law, partly because of its positive implications for a theory of social evolution and partly because it cannot be studied "in the field." Diamond (*Primitive Law*) is an exception, being virtually the only contemporary anthropologist who has attempted to bring Archaic Law into juxtaposition with contemporary primitive law. He fails to emphasize, however, the most important distinguishing mark of Archaic Law when it is compared with most contemporary primitive law, namely, its emphasis on the central role of the court, that is, of formal adjudication (including both litigation and judgment) in the legal order.

28. J. E. A. Jolliffe, *The Constitutional History of Medieval England,* 3rd ed. (London, 1954), p. 24. See also Fritz Kern, *Kingship and Law in the Middle Ages,* trans. S. B. Chrimes (Oxford, 1939), p. 151: "Law [in the early Middle Ages] is old; new law is a contradiction in terms . . . all legislation and legal reform is conceived of as the restoration of the good old law which has been violated."

29. On the monastic movement in this period, see Christopher Dawson's excellent short treatment in *The Making of Europe: An Introduction to European Unity* (1932; New York and Cleveland, 1956), pp. 176–186. For a more detailed account, see Brendan Lehane, *The Quest of Three Abbots* (New York, 1968).

30. A story told by Anglo-Saxon chroniclers concerns the message of the Roman missionary Paulinus to the pagan king of Northumbria and his followers in the early seventh century. When Paulinus finished speaking, a sparrow is said

to have flown through the banquet hall, and an old counselor spoke. "The life of man," he said, "is like a sparrow's flight through a bright hall when one sits at meat in winter with the fire alight on the hearth, and the icy rain-storm without. The sparrow flies in at one door and stays for a moment in the light and heat, and then, flying out of the other, vanishes into the wintry darkness. So stays for a moment the life of man, but what is before and what after, we know not. If this new teaching can tell us, let us follow it." Bede, *Historia ecclesiastica gentis Anglorum,* ed. Charles Plummer (Oxford, 1896), II, 13.

31. See Heinrich Boehmer, *Das germanische Christentum,* in *Theologische Studien und Kritiken,* 86 (Halle, 1913), 165–280.

32. See Marc Bloch, *Feudal Society,* trans. L. A. Manyon (London, 1961), p. 83; R. Howard Bloch, *Medieval French Literature and the Law* (Berkeley, Calif., 1978), p. 19.

33. The Venerable Bede, writing 130 years later, said of Ethelbert that "among other benefits that he conferred upon his people, he enacted judgments for it with the advice of his councillors according to the examples of the Romans" ("decreta illi iudiciorum iuxta exempla Romanorum cum consilio sapientium constituit"). Bede, *Historia Ecclesiastica,* II, 5. Wallace-Hadrill points out that the phrase "iuxta exempla Romanorum" should not be taken to mean that the legislation was enacted after the manner of the Romans "but rather that Ethelbert followed . . . the Salic Law and various Burgundian, Gothic, and Lombard examples, which Augustine had brought with him from Italy." See J. M. Wallace-Hadrill, *Early Germanic Kingship in England and on the Continent* (Oxford, 1971), p. 37. Wallace-Hadrill adds that at least 19 of Ethelbert's 90 chapters have parallels in the Lex Salica, and that there are parallels with the other Germanic codes as well. He writes (p. 39): "The bringing of exempla witnessed the link that existed in Roman minds between conversion and law; it was so in Gaul, in Spain, and in Italy; and certainly in Kent."

Nevertheless, two leading English legal historians, in their efforts to disprove foreign influences on English law, have gone so far as to claim that Ethelbert's laws were "entirely pagan in origin" and were "probably" promulgated before the introduction of Christianity into England in 597. Henry G. Richardson and George O. Sayles, *Law and Legislation from Ethelbert to Magna Carta* (Edinburgh, 1966). In refuting this view, Wallace-Hadrill points out that Ethelbert's laws were within the body of a legal tradition that included Frankish, Burgundian, and other Germanic laws. Pope Gregory the Great, in sending a mission of forty men (plus interpreters), headed by Augustine, to accomplish the conversion of Ethelbert, wrote to the English king that by turning to the true faith he would be blessed by God even as the Emperor Constantine had been blessed. As Wallace-Hadrill writes (p. 29), the pope thereby "meant it be understood that the new convert was entering the family of Catholic kings of whom the emperor [in Constantinople] was the father. Papal and imperial correspondence of the period leaves no doubt about this . . . Politically this might mean little or nothing. But one certain consequence would be that the new convert would enter into the tradition of written law of which the emperor was the fountainhead. This is one reason why Aethelberht's laws must be dated after his conversion. Lawbooks were a Roman, and specifically a Christian-Roman, gift to the Germanic kings." See also A. W. B. Simpson, "The Laws of Ethelbert," in M. S. Arnold, T. A.

Green, S. A. Scully, and S. D. White, *On Laws and Customs of England: Essays in Honor of Samuel E. Thorne* (Chapel Hill, N.C., 1981), pp. 3–17.

34. See George Vernadsky, *Medieval Russian Laws* (New York, 1947).

35. Alfred also included in his laws the golden rule, do not unto others what you would not have them do unto you, with the addition: "From this one doom a man may remember that he judge everyone righteously; he need heed no other doom book." The laws of Alfred may be found in Attenborough, *Laws*, pp. 62–93.

36. See Dawson, *Making of Europe*, pp. 190–201. Under Charlemagne the Frankish state "was to an even greater extent than the Byzantine Empire a *church-state* . . . The King was the governor of the church as well as of the State, and his legislation laid down the strictest and most minute rules for the conduct of the clergy and the regulation of doctrine and ritual. . . The government of the whole Empire was largely ecclesiastical, for the bishop shared equally with the court in the local administration of the 300 counties into which the Empire was divided, while the central government was mainly in the hands of the ecclesiastics of the chancery and of the royal chapel . . . The control and supervision of the local administration was ensured by the characteristic Carolingian institution of the Missi Dominici, who went on circuit through the countries of the Empire, like the [later] English judges of assize, and here, too, the most important missions were entrusted to bishops and abbots" (p. 190). Dawson quotes Alcuin, the great Anglo-Saxon adviser of Charlemagne, who wrote that there were three supreme powers in the world — the Papacy at Rome, the Empire at Constantinople, and the royal dignity of Charles — and of these the last was highest because Charles had been appointed by Christ as the leader of the Christian people (*populus Christianus*). Alcuin changed the phrase *imperium Romanorum* in the church liturgy to *imperium christianum,* referring to Charles's own empire, which transcended both Rome and Romans.

On the "sacral kingship" in England, and on Alfred's role as head of the church, see William A. Chaney, *The Cult of Kingship in Anglo-Saxon England* (Berkeley and Los Angeles, 1970), esp. chap. 6, "Sacral Kingship in Anglo-Saxon Law." Chaney writes that "the most fundamental concept in Germanic kingship is the indissolubility of its religious and political functions . . . [The king] is not a god and not all-powerful, but he is filled with a charismatic power on which his tribe depends for its well-being. This is the king's mana . . . [which] permeates not the king alone but the entire 'royal race,' the whole kin from among whom the folk elect him" (pp. 13, 15). The sacral kingship was carried over into the Christian period; there was no division between the secular and spiritual spheres, and the king was Christ's deputy in both, who "must legislate on ecclesiastical as well as on secular matters — that is, on the totality of his kingdom's well-being under God and the king" (p. 192). "The king was still the head of the folk under divine auspices, and a separation of religion and royal function was as unthinkable as under paganism . . . The ruler was expected to play a theological and eschatological role for his folk" (p. 247).

37. VIII Aethelred 2, in Agnes J. Robertson, ed., *The Laws of the Kings of England from Edmund to Henry I* (Cambridge, 1925), p. 119.

38. Ibid., p. 43.

39. Rudolph Sohm, "Fränkisches Recht und römisches Recht," *ZSS (rom)*, 1 (1880), 1.

Notes to Pages 67–70

40. See Ernst Levy, "Reflections on the First Reception of Roman Law in Germanic States," *Gesammelte Schriften,* I (Cologne, 1963), 201–209; Levy, "Vulgarization of Roman Law in the Early Middle Ages," ibid., 220–247; Levy, *West Roman Vulgar Law: The Law of Property* (Philadelphia, 1951); Levy, *Weströmisches Vulgarrecht: Das Obligationenrecht* (Weimar, 1956).

41. See Loyn, *Anglo-Saxon England*, p. 292. "The presence of a kin capable of vouching for [a man's] good behavior, and of taking vengeance if he were wronged or slain, is all-important . . . If a man was in prison, his kindred fed him. If captured by his enemies after taking sanctuary, after siege in his own house, or after peaceful surrender in open country, his kindred were to be informed within thirty days. If he was taken in theft or accused of witchcraft or incendiarism, his kindred could stand surety for him. If the kindred refused to do so, he was condemned to penal slavery or to death. If he was slain during his first year as a penal slave, his kinsmen were to receive his wergeld . . . In case of death at young age the kindred took on responsibility for maintaining the heir . . . The kindred certainly possessed extensive authority over landed property . . . But for all its importance in these social matters, in ensuring a man's standing in law, in providing him with compurgators who would swear to his innocence or to his good name in court, the kindred took on its most spectacular aspect, and also its most significant, in relation to two closely related institutions: the payment of wergeld and the waging of vendettas. If a man were killed by violence then his kindred had the right to wage a feud against the slayer's kindred. Such a feud could be composed. The spear could be bought off; and the wergeld was the sum payable by kindred to kindred for this composition. It was the blood-price." Loyn is describing Anglo-Saxon law, but his description is equally applicable to Frankish law and the laws of all the peoples of Europe between the fifth or sixth and the tenth or eleventh centuries.

42. Kern writes: "[Customary law] quietly passes over obsolete laws, which sink into oblivion, and die peacefully, but the law itself remains young, always in the belief that it is old. Yet it is not old; rather it is a perpetual grafting of new onto old law, a fresh stream of contemporary law springing out of the creative wells of the sub-conscious, for the most part not canalized by the fixed limits of recorded law and charter . . . Customary law resembles the primaeval forest which though never cut down and scarcely changing its outline, is constantly rejuvenated, and in a hundred years will be another forest altogether, though outwardly it remains the same 'old' wood, in which slow growth in one part is accompanied by an unobserved decay elsewhere." Kern, *Kingship and Law,* p. 179.

43. There is a relatively small but valuable body of literature in English on the penitentials, including John T. McNeill and Helena M. Gamer, *Medieval Handbooks of Penance: A Translation of the Principal Libri Poenitentiales and Selections from Related Documents* (New York, 1938); Thomas P. Oakley, *English Penitential Discipline and Anglo-Saxon Law in Their Joint Influence* (New York, 1923); John T. McNeill, *The Celtic Penitentials and Their Influence on Continental Christianity* (Paris, 1923); and several articles by McNeill cited in the introduction to *Medieval Handbooks.* The role of the penitentials in the monastic movement of the sixth to tenth centuries is vividly portrayed in Lehane, *Quest of Three Abbots.*

44. See Bernhard Poschmann, *Penance and the Anointing of the Sick,* trans. Francis Courtney, S. J. (New York, 1964), p. 104.

45. Ibid., p. 64. See the Penitential of Cummean (ca. 650), in McNeill and Gamer, *Medieval Handbooks,* p. 98.

46. Boniface, the Anglo-Saxon monk who played a principal role in the conversion of what is now Germany, opposed the Celtic emphasis on private penance. A capitulary of Charlemagne of 813 contained the demand for "open sin, open confession," and in 847 the Council of Mainz ruled that there should be public penance for public crimes; but McNeill, *Celtic Penitentials,* p. 173, indicates that these provisions were not regularly enforced. Yet public penance continued to be practiced, at least as a wholly voluntary matter. Thus one tenth-century Frankish penitential states: "At the beginning of Lent all penitents who are undertaking or have undertaken public penance shall present themselves to the bishop of the city before the doors of the church, clad in sackcloth, with bare feet, with their faces downcast toward the earth." Regino's Ecclesiastical Discipline, Canon 295, in McNeill and Gamer, *Medieval Handbooks,* p. 315.

47. See Oakley, *Penitential Discipline,* p. 169. In cases of homicide, in addition to the usual types of penance the offender was required to satisfy the friends of the slain (this probably refers to wergeld) and to render service to the father and mother.

48. Cf. McNeill, *Celtic Penitentials,* p. 185. The earlier formulae were in the subjunctive: "Ipse te absolvat" or "Absolvat te sanctus Petrus et beatus Michael archangelus." In the first part of the thirteenth century it was common to use the declaratory formula, "Ego absolvo te auctoritate domini Dei nostri Jesu Christi et beati Petri Apostoli et officii nostri."

49. See McNeill and Gamer, *Medieval Handbooks,* p. 323. The formula "medicine for souls" goes back to earlier times. Thus the Penitential of Cummean starts with the words: "Here begins the Prologue of the health-giving medicine of souls" (ibid., p. 99).

50. This was the formula of Alexander of Tralles (525–605), the greatest medical authority of the period. Ibid., p. 44.

51. Penitential of Columban (ca. 600), A. 12, ibid., p. 251.

52. Ibid., p. 223.

53. Robert C. Mortimer, *Western Canon Law* (London, 1953), p. 28.

54. VI Aethelred 50, in Robertson, *Laws of the Kings,* p. 104.

55. See Dawson, *Making of Europe,* p. 190.

56. *Leges Henrici Primi,* ed. and trans. L. Downer (Oxford, 1972), pp. 81, 101, 143, 173, 177, 271.

57. Quoted in Doris M. Stenton, *English Justice between the Norman Conquest and the Great Charter, 1066–1215* (Philadelphia, 1964), p. 7.

58. Ibid., p. 8.

59. Stephen D. White, " 'Pactum . . . regem vincit et amor judicium,' The Settlement of Disputes by Compromise in Eleventh-Century Western France," in *American Journal of Legal History,* 22 (1978), 301–302.

60. Max Gluckman, *Custom and Conflict in Africa* (Oxford, 1955), pp. 1, 5.

61. Wallace-Hadrill, *Early German Kingship,* p. 151.

62. Kern, *Kingship and Law,* p. 180. Kern speaks of "medieval" law, but he is clearly referring to the folklaw of the Early Middle Ages, that is, the period prior to the late eleventh century.

63. The story is told in Robert E. Ornstein, *The Psychology of Consciousness.*

64. On the intuitive (including mystical and poetic) and the analytical as two complementary aspects of consciousness, and their relationship to the two hemispheres of the brain and the two sides of the body, see Ornstein, *Psychology of Consciousness.* See also Jerome Bruner, *On Knowing: Essays for the Left Hand* (Cambridge, Mass., 1962), pp. 2–5. Bruner relates the symbolism of the right hand to action, to law, and to science, and the symbolism of the left hand to sentiment and intuition and to heart. He notices the connection between the word for law in French — *droit* — and the word for the direction, "right." (The same is true of the German word *Recht,* the Russian word *pravo,* and the English word "right," which once meant law in the large sense, as in the old expression "common Right," and which still means a legally protected claim, as in "a property right" or a "contract right.") Bruner understands, however, that scientific knowledge — and presumably law as well — cannot be reached only with the right hand. He writes in his introduction: "Since childhood, I have been enchanted by the fact and the symbolism of the right hand and the left — the one the doer, the other the dreamer. The right is order and lawfulness, *le droit.* Its beauties are those of geometry and taut implication. Reaching for knowledge with the right hand is science. Yet to say only that much of science is to overlook one of its excitements, for the great hypotheses of science are gifts carried in the left."

65. See Paul Bohannan, *Justice and Judgment among the Tiv* (London, 1957).

66. Diamond, *Primitive Law,* pp. 61, 195, 317 (n. 10), 320.

67. See Henry Sumner Maine, *Ancient Law: Its Connection with the Early History of Society and Its Relation to Modern Ideas* (Boston, n. d.), p. 15.

68. Diamond, *Primitive Law,* pp. 47–48. Diamond also criticizes Maine for stating that the early codes "were mere collections of existing customs" (p. 45) and that in general "law is derived from pre-existing rules of conduct which are at the same time legal, moral, and religious in nature" (p. vii). Indeed, Diamond considers the latter proposition to be so discredited that criticism of it is "hardly necessary in these days" (ibid.). But Maine was almost always much more careful in his statements than his critics recognize. In the first place, he was speaking not of the Germanic codes but of the ancient Roman, Greek, and Hindu codes (the Twelve Tables, the Attic Code of Solon, the Law of Menu). In the second place, the proposition that historically "law" (here Maine does not say "codes") is "derived from" preexisting rules of conduct is self-evident, unless one is to assume that the earliest legal rules sprang full-blown from the head of some lawmaker. That those preexisting rules of conduct were moral and religious as well as legal in nature is what Diamond considers absurd; however, his argument is based on a confusion of "moral and religious" with "priestly" or "ecclesiastical." Maine's and Diamond's views are discussed further in notes 69 and 70.

69. Dennis Lloyd, *The Idea of Law* (London, 1970), p. 235. Lloyd writes (p. 232): "At one time the view commonly held was that in early society it was impossible to differentiate between legal, moral, and religious norms, since these were so closely interwoven into a single texture . . . The fact, however, that customary observances may draw upon the religious beliefs of the community and obtain from them a good deal of their binding quality, does not mean, as was supposed by earlier writers such as Sir Henry Maine, that it is not possible to distinguish between religious and secular rules in a primitive society . . . Rules which constitute religious taboos of the community, violation of which will draw

upon the offender direct punishment at the hands of supernatural powers, are often distinguished from rules which regulate the social and economic organization of the community and whose enforcement is in the hands either of some secular authority — the tribe or clan itself, the chieftain, or group of elders — or the next-of-kin of an injured person." The reference to Maine is misplaced because Maine never wrote that it is not possible in early societies to distinguish religious taboos enforceable by supernatural sanctions from rules of the social and economic organization enforceable by the tribe or the kindred. What he wrote was that the "secular" rules (as Lloyd, Diamond, and others call them) drew — as Lloyd admits — upon the religious beliefs of the community and obtained from them a good deal of their binding quality; drew upon them so heavily, indeed, that the rules and beliefs were, in Lloyd's excellent phrase, "interwoven into a single texture."

The difference between Diamond and Maine, and to a lesser extent between Lloyd and Maine, arises less from a difference in identification of the salient facts than from a difference in concept of the nature and purpose of law. Both Diamond and Lloyd consider the hallmark of law to be the imposition by governmental officials of sanctions for breaches of rules. Thus Lloyd writes (p. 235): "Broadly speaking . . . the vital contrast between primitive custom and developed law is not that the former lacks the substantive features of law, or that it is unsupported by sanctions, but simply that there is an absence of centralized government . . . there are no centralized organs either for creating law or for enforcing it." Diamond's definition of law, given in the text, is also essentially positivist: law consists of rules laid down and enforced by the state. Maine, however, considers the essential feature of law to be the existence of a group of men — in effect, judges — who have "exclusive possession of the principles by which quarrels are decided" (*Ancient Law,* p. 11). Maine was one of the first to show that a positivist definition of law excludes much of primitive law from consideration — and that, on the contrary, a definition which embraces all custom, regardless of its source and nature, leaves hardly anything out of consideration. Thus Maine, who in fact wrote little about Germanic folklaw, would probably have found its origin not primarily in the early codes, as Diamond does, but in the decisions, the dooms, of the folkmoots, which the codes reflected and guided. The rules of the Germanic codes, Maine would probably have said, were "derived from" preexisting rules of conduct which were at the same time legal, moral, and religious in nature. What made the codes "law" was the fact that they consisted of judgments and dooms that reflected and guided the knowledge of those charged with declaring and applying custom in cases of conflict. However, by showing that the Frankish and Anglo-Saxon dooms were an integral part of a religious system — the system of *wyrd* and *lof,* and of ordeals and compurgation — I believe I have demonstrated not only that they were "derived from" preexisting rules of conduct that were at the same time legal, moral, and religious in nature, but that in fact they themselves were "interwoven" with moral and religious beliefs "into a single texture."

Because of his definition of law, Diamond is led to treat the Germanic codes as themselves "the" law — instead of as part of a larger legal (and indeed, moral and religious) order. He goes so far as to argue that what was not in the codes could not have been important in the law, referring particularly to the fact that the

early codes contained little on procedure. Thus he states (p. 61) that "to the barbarian of the day rules of law and not the procedure were the essence of the matter—a simple truth that might have appeared self-evident but for a widespread
view of primitive law which well-known dicta of Maine have helped to spread
—namely that to early man [in Maine's words] a rule of procedure predominates
in importance over a rule of substance, so that substantive law has at first the
look of being gradually secreted in the interstices of procedure." The only basis
for saying that the matter is "self-evident" is that there is little about procedure in
the codes. However, the assumption that the codes were intended to deal with all
important aspects of the law is wholly unfounded. They were chiefly intended to
deal with those aspects of the law which required a statement of substantive
rules. The overwhelming majority of the provisions of the codes dealt with
homicide, wounding, sexual offenses (rape, adultery, and seduction), and theft.
Many things besides procedure were wholly omitted or hardly touched on. In
some codes, treason, for example, was not covered. Feudal relations generally
were omitted. Land law was hardly mentioned. The truth is that the formulation
of substantive rules stating the precise amounts of money to be paid for various
forms of injuries was an important part of the procedure of negotiating the settlement of interclan and interhousehold conflict. Thus it can be said, with Maine,
that the law of the codes does indeed have "the look of being secreted in the interstices of procedure."

70. Diamond, *Primitive Law,* p. 326 and elsewhere, states that law and religion
have two points of contact in primitive societies: first, certain wrongs may be so
abhorrent that they become both violations of law and breaches of religious
norms, and second, religious sanctions or the belief in magic may be used in legal
procedures to ascertain truth by the application of an ordeal or some other mode
of divination. Otherwise, he says, the law is wholly secular and essentially
unaffected by religion. These conclusions follow, of course, from his definition of
law. (See notes 68 and 69).

71. See Fung Yu-Lan, *A History of Chinese Philosophy,* trans. Derk Bodde, 2
vols. (Princeton, N.J., 1953). Heaven, that is, the natural universe, was said to
be in interaction with human affairs; heaven determines the virtuous and
punishes the wicked (ibid., II, 500–508). A good short summary of the meanings
of *fa* and *li* may be found in Derk Bodde and Clarence Morris, "Basic Concepts
of Chinese Law," in James T. C. Liu and Wei-ming Tu, eds., *Traditional China*
(Englewood Cliffs, N.J., 1970), pp. 92–108. The heavenly li, rooted in innate
human feeling, prescribe modes of behavior for the major human relationships of
father and son, ruler and subject, husband and wife, elder and younger brother,
friend and friend, whereas fa (law) obliterates the relationships by imposing a
forced uniformity. The li, created by the sages of antiquity in conformity with
human nature and with cosmic order, have universal validity, whereas fa is
merely the ad hoc creation of modern men. The rites and ceremonies of the li
give poetry and beauty to life, whereas fa is mechanistic and devoid of emotional
content. I am indebted to Y.C. Liu for an understanding of these insights.

2. The Origin of the Western Legal Tradition in the Papal Revolution

1. The concept of the Papal Revolution as a fundamental break in the
historical continuity of the church, and as the first of the great revolutions of

Western history, was pioneered by Eugen Rosenstock-Huessy in *Die europäischen Revolutionen* (1931; 3rd ed. rev., Stuttgart, 1960), and in *Out of Revolution: The Autobiography of Western Man* (New York, 1938). See also his *Driving Power of Western Civilization: The Christian Revolution of the Middle Ages,* preface by Karl W. Deutsch (Boston, 1949). Among church historians, see in addition Gerd Tellenbach, *Libertas: Kirche und Weltordnung im Zeitalter des Investiturstreites* (Stuttgart, 1936), trans. with intro. by R. F. Bennett as *Church, State, and Christian Society at the Time of the Investiture Contest* (London, 1959) (reprinted as a Harper Torchbook, New York, 1970). Tellenbach states (p. 111) that the movement to liberate the church from royal and other lay control, which he dates from 1058, constituted "a great revolution in world history," and that Pope Gregory VII "stands at the greatest — from the spiritual point of view perhaps the only — turning-point in the history of Catholic Christendom . . . He was at heart a revolutionary; reform in the ordinary sense of the word . . . could not satisfy him" (p. 164). In David Knowles and Dmitri Obolensky, *The Christian Centuries,* vol. 2, *The Middle Ages* (New York, 1968), p. 169, the authors state that in the course of the Gregorian Reform "there emerged in the West, for the first time, an organized class, the clergy or great body of clerks, tightly bound together under bishops who themselves were tied tightly to the bishop of Rome, with a law and interest that separated them from the laity, who were to occupy a lower place." "Speaking loosely," the same authors write (p. 260), "it may be said that it was the Gregorian reform that finally separated the clergy from the laity as two divisions within the church. This separation was emphasized more and more, and in a short time 'the church' and 'churchman' came to stand for the clergy as opposed to the laity." Even so strong a believer in the unbroken continuity of Roman Catholic history as Walter Ullmann, who wrote that Gregory VII was attempting "the translation of abstract principles into concrete government actions," nevertheless characterized the Gregorian Reform as "the first concrete application of these principles." Walter Ullmann, *The Growth of Papal Government* (London, 1955), p. 262. Ullmann wrote that the papacy in the second half of the eleventh century was not "a mere 'Reform' papacy" — it did not "restrict its objectives to the removal of certain evils and abuses." "What the papacy attempted was the implementation of the hierocratic tenets . . . " In other words, it was concerned not with "mere reform" but with revolution.

In his classic study, *Western Society and the Church in the Middle Ages* (Harmondsworth, 1970), R. W. Southern states (p. 34) that within sixty or seventy years after 1050 the outlook on western Europe's economic condition, religious ideals, forms of government, and ritual processes "had changed in almost every respect." "The secular ruler had been demoted from his position of quasi-sacerdotal splendour, the pope had assumed a new power of intervention and direction in both spiritual and secular affairs, the Benedictine Rule had lost its monopoly in the religious life, an entirely new impulse had been given to law and theology, and several important steps had been taken towards understanding and even controlling the physical world. The expansion of Europe had begun in earnest. That all this should have happened in so short a time is the most remarkable fact in medieval history."

An illuminating essay by Yves Congar states that "the reform begun by St. Leo IX (1049–1054) and continued with such vigour by St. Gregory VII represents a decisive turning point from the point of view of ecclesiastical doctrine in general and of the notion of authority in particular." Congar points out that the search for legal texts to support Gregory's position marked the beginning of the science of canon law, and that the mystique of Gregory's program lay in its translation of absolute justice, or divine law, into a new system of church law, at the heart of which was the legal authority of the pope. "One is actually obeying God when one obeys his representative," Congar writes. From the eleventh century onward, he states, ecclesiastical authority, and especially the supreme authority of the pope, came to be stated in legal terms. It was then, for example, that the term "papal curia" was first used to refer to the papal household as a law court, with authority to review automatically the judgments handed down in all bishops' courts. Yves Congar, "The Historical Development of Authority in the Church: Points for Christian Reflection," in John M. Todd, ed., *Problems of Authority: An Anglo-French Symposium* (London and Baltimore, 1962), pp. 139–140.

The great French social and economic historian Marc Bloch writes: "The Gregorian reform was an extraordinarily powerful movement, from which, without exaggeration, may be dated the definite formation of Latin Christianity; and it was no mere coincidence that this was the very moment of the final separation between the eastern and western churches. Varied as were the manifestations of this spirit — a spirit more revolutionary than contemporaries realized — its essence may be summed up in a few words: in a world where hitherto the sacred and profane had been almost inextricably mingled, the Gregorian reform proclaimed both the unique character and the supreme importance of the spiritual mission with which the church was entrusted; it strove to set the priest apart from and above the ordinary believer." Marc Bloch, *Feudal Society*, trans. L. A. Manyon (London, 1961), p. 107. Bloch also suggests at various points that the revolutionary spirit within the church was connected with a major social-economic transformation which took place at the same time, separating what he calls "the first feudal age" from "the second feudal age." "A series of very profound and very widespread changes occurred toward the middle of the eleventh century," he writes (p. 60), which "affected all the graphs of social activity." In addition to spiritual and social-economic changes, Bloch points also (p. 107) to "an immense cultural development" at this time and to a new way of thinking about society. Here he stresses the importance of the revival of jurisprudence in the latter part of the eleventh century, which "led to the recognition that the realities of social life were something that could be described methodically, and consciously worked out." The new legal education "inculcated the habit of reasoned argument no matter what the subject under discussion." As a result, by the end of the twelfth century "men of action had at their disposal a more efficient instrument of mental analysis than that which had been available to their predecessors."

During the recent reform movement initiated by Pope John XXIII, an increasing number of Roman Catholic advocates of radical change began to refer to Pope Gregory VII as the initiator of a new era in church history, one which they saw drawing to a close. See Hans Küng, *The Church* (New York, 1967), p. 384.

Among secular historians the significance of the Papal Revolution has been in part illuminated and in part obscured by the rediscovery of the "twelfth century" as the formative period of modern Western institutions, thought, art, etc. The English-language literature goes back to C. H. Haskins's *Renaissance of the Twelfth Century* (Cambridge, Mass., 1927). See also Marshall Claggett, Gaines Post, and Robert Reynolds, *Twelfth-Century Europe and the Foundations of Modern Society* (Madison, Wis., 1961); Colin Morris, *The Discovery of the Individual, 1050–1200* (New York, 1972); Sidney R. Packard, *Twelfth-Century Europe: An Interpretive Essay* (Amherst, Mass., 1973); Norman F. Cantor, *Medieval History: The Life and Death of a Civilization* (New York, 1963). The author of the last work speaks of the Gregorian reform as "the first of the great world revolutions of western history," which he places in a series with the Reformation, the French Revolution, and the Russian Revolution. This correctly identifies the period of fundamental change as about 1050 to 1150, rather than 1100 to 1200.

As Marc Bloch has written, "The appearance of the great epic poems in eleventh century France may be regarded as one of the signs that heralded the immense cultural development of the succeeding age. 'The twelfth century renaissance' is the phrase frequently used to describe this movement; and with the necessary qualification that the word 'renaissance,' literally interpreted, is apt to suggest a mere revival, rather than a new development, the formula is valid—provided it is not understood in too exact a chronological sense. For though the movement only reached its full development in the course of the twelfth century, its earliest manifestations, like those of the demographic and economic changes that accompanied it, date from the two or three decades immediately preceding the year 1100." Bloch, *Feudal Society*, p. 103.

Joseph R. Strayer attributes to Gregory VII, and to the developments of the late eleventh and twelfth centuries associated with his name, the origin of the idea of the modern secular state. See his *On the Medieval Origins of the Modern State* (Princeton, N.J., 1970), p. 22. This is one of the main themes of my book.

Revolutionary changes in the constitutional and legal structure of European polities in the period after the Investiture Struggle are traced in detail in Heinrich Mitteis' important book, *Der Staat des hohen Mittelalters: Grundlinien einer vergleichenden Verfassungsgeschichte des Lehnzeitalters,* 4th ed. (Weimar, 1953), translated by H. F. Orton under the title *The State in the Middle Ages: A Comparative Constitutional History of Feudal Europe* (Amsterdam, 1975). Mitteis does not hesitate to speak of a "constitutional revolution" during this period and of a "revolution in political thought" as well as of "revolutionary changes" in law. Much of the same ground is covered in Walter Ullmann's important book, *Law and Politics in the Middle Ages* (London, 1975), although Ullmann does not make such a sharp division between the periods before and after the Investiture Struggle.

See also Peter Brown, "Society and the Supernatural: A Medieval Change," *Daedalus,* Spring 1975, p. 133, where a catalogue of fundamental changes is given that could serve as a table of contents of the present chapter. Brown writes (pp. 133–134) of "the sudden emergence of a new relationship between the clergy and laity in the time of the Investiture Contest (a contest connected with the name of one great pope—Gregory VII [1073–1085]—but in reality a process as widespread and ineluctable as a change in the tide of Western society). In the course of the eleventh century the feudal knightly class emerges as a distinct group, while, in the twelfth century, the facts of urban life and of a new-style mercantile professionalism had come to stay . . . We find novel departures in forms of law and organization: the emergence of written codes after centuries of customary, oral law, the reception of Roman law at the Schools of Bologna, and the codification of the canon law and theology of the Christian church (in the *Decretum* of Gratian, *ca.* 1140, and the Sentences of Peter the Lombard, *ca.* 1150) . . . Innumerable novel ventures in administration and constant experimentation in new forms of social organization cover the face of Europe of the twelfth century. Finally . . . we find a probing of modes of self-expression."

Despite this array of authority, the conventional view remains one of skepticism concerning any fundamental break in the historical continuity of Europe during the so-called Middle Ages. Sidney R. Packard writes: "Although a comparison of European governments in 1100 and in 1200 will reveal many and important differences, the attempts of some writers to dream up yet another 'revolution' in this area seem to rest on the shakiest of evidence." Packard, *Twelfth-Century Europe,* p. 321. Perhaps even such faith in the perpetual gradualness of change may be upset by the very substantial evidence, presented here, of the emergence of new legal systems throughout Europe in the century and a half between about 1075 and 1225.

2. Brown, "Society and the Supernatural," p. 134.

3. Emperor Henry III justified his deposition of three popes in 1046 on the ground that he was the vicar of Christ. See Southern, *Western Society,* pp. 104–105. Later Henry IV wrote to Pope Gregory VII: "You have dared to touch me . . . whom, according to the traditions of the Holy Fathers, God alone can judge." See Geoffrey Barraclough, "The Investiture Contest and the German Constitution," in Schafer Williams, ed., *The Gregorian Epoch: Reformation, Revolution, Reaction?* (Lexington, Mass., 1964), p. 63.

4. See Rosenstock-Huessy, *Out of Revolution,* p. 506. David Knowles writes that Cluny did not become fully centralized until the eleventh century, and that in practice it was much more loosely organized than the Cistercian order became in the twelfth century. Quoted in Williams, *The Gregorian Epoch,* p. 39.

5. See F. L. Ganshof, *The Imperial Coronation of Charlemagne* (Glasgow, 1971).

6. Brian Tierney, *The Crisis of Church and State, 1050–1300, with Selected Documents* (Englewood Cliffs, N.J., 1964), pp. 13–14. Documentation supporting much of this chapter can be found in Tierney's book. See also Brian Tierney and Sidney Painter, *Western Europe in the Middle Ages, 300–1475* (New York, 1978).

7. Tierney, *Crisis of Church and State,* p. 227.

8. R. F. Bennett, in his introduction to Tellenbach, *Church, State,* pp. xiv–xv.

9. Quoted by Orville Prescott, *Lords of Italy: Portraits from the Middle Ages* (New York, 1972), p. 43.

10. K. J. Leyser, "The Polemics of the Papal Revolution," in Beryl Smalley, ed., *Trends in Medieval Political Thought* (Oxford, 1965), p. 53.

11. Quoted ibid., p. 42. See also Karl F. Morrison, *Tradition and Authority in the Western Church, 300–1140* (Princeton, N.J., 1969), pp. 294–295: "Leo IX had witnessed violent protests against his prohibitions of [simony and nicolaism] at synods in Rome and Mantua. But Gregory's decrees against simony prompted resistance of that sort throughout Europe . . . A similar reaction met his decrees on clerical celebacy. In 1059, Peter Damian's attempt to enforce clerical celibacy in Milan led to a popular uprising, and the Roman clergy under Stephen IX considered clerical continence 'vain and frivolous.' When the Bishop of Brescia

read Nicholas II's prohibition of marriage among the clergy, his clergy beat him to the point of death. Gregory's decrees met the same reception. For his defense of Gregory's prohibition, an abbot was set upon in the Synod of Paris, and the Archbishop of Rouen's clergy stoned him out of his church. The clergy of Cambrai was in open rebellion. Similar conditions prevailed in some German churches."

12. The Latin text of the *Dictatus Papae* is in Karl Hofmann, *Der Dictatus Papae Gregors VII* (Paderborn, 1933), p. 11. The *Dictatus Papae* may be found in English translation in S. Z. Ehler and J. B. Morrall, *Church and State through the Centuries* (London, 1954), pp. 43–44, reproduced in Tierney, *Crisis of Church and State,* pp. 49–50.

13. See Augustine Fliche, *La réforme Gregorienne,* II (Paris, 1933), 202. It is now generally supposed that the twenty-seven propositions were a table of contents for a subsequent documented text, which, however, was never written.

14. The letter is reproduced in Tierney, *Crisis of Church and State,* pp. 59–60.

15. The decree is reproduced in *The Correspondence of Pope Gregory VII: Selected Letters from the Registrum,* ed. and trans. Ephraim Emerton (1932; reprint ed., New York, 1969), p. 133.

16. Gregory wrote to William the Conqueror: "If I, therefore, am to answer for you on the dreadful day of judgment before the just Judge who cannot lie, the creator of every creature, bethink you whether I must not very diligently provide for your salvation, and whether for your own safety you ought not without delay obey me, so that you may possess the land of the living." Quoted in James Bryce, *The Holy Roman Empire* (New York, 1886), pp. 157–158.

17. Gabriel Le Bras, "Canon Law," in C. G. Crump and E. F. Jacob, eds., *The Legacy of the Middle Ages* (Oxford, 1926), pp. 333–334.

18. See E. Bernheim, "Politische Begriffe des Mittelalters im Lichte der Anschauungen Augustins," *Deutsche Zeitschrift für Geschichte,* n.s. 1 (1896–1897), 7. (The pope as Christ's vicar on earth is "debitor justiciae in omnibus qui in Christo sunt — curia totius christianitatis.")

19. This is a major theme of Rosenstock-Huessy's *Out of Revolution.*

20. Southern, *Western Society,* p. 27. Southern points out (ibid.) that "both the Greek and the Islamic systems were immensely richer, more powerful, and intellectually more sophisticated than that of Western Europe. The West was the poor relation of Byzantium."

21. From 1074 on, Pope Gregory VII promoted the idea of an army organized under the papacy that would free the Christians of the East from domination by the Turkish infidels. In launching the First Crusade, Pope Urban II considered that he was following in the path charted by Gregory. See Carl Erdmann, *Die Entstehung des Kreuzzugsgedankens* (Stuttgart, 1936), pp. 149–153, 210–211, 285–286, 308–309. One purpose of the crusades, beyond the liberation of the burial place of Christ from the Moslem infidels, was to export the Papal Revolution to Eastern Christendom. In some instances, Eastern Orthodox Christians were engaged in battle by the crusaders. The pope declared his supremacy over Constantinople and the entire Christian world. Ultimately, however, this purpose was not achieved. In 1099 the crusaders founded the Kingdom of Jerusalem, subordinate to the papacy. However, the Second Crusade (1147–1149) was altogether without result; and the Third Crusade

(1189–1192), although it succeeded in taking Acre, was unable to retake Jerusalem, which had been captured by Saladin in 1187. The Fourth Crusade, launched in 1199, culminated in an attack on Constantinople in 1203 and the deposition and replacement of the emperor by the crusaders. (Jerusalem was not even approached.) There were four more crusades in the thirteenth century, all of them substantial failures (although Frederick II regained Jerusalem for a short time in 1228–29). Nevertheless, the crusades accomplished important domestic political results. They reflected and kept alive the ideology of the Papal Revolution. They expanded trade and contributed to the development of great Italian trading cities such as Venice, Genoa, and Pisa. They strengthened the power of the papacy. Finally, they helped to create a class of military aristocracy—the knights—which was Christian and European in character.

22. Southern, *Western Society*, pp. 34–35. Southern adds: "There was no single outstanding technical innovation behind this expansive movement, but a combination of many circumstances: growing accumulation of capital, rising population, the return of the Mediterranean to Western control, the political decline of the Greek and Moslem empires, all helped to open up ever-enlarging prospects to the West." More specifically, Southern mentions the settlement of waste lands, the improvement of rivers, roads, and canals, and the organization of markets and credit. "Colonization began on all the frontiers of Western Europe, and with colonization there began the familiar process of military aggression. For the first time in its history Western Europe became an area of surplus population and surplus productivity . . . For two centuries after 1100 the West was in the grip of an urge for power and mastery to which there appeared no obvious limit." Southern's view that "there was no single outstanding technical innovation behind this expansive movement" is disputed by Lynn White (see note 23).

23. Lynn White, *Medieval Technology and Social Change* (Oxford, 1961), pp. 57–69. White points to the importance of the invention of the horse collar, which made it possible for the first time to use horse power on a large scale (pp. 72–76). The wider use of farm horses was connected with the introduction of a spring planting and a triennial crop rotation, which made it possible substantially to increase the food supply. M.-D. Chenu writes concerning technological advances in the twelfth century that "the production of energy made enormous strides with the perfecting and spread of machines to harness waterpower and to produce circular motion: mill wheels; hydraulic wheels, which enabled one horse to do the work that formerly required twenty-five; windmills, first used in Europe in 1105; machines that could store power through a system of weights and geared wheels . . . New means of transport and travel gave men increased freedom: the early invention of the draft collar for horses or oxen transformed rural life; the use of the keel and rudder dates from 1180; and the compass allowed long voyages by sea . . . The mechanical clock began to rationalize time . . . " M.-D. Chenu, *Nature, Man, and Society in the Twelfth Century*, ed. and trans. Jerome Taylor and Lester K. Little (Chicago, 1968), p. 43 (first published 1957 as *La théologie au douzième siècle*).

24. See chapter 3 on the origins of Western legal science. Chenu, *Nature, Man, and Society*, pp. 16–17, points out that Abelard, in the early decades of the twelfth century, made a "rigorous distinction" between those things that were attributable to the creative activity of God in constituting the world, on the one

hand, and, on the other hand, the "natural causes" which "account for the constitution or development of those things that originate without miracles." He spoke of the latter as *vis naturae* ("the force of nature") and *naturales causae* ("natural causes").

25. See Marc Bloch, *Feudal Society,* pp. 93, 103. A pathbreaking study of interconnections between the new literature of the late eleventh and early twelfth centuries and the contemporaneous development of law is R. Howard Bloch, *Medieval French Literature and Law* (Berkeley, 1977).

26. Charlemagne had amended the Nicene Creed by inserting the words, "and from the Son" (*filioque*), after the words, "I believe in the Holy Spirit . . . who proceeds from the Father." This was offensive to the Eastern Church both because it represented a new conception of the Trinity and because it was a unilateral amendment of the most important declaration of the most important ecumenical council in the history of the church. See Chapter 4 at note 28.

27. Peter Brown, in Smalley, *Trends,* p. 11.

28. Ibid., p. 12.

29. *De Civitate Dei* 1. 35. 46. See R. A. Markus, *Saeculum: History and Society in the Theology of St. Augustine* (Cambridge, 1970), pp. 20–21: "one of the fundamental themes of his reflection on history [is] that since the coming of Christ until the end of the world, all history is homogeneous, that it cannot be mapped out in terms of a pattern drawn from sacred history." See also G. L. Keyes, *Christian Faith and the Interpretation of History* (Lincoln, Nebr., 1966), pp. 177–178: The Christian "has no hope of an earthly state much better, from a Christian point of view, than the one he sees before him, much less of a progressive realization of the Kingdom of God on earth."

30. Quoted in Tierney, *Crisis of Church and State,* pp. 68–69, 71.

31. Quoted in Eugen Rosenstock-Huessy, *Soziologie,* II (Stuttgart, 1958), 663.

32. Quoted ibid., p. 662.

33. See *Policraticus: The Statesman's Book of John of Salisbury,* trans. John Dickinson (New York, 1963), p. 9.

34. K. J. Leyser, in Smalley, *Trends,* p. 60.

35. See Chenu, *Nature, Man, and Society,* pp. 162–201. Chenu states (p. 162) that "it was not the least splendid achievement of Latin Christendom in the twelfth century to awaken in men's minds an active awareness of human history." See also R. W. Southern, "Aspects of the European Tradition of Historical Writing. 2. Hugh St. Victor and the Idea of Historical Development," *TRHS,* 5th ser., 21 (1971), 159. Walter Freund stresses the use of the concept of modernity in the writings of Peter Damian, John of Salisbury, Walter Map, and other twelfth-century authors. Walter Freund, *Modernus und andere Zeitbegriffe des Mittelalters* (Cologne, 1957). He traces this in part (p. 60) to the belief of the Gregorian reformers of the late eleventh century that they were entering wholly new and unprecedented times.

36. See Geoffrey Barraclough, *The Origins of Modern Germany* (Oxford, 1947), p. 114: "Turning its back on the old Gelasian theory of the harmonious cooperation of the two great powers [spiritual and secular], the Hildebrandine party sought a separation of Church and State, involving a complete change in the position of the king in Christian society. It did not necessarily mean his subordination to the pope, although Gregory soon drew this positive conclusion from

his own arguments; but it did mean necessarily that the king's sacerdotal position and character were challenged. For Gregory, the king was a removable official."

In 1302 Pope Boniface VIII carried Gregory's view still further, stating: "He who denies that the secular sword is in the power of Peter does not understand the words of the Lord." This view corresponds to the doctrine of the "plenitude of power" (*plenitudo potestatis*) of the pope as vicar of Christ on earth. However, whereas the spiritual sword was wielded by the pope directly, the secular sword was wielded through the agency of kings and princes. Southern, *Western Society,* p. 143. See also Tierney, *Crisis of Church and State,* pp. 183, 188–189. See Chapter 7.

37. On the transformation of the nature of episcopal authority as a result of the Investiture Struggle, see generally Robert L. Benson, *The Bishop-Elect: A Study in Medieval Ecclesiastical Office* (Princeton, N.J., 1968). Benson analyzes much of the source material that forms the basis of this chapter.

38. The first phrase is from Rosenstock's *Europäischen Revolutionen* (1931). The second is from Tellenbach's *Libertas: Kirche und Weltordnung* (1936). The phrase used by the eleventh-century reformers was simply "right order."

3. The Origin of Western Legal Science in the European Universities

1. See Samuel E. Thorne, ed. and trans., *Bracton on the Laws and Customs of England,* I (Cambridge, Mass., 1968), xxxvi. Thorne convincingly refutes Maitland's view that Bracton was a "bad Romanist."

2. Haskins writes: "There were other centres of legal study before Bologna, such as Rome, Pavia, and Ravenna, there were Bolognese jurists before Irnerius, notably Pepo, 'bright and shining light of Bologna,' who is found perhaps in 1065 and certainly in 1076 in the decision of the very case where the Digest first reappears . . ." Charles Haskins, *The Renaissance of the Twelfth Century* (Cambridge, Mass., 1927), p. 199. Nevertheless, as Haskins also states, it was Irnerius who "separated law finally from rhetoric and gave it full status as an independent subject of study, based no longer upon extracts and outlines but upon the text of the Corpus Juris, the whole of which could now be used to explain every part." This last phrase is the key to the present chapter.

The best account in English of the law school at Bologna is Hastings Rashdall, *The Universities of Europe in the Middle Ages* (Oxford, 1936), I, 87–267. The classic work on the subject remains Friedrich Carl von Savigny, *Geschichte des römischen Rechts im Mittelalter,* 2nd ed., III (Heidelberg, 1834), 137–419. An excellent short account is that of David Knowles, *The Evolution of Medieval Thought* (New York, 1962), pp. 153–184. An invaluable study not only of law teaching at Bologna but also of the transplantation of the Bologna system to other European universities is Helmut Coing, ed., *Handbuch der Quellen und Literatur der neueren europäischen Privatrechtsgeschichte,* I (Munich, 1973), 39–128.

3. Odofredus in the early thirteenth century reported that there were 10,000 students at Bologna. This figure is doubted by some leading scholars, and an estimate of 1,000 is given in Coing, *Handbuch,* p. 81. However, the estimate of 10,000 is not doubted by other leading scholars, including: P. Heinrich Denifle, *Die Entstehung der Universitäten des Mittelalters bis 1400* (Berlin, 1885), p. 138; and Albano Sorbelli, *Storia della Università di Bologna,* vol. 1, *Il Medioevo: Secc. XI–XV* (Bologna, 1944), p. 209.

4. Rashdall, *Universities of Europe,* pp. 159–160.

5. See generally ibid., pp. 50–54, 275–278. See also note 7.

6. Ibid., pp. 159–160.

7. The University of Paris received certain privileges from King Philip in 1200 and its first statute from the papal legate in 1215. Its origins go back to Abelard in the early twelfth century.

8. See S. P. Scott, ed., *The Civil Law,* 17 vols. (Cincinnati, Ohio, 1932). Manuscripts of the Code and the Novels had survived in the West, and the Institutes of Gaius, upon which the Institutes of Justinian were patterned, had also survived. But the Digest, which was by far the most important of the four books, had disappeared.

9. D. 42.16, Concerning the Interdict Vi et Armata ["By Force and by Armed Force"]. The Latin text of Justinian's compilation may be found in Paul Krueger, Theodor Mommsen, Rudolf Schoell, and Wilhelm Kroll, eds., *Corpus Iuris Civilis* (Berlin, 1954–1959).

10. John P. Dawson, *The Oracles of the Law* (Ann Arbor, Mich., 1968), pp. 114–115.

11. Ibid., pp. 116–117.

12. Paul Vinogradoff, *Roman Law in Medieval Europe* (Oxford, 1929), p. 59.

13. Odofredus, quoted in Savigny, *Geschichte,* p. 553.

14. In its contemporary usages the concept of the dialectic as a method of synthesis of opposites is derived from Hegel. However, the tradition of thought goes back to Abelard.

15. Haskins, *Renaissance,* p. 53.

16. See Knowles, *Evolution,* p. 162.

17. Peter Abailard, *Sic et Non: A Critical Edition,* ed. Blanche Boyer and Richard McKeon (Chicago, 1976). In the prologue Abelard indicates several possible ways of reconciling the contradictions (for example, the same words may have been used in different senses); but his followers, if not he himself, recognized that a mechanical reconciliation might be impossible and that the meaning of contradictory passages was often to be found only in the interconnections and purposes of the whole body of scriptural and patristic writings. See Martin Grabmann, *Die Geschichte der scholastischen Methode,* II (Freiburg, 1911), 168–229.

18. John Herman Randall, Jr., *Aristotle* (New York, 1960), p. 33.

19. Ibid., p. 54.

20. Aristotle, *Topics,* 1.1. 100^a25–100^b23; $1.12.105^a10$–19, in Richard McKeon, ed., *The Basic Works of Aristotle* (New York, 1941), pp. 188, 198.

21. See Ludwig Wittgenstein, *On Certainty,* ed. G. E. M. Anscombe and G. H. von Wright (New York, 1969).

22. See Wolfgang Kunkel, *An Introduction To Roman Legal and Constitutional Law,* trans. J. M. Kelley, 2nd ed. (Oxford, 1973), pp. 98–103.

23. Carl J. Friedrich, *Transcendent Justice: The Religious Dimension of Constitutionalism* (Durham, N.C., 1964), p. 5.

24. Kunkel, *Introduction,* pp. 84–86, 95–124.

25. Fritz Schulz, *History of Roman Legal Science* (Oxford, 1946), pp. 57–58.

26. Fritz Schulz, *Principles of Roman Law* (Oxford, 1936), p. 53; Peter Stein, *Regulae Iuris: From Juristic Rules to Legal Maxims* (Edinburgh, 1966), p. 36.

27. Schulz, *Roman Legal Science,* p. 94.

28. Ibid., p. 95.

29. Stein, *Regulae,* p. 36.

30. Ibid., pp. 45–46.

31. Ibid., p. 37.

32. Ibid., p. 41.

33. Ibid., p. 48.

34. Ibid. See also Dietrich Behrens, "Begriff und Definition in den Quellen," *ZSS (rom),* 74 (1957), 352.

35. D. 19.1.11.1.

36. Stein, *Regulae,* p. 118.

37. Thus, according to D. 50.17.67, "Whenever a sentence has two meanings, that should be accepted which is better adapted to the case," while according to D. 50.17.114, "When words are ambiguous, their most probable and ordinary signification should be adopted." According to D. 50.17.125, "Defendants are regarded with greater favor than plaintiffs," while according to D. 50.17.126, "When a question arises with reference to the claims of two persons, the position of the possessor is preferable."

38. Stein, *Regulae,* p. 70.

39. Theodor Viehweg, *Topik und Jurisprudenz,* 5th ed. (Munich, 1954), p. 74.

40. Quoted in Schulz, *Principles,* pp. 51–52; see Max Weber, *Economy and Society,* ed. Guenther Roth and Claus Wittich, II (New York, 1968), 787. See also Viehweg, *Topik,* pp. 46–61. But see Stein, *Regulae,* pp. 74–89.

41. Schulz, *Roman Legal Science,* pp. 43–48.

42. Ibid., p. 65.

43. Quoted in Stein, *Regulae,* p. 157.

44. Peter Abelard, *Dialectica,* ed. L. M. de Rijk (Assen, Netherlands, 1956), p. 263.

45. See William and Martha Kneale, *Introduction to Logic* (Oxford, 1968). The authors of this leading text consider that Abelard is one of the four most important persons in the development of logic, the others being Aristotle, Leibniz, and Frege. See pp. 202–203, 245, 320, and 511. I am indebted to Manuel Lourenço for directing me to this work and for guiding me in the intricacies of existential generalization.

46. For example, whereas the Justinian texts made passing references to "the nature of a contract" in a very limited sense, the glossators translated *natura* ("nature") as "substance," and debated whether the *naturalia* of a contract could properly be excluded by express agreement. In the fourteenth century Baldus developed an elaborate theory which distinguished among the *substantialia,* i.e., those elements of a contract which give it its "being," and without which it cannot exist (e.g., in a contract of purchase and sale, the thing sold and the price), the *naturalia,* i.e., those elements which are inferred from the contract and which may be altered by express terms, and the *accidentalia,* i.e., those elements which derive solely from the express ordination of the parties. See Baldus, D. 2, 14, 7, 7. no. 1; Gl. *Extra naturam* D. 2, 14, 7, 5. Cf. Helmut Coing, "Zum Einfluss der Philosophie des Aristoteles auf die Entwicklung des Römischen Rechts," *ZSS (rom),* 69 (1952), 24–59. Although he cites this passage from Baldus, Professor Coing does not distinguish medieval European from Byzantine legal reasoning but rather traces the influence of Aristotle as though it had moved in a straight line.

A brilliant example of the way in which the glossators used a maxim to derive a wide variety of specific kinds of results may be found in Gerhard Otte, *Dialektik und Jurisprudenz* (Frankfurt am Main, 1971), pp. 214–215.

47. Even today it is disputed whether Aristotle was a realist or a nominalist or something in between, sometimes called a conceptualist. A conceptualist views the essence of things (universals) as existing *in* those things, rather than as existing separately from them (realism) or as not existing at all (nominalism). This position is fairly close to that of Abelard, and it is implicit in the view that legal rules are generalizations of specific decisions.

48. What is known of Gratian's biography is recounted in Stephan Kuttner, "The Father of the Science of Canon Law," *The Jurist,* 1 (1941), 2–19.

49. *Decretum*, in E. Friedberg, ed., *Corpus Iuris Canonici*, vol. 1 (1879; reprint ed., Graz, 1959).

50. See Migne, *PL* 140. 539–1058. Burchard died in 1025.

51. Migne, *PL* 166. 47. Ivo lived from about 1040 to about 1115.

52. Other canonists and theologians upon whom he relied for his dialectical method are referred to in Stanley Chodorow, *Christian Political Theory and Church Politics in the Mid-Twelfth Century: The Ecclesiology of Gratian's Decretum* (Berkeley, 1972), p. 2, n. 3.

53. See Stephan Kuttner, *Harmony from Dissonance: An Interpretation of Medieval Canon Law* (Latrobe, Pa., 1960).

54. *Decretum,* Dist. 9, c. 1.

55. Ibid., Dist. 9, dict. post c. 11.

56. Ibid., Dist. 1, c. 2.

57. Ibid., Dist. 9, c. 2.

58. Fritz Schulz may be right that such classical Roman law texts as, "What has pleased the prince has the force of law," and, "The prince is absolved from the laws," are to be construed narrowly, and that only in the postclassical period did the emperor come to be above the laws generally. See Schultz, "Bracton on Kingship," *English Historical Review,* 60 (1945), 136. Nevertheless, no statement of any Roman jurist claiming that the emperor was bound by the laws has survived (or as Peter Banos has said, perhaps no jurist ever made such a statement and survived). The position taken in the text is supported, rather than refuted, by the provision of Justinian's Code 1.14.4: "It is a statement worthy of the majesty of a reigning prince for him to profess to be subject to the laws; for Our authority is dependent upon that of the law."

59. *Decretum,* Dist. 10, c. 1 and Pars II.

60. Ibid., Dist. 11, Pars I. An analysis of the originality of Gratian's exposition of the sources of law may be found in Jean Gaudemet, "La doctrine des sources du droit dans le Decret de Gratien," *Revue de droit canonique,* 1 (1951), 6. Stanley Chodorow is undoubtedly right in stressing that the key to Gratian's approach to the hierarchy of laws is that he viewed the church as a juridical community, analogous to other juridical communities. Stanley Chodorow, *Christian Political Theory,* p. 97. For that reason he looked primarily to the political authority of the author of a law or legal principle to determine its place in the hierarchy.

61. Gabriel Le Bras, "Canon Law," in C. G. Crump and E. F. Jacob, eds., *The Legacy of the Middle Ages* (Oxford, 1926), pp. 325–326.

62. *Decretum,* Dist. 9. c. 1.

63. Ibid., Dist. 37, translated in A. O. Norton, ed., *Readings in the History of Education* (New York, 1971), pp. 60–75.

64. A different kind of synthesis, involving the simple choice of one of two contradictory solutions, is characteristic of the philosophical method of Thomas Aquinas (late thirteenth century), who in that respect took a step backward.

65. See Frederick H. Russell, *The Just War in The Middle Ages* (Cambridge, 1975).

66. See Hermann Kantorowicz, "The *Quaestiones Disputatae* of the Glossators," *Tijdschrift voor Rechtsgeschiedenis/Solidus Revue d'histoire du droit,* 16 (1939), 5.

67. Ibid., p. 23.

68. Ibid., pp. 55–56. Kantorowicz lists the following: *titulus, rubrica, summaria, exordium, casus, causa, materia, thema, ponere, queritur, questio, controversia, disputatio, actor, argumentum, decisio, definitio, determinatio, iudicum, sententia, responsum, distinctio, divisio, problema, solutio,* and others. But see Fritz Pringsheim, "Beryt und Bologna," in *Festschrift für Otto Lenel* (Leipzig, 1921), pp. 204, 252. Kantorowicz points out that Pringsheim (who was writing nearly two decades earlier) erred in attributing many of these terms to the Roman law that had developed in the East *after* the time of Justinian.

69. Kantorowicz, "The *Quaestiones Disputatae,*" pp. 1–6.

70. Ibid., p. 43.

71. Ibid., pp. 5 — 6.

72. See Schulz, "Bracton on Kingship," pp. 43–44.

73. An early example — perhaps the first — of the application to natural phenomena of the methods of modern science previously developed in law may be seen in the work of Robert Grosseteste (1168–1253), who taught at Oxford in the first decade of the thirteenth century and was Bishop of Lincoln from 1235 until his death. In his experimental investigations of optics, sound, heat, astronomy, and other natural phenomena Grosseteste built especially on Aristotle's distinction between "the fact" (*quia*) and "the reason for the fact" (*propter quid*). To this he added the method of breaking down an observed phenomenon into its component elements, reconstructing the phenomenon theoretically, and comparing the theoretical reconstruction ("composition") with the component elements ("resolution") in order to test the validity of the principles employed. In the words of a modern writer on Grosseteste's position in the history of science: "Gratian used the same logical method to reform canon law." A. C. Crombie, "Grosseteste's Position in the History of Science," in D. A. Callus, ed., *Robert Grosseteste, Scholar and Bishop: Essays in Commemoration of the Seventh Centenary of His Death* (Oxford, 1955), p. 100. Grosseteste's pupil, Roger Bacon (c.1220–c. 1292), wrote of Grosseteste that he and other contemporary scientists "were aware that the power of mathematics is capable of unfolding the causes of all things, and of giving a sufficient explanation of human and divine phenomena." Francis S. Stevenson, *Robert Grosseteste, Bishop of Lincoln: A Contribution to the Religious, Political, and Intellectual History of the Thirteenth Century* (London, 1899), p. 51. Stevenson adds that by "the power of mathematics" Bacon probably meant what would be labeled now (1899) "the reign of law," and that "ample recognition of that is found in Grosseteste's writings." See A. C. Crombie, *Grosseteste, Bacon, and the Birth of Experimental Science, 1100–1700* (Oxford, 1953). p. 10.

74. "Causa est civilis disceptatio de certo dicto vel facto certae personae." See

Alessandro Giuliani, "The Influence of Rhetoric on the Law of Evidence and Pleading," *Juridical Review,* 62 (1969), 231.

75. Ibid., pp. 234–235. These rules of relevance were applied first to the propositions (*positiones*) to which parties and witnesses swore oaths and later to the allegations (*articuli*), proved through witnesses and documents, which gradually replaced the older form as oaths were devalued.

76. Ibid., p. 237.

77. Alexander Koyre, *From the Closed World to the Infinite Universe* (Baltimore, 1976).

78. Joseph Needham, in seeking answers to the question why modern science did not develop in traditional Chinese civilization (or Indian) but only in Europe, emphasizes the importance, on the one hand, of Babylonian, Stoic, and Judaic conceptions of a body of laws laid down by a transcendent God and covering the actions both of men and of the rest of nature, and, on the other hand, of the sharp separation, only made in the late sixteenth and seventeenth centuries, between human natural law and nonhuman laws of nature. (The Chinese, by contrast, did not have a concept of law that was applicable to nonhuman phenomena.) Needham attributes the West's shift to a belief in a separate body of laws of nature principally to the rise of royal absolutism at the end of feudalism and at the beginning of capitalism. The fact that Roger Bacon had used the expression "laws of nature" in the thirteenth century only supports this thesis, Needham states, since the critical fact is that Bacon's concept "remained dormant until at the Renaissance a new political absolutism and a new birth of experimental science brought it again into the limelight of discourse." See Joseph Needham, *The Grand Titration: Science and Society in East and West* (London, 1969), pp. 310–311. Needham's explanation is only partly true. That something new happened in the West, both in science and in society, in the sixteenth and seventeenth centuries is an undoubted fact. It is truc also that physical nature then came to be viewed as having its own laws, which were thought to be quite distinct from the moral laws of human nature. But it is highly misleading to say that Bacon's idea—and Grosseteste's before him—that there were laws of matter and light, and other laws of nature, "simply did not win general acceptance in his day" (ibid., p. 310). Grosseteste's and Bacon's theories were characteristic of scientific thought in their time (see note 73). They were part of a scientific world view that was quite different from that of the ancient Babylonians, Greeks, and Hebrews, and quite different also from that of the Christians—whether of the East or of the West—prior to the twelfth century. It was a scientific world view that, by analytically separating the world from God, the temporal from the eternal, "natural causes" (in Abelard's words) from the miraculous (see chapter 2, note 24), permitted—indeed, required—a systematization of the laws applicable to each of the two spheres. This paved the way for a later analytical separation, within the world, of nature from man, which in turn permitted and required a systematization of the laws applicable to each of those two spheres. The methods of systematization remained basically similar. Thus the rise of modern scientific thought should be traced first to the separation of the ecclesiastical and the secular authorities in the late eleventh and twelfth centuries and only second to the events of the sixteenth and seventeenth centuries (including the rise of absolute secular monarchies).

79. See André F. Cournand and Harriet Zuckerman, "The Code of Science: Analysis and Some Reflections on Its Future," *Studium Generale*, 23 (1970), 941, 945–961. I am indebted to Grace Goodell for calling this invaluable essay to my attention.

80. Ibid., p. 945.

81. See Harold J. Berman, "The 'Right to Knowledge' in the Soviet Union," *Columbia Law Review*, 54 (1954), 749.

82. See Chapter 4. Heresy had been denounced by the church from the first century on, and it had been persecuted at various times by both secular and ecclesiastical authorities. However, it did not assume the character of a legal offense until the Papal Revolution established the Western church as a legal entity. See generally Herbert Grundmann, *Ketzergeschichte des Mittelalters* (Göttingen, 1963). Valuable documentary sources are given in English translation in R. I. Moore, *The Birth of Popular Heresy* (London, 1975), and Jeffrey B. Russell, *Religious Dissent in the Middle Ages* (New York, 1971).

83. Robert K. Merton, "Science and the Democratic Social Structure," *Social Theory and Social Structure* (1942; reprint ed., New York, 1957), pp. 550–561.

84. Historians of ideas sometimes turn things the other way around. See *A Scholastic Miscellany: Anselm to Ockham*, ed. and trans. Eugene R. Fairweather (New York, 1956): "Indeed, the whole history of medieval thought can be organized in terms of the progressive rediscovery of Aristotle." In fact, the major works of the founding fathers both of the new theology and the new legal science, especially Abelard and Gratian, just antedated the translation of Aristotle's major works on logic. This is not to say that Aristotle's theories of logic, as they had been transmitted by Boethius in the sixth century, were unimportant. But the question remains, why did they suddenly acquire a new significance? Why was it suddenly felt to be necessary that his major works on logic be translated?

85. European Jews in the late eleventh, twelfth, and thirteenth centuries in Europe lived under conditions that changed dramatically from place to place and time to time. In some places and times they were the objects of terrible persecution and official banishment; in others they lived in peace with their neighbors and achieved prosperity and even political influence. Throughout this period the Jews preserved their own law and their own courts and also were subject to royal law. They were often specifically protected in royal peace statutes and in urban charters of liberties.

While a direct influence of Jewish law on Western law cannot be identified, Jewish thought did contribute to the general intellectual climate of the times. This came about in two ways. First, there was the influence of Jewish thought directly—in particular, the allegorical tradition of reasoning present in the Midrash, which was in general use among Jewish thinkers, as well as the rational school centered around Rashi (1040–1105) in northern France and a century later around the writings of Moses Maimonides (1135–1204). As Beryl Smalley has pointed out, Rashi's impact on several important thinkers of the late eleventh and early twelfth centuries can be directly identified, while both Thomas Aquinas (1225–1274) and Albertus Magnus (c. 1200–1280) were influenced by Maimonides. See Beryl Smalley, *The Study of the Bible in the Middle Ages* (Notre Dame, 1978), especially pp. 149–172, on the influence of Rashi; on Maimonides see Wolfgang Kluxel, "Die Geschichte des Maimonides im lateinischen

Abendland als Beispiel eines christlichjüdischen Begegnung," in *Judentum im Mittelalter, Miscellanea Mediaevalia,* IV (Berlin, 1966).

The second form of influence was more subtle. As Christian scholars sought contacts with Jewish intellectuals in order to clarify their understanding of the Old Testament, they found that the Jews frequently had translated words and phrases differently and had interpreted passages in a wholly different way. This forced the Christians to reexamine their sources and their arguments, and often to devise new explanations to counter Jewish knowledge and criticism. Smalley, *The Study of the Bible,* pp. 364–365. In this way, as Robert Chesler has put it, "the very existence of a separate intellectual tradition alongside that of Christian Europe forced a confrontation of weaknesses, and an excitement of ideas, that otherwise might not have been possible."

Nevertheless, neither Jewish thought nor Jewish law seems to have had any substantial influence on the legal systems of the West, at least so far as the surviving literature shows. Smalley, p. 157, n. 2, cites L. Rabinowitz, *The Social Life of the Jews in Northern France in the XII–XIV Centuries as Reflected in the Rabbinical Literature of the Period* (London, 1938), to the effect that "cases of Christians becoming learned in the Jewish law are known." However, Rabinowitz actually gives only one example, that of a Christian who studied Jewish law while becoming a convert to Judaism.

One basic reason for this may have been the absence in Judaism of a separation between spiritual and secular law: for the Jews of the twelfth century, every part of Jewish law was rooted in the Bible as the sacred word of God and in the character of the Jewish community as a chosen vessel of divine will. Also the intense casuistry of the Talmud may have helped to make it seem alien to Western legal thought, which stressed the systematization of legal principles.

Perhaps for similar reasons, the influence of Islam on Western law was negligible in the eleventh and twelfth centuries. While Europeans were interested in Islamic civilization, they limited their studies of it at that time primarily to astronomy, astrology, mathematics, and medicine. In the late eleventh century—to cite one example—Constantinus Africanus, a Tunisian Christian in the service of Robert Guiscard, Count of Apulia, translated medical works from Arabic into Latin and presented them to the University of Salerno. It was only in the later thirteenth century, after the major directions of Western law had been determined, that Arabic philosophy became influential among theologians such as Thomas Aquinas and Roger Bacon. See Johann Fueck, *Die arabischen Studien in Europa, bis in den Anfang des 20. Jahrhunderts* (Leipzig, 1955); R. W. Southern, *Western Views of Islam in the Middle Ages* (Cambridge, Mass.); F. Wuestenfeld, *Die Uebersetzungen arabischer Werke in das Lateinische seit dem XI Jahrhundert* (Göttingen, 1877).

An exception was provided by Peter the Venerable (1092–1157), Abbot of Cluny. Once Peter traveled to Iberia to mediate a quarrel between Castile and Aragon, and while there he found two men with a knowledge of Arabic working on astrology. They returned with Peter to Cluny, where one of them translated the Koran into Latin, although with many gaps and mistakes, while the other translated a tract on the teachings of Mohammed. Peter sent these works to Bernard of Clairvaux, but his efforts did not lead to a wider study of the Koran. As R. W. Southern has written, the translation of the Koran was "an end rather than a beginning. The serious study of Islam was not an object that commended itself to the contemporaries or immediate successors of Peter the Venerable." Southern, *Western Views,* pp. 33–37.

It was only in the following century that, due to the work of Arabists such as Raymundus Martini and Ramon Lull, Arab philosophy became generally available and known in the West and came to influence a wide variety of scholars. Even then, Western legal systems seem to have remained largely unaffected by Islamic thought. See Deno J. Geanakoplos, *Medieval Western Civilization and the Byzantine and Islamic Worlds* (Lexington, Mass., 1979), p. 159.

86. Knowles, *Evolution,* pp. 80−81.

87. Roberto Unger has attributed the emergence of the concept of law as an autonomous system in European history to the convergence of a theology of transcendence, a belief in group pluralism, and the idea of the liberal secular state. See Roberto M. Unger, *Law in Modern Society: Toward a Criticism of Social Theory* (New York, 1976), pp. 66–76, 83–86, 176–181. There are some striking parallels between his analysis and the account given here, despite the sharp contrast between his more philosophical and this more historical interpretation. However, in dating the origins of the Western concept of an autonomous legal system from the seventeenth century, and in linking it with the emergence of a positivist political and legal theory, Professor Unger has avoided the crucial questions of the political and legal character of the church and the interrelations of church and state, questions which were central to Western political and legal thought from the late eleventh to the nineteenth centuries and which, in disguise, still haunt Western secular religions, including both liberalism and socialism. See Harold J. Berman, *The Interaction of Law and Religion* (New York, 1974).

88. A similar belief in the interdependence of form and substance in legal thought, but a different view of the nature of each, has been presented by Duncan Kennedy in his article, "Form and Substance in Private Law Adjudication," *Harvard Law Review,* 89 (1976), 1685. Professor Kennedy asserts that in contemporary American private law adjudication all *forms* of law fall into two opposed categories, namely, "rules," which are relatively narrow and specific and are supposed to operate with objectivity and generality, and "standards," such as fairness, reasonableness, and due process, which are relatively broad and which permit persons and situations to be dealt with on an ad hoc basis. Professor Kennedy further asserts that all *substantive goals* of law fall into two opposed categories, namely, "individualism," which he identifies with self-interest, party autonomy, and reciprocity, and "altruism," which he identifies with sharing, sacrifice, and communal involvement. To complete the circle, Professor Kennedy asserts that a preference for legal argument cast in the form of rules is connected with the substantive goal of individualism, while a preference for legal argument cast in the form of standards is connected with the substantive goal of altruism. There is an overlap, he writes (p. 1776), but at "a deeper level . . . the individualist/formalist and the altruist/informalist operate from flatly contradictory visions of the universe." This analysis represents a sharp break with the traditional Western conception that conflicting rules and standards (as well as other conflicting forms of legal utterance, such as doctrines, concepts, and analogies) are ultimately reconcilable by the legal system as a whole. Similarly, it breaks with the traditional Western belief that conflicting purposes of law, including not only individualism and altruism but also other polar values (for example, diversity and

unity, change and continuity, freedom and equality) are ultimately reconcilable within the values of the whole legal system. Moreover, it is a postulate of traditional Western legal thought that the extent to which a particular purpose of law is served by a particular legal form cannot be answered in the abstract but can only be answered in a historical context. In some societies (for example, Communist societies) and in some areas even of so-called private law (for example, community property law) the rules may be more altruistic and the standards more individualistic, in Professor Kennedy's sense of those words.

By reducing the framework of analysis to a series of dualisms, which are themselves ultimately reduced to a single dilemma, Professor Kennedy gives dramatic expression to a widespread skepticism regarding legal rules and a widespread faith in what has been called the "adhocracy" of decisions based on legal standards. Contemporary Western man finds it hard to believe in rules since he tends to view them in isolation from the entire system of which they are integral parts. He finds it easy to believe in values since he sees them unencumbered by the rules required for realizing them in various types of cases. This "antinomy of rules and values" has been exposed by Roberto Unger as a dead end of modern liberal thought. See Roberto M. Unger, *Knowledge and Politics* (New York, 1975), pp. 88–100.

One purpose of exploring the origins of Western legal thought in the eleventh and twelfth centuries is to show, by implication, the contrast between the synthesizing legal science which is at the root of the 900-year-old Western legal tradition and the fragmenting jurisprudence that has become prominent, if not dominant, in the West in the twentieth century.

4. Theological Sources of the Western Legal Tradition

1. *Encyclopedia Britannica*, 1969 ed., s.v. "myth."

2. The phrase is from the *Book of Common Prayer*. Its source is Ezek. 18:23.

3. See Ps. 98:8–9; Jer. 23:5; Mic. 4:3; Amos 5:18; Zeph. 3:8–11, and 1:15.

4. Nicene Creed (A. D. 325). See J. N. D. Kelly, *Early Christian Creeds* (New York, 1950), pp. 215–216.

5. Matt. 25:31–46.

6. See the Preamble of the *Ecloga* (a collection of laws promulgated by the Byzantine emperors about A.D. 740), in Edwin H. Freshfield, *A Manual of Roman Law: The Ecloga* (Cambridge, Mass., 1926). The opening paragraph states: "A selection of laws arranged in compendious form by Leo and Constantine, the wise and pious Emperors, taken from the Institutes, the Digests, the Code, and the Novels of the Great Justinian, and revised in the direction of greater humanity, promulgated in the month of March, Ninth Indiction in the year of the world 6234."

7. See Jaroslav Pelikan, *The Christian Tradition*, vol. 2, *The Spirit of Eastern Christendom, 600–1700* (Chicago, 1974), pp. 279–280. Orthodoxy never developed theories concerning merits, satisfaction, purgatory, and supererogatory works. Some Eastern theologians have introduced ideas somewhat similar to that of purgatory, but these have never been widely accepted in the Eastern Church. The doctrine of eternal damnation is rejected and, in general, legal thinking plays a minor role in Eastern theology.

8. Eugen Rosenstock-Huessy, *Out of Revolution: The Autobiography of Western Man* (New York, 1938), pp. 509–510.

9. These were "partial indulgences," normally given in terms of years,

months, days, or "quarantines" (Lenten periods). The term of the indulgence referred *not* to the time of punishment but to the time of penance; i.e., an indulgence of six years corresponded in value to six years lived under the penitential disciplines of the early church.

10. John T. McNeill and Helena M. Gamer, *Medieval Handbooks of Penance* (New York, 1938), p. 17. See Bernard Poschmann, *Penance and the Anointing of the Sick* (New York, 1964), chap. 1, n. 41a, pp. 147–149. Poschmann states (p. 148) that the word "absolution" (*absolvere*) entered the liturgy of penance quite late and that for a long time it was identified with the sinner's own works of penance. He sees as a "basic difficulty" of the earlier practice the fact that "the forgiveness of sins [was viewed prior to the eleventh century as] primarily the effect of personal works of penance," so that no "scope. . . remained for a real act of absolution" and "in the last analysis absolution appears devoid of content." This interpretation of the earlier practice perfectly reflects the viewpoint of the reformers of the eleventh and twelfth centuries.

11. *De Vera et Falsa Poenitentia*, Migne, *PL*. 40.1113, written c. 1050 A.D. and wrongly attributed to St. Augustine. This essay was widely used in the next century by Gratian and other canonists. In the sixteenth century it was extensively commented on by Erasmus and others; it was repudiated by Luther. The passage quoted in the text is at p. 1129.

12. Ibid.

13. *De Vera et Falsa Poenitentia*, chaps. 10, 18, Migne, *PL* 40.1122, 1128. Poschman, *Penance*, p. 158, n. 3, states that the identification of the power to impose temporal punishment with the power to impose eternal punishment adds nothing new to traditional teaching. But this misses the point made by the author of the tract, namely, that the temporal punishment in question is temporal punishment in this world and not temporal punishment in the next world (purgatory).

14. See George H. Williams, *Anselm: Communion and Atonement* (St. Louis, 1960), p. 18.

15. Poschmann, *Penance,* pp. 156–183, esp. pp. 178–179.

16. On the controversy between Lanfranc and Berengar there is a large literature, including useful discussion with citation of authorities in Hasso Hofmann, *Repräsentation: Studien zur Wort- und Begriffsgeschichte von der Antike bis ins 19. Jahrhundert* (Berlin, 1974). See Joseph Ghellinck, *Le Mouvement théologique du douzième siècle* (Bruges, 1948), p. 72. See also R. W. Southern, *Saint Anselm and His Biographer* (St. Louis, 1960), p. 21. Berengar finally recanted his views in 1080, some twenty-one years after they had been officially denounced.

17. The word "transubstantiation" (which was unknown to the Eastern Church) only became current in the mid-twelfth century; the doctrine of transubstantiation was not officially adopted until the Fourth Lateran Council of 1215. However, the elevation of the host appeared in the mass in the early twelfth century. See Colin Morris, *The Discovery of the Individual, 1050–1200* (New York, 1972), p. 142. In the thirteenth century the wine was withheld from the laity, except for the most worthy.

The change of the "substance" of the bread and wine into the mystical body and blood of Christ takes place, according to St. Thomas Aquinas, "in the last instant of the pronouncing of the words [*Hoc est corpus meum*]." *Summa Theologica,* pt.

III, qu. 75, art. 7, reply obj. 3. "The perfection of this sacrament does not lie in the participation of the faithful but in the consecration of the elements." Ibid., pt. III, qu. 80, art. 12, reply obj. 2. This distinguishes it from all other sacraments. Ibid., pt. III, qu. 73, art. 1. The withholding of the cup from the laity does not affect its validity, provided that the priest who consecrates receives both the wafer and the wine. Ibid., pt. III, qu. 80, art. 12, reply obj. 2.

18. In 1264 Pope Urban established the holiday of Corpus Christi, celebrating the elevation of the host. Rosenstock-Huessy calls it "the Church holiday of the Papal Revolution." *Die europäischen Revolutionen,* 2nd ed. (Stuttgart, 1951), p. 168. It remains to this day one of the great popular holidays in all places where the population is predominantly Roman Catholic.

Of the doctrine of transubstantiation, the great German historian Ranke wrote: "The prerogatives of the priesthood are also essentially connected with this article of faith." Leopold von Ranke, *Deutsche Geschichte im Zeitalter der Reformation* (Leipzig, 1867), p. 157.

19. As George Williams has shown, the pre-Anselmian theory of redemption was related predominantly to the mystery of baptism, through which man is liberated from death and the demonic by identification with the resurrection of Christ. The stress in baptism is on rebirth and renunciation of the demons of one's preconversion life. Anselm and his successors, on the other hand, related atonement primarily to the mystery of the eucharist, which, in contrast to baptism, is a repetitive sacrament, and which in the eleventh century had come to be preceded by the sacrament of penance. Henceforth, the eucharist was thought to liberate from sin. "The concern is no longer with the renunciation of the demons of one's preconversion life but with the fulfillment of penance for one's post-baptismal sins." Williams, *Anselm,* p. 13. Williams points out (p. 24) that under the new theory the eucharist "makes possible a greater degree of participation in redemption in the measure that actual sacramental incorporation into Christ is superior to sacramental rebirth." But note that sacramental incorporation into Christ was conceived in terms of identification with Christ on the cross, not with the risen Christ. Thus the centrality of the eucharist in the second millennium of the history of the church, as contrasted with the centrality of baptism in the first millennium, is connected with the later emphasis on the incarnation of God in human history as contrasted with the earlier emphasis on the deification of man in the kingdom of heaven.

20. See Pelikan, *Christian Tradition,* II, 138. Pelikan states that the centrality of the resurrection of Christ to the Eastern doctrine of the atonement was emphasized both in the liturgy and in the writings of theologians: "the very words of institution were amplified to include the command: 'For as often as you eat this bread and drink this cup, you proclaim my [Christ's] death and *you confess my resurrection*' . . . The resurrection was presented in the liturgy as a decisive part of an atonement that consisted in Christ's victory, through both crucifixion and resurrection, over the powers of death and Hades." Pelikan states that the Eastern "liturgical theologians" further developed the same themes: "the language of the liturgy made the themes of battle and victory a natural way of describing the way of salvation."

21. Petrus Lombardus, *Sententiarum Libri Quatuor,* Migne, *PL* 192.519. In Book Four, Dist. II (col. 841), the author simply states: "We now come to the

sacraments of the new law, which are baptism, confirmation, the blessing of the bread, i.e., the eucharist, penance, extreme unction, ordination, marriage." He does not explain or offer authority to support this list, which thereafter was taken for granted as the complete list of sacraments. It should also be noted that Peter Lombard (col. 839) defines a sacrament not only in the terms of St. Augustine, as "a sign of the grace of God," but also as a "cause" of the grace which it signifies. In the East, on the contrary, until very much later, and to a certain extent even today, no sharp distinctions were or are drawn between the various ways in which divine grace may be visibly manifested. The presence of the saints in the icons, the lighting of candles, and indeed, any and every part of the liturgy is a mystery (and hence a sacrament) with miraculous grace-giving power. The church itself is a sacrament; and the building is a house where God himself dwells and his presence can be felt. In the West, however, such mysteries came to be called "sacramentals," as contrasted with "sacraments," and only certain specific rites, performed in specific ways, were considered to operate sacramentally, *ex proprio vigore* ("by their own force").

22. St. Augustine provided wisdom for all subsequent ages; however, it is incorrect to identify him, as some have done, with scholasticism, despite the fact that both St. Anselm, who is often called the founder of scholastic theology, and St. Thomas Aquinas, its most famous exponent, considered themselves to be Augustine's disciples. The main difference between them and Augustine is that Augustine made no sharp separation between reason and faith, and he always sought knowledge not for its own sake but for the sake of union with God. In that respect he was in the tradition of Eastern Christian theology, which "has never made a sharp distinction between mysticism and theology, between personal experience of the divine mysteries and the dogma affirmed by the Church." Vladimir Lossky, *The Mystical Theology of the Eastern Church* (London, 1957), p. 8. Lossky states (p. 104): "The theology of the Orthodox Church . . . has never entered into alliance with philosophy in any attempt at a doctrinal system; despite all its richness, the religious thought of the East has never had a scholasticism. If it does contain certain elements of Christian gnosis . . . the speculation is always dominated by the central idea of union with God and never acquires the character of a system." In this perspective, Lossky places St. Augustine among the authoritative church fathers of the first five centuries of the Christian era, whose theology prevailed in both the Eastern and the Western churches prior to the eleventh century.

St. Augustine himself follows Greek usage in defining theology as an "account or explanation of the divine nature." See *City of God* (trans. Marcus Dods) 8.1 and 6.8. However, that account or explanation is given by him in terms of a philosophy which he identifies with wisdom and whose truths he tests by revelation. Thus he writes that of all the philosophers the Platonists have excelled in "that part of theology which they call physical, that is, natural," and he refers especially to the Platonist argument that behind the changeable forms of body and mind there must exist a first form, unchangeable and not admitting of degrees of comparison, which is God. *City of God,* 8.6. This insight he praises as conforming to the account in Exodus in which God, when asked by Moses for his name, replied: "I am who am; and thou shalt say to the children of Israel, He who *is* sent me unto you." St. Augustine finds the similarity so great between the

God of Moses, who *is*, and the immutable form which Plato sees as standing behind all phenomena, that he is "almost inclined" to believe that Plato must have read the Bible. *City of God*, 8.11.

Yves Congar has written that Augustine believed that a "true theology" would lead the pagans to Christianity. "But this true theology for him is still only a philosophy like Platonism . . . Indeed, it seems we must wait for Abelard before the term *theologia* receives the meaning it has for us." Yves Congar, *A History of Theology* (New York, 1968), p. 32. Etienne Gilson also emphasizes—indeed, overemphasizes—the role of Platonism in St. Augustine's thought; when he turns to St. Anselm, however, who repeatedly said that his only ambition was to restate what his master Augustine had already stated, Gilson confronts the great difference in the method of thought of the two men. Anselm and his disciples, Gilson writes, "remain famous in the history of theology for their recklessness in giving rational demonstrations of all revealed truths . . . This bold ambition to procure necessary reasons for the revealed dogmas had never entered the mind of Augustine." Etienne Gilson, *Reason and Revelation in the Middle Ages* (New York, 1938), p. 27.

Not only St. Augustine but virtually all of the theologians of the first millennium of church history, both in the East and the West, would have agreed with Lossky that a "theology of concepts" is to be avoided at all costs since it will defeat the very goal of theology, which is "ascent toward the infinite." The Eastern attitude of mind "refuses to form concepts about God," he writes. It "utterly excludes all abstract and purely intellectual theology which would adapt the mysteries of the wisdom of God to human ways of thought. It is an existential attitude which involves the whole man: there is no theology apart from experience; it is necessary to change, to become a new man . . . The way of the knowledge of God is necessarily the way of deification." Lossky, *Mystical Theology*, p. 39. The Western theologians of the late eleventh century and thereafter reflected a different attitude. They sought to conceptualize theology, to fit divine attributes into human ways of thought. For them theology was to be divorced from mysticism and from personal spirituality. Anselm, for example, was a mystic and poet, but he put that to one side when he set out to prove divine mysteries "by reason alone." He sought to encompass the divinity in human categories—to bring God down to earth rather than to carry man up to heaven. For the scholastics of the late eleventh and the twelfth centuries the way of the knowledge of God was the way of incarnation, not deification.

On Anselm as "the creator of scholastic theology," and on Abelard as the person responsible for popularizing the word *theologia* "in the new sense," see Ghellinck, *Mouvement théologique*, p. 83.

23. Anselm, *Proslogion, seu Alloquium de Dei Existentia*, Migne, *PL* 158.225. See M. J. Charlesworth, *St. Anselm's Proslogion* (Oxford, 1965), including text with English translation. On Anselm generally, see Southern, *Saint Anselm*. St. Augustine had written that "you should understand what you believe" (*quod credis intelligans*), and had quoted Isaiah as saying, "If you will not believe, you will not understand" (*nisi credideritis, non intelligetis*). See L. Schoop, ed., *The Fathers of the Church: A New Translation*, II (New York, 1953), 300, 301–302. However, St. Augustine's emphasis was upon bringing the light of reason, or understanding, to bear upon what is known by faith, whereas St. Anselm's emphasis was upon

rational proof, or demonstration, of revealed truths. Augustine's "intelligere" is closer to wisdom; Anselm's is closer to science. (Isaiah's meaning was quite different from both.)

24. Anselm, *Cur Deus Homo,* Migne, *PL* 158.359–431. See John McIntyre, *St. Anselm and His Critics: A Reinterpretation of the Cur Deus Homo* (Edinburgh, 1954).

25. "By His death on the Cross He satisfied the justice of God, freed us from sin, broke the power of Satan and restored us to grace. Heaven from that time on was opened for all. But to enter we must participate in the redemption . . . *The Resurrection of Christ is linked in Scripture with His death: it is an integral, although not an essential, element of the Redemption.* By His death Christ liberated us from sin and opened the gates of heaven; by His Resurrection He prefigured and restored to us a life which had been lost by Adam's sin . . . It is true, of course, that Christ merited for us by His death the remission of sin, justification and glory, but in the plan of Divine providence it was only after the Resurrection that the Apostles were to go forth and preach the faith, through which alone we can be justified." Rev. J. S. Considine, "The Passion, Death, and Resurrection of Christ," in St. Thomas Aquinas, *Summa Theologica,* 1st complete Amer. ed., trans. Fathers of the English Dominical Province (New York, 1948), III, 3426, 3436 (italics added). See also Williams, *Anselm,* p. 9, where the author convincingly explains *Cur Deus Homo* as a eucharistic theory.

26. William J. Wolf, *No Cross, No Crown: A Study of the Atonement* (New York, 1957), pp. 19–20.

27. See Williams, *Anselm,* p. 25. There were parallel changes in modes of worship. Thus Morris, *Discovery of the Individual,* p. 142, states that in the twelfth century "a new position of prayer was widely adopted, which subsequently became conventional; kneeling with the hands together. It was the position of homage, and its use expressed the personal loyalty which the believer felt for his Lord." Before then people had prostrated themselves, as is still done in the Eastern Church.

28. See Chapter 2, note 26. In 809 Charlemagne had used the *filioque* clause as part of the creed in his own imperial chapel; Pope Leo III would not accept this amendment of the creed in Rome, although he did accept the doctrine which it reflected. It was only in 1014 that the liturgy was changed at St. Peter's to include the filioque clause. This was a principal cause of the schism between the Eastern and Western parts of the church in 1054, and it still remains an obstacle to their reunion. See Kenneth Scott Latourette, *A History of Christianity,* I (New York, 1975), 303; see also Pelikan, *Christian Tradition,* II, 183–198.

29. See also *Proslogion,* chaps. 9–11, Migne, *PL* 158.231–234.

30. *De Vera et Falsa Poenitentia,* chap. 10, Migne, *PL* 40.1122.

31. Ibid.

32. Ibid.

33. See Southern, *Saint Anselm,* p. 98.

34. See Robert D. Crouse, "The Augustinian Background of St. Anselm's Concept of Justitia," *Canadian Journal of Theology,* 4 (1958), 111.

35. In *Cur Deus Homo,* Anselm asks whether it would be fitting for God to remit sins by mercy alone, without requiring any satisfaction or punishment. He states that "it is not fitting for God to remit anything in His realm irregularly (*inordinatum*)," and that to treat the guilty and the not guilty equally would "not be

proper for God." He then adds: "Observe this also. Everyone knows that the justice of men is under law . . . But if sin is neither discharged nor punished, it is subject to no law . . . Injustice, therefore, if it is remitted by mercy alone, would be more free than justice, which seems very improper." *Cur Deus Homo,* bk. 1, chap. 12, Migne, *PL* 158.377. Anselm returns to this question in bk. 1, chap. 24, stating that for God simply to forgive man's disobedience would be to make man blessed on account of his sin. "Truly such mercy on the part of God would be contrary to himself, it is impossible for his mercy to be of that sort." This leads Anselm's pupil to say, "If God follows the method of justice, there is no escape for a miserable wretch; and God's mercy seems to perish." To this Anselm replies, "You asked for reason, now accept reason. I do not deny that God is merciful . . . But we are speaking of that ultimate mercy by which he makes men blessed after this life. And I think that I have sufficiently shown by the reasons given above that blessedness ought not to be given to anyone unless his sins are wholly remitted, and that this remission ought not to be done except by the payment of the debt which is owed because of sin [and] according to the magnitude of sin." Migne, *PL* 158.397–398.

36. See Gottlieb Söhngen, *Grundfragen einer Rechtstheologie* (Munich, 1962), and "Rectitudo bei Anselm von Canterbury als Oberbegriff von Wahrheit und Gerechtigkeit," in H. K. Kohlenberger, ed., *Sola Ratione: Anselm-Studien für Pater Dr. h.e. F. S. Schmitt* (Stuttgart, 1970).

37. On post-Reformation theories of vicarious punishment, see Wolf, *No Cross, No Crown*, p. 109. Both Luther and Calvin shared many of Anselm's ideas concerning the atonement. However, Calvin shifted the ground from the necessity to atone for the dishonor done to God to the necessity to atone for the violation of his law. The crucifixion therefore was seen by Calvin as the transfer to Christ of man's entire guilt and punishment. Calvin's ideas were successively reduced by his followers to a view of God as "consummately and perfectly just, from which it follows that He approves no iniquity, nor leaves any unavenged." See Theodorus Beza, "Confessio," *Theol. Tract.,* II, 2, quoted in Hugo Grotius, *A Defence of the Catholic Faith concerning the Satisfaction of Christ against Faustus Socinus,* trans. with notes and hist. intro. by F. H. Foster (Andover, Mass., 1889), p. xiv. In answering Socinus's argument that since God is the offended party, and not a judge administering a body of law enacted by others, he may simply forgive the offenses done to him, Grotius distinguished between God acting in a private capacity and God acting in a public capacity; it was as a sovereign that he exacted punishment. Foster points out that this "governmental" theory went over to the English Calvinists and thence to the American colonies, where Jonathan Edwards, for example, emphasized that "when moral creatures are brought into existence, there must be a moral government . . . In order to be a moral government, there must be a penalty . . . If a penalty be denounced, indeed, but never inflicted, the law becomes no law . . . If God maintains the authority of His law by the infliction of penalty, it will appear that He acts consistently in the legislative and executive parts of His government . . . But if the authority of the law be not supported, it will rather encourage and invite to sin than restrain from it." Thus the crucifixion is seen as necessitated by divine law. The sufferings of Christ are substituted for the punishment of sinners in order to provide an example which will have the effect of making men more obedient than punishment would have

made them. Grotius, *Defence,* p. li. This "subjective" or "exemplar" theory was advocated by Abelard but was generally rejected prior to the Reformation.

38. *Cur Deus Homo,* bk. 1, chaps. 13–14, Migne, *PL* 158.379, 381.

39. See St. Thomas Aquinas, *Summa Theologica,* pt. II–II, qu. 62, arts. 3, 6.

40. See Svend Ranulf, *Moral Indignation and Middle Class Psychology* (New York, 1964).

41. *De Vera et Falsa Poenitentia,* chap. 20, Migne, *PL* 40.1129–30.

42. The phrase is that of Justice Oliver Wendell Holmes, referring to what he would say to a criminal about to be executed. See Harold J. Berman, *The Interaction of Law and Religion* (New York, 1974), p. 168, n. 18.

43. "Non enim consisteret peccatum, si interdictio non fuisset." Peter Lombard, *Sententiarum Libri Quatuor,* Migne, *PL* 192.734.

44. Peter Abelard, *Ethica, seu Scito Te Ipsum,* chaps. 5–7, 12, Migne, *PL* 178.647–653; D. E. Luscombe, ed., *Peter Abelard's Ethics* (Oxford, 1971), pp. 38–49, 55. See Stephen Kuttner, *Kanonistische Schuldlehre von Gratian bis auf die Dekretalen Gregors IX* (Vatican City, 1935), pp. 4–6, 19–20. On Gratian, see Kuttner, "The Father of the Science of Canon Law," *Jurist,* 1 (1941), 2. Gratian's monumental treatise, *A Concordance of Discordant Canons (Concordia Discordantium Canonum),* is generally recognized as having marked the first separation of canon law from theology. It is of interest that the monk Gratian was a teacher of "practical external theology" (*theologia practica externa*) in Bologna. See Hans Erich Feine, *Kirchliche Rechtsgeschichte,* I (Weimar, 1950), 228. Gratian was strongly influenced by Abelard, who had been strongly influenced by Anselm.

45. In modern systems of criminal law it is often provided that an act, to be punishable, must constitute a harm to an interest which society wishes to protect. The Soviet system of criminal law has gone further than others in this direction by making the criminality of an act hinge on its "social danger." This closely resembles the canonist conception that to constitute an ecclesiastical crime an act must constitute a *scandalum* against the church. If the social danger (or *scandalum*) must itself constitute a social *harm* in order for the act to be punishable, there is no special vice or virtue in the terminology of social *danger* (or outrage); if, however, a mere *tendency* to cause harm is sufficient to make the act punishable (or a mere sense of social vexation), the question arises whether it is justified that the criminal law intervene. See Harold J. Berman, *Soviet Criminal Law and Procedure: The RSFSR Codes,* 2nd ed. (Cambridge, Mass., 1972), pp. 21, 37.

46. See Kuttner, *Kanonistische Schuldlehre,* p. 189.

47. Abelard's views of sin were condemned by Pope Innocent II at the Council of Sens in 1140. See Luscombe, *Peter Abelard's Ethics,* pp. 9n, 15n, 21n, 24n, 38n, 46n, 63n, 126n. The condemnation was directed, however, to individual propositions taken out of context or exaggerated. Abelard's main contribution, namely, his emphasis on intention as the factor that makes an act morally good or bad, was generally accepted in the canon law. Thus if an executioner hangs a man out of obedience to law, he has done nothing sinful, although if he hangs him out of motives of personal enmity he has committed a sin. (The canonists invented the category *malum in se* to describe acts that are sinful regardless of intention, but in fact they are acts whose intention is also invariably sinful.) Abelard's distinction between an inclination to commit a sin and an internal consent to commit it was also accepted: a bad inclination, he said, does not necessarily in

volve a contempt or disregard for the divine will. However, even the internal consent, or decision, to commit a sin, though punishable in the heavenly forum of the church, should not be punished by a court, Abelard said (and here he was followed generally by the canonists, though not entirely), unless it manifests itself in an external act. Abelard states that it is the works of sin, rather than sin itself, that are punished on earth. This leads not only to a higher standard of culpability, as indicated in the text, but also to a lower standard, where mundane considerations dictate harsher treatment. Thus a mother who negligently kills her child should receive a heavy punishment, "not for the fault which she committed but so that subsequently she or other women should be rendered more cautious in providing for such things." Similarly, lesser sins that are public may be more severely punishable than greater sins that are secret, since public sins tend by their example to encourage others to sin. "For whatever can redound to the common ruin or public detriment should be punished with greater correction . . . and the greater the *scandalum* with men the greater the punishment which it incurs among men even though a lighter fault has preceded it . . . These proceedings are in accordance not so much with the obligation of justice as with the practicalities of government, so as to ensure, as we have said, the common utility of preventing public injuries." Ibid., pp. 38–39, 42–43, 44–45.

48. Kuttner, *Kanonistische Schuldlehre*, pp. 25–28, goes back and forth on this. The best proof of the validity of the statement in the text is the overwhelming concern with *contemptus*. See the discussion at note 50.

49. Ibid., pp. 377–379.

50. Ibid., pp. 28–38.

51. Gabriel Le Bras, "Canon Law," in C. G. Crump and E. F. Jacob, eds., *The Legacy of the Middle Ages* (Oxford, 1926), p. 357.

52. Perhaps the best description of the cult of the Virgin Mary in the eleventh and twelfth centuries remains Henry Adams's *Mont-Saint-Michel and Chartres* (New York, 1913).

53. See (from the twelfth century) *The Art of Courtly Love by Andreas Capellanus*, with intro., trans., and notes by J. J. Parry (New York, 1941).

54. See Udo Wolter, *Ius Canonicum in Iure Civili* (Cologne, 1975), p. 45; see also Helmut Coing, "English Equity and the Denunciato Evangelica of the Canon Law," *Law Quarterly Review*, 71 (1955), 223.

5. Canon Law: The First Modern Western Legal System

1. See Matt. 18:15–17; 1 Cor. 5:1–5, 7:12–8:13, 11:5–16; Acts 1:23–26, 2:44–45, 4:32, 15:5–29, 16:4.

2. For English translations see *The Didache,* ed. and trans. J. A. Kleist (Westminster, Md., 1948); R. H. Connolly, *Didascalia Apostolorum*, ed. and trans. R. H. Connolly (Oxford, 1929); *The Statutes of the Apostles or Canones Ecclesiastici*, ed. and trans. G. W. Horner (London, 1904). For commentary and bibliography, see Johannes Quasten, *Patrology*, I (Westminster, Md., 1950), 29–39, and II (1953), 119–120, 147–152; Erik Tidner, *Sprachliches Kommentar zur lateinischen Didascalia Apostolorum* (Stockholm, 1938).

3. The third-century North African councils determined, among other things, what was to be done with "lapsed" Christians who faltered under persecution but afterwards repented. The Council of Arles (314 A.D.) ruled that no one should be

rebaptized. At Nicaea the bishops exercised far broader powers, including the power to confirm old customs (e.g., canon 4 concerning the election of bishops and canon 6 preserving the prerogatives of the patriarchal sees of Alexandria and Antioch), to abrogate prior customs (e.g., canon 15, abolishing the custom of migratory bishops, priests, and deacons), and to enact new rules to meet new situations (e.g., canon 18 dealing with the liturgical role of deacons and canon 17 ordering the rebaptism of Paulianists wishing to return to the church). See *The Disciplinary Decrees of the General Councils,* ed. and trans. H. J. Schroeder (St. Louis, 1937), pp. 8–58.

4. The first collection of canons, made by Bishop Meletios of Antioch (d. 381), consisted of canons of five local councils of the fourth century. At the Council of Chalcedon (451), which was the fourth general (ecumenical) council — the second was at Constantinople in 381 and the third at Ephesus in 431 — a collection of 104 canons was approved, including canons issued at Nicaea and Constantinople as well as canons from the compilation of Bishop Meletios. In the early sixth century Emperor Justinian decreed: "We receive the religious teachings of these four synods [Nicaea, Constantinople, Ephesus, and Chalcedon] as sacred scripture and we observe the canons [enacted by them] as laws." Just., Nov. 131. Thereafter four other general councils were held in the East, one in 553 (Constantinople II), one in 680 (Constantinople III), one in 787 (Nicaea II), and one in 869 (Constantinople IV); however, the ecumenical character of the last is disputed. In 692 the Quinisext Council, also called the Council in Trullo, issued a collection of canons to supplement those of the fifth and sixth (hence "quinisext") general councils (Constantinople II and III); the "Trullan" collection was disputed in the West but remained a basis for subsequent Eastern collections, including canons of the Photian synod held in Constantinople in 879 to nullify the acts of the council of 869. The Photian collection is generally considered to represent the terminal point in classic Oriental canon law. See P. A. de Lagarde, *Reliquiae Iuris Ecclesiasticae Antiquissimae Graece* (Leipzig, 1856); J. A. Zallinger, *Des canons et des collections canoniques de l'Église grecque* (Paris, 1858); J. B. Pitra, *Iuris Ecclesiastici Graecorum Historia et Monumenta,* I (Rome, 1864). See also note 5.

Eastern collections formed the basis of early Western collections of canons, of which the first of importance was the *Collectio Dionysiana,* compiled at Rome about 500 A.D. This was later reproduced and circulated in various versions, of which one, called the Hadriana, was sent to Charlemagne by Pope Hadrian in 774. Another important collection, known as the Hispana, was made in Spain in the seventh century. Later it was attributed to St. Isidore of Seville. It included Gallic and Spanish synodal legislation. It is not to be confused with the Pseudo-Isidore, or False Decretals, a ninth-century Frankish forgery which was also attributed to St. Isidore of Seville (see chapter 2). The Pseudo-Isidore was based partly on the Hispana. One of its author's chief purposes was to combat the subjection of bishops to the secular authorities and to archbishops who were tied to the secular authorities. In that connection, ancient canons were forged purporting to enhance the authority of the Bishop of Rome, and these were hailed by the papal party in the eleventh and twelfth centuries as a manifesto of papal supremacy. Although the authenticity of the Pseudo-Isidore was occasionally doubted, it remained authoritative until the sixteenth century, when Erasmus and others finally proved it to be spurious. Both the Hispana and the Pseudo-Isidore are an advance over earlier compilations of canons in that the texts, though still arranged chronologically, are also subdivided under some subject-matter headings. However, the first collection of canons that was arranged to a considerable extent according to subject matter (sacraments, liturgy, moral offenses, etc.) was the *Decretum* of Burchard, Bishop-Prince of the Frankish-German city of Worms, dated 1010. See generally Paul Fournier and Gabriel Le Bras, *Histoire des collections canoniques en Occident,* I (Paris, 1931); Alfonso van Hove, *Prolegomena ad Codicem Iuris Canonici* (Rome, 1945).

5. It is often forgotten that a great deal of Roman law, not only in ancient times but also in the classical and postclassical periods, was of a religious character. Eventually, the Greek word for law, *nomos,* corresponding to the Latin word *lex,* was fused with *canon* in the word *nomocanones,* which was the title of collections issued periodically by Byzantine emperors between the sixth and tenth centuries, combining secular and ecclesiastical rules. These are sometimes neglected by students of the earlier canon law, as are canons issued by the emperor in the West between the eighth and tenth centuries. The *Nomokanon in Fifty Titles* and the *Nomokanon in Fourteen Titles* are discussed in J. A. B. Mortreuil, *Histoire du droit Byzantin,* I (Paris, 1843), 217, 481; see also Zachariae von Lingenthal, *Die griechische Nomokanon,* in *Memoires de l'academie imperiale des sciences de S. Petersburg,* VII (St. Petersburg, 1977), 2. The *Ecloga,* promulgated by Emperor Leo III about 726, is reproduced in Greek and in English translation in E. H. Freshfield, *Roman Law in the Later Roman Empire; The Isaurian Period: The Ecloga* (Cambridge, 1932). See also Mortreuil, *Histoire,* I, 357–372.

6. Rudolph Sohm, *Das altkatholische Kirchenrecht und das Dekret Gratians* (Leipzig, 1914).

7. Stephan Kuttner, "Some Considerations on the Role of Secular Law and Institutions in the History of Canon Law" (Paper read at the Conference on Law and the Humanities held by the American Council of Learned Societies, Dumbarton Oaks, April 12–13, 1950), p. 356. Professor Kuttner adds: "The contrast which Sohm *should* have pointed out was between two different modes of legal thought, i.e., between the dialectical rationalization of the twelfth, and the linear traditionalism of the earlier centuries."

8. *Dictatus Papae,* chap. 7. See chapter 2 at note 12.

9. See Gabriel Le Bras, Charles Lefebvre, and Julius Rambaud, *Histoire du droit et des institutions de l'Église en occident,* vol. 7, *L'Age classique: Source et theorie du droit, 1140–1378* (Paris, 1965), p. 133.

No attempt is made here to rescue another major part of Sohm's thesis, namely, that Gratian's treatise belongs to the earlier era of "old-Catholic law," that it is essentially an exposition of sacramental law, and that only after Gratian was a sharp distinction made between sacramental power (the power of orders) and jurisdictional power. On the contrary, Gratian stresses the legislative and judicial jurisdiction of the pope and of bishops as something that proceeds from their office rather than from their sacramental powers. Stanley Chodorow states that he stands with Sohm on this point. See Chodorow, *Christian Political Theory and Church Politics in the Mid-Twelfth Century* (Berkeley, 1972), pp. 8–16. But he, too, emphasizes (pp. 65, 137) the fact that Gratian treats the church as a "juridical community," and assigns to the pope all legislative power and supreme judicial power.

10. See Peter Stein, *Legal Evolution* (New York, 1980). Stein states (p. ix) that "legal evolution has a history of its own, which begins in the eighteenth century." In an otherwise excellent study, he ignores the fact that the "historical school" of legal philosophy (Burke, Savigny, and others), which preached legal evolution, rested on a conscious tradition dating from the twelfth and thirteenth centuries.

11. The *Corpus Juris Canonici,* as it was called in the thirteenth century and thereafter, was established officially and formally in 1580 as consisting of the following texts: (1) the *Decretum* of Gratian (c. 1140); (2) the *Liber Extravagantium* (usually called *Liber Extra*), a collection of decretals issued by Pope Gregory IX (1234); (3) the *Liber Sextus Decretalium* (or *Liber Sextus*), a collection of decretals issued by Pope Boniface VIII (1298); and (4) the *Clementinae,* a collection of decretals of Pope Clement V (1305–1314) and the Council of Vienne (1311–1312), issued in 1314 and transmitted to the universities by Pope John XXII in 1317. In addition, although not officially included, these two texts, which were unofficially compiled shortly after the reign of Pope John XXII, are usually considered to be part of the *Corpus Juris Canonici:* (5) the *Collectio Viginti Extravagantium* of John XXII (1316–1334); and (6) the *Extravagantes Communes.* (The term *extravagantes* refers to decretals that "wander outside" the basic texts — *decretales extra decreta vagantes.*) In addition to these basic texts of the classical canon law there were authoritative standard glosses, commentaries, and summae, of which the *Summa* of Huguccio (c. 1190) and the *Glossa Ordinaria* of John the German (Joannes Teutonicus) (c. 1215–1217) were the most important.

The *Clementinae* of 1317 was the last official collection of canon law before the Council of Trent (1545–1563), which did not (contrary to the expectations of many) result in the promulgation of a general codification of canon law but did enact several important sets of regulations, such as those on the duties of clerics, on benefices, on religious orders, on marriage, and on penitential discipline and criminal proceedings. The general effect of the Council of Trent was a sharply increased centralization of power in the papacy and an expansion of the legal jurisdiction of the papal curia.

The formal structures and rules of canon law did not undergo substantial changes in the centuries after the Council of Trent. In 1904, Pope Pius X established a commission to draft a new Code of Canon Law; in 1914 the work of the commission was completed and in 1914 Pope Benedict XV promulgated the new *Codex Juris Canonici,* to take effect on May 19, 1918. The new Code was essentially a further systematization of the canon law of the twelfth to fourteenth centuries, as revised by the Council of Trent.

On January 25, 1959, shortly after assuming the papacy, Pope John XXIII (1958–1963) announced that he would call a new ecumenical council for the purposes of reforming the Roman Catholic Church and of promoting deeper unity among the divided Christian churches of the world (which were invited to send observers to the forthcoming council); and further, that he would establish a commission to achieve "the expected and desired modernization of the Code of Canon Law." John XXIII, Allocution of Jan. 25, 1959, *Acta Apostolicae Sedis* (Rome, 1959), pp. 51–68. This commission was constituted on March 28, 1963, and was charged with producing an entire revision of the Code in keeping with the reforming spirit of the decrees of the Second Vatican Council of 1962–1965.

12. Charles P. Sherman, "A Brief History of Medieval Roman Canon Law," *Canadian Law Times,* 39 (1919), p. 638. The following statement by Sherman (p. 649) reflects conventional nineteenth-century Western conceptions — still unfortunately shared by many, though convincingly refuted by virtually all contemporary specialists in the field: "The Corpus Juris Canonici is the eldest daughter of the Corpus Juris Civilis of the Roman Emperor Justinian . . . The great problems of law and jurisprudence were thought out once for all by the Roman lawyers, and their labours are recorded in the Corpus Juris Civilis; the Canonists embodied many of their solutions literally or indirectly in the Corpus Juris Canonici, and with them saved civilization in Europe until Europe was ready [in the sixteenth century and thereafter] to go to the pure fountains of the Roman law."

13. See Robert E. Rodes, Jr., *Ecclesiastical Administration in Medieval England: The Anglo-Saxons to the Reformation* (Notre Dame, Ind., 1977), p. 66. In a book that contains valuable insights, but is quite wrong on this point, Professor Rodes states: "[The canonists'] descriptions of how the law operates, their theoretical speculations on the nature of the law, their manner of classifying legal enactments as to subject matter or sources were all taken directly or indirectly from the Roman jurists." Rodes cites as the most important example the principle of the primacy of the pope, which, he states, "was given its juridical form of the *plenitudo potestatis* through the analogy of the place of the emperor in Roman law." It is, of course, true that the canonists relied partly on Roman texts referring to the supremacy of the *princeps* in order to justify the supremacy of the pope as "prince" of the church. However, it was precisely "theoretical speculations on the nature of the law" and on "plenitude of power" that were missing from the Corpus Juris Civilis and that were supplied by the canonists.

14. See Udo Wolter, *Ius Canonicum in Iure Civili* (Cologne, 1975).

15. The first Frankish emperor, Charlemagne, crowned in 800, took the title "Charles, most serene Augustus, crowned by God, great and pacific emperor, governing the Roman empire." In the West at that time, "Roman empire" did not have a strong territorial connotation but referred primarily to the peoples of Western Christendom; the phrase "Christian empire" was more often used than "Roman empire." The East Frankish ruler Otto II (d. 983) was the first to call himself "Roman emperor," and after the founding of the Salian dynasty by the Saxon Conrad II in 1024, the term "Roman Empire" was used in 1034 for the first time to refer to the lands under his rule. Under Emperor Frederick I (Frederick Barbarossa) (1152–1190) reference was made for the first time to the "Holy Empire," but the precise phrase "Holy Roman Empire" was not used until 1254. Only after two hundred years — under Frederick III (emperor from 1452 to 1493) — did the title "Holy Roman Empire of the German Nation" finally evolve. Yet it is surely fair to say that the "Roman Empire" of the Salian and Hohenstaufen dynasties was essentially German, not Roman. See notes 16 and 17.

16. The view is still held by some that the Germanic peoples of the West "received" the Roman law in the eleventh and twelfth centuries as a result of the belief that the mantle of Roman imperial authority had fallen on the Frankish emperor Charlemagne and his successors. Even Paul Koschaker states that for the glossators the authority of the texts of Justinian rested on the fact that the im-

perium Romanum continued to live in the empire of the Saxon ruler Henry IV and his successors. See Koschaker, *Europa und das römische Recht,* 3rd ed. (Munich and Berlin, 1958), pp. 70–71. Yet in fact, even within the "Roman empire" of the German kings, Roman law prevailed directly only to the extent that it was construed as latent, subsidiary law, which "came into play where territorial statute and custom left room for it"; otherwise, its influence on secular law was indirect, in that its terminology and concepts were used as a basis for interpreting statute and custom. See Kuttner, "Role of Secular Law," p. 353. As Kuttner points out, it was above all the canon law that served as an instrument of the "reception" of Roman law. This is not to say that Roman law was not considered to be a living law or that emperors did not sometimes pretend that the ancient Roman Empire still survived in their persons. See note 17.

17. Emperor Frederick Barbarossa at the Diet of Roncaglia in 1152 proclaimed a new law concerning the rights of universities and ordered that it be placed in the appropriate section of the Corpus Juris Civilis of Justinian. Indeed, the entire series of decrees issued at Roncaglia were promulgated in a manner reminiscent of Roman imperial legislation. This, however, is a rare if not unique example, and Frederick Barbarossa eventually had to give up his dream of restoring a Byzantine style of rule. See chapter 14.

18. In an extraordinary aside, Maitland says, "The Decretum is sad stuff when set beside the Digest"—meaning that the intellectual quality of Gratian's work is hardly equal to the jurisprudence of the classical Roman jurists. Sir Frederick Pollock and Frederic William Maitland, *History of English Law,* 2nd ed. (1898; reprint ed., Cambridge, 1968), 24. No doubt Maitland had in mind not the Digest as such but the Digest as reconstructed by the medieval Romanists into a more tightly woven, integrated set of concepts and definitions, laid down once and forever, containing intricate solutions to intriguing problems of legal logic. By that standard, any system of law will seem "sad stuff" if its purpose is to reflect actual conditions in society and thus to change in order to meet new situations. The reason the remark is extraordinary is that Maitland was not one to place a high value on legal logic for its own sake, and he would never have accepted a similar judgment upon his own beloved English common law.

19. "It is difficult to pinpoint exactly when the [formal] recognition [of the pope's *plenitudo potestatis*] occurred, but it had certainly begun when Simon of Bisignano wrote his *Summa* (1177–79) . . . and was finally rounded off in the pontificate of Innocent III. The evolution of the term in this period reveals in microcosm a whole process of the formation of canonist doctrines." John A. Watt, *The Theory of Papal Monarchy in the Thirteenth Century: The Contribution of the Canonists* (New York, 1965), p. 78.

20. *Decretum,* Dist. 19, c. 9, incorporating an early text which stated that Pope Anastasius, because of heresy, was struck down by the divine will. See note 21.

21. Ibid., Dist. 29, ante c. 1. Gratian raised the question whether the words of such great "expositors of sacred scripture" as St. Jerome and St. Augustine were to be preferred to the decretals of a pope. He concluded that the church fathers were to be preferred in expositions of sacred scripture, but not in settling legal affairs, where "not only knowledge but also power is necessary." Gratian did not use the word *jurisdictio* to distinguish the legal authority of the pope, but instead used the phrase *executio potestatis* ("execution of power"), to which he gave

substantially the same meaning as his successors gave to *jurisdictio* in their analysis of the pope's power to decide disputes, including doctrinal disputes. As Brian Tierney states, "the authority that the canonists attributed to the pope in matters of faith was the authority of a supreme judge, not that of an infallible teacher. [Gratian's successor] Huguccio considered the case of a pope who was a learned theologian. If he contradicted another theologian his status as pope did not lend any additional weight to the views he expressed as a teacher; but all were bound to hold what he laid down as pope *in the decision of cases*. If the pope erred in deciding a case involving a matter of faith the canonists were confident that the error would be corrected by the pope himself or by a successor (as in the case of Anastasius [see note 20]) before the whole church had been led astray." Brian Tierney, *Origins of Papal Infallibility, 1150–1350* (Leiden, 1972), p. 42. Tierney has shown that there was no theory of papal infallibility prior to the end of the thirteenth century, and that when the theory emerged it was advanced as a limitation on papal authority: it meant that the infallible utterances of prior popes could not be reformed by the pope in power at any given moment. See also Tierney, *The Foundations of the Conciliar Theory* (Cambridge, 1955).

22. The title "cardinal" had various meanings prior to the mid-eleventh century. At that time the reforming popes assigned to "cardinal" bishops and priests of the 28 neighboring churches that served the four great basilicas of Rome administrative, and not only (as before) liturgical, functions in the Roman Church. Also non-Romans were elevated to be cardinals, including, for example, Humbert of Silva Candida, one of the leading reformers. Thus cardinal bishops and priests became for the first time an administrative corps of the papacy. By decree of Nicholas II in 1059 they became papal electors as well. See Stephan Kuttner, "*Cardinalis:* The History of a Canonical Concept," *Traditio,* 3 (1945), 129–214; *New Catholic Encyclopedia,* 1967 ed., s.v. "cardinal."

23. Yves Renouard, *La Papauté à Avignon* (Paris, 1954), p. 29. The year 1378 marked the beginning of the Great Schism (1378–1417), when two papal courts (and for a time, three) reigned in competition with one another. Prior to that time, from 1309 to 1377, the seat of the papacy was not Rome but Avignon, in southern France; this period became known as the Babylonian captivity of the Church of God.

24. See Gabriel Le Bras, *Institutions ecclésiastiques de la Chrétienté médiévale* (Paris, 1964), pp. 346–348.

25. The authority of the papal legate was first proclaimed as a general principle in the *Dictatus Papae,* in which Gregory VII decreed (Dictatus IV): "That his [i.e., the Roman Pontiff's] legate, even if of lower grade, takes precedence, in a council, of all bishops and may render a sentence of deposition against them." Eventually, papal legates derived their powers from their specific commissions.

26. Le Bras, *Institutions,* p. 414.

27. Ibid., p. 419. Le Bras states: "The clergy viewed with mistrust the insertion into its temporal administration of this body usually composed of laymen. It appeared that a fundamental principle of the canon law was being violated [namely, the canon that "laymen, no matter how devout they may be, have no authority to dispose of ecclesiastical property"]. Some [local] councils protested. However, the ancient custom of participation by parishioners in the temporal life of the parish community eventually brought about the acceptance of the

body of *fabriciens,* who, by the 14th century, were among the normal institutions of Christendom."

28. Maitland argues that the church was a federal structure, in which there was a dual subordination of the bishopric: to the archbishopric, on the one hand, and to the papacy, on the other. Similarly, there was a dual subordination of the individual parish: to the bishopric and to the papacy. Thus each archbishopric was, in effect, a state within a federal union of states. F. W. Maitland, *Roman Canon Law in the Church of England* (Cambridge, 1898), pp. 101–105.

One difficulty with this analysis is that the central authority, that is, the papacy, was omnicompetent; there were no matters reserved exclusively to the "states." On the other hand, if the church in the twelfth and thirteenth centuries is to be considered as a unitary state, as contrasted with a federation, it surely was made up of a very large number of diverse subunits, each having considerable autonomy.

29. George Size, "Thoughts on the Government of the Church in the Classical Period," (ms in the possession of the author, 1978), p. 4.

30. *Glossa Platina ad Dist. 19, c. 19,* quoted in Tierney, *Papal Infallibility,* p. 32. The Latin word *arbitrium,* translated here as "will," is translated by Tierney as "judgment."

31. Paul Hinschius, *Das Kirchenrecht der Katholiken u. Protestanten in Deutschland,* III (Berlin, 1883), 769.

32. *Decretum,* Dist. 40, c. 6.

33. Tierney, *Conciliar Theory,* p. 57. In the early thirteenth century, the canonist Alanus, anticipating the more extreme conciliar theories of the fourteenth and fifteenth centuries, wrote: "It is true that only for heresy can a pope be judged against his own will . . . but that is so in this crime because in matters that pertain to faith he is less than the college of cardinals or a general council of bishops." *Glossa ad Dist. 40 c. 6,* quoted in Tierney, *Papal Infallibility,* p. 52.

34. Huguccio's theory is cited in Tierney, *Papal Infallibility.* It was not accepted in the *Glossa Ordinaria.* Huguccio argued that Gratian mentioned heresy only by way of example or else because the pope could be accused of heresy even when it was not notorious.

35. Tierney, *Papal Infallibility,* p. 48.

36. Ibid., pp. 51, 53, 89.

37. Tierney, *Conciliar Theory,* p. 97.

38. A concise survey of Roman corporation law may be found in W. W. Buckland, *A Text-Book of Roman Law from Augustus to Justinian,* 2nd ed. (Cambridge, 1932), p. 175. For an excellent analysis of the relationship of Roman legal concepts of the corporation to modern Western concepts, see P. W. Duff, *Personality in Roman Private Law* (Cambridge, 1938).

39. Otto von Gierke, *Das deutsche Genossenschaftsrecht,* 4 vols. (Berlin, 1868–1913).

40. See Pierre Gillet, *La personnalité juridique en droit ecclésiastique spécialement chez les Décretistes et les Décrétalistes et dans le Code du droit canonique* (Malines, 1927), p. 61. Gillet analyzes the theories of the glossators, that is, of the Romanists, but those theories were essentially the same as the theories of the canonists, and many of them were derived from canonist writings. Gillet states that the term "corporation" was applied to all kinds of associations, ecclesiastical and secular,

that were "formed for preserving to each his justice" (p. 70). The various Latin words *universitas, collegium, corpus,* and *societas* were used as synonyms; also religious and civil "foundations" were considered to be corporations. The association had to have at least three members in order to qualify as a corporation. There was no requirement of a charter or of a particular form of organization.

According to Plöchl, a conclusive answer was not given in this period to the question as to how far the consent of higher ecclesiastical authorities was required to invest individual ecclesiastical entities with legal personality. Willibald M. Plöchl, *Geschichte des Kirchenrechts,* I (Vienna, 1953), 175.

41. Plöchl, *Geschichte,* p. 73.

42. See Gierke, *Genossenschaftsrecht,* vol. III. The contrast is undoubtedly exaggerated by Gierke, of whom it has been said that he "is an artist who delights in emphasizing the dependence of Roman corporations on the State, to make sharper the contrast with the free German Genossenschaft of which he is the historian and prophet." Duff, *Personality,* p. 118.

43. Gillet, *La personnalité juridique,* p. 76.

44. Ibid., pp. 77–78. See Walter Ullmann, "The Delictal Responsibility of Medieval Corporations," *Law Quarterly Review,* 64 (1948), 77.

45. Gierke's thesis that the "fiction" theory of the corporation (namely, that it is an artificial person which derives its existence and its powers from the political authority) originated in the thirteenth century, in a decretal of Pope Innocent IV, has now been thoroughly disproved. See Gillet, *La personnalité juridique,* p. 163; Duff, *Personality,* pp. 221–224; Tierney, *Conciliar Theory,* p. 98. Gillet shows that the fiction theory of the canonists is not what Gierke thought it to be. The canonists said that the members of a corporation (*universitas*) are considered by law (*finguntur*) to form one person. The famous text of Pope Innocent IV, which Gierke treats as the establishment of the fiction theory, states: "Collegium in causa universitatis fingatur una persona" — the "collective" in a matter involving the corporation "is treated as if it is" one person. But this is not to say that the corporation exists as an abstract entity independently of its members, or that the "essence" of the corporation is in the collective and the "accidents" are in the individual members. Neither Innocent IV nor the other canonists developed such theories, nor are they necessarily implicit in the view that "legal personality" can be attributed to a collective or a group or, for that matter, to a fund. The canonists of the twelfth to thirteenth centuries were not, as Gierke supposed, "exaggerated realists." On the contrary, the corporation law developed by them reflects a moderate nominalist view (see note 48). Equally important, it reflects the view that the legal capacity and the legal rights and duties of a group, like the legal capacity and legal rights and duties of an individual, are derived from the same sources from which all law is derived, including divine law and natural law as well as the positive law of the church and of the secular polities. Innocent IV would have said that to give the capacity to own property, to make contracts, and to sue and be sued to a group is no more artificial or "fictitious" than it is to give such capacity to an individual.

46. This point is made by Tierney, *Conciliar Theory,* p. 101.

47. Ibid., pp. 96, 101.

48. Tierney calls it a "moderate realist" position (ibid., p. 102). In that connection, however, he quotes the statement of the great fourteenth-century jurist Bartolus: "All philosophers and canonists [believe] that the whole does not differ

really [*realiter*] from its parts"—which is a classic statement of the nominalist view. See chapter 3.

49. Ibid., p. 108.

50. Ibid. Tierney notes that at first there was a tendency to confuse the two terms "advice" (*consilium,* "counsel") and "consent" (*consentio*).

51. Ibid., p. 111.

52. Ibid.

53. Ibid., p. 117. An excellent example of the legal method of the canonists, used by Tierney (ibid., pp. 103–104), is a passage of Bernardus Parmensus dealing with the question whether a bishop could sue or answer a charge in a court of law without the consent of his chapter. "He first put forward the inevitable organic metaphor—prelate and chapter could not act separately since they were one body . . . But he went on to cite a whole series of Roman law texts that would seem to point to the opposite conclusion . . . Then he proceeded to his own conclusion, suggesting that the prelate could act alone in certain types of cases where the interests of his church could not possibly be injured, and remarking incidentally that the rules of Roman law were not binding in ecclesiastical cases: *Nec in rebus ecclesiasticis stamus legibus illis sed canonibus* . . . He put forward the Roman law tenets as if to show that the organic metaphor did not provide the only way of approaching the problem, but then forged ahead to the solution that seemed to him most likely to promote the well-being of the Church." Tierney rightly concludes that the method of dealing with concepts and texts exemplified in this passage "takes us to the heart of the canonists' achievement." "The maintenance of orderly life in the Church—nothing less— was the real task that the canonists faced in dealing with the flood of litigation, usually petty in itself, concerning the authority of ecclesiastical corporations and the rights of their various members. It was a considerable intellectual achievement that they both solved the immediate problems and, in the process, evolved a subtle and harmonious theory of corporation structure." It was Bernardus Parmensus, incidentally, who first established the triple classification of rights pertaining to the prelate, rights pertaining to the chapter, and rights held jointly by the prelate and the chapter together.

54. The maxim—*Quod omnes tangit omnibus tractari et approbari debet*—referred to the rule that when several guardians (*tutores*) had an undivided guardianship (*tutela*), their joint administration could not be dissolved without the consent of all. The Romanists and canonists of the twelfth and thirteenth centuries put this rule together with various other rules found in the Digest requiring consent by all persons sharing common rights, especially those of a procedural nature where suit was brought by or against one of such persons. Characteristically, they then applied the principle which they found to underlie these various rules to transactions involving a corporation or other community, where the transaction was for the common utility and therefore, they concluded, the consent of all the members, or a majority of them, or the "sounder part" (*sanior pars*) was required. The scope of the doctrine was limited somewhat, however, by its derivation from, and continued association with, procedural requirements. An interesting discussion may be found in Gaines Post, *Studies in Medieval Legal Thought* (Princeton, 1964), chap. 4, "A Romano-Canonical Maxim, *Quod Omnes Tangit*, in Bracton and in Early Parliaments."

6.   Structural Elements of the System of Canon Law

1. On the canon law of marriage in the twelfth and thirteenth centuries, see
A. Esmein, *Le mariage en droit canonique*, 2 vols. (Paris, 1891); Gabriel Le Bras,
"La doctrine du mariage chez les théologians et les canonistes depuis l'an mille,"
in *Dictionnaire de théologie catholique*, IX (1926), 2123-2317; Willibald M. Plöchl,
Geschichte des Kirchenrechts, II (Vienna, 1955), 267-298.

2. Gabriel le Bras, "Canon Law," in C. G. Crump and E. F. Jacob, eds., *The
Legacy of the Middle Ages* (Oxford, 1926), p. 345. This essay remains an extremely
useful summary of the main features of canon law, including the law of marriage, in the period prior to the sixteenth century.

3. On the canon law of inheritance in the twelfth and thirteenth centuries, see
Henri Auffroy, *Évolution du testament en France des origines au treizième siècle* (Paris,
1899); Jerome Hannan, *The Canon Law of Wills* (Washington, D. C., 1934).

4. Sir Frederick Pollock and Frederic William Maitland, *History of English
Law*, 2nd ed. (1898; reprint ed., Cambridge, 1968), I, 314. The post-obit gift
was not only an Anglo-Saxon device; it was known to the Normans and had
parallels among other Germanic peoples.

5. Just., Nov. 131.9, and 131.11.1 and 2. See generally Hannan, *Wills*,
p. 334; F. H. Lawson, *The Roman Law Reader*, (New York, 1969), pp. 81-83,
234. See also Demetrios Constantelos, *Byzantine Philanthropy and Social Welfare*
(New Brunswick, N.J., 1968).

6. Pollock and Maitland, I, 338-339.

7. See Hannan, *Wills*, pp. 274-275.

8. G. D. G. Hall, ed. and trans. *The Treatise on the Laws and Customs of England
Commonly Called Glanvill* (London and Edinburgh, 1965), p. 70.

9. On the canon law of property in the twelfth and thirteenth centuries, see
Plöchl, *Geschichte*, p. 396; Hans Erich Feine, *Kirchliche Rechtsgeschichte*, I (Weimar,
1950), 310, 327.

10. *Decretum*, C. 3 q. 1 c. 2.

11. See Francesco Ruffini, *L'Actio Spolii* (Turin, 1889), p. 327.

12. Ibid., p. 244.

13. See Just., C. 8.4.1.

14. See D. 48.16.1.

15. Just., I. 4.15.6.

16. On the canon law of contracts in the twelfth and thirteenth centuries, see
Plöchl, *Geschichte*, p. 399; Timothy Lynch, *Contracts between Bishops and Religious
Congregations: A Historical Synopsis and a Commentary* (Washington, D. C., 1947);
Alfred Söllner, "Die causa im Kondiktionen-und Vertragsrecht des Mittelalters
bei den Glossatoren, Kommentatoren und Kanoniken," *ZSS* (*rom*), 77 (1960),
182-269.

17. D. 2. 14. 7. 1.

18. James R. Gordley, "The Search for a General Theory of Contract," (ms in
the possession of the author, 1979), p. 48.

19. Ibid.

20. Söllner, "Causa," p. 240.

21. Just., C. 4. 44. 8. The full text is given in Latin and in English translation, together with an analysis of it, in Kenneth S. Cahn, "The Roman and

Frankish Roots of the Just Price of Medieval Canon Law," *Studies in Medieval and Renaissance History*, 6 (1969), 1.

22. Eduardus Bocking, ed., *Corpus Legum sive Brachylogus Iuris Civilis (Berlin, 1829)*, pp. 98–99, quoted in Cahn, "Roman and Frankish Roots," p. 18, n. 15.

23. In a decretal of Pope Alexander III (1159–1181) it was held that in the case of a wood sold by the canons of Beauvais to the abbey of Chaalis, which was judged by the Bishop of Arras to have been purchased for less than half the just price, the buyer was not required (as the bishop had decided) to take back what it had paid and return the property but was given the option of paying what was lacking of the just price. Gregory IX, *Decretals* 3. 17. 3, cited by Cahn, "Roman and Frankish Roots," p. 25, n. 40.

24. See J. R. Gordley, "Equality in Exchange," *California Law Review*, 69 (1981), p. 1640.

25. Ibid. See also John T. Gilchrist, *The Church and Economic Activity in the Middle Ages* (New York, 1969), p. 274.

26. See John Noonan, Jr., *The Scholastic Analysis of Usury* (Cambridge, Mass., 1957), p. 11.

27. Ibid., p. 506.

28. Decretum, C. 14. q. 4, and 46, cc. 9 and 10.

29. Gilchrist, *Economic Activity*, p. 107.

30. On the canon law of procedure and evidence in the twelfth and thirteenth centuries, see Plöchl, *Geschichte*, I, 88–90, and II, 311–338; R. B. Clune, *The Judicial Interrogation of the Parties*, CLS, no. 269 (Washington, D. C., 1948); Allessandro Giuliani, "The Influence of Rhetoric on the Law of Evidence and Pleading," *Juridical Review*, 62 (1969), 231–251.

31. *De Vera et Falsa Poenitentia*, Migne, *PL* 40.1129.

32. Giuliani, "Rhetoric."

33. See Helmut Coing, "English Equity and the Denunciatio Evangelica of the Common Law," *Law Quarterly Review*, 71 (1955), 233.

34. Mauro Cappelletti and Joseph M. Perillo, *Civil Procedure in Italy* (The Hague, 1965), pp. 35–36.

35. The canonists stated that the burden of proof of an assertion rested on the party making the assertion. This may be one source of the doctrine of the presumption of innocence. With the virtual replacement of oral procedure by written procedure, however, the judges began to require the accused persons to give explanations in response to charges against them, leading (according to M.J. Essaid) "to a virtual presumption of guilt." See M.J. Essaid, *La présomption d'innocence* (Rabat, 1971), p. 26, n. 15.

7. Becket versus Henry II

1. See Z. M. Brooke, *The English Church and the Papacy from the Conquest to the Reign of John* (Cambridge, 1952), chap. 12, "Stephen. The 'freedom of the Church.'"

2. Ibid., pp. 188–190.

3. See Beryl Smalley, *The Becket Conflict and the Schools* (Oxford, 1973), p. 122; Charles Duggan, "The Becket Dispute and the Criminous Clerks," *Bulletin of the Institute of Historical Research*, 35, no. 91 (May 1962), 1–28; James W. Alexander, "The Becket Controversy in Recent Historiography," in *The Journal of British*

Studies (Hartford, Conn.), 9 no. 2 (May 1970), 1–26. Alexander effectively refutes the older anti-Becket position taken by H. G. Richardson and G. O. Sayles in *The Governance of Medieval England* (Edinburgh, 1963).

4. George Greenaway, ed. and trans., *The Life and Death of Thomas Becket Chancellor of England and Archbishop of Canterbury Based on the Account of William Fitzstephen His Clerk with Additions from Other Contemporary Sources* (London, 1961), p. 22 (Greenaway's account is strongly pro-Henry).

5. Sidney R. Packard, *Twelfth Century Europe: An Interpretive Essay* (Amherst, Mass., 1973), p. 286.

6. Sir Frederick Pollock and Frederic William Maitland, *The History of English Law*, 2nd ed. (1898; reprint ed. Cambridge, 1968), I, 449.

7. The position taken here is supported by many authorities, including those cited in note 3, but is not a popular position among English political and legal historians, including those cited in notes 4 and 5. A well-known biography of Henry II, which lays the blame for the conflict squarely on Becket's intransigence, greatly understates Henry's demands — and consequently also understates the concessions made by Henry after Becket's martyrdom. See W. L. Warren, *Henry II* (Berkeley and Los Angeles, 1973), pp. 462–464, 477–482, 538–548. To disagree with the pro-Henry view is not to say that there was not ample room for compromise on Becket's part as well. Both Becket and Henry locked themselves into extreme positions from which they were unable to extricate themselves. To argue, however, as Warren does, that Becket was a belated Gregorian, out of step with his time and doomed to failure, is to ignore the fact that Pope Gregory VII's revolution was very much alive throughout the twelfth century. Not only Becket but also Pope Alexander III strongly denounced the Constitutions of Clarendon, charging Henry with "usurping . . . the powers which belong to Jesus Christ" and "confounding church and state." Quoted ibid., pp. 524, 527.

8. See Smalley, *Becket Conflict*, pp. 124–125.

9. See David Knowles, *Thomas Becket* (London, 1970), pp. 18–84.

10. Pollock and Maitland, I, 454, 455, 443, 447.

11. Greenaway, *Life and Death of Thomas Becket*, p. 19.

12. We owe the peculiar English doctrine of benefit of clergy to the martyrdom of Becket. Its subsequent development was curious, to say the least. The usual test of clerical status was the ability to read, and this swept more and more people into the immunity as time went on. To check abuses, the rule developed that the benefit could be used only once — whether or not the convicted clerk was deprived of his clerical status after the first offense. To make this rule easier to enforce, it was enacted in 1490 that a clerk convict should be branded on the thumb. (This practice is said to be the origin of the phrase "rule of thumb.")

"The Reformation," Plucknett writes, "would at first sight seem to have been a convenient moment for abolishing so troublesome a relic of Rome, but in fact policy fluctuated." In 1547, benefit of clergy was extended to bigamists — previously, because a clerk in lower orders, though permitted to marry, lost his clerical status upon committing the sin of marrying twice, or marrying a widow, bigamists had been excluded from clerical immunity — and also to peers of the realm, whether they could read or not. (Peers were also excused from the branding.) In the seventeenth century the benefit was also extended to women. "In

1707 all the world were admitted, by the abolition of the reading test, or 'neck verse.' "

"As a matter of fact," Plucknett comments, "all this means that the nature of benefit of clergy had undergone a radical change. In 1576 it was enacted that clerks convict should no longer be handed over to the ordinary, but should be forthwith discharged, and so the last connection of the benefit with either Church or clergy was severed, but the same act authorized one year's imprisonment before discharge, at the discretion of the court. Even before the Reformation, Parliament had ventured to enact that petty treason should no longer be clergyable . . . After the Reformation a long line of statutes made murder, piracy, highway robbery, rape, burglary and a host of other crimes non-clergyable. The result was important. The gap between felony and misdemeanor was much too large, and by using the benefit of clergy Parliament was able to make some crimes capital for a first offense (non-clergyable) and others capital only for a second felony (clergyable). Thus a rough classification of crimes into more than the two medieval categories became possible. This process was carried further by developing the policy of the Act of 1576, and condemning persons convicted of clergyable larceny to transportation for seven years. Thus the survival of clergy greatly modified the harshness of the penal law and permitted the growth of a graduated scale of punishment." Benefit of clergy was finally abolished in England in 1827. Theodore F. T. Plucknett, *A Concise History of the Common Law*, 5th ed. (Boston, 1956), pp. 439–441.

13. Frederic W. Maitland, *Roman Canon Law in the Church of England* (London, 1898), pp. 56–57.

14. "While the theory of the royal prerogative would maintain that the king has always the right to forbid church courts to hear pleas that are of royal jurisdiction, nevertheless the writ of prohibition as a legal instrument is always moved for by the litigant." G. B. Flahiff, "The Writ of Prohibition to Court Christian in the Thirteenth Century," part II, *Medieval Studies*, 7 (1945), 232.

15. Ibid., p. 257.

16. Ibid., p. 237.

17. Ibid., p. 241, n. 71.

18. Ibid., pp. 243–244.

19. Ibid., pp. 244–245.

8. The Concept of Secular Law

1. The Latin text of the *Policraticus*, edited by C. C. Webb, was published by Oxford University Press in 1909. There is an English translation, entitled *The Statesman's Book of John of Salisbury, Being the Fourth, Fifth, and Sixth Books, Selections from the Seventh and Eighth Books, of the Policraticus*, trans. with intro. by John Dickinson (New York, 1963). John of Salisbury has been called by a leading historian "the most accomplished scholar and stylist of his age." David Knowles, *The Evolution of Medieval Thought* (New York, 1962), p. 135. Born in England in 1115, Salisbury studied for twelve years at Chartres under Abelard, Gilbert de la Porree, and other great masters. In the late 1140s he served in the papal court, and later for many years in the entourage of Archbishop Thomas Becket. He was exiled by King Henry II in 1164 but was present at Canterbury in 1170 when

Becket was murdered. He was Bishop of Chartres from 1176 until his death in 1180. The *Policraticus* is dedicated to Becket.

2. See George H. Williams, *The Norman Anonymous of 1100 A.D.*, Harvard Theological Studies, vol. 18 (Cambridge, Mass., 1951).

3. Ibid., p. 173.

4. Dickinson, *Salisbury*, p. lxxxi.

5. Ibid., pp. lxxx–lxxxi.

6. Ibid., p. lxxxii.

7. Aristotle's *Politics* was translated about 1260. Aquinas's *De Regimine Principum* was written in 1266.

8. John of Salisbury's *Metalogicon*, written in the same year as the *Policraticus* (1159), drew on Aristotle's *Analytica Priora* and *De Elenchis Sophisticis*, which had been translated between 1128 and 1140.

9. R.W. Carlyle and A.J. Carlyle, *A History of Medieval Political Thought in the West*, 6 vols. (London, 1903–1936), II, 2; III, 140, 142–143, 146.

10. See Dickinson, *Salisbury*, p. xl.

11. Ibid., p. xxii.

12. Carlyle, *Medieval Political Thought*, IV, 333.

13. Ibid.

14. "St. Augustine is indifferent towards the state as community and territory . . . And yet, [he] does accept certain elements of the ancient notion of the state, namely the ideas of law and justice, order and peace which the Roman Republic and the Roman Empire had tried to make a reality within their limited conception of the true aims of mankind . . . Thus terrestrial imperium and terrestrial regnum, insofar as they are evaluated in a positive sense by St. Augustine, are for him not states as communities or territories, but forms and functions of just government in the mixed condition in which the City of God finds itself on this earth." Gerhard B. Ladner, "Aspects of Medieval Thought on Church and State," *Review of Politics*, 9 (1947), 403–422.

15. Quentin Skinner, *The Foundations of Modern Political Thought*, vol. 2, *The Age of Reformation* (New York, 1978), p. 353. See note 17.

16. *Ergo est . . . princeps potestas publica* . . . Webb, *Policraticus* 5.1. See Gaines Post, *Studies in Medieval Legal Thought: Public Law and the State, 1100–1322* (Princeton, N.J., 1964), p. 515, n. 42. Post strongly supports the view that the modern concept of the state is rooted in the legal thought of the late eleventh, twelfth, and thirteenth centuries.

17. The words in italics are those omitted from the quotation given in the text at note 15. The italics are supplied.

18. There is, of course, a huge literature on the emergence of the modern concept of the state. See Skinner, *Modern Political Thought*, II, ix–x: "The decisive shift was made from the idea of the ruler 'maintaining his state'—where this simply meant upholding his own position—to the idea that there is a separate legal and constitutional order, that of the State, which the ruler has a duty to maintain." But that shift was first made not in the sixteenth century, as Skinner maintains, but in the late eleventh and twelfth centuries, and is reflected in the writings of John of Salisbury.

Skinner goes on, however, to adopt a definition of the state (which he attributes to Max Weber) as "the sole source of law and of legitimate force within its own territory and as the sole appropriate object of its citizens' allegiances." By this definition, it is doubtful that even today the United States of America would qualify as a state, since it is governed in part by international law (including international customary law as well as international treaties and agreements) and its citizens may have other allegiances (for example, religious allegiances).

19. Dickinson, *Salisbury,* p. 335.

20. Ibid., pp. 4–5.

21. Ibid., p. 351.

22. Ibid., p. 212.

23. Ibid., p. 213.

24. Ibid., p. 258.

25. Ibid., p. 85.

26. Ibid., pp. lxxiii–lxiv (quoting *Policraticus* 3.15).

27. It was argued by some that the consecration ceremony, which required clerical participation, was a sacrament by which the ruler was constituted in his office—and by others that it merely confirmed his selection. Similarly, it was argued by some that excommunication or lapse into heresy or schism deprived a ruler's commands of their lawful authority—and by others that the lawfulness of such commands depended on their nature and purpose and not on the presence or absence of ecclesiastical censure of the ruler. Thus Gratian cited a letter written by Gregory VII in which Gregory justified his actions against Henry IV by referring to the participation of Pope Zachary I in the deposition of Childerich III, the last Merovingian king, when Zachary freed the Franks from their oaths of allegiance to Childerich so that they could swear fealty to his successor without perjury. Gratian's pupil Rufinus later discussed this case in terms of the nature of the oath sworn to Childerich, and more particularly, whether it was given to the king in his capacity as a private person or by virtue of his office.

28. Dickinson, *Salisbury,* p. 84.

29. Ibid.

30. Ibid., p. 65.

31. Ibid., p.9.

32. Ibid., p. 84.

33. Ibid., p. xliii.

34. Ibid., p. 191.

35. Ibid., p. 65.

36. Ibid.

37. Carlyle, *Medieval Political Thought,* I, 63–70, 125–131. As late as the 1080s the papal party had invoked the compact theory to challenge the authority of the emperor, whose "cruel tyranny over his subjects," it was said, had made it clear that "the people are free from his lordship and from subjection to him since it is evident that he first broke the compact by virtue of which he had been appointed." Manegold of Lautenbach, quoted in Brian Tierney, *The Crisis of Church and State, 1050–1300* (Englewood Cliffs, N.J., 1964), p. 79. Manegold adds, "To take an example from a meaner sphere, if a man hired someone for a fair wage to look after his swine and then found that he was not caring for them but stealing, killing and destroying them, would not the man withhold the promised wage from him and remove him ignominiously from his task of caring for

the swine?" Later in the same document (p. 80) Manegold states: "Since then no one can make himself an emperor or king, the people raise some man above themselves for these reasons, to rule and govern them by virtue of his just authority, to apportion to each his own, to protect the good, to repress the wicked and to deal out justice to all. If, however, he breaks the compact by which he was elected . . . reason justly considers that he has absolved the people from their duty of submission to him since he himself first broke the bond of mutual fidelity by which he was bound to them and they to him." John of Salisbury, though a supporter of the papal revolution and a foe of royal tyranny, did not take up this "left-wing" argument.

38. Aristotle, *Politics* 1.1, in *The Basic Works of Aristotle*, ed. Richard McKeon (New York, 1941), p. 1127.

39. Ladner, "Aspects of Medieval Thought," pp. 411–416.

40. See Myron P. Gilmore, *Argument from Roman Law in Political Thought, 1200–1600* (Cambridge, Mass., 1941), pp. 15–36.

41. D. 2.1.1 and 1.16.7.2. See John W. Perrin, "Azo, Roman Law, and Sovereign European States," *Studia Gratiana*, 15 (1972), 92–94, 97–101.

42. Perrin, "Azo," p. 93.

43. Ibid., p. 95.

44. Ibid., p. 93.

45. See Joseph R. Strayer, *On the Medieval Origins of the Modern State* (Princeton, N.J., 1970), p. 21.

46. See Ernst H. Kantorowicz, *The King's Two Bodies: A Study in Medieval Political Theory* (Princeton, N.J., 1957), pp. 143–192.

47. Fritz Kern, *Kingship and Law in the Middle Ages*, trans. S. B. Chrimos (Oxford, 1939), pp. 83–84.

48. See Ralph E. Giesey, *The Oath of the Aragonese and the Legendary Laws of Sobrarbe* (Princeton, N.J., 1968).

49. Magna Carta, 17 John (1215), chaps. 12, 17, 38, 39, 40, 41, 42, 45.

50. Golden Bull, chaps. 1, 2, 3, 9, 14, 16, 23, 28. For the full text of the Golden Bull of 1222 see Henrik Marczali, *Enchiridion Fontium Historiae Hungarorum* (Budapest, 1902), pp. 134–143. See C. M. Knatchbull-Hugessen, *The Political Evolution of the Hungarian Nation*, I (London, 1908), 19–30.

51. See Lord Dicey's definition as qualified by Roberto M. Unger, *Law in Modern Society: Toward a Criticism of Social Theory* (New York, 1976), pp. 273–274. Unger calls the rule of law a "legal order," which he contrasts with "customary law," on the one hand, and "bureaucratic law" on the other. This leads him to the erroneous view (p. 54) that "the legal order emerged with modern European liberal society," that is, not until the seventeenth century.

9. Feudal Law

1. Marc Bloch divides feudalism into the "first feudal age," from the eighth to the mid-eleventh century, and the "second feudal age," from the mid-eleventh to the fifteenth century. "There were," he writes, "in a word, two successive feudal ages, very different from one another in their essential character." Bloch, *Feudal Society* (London, 1961), p. 60. Similarly, Georges Duby considers the eleventh century to be the critical period in the emergence of Western feudalism, and he calls the years from 1070 to 1180 "the century of great progress," in which

feudalism as a system was established throughout Europe. Georges Duby and Robert Mandrou, *A History of French Civilization*, trans, J. B. Atkinson (New York, 1958), p. 59; see also Duby, *The Early Growth of the European Economy* (London, 1974). Compare Rodney H. Hilton, *Bond Men Made Free: Medieval Peasant Movements and the English Rising of 1381* (London, 1973), pp. 14–16; David Herlihy, ed., *The History of Feudalism* (New York, 1970), p.3.

2. See Jean Richard, *The Latin Kingdom of Jerusalem*, vol. A (New York, 1979), 67, where the Kingdom of Jerusalem is described as "such a Utopia as the purest theoretician of feudal law might have dreamed of."

3. Bloch, *Feudal Society*, pp. 62–63.

4. For an excellent analysis of these invasitons, see ibid., pp. 3–56.

5. Duby and Mandrou, *History of French Civilization*, p. 43.

6. See Herlihy, *History of Feudalism*, pp. xiv–xv. Duby and Mandrou, *History of French Civilization*, p. 47, state that "by the beginning of the eleventh century men were forced to obtain a clear awareness of [the duties called forth by homage]." See also Bloch, *Feudal Society*, pp. 219–224.

7. The English development is analyzed by Samuel Thorne, "English Feudalism: Estates in Land," *Cambridge Law Journal* 17 (1959), 193–209.

8. The development of the heritability of fiefs in various parts of Europe is discussed in F. L. Ganshof, *Feudalism* (New York, 1964), pp. 133–136.

9. Bloch, *Feudal Society*, p. 195.

10. Ibid., p. 197.

11. Ganshof, *Feudalism*, p. 78, states that the kiss "was simply a way of confirming the obligations contracted by the two parties, just as it was used to confirm other forms of contract." The word "simply" may be misleading. The entire ritual by which the contract was formed effectively symbolized the obligations incurred by the parties. In the phrase of the Oxford philosopher John Austin, the words and acts were "performative utterances." They brought into being what they symbolized.

12. Friedrich Heer, *The Medieval World: Europe, 1100–1350* (New York, 1961), p. 37.

13. *MGH*, Legum IV, I, pp. 90–91. This and later feudal statutes were collected in about 1100 in the *Consuetudines Feudorum* (later called *Libri Feudorum*). Undoubtedly Conrad's statute was known to those who drafted the Magna Carta. See Walter Ullmann, *Law and Politics in the Middle Ages* (London, 1975), pp. 216, 219.

14. Sir Frederick Pollock and Frederic William Maitland, *History of English Law*, 2nd ed. (1898; reprint ed., Cambridge, 1968), I, 589.

15. Philippe de Beaumanoir, *Coutumes de Beauvaisis*, ed. A. Salmon, 2 vols. (Paris, 1970), I, secs. 294-301.

16. Bloch, *Feudal Society*, p. 227 states: "The contract of vassalage bound together two men who were, by definition, on different social levels."

17. Heer, *Medieval World*, p. 40.

18. See Herlihy, *History of Feudalism*, p. 98.

19. Ibid., p. xv. On the *Libri Feudorum* see Heinrich Zoepfl, *Deutsche Rechtsgeschichte* (Stuttgart, 1858), pp. 120-126; Walter Ullmann, *Law and Politics in the Middle Ages* (London, 1975), p. 217.

20. Other early sources of feudal law were the *Statute* of Count William II for the county of Forcalquier in Provence (1162), the *Assie au Comte Geoffroy* for Brit-

tany (1185), and the *Charte féodale* for Hainault (1200). References may be found in Ganshof, *Feudalism*, p. 68.

21. Bloch, *Feudal Society*, pp. 181–189.

22. Beaumanoir, *Coutumes de Beauvaisis*, sec. 146.

23. See Frederic William Maitland, "The Mystery of Seisin," *Law Quarterly Review*, 2 (October 1886), 481–496.

10. Manorial Law

1. See Rodney H. Hilton, *Bond Men Made Free: Medieval Peasant Movements and the English Rising of 1381* (London, 1973), p. 61.

2. The term *manerium* was introduced into England by the Normans in 1066, but the institution itself had existed there for a long time. The Scandinavian peoples, however, never developed a manorial system; those Norsemen (Normans) who settled in the western part of the Frankish Empire in the early tenth century adopted it from the Franks.

3. Philippe de Beaumanoir, *Coutumes de Beauvaisis*, ed. A. Salmon, II (Paris, 1970), secs. 1451–53, and Georges Hubrecht, "Commentaire historique et juridique," ibid., III (Paris, 1974), pp. 184–186.

4. By feudal and manorial law, a serf could not enter into holy orders without permission of his lord, and by canon law no person could enter holy orders unless he was free. Nevertheless, the pressure to free a serf who wished to enter into holy orders, or to permit a serf to send his children to study for holy orders, must have been substantial, as shown by the fact that a considerable number of the clergy were ex-serfs.

5. See note 4. Again, permission of the lord was required, but to withhold such permission was to risk eternal damnation.

6. Canon lawyers unanimously agreed that slavery was contrary to natural law, although there was also general agreement that it was lawful under positive law. "The Church gave the weight of its authority to the provisions of the Roman law which restrained the arbitrary power of the master and protected the slave, and lent the sanction of its own penalties to the enforcement of those laws, while in relation to the marriage of the slave it went further than [the Roman law of Justinian]." R. W. Carlyle and A. J. Carlyle, *A History of Medieval Political Thought in the West*, II (London, 1909), 129. Thus marriage between a free person and a slave was valid under canon law. Gratian reproduces a statement by St. Gregory the Great "in which he describes the purpose of the Incarnation as being to break the chain of slavery by which men are bound and to restore them to their primitive liberty; and urges that it is therefore a good action to give back to men who in the beginning were brought forth by nature free and whom the law of nations had subjected to the yoke of slavery, that liberty in which they had been born." Ibid., p. 135. See also Marc Bloch, *Feudal Society*, trans. L.A. Manyon (London, 1961), p. 259.

7. Hilton, *Bond Men*, p. 65.

8. Perry Anderson, *Passages from Antiquity to Feudalism* (London, 1974), pp. 149, 185.

9. Hilton, *Bond Men*, pp. 69–70.

10. Achille Luchaire, quoted in Maurice Dobb, *Studies in the Development of Capitalism* (London, 1946), p. 46.

11. Ibid., p. 46.

12. Ephraim Lipson, *Economic History of England*, 7th ed., I (London, 1937), 92–94.

13. Anderson, *Passages*, pp. 152–153.

14. Beaumanoir, sec. 1043.

15. Ibid., sec. 295.

16. See John P. Dawson, *A History of Lay Judges* (Cambridge, Mass., 1960), p. 194.

17. Rodney H. Hilton, *A Medieval Society* (London, 1966), pp. 150–151.

18. See W. O. Ault, *Open-Field Farming in Medieval England: A Study of Village By-Laws* (London, 1972), pp. 145–174, where manorial court rolls are reproduced in modern English translation.

19. Ibid., p. 151. This case arose in 1290 but it could as easily have arisen 150 years earlier.

20. Ibid., p. 157.

21. Ibid., pp. 81–144, where such by-laws are reproduced.

22. Anderson, *Passages*, p. 148.

23. In 1702 Lord Holt held that a Negro could not be sold under English law, and that "as soon as a negro comes into England he becomes free; one may be a villein in England, but not a slave." *Smith* v. *Brown and Cooper*, 2 Salk. 666 (1702).

24. Beaumanoir, sec. 15.

25. *Encyclopaedia Britannica*, 1969 ed., s.v. "serfdom and villeinage," 246–247 (Rodney H. Hilton).

11. Mercantile Law

1. See generally Robert S. Lopez, *The Commercial Revolution of the Middle Ages, 950–1350* (Englewood Cliffs, N.J., 1971); Robert S. Lopez and Irving W. Raymond, eds., *Medieval Trade in the Mediterranean World: Illustrative Documents with Introductions and Notes* (New York, n.d.); Raymond de Roover, *Business, Banking, and Economic Thought in Late Medieval and Early Modern Europe* (Chicago, 1974).

2. See Norman J. G. Pounds, *An Historical Geography of Europe, 450 B.C.–A.D. 1330* (Cambridge, 1973).

3. See Lopez, *Commercial Revolution*, chap. 3.

4. Henri Pirenne, *Economic and Social History of Medieval Europe* (New York, 1937), pp. 48–49.

5. Ibid., p. 14. The statement is quoted by Pirenne from Levin Goldschmidt, *Universalgeschichte des Handelrechts*, I (Stuttgart, 1891), 139: "Homo mercator vix aut numquam potest Deo placere." Pirenne fails to mention that it was said first by St. John Chrysostom in the third century A.D., and that the quotation continues: "therefore no Christian ought to be a merchant, and if he wishes to be one he should be cast out of the Church of God." This reflects the spirit of monasticism prior to the late eleventh century, but it hardly reflects the spirit of the crusading Roman Church of Gregory VII and his successors.

6. Pirenne, *Medieval Europe*, p. 28. Pirenne quotes an episode from the life of St. Gerald of Aurillac, who died in 909, without noting that there was a shift two centuries later. He writes (pp. 28–29): "From the beginning to the end the Church continued to regard commercial profits as a danger to salvation. Its ascetic ideal, which was perfectly suited to an agricultural civilization, made it always suspicious of social changes, which it could not prevent and to which

necessity even compelled it to submit, but to which it was never openly reconciled. Its prohibition of interest was to weigh heavily on the economic life of later centuries. It prevented the merchants from growing rich with a free conscience and from reconciling the practice of business with the prescripts of religion. For proof of this we need only read the many wills of bankers and speculators directing that the poor whom they had defrauded should be repaid and bequeathing to the clergy a part of the property which at the bottom of their hearts they felt to be ill-gotten." But this is based on a wrong psychological theory as well as a greatly oversimplified view of the church's position.

7. Max Weber first propounded his thesis connecting the rise of capitalism with the Reformation in "Die protestantische Ethik und der Geist des Kapitalismus," *Archiv für Sozialwissenschaft und Sozialpolitik*, vols. 20 and 21 (1904–05). The English translation was published as *The Protestant Ethic and the Spirit of Capitalism*. In the meantime, the Weber thesis had been elaborated by Ernst Troeltsch in *Die sozialen Lehren der christlichen Kirchen und Gruppen* (Tübingen, 1912), and sharply attacked by Werner Sombart in *Der Bourgeois* (Munich, 1913). In *Religion and the Rise of Capitalism* (New York, 1926), R. H. Tawney followed the Weber thesis in dating the rise of capitalism from the time of the Reformation, while assigning greater importance to concurrent social and economic developments. Other scholars, however, have stressed that capitalism antedated the Reformation. See H. M. Robertson, *Aspects of the Rise of Economic Individualism* (Cambridge, 1933); Amintore Fanfani, *Catholicism, Protestantism, and Capitalism* (New York, 1935). For a recent article defending the Weber thesis, see Ehud Sprinzak, "Weber's Thesis as an Historical Explanation," *History and Theory*, 11 (1972), 294. Excerpts from many of the above materials appear in Robert W. Green, *Protestantism and Capitalism: The Weber Thesis and Its Critics* (Boston, 1959).

8. See also Mark 10, 23–25 ("How hard it will be for the wealthy to enter the kingdom of God!"). The emphasis throughout is not on the evil of having wealth but on the evil of loving wealth.

9. See chapter 5.

10. See Henri Pirenne, *Medieval Cities: Their Origins and the Revival of Trade*, trans. Frank D. Halsey (Princeton, N.J., 1925), pp. 157, 158.

11. Quoted in F. M. Burdick, "Contributions of the Law Merchant to the Common Law," *Select Essays in Anglo-American Legal History*, III (Boston, 1909), 50.

12. Gerard Malynes, *Consuetudo vel Lex Mercatoria, or the Ancient Law Merchant* (London, 1622), from the Preface, "To the Courteous Reader."

13. William Blackstone, *Commentaries on the Laws of England* I (Portland, 1807), 273.

14. William Mitchell, *An Essay on the Early History of the Law Merchant* (Cambridge, 1904), p. 7.

15. Ibid., p. 9.

16. See Levin Goldschmidt, *Universalgeschichte des Handelsrechts*, I (Stuttgart, 1891), 119.

17. Ibid.

18. Magna Carta, 17 John (1215), chap. 41. The chapter continues: ". . . except in time of war, such merchants as are of a country at war with Us. If any such be found in Our dominion at the outbreak of war, they shall be attached, without injury to their persons or goods, until it be known to Us or Our Chief

Justiciary how Our merchants are being treated in the country at war with Us, and if Our merchants be safe there, then theirs shall be safe with Us."

19. Hubert Hall, ed., *Select Cases concerning the Law Merchant*, III (London, 1932), 175.

20. Goldschmidt, *Universalgeschichte*, pp. 180–182.

21. See Mitchell, *Essay*, pp. 14–16. Mitchell writes: "At Marseilles, where the existence of commercial judges dates from the twelfth century, it was their duty to decide cases and disputes 'summarily, without regard to the subtleties of the law.' The German Hanse, the English and French Admiralty all administered summary justice. For the passing stranger or the foreign merchant en route a specially prompt justice was generally the rule."

22. The document is reproduced in G. F. Sartorius Freyherrn von Waltershausen, *Urkundliche Geschichte des Ursprunges der deutschen Hanse*, ed. J. M. Lappenberg, II (Hamburg, 1830), 3. It is in the form of a command by Henry to his justiciars, sheriffs, and "all his servants and faithful" in France and England, to "keep and maintain and protect the citizens and merchants and men of Cologne and all their property [*res*] and possessions . . . as my own [*sicut meas proprias*]." A second document, printed on page 4 of the same volume, reaffirms the command to keep and maintain and protect the "men and citizens of Cologne, as my men and friends, and all their property and merchandise and possessions" and adds that "you shall not exact from them any new customs or rights which they . . . were not accustomed to perform." The two laws were issued at Woodstock and Northampton, respectively, but are not dated. (Henry II ruled from 1154–1189.) Presumably the government of the city of Cologne reciprocated by extending similar protection to English merchants there.

23. See Chapter 6.

24. The decree is reproduced in translation in Lopez and Raymond, *Medieval Trade*, pp. 276–277. It states that the doge and alderman consider "that if instruments of exchange and other trade contracts, in or without writing, could not be enforced because of impediments of this kind, this would result in great loss and inconvenience to the Genoese citizens and merchants, who ordinarily make such contracts, and that otherwise no trade could be carried on nor ships be sent on their voyages."

25. Goldschmidt, *Universalgeschichte*, pp. 170–171.

26. Statute of the Staple, 27 Edward III (1353).

27. Mitchell, *Early History of Law Merchant*, pp. 14–17, 20.

28. Decretal "Saepe Contingit" of Pope Clement V (1306), *Corpus Juris Canonici, Decretalium Collectiones* (Leipzig, 1881), p. 1200.

29. "Item propter personas qui celeren habere debent iustici iusticiam, sicut sunt mercatores quibus exhibetur iustitia pepoudrous." Bracton, *De Legibus et Consuetudinibus Angliae*, fol. 333, in Samuel Thorne, *Bracton on the Laws and Customs of England*, IV (Cambridge, Mass., 1977), 63.

30. In German and French law, the right of the good-faith purchaser of goods against the true owner is expressed in the maxims "Hand wahre Hand" and "Meubles n'ont point de suite." In English law the doctrine is confined to transactions in the "open market" (market overt).

31. Goldschmidt, *Universalgeschichte*, p. 133, calls this "die Materialisierung

des Besitzrechts." It applied to land as well as to chattels.

32. The sea loan (*foenus nauticum*) was an unsecured loan made to a merchant who was shipping goods overseas, repayable on condition that the vessel returned safely. Interest rates were very high; in the eleventh and twelfth centuries they were generally 50 percent. The Western jurists invented a variation of this, the *respondentia*, which required interest and principal to be repaid if the cargo reached its destination, regardless of what happened to the vessel. The bottomry loan, though repayable only if the vessel returned, was less expensive since it was secured by transfer to the lender of the seller's lien on the cargo and the seller's interest in the vessel itself. The sea loan was criticized as usurious and was finally condemned by Pope Gregory IX in 1236. See Raymond de Roover, "The Organisation of Trade," in *Cambridge Economic History of Europe*, ed. M. M. Postan, E. E. Rich, and Edward Miller, III (Cambridge, 1963), 54.

33. Most of this list may be found in Goldschmidt, *Universalgeschichte*, beginning on p. 133.

34. "Vel ei cui ordinaverit." Ibid., p. 135, n. 145. Goldschmidt cites Heinrich Brunner to the effect that "order" paper had been used in Italy since the sixth century in various stereotyped formulas, but Goldschmidt states that in the form that corresponds to modern usage ("to X or order" or "to the order of X") it first appeared in Italy in the twelfth century and in Germany in the thirteenth century. Bearer paper had been used in Italy as early as the ninth century, according to Goldschmidt, but in Flanders and France only since the end of the thirteenth century and in Germany since the beginning of the fourteenth century.

35. Lopez, *Commercial Revolution*, p. 72.

36. Goldschmidt, *Universalgeschichte*, p. 306.

37. Ibid., p. 176.

38. Lopez, *Commercial Revolution*, p. 73.

39. De Roover, "*Organisation of Trade*," p. 50.

40. Ibid.

41. See W. A. Bewes, *The Romance of the Law Merchant* (London, 1923), pp. 20, 21.

42. See F. Edler de Roover, "Early Examples of Marine Insurance," *Journal of Economic History*, 5 (1945), 172, 183, 198.

43. New credit devices were invented which are to be found neither in the Graeco-Roman world nor among the Germanic peoples, although there were some parallels among the Arabs. Lopez sees the development and expansion of credit as fundamentally an outgrowth of the same cooperative spirit that led to the creation of the urban communes in this period. See Lopez, *Commercial Revolution*, pp. 71–73.

44. Goldschmidt, *Universalgeschichte*, p. 36. Goldschmidt argues that types of legal transactions, like the law itself, are subject to a "double law of development," namely, a "law of unfolding (differentiation)" and a "law of simplification." By the second law he apparently means conceptual simplification, or increasing generalization. This law seems doubtful, particularly as applied to commercial transactions, which seem to become not only more and more complex (which is perhaps part of their "differentiation") but also less and less susceptible of conceptual integration.

12. Urban Law

1. Henri Pirenne, *Medieval Cities: Their Origins and the Revival of Trade*, trans. Frank D. Halsey (Princeton, N.J., 1925), p. 56.

2. See Lewis Mumford, *The City in History: Its Origins, Its Transformations, and Its Prospects* (New York, 1961), p. 253.

3. Robert S. Lopez, "The Trade of Medieval Europe: The South," in *Cambridge Economic History of Europe*, ed. M. M. Postan, E. E. Rich, and Edward Miller, II (Cambridge, 1963), 297–298. See also R. S. Lopez, *The Birth of Europe* (New York, 1967), pp. 260–262.

4. "Omnes burgenses et tota communa liberorum hominum habeant wambais et capellet ferri et lanceam." Assize of Arms, art. 3, in William Stubbs, ed., *Select Charters and Other Illustrations of English Constitutional History*, 9th ed. rev. (Oxford, 1951), p. 153. Stubbs comments: "The use of the words *communa liberorum hominum*, in Article 3 . . . gives a sort of clue to the political tendency of the whole Act."

5. See Maxime Rodinson, *Marxism et Monde Muselman* (Cambridge, Mass., 1972), p. 106. A different view is stated by Ira M. Lapidus, *Muslim Cities in the Late Middle Ages* (Cambridge, Mass., 1967).

6. See Norman J. G. Pounds, *An Historical Geography of Europe, 450 B.C.–1330 A.D.* (Cambridge, 1973); J.C. Russell, *Late Anceint and Medieval Population, Transactions of the American Philosophical Society*, vol. 48, pt. 3 (Philadelphia, 1958), pp. 60–62; Lopez, *Birth of Europe*, pp. 258–270; Lopez, "Trade of Medieval Europe," pp. 293–304.

7. Lopez, "Trade of Medieval Europe," p. 303.

8. Mumford, *City in History*, p. 260.

9. See Wilhelm Reinecke, *Geschichte der Stadt Cambrai bis zur Erteiling der Lex Godefridi (1227)* (Marburg, 1876).

10. See Albert Vermeesch, *Essai sur les origines et la signification de la commune dans le nord de la France (onzième et douzième siècles)* (Heule, Belgium, 1966).

11. See L. H. Labande, *Histoire de Beauvais et de ses institutions communales jusqu'au commencement du quinzième siècle* (Paris, 1892), pp. 62, 64; Carl Stephenson, *Borough and Town: A Study of Urban Origins in England* (Cambridge, Mass., 1933), p. 37. The date of the charter of Louis VI is not known; it may have been 1122. Also, the precise year of the establishment of the commune is not known, although it is sometimes given as 1099.

12. Lancelin de Bulles, one of the leading landowners, appropriated much of the episcopal demesne for his own use and succeeded in having his son Fulk elected bishop in 1089. See Labande, *Histoire de Beauvais*, chap. 4.

13. Ibid.

14. Stephenson, *Borough and Town*, p. 38. See also Charles Petits-Dutailles, *Les Communes françaises* (Paris, 1947).

15. Stephenson, *Borough and Town*, pp. 29, 30. See also Rodney H. Hilton, *Bond Men Made Free* (London, 1973), p. 81; Maurice Prou, *Les coutumes de Lorris et leur propagation aux douzième et treizième siècles* (Lorris, 1884).

16. D. Ainé, *Histoire de Montauban* (Montauban, 1855); Stephenson, *Borough and Town*, p. 32.

17. Stephenson, *Borough and Town*, pp. 30, 31.

18. Ibid., p. 34.

19. Ibid., p. 35.

20. Stephenson reports that Saint-Omer had to surrender its right the following year, but that the citizens were then given the right to collect their own taxes for a fixed rent. Ibid.

21. Ibid., p. 24.

22. The information contained in this section is derived from the following books: Paul Strait, *Cologne in the Twelfth Century* (Gainesville, Fla., 1974); Richard Koebner, *Die Anfänge des Gemeinwesens der Stadt Köln* (Berlin, 1922); Thea Buyken and Hermann Conrad, *Die Amtleutebücher der Kölnischen Sondergemeinden* (Weimar, 1936); Carl Hegel, *Die Chroniken der deutschen Städte vom 14. bis ins 16. Jahrhundert*, vol. 12, *Köln* (1875; reprint ed., Göttingen, 1968); Elisabeth Rütimeyer, *Stadtherr und Stadtbürgerschaft in den rheinischen Bischofsstädten: Ihr Kampf um die Hoheitsrechte im Hochmittelalter* (Stuttgart, 1928); Arnold Stelzmann, *Illustrierte Geschichte der Stadt Köln*, 3rd ed. (Cologne, 1962); Edith Ennen, *Die europäische Stadt des Mittelalters*, 2nd ed. (Göttingen, 1975). See also Friedrich Lau, *Entwicklung der Kommunalen Verfassung und Verwaltung der Stadt Köln bis zum Jahre 1396* (Bonn, 1898).

23. Stephenson, *Borough and Town*, pp. 33–35. See also Franz Beyerle, *Untersuchungen zur Geschichte des aelteren Stadtrechts von Freiburg im Breisgau* (Heidelberg, 1910), p. 75.

24. M. V. Clarke, *The Medieval City State: An Essay on Tyranny and Federation in the Late Middle Ages* (London, 1926), pp. 15–16.

25. A complete list of mother cities and daughter cities is given in Hans Reichard, *Die deutschen Stadtrechte des Mittelalters* (Berlin, 1930), pp. 76–79.

26. This is all the more important because the city of Magdeburg was almost entirely destroyed by fire in 1631 and its archives were totally consumed, so that virtually all the information that is available concerning the Magdeburg law comes from archives of other cities that received that law. See Georg Piltz, *Magdeburg: Stadt am Strom* (Dresden, 1954), pp. 52–54; F. A. Wolter, *Geschichte der Stadt Magdeburg von ihrem Ursprung bis aud die Gegenward*, 3rd ed. (Magdeburg, 1901), p. 162.

27. The nine articles of the first Magdeburg law, in Latin, are reproduced in Paul Laband, *Magdeburger Rechtsquellen zum akademischen Gebrauch* (Königsberg, 1869), pp. 1–3.

28. The Breslau and Görlitz laws of 1261 and 1304, respectively, in old German, are reproduced ibid., pp. 14–31, and in Ernst Theodor Gaupp, *Das alte Magdeburgische und Hallische Recht: Ein Beitrag zur deutschen Rechtsgeschichte* (Breslau, 1826), pp. 229–323.

29. Paul Laband, *Das Magdeburg-Breslauer systematische Schoeffenrecht aus der Mitte des XIV. Jahrhundert* (Berlin, 1863).

30. Stephenson, *Borough and Town*, p. 120.

31. Ibid., pp. 152, 153, 165, 166.

32. Ibid., p. 143.

33. Ibid., p. 180. See also Christopher N. L. Brooke, *London, 800–1216: The Shaping of a City* (London, 1975); Mary Bateson, "A London Municipal Collection of the Reign of John," *English Historical Review*, 17 (1902), 480–511, 707–730.

34. Charter of Henry I to the Citizens of London, Stubbs, *Select Charters*, pp. 107–108.

35. In 1086 York had a body of burgesses and four *judices* over them, according to Domesday Book; this probably represented a survival of pre-Conquest institutions. In the 1170s there was an unsuccessful attempt to set up a commune at York. In 1203 York received a charter from the king, and thereafter claimed the status of a commune, as did Winchester, whose guild merchant had received grants of liberties and customs from Henry II and possibly from Henry I. New charters for Winchester issued by Richard and John secured to its citizens immunity from process outside the city walls and an autonomous city overnment. See Peter Werham, *York* (London, 1971), pp. 62–83; G. W. Kitchin, *Historic Towns: Winchester* (London, 1891), p. 163; B. B. Woodward, *History of Winchester* (Winchester, [c. 1900]); J. E. A. Joliffe, *The Constitutional History of Medieval England* (London, 1937), pp. 321–326.

Mention should also be made of the Cinque Ports, which consisted originally of five towns (Hastings, Romney, Hyth, Dover, and Sandwich), although over thirty towns joined at various times. The towns gave an annual service of ships to the crown for defense, in return for communal privileges. The roots of this arrangement go back to the early years of the twelfth century; it was officially defined under Henry II. In 1205 the towns first received individual charters. In 1260 a general charter was issued to the towns collectively. There seems, however, to have been no formal written document of federation or other formal constitution. The abundant privileges enjoyed by the towns included a common court of justice, freedom from tolls and other burdens, freedom from jurisdiction outside their limits, and annual fairs. See K. M. E. Murray, *Constitutional History of the Cinque Ports* (Manchester, 1935), pp. 1–27.

36. The full text of the Ipswich Charter appears in Charles Gross, *The Gild Merchant: A Contribution to British Municipal History*, 2 vols. (Oxford, 1890), II, 115–116. The phrase used to designate the life tenure of the provosts—that they shall serve "on good behavior" (*quamdiu se bene gesserint*)—was used also in the seventeenth century after the English Revolution to designate life tenure of judges and was embodied in the Act of Settlement of 1701.

37. The following description is drawn from the Domesday Book of Ipswich, as reproduced in Gross, *Gild Merchant*, II, 115–123. See also ibid., I, 23–26 and Stephenson, *Borough and Town*, pp. 174–178.

38. Domesday Book of Ipswich, in Gross, *Gild Merchant*, II, 122–123.

39. See Helen M. Jewell, *English Local Administration in the Middle Ages* (New York, 1972), p. 53. The author rightly stresses also the importance of the exemption of burgesses from attendance at shire and hundred courts, implying the right to have a court of equivalent competence for themselves within the borough. This right of the borough to judge itself (together with the right to "farm" the annual tax due to the crown) was granted to London in perpetuity in 1131. However, the crown always maintained the jurisdiction of the royal courts of Common Pleas and King's Bench over felonies and over disputes concerning freehold land. When these courts traveled on circuit, they were required in some places to come within the confines of the borough to judge; normally, however, twelve jurors from the borough had to attend the circuit ("eyre") session, along with juries from the hundreds.

40. See generally Alfio Natale, *Milano medievale, da Attila ai Torriani* (Milan,

1964); Cesare Manaresi, ed., *Gli Atti del Comune di Milano fino all'anno MCCXVI* (Milan, 1919).

41. Quoted in Eugen Rosenstock-Huessy, *Out of Revolution: The Autobiography of Western Man* (New York, 1938), p. 571.

42. For these and other data about communal self-government in this period, see *Encyclopaedia Britannica*, 1969 ed., s.v. "commune (medieval)" (D. P. Waley).

43. Ibid., p. 199.

44. Rosenstock-Huessy, *Out of Revolution*, p. 573.

45. Francesco Calasso, *Medio Evo del Diritto*, I (Milan, 1954), 422.

46. Ibid.

47. See *Constituta Legis et Usus Pisanae Civitatis*, in Francesco Bonaini, ed., *Statuta inediti della Citta di Pisa*, II (Florence, 1870), 643–1026. (The *Constitutum Legis* occupies pp. 647–809; the *Constitutum Usus* occupies pp. 810–1026.)

48. Friedrich Heer, *The Medieval World* (New York, 1962), p. 74.

49. See Franco Valsecchi, *Le Corporazioni nel'organismo politico del medio evo* (Milan, 1931), pp. 21–23.

50. Franz Wieacker, *Privatrechtsgeschichte der Neuzeit* (Göttingen, 1967), p. 51.

51. Statute of the Staple, 27 Edward III (1353).

52. John H. Mundy and Peter Riesenberg, *The Medieval Town* (New York, 1958), Document No. 43, pp. 163–164.

53. See Harvey Cox, *The Secular City* (New York, 1965).

54. See Max Weber, *The City*, trans. and ed. Don Martindale and Gertrud Neuwirth (New York, 1958). In his preface (pp. 21, 34–40, 43–45) Martindale contrasts American and European scholarship in the field of urban sociology, indicating that American sociologists tend to view the contemporary city from a geophysical and ecological perspective and are chiefly concerned with the disintegrating effects of urban social structure on family ties, local associations, culture, caste, and status, and the substitution of an order resting on occupation and vocational interests. In Europe, by contrast, sociologists like Simmel and Durkheim have emphasized the social-psychological characteristics of the city (its exaltation of punctuality, calculability, and exactness, its "blasé" attitude, its superficiality, its anomie or normlessness), while others, following Fustel de Coulanges and Weber, have taken a historical and comparative approach. Martindale shows how knowledge concerning the historical development of the institution of the podestà system might have helped Americans in the early twentieth century to avoid misunderstanding the role of the mayor and city council and of the city manager in American cities.

55. Weber, *City*, pp. 54–55.

56. See William Bennett Munro, *The Government of American Cities* (New York, 1926).

57. Weber, *City*, p. 91.

58. Ibid., pp. 92, 93.

59. Ibid., p. 94.

60. Ibid., p. 96.

61. Ibid., p. 97.

13. Royal Law: Sicily, England, Normandy, France

1. Joseph R. Strayer, *On the Medieval Origins of the Modern State* (Princeton, N.J., 1970), p. 22.

2. Ibid., p. 33.

3. Heinrich Mitteis, *The State in the Middle Ages*, trans. H. F. Orton (Amsterdam, 1975), p. 307. See also Strayer, *Medieval Origins*, p. 12: "The modern state, wherever we find it today, is based on the pattern which emerged in Europe in the period 1100–1600."

4. Mitteis, *State*, pp. 307–308.

5. James M. Powell, ed. and trans., *The Liber Augustalis or Constitutions of Melfi Promulgated by the Emperor Frederick II for the Kingdom of Sicily in 1231* (Syracuse, N.Y., 1971), p. xxxviii.

6. See Orville Prescott, *Lords of Italy: Portraits from the Middle Ages* (New York, 1972), p. 3.

7. Quoted in David C. Douglas, *The Norman Achievement, 1050–1100* (Berkeley and Los Angeles, 1969), p. 105.

8. Ibid., p. 143.

9. Mitteis, *State*, p. 172.

10. Roger II succeeded to his father's title as Count of Sicily. After he had acquired Calabria and Apulia, Pope Honorius invested him as Duke of Apulia. When Honorius died in 1130, two rival popes were elected. Roger, anxious to be a king, supported the weaker of the two, Anacletus, who promptly anointed and invested him as King of Sicily, Apulia, and Calabria. In 1139, Anacletus having died, Pope Innocent II, successor to Honorius, added his own investiture of Roger as king. The story is told very well in Prescott, *Lords of Italy,* p. 83.

11. See H. G. Creel, *The Origins of Statecraft in China*, vol. 1, *The Western Chou Empire* (Chicago and London, 1970), p. 12, citing a book by a Muslim geographer, written at Roger II's court in 1154, which "devotes far more space to the government of China than to that of any other state."

12. See generally Ferdinand Chalandon, *Histoire de la Domination Normande en Italie et en Sicile* (New York, 1960); Douglas, *Norman Achievement*; Claude Cahen, *Le régime féodal de l'Italie normande* (Paris, 1940).

13. See Charles H. Haskins, "England and Sicily in the Twelfth Century," pt. 3, *English Historical Review*, 26 (October 1911), 641, 655, 663–664.

14. Heinrich Mitteis, *Der Staat des hohen Mittelalters* (Weimar, 1953), p. 238. This is badly translated in Mitteis, *State*, p. 226.

15. This was a collection of hundreds of legal rules in the Germanic style, showing some influence of surviving Roman law, but without the kind of systematization and integration that characterize the Western legal tradition from the twelfth century on. See *Liber Legis Langobardorum Papiensis Dictus, MGH*, Legum III, p. 290.

16. Max Hofmann, *Die Stellung des Königs von Sizilien nach den Assisen von Ariano (1140)* (Münster, 1915), pp. 39, 155, 174.

17. The text of the Assizes of Ariano is reproduced in Francesco Brandileone, *Il diritto romano nelle leggi normane e sveve del regno di Sicilia* (Turin, 1884).

18. Hofmann, *Stellung*, p. 65.

19. Ibid., p. 72.

20. Quoted in Thomas C. Van Cleve, *The Emperor Frederick II of Hohenstaufen: Immutator Mundi* (Oxford, 1972), p. 241.

21. See Haskins, "England and Sicily," pp. 642–643.

22. Ibid., pp. 644–645.

23. Ibid., pp. 647–648.

24. See Hofmann, *Stellung*, p. 85.

25. Prescott, *Lords of Italy*, p. 164. Prescott adds that Frederick also forbade the building of new private castles and that he himself built, during his long reign, sixty new castles at strategic locations. Prescott's account of the exploits of Roger II, Frederick II, and the other rulers of southern Italy in the period from the late eleventh to the early fourteenth century is certainly the most vivid and possibly the best short account that has been written on the subject.

26. Powell, *Liber Augustalis*. Specific citations to this work are given in the text.

27. Quoted by Prescott, *Lords of Italy*, p. 166.

28. Powell, *Liber Augustalis*, p. xx.

29. Ibid., p. xxi.

30. Quoted by Prescott, *Lords of Italy*, p. 167.

31. See Douglas, *Norman Achievement*, pp. 105–106.

32. Ibid., p. 144.

33. William's decree is reproduced in William Stubbs, *Select Charters and Other Illustrations of English Constitutional History from the Earliest Times to the Reign of Edward I* (Oxford, 1913), pp. 95–99.

34. Ibid., pp. 99–100.

35. See Z. N. Brooke, *The English Church and the Papacy* (Cambridge, 1931), pp. 154–155.

36. Ibid., pp. 155, 166–167, 174, 187–189, 198–199, 211-212.

37. See W. L. Warren, *Henry II* (Berkeley and Los Angeles, 1973); Amy Kelly, *Eleanor of Aquitaine and the Four Kings* (Cambridge, Mass., 1950); Jacques Boussard, *Le Gouvernement d'Henri II Plantagenet* (Paris, 1956).

38. Walter Map, *De Nugis Curialium*, ed. M. R. James (Oxford, 1914), p. 261.

39. Ibid., p. 277.

40. Doris M. Stenton, *English Justice, 1066–1215* (Philadelphia, 1964), p. 53.

41. Other feudal incidents (in addition to knight's service) included: (1) relief — a sum of money payable by the heir for permission to renew the ties to the lord broken by the death of the heir's predecessor; (2) primer seisin — the lord's right of first possession of the land until the relief was paid; (3) wardship — the lord's right to administer the estate and appropriate the revenues as long as the heir was a minor or an unmarried woman; (4) marriage — the lord's right to choose the heiress's husband, provided she consented; (5) escheat — the return of the land to the lord if the holder was no longer able to render services because he had been outlawed or imprisoned for a felony or because the line of succession had come to an end; (6) fine on alienation — a fee payable to the lord upon the sale or gift of the land by the holder to another; (7) aids — payments to help the lord meet various obligations. In 1215 Magna Carta reduced the number of aids to three: the ransoming of the lord's person from captivity, the knighting of his eldest son, and the marriage of his eldest daughter.

42. See Charles H. Haskins, *Norman Institutions* (Cambridge, Mass., 1918), p. 155.

43. See Haskins, "England and Sicily," pp. 651–655.

44. See ibid., pt. 1, July 1911, pp. 438–443; cf. *Dialogus de Scaccario* (*The Course of the Exchequer*), ed. and trans. Charles Johnson (New York, 1950), pp. 35–36.

45. The full passage is quoted in T. F. T. Plucknett, *A Concise History of the Common Law*, 5th ed. (Boston, 1956), p. 148.

46. The phrase is Maitland's. See F. W. Maitland, *The Constitutional History of England* (Cambridge, 1965), pp. 106–107.

47. Strayer, *Medieval Origins*, p. 34.

48. Ibid.

49. R. C. van Caenegem, *Royal Writs in England from the Conquest to Glanvill* (London, 1959), p. 200.

50. Ibid., p. 199.

51. See ibid., p. 444.

52. G. D. G. Hall, ed. and trans., *The Treatise on the Laws and Customs of the Realm of England Commonly Called Glanvill* (London, 1965), p. 167.

53. The Assize of Clarendon is discussed and important parts of it are translated in Plucknett, *Concise History*, pp. 112–113.

54. Course in Development of Legal Institutions, Harvard Law School, 1968.

55. On the abolition of ordeals and the introduction of the trial jury in criminal cases, see Plucknett, *Concise History*, pp. 118–126. Plucknett shows the resistance to the abolition of the ordeal in England, the hesitation over the substitution of inquest procedure, and the rejection of the option of interrogation of parties and jurors by the courts.

56. See Frederic William Maitland, *The Forms of Action at Common Law* (Cambridge, 1965).

57. See Chapter 6, notes 10 and 11.

58. Sir Frederick Pollock and Frederic William Maitland, *History of English Law*, 2nd ed. (1898; reprint ed., Cambridge, 1968), I, 146.

59. Joüon des Longrais, *Henry II and His Justiciars: Had They a Political Plan in Their Reforms about Seisin?* (Limoges, 1962). A similar acheivement had been attempted some fifteen years earlier by the newly elected German king Frederick Barbarossa. In his "peace statute" of 1152, Frederick provided "that a possessory dispute between two vassals of the same lord should be brought before the royal judge, so that the feudal court was limited to the question of ownership, which frequently was not raised; we know from contemporary documents that the question of possession was resolved by inquest procedure. Exactly like Henry II of England, Frederick sought to create a royal possessory procedure and thereby to limit the jurisdiction of the nobility." Mitteis, *Der staat des hohen Mittelalters*, p. 254. Frederick, however, could not create a procedural judicial system capable of realizing his ambitions, and eventually decided to encourage the development of princely jurisdiction within the individual territories that made up the German empire. See Chapter 14.

60. Hall, *Treatise Called Glanvill*, p. 1.

61. J. E. A. Jolliffe, *The Constitutional History of Medieval England* (London, 1961), p. 206.

62. See Charles H. Haskins, *Norman Institutions* (Cambridge, Mass., 1918), p. 58; see also Charles Petit-Dutaillis, *The Feudal Monarchy in France and England from the Tenth to the Thirteenth Century*, trans. E. D. Hunt (London, 1936), p. 162.

63. Haskins, *Norman Institutions*, p. 192.

64. Ibid., pp. 192–193.

65. See Ernest-Joseph Tardiff, *Coutumiers de Normandie*, 2 vols. (Rouen, 1881–1903).

66. See Maurice Jallut, *Philippe Auguste, fondateur de l'unite française* (Paris, 1963); Achille Luchaire, *Philippe Auguste* (Paris, 1884).

67. *Chronique rimée de Philippe Mouskès*, publ. Baron de Reiffenberg, II (Brussels, 1838), 427 ss. 23735–23738.

68. The following account is supported by the factual materials—though not always by the interpretations—found in Francois J. M. Olivier-Martin, *Histoire du droit français des origines à la révolution*, 2nd ed. (Paris, 1951); Émile Chénon, *Histoire générale du droit français public et privé des origines à 1815*, I (Paris, 1926); Mitteis, *Der Staat des hohen Mittelalters*; Ludwig Buisson, *König Ludwig IX, der Heilige und das Recht* (Freiburg, 1954); Petit-Dutaillis,*Feudal Monarchy*.

69. Olivier-Martin, *Histoire*, p. 225.

70. Thomas Aquinas, *Summa Theologica*, pt. II–I, qu. 90–97.

71. John P. Dawson, *The Oracles of the Law* (Ann Arbor, Mich., 1968), p. 276.

72. Ibid., p. 268.

73. See Olivier-Martin, *Histoire*, p. 114. See note 87.

74. Philippe de Beaumanoir, *Coutumes de Beauvaisis*, ed. A. Salmon, 2 vols. (Paris, 1970), I, sec. 683.

75. Henry Sumner Maine, *Ancient Law* (1861; 3rd Amer. ed., New York, 1888), p. 24.

76. "By the year 1296—some thirty-five to forty years after it had begun to emerge as a distinct branch of the *Curia Regis*—a royal ordinance fixed [the] regular membership [of the Parlement of Paris] at fifty-one judges. Twenty-three years later, in 1319, the official total was sixty-seven . . . in 1345 [the membership] was stabilized at about eighty . . . the contrast with England is especially striking . . . between 1300 and 1500 the permanent judges of the King's Bench and Common Pleas totaled normally not eighty but eight or nine judges." Dawson, *Oracles*, p. 274.

77. See Beaumanoir, *Coutumes*, I, sec. 1: "Ci commence li livre des coustumes et des usages de Beauvoisins."

78. ". . . chascuns barons est souverains en sa baronie . . . li rois est souverains par dessus tous et a de son droit la general garde de tout son roiaume, par quoi il puet fere teus establissemens comme il li plest pour le commun pourfit, et ce qu'il establist doit estre tenu." Beaumanoir, *Coutumes*, II, sec. 1043.

79. Beaumanoir's treatment of the role of *procureurs* and avocats in the bailiff's court is summarized in Georges Hubrecht, "Commentaire historique et juridique," in Philippe de Beaumanoir, *Coutumes de Beauvaisis*, III (Paris, 1974), chaps. 4 and 5. Dawson, *Oracles*, pp. 282–285, discusses the functioning of the procureurs and avocats in the Parlement of Paris.

80. Beaumanoir, *Coutumes*, II, secs. 1122–1223.

81. Ibid., I, secs. 954–988.

82. Ibid., II, sec. 999. Beaumanoir's phrase *Convenance vaint loi* is a translation of the Latin expression *conventio vincit legem*, which was often used throughout Europe at that time and is to be found a century earlier in Glanvill. The meaning was that the will of the parties superseded those (nonmandatory) provisions of law which defined contractual obligations "unless otherwise agreed." A contrary interpretation is given in an otherwise rewarding essay on Beaumanoir in M. E. Tigar and M. R. Levy, *Law and the Rise of Capitalism* (New York, 1977), p. 145.

83. Beaumanoir, *Coutumes*, II, sec. 1000.

84. Ibid., II, secs. 823–936. Dawson emphasizes the local character of the French customary law of crime, civil obligations (contract and tort), and criminal

and civil procedure, stating that virtually the entire body of French *royal* customary law consisted of land law, property rights of married persons, inheritance, gifts, and testaments. Yet the criminal law as stated by Beaumanoir hardly gives the impression of being specific to Beauvais. The law of treason, counterfeiting, and heresy, for example, is discussed in the same context as the law of homicide, arson, robbery, and other crimes. Also, the contract law presented by Beaumanoir is hardly to be viewed simply as the local custom of Beauvais. It seems rather to be customary (in the sense of nonenacted) law, applicable in appropriate cases in any courts in France, including the royal courts. Dawson's analysis is well adapted to a later time, when the need first developed to harmonize and unify the diverse customs of the various parts of France. See Dawson, "The Codification of the French Customs," *Michigan Law Review*, 38 (1940), 765.

85. Olivier-Martin, *Histoire*, p. 233.

86. Bracton transcribed some two thousand cases from the plea rolls; these are collected in Bracton's *Note Book*, edited by Maitland. No similar notebook of Beaumanoir has been discovered; however, he makes reference — though not by name — to hundreds of cases in his treatise. His use of case law (in French, *jurisprudence*) has been described as follows: "Sometimes he starts by expounding a customary rule and cites a judicial decision to illustrate it. Sometimes he does the reverse: proceeding from a judicial decision which he has seen rendered, he points out the principle of which the judgment is an application . . . As evidence of a custom recently contested, [Beaumanoir] invariably refers only to one judicial decision, undoubtedly because the single precedent suffices because it is decisive." Hubrecht, "Commentaire," p. 4.

87. Beaumanoir, sec. 31. The interpretation of this passage to refer to "similar" cases, and not only to "the same" case, is supported by Hubrecht, "Commentaire," p. 19. Hubrecht adds: "Thus case law [*jurisprudence*] is applied in conditions analogous to those of English law, and the judge can decide directly without calling upon the [suitors]." Another passage in Beaumanoir may seem at first to contradict the view that the author, or the law that he analyzes, placed a high value on consistency of judicial decisions. The passage in question (sec. 1880) states that a judge should disqualify himself in a case if he had taken part in a similar case, to avoid the suspicion that he might be inclined to reaffirm what was decided before even if it was erroneous. On a closer reading, it appears that the passage refers to a prior case in which the judge had participated as a party, rather than to a case in which he had participated as a judge. This interpretation is supported by the fact that the following section (sec. 1881) requires a judge to disqualify himself if he had appeared in a similar case as a witness. See also Hubrecht, "Commentaire," p. 4.

88. "France and England entered the later Middle Ages with a common fund of legal and political institutions. Much of the area that was to be included in modern France was united with England under a common sovereign; political institutions were shaped by the same basic forms of feudal organization; private law was largely composed of unformulated popular custom, remarkably similar even in detail. As early as the thirteenth century the tendencies toward divergence, both in law and government, had made themselves apparent." Dawson, "Codification," p. 765. Professor Dawson is writing here from the

perspective of the sixteenth to the nineteenth centuries. If the same facts were to be written from the perspective of the eleventh and twelfth centuries, the last sentence might read: "As late as the thirteenth century the similarities predominated over the differences."

14. Royal Law: Germany, Spain, Flanders, Hungary, Denmark

1. Heinrich Mitteis, *Der Staat des hohen Mittelalters* (Weimar, 1953), p. 155. An alternative translation may be found in Mitteis, *The State in the Middle Ages*, trans. H. F. Orton (Amsterdam, 1975), p. 149.

2. Mitteis, *Der Staat*, p. 201.

3. Ibid., p. 256ff.

4. Ibid.

5. See Peter Munz, *Frederick Barbarossa: A Study in Medieval Politics* (London, 1969), pp. 250–251. A somewhat different version is given by Carl Erdmann, "Der Prozess Heinrichs des Löwen," in Theodor Mayer, ed., *Kaisertum und Herzogsgewalt im Zeitalter Friedrichs I* (Leipzig, 1944), pp. 348–353.

6. Mitteis, *State*, p. 335.

7. Ibid., pp. 225–233, 310. See also Albert Brackmann, "Die Wandlung der Staatsanschauungen im Zeitalter Kaiser Friedrichs I," *Historische Zeitschrift* 145 (1932).

8. In 1111, Pope Pascal II's Privilege listed as regalia imperial rights connected with cities, duchies, margraveships, countdoms, coins, tolls, markets, imperial and ecclesiastical patronage, hundred courts, and some others. Hermann Conrad, *Deutsche Rechtsgeschichte*, 2nd ed. (Karlsruhe, 1962), I, 369–376.

9. Heinrich Appelt, "Friedrich Barbarossa und das römische Recht," *Römische historische Mitteilungen*, 5 (1961–62), 18–34; H. Koeppler, "Friedrich Barbarossa and the Schools of Bologna," *English Historical Review*, 54 (1939), 577–607.

10. Munz, *Barbarossa*, pp. 122–124.

11. See Günther Schmidt, *Das Würzburgische Herzogtum und die Gräfen und Herren von Ostfranken vom 11. bis zum 17. Jahrhundert*, Quellen und Studien zur Verfassungsgeschichte des deutschen Reiches im Mittelalter und Neuzeit, vol. 2 (Weimar, 1913), pp. 1–52. Schmidt states that it was not a question of naked power or of owning large amounts of land in the duchy but the ability to give justice that characterized the emerging territorial states of Germany. On Austria, see Heinrich Appelt, *Privilegium Minus: Das staufische Kaisertum und die Babenberger in Österreich* (Vienna, 1973). See also E. E. Stengel, "Land- und lehnrechtliche Grundlagen des Reichsfürstenstandes," in *Abhandlungen und Untersuchungen zur mittelalterlichen Geschichte* (Cologne, 1960).

12. See Walter Ullmann, "The Pontificate of Adrian IV," *Cambridge Historical Journal*, 11 (1955), 243.

13. Munz, *Barbarossa*, p. 31.

14. Ibid., p. 372.

15. Joachim Gernhuber, "Die Landfriedensbewegung in Deutschland bis zum Mainzer Reichslandfrieden von 1235," *Bonner Rechtswissenschaftliche Abhandlungen*, 44 (Bonn, 1952), 72–102.

16. Ibid., p. 74.

17. Lorenz Weinrich, ed. and trans., *Quellen zur deutscher Verfassungs-Wirtschafts-, und Sozialgeschichte bis 1250*, Ausgewählte Quellen zur deutschen

Geschichte des Mittelalter, vol. 32 (Darmstadt, 1977), pp. 166–167. Only a digest of the 1103 land peace has survived.

18. Ibid., p. 214. Emphasis added.

19. Ibid., p. 216.

20. Mitteis, *State,* p. 243.

21. Weinrich, *Quellen,* pp. 246–259.

22. Frederick issued this statue at the request of the four doctors, as a reward for their services at the diet. It is the only instance of an express addition to Justinian's laws by a German emperor.

23. In 1186 Frederick issued his Peace Writ against Arsonists, consisting of twenty-three articles, some quite long. This was a sophisticated document attempting to bring arson, a serious threat to the royal peace, under imperial control.

24. The Landfriede movement did not totally cease between 1186 and 1235, but neither did it make substantial progress. The most important of the Landfrieden issued by Henry VII, the Truce of Henry of 1224, represented a regression to an earlier form; there was no mention of jus or lex, and many of the regulations only renewed traditional limitations on the feud. The other two principal enactments of this period, the Treaty with the Ecclesiastical Princes of 1220 and the Statute in Favor of Princes of 1232, did not purport to be Landfrieden but were merely concessions of Frederick II to the ecclesiastical and lay princes.

25. Weinrich, *Quellen,* pp. 462–483.

26. See James M. Powell, ed. and trans., *The Liber Augustalis or Constitutions of Melfi Promulgated by the Emperor Frederick II for the Kingdom of Sicily in 1231* (Syracuse, N. Y., 1971), I, 8, "Mainzer Landfriede 5."

27. See Heinz Angermeier, *Königtum und Landfriede im deutschen Spätmittelalter* (Munich, 1966), pp. 27–29.

28. The reforms of Frederick II meant that the court decisions would be collected and safeguarded in a single place, "so that a legal framework for the most varied relations of public life, a norm for the speaking of law, could be established." R. Scholz, *Beiträge zur Geschichte der Hoheitsrechte des deutschen Königs zur Zeit der ersten Staufer, 1138–1197,* Leipzig Studien, vol. 24, (1896), p. 26.

29. Karl August Eckhardt, ed., *Sachsenspiegel V: Landrecht in hochdeutscher Übertragung* (Hannover, 1967), prolog and III, 78, no. 2. There is no edition of the *Lehnrecht* in modern German (although there is a modern edition in old German).

30. "The Pope may not ban the emperor except for heresy, abandonment of wife, or destroying God's house." Eckhardt, *Landrecht* 1.1; 3.57.1.

31. "The ban hurts the soul but takes no life or reduces no one in *Landrecht* or *Lehnrecht* unless it is followed by royal outlawry." Eckhardt, *Landrecht* 3.63.2.

32. "The judge can judge any kind of complaint within his court's jurisdiction, wherever he is, except when one complains concerning his own land or charges a crime against a free man; that the judge cannot judge except at a genuine local judicial assembly and under royal ban." Eckhardt, *Landrecht* 1.59.1.

33. Eckhardt, *Landrecht* 3.57.2. The *Sachsenspiegel* stated that the cupbearer was entitled to the seventh vote, but since the possessor of that office, the King of Bohemia, was not a German, he had no electoral voice. However, in 1290 Emperor Rudolf, relying on the authority of the *Sachsenspiegel,* granted the vote to Bohemia, thus fixing the seven electors until the mid-seventeenth century.

34. Eckhardt, *Landrecht* 2.66.1.

35. See Adolf Laufs, *Rechtsentwicklung in Deutschland* (Berlin, 1978), pp. 21–22, citing Eckhardt, *Landrecht* 2.13.1, dealing with different types of punishment for thieves. See also Gerhard Kallen, "Friedrich Barbarossa's Verfassungsreform und das Landrecht des Sachsenspiegels," *ZSS (germ)*, 71 (1938), 560; Hans von Voltellini, "Ein Beitrag zur Quellenkunde des Sachsenspiegels Landrecht," *ZSS (germ)*, 71 (1938), 548.

36. Laufs, *Rechtsentwicklung*, citing Eckhardt, *Landrecht* 2.69.

37. Its impact on city law can be seen especially in the development of the Magdeburg Law, the Görlitz Codex of the early fourteenth century, and the Breslau Landrecht of 1356; it continued to accompany the Germans as they moved east, while traces can also be seen in the Netherlands. It was glossed repeatedly, notably by the Brandenburg knight and jurist Johann von Buch (trained at Bologna) after 1325, and by Nicholas Wurm, also trained at Bologna, around 1400. In general, see Herman Conrad, *Deutsche Rechtsgeschichte*, I (Karlsruhe, 1954), 477–479; Richard Schröder and Eberhard Freiherr von Künssberg, *Lehrbuch des deutschen Rechtsgeschichte*, 7th ed. (Berlin, 1932), pp. 722–725.

38. Hans Fehr, "Die Staatsauffassung Eikes von Repgau," *ZSS (germ)*, 50 (1916), 159.

39. The *Schwabenspiegel*, written in 1274–75, was the most influential lawbook in southern Germany. It drew from Bavarian folklaw, imperial law, the peace statutes, Roman law, and canon law. It took a pro-papal position as compared to the pro-imperial stance of the *Sachsenspiegel*. The *Deutschenspiegel*, also written in 1274–75, relied heavily on the *Sachsenspiegel* but made greater use of canon law and Roman law. It did not have a significant impact. The *Frankenspiegel*, written in Hesse between 1328 and 1338, was strongly pro-imperial. A number of lesser works also apppeared in the fourteenth century. See Conrad, *Deutsche Rechtsgeschichte*, p. 479.

40. Geoffrey Barraclough, trans., *Medieval Germany, 911–1250: Essays by German Historians*, I (Oxford, 1938), 104.

41. Ibid., p. 76.

42. Mitteis, *Der Staat*, p. 330.

43. *MGH*, Legum IV, I, p. 222.

44. Barraclough, *Medieval Germany*, I, 105.

45. "Confoederatio cum principibus ecclesiasticus" and "Statutuum in favorem principuun," in Weinrich, *Quellen*, pp. 382, 434.

46. Ruth Hildebrand, "Der sächsische 'Staat' Heinrichs des Löwen," *Historische Studien* (Berlin), no. 302 (1937), pp. 371–392.

47. Karl Jordan, *Heinrich der Löwe: Eine Biographie* (Munich, 1979), p. 148.

48. Max Spindler, *Die Anfänge der bayerischen Landesfürstentums*, Schriftenreihe zur bayerischen Landesgeschichte, vol. 26 (Munich, 1937). In general see Eugen Wohlhaupter, *Hoch- und Niedergericht in der Mittelalterlichen Gerichtsverfassung Bayerns*, vol. 12, pt. 2, of *Deutschrechtliche Beiträge*, ed. Konrad Beyerle (Heidelberg, 1929); Wolfgang Schnelbogl, *Die innere Entwicklung der bayerischen Landfrieden des 13. Jahrhunderts*, vol. 13, pt. 2, of *Deutschrechtliche Beiträge*, ed. Konrad Beyerle (Heidelberg, 1932).

49. Spindler, *Anfänge*, p. 116.

50. Ibid., p. 120.

51. Ibid., pp. 166–167.

52. Ibid., pp. 176–184.

53. Ibid., p. 167.

54. Reckesvinth also abrogated all use of Roman law except for purposes of study. This included the suppression of the Lex Romana Visigothorum, or Breviarium Alarici, a pre-Justinian compendium (issued by Alaric II in 506) that became the leading text of its kind.

55. See Eugen Wohlhaupter, *Studien zur Rechtsgeschichte des Gottes- und Land-friedens in Spanien*, vol. 14 of *Deutschrechtliche Beiträge*, ed. Konrad Beyerle (Heidelberg, 1933).

56. Juan Beneyto Perez, *Manual de Historia del Derecho* (Madrid, 1960), pp. 101–128; E. E. von Kleffens, *Hispanic Law until the End of the Middle Ages* (Edinburgh, 1968), pp. 238–268.

57. Spain's oldest university, Palencia, was founded between 1208 and 1214. In 1239 it was moved to and merged with the University of Salamanca, founded perhaps a dozen years earlier. Salamanca became an important center for the study of both Roman and canon law.

58. Beneyto Perez, *Manual*, pp. 110–123; von Kleffens, *Hispanic Law*, pp. 147–236.

59. Leopold A. Warnkönig, *Flandrische Staats- und Rechtsgeschichte bis zum Jahr 1305*, I (Tübingen, 1835) 127. See also Henri Pirenne, *Geschichte Belgiens*, I (Gotha, 1899); Raymond Monier, *Les Institutions centrales du Comte de Flandre de la fin du neuvième siècle à 1384* (Paris, 1949).

60. Warnkönig, *Flandrische Rechtsgeschichte*, p. 149.

61. Ibid., pp. 160–162.

62. On Hungary, see Thomas von Gogyay, *Grundzüge der Geschichte Ungarns*, I (Pest, 1851), 66–125; Dominic Kosary, *A History of Hungary* (Philadelphia, 1906), pp. 50–61; E. Pamlenyi, ed., *A History of Hungary* (Budapest, 1973), pp. 29–61.

63. See T. K. Derry, *A History of Scandinavia* (Minneapolis, Minn., 1975); John Danstrup, *A History of Denmark* (New York, 1947).

64. *Das jutsche Low, aus dem Dänischen übersetzt von Blasius Eckenberger*, ed. N. Falck (Altona, 1819).

65. Danstrup, *Denmark*, pp. 28–31. Portions of the preamble are taken directly from the canon law.

66. Derry, *Scandinavia*, p. 66.

67. Aristotle, *Nicomachean Ethics*, 5.10.1137[b] 11–28, in Richard Mckeon, ed., *The Basic Works of Aristotle* (New York, 1941), p. 1020.

Conclusion

1. See Robert C. Tucker, "The Marxian Revolutionary Idea," in *Revolution*, ed. Carl Friedrich, *Nomos*, no. 8 (1966), pp. 217–246, esp. p. 219.

2. Ibid., pp. 223–224.

3. Christopher Hill, "A Comment," in Rodney Hilton, ed., *The Transition from Feudalism to Capitalism* (London, 1976), p. 121.

4. Ibid.

5. Letter to Conrad Schmidt, Oct. 27, 1890, in Karl Marx and Friedrich Engels, *Selected Works*, III (Moscow, 1966), pp. 492–493.

6. Perry Anderson, *Passages from Antiquity to Feudalism* (London, 1974), p. 153.

7. Hilton, *Transition*, pp. 9–30 (quotation, p. 18).

8. W. W. Rostow, *The Stages of Economic Growth* (Cambridge, Mass., 1960), pp. 4–7.

9. See David Herlihy, ed., *The History of Feudalism* (New York, 1970), pp. 3, 34.

10. Perry Anderson, *Lineages of the Absolutist State* (London, 1974), p. 403. The East German Marxist Rudolf Bahro also sees Western feudalism as a unique economic form which had within it "an immanent tendency of transformation" into capitalism. Bahro states: "Feudalism-capitalism is essentially a single development." *The Alternative in Eastern Europe*, trans. David Fernbach (London, 1978), p. 66.

11. *Max Weber on Law in Economy and Society*, ed. Max Rheinstein (Cambridge, Mass., 1966), p. 297.

12. *Proceedings of the First Conference of German Sociologists*, 1910, quoted in Max Weber, *Economy and Society*, ed. Guenther Roth and Claus Wittich (New York, 1968), I, lxiv.

13. Max Weber, *Gesammelte Aufsatzen zur Religions-soziologie* (Tübingen, 1920), p. 1.

14. This conclusion can be supported by many quotations from Weber's writings, although other quotations can be found to qualify and even refute it. In fact, Weber's historical writings are quite confused and inconsistent, though his theoretical analysis is just the opposite.

15. Rheinstein, *Max Weber*, p. 304.

16. Ibid., p. 305.

17. See Donald R. Kelley, "The Metaphysics of Law: An Essay on the Very Young Marx," *American Historical Review*, 83 (April 1978), 350–367.

18. Rheinstein, *Max Weber*, pp. 63–64.

19. Ibid., p. 303.

20. Weber, *Economy and Society*, pp. 226–227 and 1070.

21. Ibid., p. 242.

22. Ibid., p. 244.

23. Ibid., p. 246.

24. Ibid., p. 76.

25. Ibid., p. 86.

26. Rheinstein, *Max Weber*, pp. 304–305.

27. Ibid.

28. Kent V. Flannery, "The Cultural Evolution of Civilizations," *Annual Review of Ecology and Systematics*, 3 (1972), 399, 407.

29. See Grace Goodell, "From Status to Contract: The Significance of Agrarian Relations of Production in the West, Japan, and in 'Asiatic' Persia," *European Journal of Sociology*, 21 (1980), 285–325, esp. 288–291.

30. Rodney H. Hilton, *Bond Men Made Free: Medieval Peasant Movements and the English Rising of 1381* (London, 1973), pp. 70–71, 74–75.

31. Goodell, "From Status to Contract," p. 298.

32. Octavio Paz, "Reflections: Mexico and the United States," *The New Yorker*, September 17, 1979, pp. 138, 153.

Acknowledgments

I started writing this book in 1938, as a graduate student in legal history at London School of Economics. I had gone to London under the inspiration of Eugen Rosenstock-Huessy, to study the impact of the English Revolution of 1640–1689 on the development of English Law. T. F. T. Plucknett, the dean of English legal historians in the period after the First World War, told me that I would not understand a word of English legal history unless I started in the twelfth and thirteenth centuries with Glanvill and Bracton. I took his advice, but I also followed R. H. Tawney's course in seventeenth-century English history. These three men were all great Europeans, though they came from very different times: Plucknett's thought was rooted in the twelfth to seventeenth centuries, Tawney's in the seventeenth to twentieth, Rosenstock-Huessy's in the aftermath of what he called the World War Revolution. I would like to think that this book builds on the work of all three.

In the intervening decades I have been helped by a multitude of student research assistants as well as by many colleagues and friends. I will mention only three, whose assistance is reflected graphically in these pages: Carmen Arevalo, who prepared the maps; Robert Chesler, who prepared figure 2; and George Size, who prepared figure 1.

Grateful acknowledgment is made to Houghton Mifflin Company for granting permission to reprint a portion of "The Metaphors" from *The Human Season* by Archibald MacLeish, copyright © 1972 by Archibald MacLeish, and to the British Library for granting permission to quote from an Anglo-Saxon poem found in Cotton Manuscripts, "Maxims."

I should also like to thank the National Humanities Center for providing a most congenial environment in which to finish the manuscript and to plan its sequel.

Index